Sociology

SOCIOLOGY

RODNEY STARK

University of Washington

Wadsworth Publishing Company
Belmont, California
A Division of Wadsworth, Inc.

Sociology Editor: Sheryl Fullerton
Production Editor: Patricia Brewer
Designer: MaryEllen Podgorski
Print Buyer: Barbara Britton
Photo Researcher: Barbara Hodder
Illustrators: Mary Burkhardt and Lisa Sliter
Compositor: Graphic Typesetting Service, Los Angeles

Cover painting: Lorenzetti, *Buongoverno in citta*. Siena, Palazzo Pubblico

Illustration credits appear on pp. 544–545.

A study guide has been specially designed to help students master the concepts presented in this textbook. Order from your bookstore.

Printed in the United States of America

2 3 4 5 6 7 8 9 10
89 88 87 86 85

ISBN 0-534-03126-9

Library of Congress Cataloging in Publication Data

Stark, Rodney.
   Sociology.

   Bibliography: p.
   Includes indexes.
   1. Sociology.   I. Title.
HM51.S89625   1985   301   84–17363
ISBN 0–534–03126–9

About the Author

Rodney Stark grew up in Jamestown, North Dakota, and received his Ph.D. from the University of California, Berkeley, where he held appointments as a research sociologist at the Survey Research Center and at the Center for the Study of Law and Society. Since 1971 he has been Professor of Sociology at the University of Washington. He is the author of eleven books and scores of scholarly articles on subjects as diverse as shoplifting, anti-Semitism, police riots, and suicide. However, the greater portion of his work has been on religion and especially on religious movements. His most recent book, with William Sims Bainbridge, is *The Future of Religion: Secularization, Revival, and Cult Formation,* published in 1985 by the University of California Press.

Brief Contents

Detailed Contents

■ Marks over-the-shoulder sections.

PART TWO
INDIVIDUALS AND GROUPS   94

PART THREE
STRATIFICATION AND CONFLICT   198

Preface

Over the past several decades, introductory sociology has become a subject unto itself. The leading textbooks offer only shadows and faded memories of the field that sociologists actually pursue. In part this may reflect a compulsion to imitate success, to produce books that run no risk of being out of tune with the market. In part, too, this is because textbook authors rely on one another as primary sources—the same examples seem to appear in many of the books.

Worse yet, every leading text includes the same array of obsolete topics and illustrations. For example, zonal theories of the structure of cities were discarded by urban sociologists as a dead end in the late 1950s! Yet the leading texts continue to advise students that all cities are like Chicago used to be. Meanwhile, many of the new and significant developments in sociology have yet to penetrate the introductory textbook culture. For example, the word *deterrence* is not even in the index of any leading text, despite the fact that articles on deterrence have been crowding the deviance and criminology journals for a decade. Or no attempt is made to deal with world system (or dependency) theory, although this is *the* topic among sociologists of social change and modernization.

Major introductory texts also treat "theories" as but names to be rattled off, not as intellectual schemes to be *used to explain social phenomena*. Words like *functionalism* or *conflict theory* are used only as labels—of the same order as *liberal*. In fact, sociology textbooks are essentially elaborate lists of concepts fleshed out with a vast clutter of "facts" and "findings."

If sociology is no more than a set of peculiar names to be imposed on common-sense observations and everyday experiences, it isn't worth much. By presenting sociology as merely a wordlist and by not showing sociological *concepts in action*—being used to *do* sociology—the current texts subvert my aims as a teacher.

Twice each year I teach introductory sociology to a class of more than 700 students. I do it because I am shamelessly enthusiastic about being a sociologist. My goal each quarter is to share that enthusiasm, to let students see for themselves why I have so much fun doing sociology. I can't do that with a book that fails to reveal contemporary sociology— a book that would leave even me wondering how anyone could stand to be a sociologist.

Simply to fill a textbook with up-to-date citations from major journals does not make up for failures to include the major theoretical and empirical issues that give these same journals an intelligible and exciting content. Hence, to offer only definitions of concepts such as religion or the family, and then to shovel in a recent assortment of little facts, invariably results in chapters that ignore everything that attracts sociologists to these topics. Why shouldn't freshmen be let in on real contemporary sociology?

If we are to do better, we must have texts that do not substitute *descriptions of social problems* for explanations of how societies operate. No description of poverty and privilege, no matter how lengthy or well written, can substitute for a clear presentation of *theories of stratification*. Nor can vivid accounts of interracial strife replace *theories of intergroup conflict*. Our students already know poverty and prejudice exist. They would like us to try to tell them why. When we don't, they conclude it's because sociology is a failure. Nor can we hide in the claim that real sociology is too advanced for most stu-

dents. They are being asked to grasp as difficult material in many other courses—including other social science courses. Leading introductory texts in psychology, economics, and anthropology take students straight to the intellectual core of the discipline, to the major contending theories, the critical disputes, and the most active lines of research.

I wrote this book primarily so that my students could have a textbook that did not make sociology seem shallow compared with the other social sciences. Moreover, I have done my best to display sociology as an adventure—as a worthy calling pursued by original, enthusiastic, and interesting people.

"OVER-THE-SHOULDER" SOCIOLOGY

I have tried to write a book that reveals sociology as a *human activity*—as something people *do*. Whenever possible I have selected a major work in an area and, by explaining why and how it was done, I have used it as a vehicle for displaying major theoretical and empirical accomplishments of the area. I think I often have been able to make a theory come alive by letting students watch someone struggle to fashion an explanation of some aspect of social life.

By the same token, research methods only become coherent when they are put to use. Thus I have not limited discussion of methods to a hermetically sealed chapter on the subject but have tried to give students a vicarious methodological apprenticeship throughout the book. To the greatest extent possible, I have tried to place readers in a vantage point from which they can look over the shoulder of sociologists as they *do* sociology. Moreover, I have tried to show not only *what* sociologists do, but *why* we do it. And I have stressed not only the value of doing sociology but the pure fun of it.

The over-the-shoulder approach to sociology in this book clarifies how and why we do sociology and heightens reader involvement. But I refused to be a slave to that format; when it got in the way I didn't use it. Usually, the over-the-shoulder format worked best in recounting a major research study, but sometimes it did not lend itself as well to the exposition of theory.

POINT OF VIEW AND APPROACH

Sociologists considering a textbook often ask what "kind" or "brand" of sociology it reflects. What are the author's theoretical and methodological commitments? I find some difficulty framing a satisfactory answer to such questions, because I don't think I have a brand. First of all, my fundamental commitment is to sociology as a social science. Hence, I want to know how societies work and why, not to document a perspective. Moreover, in constructing sociological theories I am a dedicated, even reckless, eclectic. Competing theoretical sociologies persist, in part, not only because they tend to talk past one another, but because each can explain some aspect of social life better than the others can. Therefore, in my own theoretical writing I tend to take anything that seems to work from whatever school can provide it. The textbook does much the same, but with care to point out which elements are being drawn from which theoretical tradition.

I also have not written a book that favors either *micro* or *macro* sociology. Both levels of analysis are essential to any adequate sociology. Where appropriate, the chapters are structured to work from the micro to the macro level of analysis. And the book itself works from the most micro topics to the most macro.

Methodologically the text is equally eclectic. In my own research I have pursued virtually every known technique—participant observation, survey research, historical and comparative analysis, demography, human ecology, even experiments. My belief, made clear in the book, is that theories and hypotheses determine what methods are appropriate (within practical and moral limits). That is why there is not one chapter devoted to methods and one devoted to theory. Instead, Chapter 3 first introduces basic elements of micro theories and then demonstrates how such theories are tested through experiments and participant observation. Chapter 4 introduces social structure within the context of survey research methods. The chapter then assesses basic elements of major macro schools of sociological theory and concludes with an extended example of testing macro theories through comparative research using societies as the units of analysis. Throughout the book, the interplay of theory and research is not asserted, but *demonstrated*. No sooner do readers meet a theory than they see it being tested.

Countless publishers have stressed to me that introductory sociology textbooks, unlike texts in other fields, must *not* have an integrated structure. Since sociologists, I am told, have idiosyncratic, fixed notions about the order of chapters, books must easily permit students to read them in any order. That would be a poor way to use this book. The fact is that later chapters build on earlier ones. To do otherwise would have forced me to eliminate some of sociology's major achievements or else to write a redundant book that repeats itself each time basic material is elaborated or built upon. Clearly, some jumping around is possible—the institutions chapters work well enough in any order (and could even be omitted without harming subsequent chapters), but the basic ordering of the major parts of the book is organic. Thus, for example, the chapter on socialization expands upon material already presented in the biology chapter. And the discussion of theories of intergroup relations included in Chapter 11 is basic to the examination of models of urban segregation taken up in Chapter 18. In my judgment textbooks can only be highly flexible at the risk of being superficial (imagine a chemistry book with chapters that could be read in any order).

NO MORE "PRETTY" BOOKS

In the early 1970s I was associated with the first textbook in sociology to be lavishly illustrated. I continue to believe that good graphics can make textbooks more effective instructional tools. Yet over the past 15 years I have been very disappointed to see introductory sociology texts fill up with pointless and even condescending illustrations. The text mentions older persons, so the photo editor provides a picture of several older people in case students don't know what they look like. Further on, the text mentions minority groups so readers are provided a photo of two black college students.

I wanted this book to include a lot of art—tables, maps, graphs, drawings, and photos. But I wanted *never* to include an item just to decorate a page. From the start I had the agreement of my editors that we would never include art unless it helped expand upon substantive points or increased a student's understanding of another important time or place. This is one reason the book relies heavily on historical photos and illustrations. It seemed to me that students would learn more if they could *see* as well as read about Italian immigrants in 1890 or black slaves in 1862.

To guard against frivolous use of art, I wrote most captions before beginning the search for the right pictures to fulfill them. Then, armed with a clear notion of what I wanted to accomplish, my photo editor Barbara Hodder achieved prodigies in the archives. Again and again she found just exactly the right picture. I think the final product is a book that is not simply pretty but is effectively illustrated.

USER-FRIENDLINESS

All of what I have described so far indicates a book that intends to provide a more sophisticated look at sociology than do other leading texts. But that in no way makes it a more *difficult* book. A book is not difficult to the extent that the material it presents is easily understood. Sophisticated ideas rarely require dense prose. They merely demand that the author work over the material until it is easy to follow. Moreover, students often find books "difficult," not because the books are sophisticated, but simply because they can't stay awake while reading them.

Prose style

I can't guarantee that students will never doze while reading this book, but I do claim that my discussions, even of topics such as theories of stratification, are suitable for students everywhere. I have devoted much of my life to clear writing. I once worked as an advertising copy writer, and I spent four years as a reporter for several major newspapers. Since becoming a sociologist, I have always tried to write for the general public, even (perhaps especially) my journal articles. Perhaps of even greater importance, I have spent the past decade preparing this book—deciding what should be in it and pretesting each piece by lecturing it. If students can follow an oral presentation they will not have trouble when they have that same material available in text—when they can read and reread at their leisure rather than having to rely on rapidly taken notes.

In order to most effectively convey my sense of what it's like to do sociology, I have avoided the remote, third-person prose typical of textbooks. I wanted students not simply to watch real people enjoy doing sociology, but to know that a real person, not a computer or a committee, wrote this book. On the other hand, I loathe "with it" prose styles. What I aimed for was a style similar to the lecture style I use with my large classes—not remote and impersonal, but not too informal and intimate either. Just as a lecture benefits from some suggestion of interaction between instructor and class, so do textbooks.

Study aids

To assist readers, each chapter ends with a **complete review glossary** that includes not only concepts but also principles. For example, the glossary for the population chapter includes not only concepts such as "birth cohort" or "crude birth rate," but also a succinct restatement of "Malthusian theory" and of "demographic transition theory." The glossary is ordered in the same way as the chapter so it serves to summarize and review the chapter.

Boxed inserts of side material have become a standard feature of leading sociology texts. I decided against them. First of all, if the material is worth including it belongs in the body of the chapter. Placed in a box, the material breaks the narrative flow of the chapter and often gets skipped.

In five instances, however, I have included small essays—minichapters identified as **Special Topics**. I did this because I wanted to amplify and apply materials from several chapters to give them extra emphasis. For example, so much coverage is given to sex roles within various chapters that it did not make sense to devote a whole additional chapter to that topic. On the other hand, it is a topic that deserves special treatment and that also provides a fine opportunity to apply many of the major points developed in the chapter on socialization. So sex-role socialization appears as Special Topic 2, taking up about a quarter the length of a regular chapter.

Anyone who reads all of the books and articles recommended for **further reading** at the end of each chapter will know a lot of sociology. To choose them I asked myself what I had read that was of broad interest and had helped me to write the chapter. Obviously I did not think anyone would rush out and read them all. But students attracted by a particular topic may find useful follow-up reading provided in these suggestions. I also have found these works useful in composing lectures.

SUPPLEMENTS

Doing sociology in the classroom: Instructor's Resource Book

All introductory textbooks come with test items, and often these are combined in a manual with some lecture materials and things to do in class. Unfortunately, the manuals leave much to be desired, in my opinion because other people—not the authors of the textbooks—write them. The manuals often aren't helpful and they often don't support the teaching of the course because they may have been afterthoughts with little relation to the text they accompany.

Instructor's manuals aren't, despite common perceptions, just "window dressing" that publishers devise to help sell books. They're supposed to help us get the most out of a textbook and our students. For this reason I felt an obligation to write my own instructor's manual and to make sure that it gave students a chance to experience what I find so exciting about sociology—research.

I have therefore included in the Instructor's Resource Book materials to make it possible for students to do research on interesting topics in the classroom, to watch and to help out in using research to answer sociological questions. Chapters provide all the essential materials, including readings in some cases, data, and so on to lead students through original data analysis. I've set up correlations in some cases and provided suggestions for using the material.

In addition, I included in the manual other class projects, games, demonstrations, amusements, and suggestions for lectures (including large amounts of material on which I base lectures). The manual is filled with concrete suggestions that I have class-tested and that I believe usefully expand on the text discussions and enrich students' first exposure to sociology.

I decided to write my own test items, too, because I think exams are as much a part of the instructional chore as are lectures and reading assignments. And the author knows better than a free-lance test-writer what particular parts of the text aim to accomplish. I've carefully designed and devised the questions, based on my own teaching of large lecture sections, to *measure* students' understanding not just their narrow grasp of the facts. The introduction to the manual explains how the items are set up to do that. Test items are published as part of the Instructor's Resource Book and are available on Micro-Pac, the Wadsworth electronic test generation and authoring program, for the Apple II + and IIe and IBM PC.

The Study Guide

I did not write the Study Guide for students that also is available for this text. As it turned out, I felt I was much too close to the book itself to be really effective in writing condensed versions of the chapters. Fortunately, Carol Mosher, of Jefferson Community College in Louisville, Kentucky, who was a major reviewer for the book all along the way, agreed to take on this assignment.

The Study Guide is designed to accomplish several purposes: First , it includes a section on how to study using the SQ4R method, a six-step method to help students read and study more effectively. It also includes a section on taking tests.

Second, each chapter in the Study Guide is set up in the same format:

- An *overview* that highlights the important chapter topics.
- A *capsule summary* that condenses the chapter into a few paragraphs.
- A *list of key concepts, theories, studies, and contributions* with specific text page references. This section also includes specific directions, if any, for studying a particular chapter.
- *Fill-in-the-blank questions* drawn from throughout the chapter, with answers listed at the end of the Study Guide chapter. These questions, as well as the essay questions, are based on the SQ4R method and techniques.
- *Essays* that ask students to synthesize, apply, and use text concepts.

Third, for each part in the text there is a brief review of the chapters in that part, plus a suggestion for a special project that offers ways of "doing sociology." The projects have been left open-ended to allow for maximum flexibility.

ACKNOWLEDGMENTS

This book can only teach sociology to the extent that I have learned sociology. Thus, I must acknowledge many intellectual debts. First of all, I must thank my teachers at Berkeley: Kingsley Davis, Charles Y. Glock, Erving Goffman, Seymour Martin Lipset, Philip Selznick, and Neil Smelser. In graduate school I also learned much from my friends Travis Hirschi, Fred Templeton, and John Lofland. More recently, my colleagues Samuel Preston and James McCann caused me to learn some demography. And my marriage to Lynne Roberts has provided me with an ongoing tutorial in micro sociology and formal theory. My intellectual debts to my frequent co-author William Sims Bainbridge are so many and complex that neither of us any longer knows who taught what to whom. Finally, I have learned much from each and every scholar included in the bibliography, which is why they are there.

I also must express my gratitude to Steve Rutter, Vice President of Wadsworth Publishing Company, for urging me not to write a clone of other leading books. Instead, he asked me to write the best book I could and then he assigned Sheryl Fullerton as my editor to make sure I did. Pat Brewer was a tower of sanity during the production stages. After much experience with many textbook factories posing as publishers, it was a privilege to work with people who respect their profession as much as I do mine.

Of course, a most significant debt is to the thousands of students who have taken introductory sociology from me at the University of Washington. They taught me what material worked and what didn't. And it was because they were so much fun to tell about sociology that I became confident that a book like this could succeed.

When I began this task, my first problem was to discover what an introduction to contemporary sociology ought to include. The other textbooks were no help. And no lone sociologist is well informed about each of the many subfields that constitute sociology. Fortunately, scores of my colleagues were willing to help. Some gave me a quick tour of their specialty and got me pointed at the right topics and sources. Others read drafts of various chapters, and many did me the immense honor of pouncing on many glaring errors and omissions. Still others read the entire manuscript with special emphasis on making it the best possible teaching tool.

The influence of Paul J. Baker is to be found in

every chapter. I suspect he is the most widely informed sociologist alive, and he was an extraordinary "sidewalk superintendent" throughout the project. I also am indebted to Ann S. Sundgren, Tacoma Community College, for assessing each chapter from the point of view of students and in terms of how to teach from it. Carol Mosher not only gave me thoughtful critiques of each chapter, but then compiled the many reviews of specific chapters or parts of the book. I also wish to thank the many other scholars who helped me with the project. These include Mary Frances Antolini, Duquesne University; David M. Bass, University of Akron; H. Paul Chalfant, Texas Tech University; Gary A. Cretser, California Polytechnic University at Pomona; Stephen J. Cutler, University of Vermont; Kay Denton, University of Utah; Thomas Egan, University of Louisville; Avery M. Guest, University of Washington; Geoffrey Guest, SUNY at Plattsburgh; Faye Johnson, Middle Tennessee State University; Frederick R. Lynch, University of California at Los Angeles; Shirley McCorkell, Saddleback Community College; Jerry L. L. Miller, University of Arizona; Barbara Ober, Shippensburg State University; Vicki Rose, Southern Methodist University; James F. Scott, Howard University; David A. Snow, University of Texas at Austin; Steven Stack, Pennsylvania State University; Kendrick S. Thompson, Northern Michigan University; and Susan B. Tiano, University of New Mexico.

Rodney Stark

Sociology

Percentage of 18–24-year-olds currently enrolled in college, 1982. National = 41.2 percent.

More than 40 percent of people like you now enroll in college, a higher percentage than completed high school 50 years ago. In Chapter 15 we shall examine why and how this change took place and the impact it has had on the economy. Here we can begin to explore sociology by peeking behind this simple statistic. If we examine college enrollments for each of the census regions, we see that going to college is more common in some parts of the nation than in others. The Pacific region has the highest rate (52.6 percent), and the East South Central region has the lowest (32.3 percent). College enrollments are lower in the southern regions than in other parts of the nation. Why? Mostly because of money. Although the South is currently undergoing very rapid economic development, the average southern family still earns substantially less than families elsewhere. The lower a family's income, the less likely the children will attend college.

Pacific 52.6

Mountain 43.7

West North Central 40.2

East North Central 41.3

Middle Atlantic 40.8

New England 46.6

West South Central 35.4

East South Central 32.3

South Atlantic 35.9

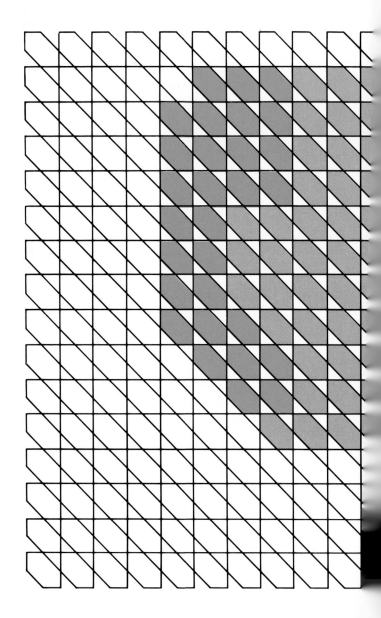

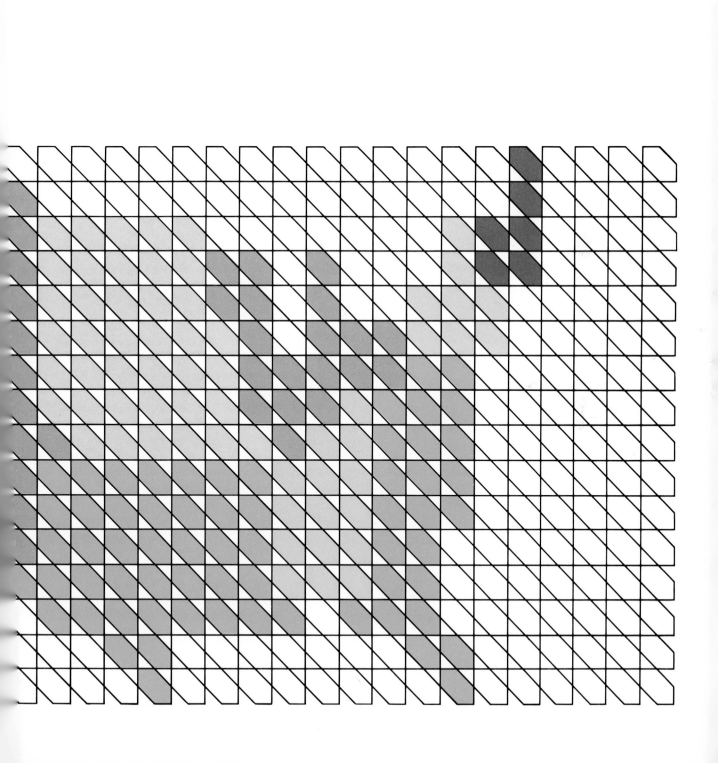

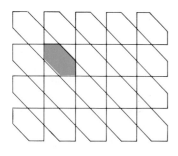

The best title ever given an introductory sociology textbook is *Invitation to Sociology* by Peter Berger (1963). That title indicates that all good introductory textbooks and all good introductory courses aim to do more than simply expose students to basic principles of a field. They also aim to recruit: to encourage some students to make that field their life's work.

The best way to invite students to become sociologists is to present the field not simply as a subject, but also as an activity. People don't merely study sociology, they *do* sociology. I do it nearly every day, and in this book I want you to watch sociology being done.

No scholarly field consists primarily of a collection of books and journals in libraries. Every field consists of people, and it exists only because those people think, do research, and write down their conclusions. An effective introduction to a field will emphasize why people asked certain questions and how they pursued answers as much as what their published conclusions were. In this book I will avoid presenting sociology mainly in its published and public form. Instead, I invite you backstage to look over the shoulders of people as they do sociology. From that vantage point you will not only gain a clearer view of basic sociology, but also sense what it is like to be a sociologist. You will see not only what sociologists have achieved, but also some of what we hope to do—the engrossing mysteries and opportunities ahead.

A Sociological Sampler

CHAPTER PREVIEW

CHAPTER PREVIEW

As an introduction to sociology, this book must first define the field and suggest the difference between sociology on the one hand and psychology, economics, anthropology, and the other social sciences on the other. We need not linger over these matters, because the whole book is meant to reveal what sociology is. In the rest of this chapter, we deal with several basic philosophical issues having to do with whether a *scientific* sociology is possible—or even desirable. Even here, however, I shall try to keep my promise to let you see sociologists at work. Taken as a whole, this chapter sets the stage for the rest of the book and offers samples of what sociology is like, and why and how people pursue it.

WHAT IS SOCIOLOGY?

Sociology is one of several related fields known as the **social sciences**. They share the same subject matter: human behavior. They are called *social* sciences because the human is not a solitary beast. Our daily lives intertwine with the lives of others—what we do, even much of what we hope, is influenced by those around us. To study ourselves, we must study our social relations. In fact, as we shall see in Chapter 6, the process by which newborn infants are transformed into competent adults is called *socialization*. Learning to speak, learning to control our impulses, or even learning to play games is learning how to be social.

Despite their common subject matter, there are a number of different social sciences. Psychologists, economists, anthropologists, criminologists, political scientists, and even many historians, as well as sociologists, are social scientists. Divisions among these fields are often hazy. Indeed, sometimes it is impossible to tell to which field a social scientist's work belongs. The field may be determined merely by the university department in which the person is trained or employed. Nevertheless, the following rules of thumb may help you to distinguish sociologists from other social scientists.

Sociologists differ from psychologists because we are not concerned so exclusively with the individual, with what goes on inside people's heads. We are more interested in what goes on *between* people. Sociologists differ from economists by being less exclusively interested in commercial exchanges—we are equally interested in the exchange of intangibles such as love and affection. We differ from anthropologists primarily because the latter specialize in the study of preliterate or primitive human groups, while we are primarily interested in modern industrial societies. And while most criminologists are trained in and employed in sociology departments, they specialize in illegal behavior, while sociologists are interested in the whole range of human behavior. Similarly, political scientists focus on political organization and activity, while sociologists survey all social organizations. Finally, sociologists share with historians an interest in the past but are equally interested in the present and the future.

These contrasts make it evident that sociology is a broader discipline than the other social sciences. In a sense, the specialty of sociologists is generalization: to find the connections that unite the various social sciences into a comprehensive, integrated science of society. When I had to decide which social science to pursue, I chose sociology precisely because of its greater scope and grand aspirations. Moreover, to be a sociologist is to be free to do psychology, economics, anthropology, political science, criminology, or history as the need arises and to not worry about it.

Yet sociologists do have a distinctive subject matter—a turf of their own. Sociologists study the patterns and processes of human social relations. Some of us concentrate on small groups and the patterns and processes of face-to-face interaction between humans. This part of sociology is known as **micro sociology**—*micro* means "small," as in *microscope*. Micro sociologists look at life close up. Others of us concentrate on larger groups, even on whole societies. From this viewpoint the individual is simply one small dot among many dots that help form a larger picture, much as do the dots on a TV screen. This larger-scope sociology is known as **macro sociology** (*macro* means "large"). Macro sociologists attempt to explain the fundamental patterns and processes of large-scale social relations.

As we shall see in Chapters 3 and 4, macro and micro sociology are closely connected, for societies shape the individual and the small group and, in turn, are shaped by them. Suppose sociologists set out to study military battles. Micro sociologists would concentrate on small groups of soldiers, while macro sociologists would concentrate on larger groups, including whole armies. But it is clear that to understand a battle, one would need to know both micro and macro levels of events: how the great masses of troops were assembled and directed and how the troops reacted and fought. Brave troops have been defeated because of a poor plan of battle, and brilliant plans have failed when the troops ran away.

But whether one pursues sociology at the micro or the macro level, the primary focus is not on individuals and individual behavior but on *social behavior*. Since sociologists specialize in studying what goes on between people, the primary subject of sociology is the group. Thus, the true difference between micro and macro sociology is in the size of the groups studied.

GROUPS: THE SOCIOLOGICAL SUBJECT

A **group** consists of two or more persons who maintain a stable pattern of relations over a significant period of time. Some groups, such as a married couple, are tiny. Other groups, such as the workers in a factory, are large. However, not just any gathering of people qualifies as a group in the sociological sense.

In everyday speech we often refer to ten people standing on the corner waiting for the walk light as a "group." But sociologists would call them an **aggregate** of individuals. They have come together only briefly and accidentally. They are not acquainted with one another, and they may not even notice one another. For sociologists, people constitute a group only when they are *united by social relations*. If the ten people waiting for the walk light were all members of the same family or Girl Scout troop, then they would be a group in the sociological sense of the term.

Dyads and triads

The smallest sociological group is the **dyad**: a pair of individuals who engage in social relations. As we shall see in Chapter 3, an analysis of the basic properties of two-person relationships gives sociology the tools for building a theory of human interaction—for explaining how we influence one another and thereby construct and enforce rules governing social life. Much of our behavior is governed by our need to exchange with others, whether we exchange apples or affection. Such exchanges are possible only if we can anticipate how the other person will respond and vice versa.

However, if the dyad is the fundamental building block of sociology, it is not its primary object of

A crowd like this one, gathered in the park on a summer afternoon listening to folk music, is not a group, but an aggregate. Groups are united by social relations, while most of these people are strangers to one another. Notice, however, that within *this aggregate are a number of small groups.*

interest. Human social relations do not consist mainly of isolated pairs, but of multiple relations involving every individual with a number of others. And, as soon as we shift our focus from dyads to social relations involving three or more individuals, some very interesting and complex patterns emerge. As a preview, let's consider **triads**: social relations among three persons.

Triads include not one but three relationships. That is, relationships exist between A and B, B and C, and A and C. Many rules about the behavior of triads have been established. Let's consider two of them.

Transitivity Triads demonstrate the **transitivity** rule governing human relations (Figure 1-1). The rule is simple: Relations among members of a group will tend to be balanced or consistent. This idea is captured by everyday sayings such as "Any friend of yours is a friend of mine," "My enemy's friends are my enemies," "Your enemies are my enemies," and "If you like her, you're no friend of mine." From this it follows that in any triad, if A likes B and B hates C, A will tend to hate C. Or, if A likes B and B likes C, then A will tend to like C. Also, if A hates B and B likes C, A will tend to hate C. Such patterns of relations in a triad are said to be transitive, because

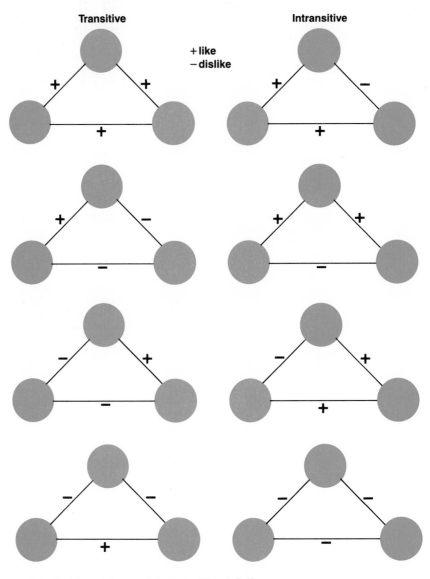

Transitive   **Intransitive**

+ like
− dislike

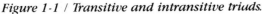

Figure 1-1 / Transitive and intransitive triads.

Relations in a triad are transitive, or balanced, when no two members have opposite or inconsistent relations with the third—when there exists no pair who like one another and have opposite feelings toward the third person. In the four examples on the left, persons who like one another share the same opinion of the third member of the triad—in the top example by liking the third member, in the other three examples by both disliking the third. Triads are intransitive when one member tries to be friends with two who dislike one another, as in the top three examples on the right. Micro sociologists predict that these intransitive triads will tend to break up, because the member who likes both is subject to great pressure to choose between them. The intransitivity of the bottom example on the right is not so obvious, for here all three members dislike one another. The intransitivity arises because of the rule "enemies of my enemies are my friends." In this situation, if the trio remains in contact, two members are apt to begin to like one another because of their mutual dislike of the third, and thus they may form a coalition against the third person.

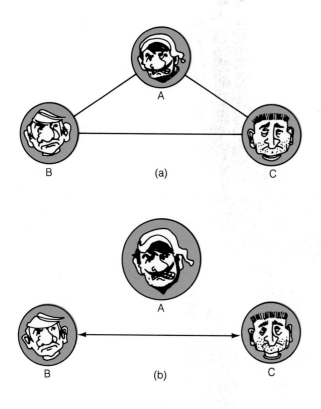

Figure 1-2 / Coalition formation in triads.

In his major work on coalitions in triads, Theodore Caplow (1968) examined relations among three hypothetical smugglers, Ahab, Brutus, and Charlie, who meet on a lonely island to divide their goods. Because they are wicked fellows, they are as willing to cheat one another as to cheat the tax collector. Each is open to a deal to gang up on the third smuggler and steal his goods. In the first condition, each smuggler is of equal fighting ability, as indicated by the size of the circles in diagram (a). When this is the case, it is impossible to predict which pair may form a coalition against the third.

Now let's suppose that Ahab is a real brute, able to beat up either Brutus or Charlie but not quite able to beat up both at the same time (b). Now we can predict that neither Brutus nor Charlie will agree to combine forces with Ahab: If they did, as soon as they helped Ahab beat up the third member, they would then be at the mercy of Ahab, who could always take all of the goods. Therefore, we can predict that Brutus and Charlie will always combine to rob Ahab. In this way they can split Ahab's goods and need not fear being robbed by one another, since they are too evenly matched. Ahab's superiority ensures that he will always end up the victim.

there are no strains on relationships between any pair due to contrary relations with the third person (Heider, 1946; Newcomb, 1953; Davis and Leinhardt, 1972).

Now suppose two members of a triad in which all three persons who had liked one another suddenly have a falling out. For example, suppose A and B get mad at each other while both remain close friends of C. What now exists is an *intransitive* triad, often found in everyday life in what has been called the "eternal triangle." Now when A exchanges with C, B will be resentful and possibly jealous—"Why does my friend like my enemy?" Similarly, when B exchanges with C, A feels betrayed.

Intransitive triads are *unstable* and usually break up. The resentment that A and B direct toward C will force C to drop one or both relationships.

Coalition formation If C breaks off with B and joins A as an enemy of B, we say that A and C have formed a **coalition**: They have combined to oppose

someone else. Now let's introduce power into the triad. Sociologists define power as the ability to get one's way over the opposition of others (see Chapter 9). Many things cause some people to be more powerful than others, but here let us limit our attention to physical strength. If all three members of a triad are of equal physical strength, it is not possible to predict whether C will choose to combine with A or with B. Either choice is equally likely.

However, suppose A is much stronger than either B or C and could beat up either of them, while B and C are about equally matched. Suppose, too, that A is not strong enough to beat up both B and C. We can then predict that B and C will form a coalition (Caplow, 1968). Why? If B combined forces with A, then B would still be at the mercy of A, even though the pair could easily dominate C. The same applies if C combines with A. But if B and C combine, they are safe from A, and neither is risking domination by the other since they are equally strong. Figure 1-2 illustrates the principle of coalition formation.

Transitivity and coalition formation are but two of a multitude of principles governing social relations in small groups. I have discussed them here to offer a sample of what micro sociologists study. However, principles such as these are not limited to the behavior of triads. The intimate connections between micro and macro sociology can be seen if we realize that rules such as those above apply equally well to large groups. To illustrate, let's see how intransitivity and coalition formation shape the internal structure of larger groups.

Networks

All groups consist of social relations among members, whether the group contains three or three thousand members. The patterns of relations among members of a group are often called **social networks**. Ideally, even a large group is transitive, with all members liking one another. However, frequently this is not the case. Some members do not like others, and thus relations inside a group can become intransitive. And just as intransitivity can lead either to the breakup of a triad or to coalition formation, so can it cause people in large groups to readjust their relations. This leads to the formation of internal clusters within the network of the group—clusters composed of persons who like one another and have few friends outside their own cluster. These clusters are often called internal factions or **cliques**. When a pattern of cliques has developed, transitivity is restored: People no longer attempt to remain friends with people who are also friendly with their enemies.

To study the structure of group networks, sociologists often use **sociograms** to chart relationships within a group (see Figure 1-3). For example, a sociologist may ask members of a fourth-grade class, a sorority, or a business office to list the individuals whom they like or admire most in the group (or whom they dislike most). The lines of friendship can then be drawn on a chart. Usually several individuals stand out as "sociometric stars" because they are often chosen as the most liked. If these stars also like one another, then an integrated network exists. People who admire one star will also tend to like

another star as well as group members who like other stars.

For example, suppose George and Mary are the two most popular kids in the fourth grade and also like each other. Then those who like George will also tend to like Mary and the other kids who regard Mary as the star. Many bonds of friendship exist between members, and no clear lines of separation exist within the group.

Intransitivity arises, however, when two stars become enemies—when, in our example, Mary and George suddenly decide they can't stand each other. For then they impose strains between their respective followers just like the strains created in the triad when A and B got mad at each other. And, just as the intransitive triad led to a coalition, so, too, does intransitivity in larger networks produce a choosing up of sides. Such networks display clearly separated patterns of social relations: distinct cliques or factions. When more than two such internal factions exist, coalition formation is likely: Several factions will cooperate against other factions. Here, too, the coalition rule outlined above applies. But, whether or not coalitions form, internal factions always threaten to produce internal conflict, and in some cases they can cause the group to break up.

Primary and secondary groups

Not all groups are of equal importance to their members. For example, we will more willingly withdraw from a group made up of persons working in our office than from one made up of family or intimate friends. This distinction is captured by the notions of primary and secondary groups.

Primary groups are characterized by great intimacy among the members. People in these groups do not merely know one another and interact frequently, but they know one another well and have strong emotional ties. As a result, people gain much of their self-esteem and sense of identity from primary groups—as we shall consider in depth in Chapter 3. For example, when retired athletes report how much they miss belonging to a team, they are telling of the pains of leaving a primary group.

The family is the most common primary group,

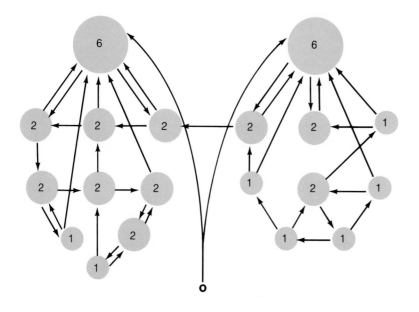

Figure 1-3 / A sociogram of a small group.

Each member of this group was asked to name his or her two best friends. By the use of arrows, the sociogram shows who chose whom. In this group there are two very isolated cliques, each headed by a "star." The numbers show how many times each person was chosen as a best friend. The two stars were chosen six times, while most others were chosen only twice. Only one person reported a best friend in the other clique. One poor soul was chosen by no one and selected the two stars as his or her best friends.

but many other groups can also become so. Indeed, Charles H. Cooley, who coined the term *primary group,* said a group is primary if its members refer to themselves as "we." Primary groups involve "the sort of sympathy and mutual identification for which 'we' is the natural expression" (Cooley, 1909).

Secondary groups consist of less intimate social networks within which people pursue various collective goals but without a powerful sense of belonging. Business organizations, political parties, even model railroad clubs are typically secondary groups. People find it relatively easy to switch from one secondary group to another and refer to themselves and group members as "we" only in a mild sense of the term. However, as we shall see in Chapter 19, primary groups often form *within* secondary groups, which can produce internal strains. For example, a group of close friends within a business

may promote one another to the disadvantage of other employees and perhaps cause the company to operate less efficiently.

Groups, then, are the primary subject matter of sociology. The aim of sociologists is to construct a science of groups, of human social relations. However, not everyone believes that it is possible to achieve a science of social relations.

CAN SOCIOLOGY BE SCIENTIFIC?

Can there really be social *sciences*? Anyone who asks that question is usually comparing the achievements of the physical and natural sciences (such as physics and chemistry) with those of the social sciences.

The family is the most common primary group, characterized by intimate, life-long attachments. In fact, conflicts among family members cause so much anguish because it is so difficult to "quit" belonging—even many divorced couples must remain in close contact because they remain parents.

From this perspective, the social sciences may appear less scientific, since they do not possess as general or powerful theories expressed in precise mathematical form. But this is to mistake scientific achievement for the scientific method.

Science is not a set of discoveries, but a method of discovery. A field is not scientific because of *what* it has achieved, but because of *how* the field is conducted. Science is a *method* by which theories are formulated and then tested against appropriate observations. In Chapters 3 and 4 we shall see what theories are and observe them being tested. There we shall see that sociologists can observe the rules of scientific method as fully as physicists or biologists. If the latter two types of scientists have achieved more potent results, one reason is that they have pursued their research in a truly scientific way far longer than social scientists have. A second reason, in my judgment, is that the social sciences confront a more difficult subject matter than do the natural and physical sciences. The difference can be summed up in a phrase: *Bacteria don't blush.*

STUDYING SELF-AWARE SUBJECTS

Suppose a chemistry teacher regularly demonstrated that, when two harmless chemicals are mixed

Compared with families, people are much less deeply attached to a secondary group like this bellringer's musical society. People are quitting or joining all the time. However, people often will forge primary ties with another member or two—members have even married. Thus, secondary groups are not without close interpersonal bonds: it is simply that the average relationship in secondary groups is less close than is the average in primary groups.

together, they explode. Then one day, just as the demonstration was about to begin, one of the chemicals said to the other, "I'm really getting sick of this. Today, let's not explode. Let's do something different. How about helping me make a huge stink instead?" If this could ever happen, chemistry would be a very different field. However, such things routinely happen in the social sciences. Unlike chemicals, people are able to choose among various possible actions. Moreover, they are self-aware. They often know when someone is looking at them, and, unlike bacteria under a biologist's microscope, people often do blush when they are looked at. Social scientists must overcome the problem of disturbing what they look at—of being misled because people

sometimes act differently when they know they are being observed. While this makes the social sciences difficult, it also makes them fun. People are more interesting than bacteria or isotopes—at least to me. And part of the pleasure of doing sociology is finding ways to keep people from outsmarting your research procedures. A few examples may help demonstrate this point.

Unobtrusive measures

Sociologists don't always need to observe what people do *at the time they are doing it* in order to obtain a good record of what they did. A good deal of human behavior leaves clear traces. When sociologists examine such traces, they need not worry that self-conscious subjects altered their normal behavior.

For example, one sociologist who wanted to know what radio station people really listened to while driving arranged to have auto mechanics note the dial position of radios in the cars that they serviced (Webb, et al., 1966).

Recently, my colleague William Sims Bainbridge and I were interested in geographic patterns in occult and metaphysical beliefs and practices (Bainbridge and Stark, 1980; Stark and Bainbridge, 1985). We might simply have used a national opinion poll to ask people about such beliefs, and in fact we did use Gallup poll results. But we also knew that we could find many traces of such interest that did not depend upon people being truthful.

One such trace was in the *Yellow Pages* under the listing for "Astrologers" (see Figure 1-4). By looking in the *Yellow Pages* of every major city in the United States, we could easily count how many people offered astrological services to the public. By dividing the number of listings for each city by its population, we identified cities with higher and lower rates of professional astrologers—good evidence of the level of belief in astrology existing in each city (see Figure 1-5).

When astrologers took out listings in the *Yellow Pages,* they were not worried that Bainbridge and I were looking. Nor were we looking when people selected an astrologer by consulting the *Yellow Pages*

Figure 1-4 / Computing an unobtrusive measure.

Suppose you wanted to know how the popularity of astrology differed among American cities and regions. One way to find out would be to conduct opinion polls in various parts of the country, asking people if they believed in astrology. That would be very expensive. The results of the polls would also be subject to error if many people were unwilling to admit to strangers that they accept astrology. However, an unobtrusive measure of belief in astrology can be obtained by consulting the Yellow Pages *in the nation's cities. There one can discover the number of astrologers in a given city or area who have a business listing. Below is the "Astrologers" section of the Seattle, Washington,* Yellow Pages *for 1981–82.*

As you can see, there are eighteen separate listings for astrologers in Seattle. By itself, that total isn't very helpful. To compare the figure with those of other cities, population must be taken into account. By dividing the total number of astrologers by the population of the city in which they practice, a rate can be obtained. Notice, however, that one of these listings is not actually in Seattle. The International College of Astrology is in Auburn, so we must eliminate it. (By checking phone exchanges—the first three numbers—it is possible to select those listings in the city being studied, since prefixes have specific geographic boundaries.) You will also notice that several listings have the same phone number. For the sake of accuracy, calls were made to these listings to make sure that they represented several astrologers in a "group practice," not one astrologer using two listings.

By these means we can see that in 1981–82, Seattle had seventeen persons or firms whose astrological practice was sufficiently active to warrant a business listing. Divided by the population of the city, this produces a rate of professional astrologers of thirty-five per one million residents, making Seattle one of the top U.S. cities in terms of astrological interest.

When similar procedures were applied to the Yellow Pages *for the entire nation, regional patterns of astrological interest were charted, as shown in Figure 1-5.*

Astrologers

ADVANCED ASTROLOGICAL SERVICES
Counseling-Specializing In Horary & Comparison Charts-By Appointment Only
15346 Stone N ---------- **364-3198**
American Institute Of Astrology --------- 362-2606
Astrological Counseling 16735 10th NE --- 362-4517
ASTROLOGY CENTER OF THE NORTHWEST
Bookstore-Computer Calculated Horoscopes-Classes-Herbs
522 NE 165th ---------- **363-5313**
ASTROLOGY ET AL
BOOKS—CLASSES—HERBS
Professional Counseling
4728 University Wy NE ----------**524-6365**

5TH ELEMENT THE
Astrology & Tarot
Consultations By Appt.—Books
Open 10-5 Mon thru Fri
7527 Lake City Wy NE ----------**522-4535**

Green Jeff 4728 University Wy NE --------**524-6365**
HUGHES DOROTHY B 2322 6th------**622-7866**
INTERNATIONAL COLLEGE OF ASTROLOGY
Horoscopes By Appointment Or Mail
Astrology Home Courses-Books
4248 A Southeast Auburn ---------**833-2361**
Jinni --------------------------------**524-3114**
Meehan Rosalie M
Rosalie M Meehan-Room 819
1932 1st----------**622-4770**
Moy Barbara Assoc 1331 3d-------------**625-0575**
MYRON & CORN
Bruce I Myron
Johanna E – Savannah Corn
By Appointment-Bank Cards Accepted
Smith Tower ----------**622-2554**
Nalbandian Margaret
4728 University Wy NE ----------**524-6365**
REFLECTING POND
Books For Creative Living
Astrological Services By
David Vikaso Pond
6211 Roosevelt Wy NE ----------**527-4333**

ROBERTSON MARC & ASSOCIATES
----------**324-3480**
Search Astrology And The Arts ----------**523-1970**
Wickenburg Joanne ----------**523-1970**

and thereby insured that the listings be continued.

Measures of activity made in this way are called **unobtrusive measures**. They gain information without disturbing the objects of the research.

Of course, sociologists do not rely on traces of unobserved behavior alone. Most of the time when we examine what people believe and do, they know we are looking. In fact, we often ask them to tell us what we want to know. We are able to trust such data because a great deal of effort has gone into checking to see if they are accurate and into finding ways to increase their accuracy.

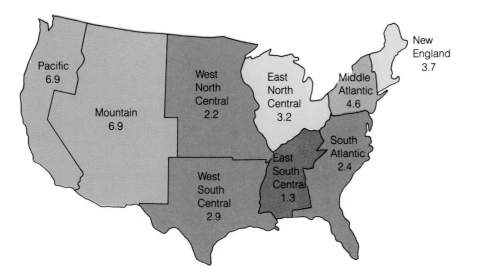

*Figure 1-5 / **Regional rates of astrologers listed in the** Yellow **Pages.***

The numbers indicate the professional astrologers per million population in metropolitan areas. Professional astrologers are much more prevalent in the western United States than elsewhere in the country. In Chapter 13, we shall see that this same pattern applies to many measures of religious and mystical novelty, both now and at the turn of the century. We shall also see why this marked regional pattern exists.

Validation

To ensure that they are getting accurate information, sociologists frequently conduct **validation research**. One way to assess validity is to test data against some independent standard of accuracy.

For example, it is often possible to obtain data known to be accurate, but it can be expensive and difficult to do so. We could determine the exact ages of a sample of American adults by checking official documents (driver's licenses, birth records, and the like), but it is much cheaper simply to ask them their age. To make sure that this information is accurate, we can periodically test the information so obtained by checking it against official records. If what people tell us is close enough to the information obtained when we check up, we feel confident in the information that is not checked. In this case, studies found that people gave more accurate answers when they were asked their year of birth rather than their age. So that's how we usually ask the question now.

In Chapter 7 we shall examine the results of many studies of delinquency. Most of these studies are based on *self-reports*. That is, samples of teenagers were interviewed or asked to fill out questionnaires, and some of the questions pertained to various illegal acts: "Have you ever stolen things from a store?" "How often have you done this?" "When was the most recent time you did this?"

The conclusions drawn from such studies obviously depend upon the validity of people's answers. Since a lot of people may lie, the accuracy of self-reports on delinquency has repeatedly been subjected to stringent validity checks. For example, in his delinquency study Travis Hirschi (1969) asked boys in Richmond, California, whether they had ever been picked up by the police. Later he checked every boy out through the police identification bureaus in the area. He found that only a tiny number of the boys actually having a juvenile record had denied being picked up. Other sociologists have interviewed teenagers about their delinquency and then

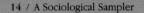

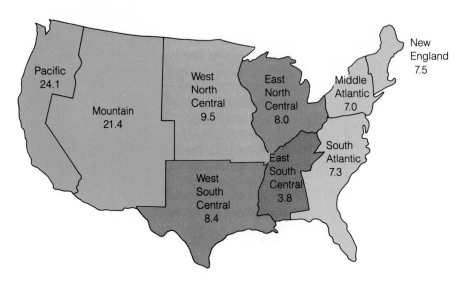

*Figure 1-6 / **Validating the astrologer rates.***

Fate *magazine subscribers per million population are shown. The astrology rates based on listings in the* Yellow Pages *were used as an unobtrusive measure of interest in novel religious and mystical beliefs and practices. A second measure of such interest can be found in the subscription lists for* Fate *magazine, the nation's leading periodical devoted to mystical and occult phenomena. With the number of* Fate *subscribers in each state, regional rates could be computed. Notice how closely they correspond with the regional rates for astrologers—again the Mountain and Pacific regions tower over the others. When a variety of measures obtained independently show the same thing, our confidence in the validity of each is greatly increased.*

reinterviewed them with a lie detector. They also found the initial interview data to be very accurate (Clark and Tifft, 1966).

Recently a huge test was made of the validity of a number of different self-report measures of delinquency. In this test, answers from these measures were checked against official police and court records, against answers given while hooked to a lie detector, and even against reports from each person's friends. Again, the self-report data were found to be valid (Hindelang, Hirschi, and Weis, 1981).

A second way to assess the validity of sociological data is to compare results when different measures are used. For example, in our research on occultism, Bainbridge and I found very high agreement between the *Yellow Pages* data on astrologers, *Fate* magazine subscribers (see Figure 1-6), and many similar measures (including the results of public opinion polls). Any questions raised about the validity of any one of our measures lose their force when various measures collected in various ways all tell the same story.

So far this chapter has tried to explain something about what sociology is and how it is done. Now it is time to see someone *do* some sociology. The following example was selected for several reasons. First, it illustrates the connections between micro and macro sociology. Second, it shows how difficult problems of research can be overcome by originality and reflection. Third, it deals with issues concerning the quality of interpersonal relations, of networks, in modern societies—issues that will be central throughout this book. Finally, it may let you see why I think sociology is not only interesting but also fun.

IT'S A SMALL WORLD: STUDYING NETWORKS

 As we shall see in Chapter 18, cities are rather new in human history, large cities are very new, and urban societies—in which the majority of people live in cities rather than rural areas—did not exist until this century. Rapid social change always causes alarm, as people worry about whether the changes will be harmful. For instance, during the nineteenth century, cities grew rapidly and huge numbers of people migrated from rural areas, heralding the shift to urban societies. Many people became greatly concerned that city life would destroy human relations and make people miserable. Most social critics believed that urban life caused people to become lost in a sea of strangers; they believed that modern cities were too big, too crowded, and too unsettled to allow individuals to form and maintain intimate ties (Wirth, 1938). Since sociologists regard interpersonal attachments as the basic structure of social life, they understandably became very alarmed about the shift to city living. And, by the 1940s, the belief that people in cities lack attachments was elaborated into what were called *mass society theories.*

Mass society theories

Mass society theories were used to explain a great many social problems, from crime, suicide, divorce, and alcoholism to the success of radical political movements such as the Nazi and Communist Parties (see Chapters 18 and 20).

But no sooner had social scientists largely accepted mass society theories than these theories came under serious criticism. Social scientists increasingly realized that the image of city people as lonely, isolated social atoms did not square with sociologists' own personal experience of city life. These sociologists still visited relatives frequently and had many close friends. Maybe most city people did.

Soon research evidence of many kinds began to support the personal experience of sociologists. For example, the first studies of political behavior, based on public opinion polls, revealed that people did not fit the image of isolated individuals vulnerable to propaganda appeals through the mass media. Instead, people placed little importance on the media in reporting how they decided how to vote—most said they made up their minds through discussions with family and friends (Lazarsfeld et al., 1948; Berelson et al., 1954). But these were precisely the kinds of ties that urban Americans were supposed to lack. As research continued, it became obvious that a vast majority of the people living in the largest cities had many stable and intimate ties to family and friends (Fischer, 1976). In this sense, at least, mass society theories were based on a faulty perception; the rise of cities had not overwhelmed human relations.

At this point, those dedicated to mass society theories revised their views. They admitted that most people were still linked to a group of intimate friends, but they argued that these groups were isolated: They were but islands of intimacy adrift in an ocean of strangers. That is, whereas rural villages were united by links of intimacy that connected the whole community, in modern cities people were connected only to fragments of the overall community, and each of these fragments was isolated. The members of these groups were overwhelmed by a sense of powerlessness and anonymity. Thus, mass society theories were revised to accommodate contrary research findings (Kornhauser, 1959).

Obviously, mass society theorists were correct in arguing that an individual can know every inhabitant in a village of 500 but not every resident in a city of 500,000. But many sociologists began to wonder whether that really meant that cities were composed of large numbers of small, isolated groups. Perhaps these groups were not closed and isolated but were interlocking, so that most people were connected to *chains of attachments* indirectly linking them to huge numbers of other individuals. The issue then became: Are cities collections of small, closed networks of intimacy, or are they huge chains connecting the community as a whole?

At first, this seemed a very difficult question to assess by research, but eventually the means to settle the issue arose from a common everyday experience. Time and again we meet a total stranger only to discover after some conversation that we

Sociologists now recognize that even in the largest modern cities most people do not experience daily living as a faceless member of a mass of strangers. Like these men playing checkers in a park in New York City, most people spend most of their time surrounded by family, friends, neighbors, co-workers, and others with whom they maintain long-term patterns of interaction.

have a good friend in common. Travelers frequently tell of meeting someone far from home who turns out to be a close friend or relative of one of their close friends. This common observation from everyday life prompted Stanley Milgram (1967) to conduct his famous "small world" research.

Milgram's method

Milgram knew how often complete strangers discover that they have mutual friends and acquaintances. Therefore, he suggested that American society more closely resembled one big friendship network than a multitude of isolated subgroups. But

how could he see whether or not this was true? He couldn't simply obtain a list of the friends of every American and then check all these lists for duplicated names. Not even the most powerful computers could deal with that task, even if it were possible to get an accurate list from every citizen. But, he reasoned, what if he selected individuals at random in various parts of the country and tried to find out if they were in fact linked into a common friendship chain? If so, how far apart on that chain are most people?

From this starting point, Milgram invented an extremely clever and simple research method—and with a total budget of only $680. First, he selected a number of individuals from throughout the United States to serve as receivers. Next, he selected a number of other individuals from throughout the United

States to act as senders. Then, he prepared letters addressed to the receivers that he distributed to the senders. However, instead of simply asking the senders to mail the letters to the addressee, he told each sender to mail the letter to someone he or she knew personally ("on a first-name basis") who might know the receiver. Each sender was to tell these personal acquaintances that if they didn't know the receiver, they should send the letter on to someone else whom *they* personally knew who might know the receiver.

Arrangements were made to record each person through whom a letter was passed on its way to each receiver. Since senders and receivers had been selected at random in various parts of the country, there was no reason to suppose that any sender had heard of any receiver before being given the letter. What Milgram's study was designed to determine was whether most senders did belong to a chain of friendships that led to the receivers; that is, did the letters ever reach their destination? And, if they did, how many links between most senders and receivers existed along this friendship chain?

The results powerfully supported Milgram's belief that it is a small world. Not counting those letters that were not received because an intermediary did not send it on, the vast majority of the letters did reach their designated receiver. Moreover, it took an average of only *five* links on the friendship chain for a letter to get from sender to receiver. How did people go about getting the letters to the receivers? In the same way that strangers uncover mutual friends. If a sender in California, for example, had a letter addressed to someone in New Hampshire, he or she usually proceeded by asking, "Who do I know in New Hampshire?" If the sender knew someone there, he or she sent the letter on to them, much as a stranger learning that another stranger is from New Hampshire might ask, "Do you know my friend Charlie Adams? He lives in Dover, New Hampshire." Senders who didn't know someone in the city or state in which the receiver lived sent the letter to a friend who they thought might have friends in that area. In this fashion, letters were transmitted from friend to friend and thus left a recorded trail of the connections that tie Americans to one another.

While Milgram's study dealt another severe blow to mass society theories, their underlying thesis—that humans lacking intimate ties to others are subject to all manner of problems—remains a central tenet of modern sociology. Although mass society theorists incorrectly assumed that city life had left most people without adequate social relations, the fact remains that some people in modern societies are unattached and isolated. In Chapters 7 and 18, we shall see the serious consequences resulting from a lack of attachment. Here, I have attempted only to offer a glimpse of good sociology and how and why it was done—to show how scientific procedures are used to test our beliefs. In fact, the purpose of scientific research is to test what we believe about the world, especially scientific theories about how the world works.

BIAS

As we shall see in Part Two, the essence of the scientific method is systematic skepticism. Nothing is to be taken for granted. Every step of logic in an argument and every set of facts produced by research are to be tested, checked, and retested. Moreover, the proper approach to research is to try to *disprove* those things that the researcher actually believes to be true.

Scientists must be willing to lay their opinions and beliefs on the line: to subject them to rigorous tests and accept the test results. However, that is not to say that scientists must free themselves from their personal biases, commitments, or hopes in order to function properly. The image of scientists as neutral, unemotional beings, like Mr. Spock in *Star Trek,* is romantic nonsense. All human beings are inescapably biased; we all have deep personal beliefs. The scientific method does not aim to strip scientists of their fundamental humanity or to make them into computers, but to prevent our personal biases from distorting our work. The scientific method consists of rules that, if followed, lead us to the facts, regardless of what we might hope or believe the facts to be. Some of the most important moments in scientific progress have occurred when research turned up results very different from those expected by the researchers.

It would be naive to suggest that scientists never distort their findings or cheat in an effort to support their own convictions. But the public nature of science weakens this temptation and eventually exposes those who cannot overcome their biases. Scientists must report not only what they found but also how and where they found it. This lets others check the results and even repeat the research to see if they obtain the same results.

Personal bias is possibly a more serious problem for social than for natural and physical scientists. Few of us grow up with deep convictions about what color a shark's liver ought to be or about the proper behavior for atomic particles. But we all grow up with many firm beliefs about what people are like and how they ought to behave. Hence, social scientists have to try harder to lay their beliefs aside and look carefully at how things really are.

But this, too, offers some advantages. Social scientists are intimately familiar with their fundamental subject matter: people. In an important sense, every competent human being is something of a social scientist. If we were not very good at predicting one another's behavior, social life would be impossible. We would not dare to be in contact with one another if we did not have relatively accurate notions about what makes people tick. Thus, students in introductory sociology have a head start on students taking their first course in biochemistry.

Then why aren't the social sciences far more advanced than sciences such as chemistry and physics? The answer is that common sense and everyday experience take us only so far in understanding human relations. To go further, science is required. And we have applied scientific procedures to human relations for only a relatively short time.

THE ORIGINS OF SOCIOLOGY

Even primitive tribes have understood a great deal about human behavior and the structures and processes governing social life. Yet the physical and natural sciences began centuries before anyone attempted to pursue the social sciences.

It is impossible to date precisely when the social

Adam Smith.

sciences began. Some trace their origins to philosophy and thus back to the Middle Ages or even ancient Greece. But simply to wonder about how social life operates or to assert doctrines about human nature is not social science. Science involves two essential elements. First, its explanations must take the form of *theories,* a term we shall explore fully in Chapter 3. Second, theories must be the object of *testing by systematic research.*

We have already looked at sociologists attempting to use research to discover if certain statements about social life are correct. In Chapters 3 and 4 we shall examine research procedures in depth and see the connection between theories and research. Here, I simply want to point out that philosophers such as the ancient Greek Plato did not really formulate social theories, nor did they, or anyone else at that time, attempt to do social research. For these reasons I regard the economist Adam Smith as the first real social scientist. In his great book *The Wealth of Nations,* published in 1776, he attempted to state formal theories about economic behavior and to use data to test his theories. For this reason, economists regard Smith as the founder of the science of economics (Heilbroner, 1961).

But it was still another century before the other

Wilhelm Wundt.

W. E. B. DuBois.

social sciences emerged. For example, it was not until 1879 that Wilhelm Wundt started the first laboratory devoted to psychological research in Germany. At about this same time, Cesare Lombroso, an Italian physician, began to collect observations on convicts and founded modern criminology. In 1880, Karl Marx made one of the first efforts to conduct an opinion survey in England by distributing 25,000 questionnaires to workers (although hardly any were filled out and returned). In the United States in 1898, W. E. B. Du Bois, one of the nation's leading black intellectuals, became the first person to conduct a systematic field study of urban life.

Sociology is so new that no one even suggested such a field until the French philosopher Auguste Comte did so in the 1830s. For a long time sociology remained but a suggestion, for although Comte urged others to do sociology, he never got around to doing any himself. Virtually no one else did either, until the twentieth century. The first department of sociology in the United States was opened at the University of Chicago in 1892, and only slowly did other major universities follow suit. Harvard did not have a sociology department until 1930, Berkeley and Johns Hopkins did not until the 1950s.

Despite this history, sociology is dominated by

Americans: A substantial majority of the world's sociologists were educated in the United States, and most live and work here, too. Still, only a few thousand Americans call themselves sociologists, and perhaps no more than two thousand people regularly attempt to construct sociological theories or do sociological research. Little wonder, then, that a field that is only a hundred years old and pursued by a small band of scholars cannot yet match the achievements of much older and larger sciences such as physics and chemistry. Nevertheless, much has been achieved— as will be evident as you read this book.

I find it very attractive and exciting to take part in a new, small field. There is so much to be done that new things happen all the time. Furthermore, it is very satisfying to be able to meet and know a substantial proportion of those active in the field. In fact, it is only because sociology is a small, intimate field that I could attempt to write an introductory book that views the subject from backstage.

While I do not trace the origins of modern social sciences back to early philosophers, a very fundamental philosophical issue long delayed the development of the social sciences. It is an issue that lingers still and that often troubles students. But in reality it is a nonissue based on illogic.

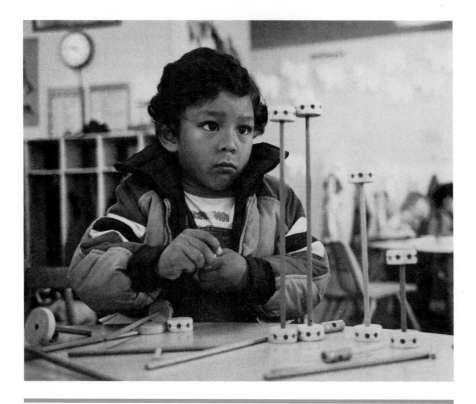

Choosing is the essential feature of human existence. Whether we are building with tinker toys or composing music, throughout our lives we attempt to make good choices and to learn from our mistakes.

FREE WILL AND SOCIAL SCIENCE

For many centuries a major dispute in theology concerned individual responsibility. According to the doctrine of religious determinism (or fatalism), all human actions are preordained, determined by the gods or God; humans are helpless to alter their fates. But, if this were so, how could humans be asked to observe moral codes? If our actions are not ours to choose, how can we be blamed for our evil deeds? Early Christian theologians dealt with this problem by declaring that each individual possesses **free will**. God did make the world and create humans, they argued, but He did not create robots required to do His bidding. Instead, He gave humans the capacity to choose freely among alternatives, and He can

therefore reward those who choose good and condemn those who choose evil.

This was a very powerful religious idea. God was no longer to be regarded as capricious, unjust, and terrible—as He must be so long as He is responsible for what we do, whether good or evil. Instead, it was possible to conceive of a God of mercy, justice, and absolute virtue—a God who gave humans life and choice and asked only virtue in return.

But what does the doctrine of free will have to do with social science? It mistakenly led to the conclusion that because humans possess free will, it is impossible to construct scientific theories to predict and explain their behavior! Thus, it was assumed that if it were possible to achieve social science, then humans must not possess free will; if their behavior is lawful and predictable, then it is inescapable and preordained. If we can predict who will commit crimes, then criminals can't choose good over evil and therefore bear no personal responsibility for their deeds.

In fact, social scientists have sometimes echoed this view, suggesting, for example, that there are no "bad" people in prison, only "sick" people. But, as we shall see in Chapters 7 and 8, sociological theories of crime do not assume that criminals have no choices. Instead, they concentrate on how different people have a different basis for making choices and different alternatives from which to choose. This is contrary to an image of human robots programmed to steal and kill.

Similarly, the first assumption of virtually all social science theories is the same: Humans possess the ability to reason and therefore to select among different lines of action. Social science proceeds from this starting point by postulating that the choices people make can be predicted and explained by assuming that they will *attempt* to do the most reasonable thing, given their circumstances, information, and preferences. That is, people will seek to do things they find rewarding and to avoid things they find unrewarding or costly. In Chapter 3 we shall see how this simple assumption about human behavior quickly leads to explanations of why and how codes of morality come to exist and why these, in turn, shape individual calculations about what choices are rewarding. Here, let us concentrate on the fact that it is only because people's choices are predictable that it is possible to claim that they have free will.

If people's behavior is not predictable, it must be random. That is, if knowledge of their past actions and their present situation tells us nothing about what people will do next, then the human mind does not reason, but operates like a slot machine or a pair of dice. For only then can there be no consistent patterns between past and future behavior, no link between circumstance and action. Such people would indeed be unpredictable and would frustrate all attempts at social science. But such people would not be human. And surely they could not be judged for their acts or be said to possess free will, for they would have no capacity to choose and no reasoning power at all.

Let's approach this matter in another way. Suppose I set up a money store and offered to sell gen-uine $20 bills for 35¢ each. As soon as people made sure that there was no hidden gimmick, that they really could buy money from me at a huge discount, I'm sure I would have more customers than I could handle. When I predict that people will opt for a good deal, I am not reducing them to predetermined robots lacking the power of choice. I am merely saying that by assuming people can select reasonable choices, it is often very easy to predict what they will choose to do.

Free will is the essential assumption of social science. We do not assume that humans are puppets, but that they are reasoning, feeling organisms who learn from experience, who respond to the world around them, who have the power to love, hope, dream, and plan. The goal of social science is to understand why and how humans have these capacities. Moreover, it is because humans can include the findings of social science in making their choices that social science is worthwhile. Social science is not dehumanizing. Rather, it is in some ways the most humanizing of disciplines—it asks what the nature of humanity is and how human life can be enhanced.

CONCLUSION

The purpose of this book is to introduce sociology not simply as a subject but as an activity. In letting you see what sociologists do, I hope to convey more effectively what we know, but I also hope to show why and how we go about our trade. In this way I hope to enlist some of you to do sociology.

This chapter has attempted to lay an introductory basis for the chapters to come and to engage your interest and curiosity: to serve as an attractive invitation to the rest of the book. Rather than teaching you a first lesson in sociology, it was designed to offer sample previews of what is to come, just as TV previews are meant to encourage you to tune in a new show.

I know very well that not every part of every chapter or even some whole chapters will arouse your interest or stir your imagination. That is no surprise.

Although every topic included in this book is of primary interest to some group of sociologists, probably no professional sociologist is especially interested in *all* of these topics. To be candid, I'm less interested in some of them than in others. However, since this book is an introduction to the whole field of sociology, it must cover all active topics in the field. In addition, it is important that you have a chance to sample and explore all of these topics, but it is not necessary that you find each topic of special interest. Any one of the chapters that follow contains enough important, unsolved problems to provide you with a life's work. Indeed, except for Chapter 2, every chapter covers an area of sociology to which any major department of sociology offers at least one whole course and sometimes two, three, or even four advanced courses.

In a sense, then, this book is a sociological sampler whose aim is to survey what sociologists do. In this way you can discover for yourself what kind of sociology most appeals to you.

Finally, I have asked you, as a reader of this book, to explore sociology with me. Although we probably will never meet, we nevertheless will spend a good deal of time together over the next several months. I have made a serious effort to let our author–reader interaction be more intimate than is usual in college textbooks. I want you to share in the fun I have in being a sociologist and telling you about it. For this reason, from time to time I let you look over my shoulder as I do some sociology. Hence, while many of my studies are reported in other introductory textbooks, my work will receive more space in this one. Since I am presuming to tell you what sociology is and how it is done, it seems fair to let you see for yourself what kind of sociologist I am. But I have also chosen to let you watch me work because it was by doing these studies that I truly became a sociologist. Letting them see my work is the most effective way I have found to reveal to my students what being a sociologist means to me.

Review glossary

Sociology The scientific study of the patterns and processes of human social relations. (p. 3)

Social sciences Those scientific fields devoted to the study of human behavior, including sociology, psychology, economics, political science, anthropology, criminology, and some branches of history. (p. 3)

Micro sociology The study of small groups and of face-to-face interaction among humans. (p. 4)

Macro sociology The study of large groups and even of whole societies. (p. 4)

Group Two or more persons who maintain a stable pattern of social relations over a significant period of time. (p. 4)

Aggregate A collection of people lacking social relations; for example, pedestrians waiting for a green light. (p. 4)

Dyad The smallest possible group, consisting of only two people. (p. 4)

Triads Groups with three members. (p. 5)

Transitivity A group property that exists when relationships among members of a group are balanced in such a way that no two people when paired disagree in their feelings toward other group members. That is, the two people in all pairs of friends either both like or both dislike other group members. (p. 5)

Coalition What is formed when two or more persons join forces to oppose someone else. (p. 7)

Social networks Patterns of relationships among members of a group. (p. 8)

Cliques Factions within a group; groups within a group. (p. 8)

Sociograms Charts showing the social networks within a group. (p. 8)

Primary groups Groups whose members have close and intimate relations with one another. (p. 8)

Secondary groups Groups whose members have only limited emotional attachments to one another. (p. 9)

Science A method through which theories (or explanations) are tested and refined on the basis of objectively and carefully collected observations. (p. 10)

Unobtrusive measures Techniques used to measure behavior in such a way as to not disturb the behavior of the subjects. (p. 12)

Validation research Studies conducted to determine whether particular measures used in research are accurate. (p. 13)

Mass society theories Attempts to explain many social problems, such as suicide and divorce, as the result of a breakdown in social relations caused by a shift from rural and village life to life in large cities. People who lack attachments to others are, in fact, more prone to suicide, alcoholism, divorce, and criminality, but the prediction that most people in big cities would show a lack of attachments has turned out to be false. (p. 15)

Free will The philosophical and theological doctrine that humans possess the capacity for choosing among alternatives and, therefore, can be held responsible for the choices they make. (p. 20)

Suggested readings

Berger, Peter L. *Invitation to Sociology*. New York: Doubleday, 1963.

Caplow, Theodore. *Two Against One: Coalitions in Triads*. Englewood Cliffs: Prentice-Hall, 1968.

Homans, George C. *The Nature of Social Science*. New York: Harcourt, Brace & World (Harbinger Books), 1967.

Collins, Randall, and Michael Makowsky. *The Discovery of Society*. New York: Random House, 1978.

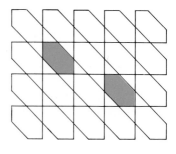

■ The starting point of all sciences is classification. For example, chemists have classified elements with similar atomic structure into the groups we see in the periodic table of the elements. In biology, all living organisms are classified into species.

This scientific classification is based on concepts. **Concepts** are names used to identify some set or class of things that are said to be alike. For example, whenever biologists encounter an animal that is warmblooded, gives birth to living offspring (as opposed to laying eggs, for example), and suckles its young, they agree that this animal is a member of the class called mammals. The word *mammal* refers to an important biological concept.

Scientific concepts are **abstractions**; that is, they are ideas, not things. The concept of mammal is separate from the specific animals described by this concept. We can see animals that belong to the class called mammals, but we cannot see or touch the concept of mammal—it exists only in our minds. Thus, the concept of mammal includes all animals having certain characteristics, including all that ever existed, now exist, will exist, or could exist.

Concepts allow us to take the world apart and to classify the various pieces. Because each concept is an abstraction, it can be used to group together a huge array of things that may have superficial differences. For example, no two mice are the same, but each is a mammal. Dogs are very different from cats, but each is a mammal. Concepts permit us to simplify the world by taking it apart and sorting it out.

Concepts are the building blocks of any science and serve as a common vocabulary. That is why introductory textbooks usually begin by explain-

Using Sociological Concepts:
A Comparative Study of Ethnic Mobility

ing and defining concepts: to provide students with a sufficient vocabulary so that they can follow discussions containing specialized terminology. And that is the purpose of this chapter: to provide readers with a working vocabulary of key sociological concepts.

However, it is very boring to memorize a list of concepts, and even sociologists don't sit around running a list of concepts through their minds. Concepts are not meant to be recited but to be used; and, of course, using them is the best way to learn them. ■

Despite the fact that this question is used as a vehicle for explaining basic sociological concepts, the chapter is not merely an exercise in learning concepts. You will also investigate a sociological question of genuine concern, as it has been pursued by real sociologists, and you will examine the best and latest answers that these sociologists have been able to uncover. By the end of the chapter you will have a working sociological vocabulary, know some significant sociology, and be able to judge for yourself whether sociologists are up to anything worthwhile.

CHAPTER PREVIEW

This chapter introduces many of the major concepts of sociology as it analyzes an important sociological question: Why did two groups of immigrants to the United States achieve economic and social success at such different rates?

In the late nineteenth century, large numbers of Jews and Italians immigrated to the United States. Members of both groups were very poor when they arrived, and both groups faced considerable hostility from groups that had been in America longer. Both Jews and Italians ultimately rose from poverty to achieve economic equality and social acceptance, but Jews achieved this much faster than Italians. Why? As you will see, the answers to this question shed light on the present plight and probable fate of disadvantaged racial and ethnic minorities in the United States today.

SOCIETY AND CULTURE

President Franklin Delano Roosevelt once shocked a convention of the Daughters of the American Revolution by greeting them as "fellow immigrants." Despite the fact that the United States is a nation of immigrants, descendants of some groups who arrived here early like to think of themselves as true Americans and to dismiss as "foreigners" groups who immigrated later. In this chapter we shall analyze the American experience of two groups—Jews and Italians—who were relative latecomers to the United States. In order to do so, we must first clarify the distinction between two fundamental sociological concepts: society and culture.

As the discussion of these two concepts unfolds, you will see that regarding them as two distinct parts of social life is somewhat artificial. Society and culture never exist separately in the real world—they are rather like opposite sides of the same coin. However, as the chapter progresses, you will see that distinguishing between these two concepts helps us explain the phenomena we are studying. And that, of course, is the whole point of taking things apart.

The concept of society

Sociologists often use the terms *society* and *nation* interchangeably. However, not all nations are societies, and not all societies are nations. A better definition of **society** is a group of people who are united by social relationships. Since a society often contains many such groups, the term must also refer to a group that is relatively self-sufficient and independent—a distinct social boundary should set off members of one society from all persons and groups. Most people know which society they belong to. Furthermore, societies tend to occupy a definite physical location. Finally, most societies have existed for a relatively long time—they do not spring up overnight (Hoult, 1969).

Almost every nation in the world today meets this definition of society. Some do not, however. In some nations bitter conflicts exist because two or more societies are contained within their political boundaries. The Civil War showed that the United States was not a single society in the mid-nineteenth century, and current conflicts between French- and English-speaking persons in Canada challenge the notion of a single society there. Conversely, at times several nations have constituted a single society. Early-nineteenth-century maps show that the areas now comprising Germany and Italy were dozens of independent states. The ease with which they later merged into nations suggests that they may have been parts of a larger society long before their union.

Despite exceptions such as these, sociologists regard most modern nations as societies. However, sociologists also regard most primitive tribal groups as distinct societies. Societies can thus come in many sizes, from millions of members to as few as several dozen. The key is to look for relatively self-contained and self-sufficient human groups that are united by social relationships—relationships that

make possible coordinated activities such as earning a living and fighting a war.

In 1400, the area that is today the United States was occupied by many societies: The social and geographic boundaries between Indian tribes were rather clear-cut. Contact between the tribes was limited, and each tribe pretty much went its own way. Despite their small size, separate tribes were separate societies.

In America today, several states, such as Texas and California, are larger than many nations. These two states are each united internally by complex social relationships. However, the states' resemblance to societies ends there. Neither Texas nor California is very self-sufficient—what happens in each state is influenced greatly by what happens elsewhere in the nation. Citizens of Texas and California are closely connected to citizens of other states by bonds of family, friendship, business, and a sense of common destiny. Furthermore, Americans as a whole are bound together by a common *culture*. Indeed, all societies can be characterized on the basis of a distinctive culture.

The concept of culture

People frequently move from one society to another, and what happens to them helps us to see the distinction between society and culture. During the nineteenth century, millions of people left their homelands and came to the United States. Some of them adjusted to life in America very easily. Those who came here from England, for example, found a way of life that was very familiar. But others had to make much greater adjustments, such as learning a new language and adopting many new customs.

When we notice the problems that some immigrants have in adjusting to life in a new country, we are recognizing the fact that every society possesses a *culture*. While society is a group of people united by social relationships, their culture is their way of life. What separates Mexico from the United States, for example, is not just a political boundary. Americans and Mexicans speak different languages, eat different foods, wear different kinds of clothes,

Women taking medical examinations at Ellis Island, the reception station in New York Harbor through which most immigrants passed at the turn of the century. Looking at these women it is obvious that they are not simply entering a new society, but that they are bringing with them a way of life, a culture, that is quite different from that of the two American women performing the examinations.

observe different customs, hold different beliefs, and differ in many other ways. In sum, we can say that Mexico and the United States have different cultures.

If *society* is often synonymous with *nation, culture* is often synonymous with *civilization.* **Culture** is the complex pattern of living that humans have developed that they pass on from one generation to the next. Culture, then, is a very broad concept. While sociologists use the concept of society to identify people according to their relationships with one another and their independence from others, they use the concept of culture to identify people according to what they believe, what they do, what they know, and how they act: In short, everything that humans learn is culture. Culture can also pertain to

the various materials and objects that people learn to use. That is, *technology*, whether it be simple bows and arrows or computers, is as much a mental as a physical phenomenon. It is human knowledge that turns a stick and a string into a bow or that makes it possible to flake stones to serve as arrowheads. Technology does not exist naturally—it is created. A stick is not a club until a human picks it up and hits things with it. To the ant, a statue is only another piece of rock.

As a human creation, culture is strictly a product of human society. Every society is characterized by its culture—its distinctive way of life. Because different societies have different cultures, conflicts between societies arise from cultural differences:

What is the true religion? What is the proper form of government? Some conflicts over culture occur within societies and may be so severe as to threaten the continued existence of the society.

PATTERNS OF INTERGROUP RELATIONS

Toward the end of the nineteenth century, profound conflicts developed in the United States due to immigration. These problems arose because these new waves of immigrants came from societies whose cultures were markedly different from American culture at that time.

The earliest settlers of the United States were primarily English-speaking Protestants, and they brought their cultural heritage with them from Great Britain. Most immigrants were Protestants from Britain until 1820, when the majority of immigrants began to come from northern and western Europe, such as from Germany, Holland, and Scandinavia. However, their native cultures were similar in many ways to those of Britain and the United States. And most of these new immigrants were also Protestants. Although they had a somewhat more difficult time adjusting to American culture than did British immigrants, this second group still assimilated into American culture with relative ease.

Assimilation

The term **assimilation** refers to the process of forsaking one's native culture and adopting another. Usually the term is applied when persons adjust to new surroundings by adopting the prevailing culture as their own. For example, to be fully assimilated into American society and culture, a group of German immigrants had to come to America, learn to speak English, substitute American customs, dress, and food for German, come to regard themselves as Americans, and be accepted as Americans. Perhaps it is useful to think of assimilation in terms of

fitting into, or even disappearing into, a new culture.

Until the middle of the nineteenth century, non-English immigrants quickly became fully assimilated into American society. As a result, people began to speak of the United States as the "Great Melting Pot" in which many different cultural heritages were blended into a common culture. This notion of America persisted long after it should have become obvious that not all newcomers were being fully assimilated.

The first major signs* that the melting pot was failing to "Americanize" immigrants occurred with the first waves of Irish immigrants. They were fleeing the terrible starvation caused by the "potato famine" of 1845–46, which led to at least a million deaths in Ireland. The Irish spoke English, and in many ways their culture was similar to the culture in America. However, unlike most earlier immigrants, the Irish were Roman Catholics. For centuries, religious differences sparked conflict between the Irish and the English, and the Irish suffered under repressive and exploitative English rule. This religious conflict found fertile soil in the United States. The arrival of millions of Irish immigrants after the mid-1840s caused an outbreak of anti-Catholic anxiety in the United States, and the Irish in America found themselves the targets of prejudice and discrimination.

Prejudice and discrimination

Prejudice refers to negative or hostile attitudes toward a group; people become the objects of hatred,

---

*We shall not consider here the problems that black Americans have encountered in assimilation. They were not immigrants, since they were brought to America against their will. Although the institution of slavery prevented the social assimilation of blacks, blacks rapidly became culturally assimilated long before the Civil War ended slavery. As we shall see in Chapter 11, even by the time of the American Revolution most blacks in America were native born. They soon forgot their native languages, spoke only English, and rapidly accepted Christianity (today church membership is somewhat higher among black than among white Americans). In addition, blacks soon lost contact with most of their original African culture. Indeed, the rediscovery of their original culture—their "roots"—has been a major activity among American blacks over the past few decades.

contempt, or suspicion simply because they belong to a particular group and with no regard for their individual qualities. **Discrimination** refers to actions taken against a group, such as harassment or the denial of rights and privileges available to others.

Prejudice was evident in popular characterizations of the typical Irishman in newspapers and on the stage as a drunken, lazy, superstitious, ignorant lout. Discrimination was widespread. Merchants displayed signs in store windows reading "Irish Trade Not Solicited." Help-wanted ads often stated "Irish need not apply." During the height of anti-Catholic fervor in America in the 1850s, proposals to exclude all but native-born Americans from political office and to require a 25-year waiting period for citizenship aroused considerable popular support. During this same period, Roman Catholic priests and nuns were harassed, and several convents were burned by Protestant mobs.

Greece, and eastern European nations, such as Poland and Russia. Many had dark hair and swarthy complexions. Not only were many of them not Protestants, but they were not even Roman Catholics. Large numbers of immigrants were members of unfamiliar Eastern Orthodox Catholic churches, which featured bearded and married priests and onion-domed churches. Many others were not Christians at all— they were Jews.

These new Americans appeared very alien to eyes conditioned by the cultural traditions of western Europe and mid-nineteenth-century America. They spoke strange-sounding languages and ate strange food. And to make matters worse, they were all desperately poor. The questions arose: Would they stay poor? Would religious and cultural discrimination cause permanent economic inequality?

Accommodation and pluralism

To assimilate into American culture, the Irish would have had to give up their religion, which they refused to do. Thus, the problem had to be resolved in another way—American society had to accommodate religious differences. **Accommodation** means a decision by two or more groups to ignore some important difference between them and to emphasize their common interests. The result is **cultural pluralism**—the existence of several distinctive cultural patterns within the same society. As Protestants and Catholics resolved their conflicts, the United States became a religiously pluralistic culture. Today the United States is neither a Protestant nor a Catholic nation; both religions flourish side by side. In fact, the United States is not merely a Christian nation: Non-Christian faiths have also been accommodated.

The Irish proved to be only the first test of the capacity of American society to accommodate cultural differences. The waves of immigrants that began arriving after 1880 were markedly different from earlier American settlers in a number of ways, both cultural and physical. These immigrants came primarily from Mediterranean nations, such as Italy and

Subordinate groups and subcultures

So long as the vast majority of the Irish, Poles, Italians, and other new immigrant groups were mired in poverty with low-paying laboring jobs, these minorities were **subordinate groups**. Just by belonging to one of these groups, people were politically and economically subordinated to, or dominated by, the Protestant majority.

As time passed, these groups escaped from their subordinate positions. Catholics and Jews today have achieved economic equality with the Protestant majority and have won a full say in political decision making. However, in achieving equality, these groups retained significant portions of their original cultures. Indeed, elements of their native cultures have been incorporated into the original Anglo-American culture. For example, many Italian and Jewish foods are popular with most Americans, and many Italian and Yiddish words have entered American speech (Rosten, 1968). But even as the larger society has embraced elements of these other cultures, distinctively Jewish and Italian cultures still flourish, particularly in large cities on the East Coast. Thus, to some extent a number of cultures still exist side by side in American society.

First generation immigrants often stick to the "old ways," to their native culture, but their children inevitably begin to adapt to the culture around them. And, back in 1910, that's exactly what these immigrant kids in New York City are busy doing. In an alley between their slum tenements, beneath clotheslines hung with the family wash, it's time to play ball.

To deal conceptually with this situation, sociologists have developed the concept of subcultures. A **subculture** is a culture within a culture—in other words, a distinctive set of beliefs, morals, customs, and the like developed or maintained by a group within the larger society. A subculture may exist in harmony with the dominant culture of the society; in such cases, the subculture is accommodated. On the other hand, it may be in conflict with the dominant culture or with other subcultures. In the past, there was considerable conflict between the dominant American culture and the Jewish and Italian subcultures (as well as others). There was also conflict between these two subcultures. All of these conflicts have played a major role in American history and continue to do so. Today most conflicts of this nature are between the dominant white culture and the subcultures of such nonwhite minorities as blacks, Chicanos, and Native Americans (American Indians).

Chapter 11 argues that the primary basis for such conflicts is economic; prejudice and discrimination against a minority subculture seem to persist until that group has managed to achieve economic equality. That is, cultural differences are not accommodated until a group has "made it." Thus, to understand the situation of minority groups in America today, it is important to examine how earlier subordinate minorities became full participants in the economic life of the nation. This brings us back to the major question to be addressed in this chapter: Why did two of these groups achieve economic equality at such different rates?

JEWS AND ITALIANS: CONTRASTS IN SUCCESS

Among the masses of immigrants to the United States after 1880 were millions of Jews from eastern Europe and Italians, all of whom settled mainly in the large eastern cities. Both groups arrived with little or no money. The Jews encountered even greater prejudice and discrimination from established American groups than the Italians, yet only a few years after their parents arrived in this country, the first-generation American-born Jews were becoming well educated and rapidly achieving economic success. Few Italians did likewise. Even the second-generation Italian-Americans were not becoming very well educated, and Italians as a group remained near the bottom of the American economic ladder. Only much later did Americans of Italian descent begin to enter professional occupations in significant numbers and enjoy financial success.

There has long been considerable interest in why the Jews achieved economic success so rapidly compared with the Italians. The question is important for two reasons. First, its answer may help to combat **anti-Semitism** (prejudice and discrimination against Jews). Second, the answer might give us some clues about how today's disadvantaged minorities may (or why they may not) be able to achieve economic equality.

Anti-Semitism and Jewish success

For nearly 2,000 years, Jews have remained an unassimilated minority group, enduring as small communities of non-Christians within Christian societies that have often been hostile toward them. In good times Jews have lived in uneasy accommodation within the dominant Christian culture. In bad times they have been persecuted, expelled, vilified, and slaughtered. Even today, despite the lessons that have been learned from the horrors of Nazi Germany, where six million Jews were systematically murdered in death camps during World War II, anti-Semitism persists among some Americans (Selznick and Steinberg, 1969).

The unusual success story of Jewish immigrants has often fueled anti-Semitism in America. Bigots argue that Jewish achievement is simply evidence that Jews are unethical, money-mad, conniving, pushy, sly, and clannish. How else could they have done so well? So long as the real reasons for the rapid success of Jewish immigrants remain unknown, the anti-Semitic explanation is free to prosper. (Indeed, for a long time leaders of the Jewish community have tried to play down the actual extent of Jewish success lest they further provoke anti-Semitic feelings.) As we shall see in this chapter, Jewish success is neither mysterious nor unique.

Relevance of the past

One of the most serious problems facing contemporary American society is the subordinate position of most nonwhite minorities. Some members of these groups reject the idea that these groups can escape from economic and social woes by the same process by which earlier ethnic groups succeeded in America. These people point out that groups such as the Italians, Poles, Irish, and Jews did not have physical characteristics significantly different from those of the majority group. Nor did they have to overcome the ingrained attitudes created by the doctrine of superiority of the white race. In Chapter 11 we shall assess the appropriateness of evaluating nonwhite subordinate groups in the United States as if they were recent immigrants. However, without clearly understanding the problems faced by earlier subordinate ethnic groups and the conditions that influenced their economic progress, it is impossible to say how similar the situation of today's subordinate groups is. Furthermore, as we shall examine carefully in Chapter 11, the rapid economic success and social acceptance recently achieved by Japanese-Americans suggest that race alone does not wholly determine the fate of subordinate groups. Thus, there is at least a good possibility that understanding the past will give us insights into the present.

SOCIAL STRATIFICATION

Thus far we have spoken about success in terms of achieving economic equality. To discuss the Jews and Italians in more specific terms, we must introduce some additional sociological concepts.

The first of these is **stratification**, which refers to the unequal distribution of rewards (or things perceived as valuable) among members of a society. As we shall discuss in Chapter 9, rewards are of three major types: property, power, and prestige (or honor). In all known societies, these rewards are unequally distributed—some people have more and some have less. *Stratified* literally means layered; the term *upper crust* reflects the idea that societies are made up of layers. Sociologists identify these layers as **classes**: groups of people who share a similar *position,* or **status**,* in the stratification system. For example, one might think of a particular society as being divided into three classes: the poor, the middle class, and the rich. As we shall see in Chapters 9 and 10, some societies have more than three classes, depending on how and to whom rewards are distributed in the society and on the criteria used for analysis.

Sometimes individuals or whole groups change their position in the stratification system. Upward movement is called **upward mobility**; the reverse is called **downward mobility**. When a lawyer's son or daughter becomes a factory worker, we say that he or she has been downwardly mobile. When a factory worker's child becomes a lawyer, we say that he or she has been upwardly mobile.

These concepts of stratification help us to compare the upward mobility of Jewish and Italian immigrants in the United States. Upon arrival, both groups were concentrated in the lower class of the American stratification system. In time, many Jews and Italians rose to more privileged positions in society. When Jews and Italians were distributed at each class level at about the same proportion as that of established American groups, they had achieved equality. In other words, when a Jew or an Italian was as likely as an American of English origin to be rich *or* poor, then being Jewish or Italian no longer determined social position.

As we can see in Table 2-1, by the 1960s younger Italians actually had slightly higher average incomes than did "WASPs" (white Anglo-Saxon Protestants), and Jews had even higher incomes. These income differences were partly the result of regional economic differences (WASPs were more likely to live in rural areas and the South, where incomes were

Table 2-1 / Comparisons of U.S. heads of household, 40 years or under, by ethnic group.

	WASPs*	Italians	Jews
Average annual income	$8,360	$9,127	$10,806
Percent with white-collar jobs	40%	44%	74%

Source: Andrew M. Greely, 1974. Data based on a combination of national surveys conducted between 1963 and 1972.

*Protestants who gave their nationality as English, Scottish, or Welsh.

lower). However, the much higher proportion of Jews than of WASPs or Italians holding white-collar jobs reflects the fact that Jews were much more likely than most other ethnic groups to pursue higher education. In any event, these data show that simply being an Italian or a Jew no longer condemned a person to a low social position, or status.

Social position can be determined in two general ways. Status, or position, in the stratification system that is derived from individual merit or achievement is referred to as **achieved status**. When status is derived from inheritance, we call it **ascribed status**; that is, a person's position in society is fixed (ascribed to him or her by others) on the basis of family background or genetic inheritance. So long as women are excluded from lucrative, prestigious, and powerful positions in society, for example, their status is limited by biological inheritance.

The *caste system* in India is an extreme example of a stratification system based on ascribed status. Each level in the Indian stratification system is called a caste. Everyone is born into a caste, and the caste of the parents generally determines the position in society that their offspring will occupy, regardless of individual ability or merit.

When being an Italian or a Jew in the United States greatly restricted a person's opportunities for improving his or her social position, these groups occupied an ascribed low status. To be a Jew or an Italian was similar to having been born into a lower caste group in India. To the extent that being Jewish or Italian no longer plays any significant role in

*Throughout this text, the terms *status* and *position* are used interchangeably. You will understand why in Chapter 9, where we compare how Marx and Weber conceptualized social class. Although status implies prestige and honor in everyday speech, do not think of those qualities when you read the term in this text. Instead, think only of rank or position within a society, for a person or a group may have *low* as well as high status. Indeed, in this chapter our aim is to see how Jews and Italians escaped from their low status, or low position, in America.

determining a person's position in society, his or her status is achieved.

EXPLAINING ETHNIC MOBILITY

In explaining why Jews and Italians escaped from an ascribed low status and achieved equality with WASPs at such different rates, we shall encounter two major approaches to answering sociological questions.

The first of these emphasizes the role of *culture.* For a long time the accepted answer to our question was that the Jewish culture brought to the United States was more suited to upward mobility here than the Italian culture. We shall look over the shoulders of Mark Zborowski and Elizabeth Herzog (1962) as they assemble a detailed portrait of the culture of Jewish immigrants and connect this with rapid Jewish mobility. Then we shall examine the culture of Italian immigrants as reconstructed by Leonard Covello (1967) and see why he concluded that this culture impeded Italian mobility.

The second approach to answering sociological questions emphasizes the *social* backgrounds of the immigrants. Indeed, it relates the cultures of the Jews and the Italians to the social positions these people held in their native lands. According to this view, Jewish and Italian cultures differed because the positions of Jews and Italians in the stratification systems of their native lands also differed. Here we shall observe Stephen Steinberg (1974) as he demonstrates that much of the apparent difference in the success rates of Jews and Italians is an illusion. But we are getting ahead of our story.

Before we examine cultural explanations of Jewish and Italian success rates in America, we must introduce some more basic concepts.

CONCEPTS FOR CULTURAL ANALYSIS

For decades, the leading social science explanations of the different Jewish and Italian success rates were based on isolating critical differences in the Jewish and Italian cultures. Three major elements of culture have been stressed: *values, norms,* and *roles.*

Values and norms

Values identify a group's ideals—its ultimate aims and most general standards for assessing good and bad or desirable and undesirable. When we say people need self-respect, dignity, and freedom or that we must all stand up for our country, we are invoking values. Values are not only lofty, but quite general.

Norms, on the other hand, are quite specific. They are *rules governing behavior.* Norms define what behavior is required, acceptable, or prohibited in particular circumstances. Norms indicate that a person should, ought, or must act (or must not act) in certain ways. We have all been in situations where we were somewhat anxious about how we ought to act. Such anxiety reflects not only that we are sometimes not sure what the norms are, but also that violation of the norms will often lead to disapproval or even punishment. Conversely, conforming to the norms often brings approval and other rewards. In the next chapter we shall begin discussing a theme that runs throughout the book: Why do people conform or fail to conform to the norms?

Values and norms are related. Values *justify* the norms. For example, values of human dignity and self-respect can be invoked to explain the norm against ridiculing people who are physically handicapped. That is, calling someone a "gimp" not only is violating a norm but is also morally *wrong.* As another example, Americans value the intellectual development of the individual, as we shall see in Chapter 15. This value is the basis for many norms, including the norm that children shall be enrolled in school.

Roles

A **role** is a *collection of norms* associated with a *particular position* in a society. That is, these norms describe how we expect someone in a particular position to act or not to act.

Consider a church during Sunday services. To keep things simple, let's assume that there are three roles: minister, organist, and member of the congregation. Each person in each of these roles is expected to act in different ways. The minister is expected to lead the service in the proper sequence and to preach a sermon. The organist is expected to play appropriate selections accurately and at the right times. The members of the congregation are expected to join in hymns, prayers, and rituals at the proper moments and to sit attentively the rest of the time. A minister who gets prayers mixed up violates a norm attached to his or her role, as does the organist who plays wrong notes or the churchgoer who falls asleep.

Of course, it would be a much more serious violation of role behavior if a member of the congregation ran up and pounded on the organ or if the minister fell asleep during the services. When people blatantly disregard their roles, the integrity of the social situation is called into question. We may begin to ask ourselves, "Is that person really a minister?" "Is that person really a member of this church?" "Is this really a church service or is it a hoax?" (Goffman, 1959).

Social life is structured by roles. In virtually every social situation, we have a relatively clearly defined role to fulfill: student, friend, woman, husband, shopper, pedestrian, cop, nun, bartender, housewife, and so on. Each of these roles involves a "script" that we are expected to follow.

Some roles are thought to be more demanding than others, and some are thought to be more important than others. Virtually everyone is thought to be competent enough to fulfill the role of friend or spouse, but few are considered able to fulfill roles such as mathematician or sports star. A role that is believed to be more demanding and more important earns greater rewards than roles that are considered less demanding and less important. However, societies differ in their evaluations of various roles. For example, the role of banker is considered much more important in the United States than in the Soviet Union, while the role of chess player is more highly valued in the Soviet Union than in the United States.

Differences in the rewards attached to various roles in a particular society largely influence what roles persons will seek and what aspects of roles people will try to adopt in their own behavior. For example, if people in the most exalted roles in a society are required to demonstrate intense religious faith, then many other people in that society will attempt to do likewise.

In later chapters (especially Chapter 6) much will be said about roles—about how people learn to perform roles, about conflicts among roles, and the like. For now, it is enough to understand that different cultures can evaluate a given role quite differently.

Now we can use the concepts of values, norms, and roles to explore our sociological question for this chapter.

ZBOROWSKI AND HERZOG: JEWISH CULTURE

Over the decades, many prominent American sociologists have attributed the rapid upward mobility of Jewish Americans to cultural advantages they brought with them from eastern Europe (Slater, 1969; Steinberg, 1974). However, it was two anthropologists who assembled the most detailed and compelling cultural explanation of Jewish success in the United States.

Mark Zborowski and Elizabeth Herzog painstakingly reconstructed life in the *shtetls* of Poland and western Russia, from which the great waves of Jewish immigrants came during the latter part of the nineteenth century and the early part of the twentieth. *Shtetl* (rhymes with *kettle)* is the Yiddish word for "village" or "small town." During the centuries of life in the shtetls, the cultural traditions of ancient Judaism were transformed into the way of life brought by the Jews to America.

Outside of eastern Europe, as well, Jews lived almost exclusively in towns and cities. From early medieval times, Jews were prohibited from farming or owning land in most parts of Europe. Thus, most Jews in western Europe were required by law to live in crowded *ghettos**—neighborhoods reserved exclusively for Jews. These ghettos often were walled and the gates were locked at curfew.

Since ancient times the Jewish religion has stressed literacy for men, because each man is expected to read the scriptures and spend time studying their meaning. This tradition stimulated great respect for learning; indeed, learning became a value in Jewish communities. Because they lived in towns and cities, Jews could easily maintain schools and gather in study and discussion groups. Consequently, scholarship became "the dominant force in the Jewish culture" (Zborowski and Herzog, 1962).

These facts about Jewish culture were rather well known. What Zborowski and Herzog wanted to do was to re-create the details of shtetl life so that they could see how this "cult of scholarship" worked on a day-to-day basis and understand how the roles and norms of Jewish life reflected and sustained the values about learning and scholarship. Accordingly, they conducted very long interviews with more than a hundred elderly people who had grown up in the shtetls. (What remained of shtetl life was destroyed during World War II, when shtetl inhabitants were sent to Nazi death camps.) From these recollections by Jewish immigrants and a vast supply of letters, diaries, and life histories, Zborowski and Herzog (1962) produced a rich and compelling account of shtetl life in their book *Life Is with People.*

They discovered that the *norms* governing schooling, even in the early 1800s, were strict and demanding by modern standards. Children began school between the ages of 3 and 5 years old, and the school day began at 8 A.M. and lasted until 6 P.M. six days a week! Males who showed the greatest academic aptitude were expected to adopt the *role* of scholar and devote their lives to study and learning. In fact, scholars were so highly respected that most parents hoped their sons could become scholars. Wealthy merchants sought to gain scholars as

*The term *ghetto* originated in Venice, where the section of the city in which Jews were required to live was, in late medieval times, called the "borghetto." This word derived from the Italian word *borgo,* which meant "borough," which is a major section of a city. *Borghetto* was the diminutive form meaning "little borough." Over time the word was shortened to *ghetto,* and its use spread to all European languages. Today the term is often applied to any neighborhood occupied by an ethnic or racial minority.

sons-in-law; indeed, the life of a scholar was made possible by his marrying a woman whose family could support him as he devoted himself to full-time study.

When Jews began to immigrate to the United States in large numbers, this nation was undergoing rapid change. As we shall see in Chapters 16 and 18, **urbanization** and *industrialization* were transforming America from a nation of farmers to a nation of city dwellers who earned their livings from increasingly specialized and technical occupations. Consequently, the educational system was expanding extremely rapidly. As we shall see in Chapter 15, in 1870 there were only 52,000 college and university students in the United States. By 1920 that number had increased to almost 600,000. Thus, during the period of peak Jewish immigration, the colleges and universities were making room for and actively seeking much larger enrollments. An amazing number of these new students were the sons and daughters of Jewish immigrants (Steinberg, 1974).

Jews were accustomed to sending their children to school, exalting in their academic achievements, demanding hard study, and making family sacrifices to educate their children. Indeed, an editorial in a Jewish newspaper published in New York in 1902 boasted of the Jewish "love for education, for intellectual effort," and went on to say that "the Jew undergoes privation, spills blood, to educate his child" (quoted in Sanders, 1969).

It was not an idle boast. A 1922 study of high school students (Counts, 1922) found that for every 100 freshmen who were children of native-born, white Americans, there were 44 seniors. Thus, about 56 percent of those who began high school did not finish. Among the children of Italian immigrants, there were only 17 seniors for every 100 freshmen. But among children of immigrant Jews, there were 51 seniors for every 100 freshmen—a slight majority were graduating.

Thus, it is no surprise that by the turn of the century U.S. colleges and universities experienced waves of Jewish enrollment. Indeed, Jews soon formed a majority of the students enrolled in New York University and New York City College and constituted a very sizable minority in other eastern schools, such as Harvard and Columbia. In fact, by the 1920s many of these schools imposed quotas on

A teacher in a shtetl *school drills Jewish boys in the Hebrew alphabet. Understandably, they are more interested in the photographer than in their books. But, most of the time they were required to study long and hard.*

the number of Jews admitted. Thus, Columbia reduced its Jewish enrollment from 40 percent to 22 percent two years later. A public furor erupted over formal limits placed by Harvard on Jewish enrollment, which exceeded 20 percent by 1920. Consequently, Harvard adopted a policy of regional balance, seeking students from all forty-eight states. In effect, this policy imposed a limit on Jews by limiting enrollments from New York and other eastern states with large Jewish populations.

But despite quotas and simmering anti-Semitism, plenty of room remained in the educational system for Jewish students, and Jews rapidly made their way into high-prestige, high-paying occupations, especially professions requiring advanced degrees: medicine, law, dentistry, and education. In fact, as early as 1913 the proportions of doctors, lawyers, and college professors who were Jewish were substantially greater than the proportion of Jews in the general population (Steinberg, 1974).

Thus, Zborowski and Herzog attributed the rapid upward mobility of American Jews to the favorable fit between their learning- and schooling-oriented culture and the opportunities existing in the United States at the time of the greatest Jewish immigration.

LEONARD COVELLO: ITALIAN CULTURE

 Unlike the children of Jewish immigrants, the children of newly arrived Italians did not excel in school and did not seek higher education in order to pursue professional occupations. Italian children tended to quit school at an early age. In the mid-1930s, Leonard Covello, a young teacher and school administrator in an Italian part of New York City,

A Jewish boy delivering bundles of partly sewn men's suit coats in New York about 1910. Like other immigrants, Jewish children often had to help their families earn a living. But compared to most other immigrant groups, they were much less likely to drop out of school to take fulltime jobs.

In 1903 when this picture was taken, being a newsboy was not something a boy did only after school. He had to be on his corner all day long or lose his spot to another boy. (The Newsboy Law in New York said boys could work only from 6 A.M. to 10 P.M.) Thus it is almost certain that this Italian boy had already dropped out of school to help feed his family. At that time most Italian-American children did quit school early.

began a lengthy research project to try to understand the educational problems of Italian-American children such as "truancy, absence, cutting classes, lateness, and disciplinary problems." His research lasted until 1944, and he finally published his findings in 1967. His book, *The Social Background of the Italo-American School Child,* is a superb counterpart to the work of Zborowski and Herzog. For, by conducting his research both in Italy and among his fellow Italian-Americans, Covello drew a portrait

of the culture Italians brought to America, a culture that did not fit well with life on this side of the Atlantic.

Covello, like Zborowski and Herzog, focused his attention on education, because Italian-Americans were failing to take advantage of their educational opportunities. Dropping out of school early, they typically were forced to settle for low-paying, unskilled jobs. By the time Covello published his book, this pattern had changed dramatically. Italian-

A street scene from an Italian neighborhood in Pittsburgh at the turn of the century. The men gathered at the apple cart probably were unskilled laborers, and many of the young boys probably had quit school. The presence of the two goats illustrates the tendency of many peasant immigrants to attempt to maintain rural aspects of life, even in city slums.

Americans were staying in school and many were going to college. But it had taken many decades longer for this pattern to emerge than it had among Jews. Why?

Covello concluded that Italians had arrived in America suspicious of schools and accustomed to sending children to work at an early age. These cultural patterns were appropriate to conditions in Italy, particularly in southern Italy, from where most Italian immigrants came.

The government of Italy was controlled by the populous northern regions. Southern Italy was rural, impoverished, and exploited by northerners who regarded the south as an ignorant backwater. Consequently, southern Italy had relatively few schools. Worse yet, these few schools represented the culture of the north—even the language used in them was quite different from the common southern dialects.

Southern Italian parents regarded schooling as a

threat to their own values, especially the key value of loyalty to the family, for the schools reflected negative judgments of local life. Moreover, little of what was learned in school was of much importance to life in southern Italy. Whether they went to school or not, the children grew up to be peasants. As one old Italian father told Covello, "What good if a boy is bright and intelligent in school, and then does not know enough to respect his family? Such a boy would be worth nothing."

Furthermore, the absence of children from home while they attended school often threatened the economic well-being of the family. As another father told Covello, "If our children don't go to school, no harm results. But if the sheep don't eat, they will die. The school can wait but not our sheep."

The belief that school was not important and possibly harmful was appropriate to life in southern Italy. The things children really needed to learn had to be learned at home anyway, such as how to plant crops and tend sheep. Thus, academic learning was not a value in southern Italian culture. Nor were sending children to school and rigorous study habits norms.

Finally, the role of scholar was of little importance. The primary value was family loyalty. The most important norms concerned behavior within the family, and the father was the most important social role.

Transplanted to the United States, these cultural patterns proved inappropriate. Here the Italians did not become farmers. Instead, they found themselves in rapidly growing industrial cities where child labor was of little value and large families were an economic burden rather than an asset. Furthermore, unskilled physical labor paid low wages and offered no opportunity for advancement. Covello concluded that these cultural patterns thwarted the social progress of Italian-Americans. So long as these patterns persisted, Italians could not achieve upward mobility.

In this way, cultural studies offer an explanation of the different rates of success of Jews and Italians. There can be no doubt that these scholars described Jewish and Italian cultures accurately. Nor can one really doubt that such differences influenced social mobility. Nevertheless, by the late 1960s other scholars began to suggest that these cultural explanations did not fully explain the phenomenon. For

one thing, there was nothing unusual about the time it took for Italians to achieve economic equality. Most other immigrant groups took just as long. Thus, the real question was why the Jews had risen so fast. In addition, even though their culture was unusual in its emphasis on learning, large numbers of Jews still achieved rapid economic success without much schooling. Consequently several social scientists began to suspect that the rapid upward mobility of Jews in America may have been partly an illusion. The first person to thoroughly reassess the problem in this way was Stephen Steinberg.

STEPHEN STEINBERG: THE JEWISH HEAD START

In the early 1970s, when Stephen Steinberg began a major study of the religious and ethnic origins of college and university faculty, everyone knew that the Jews had surpassed all other immigrant groups in gaining economic success. A textbook on minority groups in America reported:

Jewish immigrants, like most immigrants, came with few skills and no money. They started in American society as workers and peddlers, and they achieved remarkable success (Kramer, 1970).

Scholars were equally certain that this achievement was due to Jewish culture.

But Steinberg was not sure that these views were wholly correct. It is true that immigrant Jews were poor when they arrived in the United States. Table 2-2 shows that only 12 percent of the Jewish immigrants from 1904 to 1910 had $50 or more upon arrival in this country, a figure that is quite close to that for the Italians, the Irish, and most other immigrants.

But, Steinberg asked, is money the whole story? What if we meet a ditch digger and an engineer who are entering the United States as immigrants? What if each has only $50 in his pocket? Are they really starting off on equal footing? Steinberg answered this question no. Obviously the engineer brings tre-

Table 2-2 / Immigrants having at least $50 upon arrival in the United States, 1904–1910.

Immigrant Group	Percentage
Jews	12%
Southern Italians	5
Irish	17
Germans	31
English	55
All other immigrants	14

Source: Reports of the Immigration Commission, vol. 3 (1911), reproduced in Stephen Steinberg, *The Academic Melting Pot* (New York: McGraw-Hill, 1974).

Table 2-3 / Occupations of Jewish and non-Jewish adults in Russia, 1897.

Occupation	Percentage Jews	Percentage Non-Jews
Professions	5%	3%
Commerce	32	3
Manufacturing and skilled trades	38	15
Service	19	16
Transportation	3	2
Agriculture	3	61
Total	100%	100%

Source: Compiled from the Russian census of 1897 and presented in Israel Rubinow, "The Economic Condition of Jews in Russia," *Bulletin of the Bureau of Labor,* no. 72 (U.S. Government Printing Office: Washington, D.C., 1907).

mendous potential economic advantages with him compared with the ditch digger, and we would be very surprised if the engineer was not making much more money than the ditch digger after a few years. Steinberg suspected that Jewish immigrants brought with them experience, training, and technical skills that qualified them for highly skilled jobs and enabled them to pursue successful business and commercial opportunities. The problem was to prove it.

Fortunately, Steinberg was able to find two vital but neglected sources of data. The first was an analysis of the economic condition of Jews in Russia and Poland (then part of Russia), based on the Russian census of 1897 (Rubinow, 1907). The second was a massive forty-one-volume report of the U.S. Immigration Commission, published in 1911.

First, Steinberg examined the Russian census. At that time Jews were required to live in a restricted region of Poland and western Russia called the Pale of Settlement. Only a few Jews were permitted to live beyond the Pale. As a result, Jews were a concentrated population. As we just saw, these Jews lived in villages and small towns, the shtetls. Correspondingly, the Russian census found that only 3 percent of Jews were farmers, while 61 percent of non-Jews were (see Table 2-3). In contrast, the Jews were heavily concentrated in higher-status occupations. Nearly a third engaged in commerce, and an even higher percentage were in manufacturing or highly

skilled trades. Five percent worked at professions such as law and medicine. Within the Pale, a third of the factories were owned by Jews, who also dominated commerce.

Of course, many of these factories were tiny operations, and much of the commerce was nothing more than selling household items door to door. What is important, however, is not how much money Jews were earning in Russia and Poland, but the training and skills involved. These occupational skills set the Jews off markedly from the non-Jewish, mainly peasant populations in eastern Europe. It could have equally set them off from most other immigrants to America, who also were mainly peasants.

Of course, it is possible that only unsuccessful Jews emigrated from eastern Europe. However, since Jews in the late nineteenth century emigrated primarily to flee severe persecution under the Russian czar, that seems unlikely. In any event, Steinberg found detailed records in the Immigration Commission reports that demonstrated the occupational advantages of Jewish immigrants.

Table 2-4 shows that the occupational backgrounds of Jewish immigrants differed from those of other immigrants. Two-thirds of Jewish immigrants worked in skilled crafts in the old country, in contrast with 15 percent of the southern Italians, 13 percent of the Irish, and 6 percent of the Poles. Even immigrants from England were less likely to have skilled occupations than the Jews. In contrast, the Jews had rarely worked as laborers, farmers, or servants, while these were the most common occupations of the Italians, the Irish, and the Poles—indeed, of all immigrants as a group.

Jews entered the country with highly skilled occupational backgrounds precisely when rapidly industrializing America offered immense opportunity for such people. Consequently, the Jews rapidly reentered their old occupations as printers, jewelers, tailors, watchmakers, cigar makers, tinsmiths, furriers, and the like. Such jobs paid much better wages than the laboring jobs available to most other new immigrants. Although the Jews arrived poor, they came with marketable skills that permitted them to escape poverty rapidly. In contrast, most other groups had to develop such skills after they arrived. Not surprisingly, it took them longer. Indeed, the majority of them arrived illiterate, while the overwhelming majority of Jewish immigrants could read and write.

Several other immigrant groups have repeated the Jewish pattern of rapid success and for similar reasons. In the late 1950s and early 1960s, a large number of Cuban refugees came to the United States to escape Castro's revolutionary government. Most of them had held middle- and upper-class positions in Cuba before the revolution. Although they came with little more than the clothes on their backs, they rapidly regained their class positions here. More recently, middle-class refugees from Vietnam have shown a similar tendency toward rapid economic advancement.

Steinberg's reassessment of the actual circumstances of Jewish immigrants does not mean that Jewish culture played no role in their success. Rather, he argued that these aspects of Jewish culture reflected the position enjoyed by Jews in the shtetls. Compared with the surrounding non-Jewish populations, the Jews of eastern Europe were middle class. Many studies have shown that middle-class people everywhere in the world are very concerned about education and push their children to do well in school (Steinberg, 1974). They are especially likely to do so if they have momentarily lost their positions in society (as had Jews, Cubans, and Vietnamese when they fled to America). As we shall see in Chapter 11,

A Jewish clockmaker at work in Poland early in this century. Most adult Jewish men who came to America had worked in commerce or in skilled trades in the old country.

education is the cheapest, most rapid, and most reliable path to economic advancement under present conditions.

Steinberg summed up his findings this way:

Jewish immigrants were not simply middle class in their values. . . . There was substance and reality behind these values. Jews did not simply have aspirations for economic mobility—they also had experiences and skills in middle-class occupations. Nor did Jews simply value education and revere learning. They were also literate as a group and had cognitive skills to pass on to their children.

Table 2-4 / Occupations of immigrants entering the United States, 1899–1910.

Previous Occupation*	Percentage					
	Jews	Southern Italians	Irish	Poles	English	All Immigrants**
Higher status						
Professions	1%	0%	1%	0%	9%	1%
Commerce	5	1	1	0	5	2
Skilled labor	67	15	13	6	49	20
Lower status						
Labor	12	42	31	45	18	36
Farming	2	35	7	31	4	25
Service	11	6	46	17	5	14
Other	2	1	1	1	10	2

Source: Adapted from the *Reports of the Immigration Commission* (1911), as reprinted in Stephen Steinberg, *The Academic Melting Pot* (New York: McGraw-Hill, 1974).

 *Excludes immigrants with no previous occupation, including most women and children.

**Also includes other groups not separately listed in the table.

Conversely, [other immigrants such as the Italians] did not simply place low value on education and occupational mobility, but were handicapped by factors related to their peasant origins.

Moreover, certain conditions faced by Italian immigrants made their progress even more difficult and contributed to their slower rate of social advancement.

REFERENCE GROUPS AND ITALIAN TRADITIONALISM

At the turn of the century, government studies revealed that, compared with Jews and many other immigrant groups, Italians seemed slow to learn English. For example, in 1911 two-thirds of the Jews who had been in the United States less than five years could speak English. The figure for Italians was only one-fourth. Even Jewish and Italian immigrants who had been in the country ten years or longer showed marked differences in their knowledge of English (Steinberg, 1974).

Obviously, it is a considerable handicap to be unable to speak the language of the country in which one is trying to earn a living. Furthermore, the children of parents who do not speak English are hindered in learning to speak it and are thus at a disadvantage in school. In fact, Covello blamed many school problems experienced by Italian-Americans in the 1930s on their poor English skills. It turns out that the reason the Italians were slow to learn English was also a reason for many of their economic problems as well.

Italians were slow not only to learn English but also to adapt to occupational conditions in the United States because most of them did not plan to become Americans. Instead, most Italian immigrants came to America to take advantage of the relatively high wages available to unskilled laborers (compared with wages back in southern Italy) and then returned to Italy with their savings to resume their old ways of life in greater comfort.

It is easy to demonstrate that this was the case. Immigration Commission statistics reveal that of Italian immigrants between 1899 and 1910, only 21 percent were females (in contrast with 43 percent of Jews). Similarly, only 12 percent of the Italian

Jewish immigrants crowd the decks of the S.S. Westernland *in about 1890, trying to escape the foul air of the jam-packed hold. Notice the many women and children, indicating that these are family groups.*

immigrants were under age 14 (compared with 25 percent of Jews). Therefore, few Italian families were coming to America; instead, it was mostly young, single men. Moreover, most of them did go back. Between 1908 and 1910, for every 100 Italians who entered the United States, 55 others left to go back to Italy. Among Jews, only 8 left for every 100 arrivals during this period. A great many Italians who ended up staying in America had probably not planned to do so. Many of them delayed their returns because of the outbreak of World War I in 1914. By the time the war ended in 1918, economic conditions in Italy were very bad, leading many Italians to stay on and

wait for a better time to go back. In the end, large numbers never did return. However, so long as they thought they would go back, they were likely to cling to their Italian culture.

To describe this situation in a more sociological way, immigrants from Italy continued to regard the folks back home as their **reference group**. This concept refers to the groups that individuals identify with, the groups whose norms and values serve as the basis for self-judgment. In an important sense, our reference groups are the audiences before whom we lead our lives—the people whose approval counts most with us.

This Italian mother and children passed through Ellis Island in 1915, on their way to join the father who had come over several years before, planning to return to Italy. But the plans changed, perhaps because of the outbreak of World War I in 1914. They probably still were not certain they would stay in America forever.

A reference group need not actually be present to influence a person's behavior. Even if no member of our reference group can actually see what we are doing, we can still act on the basis of how that group would react. This aspect of reference groups often allows sociologists to make sense out of behavior that seems out of place.

Consider a nineteenth-century British gentleman exploring the upper reaches of the Nile. He sets out by himself, accompanied by forty men from an isolated African tribe who are acting as guides and carrying the supplies. There is no other British gentleman, perhaps not even any other white man, within a thousand miles. Yet every night this explorer wears a tuxedo to dinner. His native companions think this is very strange, and if we could see him doing it, we might think it strange, too. But he doesn't care, since we are not the relevant audience. His reference group is other British gentlemen, and a gentleman always dresses for dinner. Once we know this man's reference group, we can explain and even predict much of his behavior. For example, we can be sure that he will always rise from his chair if a woman enters the room and that he will think it very vulgar to mention the price paid for a possession.

The reference group for large numbers of Italian-Americans was the inhabitants of rural villages in southern Italy. Once we know that, much of their behavior is understandable. Why reject traditional norms and values of rural Italian life if you are planning to return to it? Why act in ways that would shock the folks back home, such as making your kids go to college? Moreover, despite the fact that Italian-Americans were mostly poor compared with the average American, they were rich compared with their reference group. As time passed, however, the ties to the old country began to fade. Young Italians found it hard to use as a reference group people they had never met, who lived in a place they had only been told about. Their reference groups began to change, and they began to adapt to the culture and conditions around them. In a few years, Italians achieved rapid upward mobility.

The process and results of changing from Italian to American reference groups is pointedly illustrated by the story of Amadeo Giannini. Born in 1870, the son of an Italian immigrant, he founded a small bank in 1904 in the North Beach district of San Francisco, an Italian neighborhood. Giannini's bank made loans to the small businessmen of the neighborhood, who found it very difficult to get credit at the city's other banks. Giannini named his institution the Bank of Italy. The bank survived the 1906 earthquake and the fire that destroyed much of the city. Under Giannini's brilliant management, the policy of lending to small businessmen brought the bank considerable success.

By 1928 Giannini had become uncomfortable about his bank's name, which sounded too foreign. Besides, its customers were no longer mainly Italians. So Giannini changed the name of his bank in rather dramatic fashion: from the Bank of Italy to

A. P. Giannini in about 1906.

the Bank of America. When he died in 1949, his little neighborhood bank had grown into the largest privately owned bank in the world.

As we shall see in Chapter 11, the experience of Italians in America has the most to tell us about the situation of today's disadvantaged minority groups. Unlike the Jews, the Italians really did begin at the very bottom of the American stratification system. How they escaped these circumstances is potentially applicable to others.

CONCLUSION

The purpose of this chapter was to introduce a working vocabulary of sociological concepts in the context of an actual sociological study. We have pursued a real sociological question and watched some real social scientists attempt to provide an answer. Along the way I have tried to let you see some of the things that sociologists do and to prepare you for a survey of the great variety of topics that make up sociology. I have also organized the concepts discussed in this chapter into the Review Glossary that follows. The concepts are presented in the same order in which they appeared in the chapter so that you can review the chapter as well as make sure you know all the concepts. Keep in mind, however, that you have been only briefly introduced to these concepts. Each appears in many other chapters. At each encounter you will better understand a concept.

Review glossary

Concepts Scientific definitions that identify the members of some class of things as alike, as belonging to the same set or class. (p. 24)

Abstractions Ideas or mental constructions rather than material objects. All scientific concepts are abstractions. (p. 24)

Society A relatively self-sufficient and self-sustaining group of people who are united by social relationships and who live in a particular territory. (p. 26)

Culture The complex pattern of living—made up of customs, values, technology, and so forth—that humans have developed and that they pass from one generation to the next. (p. 27)

Assimilation The process by which an individual or a group reacts to a new social environment by adopting the culture prevalent in that environment. (p. 28)

Prejudice Negative or hostile attitudes toward, and beliefs about, a group. (p. 28)

Discrimination Actions taken against a group to deny its members rights and privileges available to others. (p. 29)

Accommodation An agreement between two groups to ignore differences between them. (p. 29)

Cultural pluralism A result of accommodation, it occurs when two or more distinctive cultures coexist within the same society. (p. 29)

Subordinate groups Groups that are politically and economically dominated by another group. Often, subordinate groups are also minority groups, but sometimes a numerical minority can subordinate a majority. (p. 29)

Following the San Francisco earthquake of 1906, the Bank of Italy occupied these temporary quarters on Montgomery Street. Today, this bank is known as the Bank of America.

Subculture A culture within a culture; a group that maintains or develops its own set of beliefs, morals, values, norms, and the like, which usually are at variance with those of the dominant culture. (p. 31)

Anti-Semitism Prejudice and discrimination against Jews. (p. 32)

Stratification The unequal distribution of rewards (or of things perceived as valuable) among members of a society; the class structure. (p. 32)

Classes Groups of people who share a similar level in the stratification system. (p. 33)

Status Any particular position within a society. (p. 33)

Mobility, upward and downward A change of level within the stratification system. (p. 33)

Achieved status A position gained on the basis of merit (in other words, by achievement). (p. 33)

Ascribed status A position assigned to individuals or groups without regard for merit, but because of certain traits beyond their control, such as their race, their sex, or the social standing of their parents. (p. 33)

Values Ideals or ultimate aims; general evaluative standards about what is desirable. (p. 34)

Norms Rules that define the behavior that is expected, required, or acceptable in particular circumstances. (p. 34)

Role A set of expectations governing the behavior of persons holding a particular position in society; a set of norms that defines how persons in a particular position should behave. (p. 34)

Urbanization A process in which the population of a society shifts its place of residence from rural areas and villages to cities. (p. 36)

Reference group A group a person uses as a standard for self-evaluation. (p. 44)

Suggested readings

Covello, Leonard. *The Social Background of the Italo-American School Child.* Leiden, The Netherlands: E.J. Brill, N.B., 1967.

Glazer, Nathan, and Daniel P. Moynihan. *Beyond the Melting Pot,* 2nd ed. Cambridge: M.I.T. Press, 1970.

Howe, Irving. *World of Our Fathers.* New York: Harcourt Brace Jovanovich, 1976.

Steinberg, Stephen. *The Academic Melting Pot.* New York: McGraw-Hill, 1974.

Zborowski, Mark, and Elizabeth Herzog. *Life Is with People: The Culture of the Shtetl.* New York: Schocken Books, 1962.

ONE

Suicides per 100,000 population, 1980.
National = 11.9.

When statistics on suicides were first collected by European governments in the late eighteenth century, everyone was surprised to discover that the rates were stable from year to year, although they differed greatly from place to place. In this map we see that suicide rates differ substantially from one part of the United States to another, but they don't change much from year to year. Until rates like these were published, suicide had been regarded as an idiosyncratic and individualistic act. But when such actions aggregated into a similar rate year after year, it was necessary to suspect that the causes of suicide did not reside wholly within the individual—that there must be social causes. Indeed, because of the solid differences between regions and nations, there must be aspects of societies themselves that cause people to take their own lives. Throughout the nineteenth century many scholars attempted to explain why the suicide rate was higher in some places than in others. Then in 1897 Emile Durkheim, one of the founders of modern sociology, produced his classic work Suicide. *In it he analyzed the ways individuals are attached to one another and how these attachments underlie the moral order of societies. In the next two chapters we shall pursue this thesis in detail, for it is the insight on which all sociological theories rest.*

Pacific 14.3

Mountain 16.2

West North Central 11.2

East North Central 10.9

Middle Atlantic 9.6

New England 9.5

West South Central 12.3

East South Central 11.6

South Atlantic 12.7

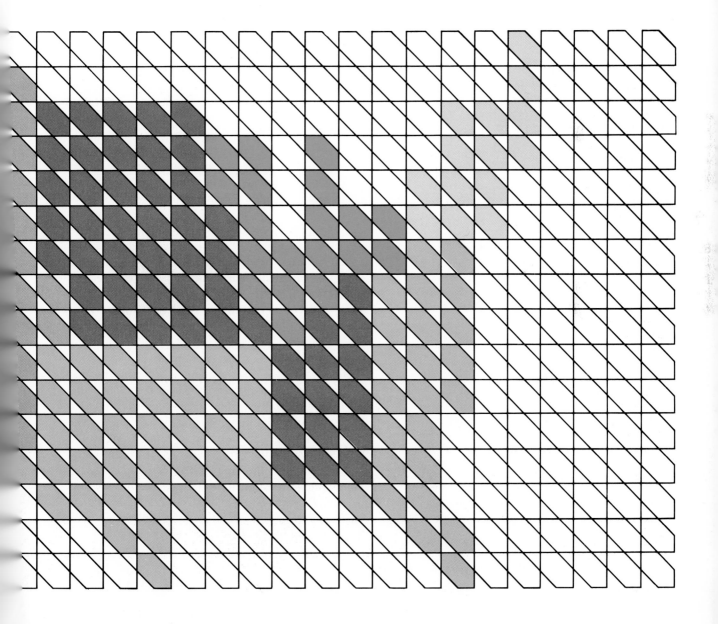

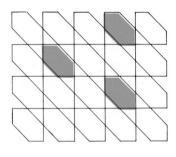

In Chapters 1 and 2 we examined basic concepts that sociologists use to analyze and classify social life. However, we can't explain how societies operate simply by taking them apart and giving names to the pieces. Although concepts identify classes of things, they don't explain anything. To give something a name does not say why it occurs.

Theories provide explanations. **Theories** are statements that say why and how several (or more) concepts are related. Since concepts are abstractions and theories are made up of concepts, theories are also abstract—the explanations they provide apply to a wide range of phenomena.

However, not just any set of statements containing concepts is a theory. To qualify as a theory, a set of statements must include or imply some conclusions that can be *empirically verified* by direct physical observation. That is, a theory must *predict* and *prohibit* certain events or conditions that can be checked. Put another way, theories must risk the possibility of being proven false.

Suppose the set of statements and concepts that physicists call the theory of gravity "predicted" that if you hold this textbook at shoulder level and then let it go, any of three things might happen: (1) The book would fall to the floor; (2) the book would remain suspended in space; or (3) the book would fly away into the clouds. That wouldn't be very useful knowledge. All possible outcomes are predicted, and none is prohibited. The theory of gravity is a theory because it predicts the first outcome and prohibits the other two. To be a theory, a set of statements must tell us what *must* happen and why, and what things *must not* happen and why.

Science consists of two primary activities: first,

Micro Sociology:
Choice and Interaction

constructing theories (trying to explain the world), and second, testing theories (trying to eliminate theories that are incorrect). Since theories predict and prohibit certain observable things, research is used to see if those things conform to the theory. However, it is very important to realize that although research can demonstrate that a particular theory is false (or at least is incomplete), no amount of research ever can prove that a theory is true. This is because theories are abstractions that apply to all possible instances of the phenomena they try to explain. It is impossible to test a theory against all possibilities: The future always holds more opportunities for the predicted or prohibited outcomes to go contrary to the theory. For example, even though every time anyone has ever dropped something it has fallen to earth, tomorrow or next year or ten centuries from now someone might drop a pencil and have it sail upward, thus contradicting the theory of gravity.

Fortunately, it is possible to *falsify,* or disprove, theories. When research yields results that are contrary to a theory, we know it is time to reject that theory or at least attempt to repair it. However, the more times a theory survives efforts to falsify it, and the greater the variety and stringency of the tests that are run against it, the more confidence we gain that the theory is valid. So although we can never be certain that a theory is true, in time we begin to take it for granted. From this discussion we can understand the fundamental rule governing all scientific research: Researchers contribute to scientific progress not by seeking evidence that will support theories but by doing their utmost to disprove them.

Because of the intimate relationship between theories and research, it is appropriate to link fundamentals of sociological theories with fundamentals of research procedures. Not only do theories direct researchers in terms of *what* research to do, but to a considerable extent theories also imply *how* that research can best be done. That is, depending on what kinds of phenomena a theory addresses, different research techniques are more appropriate. In sociology, a primary concern is whether a theory pertains primarily to micro sociology (the behavior of individuals or small groups) or macro sociology (the behavior of large-scale social phenomena). Individual humans and small groups can be studied by direct observation, through personal interviews, or in laboratory experiments. But these research techniques are more difficult, or even impossible, to apply to large-scale social phenomena. For example, we could hardly set out to observe the behavior of all Americans or to invite them into a laboratory.

Thus, we see that the distinction between micro and macro sociology has profound implications not just for *what* sociologists study but for *how* they study it. ▪

CHAPTER PREVIEW

In this chapter we shall encounter the elements of micro theories in sociology. Then we shall see the usual research techniques used to test micro theories. First, we shall examine the experimental method and see why it is the ideal way to do research. Often, however, it is impossible even for micro sociologists to use experiments. Therefore, we shall then study the principles behind several kinds of nonexperimental research styles—ways sociologists use to try to approximate the precision of experiments. In the next chapter, we shall build upon the material covered in this chapter by pursuing the elements of theories and research methods in macro sociology.

CHOICE THEORIES IN SOCIAL SCIENCE

All micro theories in social science begin with a common premise about human nature: that *people make choices* (Phelps, 1975). Thus, such theories are called **choice theories**. As we shall see, many aspects of the social and physical environment limit the options available and influence the choices people will prefer. Still, social science proceeds on the principle that, given our options and our preferences, we choose to do that which we expect to be most rewarding—whether the rewards are affection, fame, a better life for our children, money, or comic books. The idea that humans make choices is surely not new. Every normal human being ever born has been aware of the need to choose what action to take. Nor is it strange to suppose that humans prefer good choices to bad ones, good choices being those that serve our needs and bad ones those that do not.

Indeed, as was discussed in Chapter 1, it is the premise that people do choose that permits social science to recognize "free will." And it is the premise that people will try to make the best choice available that makes social science possible. If we assume that people seek to maximize the benefits of their actions, then we can hope to predict and explain their actions by examining the choices available to them. On the other hand, if people followed no rational rules in making choices and behaved randomly, social science would be impossible. But then, of course, so would human life itself.

Since the earliest efforts to explain human behavior, the "choice" or "self-interest" premise has been the fundamental starting point. Of course, it has been phrased many ways. Thomas Hobbes, an English social philosopher, put it this way in 1656:

I conceive that when a man deliberates whether he shall do a thing or not do it, he does nothing else but consider whether it be better for himself to do it or not to do it.

Modern social scientists also state the choice premise in different ways. Micro economists begin their theories with the proposition that humans seek a variety of goods. This premise gives micro economists an active human being whose behavior is rational. From this starting point they can construct laws of supply and demand. Psychologists put it another way: Behavior is shaped by reinforcement. In this way psychologists root the cause of behavior in its anticipated consequences, in the response of the social and physical environment to an individual's behavior. When psychologists say behavior is repeated because it has been reinforced, they are saying that people select their actions on the basis of past experience—we repeat actions that produce the results we desire.

Micro sociological theories also rest on the choice proposition. As Homans (1964) put it, people "are more likely to perform an activity, the more valuable they perceive the reward of that activity to be." This formulation, however, leaves something out. It was adapted directly from psychology during a period when psychologists were inclined to argue that only rewards and not punishments influenced human behavior. Perhaps they took this position because they wanted the world to be a gentler place. But the fact is that people do not only seek things they want, they seek to *avoid* things they dislike. Children do not run only to get a ball or to receive candy; they also run to avoid angry dogs, swarms of bees, and sometimes an irate parent. Hence, the formulation I prefer and use in my own theories is: Humans seek what they perceive to be rewards and avoid what they perceive to be costs. Bee stings, dog bites, and spankings are costs—things we would prefer to do without. So, too, is the loss of candy.

Although all micro social science theories begin

Thomas Hobbes.

George C. Homans.

with the same proposition, they soon go their separate ways as more propositions are added. Micro theories become truly *sociological* by the incorporation of two very important insights.

First, sociologists greatly expand the concepts of rewards and costs. For example, while economists tend to restrict these concepts to material commodities, sociologists realize that we do not live by bread alone. There are things we value immensely besides what we can put in our mouths or in our pockets. Chief among these are affection and self-esteem. We want to be loved, liked, respected, and admired.

Second, sociologists recognize that much of what we want can only be gotten from other people. Whether we seek candy, love, or learning, we must usually get it from other people. Therefore, in order to gain rewards, we must induce other people to give us rewards. However, it is costly to give up rewards: When I give you candy, I have less candy; when I provide you with a textbook, it costs me time and energy. In order to get others to reward us, we

must reward them. Perhaps nothing could be more obvious, yet throughout this book we shall trace the profound implications of this simple point.

Since humans seek rewards from one another, they are inevitably forced into *exchange relations.* That is, human beings engage in **social interaction**—they attempt to influence one another. To do this they must exchange rewards. This conclusion is implicit in the choice premise as soon as we shift our focus from the lone individual to the group.

Since, unlike micro economics, micro sociology defines *goods* as the whole range of rewards that people seek and the whole range of costs that they want to avoid, micro sociology aims to explain the whole range of social behavior by analyzing interaction and the exchanges it entails. Therefore, micro sociology consists primarily of the study of *interaction,* especially face-to-face interaction in small groups. Furthermore, micro sociological theories attempt to explain the regularities or patterns that arise out of interactions and exchanges.

As an Olympic gymnast glows in the admiration of the crowd, so do we all seek approval from those around us. Indeed, affection, not money, is the primary medium of exchange in human relations—for we must even learn to like ourselves through the reactions of others to us.

ALTRUISM

Before we examine sociological theories of interaction, it is important to review the topic of **altruism**, that is, unselfish behavior done to benefit others. Many people find they are unsettled by the assumption that humans act to increase their rewards and to decrease their costs: What about parents who sacrifice their lives to save their children, soldiers who die for their country, or people who give up a com-

fortable life to aid the sick and the poor? Many such people exist. We need not assume that by doing so they intentionally act against their own interests.

Human life and culture are immensely rich because of the incredible variety of things that people perceive as rewarding. To assume that a parent might regard the survival of his or her child as more rewarding than personal survival is a credit to the human spirit and our capacity to love. To suggest that such a parent does not act out of self-interest is to belittle such capacities; in fact, it would be reduc-

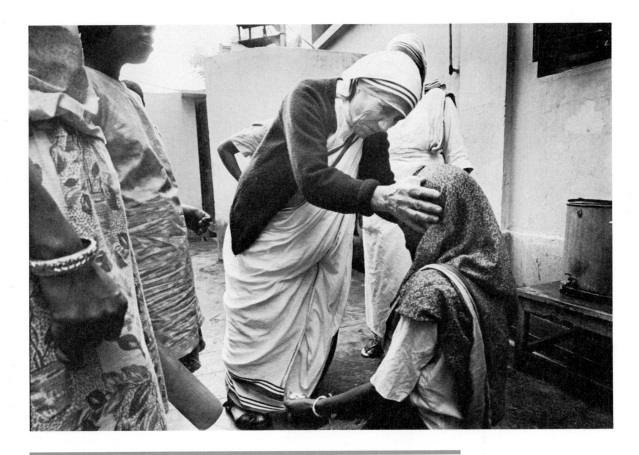

Mother Teresa has become the best-known Roman Catholic nun alive through her devoted work among India's poor. Some would argue that she is an example of an altruist, a person who acts against his or her own desires. But Mother Teresa's greatness lies in what it is that she desires—to reduce the misery of others. That is, Mother Teresa should be admired for how she finds rewards in life, not for living an unrewarding life.

ing noble action to crazy and irrational behavior. Similarly, to suggest that a soldier could not have chosen to die for his country on the basis of self-interest is to suggest that people cannot value the survival of their fellow citizens more than they value their own lives. In short, the self-interest assumption of social science is humanistic in the fullest sense. It acknowledges our capacity to find rewards in our dreams, hopes, love, and ideals. This will be clear as we examine what micro sociological theories actually predict about people.

INTERACTION THEORIES

Micro sociology seeks the causes of human behavior in the relationships between the individual and others. Indeed, sociologists assume that much of each person's individuality arises from one's interplay with the social environment, for in the absence of social relations, the human infant would develop into a dumb brute with little self-awareness.

Thus, for micro sociologists, interaction among

human beings is the fundamental social process. Interaction is the process by which we influence one another. We are endlessly tangled up in interactions, in influencing and being influenced by people around us. We act and our action affects others. They respond and their responses affect our next action. This, in turn, affects theirs. And so it goes, as we constantly adjust and readjust our activities according to feedback from our exchanges with others.

It is easy to see that human interaction consists primarily of communication. Through language, gestures, and actions we communicate with others and they communicate with us. However, unlike the grunts and hoots of animals, human communication relies heavily on symbols. **Symbols** are things that stand for or indicate another thing. The word *fish* is not a fish—it is intended to convey to a listener the idea of a fish. If humans could not use symbols, then you could know that Lake Washington is full of salmon only if someone led you to the lake and caught some salmon and showed them to you. That is exactly what a mother bear must do in order to get her cubs to learn to fish.

The use of symbolic communication can be extremely efficient, but it depends upon the ability of others to interpret or *decode* the symbols used. When we tell people we are happy, they cannot directly perceive how we feel. They must have learned to interpret the meaning of the symbol *happy.*

Theories of **symbolic interaction** have long dominated micro sociology. Their aim is to explain how interaction through the use of symbols makes and keeps people human. Sociologists who pursue these theories are often called *symbolic interactionists.* They focus on the personal, subjective meanings we attach to various symbols. How do participants engaged in interaction perceive their situations and the intentions and meanings of those around them? Is some behavior the result of misunderstandings of the meanings of symbolic communication? Indeed, do symbols mean the same things to different people? Such questions have led symbolic interactionists to conduct detailed studies of people engaged in face-to-face interactions. These researchers have also paid particular attention to children in order to learn how we develop the capacity to understand one another's use of symbols.

SYMBOLIC INTERACTION: COOLEY AND MEAD

Charles Horton Cooley (1864–1929) and George Herbert Mead (1863–1931) are considered the co-founders of symbolic interactionism. Both wondered how the human infant developed a self, and both concluded that each person's sense of self is *socially created.* In effect, we come to see ourselves as others see us; thus, we learn to view ourselves "from outside." The essence of humanness—our ability to contemplate our own existence, our past, and our future—comes to us from society.

For this reason, sociologists refer to the process by which infants develop into normal humans as *socialization.* When we judge someone to be an adequate person, we say that he or she has been adequately socialized—literally has been made social. At the start of our lives, we are not social because we are unable to understand the meaning of the behavior of those around us or to interpret the symbols they use to communicate. Therefore, we are unable to interact effectively. As will be seen in Chapter 6, if we are deprived of contact with others from birth, we fail to become socialized.

Cooley (1922) introduced the term *looking glass self* to describe the process by which our sense of self develops. Through symbolic interaction, humans serve as mirrors for one another. Whether we hold a good or poor opinion of ourselves depends upon our relationships with other people. The greater our skill is in bringing our actions into accord with theirs, the better their opinion of us is, which they reflect back to us, and the more certain we become of our own worth.

Mead (1934) carried Cooley's line of analysis considerably further. He distinguished two aspects of humans that arise out of the socialization process: the *mind* and the *self.* We must acquire certain skills in order to interact: We must learn to use and interpret symbols. Mead used the concept of **mind** to identify our *understanding of symbols,* arguing that the mind arises wholly out of repeated interaction with others.

The self also arises through social interaction. As Mead defined that term, the **self** is our learned understanding of the responses of others to our

Charles Horton Cooley.

George Herbert Mead.

conduct. Through long experience in seeing others react to what we do, we not only get a general notion of who we are but also are able to put ourselves in another's place—to see ourselves and the world as others do. Mead called this "taking the role of the other." From doing this repeatedly, we form a generalized notion of others—of what they want and expect and of how they are likely to react to us. That is, in order to know what we are like, we also have to know what they are like. Out of this tension between us and others, the self is formed.

Mead pointed out that until children develop a self, until they can take the role of the other, they cannot take an effective part in most games. In baseball, for example, children have to be able to anticipate what others will do in order to play. It is not enough that a shortstop knows to cover second when balls are hit to the right side of the infield; the other players must also know how shortstops play. To play ball, Mead wrote, a youngster must be able to put himself into "the various roles of all the participants

in the game, and govern his action accordingly" (1925). The next time you pass a soccer field where very young kids are playing, notice that they tend to be bunched around the ball. Each kid tries to get to the ball, and no one goes into position to receive a pass. It takes time for children to learn to take the role of the other, to reflect that when Tom gets the ball, I will get in position to receive a pass, and then George will break down the far side and I will cross the ball to him, and so on.

We develop a self by interacting with others, but we do not become skilled at interacting until we develop a self. In fact, Mead places the conscience in the self—in our awareness of how others will respond to our actions.

There is much more to symbolic interactionism than ideas about the origins of mind and self. From this simple starting point, we can deduce the existence of regularities, or patterns, in human interactions. Out of the process of interacting and exchanging with one another, we settle into a pat-

These two young men are doing more than simply talking, they are also shaping one another's self image. Each may be building up confidence that he is an interesting person as the other reacts favorably to what he says. Each is also probably aware of the other students who are listening in and their reactions will also count in the construction of a self.

tern of frequent interactions with certain people. We also discover and develop rules governing our interactions.

INTERACTION PATTERNS: ATTACHMENTS AND NORMS

To gain rewards, people must exchange with one another. However, self-interest limits the conditions under which people will exchange rewards. Indeed, the key insight on which Adam Smith based his economic theory is that when an exchange between two persons is voluntary, that is, when neither is being forced to yield rewards to the other, an exchange will not take place unless both persons believe they will benefit from it. When we give something to someone else, we expect a return—at the very least we expect them to appreciate our gift, to give us some degree of emotional reward. Perhaps one of the most common complaints expressed about

The saying that "old friends are the best friends" contains much sociological wisdom. The more frequently people interact and the longer the period of their interaction, the more they tend to like one another. For this reason older people shift their attachments less often and with greater reluctance than do younger people.

people is ingratitude—"After all I have done for him, is this the way he pays me back?"

Whenever we engage in an exchange with another person, we risk loss by not receiving an adequate return for what we give. That universal human problem leads to amazingly complex regularities in human interaction. When we exchange with someone and afterwards feel cheated, we tend to avoid exchanging with that person in the future. Conversely, when we exchange with someone and are satisfied with our return, we tend to seek exchanges with that person again. Consequently, over time people tend to establish stable exchange partnerships.

We make most of our face-to-face exchanges with a small number of people. Whether these exchange partners are family, friends, regular customers, or lovers, we recognize them as special to us. We have learned to count on them to provide us rewards in a "fair deal," a deal in which we also come out ahead. But they are important to us in another way as well: We have special sentiments toward them—it is these people that we like and love.

Human beings do not exchange only goods and services. Indeed, one of our major exchange commodities is sentiment. As Mead and Cooley pointed out, we can feel good about ourselves only if other people give us reason to do so. In a classic study, Miyamoto and Dornbusch (1956) found that college students' self-conceptions were remarkably similar to ratings of them made by their fellow students. Hence, people seek to interact with others who give them emotional rewards by indicating their approval and affection. There is an immense research literature demonstrating this simple point (Byrne, 1971).

Sociologists use the term **attachment** to identify a stable and persistent pattern of interaction between two people. Attachments are of special sociological interest because they are the bonds between an individual and society. That is, attachments represent something valuable to individuals—something for which people will expend costs to protect and maintain. But to keep these relationships, we must continue to make it rewarding for others to exchange with us. Common sense tells us that if we begin to cheat our friends, to abuse their affection and trust, we will soon lose them.

Although this point is self-evident, it has profound implications. Our attachments to others cause us to conform to certain expectations that they have about how we ought to behave. That is, attachments develop out of our exchanges with others only because we find exchange partners whose behavior is predictable. When we say we can count on Mary and Joe, that we can trust them, we are saying that their behavior follows certain known rules. As we saw in Chapter 2, such rules are called *norms*. The existence of norms is implicit in the possibility of attachments. If we can't predict how someone will behave, it becomes too risky to exchange with that person. Moreover, through our attachments, norms gain their force and significance. When we violate norms, we risk our attachments.

In Chapter 7 we shall see that the link between attachments and norms is central to theories of deviant behavior: People lacking attachments are free to violate norms. For now, however, our concern is with the opposite side of that same coin: to see the great costs people are willing to pay in order to preserve their attachments. When a friend says, "You know, I wouldn't do this for anybody else," that friend is demonstrating a powerful sociological "law." Human behavior is based on choice, but what we choose to do is greatly influenced by what our friends want us to do.

In the remainder of this chapter, we shall show how this major proposition of micro sociological theory applies to a variety of significant human activities. More important, we shall see how sociologists go about testing this aspect of micro theory to see if its predictions and prohibitions turn out as expected.

DOING MICRO SOCIOLOGY

At the start of this chapter, we saw that scientific theories must be testable. Theories predict or prohibit certain things that can be checked by research. Put another way, theories direct us to examine certain things and they predict what we shall find. **Research** is the process of making systematic observations. Thus, researchers test a theory by comparing the results of their observations with those predicted and prohibited by the theory.

The testable statements derived from theories are *hypotheses*. **Hypotheses** are specific predictions about the empirical or observable world. While theories are general and abstract, hypotheses are specific and concrete. For example, a portion of micro sociological theory tells us that, within human groups, strong attachments to others will result in conformity to the norms, while weak attachments will result in nonconformity. That is a very general statement. It applies to all groups, all people, all attachments, and the norms of all groups. To test such a statement, we must formulate specific predictions. That is, we must deduce hypotheses that define where we should look and what we expect to find.

For example, one of the innumerable hypotheses that we can derive from this theory is that boys in the United States who are close to their parents will be less likely to steal cars than boys who are not. We now have somewhere specific to look, some specific people to look at, and a clear idea of what the theory predicts we will find. In Chapter 7 we shall see that sociologists have confirmed this hypothesis in their research.

Remember that we can never prove that a theory is true—all we can do is test hypotheses. When the results do not agree with the theory, we know that the theory is false or at least incomplete. The more hypotheses we have tested and the more often and stringently we have tested them, the greater our confidence in the theory from which they are derived.

Since the statement that attachments produce conformity to the norms is so central to micro sociological theory, in the remainder of this chapter we shall watch from behind the scenes as several sociologists test different hypotheses derived from it. As these studies unfold, the logic of sociological research and some of its most typical features will be revealed. However, before we examine examples of research, it will be useful to establish the aim of most research: to demonstrate causation.

TESTING HYPOTHESES: CRITERIA OF CAUSATION

Most scientific hypotheses predict causal relationships. That is, they claim that something is the cause of something else. The hypotheses we examine in this chapter all predict that attachments to others will *cause* people to conform. To test these hypotheses, therefore, we need to be able to demonstrate a cause-and-effect relationship between the attachments and kinds of conformity we observe.

To claim that something causes something else, we must show that certain conditions are fulfilled. When any of these is not met, no causal relationships can exist. In order to demonstrate causation, we must show that a relationship meets three tests, or *criteria,* of causation.

Correlation

To show that something is the cause of something else, we must show that the two tend to occur in unison. That is, as one changes, the other also changes—fluctuations in the proposed cause produce fluctuations in the proposed effect. For example, to demonstrate that lack of attachments to

parents causes children to be delinquent, we must show that variations in the strength of attachments are matched by corresponding changes in delinquency. When things vary or change in unison, we say they are *correlated.*

Correlation can be either positive or negative. If one factor rises while the other declines, it is a negative correlation. This would be the case if we observed that auto theft by juveniles declined as attachments to parents rose. If both factors rise or fall together, that is a positive correlation. Either kind of correlation can demonstrate causation—indeed, a hypothesis will predict which kind is expected.

Time order

The second thing we must demonstrate in order to establish causation is **time order**, that is, that changes in the proposed cause occur *before* changes in the proposed effect—in other words, the cause occurs before the effect. This is simply to recognize that the idea of cause-and-effect makes no sense backwards. It is absurd to argue, for example, that you fell from a ladder because a friend pushed you if the push came after you had already fallen. Thus, if we observed that boys developed weak attachments to their parents only after they had stolen a car, then we would have to conclude that lack of attachments does not cause delinquency (in fact, we might suspect that misbehavior causes bad relations with parents).

Nonspuriousness

Finally, two factors often appear correlated, one seeming to be the cause of the other, when in fact they are correlated only because each is being caused by some third, unnoticed factor. If that is the case, we are observing **spuriousness**.

For example, we know that the average American marijuana smoker will live much longer than the average American who does not smoke marijuana. Therefore, marijuana smoking and life expectancy are correlated. We also can see that smoking or not smoking marijuana occurs before its alleged effect, the time of death. But even though this relationship meets the first two criteria of causation, we would be sadly misled if we believed that marijuana was the fountain of youth and took up smoking it in order to live longer. For we must not overlook the simple fact that the average American marijuana smoker is much younger than the average non-smoker. Smoking marijuana and living longer appear to be correlated only because each is correlated with age. When we examine people the same age, we do not find that marijuana smokers live longer. Correlations like this are spurious. To demonstrate cause and effect, we must establish that the correlation we observe is nonspurious: that it is not being caused by something else.

When sociologists test causal hypotheses, they must attempt to show that each of these three criteria of causation is met. In the next section, we will look over Richard Ofshe's shoulder as he tests a hypothesis and see why the experiment is the ideal method for demonstrating causation. But we will also be able to see why, despite this fact, most sociologists do not do experiments. Much of what we most need to study cannot or should not be manipulated in a laboratory. In fact, while thousands of sociological experiments have been conducted, Ofshe's is virtually the only one directly relevant to the proposition that attachments produce conformity. Let's see why, and let's also see how experiments work.

ATTACHMENTS AND CONFORMITY: AN EXPERIMENT

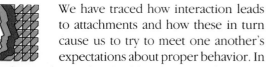

We have traced how interaction leads to attachments and how these in turn cause us to try to meet one another's expectations about proper behavior. In the late 1960s, Richard Ofshe, then a graduate student at Stanford, developed the hypothesis that, given a choice, people tend to support their friends when their friends disagree with strangers. Moreover, Ofshe

(1967, 1972) predicted that people tend to support their friends in such situations even if they don't really agree with their friends.

To test this hypothesis, Ofshe wanted to conduct an **experiment**, but this was very difficult to do. As we shall see, the power of experiments comes from being able to control what happens to those participating. Clearly, one cannot recruit a bunch of people to take part in an experiment and then randomly assign some of them to be good friends with each other. On the other hand, if we recruit some sets of friends and compare their reactions to those of other people who were recruited without friends, then randomization would be lost, and (as will be clear in the discussion below) the study would not be an experiment.

After giving some thought to these problems, Ofshe came up with a clever solution. He constructed a situation where he made some people *believe* that they were participating in an experiment with one of their friends when in fact no one else would be present. In this way he could randomly expose some people to pressure to support their friends.

Although the procedure was tricky, it was not unethical. We shall explore many experiments in this book in which deception was involved. To do experiments, researchers are required to gain approval from committees that review all proposed research involving human subjects. For such a proposal to be approved, the people must not be harmed by having been deceived (or by any other aspect of research), and when deception is involved, the actual nature of the study must be explained to the participants after they have taken part.

In his study, Ofshe recruited students from a nearby community college to be subjects in an experiment. While doing so, he told each student that another study was being planned in which friendship patterns among students would be analyzed. Ofshe then asked each of these students to name his or her four best friends on campus as possible subjects for this other study. About a month later individual volunteers were contacted and scheduled for the experiment. They were told that it was most important that they keep the appointment, since they would be taking part with two other students, and if anyone failed to show up, the session would have to be canceled.

When a student arrived for the experiment, he or she was told that the object of the study was to measure the physical responses of persons when others disagreed with their opinions. Two other students would be hooked up to devices that would record their physical reactions whenever they made a judgment that disagreed with the judgments of the others. These other two students were said to be in other rooms, and all communication was to occur electronically. The actual student subjects were told that their own physical reactions were not part of the study. Instead, they would be shown the judgments of the other two students, and their job was to register with whom they agreed when the other two students disagreed. Their judgment would then be communicated to the other two students.

The judgments to be made involved selecting the more artistically attractive of two visual patterns. After each pair had been shown, the "choice" made by the person in room 1 would appear on the upper half of the projection screen, while the "choice" of the student in room 2 would appear on the lower half. After these instructions were given, half of the subjects were told that the person in room 1 was a friend of theirs while the person in room 2 was a student they did not know. The other half of the subjects were told that both of the other participants were strangers. The experimental setup is illustrated in Figure 3-1.

Of course, there were no other subjects in the experiment. The judgments made by the other two "people" were fixed so that the same patterns occurred each time the experiment was run. What Ofshe wanted to know was the extent to which the judgments of people who thought a friend was in room 1 agreed with those of that person, and to compare this with the figures for the subjects who thought both other "participants" were strangers. Ofshe found a substantial bias by subjects toward the judgment of the person in room 1 when that person was believed to be a friend.

Now let's take Ofshe's experiment apart to see how it solves the problems of demonstrating causation. To proceed, it will be helpful to learn two terms used in research: the independent and the

Table 3-1 / The more times you flip a coin, the higher the odds against all heads.

Number of Flips	Odds Against All Heads
1	2 to 1
2	4 to 1
3	8 to 1
4	16 to 1
5	32 to 1
6	64 to 1
7	128 to 1
8	256 to 1
9	512 to 1
10	1024 to 1
11	2048 to 1
12	4096 to 1

dependent variable. A **variable** is any factor that can have two or more values. For example, in this experiment friendship was a variable that took two values: A friend either was or was not included in the "three-person" experiment. The term *independent variable* is used to indicate a cause, while the term *dependent variable* indicates an effect—we can say that variation in the dependent variable depends upon variation in the independent variable. In this study, friendship was the independent variable and bias in favor of room 1 was the dependent variable.

EXPERIMENTAL CONTROLS

Ofshe wanted to demonstrate bias in favor of a friend's judgments. Thus, he needed to put people in situations where nothing differed from subject to subject except their belief about who was in room 1. Recall that the criterion of nonspuriousness requires that all other potential causes be ruled out so that we can assume that variations in the independent variable cause the variations in the dependent variable. In experiments this is accomplished by **experimental controls**. These are measures taken to eliminate all other potential causes. This is why

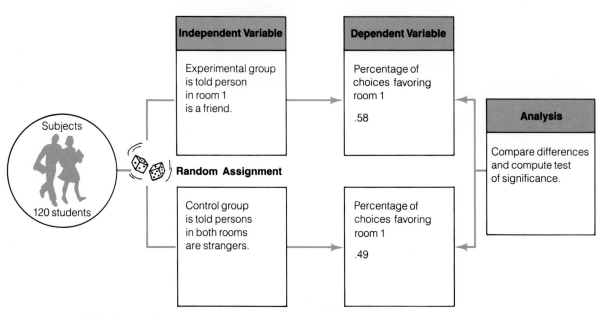

Figure 3-1 / Ofshe's experiment.

The precision of the experimental method rests in the ability of researchers to control what happens, when, and to whom. Here we see that Ofshe could randomly assign a student to either the experimental or the control group. Students in the experimental group all believed that the person in room 1 was a friend of theirs, while the person in room 2 was a stranger. Students in the control group believed that both of the other people were strangers. By comparing the results for the experimental group with those for the control group Ofshe could assess the extent to which the experimental group oversupported the choices of the person in room 1—a friend. Using a test of signifi-cance he could determine that the differences he found were unlikely to have occurred simply by chance.

Ofshe made sure that all subjects had an identical experience, saw the same patterns of responses, got identical instructions, and spoke to the same exper-imenter in the same room.

However, the experiment itself is not the only potential source of spuriousness. The subjects were not identical, since no two people are alike. Thus, differences among subjects had to be eliminated as a possible source of spuriousness. Some were males and some were females, some were older; some, doubtless, were more timid, and some might even have liked their campus friends less than others did. How could Ofshe prevent these differences from influencing his findings?

Randomization

Ofshe determined *at random* which students would be told they were taking part with a friend and which with strangers. He could have done this as easily as by flipping a coin before each student's appoint-ment and letting heads mean a friend was in room 1 and tails a stranger. Since you can't make people alike, you try to make *groups* alike; that is, by ran-dom assignment, experiments make it possible to compute the probability that groups will contain the same mix of ages, sexes, attitudes, and other traits. Because he used **randomization**, Ofshe could assume that both his groups were alike.

Time order

Experiments are ideal for establishing that causes occur before their presumed consequences, because experimenters can control *when* things happen. Ofshe arranged for students to know whether they were participating with a friend or with strangers before they were asked with whom they agreed.

Correlation

In any kind of research, it is easy to determine whether an independent variable and a dependent variable are correlated. One measures both variables and then sees if they vary together. Ofshe found that bias in favor of room 1 varied depending on the assumed relationship between the subject and the person in that room.

But there is a final matter that must be dealt with in evaluating the results of an experiment. Ofshe found a correlation in support of his hypothesis, but he still needed to know whether that correlation reflected a causal relationship or whether it could have occurred simply by chance. That is, he had to examine the probability that his results were produced by the failure of his random assignment to make the groups sufficiently alike. Here experimenters use a **test of significance**.

Significance

In determining whether to trust the results of an experiment, two things are taken into account: (1) the *number* of subjects on which the results are based and (2) the *size** of the correlation (that is,

the amount of change produced on the dependent variable). The logic involved is simple. We know that if we flip a coin many times, we eventually get about the same proportion of heads and tails. However, the fewer times we flip a coin, the greater the likelihood that we will get an unequal proportion of heads and tails. The same principle applies when subjects are randomly assigned to experimental groups. The more subjects involved, the greater the probability that potential differences between groups will be minimized. However, for any given number of subjects, the odds that a correlation is produced by random differences among the groups rather than by changes in the independent variable depend on the size of the correlation obtained. The larger the correlation is, the lower the probability that the finding is due to chance.

In this instance, when Ofshe computed the test of significance, he found that the odds were 20 to 1 against chance findings. That meets the usual standards used by social scientists.

Ofshe's study was a very strong test of his hypothesis not only because of the precision of experimental research but because it was a relatively weak situation. That is, as employed in his experiment, attachments lacked most of the power they usually possess in real life. Subjects did not know which of their friends was in room 1, they had no reason to suppose that the friend knew their identity, and they were not asked to support their friends on a matter of much importance. By the same token, they knew that the strangers were not true outsiders but were fellow students, possibly even acquaintances. Hence,

---

*The size of a correlation is expressed as a coefficient that can take any value between -1.0 and $+1.0$. When each shift in the independent variable produces a corresponding shift in the dependent variable, the correlation between them is perfect and is expressed as 1.0 (the positive or negative sign indicates whether the correlation is positive or negative). When shifts in the independent variable produce no shifts in the dependent variable, or when the fluctuations of one are random in relation to fluctua-

tions in the other, then the correlation coefficient is 0.0. Since correlations are seldom perfect (1.0), scientists must use their judgment in deciding when correlations are sufficiently large to be interesting. When correlations are based on large numbers of subjects or observations, even sociologically insignificant relationships will achieve statistical significance. For example, suppose Ofshe had run thousands of students through his experiment and discovered that a bias in favor of a friend occurred only once in every 100 opportunities. Given enough subjects, that frequency of occurrence would be statistically significant. But so slight a tendency to support friends would be sociologically insignificant. In fact, the important sociological result here would be that people essentially do not support friends in this kind of situation. In reality, of course, Ofshe found a much larger correlation and his results were both statistically and sociologically significant.

the motive to support their friends against the strangers could not have been very strong. Yet even in this weak situation, Ofshe found strong effects. Therefore, his experiment was a very demanding test of the theory.

Now suppose Ofshe had wanted to study conformity in a much stronger situation. Perhaps he might have wanted to examine the effects of deeply felt attachments, such as those between lifelong friends or lovers. He might have wanted to impose a much more demanding test on such attachments, such as asking people to accept a new religion because their friends had done so. In this case, Ofshe would have been forced to abandon the experimental method. As was already pointed out, it took originality and some deception to create even this weak attachment situation in a laboratory. But it is impossible to bring people into a lab and randomly assign them as lifelong friends or lovers, just as one could not randomly assign them to be young or old, male or female, or black or white. And, no review committee for human subjects would approve plans for an experiment to change people's religions, even if some sociologist were silly enough to propose such an experiment.

Yet sociologists need to study strong attachments, and they also need to study the effects of age, sex, and race on social behavior. And some of us even want to know about the role of attachments in religious conversion. Thus, much of our work cannot be done in the laboratory. For this reason, most sociological research is **nonexperimental research**. A number of research techniques have been been developed to try to meet the criteria of causation, even though we cannot manipulate what happens to people. In the remainder of this chapter and in the next, we shall see how this is done.

ATTACHMENTS AND CONVERSION: FIELD OBSERVATION

 A question of long-standing interest to sociologists as well as the general public is why people join new religious movements. For example, why do people in the United States from conventional religious backgrounds suddenly become Hare Krishnas or members of the Unification Church, or go to live in an ashram and study yoga with a guru from India?

When I began graduate school in 1960, that was a question that interested me. During several years as a newspaper reporter, I had been assigned to cover stories about a number of exotic new religions, including several based on revelations said to have been brought to earth by friendly aliens on flying saucers. During my first week of classes at the University of California at Berkeley, I met John Lofland, who was also interested in conversion to new religions. A great deal had been written on this topic over the years, but we found this work unconvincing. For one thing, nearly all of it seemed to have been researched in libraries, since there was very little to suggest that the authors had ever met any members of the groups they claimed to explain.

There was widespread agreement among these authors, however, that people joined a new religion because of the correspondence between the beliefs of the religion and the problems suffered by those who joined. The research procedure each scholar seemed to have followed was to study the ideology of a group in order to answer the question, What does this faith promise to do for people? Having determined this, they next asked, To whom do such promises most appeal? Thus, for example, if a new religious movement, such as Christian Science, claimed the ability to cure illness, it seemed very likely that it would most appeal to those with chronic illnesses or physical handicaps. Having deduced who ought to join a particular religious movement, these scholars seemed content to conclude that, in fact, those were indeed the people who actually did join.

But was that true? Lofland and I were not so sure. Moreover, we suspected that ideological appeals were emphasized as the cause of conversion primarily because that's about all that one can study about religious groups in the library. In the library, one can't watch anyone join a religious movement or even observe members' activities. About all one can find are books and articles written by the group to explain their ideology and works written by others to attack or criticize that ideology. But what really happens, we wondered? The only way to find out was to go out into the world and look, applying the methods of **field observation research**.

So we began looking around the San Francisco Bay Area for a group to observe. We wanted one that was new and growing but still small enough so that the two of us could closely observe most of what went on. After much hunting, we found exactly what we wanted. We discovered a group of about a dozen people who had just come to San Francisco from Eugene, Oregon, where they had been recruited to be the first American members of a new religion that had begun in Korea.

The group was led by a Korean woman, a former college professor, who had been sent to America to seek converts for a religious movement founded by Sun M. Moon. Moon was a Korean electrical engineer who believed that he had a revelation from God that Judgment Day was only a few years away. Although this group was tiny and unimpressive when Lofland and I found it, and was still very small when our study was finished, today it has become famous as the Unification Church, whose members are known to outsiders as "Moonies."

At the very start of our observational study of the Moonies, Lofland and I strongly suspected that there was much more to conversion than having a problem in life that was answered by Moonie theology. In fact, we were fairly sure that attachments played a major role. In effect, we planned to test the same proposition of micro sociological theory that Richard Ofshe tested in his experiment on attachments and conformity. We had two hypotheses in mind. First, people do not accept or join a new religion unless or until they form strong attachments with one or more members of the group. Second, people do not convert to a new religion unless their attachments to the group outweigh their attachments to persons outside the group. Quite simply, we were proposing that friendship, not ideology, played the dominant role in conversion—that joining a new religion was largely just accepting the religious beliefs and activities of one's friends.

Right away we found strong evidence to support our hypotheses. During her first months in Eugene, Miss Kim, the Moonie missionary, failed to make any converts. She attended many churches and managed to give talks to a number of women's clubs, but no one found her message attractive. But then, having moved to the edge of the city, Miss Kim became friends with a young housewife. Slowly she developed this woman's interest until one day the

John Lofland.

woman professed her belief in Kim's religious message. This woman then arranged for Kim to begin instructing two other women in the neighborhood. Soon they, too, joined. Then the husband of one of them joined, and he invited several men who worked with him home to hear Kim. They also converted. By the time the group decided to leave Eugene and attempt to build the movement in San Francisco, it had a dozen members, all of whom had been friends long before Kim met them. Thus, the initial growth of this movement had moved entirely along lines of pre-existing attachments.

Once in San Francisco, the group continued to draw some members from among their old friends in Eugene, but for some months they failed to convert anyone in San Francisco. They had no friends in that city, and they did not begin to gain new converts until they learned how to form friendships with other newcomers to San Francisco. Lofland and I spent as much time as possible with the group, watching the members convey their message to new people and waiting to see who accepted it. We soon found persuasive evidence that conversion required not only strong attachments to Moonies but also

When John Lofland and I studied them in the early 1960s, there were fewer than 30 American members of the Unification Church, sometimes called the Moonies. They have grown a lot since then, as can be seen in this photo of 2,000 couples taking part in a mass wedding ceremony held by the church in New York's Madison Square Garden. These people did not become Moonies because they were "brainwashed" or because they were desperate to find a new religion. Most joined the church primarily on the basis of their attachments to members—they accepted the religion that their close friends and relatives had accepted.

weak attachments to non-Moonies. We saw a number of people who formed strong friendships with Moonies, attended meetings regularly for a considerable time, and even professed belief in Moon's teachings, but they did not become Moonies. In each of these cases, the person had very strong attachments to outsiders who were not enthusiastic about the group. We watched people waver about joining the Moonies as they reacted to contrary influences.

People who joined were free of such pressures.

Often they were strangers themselves in the Bay Area, and their attachments were to people far away who were unaware of their evolving conversion. We even observed some people who formed strong attachments to Moonies while expressing complete disbelief in their doctrines. Several of these people moved into the apartment house owned by the group because of their friendships with members. This house also served as the Unification Church headquarters. Their decision to actually convert to the religion came months later, and then only after intimate, daily interaction with group members.

Lofland and I concluded that while elements of the Moonie doctrine did play a role in who joined—atheists never joined no matter how much they may have liked some members—the primary basis of conversion was attachment. Rather than being drawn to the group primarily because of the appeal of its doctrines, people were drawn to the doctrines because of their ties to the group.

Thus, attachments can make people accept "deviant" norms. That is, though many outsiders regard Moonies as weird, even as crazy, people willingly paid that price in order to align their behavior with that of their close friends. They were much less concerned about what the outside world thought of their actions than what their friends thought (Lofland and Stark, 1965; Lofland, 1966).

You will notice that Lofland and I could not be nearly so precise about meeting the criteria of causation in our study as we could have through an experiment. Of course, there was no way we could randomly assign people to have or not have Moonie friends and then sit back to await conversion. Nevertheless, we could meet causation criteria to some extent. First, by keeping careful records on each person who came into contact with the Moonies, we established a correlation between attachment and conversion. No one ever joined without having close attachments. Second, because we observed the group over a considerable period of time, we were able to demonstrate time order. The friendships occurred before the conversions. Indeed, in many cases the friendships had already existed for many years.

To demonstrate nonspuriousness is a much more difficult problem in nonexperimental research. There was little we could do to ensure that people who had friendships with Moonies weren't different in other significant ways from those without such friendships. We didn't notice such differences, but they might have existed. Hence, there is always an element of risk in accepting nonexperimental research findings. In Chapter 4 we shall examine some statistical procedures that help to decrease the possibility of spuriousness in nonexperimental studies, but these usually do not apply to the observational variety of nonexperimental research.

You may be wondering what Lofland and I told the Moonies we were up to while we did our study.

At first we told them nothing. We met one of their missionaries, who invited us to come and learn about their message, and we simply took her up on the offer. After a little while, however, we decided to explain to them what we were doing, since it was beginning to get awkward to sneak off to the bathroom every time we wanted to write down our observations.

Miss Kim was quite willing to let two young sociologists from Berkeley study her group. If nothing else, she thought we might compile a useful historical record. In fact, not long ago a young Moonie enrolled at a major Protestant seminary drew upon our published study and interviewed us in order to write a history of the founding of his church in America.

REPLICATION

Scientific tests of hypotheses rarely rest upon a single piece of research. Instead, the original researcher or other researchers repeat the studies to see if they obtain the same results. Such studies are called **replications**.

It usually is quite easy to replicate an experiment. For example, to replicate Ofshe's study, one would only need to create the same laboratory setup, recruit experimental subjects in the same way, and then repeat the experiment. If the result came out the same way again, we would have even greater confidence that the hypothesis is correct.

It is more difficult but even more important to replicate nonexperimental research. For example, perhaps attachments play a major role in conversion only among the Moonies but not among other groups, such as the Hare Krishnas. The only way to learn if the results that Lofland and I obtained have broad applications would be to examine conversion to many other religious groups. However, to do that might have taken Lofland and me the rest of our lives. Fortunately, sociology is not a solitary calling. Sociologists pay attention to one another's work and are often prompted to follow up on something someone else has proposed or observed.

It has been twenty years since Lofland and I published our study of conversion. In that time I have learned of more than twenty replications (for example, Gerlach and Hine, 1970; Richardson and Stewart, 1978; Snow and Philips, 1980). These replications have involved a great variety of groups, from Adventists to Zen Buddhists. While there is evidence that attachments may not play so central a role in accepting mystical beliefs when no participation in a religious group is involved (accepting the truth of astrology columns, for example), attachments have consistently been found to play the major role in explaining who converts to a new religious group.

CONCLUSION

This chapter has introduced the fundamental building blocks of micro sociological theory. We have seen that humans must interact and exchange with one another and that they therefore tend to form attachments and conform to one another's expectations. In this way, norms arise to guide and structure our behavior. Throughout the rest of the book, we shall see how this elementary theoretical scheme serves as the basis for quite elaborate theories from which a great variety of hypotheses can be derived.

In this chapter we have also begun to examine how hypotheses are tested through research. The experimental method excels in satisfying the criteria of causation, which is why it is the common research method in fields that do not require human subjects: Not only do bacteria not blush when they are being observed, but they also have no legal rights and elicit no sympathy. However, since sociologists study people, we often cannot utilize the experimental method. In this chapter we examined an observational field study and saw how it attempted to approximate the precision of experiments. In the next chapter we shall encounter more sophisticated nonexperimental forms of research. We shall also encounter macro sociological theories.

Review glossary

Theories Sets of statements that say why and how several concepts are related. For a set of statements to qualify as a theory, it must also be possible to deduce some conclusions from it that are subject to empirical verification; that is, theories must predict or prohibit certain observable events or conditions. (p. 50)

Choice theories All social science theories based on the proposition that human action reflects conscious choices. (p. 52)

Social interaction Human efforts to influence one another. (p. 53)

Altruism The name applied to behavior that is alleged to be contrary to self-interest and to occur entirely for the benefit of someone else. (p. 54)

Symbols Things used to stand for and indicate another thing. For example, the word "fish" is not really a fish, but is used to convey the thought or idea of a fish. (p. 56)

Symbolic interaction The human use of symbols to influence one another. Conversation is the most common form of symbolic interaction. (p. 56)

Mind As used by Mead, *mind* refers to the human capacity to understand symbols. (p. 56)

Self As used by Mead, *self* refers to our learned ability to gauge the responses of others to our conduct. (p. 56)

Attachment A stable and persistent pattern of interaction between two people. (p. 60)

Research The process of making systematic observations. (p. 60)

Hypotheses Specific predictions derived from theories and subject to testing by research. (p. 60)

Correlation What exists when variation in one phenomenon is matched by variations in another phenomenon, for example, when fluctuations or variations in outdoor temperatures coincide with variations in how warmly people dress. For something to be the cause of something else, the two must be correlated. (p. 61)

Time order The determination that changes in a cause occur prior to changes in its effects. (p. 61)

Spuriousness The appearance of a correlation between two phenomena because each is related to some third phenomena. For example, the number of firefighters at a fire and the amount of damage done by the fire appear to be correlated because both are related to the size of the fire. For a cause-and-effect relationship to exist, the correlation must be nonspurious. (p. 61)

Experiment A research design in which the researcher has control over the independent variable, that is, can manipulate when and how strongly the independent variable occurs, and has the ability to determine randomly which subjects are exposed to which level of the independent variable. (p. 62)

Variable Something that can take more than one value; something that varies. As used in science, the term *independent variable* is used to identify a cause, while the term *dependent variable* refers to the consequence of some cause. (p. 63)

Experimental controls Methods to ensure that nothing varies in an experiment except the independent variable, thus ensuring nonspuriousness. (p. 63)

Randomization Use of chance to assign people to experimental treatments in order to equalize groups exposed to different levels of the independent variable. (p. 64)

Test of significance A computation of the odds that a correlation occurred simply by chance; social scientists usually require that the odds against a chance finding be 20 to 1 or greater (the .05 level of significance) before they will trust a result. (p. 65)

Nonexperimental research All forms of research that are not experiments. (p. 66)

Field observation research Studies done by observing what people do in their normal situations (in contrast with observing them in a laboratory). (p. 66)

Replications Studies that repeat earlier research and thus serve both to check against chance findings and to extend the range of research findings by showing that the findings apply in another time or place. (p. 69)

Suggested readings

Blau, Peter M. *Exchange and Power in Social Life.* New York: Wiley, 1964.

Campbell, Stephen. *Flaws and Fallacies in Statistical Thinking.* Englewood Cliffs, N.J.: Prentice-Hall, 1974.

Homans, George. *Social Behavior: Its Elementary Forms.* New York: Harcourt Brace Jovanovich, 1974.

Phelps, Edmund S., ed. *Altruism, Morality, and Economic Theory.* New York: Russell Sage Foundation, 1975.

Popper, Karl R. *The Logic of Scientific Discovery.* New York: Basic Books, 1959.

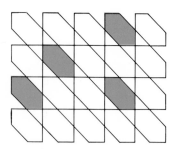

■ Suppose that you have volunteered to take part in a discussion group organized by one of your professors. When you arrive, he shows you to a booth equipped with a microphone. He explains that in order to let each participant remain anonymous, the discussion will take place over an intercom system. When it is your turn to talk, a light will come on and your mike will be open. Five other people will take part in the discussion, which will be about problems in adjusting to college. After explaining this, the professor leaves.

The discussion begins, and each person takes a turn. Suddenly one of the others, who had already mentioned that he had been a bit scared about going to college because he sometimes has epileptic seizures, begins to stammer and breathe hard into the microphone. He gasps out the word "Help." Then there is a crash, like a body falling to the floor. You can't speak to the others because your mike is not on. You don't know where your professor has gone, but he promised not to listen in. What do you do?

What you are most likely to do depends upon how many other people you believe are part of the discussion group. In the actual experiment, no one else was really present. All the other voices were simply tape recordings, including the young man who had the seizure. When this experiment was done by John Darley and Bibb Latanè (1968), some subjects were told that they would be one of two people in the discussion. Others were told there were three, and still others were told there were six (Figure 4-1). When subjects thought that they were part of a two-person group—therefore they alone knew the young man was having a seizure—*all* of them quickly left the booth to seek help. But

Macro Sociology:
Structures and Systems

when subjects thought it was a three-person group—and thus one other person was also aware of the emergency—only 80 percent left the booth to seek help, and they also took longer to respond. Subjects in the six-person situation were even slower to seek help, and only 60 percent attempted to do so.

What is going on here? Clearly, these differences in the apparent willingness of people to help someone else are not due to differences of individual character. Since people were randomly assigned to groups of different sizes, the three groups should have contained the same mix of personality types and other individual characteristics. What is going on here is **social structure**. Quite beyond individual characteristics are characteristics of the groups in which we exist, and these group features operate as structures that influence our behavior in the same way that physical structures, such as the position of doorways, do. <u>All characteristics of groups are social structures</u>.

In this instance, Darley and Latanè were conducting research on *group size* as a social structure. They had hypothesized that the larger the group believed to be present, the less an individual will feel personal responsibility to act in an emergency. And that is precisely what the results of their experiment showed.

While micro sociology focuses on the individual and his or her immediate social surroundings, macro sociology focuses on social structures. This includes features of groups, organizations, and even whole societies, how social structure is created, how one aspect of structure affects another aspect, and how these larger social collectivities function as whole systems. ■

CHAPTER PREVIEW

In this chapter we shall examine basic elements of macro sociological theories, or theories about social structure, and the typical modes of research used to test these theories. However, because people often find it a bit difficult at first to think in terms of social structure rather than in terms of the individual, it will be useful for us to sneak up on the subject. Therefore, we shall start with some recent research that began as micro sociology. However, after confusing and contradictory research findings were obtained, the research was reoriented to macro sociology in order to resolve the problems. This study will prepare the way for a discussion of macro sociological theories and also permit the most common form of sociological research to be examined: the survey. After we examine elements of macro theory, we will then see how people do macro sociological research.

DISCOVERING SOCIAL STRUCTURE

 In 1968 Travis Hirschi and I were both on the staff of the Survey Research Center at the University of California at Berkeley. He was completing a book called *Causes of Delinquency,* which has since become a classic, and I was completing a book on religious behavior in America. We had been close

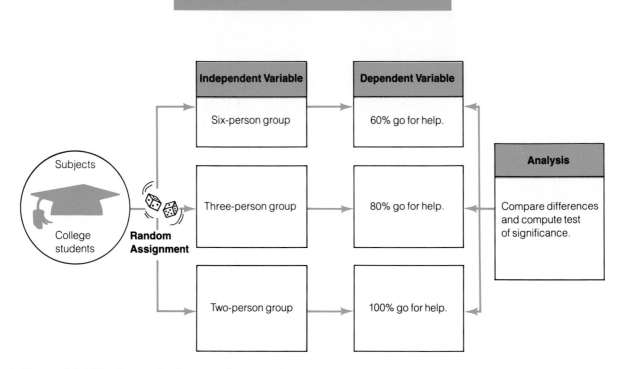

Figure 4-1 / The bystander intervention experiment.

Random assignment of subjects ensures that, although each subject differs from all others, the three groups of subjects will be alike (except for random variation). For this reason perceptions of group size, not something else, must have caused the differences among these three groups on the dependent variable—going for help. As the perceived size of the group declined, the proportion who went for help increased.

friends since we began graduate school together in 1960, and one day we decided to write a paper together to test the hypothesis that religious commitment inhibits delinquent behavior. Oddly enough, for all the many studies that had been done on delinquency, there was virtually no research on this question, despite the fact that nearly all sociologists and nonsociologists alike assumed the hypothesis to be true. Maybe that's why no one had bothered to test it. In any event, we used a method called survey research to test this hypothesis.

Religion and delinquency: survey research

Survey research has two basic elements. First, the data are collected by *personal interviews* or by hav-

ing each individual complete a *questionnaire*. Thus, if you want to know how religious people are, you ask them a series of questions about what they believe and do. If you want to know about their delinquency, then you ask them questions about violations they may have committed.

Obviously, problems can arise about whether people answer truthfully and whether they are even able to give accurate answers. For example, research has demonstrated that people do not report their TV viewing habits very accurately. To get good information about this subject, it is necessary to have people keep daily logs on what they watch. However, an immense amount of effort has gone into perfecting survey research techniques, and the data so obtained can be quite reliable when proper techniques are used and safeguards observed.

The second feature of survey research is the use

Bystander intervention, the willingness of people to go to the aid of strangers, has been a major topic in sociological research during the past several decades. Not surprisingly, people are more willing to help when they don't think it too risky to intervene, and therefore people in small towns are more often helpful than people in large cities. However, many social scientists were surprised to learn that people will more often help when they confront an emergency alone than when others are also present.

of *samples.* When we want to know about the religious behavior of the American public, we do not attempt the huge task of asking every single citizen. Instead, techniques have been developed to obtain accurate results by questioning only a selected few, or a **sample** from the larger population. If the sample is chosen properly, we can assume that the results will reflect on the whole population. Special Topic 1 describes how sampling is done.

Hirschi and I proceeded to investigate the effects of religion on delinquency on the basis of questionnaires filled out by a sample of students enrolled in junior high schools and high schools in Richmond, California, a city of about 100,000 people across the bay from San Francisco.

Our first concern was to see if there was a correlation between religion and delinquency. To do this, we first separated the data according to two categories of students: those who attended church frequently (at least once a month) and those who did not. Then we sorted each of these groups into delinquents (those who had recently committed two or more delinquent acts) and nondelinquents (those who had recently committed no more than one delinquent act). When we were finished, the results looked like those shown in Table 4-1, which shows the percentages of delinquents and nondelinquents within each religious category. It is clear that the findings seem to support our hypothesis. Frequent church attenders are much less likely to be delinquent (22 percent) than infrequent church attenders (38 percent). Thus, our results fulfilled the first criterion of causation (see Chapter 3). But what about the other two?

It is much more difficult to establish *time order* for questionnaire data than for data from experi-

Travis Hirschi.

Table 4-1 / Church attendance and delinquency.

	Church Attendance	
	Frequent	Infrequent
Delinquent	22%	38%
Not delinquent	78%	62%
	100%	100%

Source: Adapted from Hirschi and Stark (1969). The results shown here have been modified and simplified for clarity. However, they accurately reflect patterns in the actual data.

Table 4-2 / Controls for sex reveal a spurious relationship.

	Church Attendance	
	Frequent	Infrequent
Boys		
Delinquent	50%	50%
Not delinquent	50%	50%
	100%	100%
Girls		
Delinquent	10%	10%
Not delinquent	90%	90%
	100%	100%

Source: Adapted from Hirschi and Stark (1969). The results shown here have been modified and simplified for clarity. However, they accurately reflect patterns in the actual data.

ments. It is possible that people become delinquents and then become infrequent church attenders. However, other research shows that patterns of church attendance among teenagers primarily reflect family religious patterns, which are usually established long before children reach junior high. Indeed, these patterns may have been established well before a child was born. So it is reasonable to assume that the criterion of time order was met by this study.

But what about the criterion of nonspuriousness? Obviously, delinquent and nondelinquent teenagers are likely to differ in many ways other than church attendance. Could one of these other, uncontrolled factors cause a spurious correlation between church attendance and delinquency? The answer turned out to be yes.

A spurious finding

Hirschi and I knew that boys are much more likely than girls to be delinquents. We also knew that girls are more likely than boys to be frequent church attenders. So we knew we had to examine the possibility that sex differences were the real cause of the correlation in Table 4-1. We used a simple technique to check this out. First, we divided the sample into males and females. Then we examined the relationship between church attendance and delinquency separately for males and females.

The results were like those shown in Table 4-2. There we can see that boys who attend church are no less likely to be delinquent than boys who do not (50 percent of both groups are delinquents). The same holds among females: Ten percent of the girls who attend church frequently are delinquents, as are 10 percent of the girls who do not.

Thus, we must conclude that the correlation found

in Table 4-1 is spurious—religion *does not* cause people to refrain from delinquent behavior. We know a relationship is spurious if it disappears when some third variable is controlled. As a check, we tried many other measures of religiousness, including belief in heaven and hell, Sunday school attendance, and even parents' church attendance. None of these was correlated with delinquency either *when* sex differences were controlled.

Hirschi and I were astonished at these results. After all, we had set out to test something that everyone knew to be true. Frankly, we had not even been sure the study was worth the time and trouble. In fact, had the data not already been available to us (we used a fragment of the information already collected from this sample by Hirschi), we probably would not have bothered with it. However, what we found turned a lot of what everyone had believed about the world upside down . . . for a while.

After our findings were published (Hirschi and Stark, 1969), most sociologists accepted our results, and the paper was frequently cited and often reprinted. Within several years the "knowledge" that religion fails to guide teenagers along the straight and narrow was enshrined in undergraduate textbooks. But then problems began to turn up as other researchers tried to replicate our research.

Structure and a "lost" relationship

Several years after our study was published, two other scholars replicated it with a sample of teenagers from several cities in the Pacific Northwest (Burkett and White, 1974). They found that religious commitment reduced the possibility of teenagers using drugs or alcohol (which Hirschi and I had not investigated), but they, too, could find no religious effects on other kinds of delinquency. While no one could explain why religion did not influence delinquency, it still seemed that it did not.

But then two more studies yielded very different results. The first, based on a sample of teenagers in Atlanta (Higgins and Albrecht, 1977) found a very strong negative correlation between church attendance and delinquency—exactly what Hirschi and I had expected to find. The second, based on teen-

agers living in six wards (congregations) of the Mormon Church (Albrecht et al., 1977), found the same thing. At this point a fifth study that had gone unnoticed came to light (Rhodes and Reiss, 1970). Based on a sample of Nashville students, it also reported a substantial negative correlation between church attendance and delinquency.

Does religion inhibit delinquency or not? The research score stood at three to two—three studies said yes, while two said no. To shrug and say that sometimes religion does inhibit delinquency and sometimes not is not a satisfactory scientific response. When does religion have this effect, when doesn't it, and why? That was the pressing issue.

As I pondered the various studies, I began to realize that what had been conceived of as a micro sociological hypothesis had to be reformulated as a macro hypothesis. That is, I began to see that religion is not primarily an individual characteristic, a set of beliefs and practices of the particular person. Instead, it gains its power and impact on the individual as an aspect of social structure. Thus it is not religiousness alone that influences a teenager's tendency to be delinquent, but whether the majority of a teenager's friends are also religious. Thus, I was prepared to argue that in communities where most young people do not attend church, religion will not inhibit delinquency even of those teenagers who are religious.

It is in day-to-day interaction with our friends that we form our conceptions of the norms. If most of our friends are not religious, then religious considerations will rarely enter into the process by which norms are adopted or justified. Even if we are religious and do bring up religious considerations, these will not strike a responsive chord in most of our associates. In such a situation, the effect of individual religious commitment is smothered by group irreligiousness and tends to become a very "compartmentalized" component of the life of the individual—something that surfaces only in specific situations, such as in Sunday school and church. However, when most of a young person's friends are religious, then religion enters freely into everyday interactions and becomes a valid part of the normative system. In such communities, young people who are religious are much less likely to be delinquent than those who are not religious.

My next step was to test this hypothesis. If my explanation was sound, studies should find a strong negative relationship between religion and delinquency in communities where most people are religious. When studies are done in communities where most people are not religious, no correlation should be found.

As a result of other research, I already knew a great deal about the religious geography of the United States. The most striking feature is a remarkable "unchurched belt" running along the shores of the Pacific: church membership in California, Oregon, Washington, Alaska, and Hawaii is far lower than in the rest of the nation. In most of the nation, a substantial majority belongs to a church, but in the Pacific region only about a third belong (see Chapter 13).

These geographic patterns strongly supported my macro explanation of the contradictory research. Hirschi and I had found no correlation in our data from California, and Burkett and White had found none in theirs from Washington and Oregon. But studies done in Georgia, Utah, and Tennessee had found strong correlations. So I began to seek further tests of this geographic effect.

Survey studies are very expensive, and they usually collect far more data than the initial researchers can use. For that reason, computer tapes containing the original data from a survey are usually placed in public archives. I searched such archives for surveys on delinquency that had included data on religion. I found one done in Provo, Utah, which has the highest church membership rate in America. If I was right, these data ought to show a strong negative correlation, and they did. Next, I gained access to a survey of high school students in Seattle, which has one of the lowest church membership rates in the nation. Here I expected no correlation to show up, and none did.

Finally, I was able to locate a huge national survey based on samples of 16-year-old boys at eighty-seven high schools. Rather than simply relying on the geographic location of these schools, I was able to assess the proportion of religious students in each. I then hypothesized that religion would be negatively correlated with delinquency in the schools where the majority of students were religious, but that no correlation would be found in those schools (nearly all of which were on the West Coast) where most students were not. And that's exactly what the data showed (Stark, Kent, and Doyle, 1982).

Thus we meet social structure. In Richmond, Seattle, and many other West Coast cities, apparently it did not matter that some parents raised their children to be religious—at least not when it came to keeping them out of trouble with the law. This was because the surrounding social structure, in this case the irreligion of the majority, overwhelmed the effects of religion on the individual. In most of the rest of the country, however, a religious upbringing does decrease delinquency among young people, because individual religiousness is reinforced by the surrounding religious majority. Thus the expected correlation between religiousness and delinquency that got "lost" for a while, when Hirschi and I failed to find it in California, turned out to be alive and well on the other side of the mountains. Once again we see why there must be macro as well as micro sociology: Social structure is as real as personal traits, and when we fail to consider structural effects, we often can make no sense out of our research.

MACRO SOCIOLOGICAL THEORIES

Macro sociology is the study of larger social structures, and macro sociological theories attempt to explain the existence of social structures (how they arise and the causes of different kinds of structures), the relationships among social structures, and the interplay between the individual and social structures. While macro sociology has its own distinctive subject matter, it is not independent of micro sociology any more than micro sociology can ignore macro phenomena—as we have just seen. In fact, all macro theories include, either explicitly or implicitly, micro assumptions. For example, all macro theories assume that human beings operate on the basis of rational choice, or self-interest. For a specific example, when a macro theory generates the prediction that a rapid decline in the average standard of living in a society will produce political conflict, such a statement implies that people pursue rewards and try to avoid costs. When their rewards

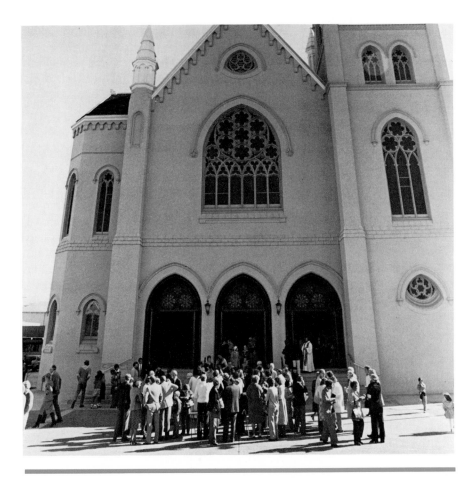

Will these children be less likely to commit juvenile crimes because they attend church? The answer to that question depends upon where this picture was taken. If it is in a city where the majority of citizens belong to a church, then going to church greatly reduces the probability of juvenile delinquency. But if it is in a city like those along the West Coast, where the majority do not belong to church, then church attendance seems to have no influence on delinquency.

fall sharply, they get unhappy. Although there are several competing schools of macro sociological theory, they make similar assumptions about micro sociology. Moreover, these schools of thought also make many common assumptions about the fundamental features of social structures. Chief among these is the assumption that the social structures found in a society are connected, for societies are social systems.

ELEMENTS OF SYSTEMS

Macro sociologists assume that societies are not chance collections of people, culture, and social structures—they assume instead that societies are systems. The idea of a **system**, whether we are discussing the solar system or a social system, has three important elements (von Bertalanffy, 1967). First, a system consists of a number of separate parts, or *structures*. The solar system, for example, primarily consists of the sun and nine planets. Second, these parts are *interdependent,* or connected, so that changes in one part produce changes in at least one other part. Third, because parts are interdependent, they tend to fall into some kind of *equilibrium,* balance or steadiness in their interrelations. No part is free to fly off on its own path, for its connections with other parts limit its actions. Let's examine how societies fulfill each of these elements of a system.

Social structures

Societies consist of innumerable structures. Here it is sufficient to note two social structures that are often treated in macro sociological theories: *institutions* and *classes*.

Institutions Sociologists recognize that social roles, groups, and activities are not randomly arranged within societies, but tend to be clustered. Moreover, each of these clusters makes fairly specific contributions to the overall welfare of a society by satisfying basic needs required for the society to exist. For example, children must be born and prepared to replace adults, or else the group will die out. Arrangements must also exist to produce and distribute goods and services among members of a society; without food, shelter, and clothing, humans cannot live.

Relatively permanent patterns, or clusters, of specialized roles, groups, organizations, customs, and activities devoted to meeting fundamental social needs are called **social institutions**. From examining many societies, both primitive and modern, sociologists have concluded that at least five basic social institutions exist in all societies: the family, the economy, religion, the political order, and education. Part Four discusses each of these institutions in detail.

Many macro theories use institutions as basic elements of social structure and attempt to relate one institution to another. For example, because the Protestant Reformation and the rise of industrial capitalism both occurred in Europe during the sixteenth century, there has been a long theoretical

debate over which might have been the cause of the other (see Chapter 16). That is, did changes in religious institutions cause changes in economic institutions, or vice versa? Indeed, a third school of thought holds that neither caused the other, but that both changed because of changes in the political institutions.

Classes Every known society has been *stratified.* That is, some members have had more power, property, and prestige than others. Classes are another major element of social structure, for, as we saw in Chapter 2, classes are groups of people having a similar position within a society's stratification system. (In Chapter 9, we shall expand this definition of classes and assess disputes about how to conceptualize stratification systems.) To explain how a society operates, macro sociologists often examine relationships among its various classes, arguing that *conflicts* among classes can cause crises in a society and be an important source of change. For example, class conflict can erupt into revolutions.

Institutions and classes are major concepts in most macro sociological theories. Indeed, many theories focus on the interplay between these social structures—for example, on how class interests shape the structure of a society's institutions.

Interdependence

Because societies are systems, the various social structures are connected; consequently, a change in one structure produces changes in some other structures. If you have a number of tiny parts spread out on a workbench—say, small gear wheels, springs, and screws—moving one part has no effect on the remaining parts. But if these parts are assembled into a watch and thus become a system, then the movement of one part affects at least several other parts, and the overall state of the system is changed.

Macro sociologists work from the assumption that societies are more like watches than like an array of disassembled watch parts. As noted above, they seek to explain why and how various social structures show **interdependence**. They do not, however, assume that every structure is related to every other structure, nor do they assume that the same degree of interdependence among structures exists

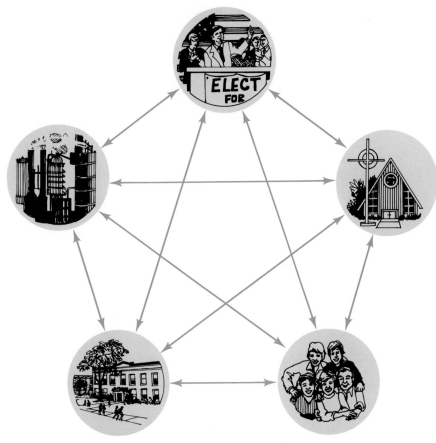

Figure 4-2 / Society as a system of institutions.

To discover why and how one social institution influences another is a major activity among macro sociologists. Will changes in family structure prompt religious or economic changes? Part Four of this book is devoted to the study of institutions.

in all societies. In fact, as we shall see in Chapter 16, sometimes so little connection exists among social structures that a society falls apart.

Equilibrium and change

The interdependence among elements of a social structure necessarily limits the possible variation in any given element. If we continue our mechanical analogy, a given element of social structure can be pulled only so far before its connections with other elements begin to limit further pulling. Such mutually limiting connections among social structures mean that the overall system tends toward a state of balance, or **equilibrium**. That is, the free movement of elements is limited by their connections with other elements. However, societies are never wholly static. Even those with the greatest equilibrium fluctuate constantly as their parts shift to remain in general alignment. This occurs, if for no other reason, because societies are *open systems*. Just as they are composed of living organisms who must interact with the physical environment, so do societies constantly react to outside forces.

Figure 4-3 / Society as a system of classes.

Imagine how different are the lives led by people living in these houses and you will begin to understand why so many sociologists think that class conflicts play the primary role in shaping societies. Part Three of this book is devoted to conflict and inequality.

There is nothing magical or mysterious about the notion that systems, including social systems, tend toward equilibrium. If we bend a cogwheel in a watch, the watch will no longer keep time. Likewise, not just any arrangement of the parts of a society will suffice to keep that society going. Societies can fall apart when their fundamental structures fail to be compatible. Equilibrium reflects the tendency for social structures to remain mutually compatible—not only when they are standing still, but also when they are *changing*. In Chapter 16 we shall pursue this in much greater detail and see that periods of very rapid social change are often dangerous times for societies because of the risk of structural misalignment and malfunction.

I have already mentioned that there are three important and sometimes competing schools of thought among macro sociological theorists. Some regard the disputes among these schools as so fundamental and vast that one must choose sides. I, on the other hand, tend to see them as more complementary than conflicting—each provides solutions to some problems that the others cannot. In any event, an introduction to the field must identify the particular emphasis and outlook of each of these major schools of macro theory.

FUNCTIONALISM

Because societies are open systems—systems that exchange with their environments—it proves useful to explain social structures on the basis of their consequences, or functions, for other parts of the system, especially as these parts come under pressure from the environment. Theories taking this form are called **functional theories**, and the school of macro sociology that favors them is called **functionalism**.

Functional theories are common throughout science. Since sociologists adopted functionalism from biology, it is useful to start with a simple biological example in order to clarify the logical structure of functional theories. Why do we have sweat glands? Biologists answer that humans have sweat glands (a physiological structure of that system called the human body) because of their function, namely, to prevent the body temperature from rising too high for our organs to survive. Such a cooling mechanism is needed because the human environment is often warm enough to endanger the organism. When the environment causes a person to overheat, the sweat glands release water stored in the body. The evaporation of this water on the surface of the body causes cooling. By explaining sweat glands in this way, biologists display the basic elements of all functionalist theories.

According to Arthur Stinchcombe (1968), functionalist theories have three components. First, there is the *part of the system* to be explained. In the above example this is the sweat glands. Second, we explain the existence of this part by identifying how it *preserves* some other part of the system from disruption or overload. In our example, sweat glands prevent other organs of the body from being damaged by high temperatures. Third, the *source* of this potential disruption or overload must be identified. In our example, this is identified as high temperatures in the environment.

Now let's apply these principles to a sociological example. When we examine primitive societies, we frequently find that the family unit is defined differently from the family in modern societies. While most Americans grow up in a **nuclear family** (one adult couple and their children), primitive societies often have **extended families**, which include several adult couples and their children. For example, in many societies the sons remain at home; when they marry, they bring their wives home to live.

Suppose we want to explain why the extended family is common among primitive societies. According to functionalism, we must see what contribution or "function" the extended family makes to some other part of such societies. Looking closely, we see that in such societies the family serves to support dependents, be they young, handicapped, ill, or elderly. To do this, the family must always include an adequate number of able-bodied adults. That is, there must be enough family members to support dependents.

However, under the conditions of life in many primitive societies, the death rate is so high that it constantly threatens the capacity of the family to support dependents. So many adults die while still young that if other adults were not on hand to assume their responsibilities, many dependents could not be supported. The extended family, by clustering adult couples into a single unit, minimizes the impact of this source of disruption (Figure 4-4). When a man dies, other men in the family remain to feed and shelter his widow and children; when a woman dies, other adult women remain to raise her children and cook for her widower. The extended family substitutes for welfare programs, retirement plans, and insurance policies; these latter programs identify what are called functional alternatives.

While functional theories attempt to explain social structures by describing their contributions to the system, functionalists do not assume that only one structural form can fulfill a particular function. For example, while all mammals die if they become too warm, many mammals, including dogs, do not have sweat glands. Instead of sweating when they get hot, dogs hang out their tongues and begin to pant. The evaporation of water from their large tongues cools the air as they inhale to keep their body temperature within tolerable limits. This is a **functional alternative** to the sweat gland—another structure by which the same function can be accomplished. By the same token, modern societies have released the family from having sole responsibility for supporting dependents by creating welfare programs. In this way the extended family has been replaced.

Nor do functional theories propose that all social structures have beneficial effects for social systems. Indeed, such theories often identify *dysfunctions,* arrangements among structures that harm or distort the system. Nor do functionalist theories assume that all social systems *ought* to survive. In discussing the survival of societies, we raise the fundamental subject matter of the second major form of macro sociological theories: social evolution.

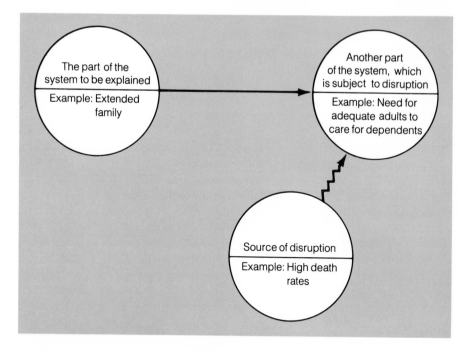

Figure 4-4 / Diagram of a functional theory.

Functional theories explain why a given part of any system exists by showing how it prevents some other system part from being disrupted. In this example the extended family is explained as a social structure designed to provide an adequate number of able-bodied adults within families to support dependent family members. Here the source of disruption is a high death rate in preindustrial societies where extended families are common. High death rates threaten the capacity of smaller families to provide for their dependents. (Adapted from Stinchcombe, 1968.)

SOCIAL EVOLUTION

Functional theories imply evolution. Thus, they do not directly answer the question of how social structures developed. For example, explaining how sweat glands or extended families make vital contributions to other parts of their systems does not tell us how they got there in the first place. Biologists use the principle of natural selection to explain the origins of sweat glands. They argue that animals with more efficient cooling mechanisms are more likely to survive and reproduce than animals with less efficient cooling mechanisms. Thus, biologists rely on evolutionary theories to explain the origins of sweat glands while relying on functional theories to explain why sweat glands are an advantage for survival.

Functional theories in sociology imply an evolutionary mechanism to explain the origins of structures just as functional theories in biology do. **Social evolutionary theories** suggest that societies with structures that enable them to adapt to their physical and social environments have a better chance of survival than societies that fail to develop such structures. Because of this selective process, certain highly adaptive social structures tend to exist in societies. For example, many primitive societies may have failed to solve the problem of sustaining dependents in the face of high death rates by failing to develop the extended family or some comparable structure. Perhaps the lack of such societies simply reflects their failure to survive.

The implicit evolutionary assumptions of functionalism have led a number of contemporary macro sociologists to construct theories about the evolution of human societies. In so doing, however, they have been careful not to simply apply biological theories of human evolution directly to explain social structure. This was a tragic failure in late nineteenth-century theories of social evolution, and the needless and objectionable substitution of biology for sociology caused sociologists to avoid the topic of social evolution for several generations.

In the late nineteenth century, social evolutionists attributed cultural differences among societies to genetic differences in their populations. Thus, if one society had advanced technology while another relied on stone axes and digging sticks, the persons in the advanced society were considered to be more highly evolved. Such conclusions provided justification for extreme racist policies. However, as we shall see in Chapter 16, these conclusions are disproven by the actual patterns of cultural development and change throughout history.

A second faulty assumption made by nineteenth-century social evolutionists was that social change is inevitable and *progressive*—that societies always change in beneficial ways. This view was so obviously incompatible with the historical record that it caused theories of social evolution to fall into disrepute. As Gerhard Lenski (1976) put it:

Not every society has grown in size and complexity. . . . Some have remained hunters and gatherers or horticulturists [simple gardeners] down to the present day. Some [societies] have even regressed from levels they achieved at an earlier time.

Evolutionary theories need not assume that all societies always evolve toward more complex cultures. Also, evolutionary theories are not meant to apply to specific cases. Instead, they apply to the population of cases. For example, no biologist believes that any *one* horse evolves. Rather, they believe that because of selection for adaptive traits, the *species* of horses changes over time. By the same token, modern social evolutionists do not apply their theories to one specific society, but to all societies. Nor do modern social evolutionists assume that the direction of change is necessarily good or beneficial. Good and bad are moral, not scientific, judgments. What modern social evolutionists do propose is that since the dawn of human history, societies have tended to become larger, to accumulate more effective technology, to become more efficient at producing food, to become more complex (in the sense of having more specialized occupations and organizations), to become more urban, and to become more powerful.

The evidence supporting these long-term trends is persuasive. Archeology reveals that the pace of change was extremely slow during the first several million years of human existence. Nevertheless, later human societies tended to be larger, more complex, and more technologically powerful than earlier societies (Lenski, 1976).

History reveals a similar pattern of social evolution. Of course, Rome fell—as have other civilizations. But the long-term trends are not obscured by the many bumps in the road of human history. Indeed, we have recently determined that the belief that Western society was ignorant and backward after the fall of Rome is much exaggerated. Instead, technological progress continued throughout the so-called Dark Ages, as medieval societies discovered or perfected much important technology unknown to the Romans (White, 1962).

Social evolutionary theories in macro sociology explain these long-range trends by referring to the pressures that the environment places on human societies. These pressures favor the survival of societies that have found the means to become larger, more complex, and more technologically advanced. Environmental pressures can result from nature. For example, if the climate turns cold, societies having fire and clothing are more likely to survive.

Environmental pressures can also come from other societies. A society with a large number of warriors equipped with better weapons will be able to seize the resources of smaller, less sophisticated neighbors. The competition for survival results in winners and losers, and hence societies will evolve in the direction of winning characteristics. In later chapters we shall examine some specific theories about the evolution of societies.

CONFLICT THEORIES

A third school of macro sociological theory focuses on the conflicts that occur within societies and how these in turn shape social structures. Where functionalists ask how a structure serves other structures in a social system and evolutionists seek the survival benefits of a particular structure, conflict theorists ask how social structure serves the interests of various competing groups within a society.

Karl Marx (1818–1883) was an early conflict theorist. He argued that social structures were created by the most powerful members of a society, the ruling class. He wrote that "the ruling ideas of any age are the ideas of its ruling class." He further argued that the ruling class constructs social structures that best serve their own interests and, conversely, that the social structure determines who will be the ruling class. Thus Marx traced the origins of social structures to class conflicts.

As we shall see in Chapter 16, Marx was also an early social evolutionist who believed that class conflicts within societies are the cause of social evolution. He argued that communist societies (which he believed would not possess a ruling class) were the inevitable outcome of social evolution, since they would not have internal class conflicts.

Many modern macro sociologists seek to explain social structures by referring to conflicts within societies, but most do not limit their attention to conflicts among different classes. Taking a very broad view of possible conflicts, they follow the lead of a great German sociologist, Max Weber (1864–1920). Weber argued that while class conflicts are a very important social influence, there are many other causes of group conflicts. For example, groups often form to pursue common aims on the basis of a great variety of cultural interests or identities (Hechter, 1978). Weber called these groups "status groups."

An ethnic group is a good example of a status group. Persons of different classes may find a common purpose and unity in their shared cultural heritage (such as a common language or shared customs), which in turn may bring this group into conflict with other ethnic groups. The present dispute between French- and English-speaking Canadians is an example of the kind of internal conflict that can shape social structure. The conflict between Cana-dian ethnic groups has produced substantial changes in many parts of Canadian society.

Conflict theories, then, are concerned with the distribution of power in societies and how various interest groups (including classes) seek and gain power and utilize their power to shape social structures. From this perspective, any society at any given moment is the result of past compromises and power struggles (Dahrendorf, 1959; Habermas, 1975). These conflicts arise from such things as class, race, region, ethnicity, religion, occupation, age, and gender; and they supply the energy and motivation for constructing and maintaining social structures.

In the remainder of this book, we shall encounter many macro sociological theories of each major school. Often they disagree, but in my judgment each tells us something important that the others don't. Therefore, the most powerful and comprehensive macro theories often contain elements from all three schools.

In the next section of this chapter, we shall look over the shoulder of a macro sociologist as he derives an important hypothesis and then tests it through research. We shall see just such a blending of the three schools of macro theory. We shall also see that good macro theories rest upon micro theories.

DOING MACRO SOCIOLOGY

Micro sociological research is usually based on individuals. As you will recall from Chapter 3, Ofshe's experiment was based on comparisons of students who took part in his study. Lofland and I studied conversion to the Unification Church by observing which individuals did or did not join. And in this chapter you have seen that Hirschi and I initially studied religion and delinquency by comparing students in Richmond, California. But when I wanted to see if social structure influenced the religion-delinquency relationship, I could no longer compare only individuals: I had to compare cities and high schools.

Individuals don't have social structures. They live within social structures, which are the properties of groups. So, macro sociological research must always be based on the comparative study of groups. Sometimes these are relatively small groups, such as new religious movements. Often they are larger groups, such as cities. Frequently macro sociological research is based on comparisons of whole societies.

However, even when macro research is based on whole societies, the logic of the **comparative research** is the same as that for research based on individuals. Correlation is demonstrated by separating societies according to the independent variable and then comparing them with respect to the dependent variable. Time order must be dealt with by showing that changes in the independent variable occurred before the changes in the dependent variable. Finally, the possibility that something other than the independent variable is causing the correlation must be addressed by controls for spuriousness. Let's watch a good macro sociologist at work.

STRUCTURE AND CONFLICT: COMPARATIVE RESEARCH

 As we have seen, a major school of macro sociology seeks to explain social structure on the basis of conflicts within societies. However, a primary interest of all macro sociologists is the basis for such conflicts. Some societies have a great deal of internal conflict, while others have relatively little. Indeed, Guy E. Swanson (1968, 1969), who surveyed a number of primitive societies, concluded that these societies have two basic forms of politics: *factional* and *communal.* Societies with factional politics contain internal groups that pursue their own special interests; decisions are reached through *competition* and *conflict* among these factions. The level of internal conflict in such societies is high and sometimes breaks out into violence. However, in communal societies, such as the Navaho Indians, internal conflicts are muffled; agreement rather than disagreement is stressed in making decisions. Hence, decisions are often delayed until general agreement is reached. The question is: How do these societies differ in other ways—what causes or reduces internal conflicts?

Jeffery Paige (1974) believed that the answer could be found in social structure. That is, he argued that not only does conflict shape social structure, but social structure can shape conflict. Paige knew from many studies that conflicts tend to break out between groups with weak attachments to each other and strong attachments internally. This principle was covered at some length in Chapter 1, where we discussed the formation of internal factions or cliques within social networks. Sometimes such factions form because of hostile feelings among a few individuals, which lead to intransitivity, but often isolated cliques form in networks simply because of their physical location. For example, cliques often arise within different locations in business organizations. Those who work in the same location have a greater opportunity to interact and form attachments. If several work areas are far apart and few people shift back and forth, there are very few attachments among persons working in different locations. If a potential conflict arises between people working in different locations, it is not muted by intergroup attachments. Instead, it pits one clique against another.

Thus, Paige reasoned, micro sociological theories about attachments combine nicely with macro sociological conflict theories to explain why some primitive societies have much internal conflict and others have very little. Structural arrangements in communal societies ought to inhibit the development of internal factions. That is, potential lines of division must be minimized by the existence of many attachments that cross these lines. In factional societies, social structures ought to promote the formation of isolated groups lacking attachments to each other.

When Paige examined primitive societies, he identified two primary bases for group formation. The first is *kinship.* Members of the same family tend to engage in constant and intimate interaction over a long period of time and hence tend to form strong attachments. The second basis for attachment is *residence.* People who live together or close by also engage in long-term interactions and therefore tend to form close attachments. Paige also found that in primitive societies conflict occurs primarily among men, particularly men of different kinship groups. Finally, Paige discovered that structural patterns of kinship and residence vary across primitive societies. In some societies the factors of kinship and

This rare photograph taken from above a valley in New Guinea shows a battle among primitive warriors armed with spears. Sometimes such battles occur between societies competing for resources, but often enough they erupt between factions within a single society. Paige's research showed that the degree of internal conflict in primitive societies was highly correlated with their rules of residence.

residence coincide. In others they cross-cut. He was about ready to formulate his major hypothesis.

In some primitive societies, the bride leaves home after marriage, and the couple take up residence with or close to the husband's family. This is called the **patrilocal rule of residence**. In such societies, male kin live in close proximity. A man's male neighbors are primarily his father, uncles, brothers, and sons. This maximizes interaction among males who are already united by ties of kinship. It also minimizes a man's interaction with males who are not his relatives. In such societies, kinship and residence structures coincide and are mutually supportive.

However, some primitive societies observe a **matrilocal rule of residence**, and newlyweds reside with or near the bride's family. Consequently, male kin in matrilocal societies are scattered and lack day-to-day interaction. After marriage, males interact mostly with males who are not their relatives.

Paige hypothesized that patrilocal societies would tend to be factional because both kinship and residence encouraged the formation of male factions. In contrast, matrilocal societies would tend to be communal, because men would retain ties to their kinsmen living elsewhere, while daily interaction created attachments to local men. Thus, the tendency to form factions on the basis of kinship would be minimized by the lack of a common residence, while the tendency to form residential factions would be minimized by kinship ties. That is, if residential factions formed, they would pit fathers against sons, brother against brother. If kinship factions formed, they would pit men against those with whom they lived and worked.

To test this hypothesis, Paige selected a sample of primitive societies, ten with patrilocal residence and ten with matrilocal residence. He then examined the levels of political conflict in each group. Of the ten patrilocal societies, eight had factional politics. Of the ten matrilocal societies, only one had factional politics. Thus he demonstrated a very strong correlation between rules of residence and political conflict, as he had hypothesized.

To argue that rules of residence cause the level of political conflict, however, Paige also needed to demonstrate time order: to show that the rules of residence were established prior to the level of conflict. Here he was blocked because pertinent data were not available.

He drew his sample of societies and the information on each from an extraordinary work called the *Ethnographic Atlas* (1967b), created by George P. Murdock and his colleagues at Yale University. The *Atlas* contains comparable information on hundreds of primitive societies. These data have been taken from field studies conducted by generations of anthropologists. Unfortunately, most of these societies existed long before anthropologists studied them. Consequently, it was impossible to determine time order on residence and conflict—both had been established long before the studies.

However, because contemporary research shows that interaction produces attachments and that anything that impedes interaction tends to encourage the formation of factions, most sociologists find Paige's hypothesized time order to be quite persuasive.

Spuriousness could also invalidate Paige's findings. That is, something else could be the cause of both rules of residence and levels of internal conflict. For example, it has been suggested by Melvin and Carol Ember (1971) that the presence of a nearby military threat from another society will cause families to keep their sons at home to provide loyal warriors and lead parents to encourage aggressive behavior in their sons, which will spill over onto internal political processes as well. This is a plausible counterhypothesis that deserves to be tested. But again, suitable data are lacking.

Clearly, Paige's hypothesis has not been fully tested against the criteria of causation. However, confidence in Paige's findings does not depend on his results alone. Paige's hypothesis is but one of hundreds derived from theories about the basis for attachments and the power of attachments to prevent conflict. Research supporting these hypotheses must be viewed as a whole, and the correlation Paige found fits into a consistent pattern of results.

CONCLUSION

In this chapter we studied social structure and saw that there is much more to human behavior than individual psychology. People act to gain rewards and to avoid costs, but social structures often determine what rewards are available and how they can be gained, thereby placing a powerful matrix upon human behavior. Thus, although attachments encourage conformity to norms, social structures can determine to whom we become attached and to whose norms we will conform.

We also examined the fundamental elements of three major schools of macro sociological theory and saw that all three work from the assumption that societies are systems. The elements of systems and of societies as social systems were also examined. Finally, we watched a macro sociologist blend elements of these schools of macro theory with a fundamental premise of micro theory to formulate a hypothesis about why different societies have different amounts of internal political conflict. We watched him test this hypothesis using whole societies as the units of analysis.

Thus we have concluded the preliminaries. We have identified key sociological concepts and elements of sociological theories and examined principles of sociological research. Now it is time to see how well sociologists have applied their theories to many major topics and what they have learned from their research.

Review glossary

Social structures Any characteristics of a group, rather than of an individual. (p. 73)

Survey research (also called public opinion polling) A common form of sociological research based on interviews of or questionnaires from a sample of a population. (p. 74)

Sample A random selection from a larger population. (p. 75)

System Any set of interdependent parts. (p. 79)

Social institutions Relatively permanent patterns or clusters of specialized roles, groups, organizations, customs, and activities devoted to meeting fundamental social needs. Five major social institutions are the family, economy, religion, political order, and education. (p. 80)

Interdependence A relationship among parts of a system such that if one part changes, at least one other part is affected. (p. 80)

Equilibrium A state of balance among system parts that is the result of interdependence. (p. 81)

Functionalist theories, Functionalism Theories that attempt to explain some part of a system by showing its consequences for some other part of the system. These consequences are called *functions;* for example, the function of the sweat gland is to keep organisms from overheating. (p. 83)

Nuclear family A family group containing one adult couple and their children. (p. 83)

Extended families Those families containing more than one adult couple. (p. 83)

Functional alternative The existence of more than one system structure that satisfies the same system need. (p. 83)

Social evolutionary theories Theories that account for the existence of a social structure on the basis of its survival benefits for societies. For example, technologically superior societies will be better able to withstand environmental challenges; hence, societies will evolve toward increased technological capacity. (p. 84)

Conflict theories Marxist conflict theories seek to explain all social arrangements as the result of class conflicts, especially the capacity of the "ruling class" to impose its interests on the whole society. Non-Marxist conflict theories examine a much wider range of conflicts within societies (for example, between groups divided by language, race, culture, and even region) and seek to show how competing groups utilize their power to shape favorable social structures. (p. 86)

Comparative research In a sense, all forms of research are comparative, since they involve comparing individuals or groups, but usually sociologists mean research involving comparisons of very large groups or even whole societies. (p. 87)

Patrilocal rule of residence A situation in which married couples live with or near the man's family. (p. 88)

Matrilocal rule of residence A situation in which married couples live with or near the woman's family. (p. 88)

Suggested readings

Babbie, Earl R. *Survey Research Methods.* Belmont, Calif.: Wadsworth, 1973.

Blau, Peter M. *Inequality and Heterogeneity: A Primitive Theory of Social Structure.* New York: Free Press, 1977.

Boulding, Kenneth E. *A Primer on Social Dynamics.* New York: Free Press, 1970.

Harris, Marvin. *Cultural Materialism: The Struggle for a Science of Culture.* New York: Random House, 1979.

Stinchcombe, Arthur L. *Constructing Social Theories.* New York: Harcourt Brace Jovanovich, 1968.

Sampling

Much sociological research depends upon finding out the distribution of certain traits or combinations of traits in particular populations. For example, Hirschi and I needed to know which students in Richmond had committed delinquent acts. We also needed to know which students went to church and which believed in hell. Only with such information could we discover whether religiousness and delinquency were correlated.

An obvious way to find out the distribution of various traits or characteristics in a population is to take a census, that is, to gather the information on every person in the population of interest. For example, if we want to know how many Americans watch football on TV, one way to find out is to ask everyone. Of course, that would be extremely expensive. In fact, it cost the U.S. government $1 billion to conduct the 1980 census. If a census were the only reliable way to get such information, very little sociological research would be possible. Fortunately, we don't have to get information on every member of a population in order to obtain valid results. Instead, we can select relatively few members of a population, find out about them, and assume that the results apply to the entire population. Such a procedure is called *sampling*.

RANDOM SAMPLES

The method of sampling requires that those included in the sample are like those who are not included.

The procedure used is identical to the means used in experiments to make sure that groups of subjects are not different. Recall that when Richard Ofshe wanted to be sure that people who thought they were evaluating a friend were not different from those who thought they were evaluating a stranger, he randomly assigned people to the groups. That made it possible to use the laws of probability to compute the odds against chance findings.

Drawing a sample from a population rests on the same principle. The aim is to make certain that people in the sample are just like those left out. To achieve this, decisions about who gets into the sample and who is left out are made randomly.

To select a simple random sample from a population, all that is needed is a complete list of the population. If we had a list of everyone in America, for example, we could put every name in a barrel, stir the names up, and then draw names until we had the total we wanted for our sample. Since every American's name would be in the barrel, everyone would have an equal chance of being selected, and because selection was random, we could calculate the probability that the sample is just like the population as a whole.

It turns out that the odds that a sample will be like a whole population depend only on the absolute size of the sample and not on the ratio of the sample size to the population size. Hence, a sample based on 1,500 cases is more accurate than one based on only 1,000 and less accurate than one based on 2,000 cases. That is true whether the population being sampled has 20 thousand or 200 million members. Thus, a sample including 1,500 persons (a common size) is equally good for describing the whole U.S. population, the population of Kansas, or the population of Fargo, North Dakota.

STRATIFIED RANDOM SAMPLES

It is impossible to choose a simple random sample of Americans, because there is no complete list. Nor is there a complete list for particular cities. The telephone book is the closest thing to a complete list of residents of a city, but it omits people who do not have phones and the large number of people with unlisted numbers. So another way must be used to sample such populations randomly. This method is called *stratified* random sampling, because the sampling proceeds through a series of levels, or strata.

The Census Bureau has divided the country into many small geographic units known as *census tracts*. Cities, for example, are made up of a number of these tracts. To select a sample of the United States, researchers essentially put every census tract into a barrel, mix them up, and then draw some out. In fact, the drawing is rigged so that the probability of each tract being drawn is equal to its portion of the U.S. population, thus ensuring that every American has the same chance to be selected. After a random set of census tracts is selected, sampling is then focused on each. Most tracts are in cities (since that is where most people live). City census tracts are made up of blocks. Again taking into account the total population of various blocks, procedures are used to select at random a sample of blocks.

Once blocks have been selected, interviewers are sent out to discover the identity of *every* person living on each of the sample blocks. From this operation a list of names emerges: names and addresses of everyone living on all of the sampled blocks. Finally, these names are subjected to random selection and a sample of Americans is obtained (when the names of those selected from rural tracts have been added). Only at this point can the actual research begin. For only when we know who is in the sample do we know who should be interviewed or be sent a questionnaire.

While samples are much cheaper than a census, they are still fairly expensive. Fortunately for sociologists, big commercial polling companies, such as the Gallup Poll, often include questions of great research value in their surveys and are extremely helpful in making their findings available to scholars. When a sociologist has funding to interview a national sample, he or she takes great care to collect data useful for many different research questions and eventually makes the data available to other researchers.

This man is conducting interviews with people on the street—a technique sometimes used by "roving reporters" for newspapers or TV. But he is not doing survey research because he is not interviewing people sampled randomly from some defined population. People do not just randomly pass down a given street. Therefore, interviews made this way will be very biased—the results will not reflect people in this city.

Percentage of Master's degrees earned by women, 1979. National = 49.1 percent.

This map of the proportion of Master's degrees awarded to women would surprise a lot of people. While nationally women have caught up with men, in the South women surpass men, while in the West they still lag behind. This challenges the widespread belief that the South clings to traditional attitudes toward women. Moreover, it is in Mississippi, often regarded as the most tradition-bound southern state, where women most surpass men—61.2 percent of Master's degrees were awarded to women there in 1979. Kentucky, with 60.6 percent, was second, In contrast, in Utah, Idaho, and North Dakota, only about a third of the Master's degrees were earned by women.

Pacific 42.9

Mountain 42.6

West North Central 45.0

East North Central 48.4

Middle Atlantic 50.9

New England 49.0

West South Central 50.6

East South Central 57.6

South Atlantic 53.8

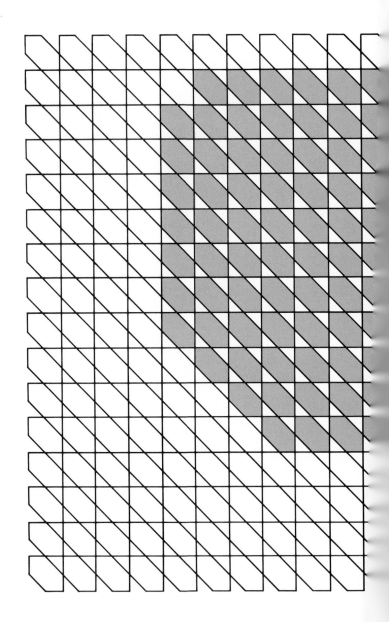

Individuals
and Groups

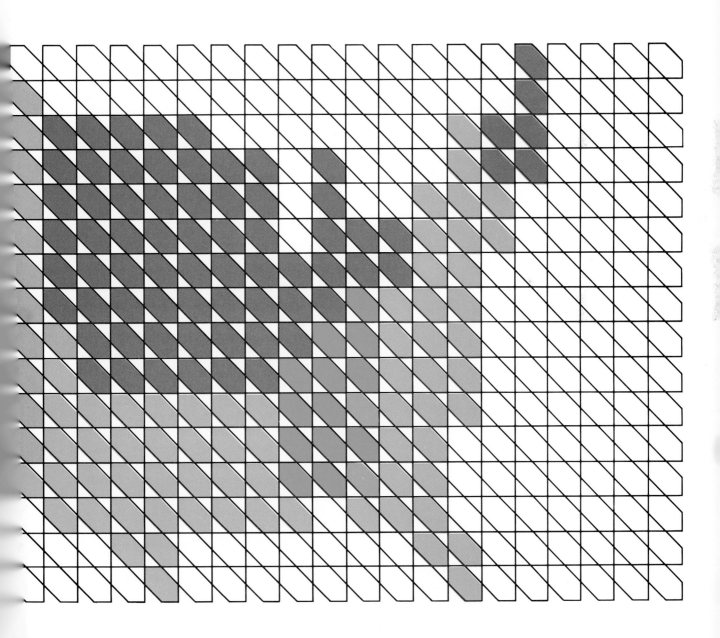

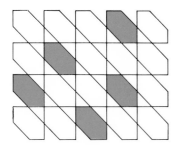

■ Early in this century many social scientists were really biologists in disguise. They argued that most human behavior was caused by inborn, or inherited, features of our biology. Major figures in psychology at the turn of the century, including Sigmund Freud, E. L. Thorndike, and John Dewey, embraced instinctual theories of behavior (Allport, 1968). An **instinct** is a form of behavior that occurs in all normal members of a species *without having been learned.* For example, a spider hatched in isolation from all other spiders will still spin webs identical to webs made by others of the same species. Thus, psychologists who proposed instinct theories of human behavior discounted the impact of the *environment*—of cultural and social influences—on human development. To them what was given to humans by heredity was final.

The major proponent of instinctual theories was the social psychologist William McDougall, who was on the faculty of Harvard before moving to Duke. In a very influential textbook of its time, *Introduction to Social Psychology* (1908), McDougall listed a number of human instincts and attempted to show how even very elaborate forms of behavior are produced by "compounds" of several instincts. Religiousness, he explained, is caused by a blend of four instincts: curiosity, self-abasement, fear, and the protective or parental instinct. Other psychologists suggested other instincts, and even different sets, and in his 1932 book McDougall revised his list and proposed that human behavior could be explained by eighteen different instincts (see Table 5-1).

Not to be outdone by psychologists, many sociologists of the period proposed biological and

Biology, Culture, and Society

hereditary explanations for cultural differences among societies. For instance, less technologically advanced societies were believed to be made up of people with inferior intellects. Others claimed that the Swedes were stubborn, the Italians were excitable, the Spanish cruel, and the Dutch obsessed with cleanliness because of their heredity. In Chapter 11 we shall examine the biological arguments employed in 1914 by E. A. Ross, president of the American Sociological Society, to urge that "biologically inferior" groups such as Italians and Jews be prevented from immigrating to the United States.

All these biological theories were simpleminded and obviously inadequate. Studies of children subjected to extreme neglect showed that they lacked even the ability to speak, let alone sophisticated thought, and thus proved that most human behavior is not instinctual (see Chapter 6). As for the "backward races," soon some of them were going to Harvard. Moreover, no one could demonstrate that humans exhibit any instinctual behavior, with the possible exceptions of a sucking response in infants and an infant's tendency to imitate facial expressions (see Figure 5-1). Soon social science books ceased to mention instincts, and even some of the major proponents of the instinct approach eventually discarded it. Soon social science textbooks made no mention of human biology at all.

By the 1930s, the social sciences were dominated by purely environmental theories. Heredity was assigned no role. Everything humans do was said to be entirely the result of cultural and social influences (White, 1949). Sometimes it was grudgingly admitted that societies and cultural patterns would be different if human biology had produced

Table 5-1 / McDougall's eighteen human instincts.

1. Food-seeking
2. Disgust
3. Sex
4. Fear
5. Curiosity
6. Protective or parental propensity
7. Gregariousness
8. Self-assertion
9. Submission
10. Anger
11. Appeal
12. Constructive propensity
13. Acquisitive propensity
14. Laughter
15. Comfort
16. Rest or sleep
17. Migratory propensity
18. A cluster of bodily needs including breathing

Source: William McDougall, 1932.

but one sex, if infants grew up in only several months, or if the average person lived for 10,000 years. But these were regarded as nothing more than silly hypothetical possibilities. The accepted view was that our biology may set some limits, but within these, human nature is essentially plastic and can be shaped into virtually any form.

As we shall see in Chapter 6, anthropologists such as Margaret Mead studied remote tribes for the express purpose of "proving" how plastic human nature really is. We shall also see that at least some of these reports probably contained as much fantasy as fact. Moreover, more careful research began

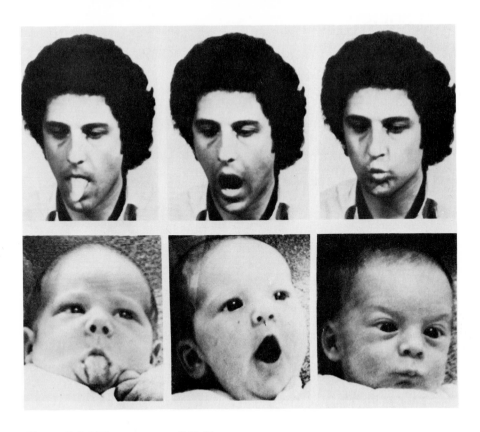

Figure 5-1 / "Same to you, fella!"

Until recently it was believed that human infants did not learn to imitate facial expressions until they were 8 to 10 months old. However, recent research has shown that infants are born with this ability. Andrew N. Meltzoff and M. Keith Moore (1977) found that newborns only 60 minutes old would imitate facial expressions. These sample photographs from video recordings show 2-week-old infants imitating (a) tongue protrusion, (b) mouth opening, and (c) lip protrusion. (Photos in Science, *October 7, 1977.)*

to show that heredity does sometimes overcome environmental influences. For example, while environmental factors can make people short, they cannot make them taller than their hereditary potential.

Today the absolute environmentalist position is judged to be as extreme as the absolute hereditarian position it was reacting against. Human beings are the result of the interplay between their biology and their social and cultural environment. To illustrate this, let us consider symbolic interaction, which was defined in Chapter 3 as the essential human capacity. Clearly, we are not born with this capacity. If no one talks to us, we never learn speech on our own. To learn the meaning of symbols takes much time and immense stimulation from the environment. However, it is equally true that our biology makes symbolic interaction possible. Only because the human brain evolved in size and complexity are we able to learn symbolic interaction skills; persons whose brains are too damaged or deficient cannot learn these skills. ■

CHAPTER PREVIEW

In this chapter we shall focus on how biology interacts with culture and society to shape human behavior. First, we shall examine several basic concepts and principles of heredity. Next, we shall explore the developing field of behavioral genetics. Here we shall find out how geneticists go about demonstrating whether a human trait is hereditary. For example, geneticists have recently found evidence for a hereditary element in such things as mental illness and intelligence.

The major portion of the chapter will address how social and cultural factors modify the fulfillment of our genetic potentials. For this discussion, we shall examine two major examples in detail and watch biologists and sociologists at work on the same question. Our first example will involve the sudden, very recent, and dramatic changes in the age of puberty and the size of human beings. The second will trace the bitter controversy over race and IQ. Our goal is to see the subtle ways in which environment and heredity combine. Finally, we shall examine recent studies that compare humans and other primates to see what similarities and differences exist. Are humans truly unique? Do only humans possess culture and language? Can animal studies provide us with useful insights?

HEREDITY

We know that cats never give birth to pups, and that the offspring of humans will always be human. The reason for this is that tiny parts of the male's sperm and the female's ovum contain an amazing amount of information that determines the kind of organism that results from the mating. Since offspring grow up to be whatever their parents' cells specify, an individual biological organism inherits its particular makeup; that is, the physical aspects of an organism are inherited.

In the case of humans, a male sperm contains twenty-three **chromosomes**, as does the female ovum. These combine to form twenty-three pairs (Figure 5-2). The specific instructions on each pair of chromosomes combine to determine various traits, such as eye color. These instructions are encoded in complex chemical chains called DNA, which are contained in tiny structures called **genes**. Each chromosome contains many genes, and humans

are estimated to have more than 1,000 genes. No two sperm and no two ova, even from the same male or female, are likely to have the same array of genes. That is why the same parents can have one child with red hair and another with brown. However, a person's hair color is determined by the particular genes he or she has received. Geneticists have worked out some precise rules of heredity, and in many cases they can often specify the odds that a given trait will show up in a child.

Two other genetic concepts will be useful in this chapter: **genotype** and **phenotype**. The sum total of the genetic instructions that an organism receives is called the genotype. However, the physical development of organisms does not always exactly follow the genetic blueprints, or genotypes. Environmental forces sometimes deflect or prevent the fulfillment of the genotype. For this reason, we refer to any specific organism as a phenotype to take into account the interplay between the genotype and the environment in physical development. In other words, the phenotype is what we see when we look at any organism. As we will see later in this chapter, for example, throughout nearly the whole period of human existence the genotype of the average person "planned" for him or her to become much taller than the environment actually permitted. In this sense, the genotype can be seen in part as a genetic potential, while the phenotype is the actual outcome of the interplay between the genotype and the environment. A second reason to distinguish between genotype and phenotype is that much of a person's genetic inheritance does not show up in his or her phenotype, but it can show up in the phenotypes of that person's children. For example, brown-eyed parents can have blue-eyed children, thus showing that both parents had a blue-eyed gene in their genotypes.

The importance of heredity to sociologists does not depend on whether some human characteristics are wholly determined by genetics, for without question some are. Blue-eyed parents, for example, can only produce blue-eyed children (although, as just mentioned, brown-eyed parents can produce blue-eyed children). The important question is what traits are determined to what degree by genetic inheritance. Do any of these traits influence human activities of interest to social science? Sociologists don't care much about eye color, but they do care

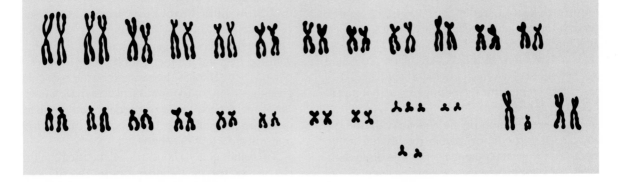

Figure 5-2 / Human chromosomes.

A photograph of the twenty-three pairs of chromosomes in a human cell. The actual hereditary information (the genes) carried by each chromosome pair is contained in DNA molecules.

very much about variations in humans that determine what people can and cannot do and how they do or do not act.

BEHAVIORAL GENETICS

Just because instinctual theories were silly does not mean that heredity plays no role in human behavior. In recent years **behavioral genetics** has been a rapidly growing field. Behavioral geneticists seek to identify human traits that influence behavior and are determined to some degree by genetic inheritance. At present, these geneticists believe that such characteristics as intelligence, many forms of mental illness, and perhaps a tendency toward impulsive and aggressive behavior have a substantial genetic basis.

To show that any particular trait is inherited, one must first demonstrate that people who are blood relatives are more alike in terms of this trait than are randomly selected, unrelated individuals. For example, David Rosenthal (1970) summarized dozens of studies which report that the mental illness known as schizophrenia clusters in families; that is, relatives of a schizophrenic are considerably more likely to become schizophrenic than are people without known schizophrenic relatives.

However, this approach has encountered major criticism. Not only do two brothers who develop schizophrenia have a similar genetic inheritance, but they also grew up in the same home with the same parents and were exposed to similar social circumstances outside the home. Opponents of behavioral genetics argue that the similar environment in which relatives are raised makes it seem as if heredity plays a part.

For this reason studies of twins, especially identical twins separated at birth, are central to research in behavioral genetics. We have seen that children of the same parents each have a unique genotype, although their genotypes are more alike than those of children with different parents or children with only one parent in common. Most twins are not identical and are the result of their mother producing two ova at the same time, both of which were impregnated by different sperm. Such twins are no more genetically similar than children born at different times to the same parents. However, once in a while, after an ovum has been impregnated, it splits in half and develops into two babies (Figure 5-3). When such splits occur, each half has the same genetic content. The results of this phenomenon, identical twins, thus have identical genotypes.

For this reason, any hereditary trait that shows up in one twin will show up in the other unless

Identical twins are genetic duplicates. As a result all dif-ferences they display can only be caused by environ-mental forces. Of course, being the same age and sex, looking the same, and having the same parents, they will tend to have very similar environments, so it is diffi-cult to know whether personality and behavioral simi-larities between them are genetic or environmental.

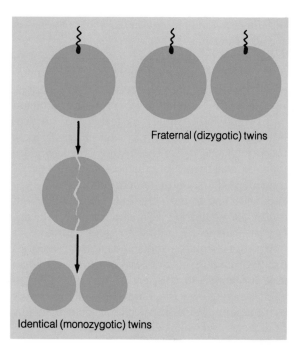

Fraternal (dizygotic) twins

Identical (monozygotic) twins

Figure 5-3 / Twins.

Identical (or monozygotic) twins occur when a fertil-ized ovum (or zygote) splits, forming two infants with precisely the same genetic inheritance. Most twins are dizygotic and occur because the mother produced two ova and both were fertilized. Such twins often are not even of the same sex and are no more similar geneti-cally than are brothers and sisters not born at the same time.

outside forces intrude. Suppose schizophrenia has a genetic basis. Then if one twin becomes schizo-phrenic, the other should, too. The same holds true if intelligence is genetic. However, studies that showed amazingly similar mental health or intelli-gence in identical twins were subject to the same criticism mentioned above. Since these twins look exactly alike and are the same age, they will have been treated in almost identical ways. Once again, similarity of environment offers a very plausible counterexplanation.

However, not all identical twins grow up in the same home. Sometimes they are adopted by two different families and grow up without even know-ing they have a twin. For some decades now, be-havioral geneticists have focused on locating such sets of identical twins. Such twins permit a more stringent test of hereditary and environmental explanations.

For example, if intelligence has no hereditary basis, the IQs of identical twins raised separately should not be more similar than IQs of randomly selected pairs of persons. In fact, a great many studies, done in different countries by many different geneticists, show that the IQs of identical twins raised apart are extremely similar, although not identical. Environ-mental factors, therefore, can and do influence intel-ligence. But the IQs of identical twins are too much alike to allow us to reject the notion that genetics also plays a major part in determining intelligence

(Erlenmeyer-Kimling and Jarvik, 1963; Omenn, et al., 1972; Lewontin, 1973).*

Studies of twins raised separately also have supported the role of heredity in many forms of mental illness, including schizophrenia and depressive disorders (Rosenthal, 1970). Work has begun only recently on possible hereditary factors in alcoholism, impulsive behavior, and aggressiveness (Schuckit, et al., 1979). These kinds of behavior are more difficult to measure than mental illness or IQ.

Many social scientists resent behavioral geneticists and cling to the belief that the environment causes all, or nearly all variation among humans. But is seems to me unwise to ignore a field conducted in a scientific manner and guided by theories that have amply explained less controversial human traits. Of course, social scientists did not feel threatened when geneticists unraveled the hereditary transmission of diseases such as sickle cell anemia or diabetes. But when geneticists discuss the heredity of mental illness or intelligence, they tread on ground social scientists were accustomed to having all to themselves. But the fact is that social scientists have as much to tell geneticists as geneticists have to tell us. This will be obvious in the next two sections of this chapter, where we shall see the immense power of the social and cultural environment to modify fulfillment of human potentials. And it is here that the combined resources of sociologists and geneticists help to illuminate many mysteries.

THE GROWTH AND PUBERTY REVOLUTIONS

Over the past several decades, it has become clear that people are getting bigger. The change has been especially obvious in sports. In the 1930s, centers selected to the all-American basketball teams sometimes were no taller than 6 feet 2 inches, the size of a good small guard today. The line of the Chicago Bears' famous "Monsters of the Midway" averaged

*There are indications that the British geneticist Cyril Burt may have faked some twin studies late in his career. However, even discarding all of Burt's studies does not weaken the evidence in favor of the role of heredity in intelligence.

less than 200 pounds in their National Football League championship season of 1933. Good high school football teams are bigger than that today.

To some degree the increase in the size of sports stars is due to the fact that players are now recruited from a much larger population, both because the U.S. population has grown and because the population enrolled in high school and college has grown even more. Thus, if a person 7 feet tall occurs only once in a million births, there will be more 7-footers when the population is over 200 million than when it is about 100 million.

However, not only sports stars have become bigger. The size of the average American has increased substantially. In fact, people in all the advanced industrial nations are bigger than their parents and grandparents. In Japan the average height has increased so much in so short a time that major changes have been required. A few years ago most of the desks in Japan's elementary schools had to be replaced by larger ones.

In addition, a second change has recently been noticed. Not only are people growing larger than before, but they are growing faster—achieving their full size at a much younger age. Data from various nations reveal that a century ago most people still grew a lot in their late teens and usually did not reach their full adult height until age 25 or even later (Tanner, 1970). Today, most people stop growing by 18 or so, and most achieve nearly their full growth much sooner than that.

Concern with the rapid shift in growth patterns led scientists to notice another change. James M. Tanner, a British physiological psychologist, found that the age at which girls begin to menstruate has also declined in recent decades. Moreover, Tanner and others noted anthropological reports that girls in remote primitive tribes, usually do not begin to menstruate until about age 17, or as much as five years later than the average age for girls in Europe and North America. Tanner suddenly suspected that the recent changes in the age of the onset of menstruation might be the very end of a truly rapid and dramatic downward trend. Could it be, he wondered, that not too long ago girls everywhere did not enter puberty until their very late teens?

These suspicions spurred Tanner and many other scientists to do a great deal of research. Many tedious searches were conducted to find old medical and school records. Across Europe, scientists reconstructed when girls typically began to menstruate during the nineteenth century. When Tanner gathered all this information together and added data for the twentieth century, a very consistent, clear, and amazing picture emerged. Data from Norway, Germany, Sweden, Finland, Denmark, Great Britain, Canada, and the United States all showed the same thing: As recently as 1850, the average girl did not menstruate until about age 17. Since that time, the age of first menstruation has rapidly declined; now the average girl in these nations begins to menstruate several months after her twelfth birthday.

The onset of male sexual maturation is not marked by so signal an event as menstruation. But since boys at present reach puberty at a later age than girls, Tanner thought it reasonable to assume that back when girls did not menstruate until age 17, boys did not begin to shave until 18 or so. This assumption has been confirmed by an unexpected source, music history. Boy choirs have long been popular in Europe, and conductors of boy choirs are always concerned with the loss of boy sopranos when their voices change at the onset of puberty. Music historians know that back when Bach (1685–1750) and Mozart (1756–1791) composed choral music, it was believed that boy sopranos could sing until the age of 18 or so. Today, boy choir singers are usually washed up by the age of 13.

Putting these facts together, we can see a dramatic change in human beings in a very short span of time. We are much bigger than our ancestors, and we grow much faster and mature much sooner than they did. Before we examine the consequences of these changes, let us attempt to see why these changes took place.

Environmental suppressors

No trained biologist could believe that these rapid changes in human physiology were caused by genetic changes. No such change could spread so far so fast. Thus, the answer had to be sought elsewhere. In fact, the answer lies in the potent capacity of environmental factors to modify genetic potential. Indeed, to ask why humans suddenly began to get so large so fast is to raise the wrong question. The right question is: What kept humans so small and delayed their maturation for so long? What we are examining is a rapid change in the phenotype of human beings that reveals the previously unfulfilled potential of the human genotype.

Much research still needs to be done to explain how the environment suppressed our natural growth patterns, but the major factors are easy to determine: inadequate nutrition (especially shortages of vitamins and proteins) and chronic poor health.

As we shall see many times in this book, one of the major impacts of the Industrial Revolution, of modernization, has been to make people healthier and longer-lived. Until modern times, most people, even farmers, ate very meager diets, deficient in vitamins and proteins. Most people had meat, eggs, or dairy products very rarely, hardly ever had fruit, and had vegetables only in summer (Braudel, 1981). They lived almost exclusively on bread and on mush and soup made from grain. As a result, their growth was stunted and their maturation delayed. Poor diet also made people more susceptible to illness and contagious diseases, the latter being most common among children. A lack of sanitation and poor personal hygiene (see Chapters 12 and 18) further contributed to poor health. For these reasons, large numbers of children, often as many as half, did not reach adulthood. Nor were those who survived strong and healthy. The average person died by age 35.

Under such privation, it is hardly surprising that human development was stunted and maturation long delayed. Then the Industrial Revolution suddenly began to change these conditions. People began to eat much more food, which was also much more nutritious (see Chapter 17). Sanitation and immunization practices eliminated many common diseases. Infant mortality declined rapidly as the average life expectancy doubled. And suddenly people got much bigger and began to mature much younger. And that, in turn, has had some profound implications.

Social consequences of early maturation

Thus far we have seen how social and cultural forces affected human biology. We shall now change our

This young American boy could almost believe that milk really is manufactured like soda pop if he could not see that the hoses from these huge milk bottles lead back to real live cows. Such modern methods have made huge improvements in nutrition. They also have reduced disease—this milk is not even exposed to the air on its way from the cow to the pasteurizing process.

point of view: How does our biology modify social and cultural patterns? Strict environmentalists would say that our biology does not greatly affect cultural patterns, that human nature is sufficiently adaptable to allow an immense range of cultural patterns. Clearly, many cultural arrangements *are* possible, since many different ones have been observed. Yet developments in the wake of the growth and puberty revolutions suggest that we are not so easily shaped. For this reason, let's look briefly at how changes in sexual norms and authority relations between adults and teenagers may be related to changes in human maturation.

Changing sexual norms Until modern times, most people 17 and under were still biological children in both size and development. Not surprisingly, they usually did not marry until they were in their early twenties. In 1890, for example, the median age at first marriage in the United States was 22 for women and 25 for men. In 1980 it was nearly the same. While the age of physical and sexual maturity fell

One aspect of this portrait of a Chinese-American man posing with his parents would be found in the huge majority of similar families—the son, born and raised in the United States, is much taller than his father. While people in industrial nations generally have been getting larger, the shift has been especially marked for Asian immigrants to Europe and America.

rapidly, the age at marriage did not. Thus, the time between maturation and marriage has grown longer and longer. Each generation has had to wait longer from the time they were sexually capable until the time they married. This put severe strains on the norms restricting sex to marriage. It is not very difficult for prepubic teenagers to refrain from sex, but it is a challenge for persons who are sexually mature to refrain from sex for more than ten years.

Clearly, this strain could not be relieved by letting people marry soon after they became sexually mature. No one believes that 13- or 14-year-olds are mature enough to marry, regardless of their physical development. Thus, the traditional means of dealing with sexuality—marriage soon after sexual maturity—became increasingly inappropriate. The result was a great shift in sexual norms. Premarital sexual behavior is now widespread and has gained considerable social acceptance (Hunt, 1974).

Of course, human biology is not the only factor involved in modifying sexual norms. Reliable methods of contraception, legalized abortion, and effective treatment for common venereal diseases have also contributed. (Indeed, the automobile and the drive-in theater probably have had significant impact, too.) The fact remains that until the twentieth century, few young teenagers were sexually mature; hence, norms of "shouldn't" were backed by the reality of "couldn't."

Adult authority Throughout most of human history, physical and social maturity have coincided. The phrase "You're not big enough to do that yet" referred to both size and maturity. When people were big enough, they were taken to be old enough. For this reason, very small adults have always had trouble being accepted as grown-ups (Truzzi, 1968). Today, however, people are big enough long before adults are willing to regard them as old enough. This has caused problems of authority, for in the final analysis, adult authority over children has always rested on the fact that adults were bigger and stronger.

Consider student-teacher relations. Until this century, even female high school teachers tended to be taller than all but their largest male students. As a result, when teachers told students to sit down or be quiet, the students were not inclined to refuse. Many authority problems in schools and in families today are exacerbated by the fact that teenagers are now of adult size. It seems that new bases of adult authority will have to develop. Kids today grow too big to be spanked long before they are old enough not to need adult supervision and direction.

Thus we have seen that biology can influence cultural and social arrangements. If this is so in these ways, then perhaps it is so in other ways as well. As we proceed on our tour of sociology, you will continue to catch glimpses of human flesh and blood in social behavior we examine. Besides social beings, humans are also biological organisms. Indeed, in the last part of this chapter we shall see how humans compare with their primate cousins. Before taking up that topic, however, we must examine how the interplay of biology, culture, and society shapes something that determines the whole of human behavior: the ability to think and to learn.

THE IQ AND RACE CONTROVERSY

Intelligence testing was begun by the French psychologist Alfred Binet (1857–1911) at his laboratory in Paris in 1906. Binet wanted to distinguish between students who lacked the ability to learn and those who were not learning because of a lack of effort. He postulated that people have an innate, or inborn, capacity for learning, and therefore the greater that capacity, the more a given individual should learn over a given period of time.

Binet set out to measure a person's **mental age** on the basis of how much that person had learned by the time he or she had reached a given calendar age. For example, variations in the ability of 8-year-olds to perform intellectual tasks will reflect variations in their innate ability to learn. Some 8-year-olds will perform as well as the average child of 9 or even 10. Such children, then, are said to have a mental age of 9 or 10, well above their calendar age. Similarly, some children will perform below their age level and thus have a mental age that is less than their calendar age.

An **IQ**, or intelligence quotient, is a person's mental age divided by the calendar age. The result is then multiplied by 100 to get rid of the decimal point. If a person's mental and calendar ages are the same, that person has an IQ of 100, which is the average IQ score. If a person's mental age is 25 percent higher than his or her calendar age (for example, a person of 8 who performs at the average for 10-year-olds), the IQ is 125. An 8-year-old who performs at the 6-year-old level has an IQ of 75. Having launched massive testing programs for French schoolchildren, Binet found that his test produced a normal distribution, the bell-shaped curve shown

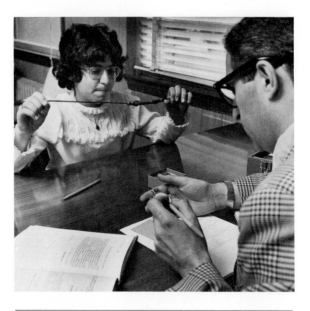

This girl is taking the Stanford-Binet IQ test. While she attempts to solve a pattern problem, the test administrator uses a stopwatch to time her. Her score for this problem depends not only on a correct solution but on how fast she performs.

in Figure 5-4. Thus, for everyone who scores 125 (25 points over the average), someone will score 75 (25 points below the average).

Binet's test was soon translated into many other languages. It was translated into English at Stanford University by Lewis M. Terman, which is why the test is known in this country as the Stanford-Binet Test of Intelligence. Since Binet developed his test more than seventy years ago, a great deal of research has been done to validate his and other IQ tests. Two facts about IQ tests are significant. First, they are very powerful predictors of school performance and occupational success. Second, test scores are very consistent over the course of a person's life. Most people score about the same when they take the test several times at different ages (Brown and Hernstein, 1975).

IQ testing has aroused opposition from some social scientists who claim it measures only environmental influences, not an innate ability. In response, supporters of IQ tests point out that what-

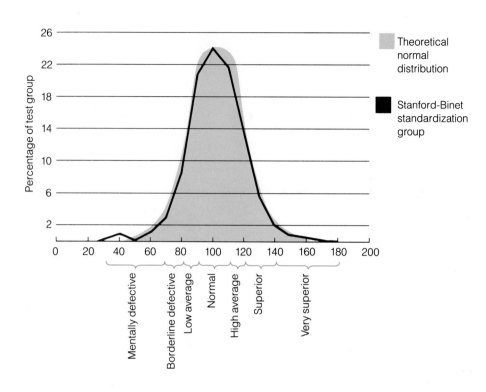

Figure 5-4 / The normal curve.

The normal curve (shown by gold shading) illustrates the theoretical distribution of IQ scores that would be obtained from a very large group of people. Note that the average score would be 100 and that 68.26 percent of all individuals would score between 85 and 115, and about 95 percent between 70 and 130. The black curve shows the IQ scores of over 2,000 children used as a standardization group for the 1937 revision of the Stanford-Binet intelligence tests. The descriptive labels often used for the various IQ intervals are given below the graph. (Adapted from Stanford-Binet Intelligence Scale by L. M. Terman and M. A. Merrill, Boston: Houghton Mifflin, 1960. Reprinted by permission of Houghton Mifflin Company. All rights reserved.)

ever the tests measure, it is something that has immense impact on how well people succeed in school and on the job. Moreover, since this quality seems to be fixed by the time children are old enough for their IQ to be measured, it does not react to environmental influences in later childhood or adulthood. Why would the environment be so potent only in the first five or six years of life, but not later? Surely much happens to people that could influence how much they learn after the age of 6. That scores remain stable suggests that IQ tests measure not

only what a person happened to learn by a given age, but also his or her underlying ability to learn. But perhaps the most powerful support for IQ tests has come from the many studies done on identical twins who were raised separately. If IQ is just the result of social and cultural influences and not heredity, then why do the IQs of identical twins who were reared apart correlate so highly?

Conflicts over the real meaning of IQ scores suddenly intensified when some social scientists claimed that blacks have less innate intelligence than whites.

Young American draftees taking the Army Alpha IQ test just after our entry into World War I in 1917. The rapid and massive influx of new troops far exceeded the available facilities at military posts, so these soldiers are sitting on the floor to take their tests. Note that a civilian is giving the test. Today the services have their own trained psychologists to supervise the many tests given new recruits.

Arthur Jensen drops a bomb

 IQ testing was widespread in the United States by World War I, and the U.S. Army developed a short test called the Army Alpha, which was given to all persons drafted for the war. The army test had been validated against the Stanford-Binet and is still regarded as a satisfactory measure of IQ. As the results of the tests were analyzed, it was noticed that the average score for black soldiers was substantially lower than that for white soldiers.

Through the years, the results of mass IQ testing continued to show a difference in the average scores of blacks and whites. Then in 1969, Arthur Jensen, a professor of educational psychology at the University of California at Berkeley, published an article in the *Harvard Educational Review.* In this article, he claimed that interracial differences in average IQ were the result of genetic differences. Jensen's reasoning was simple. First, persistent IQ differences between blacks and whites have appeared in study after study for decades. Second, obviously whites and blacks are genetically different in some respects, as evidenced by physical traits. Third, heredity is known to play a major role in the IQs of people of the same race. Jensen therefore concluded that genes affecting IQ are somewhat different between blacks and whites, causing the average black to have a lower IQ than the average white.

Understandably, Jensen's article touched off a raging controversy. If his position was true, then blacks were trapped by their heredity, not just their environment—blacks would always score lower on IQ tests, do less well in school, and occupy a lower position on the occupational ladder. Stated more bluntly, Jensen was claiming that blacks are naturally not as smart as whites. It is worth noting that Jensen was not happy about his conclusion. He didn't want it to be true, but he thought the evidence left no other explanation.

Many people rushed to condemn Jensen's findings and indeed to condemn Jensen himself (students at Berkeley demonstrated off and on for several years, demanding that Jensen be fired). Those who had always rejected the validity of IQ tests and the evidence that heredity influences intelligence found in the Jensen case new reason to attack the tests and behavioral geneticists. However, even if Jensen was wrong, haunting questions remained. Why was the average IQ score of blacks lower than that of whites? And would the difference ever disappear?

For nearly a decade, the race and IQ controversy raged on: Jensen maintained his position, and social scientists who disagreed failed to provide convincing answers to the basic questions. Then a prominent black social scientist solved most of the mystery.

Thomas Sowell solves the puzzle

 In the mid-1970s, Thomas Sowell, now at Stanford University, took Jensen's conclusions as a scientific, not a political, challenge. As he wrote in the intro-duction to his now famous study (Sowell, 1978, p. 203):

Despite the emotionally charged philosophical and political issues involved, this is ultimately an empirical question—independent of anyone's beliefs, hopes, or fears.

Sowell believed that adequate data would show that Jensen was wrong, that black–white IQ differences resulted from social and cultural differences rather than genetic differences.

Sowell started from a proposition that we shall pursue at length in Chapter 11—that in many crucial respects, the situation of most American blacks is more similar to that of recent immigrants than to that of groups long resident in the United States. Until recent times, most blacks lived in the rural South under laws and customs of segregation. The migration to northern cities, undertaken by millions of blacks since 1940, was thus more like a trip from rural Italy to the United States than from Detroit to Chicago. Sowell thus argued that the social and cultural backgrounds of most American blacks depressed their IQ scores. In fact, the model he proposed for investigating this issue of race and IQ is the same model developed to explain the growth and puberty revolutions. That is, Sowell argued that culture and society greatly stunt genetic potential. But how could he demonstrate this?

Sowell needed to compare the IQ results for blacks with those for white immigrants from deprived backgrounds during their early days in the United States. Unfortunately, World War I data from the Army Alpha testing did not identify the ethnic background but only the race of each test taker. However, Sowell remembered that earlier in this century schools routinely recorded the ethnic background of each student. (When my mother enrolled me in the first grade, the teacher asked, "And what is Rodney's nationality?" I thought the answer would be "American" but was surprised to learn that it was "Norwegian, Swedish, and German.") By the end of World War II, most schools had stopped asking this information, in part because there were no longer many first-generation Americans.

Sowell also knew that by the 1920s many schools were administering IQ tests. Did any of these records still exist? Could he get access to them? The answers turned out to be yes. Digging in dusty and

Thomas Sowell.

forgotten file cabinets and combing through store-rooms and attics, Sowell eventually discovered records from early in the century providing the ethnicity and IQ scores of more than 70,000 students. Also using some data on ethnicity and IQ that had been published between 1915 and 1925, he was able to assess the average IQ scores of many immigrants soon after they arrived in the United States.

What Sowell found confirmed his initial suspicions and dramatically proved the power of social and cultural forces to modify heredity. Around the turn of the century, the average IQ scores among recent white immigrants were well below those of white groups that had been in the country longer.

Thus, there was nothing unusual about black IQ scores. Indeed, average black IQ scores today are well above those of many white ethnic groups back in the 1920s. For example, in the 1920s Italian schoolchildren had an average IQ score of about 85 (100 is the expected average IQ). The IQs of Slovaks, Greeks, Poles, Spanish, Portuguese, Syrians, Croatians, Lithuanians, and even French Canadians also averaged below 100. Thus, sixty years ago these white ethnic groups scored at the same level as blacks were scoring in the 1940s and 1950s. Consequently, most scholars of that time were convinced that these scores also proved genetic inferiority. Indeed, laws limiting immigration, which Congress adopted in the 1920s, were justified as a means to limit the influx of "inferior" groups from eastern Europe and Mediterranean nations.

But these views of genetic inferiority were wrong. Today members of the white ethnic groups listed above score at or above the national average; as we shall see, this improvement could not have been caused by changes in their genetic makeup. Indeed, Sowell found the same pattern of low average IQs early in this century among Japanese- and Chinese-Americans, but today both groups regularly achieve average scores above 100.

Sowell made a second important discovery: Sixty years ago black students born and raised in the North had a higher average IQ than did these same groups of recent white immigrants. Moreover, throughout the century, the longer their families have lived in the North or the younger blacks were when they moved to the North, the higher their IQs. By the same token, Sowell found that the IQs of whites in poor rural areas of the South were also well below the national average, and that their IQs also rose following migration to the North.

It is impossible to attribute these improvements to genetic change. First of all, there is no plausible reason and no known genetic principle to explain why moving from one place to another would alter genetic structure. Even if a selective breeding program had been undertaken to prevent people with low IQs from having children, it would have taken centuries to produce the changes that took place in only a few decades. Instead, Sowell's findings demonstrate that, as in the cases of height and age of puberty, the environment can suppress fulfillment of the genotype, resulting in phenotypes that fall short of their potential.

Poor diets, poor health, poor schooling, and a way of life that does not require or reward abstract thinking, all can reduce intellectual capacities regardless of genetic potential. In this way, Sowell's careful scientific research demolished notions of inborn racial superiority.

But Sowell did not destroy the validity of intelligence tests. To the contrary, he argued that such tests reflect how social and cultural deprivations can damage people's abilities. Moreover, Sowell argued that intelligence testing is even more valuable for the disadvantaged than for people from privileged backgrounds. College board examinations (Scholastic Aptitude Tests, or SATs) for the first time opened high-quality colleges to students from poor high schools by enabling their talents to be compared directly with those of others. Sowell wrote (1978, p. 231):

Unusual intellectual ability among minority schoolchildren is less likely to be recognized (when objective tests are not used). Dr. Martin D. Jenkins, who pioneered the study of high-I.Q. black children in the 1930s, repeatedly found black youngsters with I.Q.s of 150 and above whose teachers were wholly unaware of their ability.

Sowell himself is a classic example of this point. He was born in the rural South and moved to Harlem in his youth. Today he is a graduate of Harvard with a doctorate from the University of Chicago, in part because intelligence testing conducted by the New York City school system revealed his exceptional intellectual talent.

HUMANS AND OTHER ANIMALS

Since the time of Darwin, biologists have regarded human beings as simply another animal species, albeit a spectacularly gifted one. Social scientists, on the other hand, have long argued that human skills are so extraordinary compared with the skills of other animals that there is little point in applying knowledge about animal behavior to human beings. Indeed, this argument was a major reason why social scientists ignored for so long the influences of human biology on social and cultural patterns.

Virtually all older introductory texts in sociology (and most current ones) refer to nonhuman species mainly to demonstrate the distinctive traits of humans and to justify an exclusive focus on them. Two primary "proofs" are usually given to demonstrate that humans are a special case, unique in the animal world. First, it is argued that only humans have *culture:* Only humans have to be educated and trained in order to fulfill normal adult roles, because only

humans have accumulated knowledge and skills that are passed down from one generation to the next. Second, only humans have *language,* or are capable of it, and only through language can culture be developed and passed on.

To conclude this chapter, we shall assess these two claims. Both arguments do much less to distinguish humans from other animals than you might believe. This is not to say that other animals have capacities that even approach those of humans; I am merely saying that the dividing line between the human animal and other animals is much less sharp than had been suspected. And if the line is less sharp, then we can apply, with caution, some studies based on animals to an understanding of human activities.

Nonhuman culture

It is widely recognized that much nonhuman behavior is *instinctual.* As mentioned at the start of this chapter, that means that the behavior is somehow programmed into the biological heritage of the species, and all normal members of the species exhibit this behavior automatically and without any learning. That some skills are purely inborn has been demonstrated by depriving a newborn organism of any chance to learn the behavior in question and then showing that the behavior is fully exhibited nonetheless. Thus, a scientist kept one group of tadpoles drugged until other tadpoles the same age had developed the ability to swim well. When awakened, the drugged tadpoles swam just as well as their experienced counterparts, despite having had no practice. Similarly, squirrels raised in an isolation cage and fed only a liquid diet will, in their first trial, bury nuts in exactly the same way as adults that had observed and practiced nut burying from infancy (Eibl-Eibesfeldt, 1970). A list of such examples can be extended almost indefinitely.

For a long time it was thought that virtually all naturally occurring animal behavior was instinctual. In recent years biologists and ethologists (students of animal behavior) have determined that a great deal of animal behavior is learned—animals deprived of the chance to learn certain skills cannot perform them.

Early clues that much animal behavior is learned

came from observing animals raised in zoos. Some species showed many bizarre characteristics, such as an inability to mate. This problem got a lot of attention because zoo directors would like most species to breed in the zoo so that the zoos can avoid the high cost of catching animals in the wild and shipping them. In time it became obvious that many animals raised apart from others of their species do not learn how to mate. Indeed, in 1975, the Sacramento Zoo in California finally resorted to showing a movie of two adult gorillas mating to their prized young gorilla pair, who seemed to want to mate but didn't know how. The film successfully provided them with the needed sex education.

The notion that many animals have to learn a great deal in order to be competent members of their species first occurred to many Americans when they read the book or saw the movie *Born Free*. *Born Free* is based on a true story about a lion named Elsa who had been raised as a pet from infancy. As she reached maturity, it became clear that no matter how close the bonds were between her and her human parents, a grown-up lion does not make a safe companion. She was simply too big and too strong. What were the parents to do? They could either lock her in a cage or set her free in the wild.

Unfortunately, Elsa had no chance to survive in the wild because she hadn't learned the techniques of being a lion. The story's interest centers on attempts to provide "remedial education" for Elsa—to train her in at least minimal wild-lion behavior, such as how to hunt, so that she could return to freedom and survive. Thus, while lions may not have culture in the sense of technology, the skills that are passed from parent to child are necessary for survival. If *culture* is defined as what must be learned, then some animals have a bit of culture.

For many scientists, some of the most overpowering evidence of animal culture came from Harry and Margaret Harlow's years of experimentation with rhesus monkeys at the University of Wisconsin. In one major experiment, the Harlows (1965) raised three groups of infant monkeys. Monkeys in the first group were raised in total isolation and fed mechanically. Those in the second group were raised in isolation cages, each with its mother. Infants in a third group were raised together but isolated from adults. Later all the monkeys were placed in a nor-

mal monkey colony, where their behavior was carefully recorded and assessed.

The behavior of monkeys raised in total isolation was extremely abnormal. They avoided all contact, cowered in corners, and never learned to engage in sex. Perhaps surprisingly, the monkeys who had been isolated with their mothers were nearly as abnormal as the first group; they also failed to learn sex or to adjust to social relations. Those raised in isolated groups without mothers showed the least abnormality and adjusted best to life in the colony, but they never became completely normal either.

These results indicate two things. First, monkeys must be exposed to monkey society from an early age, or they will fail to become normal monkeys. Second, many of the effects of isolation seem irreversible. None of the monkeys ever made up the deficits of infant isolation fully. As we shall see in Chapter 6, the effects of severe deprivation on humans bear striking resemblance to the same effects on the Harlows' monkeys.

Some social scientists object to applying the term *culture* to fighting or mating behavior, which many animals do not inherit but must learn. They would treat as culture only technology and claim that humans are the only animals who have it. If by technology we mean machines, then only humans have technology. But then are human groups without machines not in fact human?

In order to keep our ancestors in the human race, we can only equate technology with **toolmaking**—altering or adapting natural materials in order to increase the ability to achieve some goal. The earliest humans were toolmakers. A club or a sharpened rock or stick is not a very fancy tool, but it is a lot better than bare hands.

If we adopt this definition of technology, however, then we must admit that all apes have it. When enraged, apes often throw rocks or use clubs. In several experiments, apes have solved problems by employing a series of rather complex tools to reach food (Eibl-Eibesfeldt, 1970). Furthermore, apes do not only use their own individual tools. There is now considerable evidence that tools are passed on from one ape to another and from one generation to another (Wilson, 1975). Granted, ape tools are very primitive. However, several million years back our human ancestors, just down from the trees and

In another famous experiment shown here the Harlows isolated infant monkeys each with two artificial "mothers." The mother at left is made of wire and has a nipple at which the infant can nurse. The second mother has no nipple but is made of cuddly terry cloth. When the Harlows frightened an infant it fled, not to the wire mother (as Freudian theorists predicted), but to the terry cloth mother, as shown above. This was evidence that the primary tie between infants and their mothers is not based on nursing, but on cuddling.

making a living by stealing carcasses from the great cats, were making do with pretty crude tools, too. Although human culture is immeasurably more complex and powerful than animal culture, it is simply not the case that only humans have culture.

Nonhuman language

One of the main reasons why nonhuman animals cannot develop elaborate cultures is a lack of efficient communication. It is widely recognized that animals do have some capacity for communication. Cries and calls meaning "Danger!" or "I'm looking for a mate!" are widespread among animals and birds. Also, animals often communicate with gestures and body movements. Male baboons challenge others to a fight by displaying their very light colored eyelids, for example. But very little information can be communicated through such means compared with the immense amount that can be communicated quickly and accurately by human language. Lacking language, other animals have been stymied in sharing their experience and thus in accumulating and passing on knowledge. Consider how little a human parent, without speech, could teach a child. Teaching by showing is slow, and it seriously limits what can be taught. Without doubt, language is the human trait most responsible for our great superiority over other animals. If we are the kings of beasts, we talked our way into the title.

But why do only humans have language? No one is quite sure. Some have argued that sometime before evolving into humans, we must have been aquatic creatures (Morgan, 1972). A water environment impedes communicating with gestures and thus might have favored the development of vocal communication. Attempts to study the speechlike sounds made by dolphins and whales have supported this interpretation (Lilly, 1967). However, another major argument is that only humans were sufficiently intelligent to develop speech. Many careful observers of higher apes, such as chimpanzees, have long been uneasy with this claim. Through long observation of ape behavior, they are convinced that apes display considerable intelligence. Their ability to solve problems, for example, is sufficiently high to suggest that apes are smart enough to learn a language. Indeed, a number of attempts have been made to teach chimpanzees to speak. Human couples have taken infant chimps into their own homes and raised them with their own children in an effort to teach the chimps to talk. However, such efforts have been fruitless. The most celebrated case is of a chimp named Viki, who was reared by two psychologists in the late 1940s. In six years of intensive effort, they managed to teach Viki to utter only four sounds that crudely approximated English words (Hayes and Hayes, 1951).

Speaking is impossible for chimps because they lack the vocal apparatus needed to produce speech sounds. In the wild they are usually silent and produce vocal sounds only during moments of extreme excitement. To try to teach them to talk was a little like trying to teach a human to swing by the tail. And blaming their failure to talk on a lack of intelligence was a little like blaming the human inability to swing through trees on stupidity instead of an unsuitable physique.

Washoe learns to sign

 The breakthrough in determining the language-learning capacity of higher primates came in the late 1960s, when two daring psychologists at the University of Nevada realized that language does not require speech. In the wild, chimps seem to communicate mainly through gestures. While these gestures do not constitute anything like a language, Beatrice and Allen Gardiner struck upon the idea of exploiting this natural tendency of chimps by attempting to teach a chimp the American sign language (used for communication by the deaf).

In June 1966, the Gardiners obtained a year-old female chimpanzee from Africa, whom they named Washoe. Verbal speech was never used in Washoe's presence; only American sign language was used. The Gardiners also undertook teaching sign language to Washoe. They were soon successful. The chimp began to acquire a vocabulary, much as any human toddler begins to pick up words. In time Washoe began to form the simple word combinations that pass for sentences among young humans (Gardiner and Gardiner, 1969).

As word began to leak out in the scientific community of these efforts, the Gardiners were much

ridiculed and their claims quickly dismissed. But the Gardiners kept on working, and Washoe continued to develop a greater vocabulary and to fashion more sentences. Scientists were impressed when the Gardiners invited some deaf people without any previous contact with the project to come and communicate with Washoe. The scientists were sign-deaf, but the deaf people found no difficulty understanding Washoe. And Washoe understood them.

By October 1970, 5-year-old Washoe had a vocabulary of 160 signs (Fleming, 1974). Since chimps mature at much the same rate as humans, this was no minor accomplishment for her age. However, she was also getting big. A full-grown chimp weighs more than 120 pounds and is much stronger than any human male. So the Gardiners decided it was time to find her a different environment. Roger Fouts, who had studied with the Gardiners and worked with Washoe, took her with him when he joined the Institute for Primate Studies at the University of Oklahoma.

In Oklahoma, Washoe joined a number of other chimps and monkeys gathered for research on communication. A number of them were taught sign language, and Fouts and his colleagues became able to study communication among chimps (in contrast with chimp-human communication). They were especially eager to see what would happen when chimps who had learned sign language had infants. Would they teach their infants to sign?

When Washoe was sexually mature, she was allowed to mate, and the researchers waited for her to give birth. Unfortunately, she miscarried. Two subsequent pregnancies ended in miscarriage and the early death of the infant. So Fouts arranged to obtain an infant male chimp named Loulis from the Primate Research Center at Emory University. Loulis was given to Washoe to raise. Within eight days of being adopted by Washoe, Loulis began to imitate her signs. By the age of 17 months, Loulis knew ten signs, including "hug," "drink," "food," "fruit," and "give me." Thus, apes can transmit at least some language to their young.

What do chimps have to say when they learn sign language? Obviously they do not begin to recount the history and traditions of chimpanzees. Lack of language has prevented such a culture from ever developing. If chimps do develop their own history,

A chimp learns the sign for toothbrush. Most social scientists were very surprised to discover that chimps could learn sign language and carry on conversations. They have been even more surprised to find out that chimps will use *a toothbrush properly and that they will* teach their children to use them!

it can begin only now. Perhaps they will not prove to be sufficiently bright to develop and pass on a complex language or to contemplate their own existence. But before you dismiss the idea of chimps developing an elaborate culture as something that could happen only in *Planet of the Apes,* ponder the following account based on Washoe's first few days in her new Oklahoma home.

When she arrived in Oklahoma, Washoe had never seen any monkeys. Fouts therefore taught her a new sign: "monkey."

She was happy to use it for the squirrel monkeys and for the siamangs, but she concocted a different name for a rhesus macaque who had threatened her. She called him dirty monkey. *When Fouts asked her the sign for the squirrel monkeys again she quickly went back to just plain monkey. But when they returned to the macaque, it was* dirty monkey. *Before this incident, Washoe had*
used dirty *to describe only soiled objects or feces. Since her meeting with the aggressive macaque, she has applied this sign to various teachers when they refuse to grant her wishes* (Fleming, 1974).

Washoe had invented an appropriate invective for what she didn't like. And as with any human 5-year-old, her first "bad word" was the equivalent of "poop." Who then can say how much more Washoe can learn?

Animal societies

In order to better understand the connections among biology, culture, and society, many social scientists have specialized in studies of social behavior among animals. Jane Goodall (1971) has devoted years to watching a band of wild chimpanzees, while others have studied social relations among baboons, gorillas, and macaques. A major purpose of these studies is to seek basic elements of social organization by examining societies that have not been overlaid with a great deal of culture. That is, all human groups have cultures that are both elaborate and ancient. Even when we locate an isolated tribe with only Stone Age technology, we have not found people just inventing a culture. Such a group has a culture that has existed for centuries. We cannot return to the plains of Africa several million years ago to see human culture and society in its elementary forms. But if we are willing to assume that differences between humans and other primates are only of degree, not kind, then we can observe primates as substitutes for our most ancient ancestors.

A second virtue of animal studies is that we can manipulate the environment to study adaptation. Members of a primitive human tribe cannot be rounded up and moved to a new location to see what happens. But we can move animal societies—indeed, sometimes they have been moved in order to protect them from advancing human settlement. Recently social scientists moved a group of macaques from Japan to Oregon. The results were very surprising.

These macaques had long been studied in Japan, but the troop grew too large. Scientists decided to move half of the animals to a new colony in Oregon. Thus, two groups with the same genetic heritage and, in the beginning, identical social and cultural patterns now faced a different climate and a different physical environment.

The group that remained in Japan continued as before, but the Oregon troop soon began to change in remarkable ways. In the Japanese troop, dominance among males is not based on their size or ferocity. Instead, it is determined by the size and ferocity of their mothers! When young male macaques fight, their mothers quickly come to their aid, and the tougher mother beats up the other mother and her son. Thus, young males learn not to mess with some mothers' sons. This dominance carries over into adulthood. Even a quite small male will dominate larger males if his mother won his fights for him when he was young (Eaton, 1976).

In Oregon, however, this pattern rapidly disappeared. This behavior was apparently a cultural, not a biological, trait. In Oregon the macaques live in a smaller area than in Japan, where the adult males tend to congregate quite far from the females and their young and hence do not intervene in youthful quarrels. But in Oregon, when a fight breaks out, the adult males quickly move in and break it up. Thus, mothers are not permitted to win fights for their sons, and male dominance is not established by the mother's fighting ability. Instead, males establish their own dominance system by fighting as they grow up.

In Oregon the macaques also encountered snow. They responded by inventing snowballs, which they can throw so far that the handlers must be cautious during the brief periods when there is snow on the ground. The macaques also learned to roll huge snowballs and sometimes make them into piles and play on them. But so far they have not built a snowman or even a snowmacaque (Eaton, 1976).

By observing primates, social scientists have gained insights into the creation of simple social structures and the invention of culture. But there is a second reason for such animal studies. Some social scientists now believe that human biology may shape more human behavior than had been thought—like other animals, we may have some inborn behavioral traits. For example, some social scientists now suggest that aggressive behavior is partially instinctive among humans (E. O. Wilson, 1975). Intensive study of animal behavior has provided a theoretical basis for raising such issues about humans. This has led to the organization of a new academic field, *sociobiology,* in which biologists, anthropologists, sociologists, and psychologists have joined forces to study the links between biology and behavior (E. O. Wilson, 1975).

Perhaps the link between humans and other animals can best be summed up as follows: Sometimes they appear to act just like us; sometimes we appear to act just like them.

CONCLUSION

This chapter has traced the radical turnabouts in how sociologists and other social scientists have dealt with the implications of biology for society and culture. At the start of the century, many social scientists attributed most individual behavior and many cross-cultural differences to biology. Then biology was excluded from all consideration. More recently, the fascinating interactions between the biological, the cultural, and the social have been recognized. Moreover, the study of animal behavior, once the sovereign province of biology, has now attracted the interest of many social scientists. As a result, in about seventy years we have moved from the view that nearly all human behavior is produced by instincts governed by heredity to the view that much animal behavior is learned rather than instinctive.

The next chapter builds upon the interplay of biology, culture, and society as we ask how the potential humanity of newborn infants is actualized. Moreover, we shall see that the process of socialization does not simply mean growing up or how children are raised. In a significant sense, we never finish growing up. Socialization is a lifelong process.

Phenotype The observable organism as it has developed out of the interplay between the genotype and the environment. (p. 99)

Behavioral genetics A scientific field that attempts to link behavior, especially human behavior, with genetics. (p. 100)

Mental age The amount a person has learned by a given calendar age; for example, an 8-year-old who knows as much as the average 10-year-old has a mental age of 10. (p. 106)

IQ The abbreviation of *intelligence quotient,* which is mental age divided by calendar age, with the result multiplied by 100. The average IQ score is thus 100, for the calendar age of the average person is exactly equal to his or her mental age. (p. 106)

Toolmaking Altering or adapting natural materials in order to increase the ability of an organism to achieve some goal. (p. 112)

Review glossary

Instinct Any behavior that occurs in all normal members of a species without having been learned. (p. 96)

Chromosomes Complex genetic structures found in the nucleus of a cell, each containing some of the basic genetic units (genes) of the cell. Chromosomes combine in pairs; thus, in humans, 23 chromosomes from the father combine with 23 from the mother. (p. 99)

Genes The basic units of heredity within which specific genetic instructions are encoded in complex chemical chains. (p. 99)

Genotype The sum total of genetic instructions contained in an organism's genes. (p. 99)

Suggested readings

Eaton, C. Gray. "The Social Order of Japanese Macaques." *Scientific American,* October 1976.

Gardiner, R. Allen, and Beatrice T. Gardiner. "Teaching Sign Language to a Chimpanzee." *Science* (1969) 165:664–672.

Goodall, Jane. *In the Shadow of Man.* Boston: Houghton Mifflin, 1971.

Rosenthal, David. *Genetic Theory and Abnormal Behavior.* New York: McGraw-Hill, 1970.

Sowell, Thomas, ed. *Essays and Data on American Ethnic Groups.* Washington, D.C.: The Urban Institute, 1978.

Tanner, James M. "Physical Growth." In Paul Mussen, ed., *Carmichael's Manual of Child Psychology,* 3rd ed. New York: Wiley, 1970.

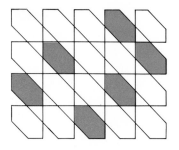

■ In June 1983, a Seattle judge gave permanent custody of a 6-year-old boy to the county welfare department. He asked that efforts be made to have the child adopted, despite protests from the child's father and mother. The judge based his decision on the fact that the child could not speak intelligibly, crawled rather than walked, and barked like a dog when people approached him. When found in his home by social workers, who had been alerted by a neighbor, the child was "filthy, smelled of urine, his teeth were rotten, he had sparse and brittle hair and a pale, pasty complexion" (Hopkins, 1983). After placement in a foster home, the boy soon became toilet trained, and he began to walk and talk.

This little boy's tragic condition was the result of isolation and almost total neglect. From infancy he had spent most of his days and nights alone in a filthy one-room home. His father was in prison, and his mother was rarely home, stopping by now and then only to feed him. Aside from his mother, he rarely saw another human being.

There have been countless cases like this, of children whose parents so neglected them and so isolated them from all human contact that when they were discovered, they acted more like wild animals than human beings. In fact, children like this are often called **feral children** (the word *feral* means "untamed"), and some people have mistakenly assumed that such children had been reared in the wild by an animal (Malson, 1972; McClean, 1978; Shattuck, 1980).

Human children cannot be raised by mother wolves, dogs, or other animals—such stories are fantasies. Unfortunately, demented or cruel human

Socialization and
Social Roles

parents can raise their children like animals. Sometimes children thought to be feral are actually victims of mental retardation or severe mental illness, not neglect. But others, like the little boy in Seattle, are born with normal capacities, for they make rapid progress once they are rescued from isolation (Davis, 1940; 1947; 1949).

Feral children demonstrate an important principle: Our biological heritage alone cannot make us into adequate human beings. Only through social relations—constant intimate interaction—can the rich cultural legacy that sets humans apart from other animals be transmitted to new humans. An infant is born without culture. Reared in isolation, a human being will not even learn to talk or walk, let alone to sing or read.

The learning process by which infants are made into normal human beings, possessed of culture and able to participate in social relations, is called **socialization**. This process, which literally means to be "made social," begins at birth and continues until death—we never cease to be shaped by our interactions with others. As we pass through life, what others expect of us and the roles we are expected to fill all change. And we change, too. ■

CHAPTER PREVIEW

In this chapter we shall examine how humans are socialized. We shall first see how infants acquire basic skills, such as speech and the ability to reason. Next we shall examine the link between culture and personality, that is, how societies shape people to fit into particular cultural patterns. Then we shall see that even within the same society, not all children are socialized alike. Instead, people are socialized differentially on the basis of the different roles that they are expected to perform as adults. Because roles are so important in socialization, at the end of the chapter we shall explore how people actually perform social roles. Immediately following this chapter, we shall apply principles of socialization by closely examining sex role socialization in modern American society.

BIOPHYSICAL DEVELOPMENT

Physicians and psychologists have done an immense amount of all the research on socialization. They have primarily aimed to discover the normal processes of the biological and physical development of infants and children to discover how these can be modified by the environment.

Years of testing infants at various ages have made it possible to determine patterns of normal development. Table 6-1 shows patterns of normal motor skill development, from the ability to turn over to the ability to walk. With reasonable parental care, children will usually learn to stand up by about the age of 8 months and to walk by about 14 months.

Statistical norms like these help parents and physicians to be alert to signs of slow development, in which case treatment or special training may be sought. But the norms also serve as a basis for

Table 6-1 / Milestones in motor and language development.

At the Completion of	Motor Development	Vocalization and Language
12 weeks	Supports head when in prone position; weight is on elbows; hands mostly open; no grasp reflex.	Markedly less crying than at 8 weeks; when talked to and nodded at, smiles, followed by squealing gurgling sounds usually called *cooing,* which is vowel-like in character and pitch-modulated; sustains cooing for 15–20 seconds.
16 weeks	Plays with a rattle placed in hands (by shaking it and staring at it), head self-supported; tonic neck reflex subsiding.	Responds to human sounds more definitely; turns head; eyes seem to search for speaker; occasionally some chuckling sounds.
20 weeks	Sits with props.	The vowel-like cooing sounds begin to be interspersed with more consonantal sounds; labial fricatives, spirants and nasals are common; acoustically, all vocalizations are very different from the sounds of the mature language of the environment.
6 months	Sitting: bends forward and uses hands for support; can bear weight when put into standing position, but cannot yet stand with holding on; reaching: unilateral; grasp: no thumb apposition yet; releases cube when given another.	Cooing changing into babbling resembling one syllable utterances; neither vowels nor consonants have very fixed recurrences; most common utterances sound somewhat like *ma, mu, da,* or *di.*
8 months	Stands holding on; grasps with thumb apposition; picks up pellet with thumb and finger tips.	Reduplication (or more continuous repetitions) becomes frequent; intonation patterns become distinct; utterances can signal emphasis and emotions.
10 months	Creeps efficiently; takes side-steps, holding on; pulls to standing position.	Vocalizations are mixed with sound play such as gurgling or bubble blowing; appears to wish to imitate sounds, but the imitations are never quite successful; beginning to differentiate between words heard by making differential adjustment.
12 months	Walks when held by one hand; walks on feet and hands—knees in air; mouthing of objects almost stopped; seats self on floor.	Identical sound sequences are replicated with higher relative frequency of occurrence and words (*mamma* or *dadda*) are emerging; definite signs of understanding some words and simple commands.

assessing whether development is impeded by particular environmental circumstances or even whether enrichment of the environment can accelerate development.

Chapter 5 mentioned the work by Harry and Margaret Harlow (1965) with infant monkeys raised in isolation. Like feral human children, monkeys raised in isolation failed to develop normal monkey skills and displayed symptoms of acute maladjustment when placed in contact with normal monkeys. Similar studies cannot be conducted on human infants, yet cases of child neglect have supplied comparable data. For example, researchers have studied infants raised in orphanages for signs of impaired development.

In a classic study, Skeels and Dye (1939) con-

Table 6-1 (continued)

At the Completion of	Motor Development	Vocalization and Language
18 months	Grasp, prehension and release fully developed; gait stiff, propulsive and precipitated; sits on child's chair with only fair aim; creeps downstairs backward; has difficulty building tower of three cubes.	Has a definite repertoire of words—more than three, but less than fifty; still much babbling but now of several syllables with intricate intonation pattern; no attempt at communicating information and no frustration for not being understood; words may include items such as *thank you* or *come here,* but there is little ability to join any of the lexical items into spontaneous two-item phrases; understanding is progressing rapidly.
24 months	Runs, but falls in sudden turns; can quickly alternate between sitting and stance; walks stairs up or down, one foot forward only.	Vocabulary of more than fifty items (some children seem to be able to name everything in environment); begins spontaneously to join vocabulary items into two-word phrases; all phrases appear to be own creations; definite increase in communicative behavior and interest in language.
30 months	Jumps up into air with both feet; stands on one foot for about two seconds; takes few steps on tiptoe; jumps from chair; good hand and finger coordination; can move digits independently; manipulation of objects much improved; builds tower of six cubes.	Fastest increase in vocabulary with many new additions every day; no babbling at all; utterances have communicative intent; frustrated if not understood by adults; utterances consist of at least two words, many have three or even five words; sentences and phrases have characteristic child grammar; they are rarely verbatim repetitions of an adult utterance; intelligibility is not very good yet, though there is great variation among children; seem to understand everything that is said to them.
3 years	Tiptoes three yards; runs smoothly with acceleration and deceleration; negotiates sharp and fast curves without difficulty; walks stairs by alternating feet; jumps twelve inches; can operate tricycle.	Vocabulary of some one thousand words; about 80 percent of utterances are intelligible even to strangers; grammatical complexity of utterances is roughly that of colloquial adult language, although mistakes still occur.
4 years	Jumps over rope; hops on right foot; catches ball in arms; walks line.	Language is well established; deviations from the adult norm tend to be more in style than in grammar.

Source: Biological Foundations of Language by Eric H. Lenneberg. Copyright 1967 by John Wiley & Sons Inc., New York. Used by permission of John Wiley & Sons, Inc.

ducted research on infants in an orphanage whose development at 19 months was judged so retarded that they were considered unfit for adoption. These infants were transferred to an institution for the mentally retarded, where Skeels and Dye arranged for each to be put under the personal care of an older, mildly retarded girl. Four years later the infants showed dramatic improvement. Their estimated IQs had risen by an average of 32 points, while similar infants who had remained in the orphanage had lost an additional 21 points over the same period.

Twenty years later Skeels (1966) did a follow-up study of these same subjects. Most of the orphans who had been mothered by retarded girls had graduated from high school and a third had gone on to college. Nearly all of them were self-supporting and

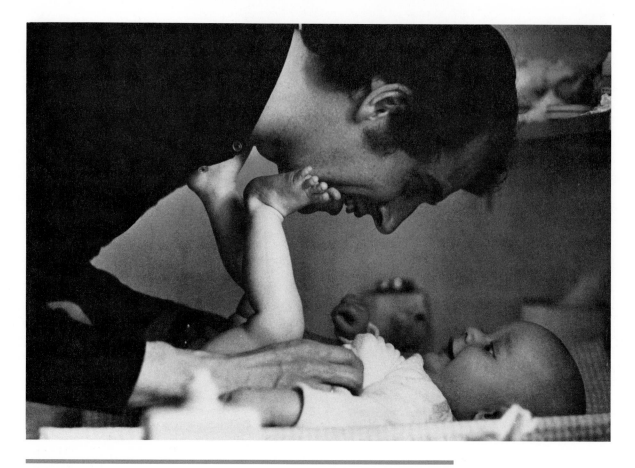

While special efforts to speedup infant development have little effect, neglect can cause development to be tragically retarded. Children need a great deal of daily interaction like this in order to fulfill their potential. This is no surprise if we remind ourselves how much each infant must master in a few short years in order to be normal.

rated as normal. However, most of the people who had been in the control group and remained in the orphanage had not progressed beyond the third grade and either remained in institutions or were not self-supporting.

Clearly, infants who lie unattended and unstimulated in crowded orphanages are deprived in much the same way as the Harlows' monkeys and feral children. As a result, despite a normal biological heritage, they fail to develop normally. Skeels and Dye's research prompted major reforms in the treatment of orphaned infants to prevent this sort of retardation. Today, most such infants are placed in foster homes rather than in institutions and thus receive more normal levels of attention. Even when infants are raised in institutions, great effort is made to handle and cuddle each one many times a day.

Can normal development be accelerated by special treatment? The answer seems to be, only a little bit. One study showed that children who have toys suspended above their cribs, such as different-colored objects that attract interest and invite handling, can reach and grasp objects about six weeks sooner than children who lack such crib toys (White, 1971). However, the infants with crib toys did not begin to look at and explore their hands as soon as those without the toys.

There seem to be two reasons why development cannot be greatly accelerated for normal infants in normal settings. First, at least in modern times, the average infant seems to receive adequate stimulation and care (for a contrast with preindustrial times, see Chapter 12). Second, development is not only a psychological and social process. Fundamental physical and mental development must occur before infants can acquire certain skills. Coaching before such development takes place is to no avail, as we shall now see.

COGNITIVE DEVELOPMENT

Learning is the key process in socialization. Thus, a primary issue in socialization theory and research is, How do we learn? Indeed, how do we learn to learn? Here we must know how the human brain operates, how it physically develops from birth, and how it builds up its capacities to solve problems and make choices.

Despite an immense amount of research and considerable theoretical progress, the brain still withholds many of its vital secrets. For example, when someone asks you if you know Bruce McElroy, you can say almost instantly whether you do. Computer experts are eager to know how humans can answer such a question so quickly. So far, the only way to answer this question with a computer is to have the computer search all names in its memory to see if "Bruce McElroy" is there. But that's not how our brain does it. We know the speed at which brain impulses travel, and people can answer too soon to have done a computerlike memory search. So the human brain must not have just a simple file of all acquaintances; instead, a single bit of information such as "knowing Bruce McElroy" must be stored in a great many different files that are interconnected in the most complex ways. But, to say that is really to say very little except that it's still a mystery.

If we don't understand exactly how the brain does many things, we do know a great deal about general patterns of what the brain can do—about the processes of learning and intellectual development. Here again, however, the brain has turned out to be a subtler and more intricate mechanism than was first suspected. We do not simply build up knowledge and learning skills in a constant, gradual way. Instead, normal cognitive development passes through a series of stages, periods of slow progress interrupted by sudden spurts. One man played the major role in discovering fundamental patterns of cognitive development, or reasoning ability, so let's go back in time and look over his shoulder.

Piaget's theory of cognitive stages

 Jean Piaget (1896–1980) was a Swiss professor of psychology who successfully challenged the conventional stimulus-response theory of how children learn. In fact, he demonstrated that strict application of the **stimulus-response (or S-R) learning theory** led to a contradiction: People could not have thought up something like the S-R theory itself if our minds operate as stated by the theory.

The S-R learning theory, which for a long time dominated psychology, proposes a simple model of learning in which humans play only a passive role. Behavior is merely a response to external stimuli, and we repeat whatever behavior has been reinforced by our environment in the past. According to this view, the brain is little more than a memory bank capable of recalling past reinforcements, but it is not an active participant in the learning process; that is, it does not construct general rules or principles to guide future behavior. For example, S-R psychology dismisses the proposition that grammatical rules are acquired in learning to talk. Instead, it postulates that language is acquired word by word and then sentence by sentence through reinforcement. One of the attractive features of this view was that it freed psychology from relying on introspection and focused research on observable behavior. While psychologists can never be sure what is going on in people's minds, regardless of what people might say is going on, they can observe what people say and do.

Piaget found this extreme form of behaviorism

The elderly man sitting on the bench, smoking his pipe, and watching the children play is Jean Piaget, the famous Swiss psychologist. Piaget's work on stages of cognitive development redirected the field.

unrealistic. If nothing but S-R learning is going on, he argued, invention is impossible. How can anyone ever say a new sentence, for example, if we only acquire language by repeating what we are taught? Any behavior that goes beyond what is present in our environment cannot possibly be a mere copy of the environment. And Piaget pointed out that we invent all the time. In fact, much of modern mathematics cannot possibly be regarded as a reflection of external reality because it has no counterpart in reality. It is a human mental creation. Thus, Piaget wrote, "To present an adequate notion of learning one first must explain how the [person] manages to construct and invent, not merely how he repeats and copies" (Piaget, 1970).

Early in his career, Piaget became convinced that the human mind develops and functions on the basis of **cognitive structures**, or general rules for rea-

soning. His initial insight into this matter came from administering Binet's IQ tests to youngsters (see Chapter 5). What struck him were the consistent patterns of wrong answers. That is, time and again kids gave the same wrong answer to a given question. Why was this? Piaget concluded that the children were applying the same, but incorrect, rule to a problem.

This led Piaget to suspect that cognitive development involves coming to comprehend a set of basic principles or rules of reasoning; normal development consists of acquiring these rules by particular ages. Thus, the difference between children who correctly answered a particular IQ test question and those who chose the same incorrect answer was that the first group had acquired the rule needed for giving a correct response, while the other group was still applying an inadequate or incorrect rule.

Thus, Piaget set out to discover basic rules of reasoning and the ages at which normal children acquire them. First, he carefully observed his own children as they grew up; then he conducted a long series of experiments with large numbers of children. In the end he proposed that cognitive development passes through four fundamental stages: (1) sensorimotor, (2) preoperational, (3) concrete operational, and (4) formal operational. In a number of experiments, he showed that humans at one stage of cognitive development cannot solve problems requiring understanding at a higher stage and cannot be taught to solve these problems before they reach that stage of development. Let us briefly examine these stages and some of the pertinent experimental evidence.

Sensorimotor stage The **sensorimotor stage** begins at birth and lasts until around the age of 2. During this period, infants discover and develop their senses and their motor skills. A major cognitive discovery during this stage is the *rule of object permanence*—the principle that objects continue to exist even when they are out of sight. Young infants immediately lose all interest in an object as soon as it is blocked from view; they do not search for it. But by about 10 months, children will search for an object when it is suddenly covered with a cloth or otherwise removed from sight: They know the rule of object permanence. However, a child takes a bit longer to begin searching for an object where it was last seen. Instead, young children will search where they last found the object.

Preoperational stage The **preoperational stage** begins at about age 2 and ends at about 7. The earliest years of this period are devoted to language learning. However, the other major task during this period is to overcome egocentrism, or, to use a symbolic interaction concept discussed in Chapter 1, to learn to take the role of the other.

During the preoperational stage, children cannot solve problems that require them to put themselves in someone else's place. In a classic experiment, Piaget and Edith Meyer-Taylor constructed a model mountain range out of clay. Children were placed by the model and asked to describe it. Then they were asked to describe how it would look from where another child was standing (from a quite different perspective). Children in the preoperational stage were unable to get the point of the request and continued to describe the model from where they stood. As George Herbert Mead pointed out, this kind of limitation prevents younger children from participating adequately in team games.

Concrete operational stage The **concrete operational stage** begins at about 7 and ends at about 12 (although many people never progress beyond this stage). In this stage children develop a number of logical principles that permit them to deal with the concrete, or observable world. One such principle is the rule of *conservation*—that is, a given amount of material does not increase or decrease when its shape is changed. Children still in the preoperational stage do not yet understand this. If you present them with identical clay balls and then flatten one of the balls, they will say that the flattened ball is smaller and contains less clay. Similarly, when such children are presented with two identical rows of checkers and then one row is clustered into a smaller space, they will say the cluster contains fewer checkers than the row.

Formal operational stage The **formal operational stage**, the final stage in Piaget's theory of cognitive development, often begins at about age 12. In previous stages children learn mainly by trying things out to see what happens. Eventually, however, some people learn to think abstractly and to impose logical tests on their ideas.

Recall from Chapter 3 the distinction between theories and hypotheses. Theories are abstract, general statements of a principle, while hypotheses are specific statements about the concrete world. In the concrete operational stage, people deal with the world only at the level of hypotheses, and they test hypotheses by examining concrete evidence. But when the formal operational stage is reached, people can formulate and manipulate theories and logically deduce from these theories that certain things are likely to be true or false. With this comes the ability to think hypothetically—to say "what if?" and then trace out the logical implications of this supposition.

People still in the concrete operational stage miss the point of hypothetical assertions and often find them distressing. Suppose someone says, "Let's assume, for the moment, that humans were of only

This boy has a very high IQ and is building a radio in school from very simple materials. He also is just about to leap forward from the concrete operational stage to the formal operational stage. When this occurs he will be able to grasp the principles of physics and not be limited to specific technological applications, such as how to assemble a radio.

That's all just idle nonsense. Let's go study families if we want to really know what goes on."

Obviously, the formal operational stage never ends. Some humans can continually refine their ability to think logically and abstractly. Unfortunately, not everyone can do so. After testing large numbers of people, researchers have concluded that perhaps half of all American adults do not reach the formal operational stage of cognitive development and thus are limited to literal interpretations of the world around them (Kohlberg and Gilligan, 1971).

Several factors may prevent people from achieving the ability for formal operations. Some people may lack the necessary intelligence. Others may not have the opportunity or the need to develop powers of abstract reasoning at this level. Although all normal humans have constant practical experience with the concrete world, many have little occasion for abstract thought.

Because of Piaget's work, few psychologists now propose that all learning is purely the result of S-R mechanisms. Even many who devote most of their own research to improving the S-R model fully acknowledge that cognitive structures influence what is learned and when (Bandura, 1974).

Piaget's theory does not reject the importance of S-R mechanisms for a great deal of what we learn. Rather it adds to this model. In particular, it adds an active human consciousness that is capable both of formulating rules of reason to interpret the constant flow of environmental stimuli and of generalizing from a few instances. For example, by falling from several objects (such as trees and bicycles), we don't only learn that it hurts to fall from these objects but we learn the general principle that falling can hurt. That saves a lot of bruises.

one sex and that every individual could bear infants. Would humans still form family units in order to make child rearing easier?" People in the formal operational stage are able to pursue such a hypothetical line of reasoning, add to it, and evaluate it. In so doing they may more fully understand why the family is a universal human institution (see Chapter 12). But people in the concrete operational stage will immediately object: "But people don't come in only one sex. Why are you saying something so stupid? How can I suppose that a lie like that is true?

Brown and Bellugi: language acquisition

 If learning is the key to socialization, language is the key to learning. Most of what we know, we were told. Thus, a major area of socialization is devoted to discovering how children develop the capacity to use and understand language. Work on this topic fills a large section in any good social science library. By watching Roger Brown and Ursula Bellugi (1964) conduct one of the landmark studies in this area, we can see a sample of this work and also understand how it supports Piaget's stage theory.

In October 1962, Brown and Bellugi began intense observation of two children whom they called Adam and Eve. Adam was studied from the age of 27 months to 36 months; Eve from the age of 18 months to 36 months. These two children were selected from an initial pool of thirty because they talked a lot and because Brown and Bellugi could understand what they said. Brown and Bellugi visited Adam and Eve in their homes every two weeks, took notes, and tape-recorded everything said by each child and by each mother as mother and child went about their normal routines. The aim of the study was to see how the acquisition of speech progresses.

A number of important findings emerged. First, Brown and Bellugi found that young children's speech is stripped of all but the most vital words. Even when young children repeat a sentence just spoken to them, they tend to retain only the nouns and verbs; they omit auxiliary verbs, articles, prepositions, and conjunctions. For example, when a mother said, "Fraser will be unhappy," the child repeated, "Fraser unhappy"; when a mother said, "No, you can't write on Mr. Cromer's shoe," the child replied, "Write Cromer shoe." Only very gradually do children begin to include more words in their sentences.

A second major finding was that not only do children repeat what parents say, but parents frequently echo their children. In so doing they expand and correct childish sentences. Thus, when Adam said "There go one," his mother echoes, "Yes, there goes one." Brown and Bellugi suggested that this interaction of repeating a phrase back and forth was a key to the development of speech. This may explain why the little boy in Seattle, mentioned in the introduction to this chapter, could not speak despite having had a fair amount of exposure to television. The TV never talks *with* you.

But perhaps the most important of Brown and Bellugi's results was clear evidence that young children experiment with speech in ways that appear to involve a search for grammatical rules. Often Adam and Eve spoke sentences that they could not possibly have heard from someone else:

"You naughty are."
"Cowboy did fighting me."
"A this truck."
"Put on it."

Brown and Bellugi believed that sentences such as these reflect a trial-and-error effort to discover the rules determining what words are allowed in which positions in sentences. Such a search for grammatical rules strongly confirms Piaget's theory of cognitive structures underlying learning. In fact, kids could hardly be speaking sentences like those above on the basis of S-R learning alone, for the sentences appear to be original. And that, of course, is Piaget's whole point. A mind is not simply a passive memory bank: Someone is in there thinking, not just recalling.

Thus far in this chapter we have examined principles of socialization that seem applicable to humans generally. There is every reason to suppose that children deep in the Amazon jungle acquire speech in much the same way that Adam and Eve did in Boston, and that such children discover cognitive rules in much the same way that Piaget found children in modern societies do. Now it is time to explore how particular cultural and social structural patterns and the socialization process interact, that is, how different child-rearing practices may be determined by and in turn sustain various aspects of different cultures and societies.

CULTURE AND PERSONALITY

Chapter 5 discussed the reaction of social scientists in the 1920s and 1930s against extreme biological determinism—theories that attributed most of human behavior to such things as instincts rather than learning. This reaction involved the equally extreme claim that biology was insignificant and that environment alone determined human behavior.

A leader of the environmentalists was Franz Boas (1858–1942), the first person ever appointed to be a professor of anthropology at Columbia University. Boas published and taught the principle of **cultural determinism**. According to this principle, regardless of how a given culture came into being,

Franz Boas.

it wholly determined the behavior of all persons who were socialized within it. Moreover, Boas argued that human nature is infinitely plastic, that cultural forces can create virtually any kind of personality type and any patterns of roles and behaviors. For example, he argued that sex roles had no biological basis but simply reflected cultural forces that blinded us to other possibilities. Moreover, Boas took the view that culture made its deep and permanent effects on people during early childhood. That is, a particular culture determined how people would think and act as a result of specific patterns of child rearing, which shaped the immature personality into the desired mold.

By postulating this powerful link between child rearing and personality, Boas was, in effect, equating culture and personality. Or, as his famous student Ruth Benedict (1934) put it, culture is "personality writ large." That is, the individual personalities of the members of a society are tiny replicas of their overall culture, while their culture is the summation of their personalities.

The major problem facing Boas and his supporters was to demonstrate exceptions to all generalizations that had been made about human behavior and personality so that they could claim that existing

patterns are only common, not necessary—that an almost infinite array of cultural and social forms is possible. That Boas and his followers strongly desired to change many norms of Western societies was a major motive in their theorizing and research (Freeman, 1983).

Today this extreme form of cultural determinism has lost much of its support. Meanwhile, however, its message has deeply penetrated our society. The mass media, for example, frequently use the great variety of cultural patterns found around the world as proof that almost any pattern is possible. Journalists still promote cultural determinism because, for decades, social science textbooks uncritically reported the claims of Boas and his students to have proved exactly that (and many texts still do). For this reason it seems useful to examine the work of Boas's most famous student to see both the carelessness of her research procedures and the obvious omissions and logical shortcomings of her conclusions.

MARGARET MEAD: THE RISE AND FALL OF CULTURAL DETERMINISM

In 1921 Margaret Mead (1901–1978) enrolled in an introductory anthropology course taught by Franz Boas. He was 64, world famous, and a dominating presence in the classroom. Within weeks Mead was committed to a career in anthropology, and the next year she enrolled in graduate studies under Boas. Soon she was devoted to proving Boas's theory of cultural determinism. Specifically, she wanted to locate a society in which something thought to be a natural and universal aspect of human behavior did not occur and thus show that culture conquers all. She focused her attention on the unrest and emotional turmoil through which Western adolescents normally pass. This was widely believed to be a normal reaction to the physical and hormonal changes of puberty. However, if she could show that somewhere adolescents passed through puberty without "this storm and stress, then the anthropologist would know . . . that this storm and stress was not inevitable" (Benedict and Mead, 1959). Or, as she posed the critical question: "Are the disturbances which vex our adolescents due to the nature of adolescence itself or to the civilization?" (Mead, 1928).

Coming of Age in Samoa

To prove that adolescent trauma is wholly cultural, Mead set out for American Samoa in 1925, when she was not yet 24. She stayed in Samoa only a few months and then returned to New York. There, working closely with Ruth Benedict, she drew upon her field notes to write the first anthropology best-seller, *Coming of Age in Samoa* (1928). The book made Mead famous, and it claimed that Boas's cultural determinism was right. In Samoa there was no adolescent trauma. It was a gentle, easy-going society. Since teenagers were permitted complete sexual freedom, they escaped guilt feelings and emotional repression; instead, they came to accept their bodies and their sexual feelings as normal and natural. Of course, men did not expect their wives to be virgins, and they displayed none of the macho, domineering style found among men in Europe and the United States. Rape was unknown—indeed, the idea of rape "is completely foreign to the Samoan mind." Relations among people were free and casual. In fact, Samoans were as casual about religion as about sex, and there was rarely any overt conflict among them over any issue.

It was a vision of paradise, complete with the tropical beauty of the South Seas. Millions have read *Coming of Age in Samoa*. Until recently it was hard to pass through college without its being required reading in some course. As a result, Mead has taught millions about the irrationality of Western culture. We can become much better people and make a much better world if we copy the Samoans and raise our children gently, permissively, and without sexual, religious, and moral hang-ups.

But now we know that this vision of paradise existed only in Mead's mind, not in the culture of Samoa (Freeman, 1983). Samoans do not have casual attitudes about sex. Instead, they have quite puritanical sexual norms, and men are very concerned that their wives be virgins. Rape is not only known

Margaret Mead poses with the daughter of a chief during her stay in Samoa in 1925. Although she is in native dress, she did not spend much time with Samoans or learn much about their culture, basing her famous research findings on romantic preconceptions about life in the South Seas.

but relatively common; in fact, reports of rapes were in the local newspapers during Mead's stay on the islands. Samoan males are very macho, as their present extraordinary overrepresentation among U.S. professional football players and boxers suggests. Moreover, rather than being casual about religion, almost all Samoans had been converted to very conservative Protestant denominations as early as the mid-nineteenth century, and religious commitment remains high among them. Finally, overt conflict is a prominent part of Samoan life (Freeman, 1983).

Mead's Samoa is almost the exact opposite of the real Samoa. How could she have gotten things so wrong? There are several answers. First, she saw what she wanted to see. Second, she saw almost nothing of Samoa. She was there only nine months and learned very little of the language. She had very little contact with adult Samoans, for she lived with an American family and made no effort to meet Samoans. In fact, her whole study was based on interviews with about two dozen adolescent Samoan girls, whom she persuaded to come to a U.S. Navy infirmary periodically for interviews and tests. Apparently, she talked with these girls from time to time for only about three months, and she held no interviews for several weeks during this period because of a serious hurricane. One does not expect books that revolutionize scientific knowledge to be based on such flimsy evidence.

Sex and Temperament

After the resounding reception given her first book, Mead was launched on a career that made her the most widely known anthropologist in her time and an international celebrity. On her next venture she was determined to show that supposed temperamental differences between men and women also have a purely cultural basis. Once again on her first try Mead discovered just the cultures needed to prove her case. In fact, her luck was so good that the groups involved lived within easy travel distance of one another on the island of New Guinea. Moreover, this study also permitted her to demonstrate another of Boas's claims—that socialization in early childhood strictly determines the adult personality.

In her second famous—and still widely read—book, *Sex and Temperament in Three Primitive Societies* (1935), Mead claimed that among the Arapesh of New Guinea, the ideal personality type for both men and women is gentle, unaggressive, responsive, cooperative, and passive—that is, both male and female Arapesh have "feminine" temperaments. Mead argued that this was the result of extremely gentle child-rearing practices in which both parents played equal roles. For example, Arapesh children were not weaned or toilet trained until they were relatively old. This avoided repres-

sion and shaped their personalities into a gentle, feminine disposition.

In contrast, among the cruel Mundugumor, Mead found the temperament of both men and women to be "masculine," that is, unrelentingly aggressive, cruel, suspicious, and violent. The Mundugumor were (and are) cannibals and treated one another almost as savagely as they did enemy tribes. Mead explained this on the basis of their brutal child-rearing practices. Mothers resented nursing their infants and used slaps and shoves to wean them at an early age. Children were cuffed and kicked whenever they displeased their parents. This, according to Mead, soon turned them into little monsters destined to become adult monsters like their parents.

From these findings, Mead concluded that male and female temperaments have no biological basis whatever. She further concluded that culture is the source of personality, imposing its marks indelibly during a person's infancy.

Once again Mead's fieldwork is very suspect. Her second husband, who accompanied her in the field, later wrote a paper on warfare among the Arapesh—the very tribe Mead had characterized as harmless, feminine types. In addition, even Mead admitted that the male Arapesh were not as gentle as the females and that the female Mundugumor were not as fierce as the males. Nevertheless, let's take Mead at her word. In doing so, we can spot some of the omissions and logical shortcomings of extreme cultural determinism.

The first shortcoming is insensitivity to physical realities. Mead tells us that the gentle Arapesh live in an almost inaccessible part of New Guinea, unsuited to growing crops. The Mundugumor, on the other hand, live on a rare tract of excellent growing land—high, well drained, and clear of the jungle. Let's pretend we know nothing about the Mundugumor except the desirability of their location and the fact that dozens of other tribes would like to live there as well. Might we not suspect the Mundugumor to be the meanest, toughest bunch of warriors on the island? If they weren't, why wouldn't tougher folks have driven them off and taken their land? This reminds us that culture isn't just the accidental result of mental processes. There is always a real world to be reckoned with that waits to impose its tests of fitness on any culture (Harris, 1979). Indeed, if the Arapesh were at all as gentle as Mead

Among New Guinea tribes such as this one Margaret Mead claimed to find proof that early child-rearing practices determine the adult personality and that human nature is essentially plastic, making virtually any cultural pattern possible. For sociologists, however, the most striking thing to be seen in this picture is differential socialization. The little boy in the foreground already is becoming a very different kind of person than the young girls in the background are becoming. This process is not limited to childhood. The adult males in this picture lead daily lives far different from those of their wives, and thus basic male-female personality differences are constantly reinforced.

portrayed them, that might explain why they ended up with the worst piece of real estate on the whole island.

But a more compelling problem is the assumption of a direct and everlasting link between early childhood socialization and adult personality. Consider this question: At what age would a child taken from the Arapesh and given to the Mundugumor still grow up with an Arapesh personality? Would it be too late to change at 2, or 5, or 15? At what age is it impossible to transform an individual? There is no clear answer because socialization is not something that happens to infants and then stops. It is a lifelong process. A lot happens between the time when children are weaned and the time when they become adults, just as a lot can happen to change people remarkably between the ages of 30 and 40 or 60 and 70.

The whole structure of Mundugumor and Arapesh life, not just early childhood experience, supported their particular styles of behavior. A Mundugumor warrior who began to mellow might end up in a neighbor's cooking pot. Being fully aware of that, he would not need to draw upon his early childhood training to remember to stay tough. Indeed, studies have failed to find any link between being frequently spanked and harshly disciplined as a child and any tendency to act in violent ways as an adult (Erlanger, 1971).

Despite these problems, however, we must recognize that the major shortcoming of the cultural determinists was that they pushed their position too far. No one would deny that cultures can differ greatly and that among these differences are great variations in how people are expected to act. For example, it is obvious that the average Mundugumor, male or female, is very different from the average German. If we acknowledge such differences, we must also acknowledge that they are produced by differences in socialization—that a Mundugumor infant sent off to be raised in Germany would become a German. Of course, early childhood socialization is not irrelevant—it simply is the start of a lifelong pattern by which, for example, Germans become and remain Germans.

The failures of the cultural determinism advocated by Boas and Mead are those of exaggeration and omission. Boas and Mead were correct in arguing that culture is extremely important in shaping humans, but they were excessive in saying that it is the *only* thing that matters. They were correct in arguing that human nature can be shaped into a great variety of expressions, but they were excessive in saying that virtually any cultural and personality pattern is possible. Finally, they were correct in arguing that child-rearing practices comprise a major aspect of the socialization process, but they were excessive in saying that only childhood socialization matters.

Suppose an adult Mundugumor warrior moved to Texas. He probably would never become just like a native Texan, but he would soon be very different from his friends back in New Guinea. Moreover, the ways in which he would change would depend a lot on the kinds of roles he assumed in Texas. Suppose he became a linebacker for the Dallas Cowboys or a cowboy on a ranch. The socialization involved in these two roles would produce rather different outcomes.

Let us now leave the South Seas and examine processes of **differential socialization**: how roles determine how people are socialized, and how this process prolongs socialization throughout an individual's lifetime.

DIFFERENTIAL SOCIALIZATION

What we have examined thus far are aspects of socialization that apply to all members of societies, the ways in which people acquire the cultural and behavioral patterns that their society expects them to master. However, in any society not all children are expected to master exactly the same culture, to develop the same basic personality, or to learn the same physical and mental skills. Instead, from infancy, children are sorted out in a variety of ways and socialized in rather different directions. This is because they are expected to lead very different lives. Put another way, they are being groomed to fill quite different social roles.

Recall from Chapter 2 that a social role is a set of shared expectations about the behavior of a person occupying a particular position in a society. A role consists of a set of norms applying to a particular position and these norms serve as a script to be followed by those people filling that position.

Every society can be conceived of as a collection of related roles. Even in very simple societies, there are a number of different positions—son, daughter, father, mother, aunt, uncle, cousin, warrior, hunter, cook, gardener, grandfather, grandmother, chief, and priest, to name but a few. Each of these positions has a unique role associated with it; the role of priest, for example, is quite different from that of hunter, although the same person may alternate between these roles.

Many social roles make major demands on those who fulfill them, and thus people must often undergo long and rigorous training before taking on such roles. Moreover, not just anyone is thought to be eligible for any role—for example, males are not qualified to be daughters. In addition, people often aspire only to some roles and not to others. In sum, some people are socialized to hold certain positions and fulfill these roles, while other people are socialized to hold other positions and perform those roles.

As we shall pursue in detail in Special Topic 2, all societies have differentially socialized people on the basis of sex: Males and females fulfill quite different sets of roles, and from infancy they are prepared to lead different lives. Although gender is the most universal and dramatic instance of differential socialization, it is but one of innumerable bases determining how people are socialized.

To illustrate this point, let's examine the differential socialization of two brothers born a year apart in England at the turn of the century. From birth, the eldest son was the legal heir to his father's title as Baron of Buncombe and to the family estate: 2,000 acres of land and Buncombe Hall, an eighteen-room Gothic manor house. The younger son would inherit no title and no estate. At most, he could hope for a modest cash inheritance. From the day of their births, these boys faced very different futures, and they knew they would play quite different roles as adults. Almost from the day of their births, they were treated differently by parents and servants.

The elder son was taught to ride and hunt and was instructed in the management of the estate. While still a lad, he rode with his father to call on the tenants who farmed various portions of the estate. On these trips he was constantly instructed in how to act like a proper lord of the manor, and he often encountered sons of tenants who were being prepared to replace their fathers and one day be his tenants.

Meanwhile, the second son was left out of most of these socialization activities. As long as he could remember, he had been aware that he would have to prepare for an occupational career—not just any career, of course, but one fit for the younger son of a baron. Usually, this meant a career in the army or in the church. Since his mother preferred that he go into the church, his father agreed that he should be prepared to become priest of the Anglican Church. As a result, he was left in the company of his mother more often than of his father, and his tutor made him study hard. The elder brother could get away with little study and with modest school achievements, but the younger brother was drilled hard in Latin, Greek, history, classical literature, and music, although, unlike his brother, he was not made to learn accounting.

At the appropriate age, each boy was sent off to a famous boarding school, but the elder was given more money to spend and was not expected to do better than passing work. The younger was pushed hard in school, since he would need to attend the university.

As an adult, the elder brother was self-confident, bold, and extremely well mannered—many regarded him as a born leader. He was a terrific rider and sportsman. The younger brother grew up to be somewhat shy. He often seemed ill at ease in large gatherings and preferred not to ride, hunt, or fish. While the elder brother spent many years as a popular and eligible bachelor and did not marry and settle down until he was past 40, the younger brother married at 25 and soon had a large family. As a father, the priest was mild and undemanding and treated all his sons pretty much the same. In contrast, the baron was soon taking his eldest son on visits to the tenants. His younger son, however, was meant for the army, so both boys did an equal amount of riding and hunting.

This is a classic case of differential socialization based on differing expectations of roles that the children would assume. Notice, too, that each brother was socialized somewhat differently to perform some of the same roles. The role of father carried a rather different script when it was combined with the role of Anglican priest instead of with the role of baron. Indeed, the role of husband was also scripted somewhat differently.

Differential socialization has long been the object of considerable sociological research. Of particular concern has been the way in which parents' expectations about their children's future influence patterns of socialization. Perhaps no one has pursued this question longer and more effectively than Melvin Kohn.

MELVIN KOHN: OCCUPATIONAL ROLES AND SOCIALIZATION

 Melvin L. Kohn is chief of the Laboratory of Socio-environmental Studies of the National Institute of Mental Health in Washington, D.C. In 1956 he conducted a study of the values guiding child-rearing practices among American parents. The results revealed some notable class differences.

Working-class parents (manual laborers and blue-collar workers) placed greater stress on such values as obedience, neatness, and cleanliness than did middle-class parents. The latter thought such values as curiosity, happiness, consideration for others, and especially self-control were more important. Both groups gave equally high importance to honesty (Kohn, 1959).

Kohn argued that these findings reflected two underlying value clusters. Working-class parents were more concerned about their children *conforming* to the expectations of others, especially expectations concerning good behavior; middle-class parents were more concerned about their children being capable of *self-expression* and independence. Put another way, working-class parents placed more importance on values involving external judgments (on pleasing others), while middle-class parents placed more importance on values involving internal judgments (on pleasing oneself).

Kohn was careful to point out that these class differences were only tendencies. Parents of all classes regarded all of these values as important in raising children. It was the emphasis given to these two clusters of values that differed among the two classes.

Kohn then asked whether these differences in how parents socialized their children affected how they actually treated their children. His research led him to identify two primary differences in child-rearing practices. The first pertained to why parents punished their children; the second to who punished them.

Kohn found that working-class families tended to punish children on the basis of what a child did. That is, if a child was prohibited from jumping up and down on the couch or yelling and then did so, the child was punished. In contrast, middle-class parents tended to be more concerned about the motives behind behavior than about rule violations as such. Thus, if a child broke a rule against yelling in the house, the parents would punish on the basis of why the child yelled. Yelling done out of anger or a loss of self-control would tend to be punished. But if it was done out of enthusiasm or happiness, middle-class parents would ignore it. In effect, working-class parents reinforce conformity to external authority, while middle-class parents reinforce self-control and self-expression.

Middle-class parents feel an obligation to be *supportive* of children in order to encourage self-expressiveness. Moreover, they feel both parents should be supportive, just as they feel both should share responsibilities for disciplining children. Working-class parents, on the other hand, tend to have a division of responsibility in child rearing. Mothers take primary responsibility for the children and tend to be the supportive parent. Fathers are delegated the responsibility of enforcing the rules. Thus, when a child is caught jumping on the bed in a middle-class family, a family conference is likely to be held. In a working-class family, the child is told, "Well, when your dad gets home, he's not going to be happy about this." Again, Kohn was careful to point out that these are only tendencies; in many middle-class families, husband and wife divide the discipline and support responsibilities, while in many working-class families, parents take equal roles in child rearing.

The next question Kohn faced, of course, was why do these different tendencies exist between working- and middle-class families? Kohn's initial answer was that these tendencies reflect a parent's own experience with how the world works. He especially emphasized work experience. Working-class parents are more successful in jobs when they observe the rules: when they are prompt, do what they are told, and show up for work looking neat and clean. Middle-class parents find they are more successful in jobs when they can work without supervision, take individual initiative, and get along well with co-workers. Parents draw upon this personal experience in deciding how to raise their own children—they raise them to succeed in the adult roles they expect children to adopt.

This interpretation led Kohn to decide that social

class as such was not the significant independent variable. Instead, he realized that the actual work conditions experienced by the parents should be the real focus of research. Although class differences are correlated with the nature of working conditions, the correlation is far from perfect. Thus, some working-class people have jobs, such as repairing home appliances, that require a great deal of self-supervision and individual initiative. Conversely, many middle-class people have jobs that are highly supervised and controlled, such as office jobs. So Kohn set out to refine his results by examining occupational, and not simply class, effects.

The results were as predicted (Pearlin and Kohn, 1966; Kohn and Schooler, 1969). Work conditions experienced by parents, not their social class, influenced whether they stressed conformity or self-expression in raising their children. This was true not just for American parents but for Italian parents as well (Pearlin and Kohn, 1966).

Kohn also demonstrated that experience with adult occupational roles not only influenced child-rearing practices but also reflected basic personality characteristics of the parents. That is, parents whose work experience placed a premium on conformity not only stressed this in raising children but had more conformist and less flexible and expressive personalities themselves (Kohn and Schooler, 1969). This raised a new question. Did correspondence between job experience and personality reflect *selection*? Were people with flexible, self-expressive personalities more likely to obtain jobs requiring little supervision and rewarding initiative and innovation? Or was this evidence of **adult socialization**? Were people changed by socialization into adult roles and thus taught to be more flexible or conformist, depending upon the conditions of their occupation?

Such a question could be answered only by a **longitudinal study,** in which observations are made of the same people at several different times. In this way, one can see what people are like before they enter a role and after they have performed it for a while. Since Kohn had already based one of his studies on a national sample of more than 3,000 employed American men, ten years later (in 1974) he arranged to reinterview them. Once again the results were striking.

Both selection and adult socialization account for the correlation between work conditions and personality. People with more flexible, self-directed personalities are more likely to obtain jobs with little supervision and much opportunity for individual initiative. Conversely, less flexible, less self-directed people gravitate toward more structured and more supervised occupations. However, people's personalities also tend to suit their jobs better as time goes by. People in highly structured jobs become less flexible and less self-directed. People in less structured jobs tend to become more flexible and self-directed (Kohn and Schooler, 1982).

The two primary lessons from Kohn's pioneering research are:

1. Children are socialized differentially on the basis of parental expectations about the roles the children will assume as adults; understandably, parents base these expectations on their own life experiences.

2. Socialization is a lifelong process. In Kohn's sample, even men 50 and older showed shifts in basic personality traits in response to changes in their occupational roles.

Thus we have seen that socialization prepares people for roles and that roles in turn shape socialization. To conclude this chapter, we must examine more closely how people go about performing social roles.

ERVING GOFFMAN: PERFORMING SOCIAL ROLES

Elizabethan playwright William Shakespeare (1564–1616) wrote in *As You Like It*:

All the world's a stage,
And all men and women merely players:
They have their exits and their entrances,
And one man in his time plays many parts.

But it was sociologist Erving Goffman (1922–1982) who most effectively analyzed social interaction from the point of view that life really is a stage and that much of the time we are putting on performances for one another.

These two men differ not only in the kind of work they do, but in the degree to which they are supervised. The white collar office worker operates in a setting where he is under the constant observation of many other people including his immediate boss (and probably even by his boss's boss). In contrast, the fisherman usually works out of sight of anyone, far out at sea. Melvin Kohn found that the degree to which people work under supervision influences their personality and the way they raise their children.

Just a few weeks ago these young men wore jeans and T-shirts and acted like most other people just out of high school. Now they wear a suit and tie every day and are rapidly trying to learn how to act mature and serious. They are undergoing several weeks of intensive training to prepare them to conduct themselves in the role of Mormon missionary for the next 18 months. Nearly half of young Mormon men (and a growing number of young women) volunteer to serve as one of the more than 30,000 unpaid missionaries their church has at work around the world. But before they go, they must be socialized into this new and demanding role.

Goffman (1961) made an important distinction between role and role performance. *Role* refers to how a person would act if he or she did only what the norms attached to a particular position directed. **Role performance,** in contrast, is "the actual conduct of a particular individual while on duty in [a] position."

Goffman pointed out that while roles do greatly shape our behavior, we rarely act only according to the script. "Perhaps there are times," he wrote, "when an individual does march up and down like a wooden soldier, tightly rolled up in a particular role." But most of the time we are not wholly confined by a role. Instead, we constantly display glimpses of ourselves, of the individual "behind" or "inside" the role. Moreover, we sometimes give an unconvincing, discreditable, incompetent, resentful, or even defiant performance.

Much like a drama teacher, Goffman identified the basic techniques for giving adequate role performances (Goffman, 1959; 1961; 1963; 1971).

First of all, Goffman examined the costumes and

props we use in role performances. Simply by wearing the appropriate clothing or carrying the right props, we can often make a convincing appearance in a role. As a young newspaper reporter, I once gained access to the medical files of a celebrated mass murderer by putting on a white coat and hanging a stethoscope around my neck. In a huge county hospital, that was sufficient proof that I was a resident physician with the right to wander onto wards and look at charts. (Such a deception would violate the role of sociologist, but not the role of reporter.)

Of course, if I had not also had the right kind of haircut, been of the appropriate age, and been able to exude the impression of bored self-confidence, someone might have asked me who I was. This illustrates Goffman's insight that a major aspect of the way we present ourselves in roles involves **impression management**—the conscious manipulation of scenery, props, costumes, and our behavior in order to convey a particular role image to others.

Goffman also pointed out that roles in life, like those in the theater, have both a *stage* and a *backstage*. Waiters in a restaurant, for example, give a stage performance to customers, and a more relaxed backstage performance in the kitchen, where they are seen only by cooks and other waiters. Professors act out their roles somewhat differently when they chat with students in the hall than when they are in front of a class.

In addition, *teamwork* is often involved in an adequate role performance. For example, a husband and wife holding a party will often prompt one another in their roles. Moreover, an effective role performance often requires that others play along. A hostess cannot play her part if the host begins to swear at her, throws his plate on the floor, takes off his clothes, or otherwise falls out of his proper role. Similarly, a parent cannot convincingly scold a child if the other parent is busy laughing at the misbehavior.

There is another kind of teamwork that plays a vital, but often little noticed, role in facilitating adequate role performances. Goffman called this **studied nonobservance.** For Goffman, this is a powerful and civilizing norm based on the acceptance of our common humanity. It is summed up by the phrase "After all, we're only human." Through nonobservance, we come to one another's aid by covering up miscues in role performance. When we are embracing a lover and his or her stomach grumbles, we pretend not to hear it. When someone unconsciously scratches inappropriately, we pretend not to see it. Day in and day out, we are careful not to notice the little slips that mar role performances. In fact, a major aspect of good manners is to not notice bad manners.

Of course, we don't ignore all failures in role performance. While actors on the stage may only risk bad reviews for a poor performance, in real life people sometimes lose their friends, their jobs, their families, and even their liberty because they have violated their roles.

Moreover, people sometimes suffer these consequences even when they have given a superb role performance—because they were acting out a **deviant role**. That is, some positions in society and their roles are against the law. Thus, while the bank officer who embezzles risks jail for an inadequate role performance, the robber who withdraws funds from the same bank risks jail for performing a deviant role. In the next two chapters we shall examine deviant behavior and deviant roles.

CONCLUSION

This chapter first studied early childhood socialization, but it soon was revealed that socialization is a lifelong process. Since socialization is the transmission of culture and the shaping of character, it does not cease so long as we continue to interact and have new experiences. Moreover, since so much socialization is aimed at preparing people for, and comes as a result of, playing new roles, socialization continues as we pass through life's successive roles.

Socialization during infancy and early childhood has received the greatest attention from social scientists, because serious failures in this period can have profound, long-lasting effects. A child who never learns to take the role of the other, for example, will never be able to play team sports; he or she may even grow up to be an egomaniac. A child who grows up in a modern society without learning to

[handwritten notes in top margin: Birth - 2, 2 - 7, 7 - 12, 12 -; Sensorimotor stage, Preoperational ", Concrete Operational "]

read is condemned to a life of marginal employment and ignorance.

However, even if early socialization is crucial, not all problems or patterns of adult behavior are rooted in childhood. Socialization failures can occur at any age and be wholly independent of anything that came before. In the next chapter we shall see that people who fall into "bad company" during their teens, or even as adults, may become socialized into new and deviant patterns of behavior. People who have successfully performed a whole series of adult roles suddenly may fail to be adequately socialized into a new one—as grandparent or retired person, for example.

Just as socialization occurs throughout our lives, so does the topic of socialization occur throughout this book. For example, when we examine social institutions such as the family, religion, school, or the economy, we also examine major sources of socialization. In fact, this textbook is part of your present socialization.

To clarify the material covered in this chapter, Special Topic 2, which follows, examines the connection between sex roles and socialization.

Review glossary

Feral children The name often applied to children who, because of severe neglect, act as if they were raised in the wild (*feral* means untamed). (p. 118)

Socialization The process of being made social, of learning to act in ways appropriate to our roles. (p. 119)

Stimulus-response (S-R) learning theory The theory in which behavior (responses) of organisms is said to be the result of external stimuli, that is, organisms only repeat behavior that has been reinforced by the environment. (p. 123)

Cognitive structures General rules or principles that govern reasoning. (p. 124)

Sensorimotor stage According to Piaget, the period from birth to about age 2 during which the infant develops perceptual abilities and body control and discovers the rule of object permanence—that things still exist even when they are out of sight. (p. 125)

Preoperational stage According to Piaget, the period from age 2 until about 7 during which a child learns to take the role of the other. (p. 125)

Concrete operational stage According to Piaget, the period from 7 until about 12 during which humans develop a number of cognitive structures, including the rule of conservation. (p. 125)

Formal operational stage According to Piaget, the time after about age 12 when some humans develop the capacity for abstract thought, that is, for using theories rather than only empirical observations. (p. 125)

Cultural determinism The claim that an almost infinite array of cultural and social patterns is possible and that human nature can be shaped into almost any form by cultural forces. (p. 127)

Differential socialization The process by which different members of the same society or even the same family are raised differently because of varying expectations about the roles that each will need to fill as an adult. (p. 132)

Adult socialization Processes by which adults are enabled to perform new roles. (p. 135)

Longitudinal study Research in which observations are made of the same people at different times. (p. 135)

Role performance The actual behavior of people in a particular role, in contrast to how they are supposed to behave. (p. 137)

Impression management Conscious manipulation of role performance. (p. 138)

Studied nonobservance The way in which people pretend not to notice minor lapses in one another's role performance. (p. 138)

Deviant role A set of norms attached to a position which, in turn, violates the norms adhered to by the larger society. For example, a proper performance of the role of burglar will deviate from other people's norms. (p. 138)

Suggested readings

Elkin, Frederick, and Gerald Handel. *The Child and Society,* 3rd ed. New York: Random House, 1978.

Freeman, Derek. *Margaret Mead and Samoa: The Making and Unmaking of an Anthropological Myth.* Cambridge: Harvard University Press, 1983.

Goffman, Erving. *The Presentation of Self in Everyday Life.* New York: Doubleday, 1959.

Goffman, Erving. *Relations in Public.* New York: Basic Books, 1971.

Kohn, Melvin L., and Carmi Schooler. "Job Conditions and Personality: A Longitudinal Assessment of Reciprocal Effects." *American Journal of Sociology* (1982) 87: 1257–1286.

Mead, Margaret. *Coming of Age in Samoa.* New York: William Morrow, 1928.

Piaget, Jean, and Barbel Inhelder. *The Psychology of the Child.* New York: Basic Books, 1969.

Sex-Role Socialization

Just how different are men and women? That has become one of the dominant questions of our time. The fundamental roles assigned to men and women have always been quite different; men have had more powerful social roles. For a long time, it was taken for granted that these role differences reflected underlying biological differences—for example, that women were by nature less aggressive than men. Today many aspects of traditional sex-role differences have disappeared, and some feminists demand an end to all differences. Such demands rest on the belief that there are no significant biological differences between men and women.

At present, neither biologists nor social scientists are sure of the extent of biological differences between the sexes or how important these differences may be in explaining differences in the behavior and abilities of men and women. Clearly, the belief that most sex-role differences are biological is incorrect. Differential socialization of males and females undoubtedly explains most of these differences. Yet biology clearly plays some part.

BIOLOGICAL DIFFERENCES

Biological differences between men and women are not limited to their sexual organs and their roles in reproduction, although, as we shall see, these differences have been important in structuring sex roles. Men and women have many other biological differences. For example, the average male is substantially larger than the average female and carries more weight in his chest and shoulders and less in his hips. Men and women also differ in the kinds and amounts of hormones produced by their bodies. Hormones influence mood and other psychological tendencies, but the extent to which hormonal differences produce psychological differences between men and women is not yet known (Weitz, 1977).

Evidence is accumulating that male and female brains function somewhat differently. The left and right hemispheres of women's brains are more integrated; thus, women who suffer strokes recover more rapidly and completely than men. This is because the undamaged half of a woman's brain can relearn tasks, such as speech, better than a man's (Durden-Smith and diSimone, 1983).

The issue, then, is not whether males and females differ biologically, but the extent to which these differences have social significance. For example, if women do more poorly on tests of mathematical ability because of biological differences, then women will always be underrepresented in science and engineering—fields that have great influence. On the other hand, if men excel in math only because of socialization differences, then male dominance in science and engineering will probably soon disappear. There has been heated debate on whether sex differences in math aptitude scores are biological or the result of socialization (Benbow and Stanley, 1980), but the issue remains unsettled. Whatever the final outcome of research on these matters, the fact remains that biology is at most a minor factor in current differences between the sexes. Even if males do tend to have greater math aptitude, the extreme underrepresentation of women in science and engineering stems primarily from cultural patterns that cause women to be less interested in these fields.

The major role played by biology in differences between the sexes is not how it determines sex roles now but how it determined them in the past, thus leading to the evolution of cultural patterns that continue to guide sex-role socialization. Therefore, before we analyze current patterns of differential sex-role socialization, let us look to the distant past to see how biology produced a sex-based division of labor and male dominance.

DESIGNING A SIMPLE SOCIETY

Imagine you have suddenly been transported back in time 100,000 years. You find yourself amidst a group of cave dwellers. Because they have been immensely impressed by your advanced knowledge, they ask you to help them redesign their whole society. So you sit down and help them prepare a list of all the vital tasks that must be performed adequately in order to sustain the group. Your aim is to divide these tasks up so that they are performed efficiently, thus providing the group with the highest possible standard of living.

As you attempt to match people to jobs, you make a profound discovery, one the cave dwellers have always known. Age and sex greatly determine to which jobs people should be assigned. It just isn't sensible to send children out to hunt wild animals or to fight enemy tribes. Nor is it feasible for women to perform tasks that separate them from their infants, since nursing is the only way infants can be fed. In addition, women are smaller than men and are often pregnant, which limits their physical mobility. You soon see that women in this society should perform those tasks that can be done close to the cave so that they can care for their infants and supervise children too young to care for themselves. Tasks far from the cave that require the greatest strength must be performed by the men. Therefore, the men will go out to hunt and fight. This division of labor is universal in primitive societies (D'Andrade, 1966; Murdock, 1949).

This is the only sensible way to divide the tasks. Unfortunately, it has many consequences. Those people most familiar with the issues involved will dominate decision making pertaining to those issues. The two most urgent areas of decision making, because they are the most difficult ones for the group to control, are hunting and fighting. Should we move in search of a better supply of game? Can we survive against the tribe on the other side of the forest? Thus, in addition to being able to dominate women by strength alone, men in simple societies gain dominance because of the particular tasks they perform. Although women's tasks are vital to the survival of the group, men's tasks involve immediate threats to survival. For example, if the women are lax in caring for their infants, the group may slowly die out. If the men are lax about defense, the group may be wiped out in a few hours.

Having designed your simple society, you soon discover something else. Different tasks call for different skills, especially for different kinds of personalities and different styles of interaction. In a world where keeping enough infants and children alive is a constant struggle, a group will have a better chance of survival if the women are tender and loving, but survival chances diminish if the men are like that. You soon realize that your society needs aggressive, somewhat cold-hearted fathers and gentle, somewhat warm-hearted mothers. But how can this be accomplished? The answer has always been differential socialization.

You must raise boys and girls differently so that they will develop different kinds of personalities and regard their differences as desirable and natural. That is, socialization will be most effective when both mothers and fathers treat sons and daughters in consistently different ways, encouraging the boys to be tough and brave and the girls to be gentle and maternal. As a result, males and females will be different.

Thus we see how sex roles came to be firmly established. Moreover, it is not surprising that these patterns of differential socialization tended to mislead people into assuming that the very different personality traits of men and women were inborn. Today, of course, many of these beliefs about the sexes have been rejected. But the fact of markedly different gender socialization remains. While differential socialization begins in infancy, it continues throughout the life cycle. It is useful, therefore, to examine sex-role socialization at various stages in life.

INFANCY

Many studies have found that, compared with men, women lack self-esteem and self-confidence (Mac-

coby and Jacklin, 1974). Since virtually all known societies prefer male children, it is probably not surprising that daughters feel less wanted. Although the preference for boys is much less marked in modern societies than in more primitive ones, which often kill female children at birth (Harris, 1979), a clear bias in favor of sons remains. In the United States, when a couple's first child is a girl, they have a second child more often and do so sooner than when the first child is a boy (Westoff et al., 1961). That clearly indicates that couples are more satisfied with sons than with daughters. It is not too surprising, then, that many little girls catch on that they were not exactly what the stork was supposed to have brought.

From the earliest days of life, an infant is not simply a child, but a boy or a girl. Boys get blue blankets; girls get pink ones. There are male and female names. Nicknames in particular reveal different conceptions of what little boys and little girls are expected to be like—Buck, Butch, Tiger, Slugger, and Sport versus Sweetie, Doll, Honey, Bunny, and Kitten.

Boys and girls play with different toys and wear different kinds of clothes. One of the earliest things any child knows is that he is a "he" and she is a "she." Once a young child accepts a gender identity, it is almost impossible to change it. Sometimes genital abnormalities cause an infant's true sex to be incorrectly identified. When this has been discovered, even at ages as young as three and four, it has proved unwise to try to change the child's mind. Instead, physicians now think it preferable to adjust surgically the child's body to his or her initial sexual identity (Green, 1974; Money and Ehrhardt 1972).

CHILDHOOD

Once a child can walk and talk, socialization speeds up. When children can talk, they can be exposed to culture more fully and efficiently. When they can walk, they can begin to learn to use their bodies for a range of activities. One of the first things children learn is that boys and girls do not use their bodies

"Like father, like son" is a saying that captures an essential truth about socialization, especially sex role socialization. It is unlikely that this father would have brought his daughter to the weight room to begin "pumping iron." As sex roles shift in modern societies, questions must be faced about what kinds of adjustments to make in how boys and girls are raised.

in the same way. Little boys are taught to run, jump, push, shove, wrestle, and pull. Little girls are taught how to walk, sit, and stand. Little boys are told not to be sissies. Little girls are sissies, which, after all, is short for "sister."

The lessons continue in school. Obviously, schools are not some external institution but are part of and reflect the culture of society. Thus, research in the early 1970s found that elementary school textbooks for reading classes gave most of their space to stories about boys and men, who alone had exciting adventures, while girls and women stayed home (U'Ren, 1971; Weitzman et al, 1972).

The same patterns occur on television. Overall, children see more men than women on TV, and male stars overwhelmingly dominate adventure shows (Miles, 1975).

TEENS

Three critical things sharply differentiate male teens from female teens. The first is the onset of secondary sex characteristics, which leads to dating. Both events intensify pressures toward differentiated sex roles. When girls begin to have breasts and boys start to shave, males and females suddenly look a lot more different than they did when they were younger. As they begin to experiment with boy-girl relationships, they attempt to appear more masculine and more feminine in other ways, as well—in dress, hairstyles, gestures, even speaking styles.

The second critical aspect of the teens is participation in organized sports. Until very recently there were almost no high school sports for girls except in a few midwestern states. It is generally believed that participation in sports, especially team sports, provides important socialization that has given men advantages in pursuing adult careers. The Duke of Wellington put so much stock in the importance of team sports in training men to be self-disciplined, cooperative, confident, and to assume leadership that, following his victory over Napoleon, he said "the battle of Waterloo was won on the playing fields" of England. In similar fashion, Margaret Hennig and Ann Jardim (1977) claimed that the lessons learned in team sports are basic to success in the managerial ranks of business.

However, there has been virtually no research to test whether sports have a significant effect on adult achievement. If they do, women have clearly been deprived of the opportunity to learn about "not giving up until the last out," "coming from behind," "shrugging off defeat," "being a team player," and "playing with pain." The recent explosion of women's sports may therefore have a considerable effect on sex roles.

The third critical development in the teen years is that the question "What are you going to be when you grow up?" takes on significance. Decisions made during the teens affect the answer to that question. For example, the decision to take math and science courses will open certain possibilities, while the decision to get married at the end of high school will close certain possibilities. Generally, career questions have been more important for boys than for girls. Boys know they must find an answer. Girls have been encouraged to adopt an answer: An adult woman should be a wife and mother.

Clearly, most girls today will become wives and mothers when they grow up, just as most boys will become husbands and fathers. But equally clearly, most girls today will also hold jobs throughout most of their adult lives. Thus, the need to plan ahead for these jobs, rather than to take whatever comes, now applies as fully to women as it has to men.

FEMALE PARTICIPATION IN THE LABOR FORCE

In 1980, 51.6 percent of American women over the age of 16 were employed (as compared with 77.4 percent of men). This was a substantial increase from 1960, when only 37.7 percent of women held jobs. Moreover, employment differences between males and females are smaller than these statistics suggest because a much larger proportion of women than men are over the age of retirement (due to the fact that women live substantially longer than men).

Although this is a very marked change, the most dramatic shifts have occurred among married women with children. Overall, married women (50.2 percent) are somewhat less likely to work than unmar-

Table 1 / Percentage of employed married American women according to age of children, 1960—1980.

Status of Children	Percentage Employed		
	1960	1970	1980
No children under 18	34.7%	42.2%	46.1%
Children 6 to 17	39.0	49.2	61.8
Children under 6	18.6	30.3	44.9

Source: U.S. Census, 1980
Note: Figures pertain to married women who are living with their husbands.

ried women (61.2 percent), but this is partly due to single women being less likely to be past the age of retirement. Table 1 shows employment rates for married women from 1960 to 1980.

Among married women, those with children between the ages of 6 and 17 are much more likely to work than women without children under age 18 or women with children under the age of 6. In part, this reflects the fact that more of the women who have no children under age 18 are past retirement age. It also reflects the fact that families with school-aged children are in greater need of the wife's income than are couples without school-age children. Not surprisingly, women are more likely to take jobs once all their children have entered school than when they still have young children to care for. Perhaps the most dramatic change over the twenty-year period, however, is the great increase in employment of women who do have children under the age of 6. In 1960, only 18.6 percent of such married women worked; in 1980, 44.9 percent worked.

What influenced this rapid shift in the proportion of working women? Some would suggest that the feminist movement played a major role. Yet major changes in female rates of employment occurred before the feminist movement. Thus, feminism was more a response to changes in the lives of women than a cause of these changes.

The primary cause of females entering the labor force was modernization and its impact on the biological basis for the traditional sexual division of labor. As we shall see in Chapter 17, a major consequence of the rise of modern industrial societies was a major decline in fertility. Not much more than a century ago, the average American woman was pregnant more than seven times during her lifetime. Today on the average, American women bear slightly fewer than two children each. Moreover, the modern woman need not stay close to an infant in order to nurse it—baby bottles and formulas can take her place. Since the average American woman has her last child by age 27, when she is in her early 30s her last child is already in school, and she can expect to live for at least another 40 years. Thus, women have been freed of the limits imposed on them by their reproductive biology, which had been the basis of traditional sex roles.

A second impact of modernization has been on the amount of labor needed in the home. Doing the laundry required several days a week when there were no automatic washers and driers and no detergents and when all clothes had to be ironed. Refrigerators and freezers have eliminated the need to shop every day, and convenience foods have reduced the time needed for cooking. Vacuum cleaners, dishwashers, and a host of appliances have reduced the time needed to keep house to a point where a full-time housekeeper is no longer necessary.

Modernization has also changed the nature of work. Muscle power is no longer essential. Few jobs today require much physical strength, which was not true even a century ago. Indeed, most jobs today involve the manipulation of information, not the physical movement of things. Thus, the kinds of work available are as suitable to women as to men.

In short, the real basis for traditional sex roles was not simply culture, or beliefs about what men and women ought to be like, but reality. When the tasks that could be assigned to women were no longer subject to women's fertility and strength, cultural patterns began to shift.

Nevertheless, culture does play a role of its own. For millions of years, human cultures have differentially socialized males and females, producing elaborate sex-role differences. Such cultural patterns do not change overnight, even if the conditions justifying them change. Moreover, it is impossible to change female roles without changing many other aspects of culture. For one thing, changing female roles necessitates corresponding changes in male roles, for the two are interdependent. Thus, if we are going to raise little girls to become a different kind of woman, we must also raise little boys to become a different kind of man. Little wonder, then, that there has been so much turmoil over matters so basic that affect everyone. Moreover, we are headed into uncharted seas. No one knows what a society with only slightly differentiated sex roles will be like—none has ever existed before.

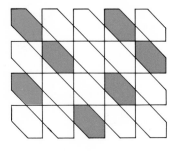

Most of us play by the rules. As we shift from role to role and from situation to situation, we usually conform to the norms that define how we are supposed to act—but not always. Each of us breaks the rules some of the time, and some of us break them a lot of the time.

When we violate norms, our behavior is called **deviance**: We deviate from, or fail to conform to, the norms. Deviance ranges from the trivial to the acute—from sleeping in class to committing murder. How others react to a deviant act indicates how serious the violation is. When people ignore or mildly disapprove of an action, the offense is minor. But when the offender is taken to jail, referred to a psychiatrist, or pursued by an angry mob, he or she has broken an important norm.

Some actions are regarded as deviant only in some societies, while other actions seem to be regarded as deviant in all societies. For example, no society condones unrestricted killing of its members or unlimited taking of goods from others against their will. On the other hand, drinking alcohol is seriously deviant in Iran, while refusing to drink in certain circumstances is slightly deviant in France.

Variations in what is defined as deviant where are of interest to sociologists, but sociologists of deviant behavior concentrate on a more basic and universal phenomenon. Although norms may differ from one society to another, all societies have norms, and all societies punish those who violate important norms. Yet, in all societies some people commit acts of serious deviance anyway. Why? Sociologists of deviance try to answer this question— why some people deviate whatever the norms may

Deviance
and Conformity

be. To do so they seek general theories of deviant behavior.

Serious deviance depends not only on the *importance* of the norm violated, but also on the *frequency* of norm violation. No one would get very upset if a student walked backward out of class, or even all the way across campus. But if that student always walked backward, day after day, this behavior would raise serious concern. Moreover, people with past records of observing the norms (such people are often described as being "of good character") will be forgiven even a very grave norm violation. For example, people with no prior police record often receive probation for quite serious crimes, such as burglary or armed robbery (see Chapter 8). On the other hand, some people with records of repeated violations may be harshly penalized for relatively minor infractions, such as being drunk in public.

People who frequently break important norms are called **deviants**. The behavior of such people is seen as a problem for others. In Chapter 8, we shall examine efforts to prevent deviance and to reform or change deviants. Here we ask, Why does deviance occur? ■

CHAPTER PREVIEW

This chapter ignores minor acts of deviance: It will have little to say about why some of your friends might have vulgar eating habits or write on lavatory walls. Rather, it will explore the causes of serious acts of deviance.

This proud husband and father is a pillar of Iranian society and has fulfilled the Muslim ideal of having four wives. In Europe and the western hemisphere he would be a criminal polygamist. What behavior will be regarded as deviant differs from society to society and even from one subculture to another with the same society. The important point for sociology is that in all societies and subcultures some people violate the norms. Theories of deviance attempt to explain why they do.

In modern societies, important norms are usually written into law; therefore, most serious acts of deviance are considered to be crimes. Since sociologists of deviance concentrate on serious deviance, they also tend to concentrate on crime, which is why many sociologists also call themselves criminologists.

However, not all sociologists of deviance specialize in crime. Many attempt to understand mental illness, for example, and while the mentally ill are sometimes subject to legal proceedings, mental illness is not a crime. Nor is alcoholism, although public intoxication and drunk driving are illegal. Both criminal and noncriminal deviance are discussed in this chapter, although crime will receive much greater attention.

Deviance is one of the most active areas of sociological study. This activity simply reflects the fact that deviance is a serious and chronic threat: The more burglars there are in our midst, the more we fear losing our belongings; the more murderers, the more we fear losing our lives. Other forms of deviance are not so threatening, but there are still widespread efforts to aid alcoholics and addicts and to treat the mentally ill. Consequently, sociologists have devoted much effort to formulating and testing theories of deviant behavior.

At present there are a number of such theories, and this chapter shall examine the more significant of these. However, simply because there are a number of theories of deviance does not mean that the field is a muddle of competing, contradictory claims. Instead, most of the theories are complementary. That is, many are directed at different aspects of the problem and thus try to answer somewhat different questions.

As a result, there are many partial theories of deviance. As we examine these, it will become evident that they suggest the outlines of a general theory. As yet, no one has attempted to construct such a general theory, but someone is bound to do so soon. Of course, not every aspect of every current theory fits with other theories or even with the basic facts of deviant behavior that have been revealed by research. As the chapter proceeds, we shall consider various theoretical disagreements and see how these square with the known facts.

Since I have chosen to work from the micro to the most macro in the overall design of this book,

in this chapter we shall begin with human biology and end with the effect of societies upon deviance.

BIOLOGICAL THEORIES OF DEVIANCE

For centuries humans have wondered why some people are chronic deviants—why some people cannot be trusted to conform to important norms. Virtually every facet of life has been blamed by someone as a cause of crime and deviance. But perhaps the oldest claim about deviance is that some people are just "born bad": Some people have an inborn personality flaw that stimulates misbehavior or prevents them from controlling their deviant urges. This view led to the start of criminology in the 1870s, when an Italian physician, Cesare Lombroso (1836–1909), began to gather systematic data on prison and jail inmates and to develop a biological theory of criminal behavior.

"Born criminals"

Lombroso believed he had found the key to criminal behavior in human evolution. His years of careful observation and measurement of prison inmates convinced him that the most serious, vicious, and persistent criminals (who he believed made up about one-third of all persons who commit crimes) were "born criminals" (Lombroso-Ferrero, 1911). **Born criminals** were less evolved humans who were biological "throwbacks" to our primitive ancestors, according to Lombroso. The born criminal is "an atavistic being who reproduces in his person the ferocious instincts of primitive humanity and inferior animals."

Because of their genetic makeup, Lombroso believed that born criminals could not restrain their violent and animalistic urges. Because the trouble was biological, he argued, little or nothing could be done to cure born criminals; society could be protected only by locking them up. However, since their criminality was not their fault, born criminals ought to be treated as kindly as possible in dignified, decent prisons.

Lombroso and his students presented a great deal of evidence to support his theory. He claimed that criminals tended to be more apelike than normal people, having abnormal skulls, huge jaws, flat noses, and long arms. Because Lombroso developed a testable theory, we know today that his theory was incorrect. His error lay in examining only prisoners and assuming that they displayed a higher proportion of physical abnormalities than nonprisoners. However, when the British physician Charles Goring (1913) measured nonprison populations, he found the same incidence of physical abnormality as Lombroso had found among convicts. Thus, Goring showed that there was no correlation between these physical characteristics and committing crimes. As Chapter 3 made clear, something cannot be the cause of something else if the two are not correlated. Lombroso's theory was therefore disproved. He is still remembered as the father of modern criminology not because he was on the right track, but because he was the first person to investigate the problem seriously.

Even though social scientists have long known that Lombroso's biological theory of criminal deviance is false, efforts to link deviance with biological causes have continued. The results to date are quite mixed.

Contemporary findings

In Chapter 5 we reviewed findings by behavior geneticists that suggest a strong link exists between heredity and forms of mental illness, such as schizophrenia and depressive states. However, although biology contributed to understanding these forms of deviance, it has not, thereby, helped explain other forms. The reason is that very few people who commit crimes are the victims of serious mental illness (Sagarin, 1975).

In the mid-1960s, scientists became very excited about findings that seemed to link crime, especially violent crime, to an extra male chromosome (Shah and Roth, 1974). Recall that normal humans have twenty-three pairs of chromosomes. One of these

Cesare Lombroso.

pairs is the sex chromosome, so called because it determines the sex of the offspring. The sex chromosome received from the mother is always an X. When the father also contributes an X, the child is female; when the father contributes a Y, the child is male. Sometimes, however, a person receives two Y chromosomes from the father, thus giving that person three sex chromosomes (XYY). Such men, known as **XYY males,** tend to be taller and have more male sex hormones than other males. It was also suspected that such men might be more aggressive. This seemed likely when a study found that this rare chromosome defect is much more common among prison inmates than men in the general population.

For several years this appeared to be a major breakthrough in linking deviance directly to biology. In fact, the defense attorney for Richard Speck, who was accused and convicted of murdering eight nurses in a rooming house in Chicago in 1968, claimed that Speck had an extra Y chromosome and thus should not be held responsible for his actions.

It was later determined that Speck had a normal sex chromosome count. In addition, a flurry of research studies failed to find any evidence that XYY males were any more inclined to commit crimes or be violent than other males. Finally, larger-scale studies showed that XYY males were not overrepresented in prison populations (Witkin et al., 1976).

A second line of research suggested a link between biology and deviance through intelligence. Many studies showed that people with lower IQs were more likely to commit criminal acts. However, it turned out that this was not because they lacked good judgment. Instead, IQ predicts who will do well in school and in a career. As we shall see, success tends to limit deviant behavior by making the costs of detection higher. That is, successful people have more to lose by being found out and are thus less likely to be deviant. When people of comparable success were compared, IQ had no influence on deviance (Hirschi and Hindelang, 1977).

As mentioned in Chapter 5, some geneticists suspect that inherited dispositions may be involved in alcohol and drug abuse (Schuckit et al., 1979). However, except for mental illness, firm links between biology and deviance have not been demonstrated.

PERSONALITY THEORY

Despite an immense amount of research, efforts to link various forms of deviant behavior to abnormal features of the personality have been disappointing (Sagarin, 1975; Liska, 1981). An assessment of ninety-four studies, which were conducted between 1950 and 1965 and meant to distinguish between criminals and noncriminals by using various personality tests, found the overall results to be weak and contradictory (Waldo and Dinitz, 1967).

The most promising line of psychological research has been on extremely aggressive behavior. Hans Toch (1969) found that men who repeatedly assaulted others had very weak self-esteem. This trait made them extremely resentful of even slight criticism or discourtesy, especially if it occurred in the presence of others. The violent rages of these men stemmed from the fear of loss of face, combined with the belief that others already held them in low esteem.

Depth interviews with men frequently convicted of assault led Leonard Berkowitz (1978) to expand on Toch's position. Berkowitz concluded that these men had such fragile self-esteem that they flew into uncontrollable rages even when no one except the offending person was present. An audience might spur them to even wilder reactions, but they could suddenly become violent even without such a spur.

Berkowitz's respondents consisted of sixty-five white males between the ages of 18 and 43; most were in their late twenties. Each was serving time in an English jail for assault, and most had served many previous sentences for violent behavior—one had twenty-seven prior convictions. Another, with fourteen previous convictions for assault, had gotten into an argument with a policeman and knocked him down. Then the man ran into his house, got a machete, and battled eight cops, wounding two of them. Why had he done it? His answer was, in effect, "Why not?" The cop "just got on me back. . . . That was it, [I] just elbowed him, brought him over me shoulder, and stamped him with me foot."

Arguments were the most common preliminary to violent outbursts by these men. The interviews showed remarkably little sign of rational calculation—of deciding whether or when to hit someone. Of course, men in jail may wish to deny responsibility for the act that got them there. Still, that these same men had repeated such behavior so often despite jail sentences strongly suggests that there is truth to their claims that these things just seem to happen to them. As one man with a long record of assault convictions put it, "At the time I'm not thinking at all, you know. It's afterwards I think this all out, but at the time I don't stop to think. At the time it seems the natural thing to do or the right thing to do" (Berkowitz, 1978).

A second approach to studying aggression through personality analysis suggests not only that the inability to control rage is a frequent cause, but that *too great* control over rage may also lead to extreme violence. Thus very passive, mild-mannered people who suppress their anger during a long period of provocation may cause others to provoke them extremely; eventually the quiet people erupt in acts

This street scene by the German expressionist George Grosz implies that conformity is but a superficial human mask—that inside us all, just beneath the surface, lurks a violent and dangerous beast ruled by dark passions and deep-seated psychological pathologies. Efforts to explain deviant behavior by uncovering its psychological basis have, however, not been very successful. Although sudden outbursts of abnormally aggressive behavior do seem to have a psychological basis, most deviance is based on conscious planning and choice.

of extreme retribution. Had they been less controlled, they might have prevented the increased mistreatment. Instead, they took it as long as they could and then earned newspaper headlines as the person who "wouldn't hurt a fly," but who suddenly took an axe to a spouse or a neighbor or went to the office one morning with a shotgun (Schultz, 1960; Megargee, 1966).

Later in this chapter we shall see that some forms of deviant behavior do seem to be acts of sudden impulse. We shall also see that sociological theories are not well suited to deal with these forms of deviance, which are probably best understood through psychology.

However, most of the deviant acts that prompt so much interest in criminology are not acts of impulse. And at least so far, personality theories have not helped much in explaining acts of deviance involving consciously made choices. We shall return to these matters toward the end of the chapter. Now we should see just what sociologists think they know about deviance.

DEVIANT ATTACHMENTS

We have already encountered the fundamental proposition on which most sociological theories of deviance are based: Our behavior is shaped through interaction with others, especially those to whom we have formed strong attachments. These attachments to others cause us to live up to their expectations about how we should act. In Chapter 3 we examined research showing the power of attachments to influence our behavior—people will even adopt a new religion to please their friends.

However, although attachments produce conformity to the expectations of others, that does not necessarily mean that we will conform to the norms of our society. What happens if our attachments are to people who themselves break norms? What if our friends are burglars or auto thieves? Questions such as these have led to the formulation of several sociological theories seeking to explain deviance on the basis of attachments to *deviant others*. These theo-

ries elaborate on the sentiments of many proverbs about falling in with "bad company."

Differential association—
social learning

Edwin H. Sutherland (1883–1950) is remembered as the most influential early American sociologist of deviant behavior. In 1924 he first proposed a theory based on deviant attachments, a theory now known as the **differential association theory**. Sutherland argued that all behavior is the result of socialization by means of interaction. That is, how we act depends on how those around us desire us to act. How much we deviate from or conform to the norms depends on differences (or differentials) in whom we associate with.

Thus, Sutherland argued, boys become delinquent because too many of their attachments are to others who engage in and approve of delinquent acts. In this view, the causes of deviance lie not in the individual but in the normal processes of social influence. However, Sutherland's differential association theory was somewhat vague. It did not precisely explain how our friends influence our behavior and teach us to conform or deviate. Therefore, in 1966 Robert Burgess and Ronald Akers reformulated Sutherland's theory into a set of precise propositions based on learning theory.

Burgess and Akers argued that Sutherland had correctly identified the source of deviant behavior: attachments to people who supported deviance. Such friends teach us to deviate by rewarding us for deviant behavior and not rewarding (or reinforcing) nondeviant (conformist) behavior. Thus, a boy may receive a great deal of attention and respect from his friends when he steals a bike or breaks a window but be ignored when he is "good."

Consider this more elaborate example. A person may have companions in the local tavern who reinforce heavy drinking and nightly visits but not staying home or abstaining. Through such a pattern of *selective reinforcement,* a person may become a habitual heavy drinker. As time goes by, such a person may become increasingly dependent on regulars at the tavern for social relations and become a problem drinker. Indeed, this may be why so many persons treated for alcohol or drug abuse resume such behavior even after hospitalization has cured their physical addiction. The patients return to the same social settings and the same sets of attachments through which they originally formed their problem behavior and quickly relearn it.

Unquestionably, differential association and learning processes play a significant role in much deviant behavior. Having assembled the findings of many studies done over a forty-year period, Maynard L. Erickson (1971) showed that the great majority of delinquent acts are done in cooperation with others. Vandalism, for example, is rarely done by a lone juvenile. Most juveniles who steal a car or burglarize a house do so in groups. And research consistently finds that delinquents tend to have delinquent friends (Liska, 1981). Yet the theory fails to explain many aspects of deviance and does not jibe with many research findings.

A major problem is research suggesting that delinquent kids end up together because others reject them (Hirschi, 1969; Jensen, 1972; Liska, 1981), not because these friends encouraged each other's delinquency. Diana Gray (1973) found that teenage girls in the process of becoming prostitutes did not begin to associate with pimps or other prostitutes until *after* they had already begun to sell sexual favors. Travis Hirschi (1969) found that only some boys with delinquent friends engaged in delinquency—those who did well in school and were attached to their parents were not more likely to engage in delinquency if they had delinquent friends than if they did not.

A second problem is that differential association–social learning theory does not address the question of why delinquent friends exist. That is, if attachments to deviant friends cause deviance, what caused the deviance of the friends? At some point someone must have begun to act in a deviant way without supportive friends. In addition, why do some people but not others have deviant friends? And why are only some people susceptible to the influence of deviant friends, as research shows?

Finally, what explains the many acts of deviance that could not possibly have been in response to the expectations of deviant friends? Many acts—indeed, many of the most serious deviant acts—are done on the sly by people who hope no one ever finds out: the man who kills his wife and hides the body, the embezzler, the secret alcoholic. Clearly, these kinds of deviance cannot be attributed to reinforcement by friends.

Here we must recognize something that will be significant at many points in this chapter: Some forms of deviance are directly rewarding. Some people enjoy the effects of alcohol or drugs and require no additional reinforcement from others. Some people enjoy peeking through windows to see others naked. As for stealing, people seldom take things they don't want or don't hope to sell. A child caught shoplifting will often explain that "it was such a neat cap gun." Granted, our friends can lead us astray. But people are perfectly capable of getting into mischief on their own.

The problems of the differential association–social learning approach are but sins of omission. That is, problems do not arise because of what the theory explains but because of what it does not explain. Other theories of deviance attempt to fill these gaps.

Subcultural deviance

One way to supply the deviant others needed by differential association–social learning theory is to recognize the existence of subcultures within a society. As we saw in Chapter 2, a subculture is a culture within a culture—a group of persons who maintain or develop a set of values, norms, and roles that are somewhat different from those of the surrounding society. As we saw in Chapter 3, sometimes subcultures arise around a new religion; those who become attached to persons in such a subculture can consequently become members themselves. In a similar fashion, a subculture can arise around drug use; in fact, during the 1960s many people were recruited to be drug users just as others were recruited to be Moonies or Hare Krishnas.

Recognition of subcultures lets us understand that deviance is often a matter of definition. An outside observer noting the behavior of a member of a subculture may regard that person as deviant. But that same person is conforming to the norms of his or

To conform to the norms of one group often is to seriously break the norms of another group. The punk rock fans on the right have gone to great pains to be "normal" in the eyes of other punks. Their dress and deportment break norms of American society in general and especially those of older professionals like the two men opposite. Of course, these men also make a considerable effort to be "normal." This helps us to be aware that some forms of deviance, such as these having to do with norms of appearance, reflect subculture conflicts. Which of these styles is seen as more acceptable often will be determined by which subculture is the more powerful.

her group. For example, the Jehovah's Witnesses are members of a religious group who, among other things, accept a norm against saluting flags (they regard it as idolatry). Many Americans observing a Jehovah's Witness refusing to salute the U.S. flag might define the behavior as deviant, but to other Jehovah's Witnesses it would be an act of conformity.

Particularly in complex modern societies, many subcultures exist, and thus some deviant behavior can be explained as conflicts over norms, or **subcultural deviance.** Public controversies over pornography, marijuana, abortion, sexual behavior, and the like are conflicts over whose norms will be represented in legal codes and public policies and whose will be judged deviant.

Some subcultural views of deviance can be summed up as "different strokes for different folks."

Thus, the norms in any society are often determined by who has the power to pass laws and set policies. Because the Jehovah's Witnesses are a tiny minority, they are unable to ban flag ceremonies. Because the majority of Americans oppose the use of narcotics, narcotics are illegal.

Subcultural theories also help explain how some forms of deviance that do not begin as conformity to the norms of a subculture can become stabilized as an individual enters into a subculture. We have seen that Diana Gray (1973) found that girls began prostitution on their own. However, in time some of them did begin to associate with pimps and prostitutes and become part of this deviant subculture. Many of the other girls soon gave prostitution up.

Although subcultural theories add to our understanding of deviance, they, too, fail to provide a full

explanation. For one thing, many forms of deviance seem to have no subcultural basis. Aside from the occasional gangland slaying, very few homicides seem to be the result of conforming to the norms of a subculture. In fact, although sociologists long attributed much serious violence to subcultures having norms that favored violence, such as juvenile gangs or working-class men, research has uniformly failed to confirm this view. Even teenage gangs turn out to be much less approving of member violence than had been supposed (Ball-Rokeach, 1973; Erlanger, 1974; Kornhauser, 1978). And that raises the major omission of subcultural theory: *deviance within any subcultural group.*

All human groups, regardless of their norms, include some members who fail to conform. Some members of juvenile gangs steal from other mem-

bers. Some gangsters squeal to the authorities. Some ministers commit adultery. Some scientists fake their results. And many people feel deeply ashamed and guilty after committing some act, which makes no sense if what they were doing was "right" according to their group norms. Subcultural explanations cannot explain deviance of this kind. Again, the solution is not to discard a theory but to add to it.

STRUCTURAL STRAIN THEORY

We now encounter a closely related group of theories that attempt to explain deviance on the basis of **structural strain**, or frustration caused by a person's position in the social structure, especially the stratification system.

The ideas underlying structural strain theories are very old. Whenever someone says that people commit crimes because of poverty or some other disadvantage, that person is invoking strain theory. Back in 1938, Robert K. Merton formulated a theory of how disadvantage can lead to deviance, and theories based on his work are called **structural strain theories**.

Merton began with the assumption that humans have a natural tendency to observe norms, a tendency instilled in us by normal processes of socialization. Indeed, this tendency is reflected by that part of our personalities often called the conscience. Because of our conscience, breaking the norms causes us to feel some degree of guilt and remorse. Yet people often act against their conscience. Why? Merton thought it was because of the terrible strain upon them.

These strains arise because people are socialized to have certain desires, or goals, and to regard certain means as proper ways to achieve these goals. However, the proper means don't work as well for some people as for others. People who are poorly placed in the stratification system will find themselves unable to achieve their goals or at least unable to achieve them as easily as people better placed in the system, if they only use legitimate means (that is, if they obey their conscience). So long as disadvantaged people stick to the rules and obey the norms, they will experience frustration because they will fail to achieve wealth, happiness, fame, comfort, influence, and all the other things socialization has taught them to value. The resulting strain forces people to use deviant or illegitimate means to achieve goals.

Merton argued that deviance is a built-in consequence of stratification. Strain theory portrays a deviant as a person torn between guilt and desire, with desire gaining the upper hand (Hirschi, 1969). In effect, Merton argued that poverty causes the poor to turn to crime, to alcohol, to drugs, and even to killing friends and relatives in order to escape their unfulfilled desires for a better life.

By itself, the structural strain theory of deviance runs into serious problems. First, the theory would seem to predict a great deal more deviance than actually occurs. Of those poorly placed in the strat-

ification system, the great majority do not commit acts of significant deviance. What distinguishes them from those who do?

Second, most of the deviant behavior committed by persons under structural strain cannot alleviate their frustrations. Most crime pays very little—even menial jobs would provide more luxury. That is, illegal behavior offers little hope for achieving goals that cannot be met by legitimate means.

Third, the theory offers no explanation for deviant acts committed by people in the privileged social positions, such as middle- and upper-class teenage delinquents. Nor does it explain why wealthy people shoplift or why bankers embezzle. Indeed, if people deviate only when driven by intense frustrations caused by societal deprivation, deviant behavior committed by privileged people is inexplicable.

Perhaps the worst problem faced by the strain theory is that a person's social class is barely, if at all, related to committing crimes. For example, dozens of research studies have failed to show that poor kids are more likely to commit delinquent acts than are kids from privileged homes (Tittle et al., 1978). It is true that class and deviance are correlated when we focus on the lowest stratum of society and the most serious offenses (Hindelang et al., 1981). But even if this correlation is best understood as a response to strain, it applies to a tiny segment of the population and a small portion of the crime and deviance that occur. We must therefore examine other explanations.

CONTROL THEORY

To formulate a more comprehensive sociological theory of deviance, the famous French sociologist Emile Durkheim (1858–1917) proposed, in effect, that we dismiss the question "Why do they do it?" and ask instead "Why don't they do it?" Since Durkheim's time, this advice has been heeded by many leading sociological and criminological theorists; this approach to deviance is known as **control theory**.

The initial assumption made by all control theories is that life is a vast cafeteria of temptation. By themselves, deviant acts tend to be attractive, providing rewards to those who engage in them. To some, theft produces desired goods and alcohol and drugs supply enjoyment. Indeed, control theorists argue that norms arise to prohibit various kinds of behavior because without these norms such behavior would be frequent.

Put another way, when we consider what things people should not be allowed to do, we don't bother to prohibit behavior that people find unpleasant or unappealing. We assume that people won't do these things anyway. Thus, we concern ourselves with things that people find rewarding and therefore might be tempted to do.

Thus, control theorists take deviance for granted and concentrate instead on explaining why people conform. Their answer is that people vary greatly in the degree of control their groups have over them. In any group, some people are rewarded more for conformity and punished more for deviance than other people are. Control theorists argue that conformity occurs only when people have more to gain by it than they have to gain by deviance.

Like strain theorists, control theorists accept that access to desired rewards is unequal among members of any society. Some people succeed, some get left out. But while strain theory argues that inequality pushes the have-nots to deviate, control theory stresses how the have-nots are *free* to deviate. In the words of the song, "freedom's just another word for nothing left to lose." Some people are free to deviate because they risk very little if their deviant behavior is detected. But for others the costs of detection far exceed the rewards of deviance.

Control theory regards the crucial element in conformity as the **social bonds** between an individual and the group. When these bonds are strong, the individual conforms. When these bonds are weak, the individual deviates. Because the strength of these bonds can fluctuate over time, control theory can explain shifts from deviance to conformity (and vice versa) over a person's lifetime. Because many bonds are not related to social class, control theory can explain both the conformity of the poor and the deviance of the wealthy. But what are these bonds between the individual and the group? They are of four kinds: *attachments, investments, involvements,* and *beliefs* (Hirschi, 1969; Stark and Bainbridge, 1985).

This famous painting by Hieronymus Bosch (1450–1516), entitled Garden of Earthly Delights, *is an allegory on temptation prompted by the painter's deep religious concerns. Bosch's vision of the human condition as an unrelenting opportunity to sin, foreshadowed the insights of modern control theory which asks not why do people deviate, but why do they ever conform?*

Attachments

We are already familiar with the concept of **attachments**—they are stable patterns of interaction between individuals. Moreover, attachments have a psychological component: We tend to like and even love those to whom we are attached. The degree to which an individual is attached to others depends upon the number and closeness of his or her bonds: how much that individual cares about others (and is cared about in return) and, therefore, how much the person cares about what others think of his or her actions. When we are strongly attached to others, we are likely to desire their continuing good opinion of ourselves and we therefore worry about how our actions will influence their regard for us. Conforming to norms helps to ensure the affection and respect of our friends—it protects our reputations.

When we are alone, we often break norms—we pick our noses, belch, and otherwise act grossly. We usually do not break these norms so freely in company. Moreover, if we knew for certain that our friends would never find out, we might even commit quite serious norm violations. Those who lack significant attachments are, in effect, *always alone*, and their friends never know about the norms they break. They do not risk relationships with others, since they have none to risk. For them, the costs of deviance are low.

By focusing on bonds of attachment, control theory is able to deal with a great many research findings about deviant behavior. The more that young people care about others—parents, friends, and teachers—the less likely they are to commit acts of delinquency (Hirschi, 1969; Liska, 1981). Conversely, delinquents are very weakly attached, even to their delinquent friends (Hirschi, 1969; Kornhauser, 1978).

Moreover, all other explanations of delinquency fail to explain why delinquency rates rise rapidly among people in their early teens and then fall rapidly as these people enter their late teens. Do people then break off with delinquent associates, join a new subculture, or suddenly cease to be poor? Hardly. What does happen to many in their early teens is that their attachments to their parents weaken. As these bonds weaken, delinquency becomes more widespread. In the later teens, people begin to form strong new attachments to peers, and delinquency declines. The same applies to people during their twenties, the age at which adults are most likely to become involved in criminal behavior. Young adults have often left family and friends and are out on their own, relatively unattached. With marriage, the birth of children, and steady employment, new attachments are formed; thus, the tendency to commit crimes falls as people get older.

Perhaps the most powerful aspect of control theory is its ability to account for weak or missing cor-

relations between social class and most forms of deviance. Close attachments are not confined to the middle and upper classes. Most poor kids love their parents, too, and most poor adults love their families and friends. Thus, most poor people have a strong stake in conformity. By the same token, many middle- and upper-class kids don't love their parents, and not all privileged people love their families and friends. Thus, their stake in conformity is low.

Durkheim answered the question "Why don't they do it?" on the basis of attachments. As he put it, "We are moral beings to the extent that we are social beings."

Investments

The idea of **investments** is simple: We are tied to conformity not only through our attachments to others but also through the stakes we have built up in life—the costs we have expended in constructing a satisfactory life and the current and potential flow of rewards coming to us. The more we have expended in getting an education, building a career, and acquiring possessions, the greater the risks of deviance. That is, we could lose our investments if we were detected in deviant behavior. An unemployed derelict may have very little to lose if caught sticking up a liquor store and a considerable amount to gain if he or she gets away with it. But it would be crazy for a successful lawyer to risk so much for so little, and most people rarely make really irrational decisions. When successful lawyers and bankers fail to resist the temptation to steal, they usually steal very large sums that seem to them to make the risks worthwhile.

Variations in investments also help account for the tendency of delinquents to reform as they reach adulthood. At age 14, most people have little investment at stake when they deviate. However, after people have begun to build normal adult lives, their investments mount rapidly.

Involvements

The *involvement* aspect of control theory takes into account that time and energy are limited. The more time a person spends on activities that conform to the norms, the less time and energy that person has to devote to deviant activities.

To a considerable extent, **involvements** are a consequence of investments and attachments. People who have families, or who play football after school, or who are engrossed in hobbies, or who are busy with careers have much less time and energy left for violating norms than people with few attachments and investments. Popular wisdom has it that "idle hands are the devil's workshop." Many studies have reported that the more time young people spend "hanging around" or riding in cars, the more likely they are to commit delinquent acts (Hirschi, 1969). The more time young people spend on schoolwork or even talking with friends, the less likely they are to get into trouble. That is, people neglect to do all sorts of things for lack of time. As we shall see in Special Topic 5, college couples even delay breaking up until between quarters or until the summer holiday, when they have more time. People also tend not to do deviant things when they are pressed for time.

Beliefs

Control theory stresses human rationality—whether people tend to deviate or conform depends on their calculations of the costs and benefits of deviance or conformity. But control theorists also recognize that through socialization we form **beliefs** not only about how the world does work but also about how it ought to work. That is, we develop beliefs about how people, including ourselves, ought to behave. This is described as the **internalization of norms**, the phrase sociologists often use instead of the word *conscience.*

We accept norms not only because our friends expect us to but also because we risk our self-respect if we deviate. The phrase "I'm not that kind of person" indicates that we hold certain beliefs about proper behavior. When a friend suggests a deviant act and assures us that nobody will know, we display internalized norms if we respond, "Yes, but *I* will know."

By themselves, our beliefs may or may not cause us to conform. As we saw in Chapter 4, individual religious beliefs lack the power to prevent delinquency unless they are supported by attachments to others who also hold religious beliefs. This fact helps us to recognize that all four elements of control theory are interconnected. Attachments are also investments—much time and energy go into building close relations with others. Attachments and investments both act as involvements: Time spent with friends or at work is time not available for deviance. In addition, our beliefs will also determine with whom we choose to become attached and what investments we decide to make.

Like other explanations of deviant behavior, control theory also cannot stand alone. It seeks to explain conformity to the norms of a social group, but it doesn't identify which group or note that conformity to the norms of one group may be deviance from the norms of another group. In combination with subcultural theory, we therefore have a more complete explanation of deviance. And control theory clearly implies and therefore requires elements of differential association–social learning theory to specify mechanisms by which attachments generate conformity.

Furthermore, none of the theories considered thus far can explain variations in the rates of deviance among societies or different regions of a single society. To accomplish this, we must examine a more macro theory of deviance.

ANOMIE AND THE INTEGRATION OF SOCIETIES

In Chapter 1 we saw that the rapid growth of large cities during the nineteenth century caused many early sociologists to fear a breakdown in human relations—that people would come to live in a world of strangers, lost and alone. Emile Durkheim, one of the founders of modern sociology, feared that as people lost their links to one another through long-standing attachments, society would suffer from **anomie**: a condition of *normlessness.* People would not know what the norms were, nor would they be motivated by their attachments to obey the norms even if they knew them, for humans would lack the moral direction provided by others. Indeed, Durkheim argued that in modern urban societies the individual is morally in "empty space." Without social ties, "no force restrains them" (Durkheim, 1897), and in such circumstances people literally lose the ability to tell right from wrong.

Durkheim contrasted conditions of city life with those of more traditional rural villages and identified the latter as "**moral communities**." He stressed two components of the moral community. The first of these is **social integration**. Here he referred to the number and intimacy of attachments enjoyed by the average person. In traditional village life, Durkheim argued, the average person was firmly anchored in an extensive network of close attachments. The second aspect of moral communities, according to Durkheim, is **moral integration**. Here he referred to shared beliefs, especially religious beliefs, that provide members of a community with a common moral conception—shared beliefs about what the norms are and why the norms are correct.

Both social and moral integration are eroded by life in large cities, according to Durkheim. People lose their attachments, and thus social integration erodes. While a single religion unites traditional communities, many competing religions flourish in cities, and each weakens the others. Thus, Durkheim concluded that cities would destroy the power of societies to control their members and therefore become locations for excessive amounts of serious deviance.

Durkheim's theory describes how macro changes in social structures could have devastating effects at the micro level. Indeed, the correspondence between his anomie theory and control theory is obvious: The sheer size and disorganization of big cities reduces the average person's attachments and beliefs. Thus, free to deviate, people would do so.

Durkheim attempted to demonstrate his thesis by showing that suicide rates were much higher in urban areas and in areas where a variety of Protestant faiths existed than in rural areas and places that remained solidly Catholic (Durkheim, 1897).

As we saw in Chapter 1, the thesis that city life inevitably produces "mass societies" in which people lack attachments and thus fall victims to anomie was not supported by research. Thus, Durkheim's predictions about the future were overly pessimistic. However, that does not invalidate his theory. Durkheim's assertions about the consequences of weak moral and social integration can be applied to the extent that societies (or different areas of societies or even different areas in a city) differ in their degree of social and moral integration. Durkheim's theory predicts that deviance rates will vary as integration varies; for example, crime and suicide rates will be higher wherever moral and social integration are lower.

During the 1930s and 1940s, many researchers attempted to test Durkheim's predictions about the relationship between integration and deviance. For example, Clifford R. Shaw and Henry D. McKay (1929, 1931, 1942) found that delinquency is much higher in urban neighborhoods with a high population turnover (residents constantly moving in and out) than in more stable neighborhoods. In neighborhoods of newcomers, social integration is necessarily lower than in places where people have had time to form attachments with their neighbors. Robert C. Angell (1942, 1947, 1949) found that cities higher in "moral integration" had lower rates of crime and suicide.

Although Durkheim's theory of integration and anomie has been repeatedly described in textbooks as a major contribution to sociological knowledge, during the 1950s and 1960s researchers seldom tested it. A major reason was the lack of good, readily available measures of social and moral integration of cities or parts of cities and the immense expense apparently required to come up with good measures.

Earlier research had many flaws because of these limits. Thus, Angell used rates of contributions to charitable fund-raising drives as a measure of moral integration on the grounds that these rates would reflect the degree of consensus on values and norms in a community. He also used these rates because they were available in reports published by charitable organizations, not because they were very appropriate for testing Durkheim's thesis. Other studies tended to be circular. Often a high crime rate was used as an indicator of weak social and moral integration, thus making it impossible to say that weak integration *caused* high crime rates. Moreover, measures of social integration, such as statistics on population turnover, were available for only a few cities—in fact, much of the research was based only on comparisons of Chicago neighborhoods.

Emile Durkheim.

Robert Crutchfield.

Only recently have problems of obtaining good measures for testing Durkheim's theory been overcome. The results have strongly supported Durkheim's predictions, but they have also consistently revealed strange correlations. These patterns have forced the concept of deviance to be reconsidered. So I invite you to watch as this research was conducted and the odd results reinterpreted.

Social integration and crime

 In 1980, while Robert Crutchfield was still a graduate student in sociology at Vanderbilt, he decided to test Durkheim's thesis about the impact of the social integration of communities on crime.

As we have seen, research on this question had long been frustrated for want of a practical way to measure the social integration of cities. How can we determine the number and intimacy of the attachments of average citizens in various cities? It is much too expensive to select large samples from a num-

ber of cities and ask individuals how many close friends they have, how often they see them, how long they have known them, and so forth.

Crutchfield therefore adopted the method used by Shaw and McKay to estimate variations in attachments among American city dwellers. Recently the U.S. Census has begun to publish statistics on population turnover for all major American cities. This is the proportion of a city's population who are recent newcomers or have recently moved to a new neighborhood within a city. Crutchfield agreed with Shaw and McKay that in cities with high rates of population turnover—where large numbers of people are always moving in, moving out, or moving around—social integration will necessarily be reduced. Attachments will be disrupted, and large numbers of people will be strangers and transients. He then computed these rates for major cities and examined whether these were correlated with crime rates (Crutchfield et al., 1983).

He found very high correlations: Cities with high population turnover (and thus low social integration) had high official crime rates, while those with low population turnover had low crime rates (Table

7-1). He also controlled for many other factors, including racial composition and poverty, to demonstrate that the relationship was not spurious. (Figures 7-1 and 7-2 give regional rates for population turnover and total crime rates.)

However, Crutchfield was not content to examine only the total crime rate. He also examined each of the seven offense rates that compose the total crime rate: burglary, larceny, auto theft, robbery, rape, assault, and homicide. The results were very strange. Burglary, larceny, and rape were strongly negatively correlated with social integration, but homicide, auto theft, and robbery were virtually uncorrelated with social integration. Since the overwhelming proportion of all reported crimes are burglary and larceny, this produced a strong correlation with the total crime rate. In fact, however, social integration seemed to affect only these two categories of offense plus rape but have no effect on the other kinds of crime. Why? For a time, no one knew.

Moral integration and crime

 While Crutchfield was reopening research on social integration, I was doing the same thing on moral integration. At the time we were unacquainted and did not learn of one another's work for another year. I was able to proceed with the first good test of Durkheim's notions about moral communities because I had figured out how to estimate accurate rates of church membership for American cities, counties, and states (see Chapter 13). Like Crutchfield, I chose to focus on major cities and see if variations in church membership correlated with variations in crime rates. I also looked at the total crime rate first and found a very high negative correlation—the higher a city's church membership, the lower its crime rate. Then I also examined the seven crime categories composing the total crime rate and found the same odd pattern (Table 7-1). Church membership reduces burglary, larceny, and rape, but it has little or no effect on homicide, assault, robbery, and auto theft (Stark, Doyle, and Kent, 1980).

Table 7-1 / Correlations between moral and social integration and crime rates.

	Moral Integration	Social Integration
Total crime rate	− .44	− .63
Burglary	− .46	− .64
Larceny	− .44	− .55
Rape	− .41	− .53
Assault	− .14	− .28
Homicide	− .12	− .26
Robbery	− .16	− .08
Auto theft	− .18	− .08

Source: Stark and Crutchfield, in press.

I learned about Crutchfield's same strange results in the next year, when I received an early draft of his paper. That fall he became a faculty member in my department, and we became friends and eventually collaborators. During our first conversations about our odd findings, neither of us could be certain they weren't simply an accident or the result of some momentary circumstance. But soon we were able to replicate both studies (Stark et al., 1983) using data for the 1920s. Once again we got the same pattern of results. At that point it was clear that something was wrong either with Durkheim's theory or with the concept of deviance. The latter seemed more likely, since the theory worked very well with some (though not all) forms of deviance.

RECONCEPTUALIZING DEVIANCE

Each sociological theory of deviance discussed in this chapter makes several basic assumptions. First of all, these theories are not directed at momentary nonconformity. Rather, they conceive of deviance as a pattern of nonconformity having significant duration. Subcultural theories, for example, treat deviance as part of a normal way of life—as conformity

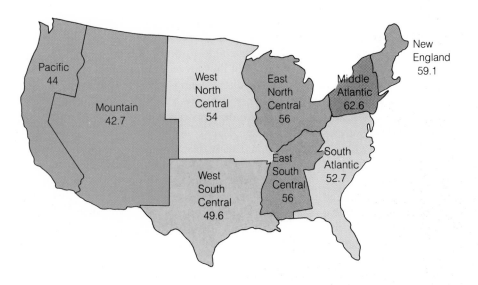

Figure 7-1 / Population stability.

Fifty-four percent of Americans have lived in the same house for the past five years, according to the 1980 Census. The map shows regional variations in this measure of population stability. Note that people in the East are less likely to have moved than are people in the West. (U.S. Bureau of the Census, 1980.)

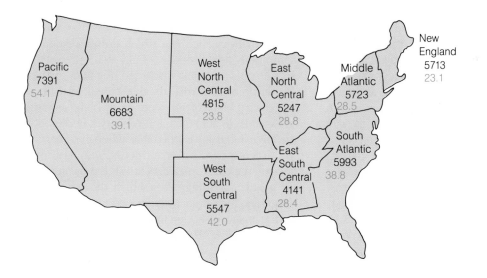

Figure 7-2 / Crime rates by region, 1981.

The national rate of reported crimes in 1981 was 5,800 per 100,000 population, including 35.6 rapes per 100,000. The map shows regional variations in the total crime rate (shown in black) and in the rape rate (shown in color).

to the norms of stable subcultures. Moreover, sociological theories of deviance assume that behavior is based on conscious motivation or at least self-awareness. Strain theory characterizes humans as driven to acts of deviance in response to thwarted desires. Control theory regards conformity and deviance as based on calculations of potential gains and losses (even if these calculations are sometimes in error).

The picture of deviant acts that emerges from all of these theories, then, is of deeds by self-aware actors who knowingly violate norms and engage in sustained periods of deviant behavior. But when we closely examine deviant acts, only some fit this description. Burglary fits. The typical burglary is committed by someone who is fully aware of the illegality of his or her actions, who planned the action in advance, who has acquired certain basic skills relevant to entering premises and selecting and selling loot, and who engages in a series of such offenses. Burglars are conscious deviants.

But this image does not fit the usual homicide. Only a minority of murders are premeditated or committed for gain. Typically, homicides occur during a sudden burst of rage, which is followed by deep remorse. In fact, of every four homicides, three involve victims who were relatives, friends, or close associates of the killer (Smith and Parker, 1980). Persons rarely repeat this form of homicide. Hence, murder often does not involve a conscious decision to violate norms or a sustained period of deviance. Instead, murderers tend to resemble the impulsively violent English men studied by Berkowitz (1978), discussed earlier in this chapter.

These reflections led Crutchfield and me to conclude that our strange results were due to the inclusion of crimes that lacked the rational elements postulated by sociological theories. We therefore proposed that deviance be reconceptualized as of two types, with sociological theories applying to only one of these types (Stark and Crutchfield, in press). These two types reflect the differences between burglars and murderers.

Intentional deviance involves rational calculation and duration. **Impulsive deviance** lacks calculation and duration. The latter category includes sudden, momentary acts of deviance that do not involve reflections about norms. For example, people tend to kill or assault one another during sudden bursts of uncontrolled (possibly uncontrollable) rage. These tend to be impulsive, even dangerous people, but they are not intentional deviants. Their morning-after feelings are typically guilt and remorse, not satisfaction with a job well done. Indeed, impulsive deviants often have a hangover the next morning.

Armed with this distinction between impulsive and intentional deviance, Crutchfield and I set out to make sense of our findings by showing that social and moral integration can limit conscious acts of deviance but not acts that were not considered.

At first glance, our new scheme did not seem to fit very well with our research results. Obviously, burglary and larceny are acts of intentional deviance for the most part, and they respond to social control as predicted by the theory. Rape, too, is usually an act of intentional deviance; most rapists are repeaters who plan ways to commit their acts without getting caught. Rape rates are also strongly influenced by social and moral integration. Homicide and assault, which are typically acts of impulse, also fit the prediction that they will tend not to be responsive to integration. But that left us with robbery and auto theft, both apparent acts of conscious, intentional deviance, but which do not respond to community integration.

We could have just discarded our new concepts at that point as a nice try that failed. Instead, we asked what kinds of acts were really being reported as instances of auto theft and robbery. Checking with the FBI, we quickly learned that although some autos are stolen by professional thieves, who strip them and sell the parts, most cars are stolen by teenagers for a little joyriding, after which the car is abandoned and recovered. Juvenile joyriding more closely fits the image of sudden impulsive action than intentional deviance. Thus, we realized that auto theft rates should be only very weakly related to community integration, which agreed with our results.

But that left robbery. Like most people, we believed that most robbers were people who had taken up a career of crime—masked gunmen who stick up store after store until arrested. As it turned out, however, this is not the kind of robber who accounts for most of the statistics. Instead, the robbery rate

The complexity facing social scientists in their efforts to explain deviance is reflected in this picture of the victim of a robbery-murder. Sociological theories can do a good job of explaining crimes that involve clear intentions to deviate. They are much less able to explain sudden, unplanned acts of impulsive deviance. Thus sociological theories are better suited to explain why someone takes up a life of armed robbery than to explain why a robber would suddenly gun down an unarmed victim.

primarily consists of a mishmash of relatively trivial and impulsive actions. When a wino shoves another wino to the ground and runs off with his bottle, that is a robbery. If one kid twists another kid's arm (or even threatens to do so) and takes his lunch money, that's robbery, too. And people who go into stores or even banks and pull a classic stickup are often drunk or deranged.

Clearly, the official robbery rate includes many intentional robberies, but the bulk of the offenses are best described as impulsive or trivial. Having learned these facts, we gained confidence in our reconceptualization. Moreover, when we computed a robbery rate based on persons serving jail and prison sentences for robbery (and who ought mainly to be intentional deviants), we found a very substantial correlation between the robbery rate and social and moral integration, as the theory would predict.

If our reconceptualization is valid, then it follows that sociological theories of deviance should apply only to instances of intentional deviance; failure to find correlations when impulsive deviance is examined leaves these theories intact. People who truthfully say "I didn't know what I was doing" or "Something just came over me and I didn't stop to think" cannot be deterred from deviance by their stakes in conformity. Moreover, it is here that an effective dividing line between sociology and psychology presents itself. Sociologists have correctly criticized psychologists for not attending to social structure and for attributing irrationality to deviants who clearly calculate the potential gains and losses of their deviance. But sociologists may have been equally naive for failing to recognize the significance of psychological factors in many forms of deviance—those that reflect impulsive, unthinking, momentary acts.

Interestingly enough, Durkheim anticipated this critical distinction before the turn of the century. He thought that acts of despair, such as suicide, reflect weak social and moral integration. Research has confirmed this prediction (Bainbridge and Stark, 1981; Stack, 1983). Durkheim also argued that "crimes of passion" would be more common in more highly integrated communities, for these occur within networks of close attachment, not between isolated strangers. This prediction still awaits adequate research.

THE LABELING APPROACH TO DEVIANCE

So far in this chapter we have assumed that the norms of any society or group are known to its members. Consequently, when people seriously violate norms, it is reasonable to ask why they did so. Now we must consider a sociological approach to deviance suggesting that this question is often inappropriate. Instead, we should ask why we label people as deviant when they break norms. Sociologists taking this approach claim that most deviance results from some persons having been identified, or labeled, as deviants. Not surprisingly, this approach is called **labeling theory**.

Labeling theorists distinguish between primary and secondary deviance. **Primary deviance** involves whatever behavior a person engaged in that caused others to identify or label him or her as deviant. **Secondary deviance** is behavior that is a reaction to having been labeled a deviant. Most labeling theorists suggest that primary deviance involves relatively transient, insignificant, quirky behavior that most people engage in from time to time. Usually such behavior is ignored by others (Lemert, 1951,

1967; Scheff, 1966; Schur, 1971). Sometimes, however, others react strongly and negatively to the primary deviance of some people, and these individuals are publicly labeled as deviant.

Having been stigmatized as deviants, many people are driven to fulfill our expectations of them. Because they have a bad name, they come to see themselves as bad, and so they do bad things. The labeling approach, therefore, concentrates on identifying and criticizing the process by which norms arise and are enforced and by which some people are labeled for behaving a certain way while others are not. The labeling approach also specifies the ways in which a label forces people to adopt a career of secondary deviance.

Allen E. Liska (1981) has identified three major ways in which labels incline people to deviate. First, a deviant label, such as burglar, alcoholic, or prostitute, limits legitimate economic and occupational opportunities. Many employers will not hire ex-convicts, for example, and some reject applicants who have been arrested even if they were acquitted (Schwartz and Skolnick, 1962). At the same time, being labeled deviant may increase illegitimate economic opportunities (serving a jail term may make a person more proficient in crime).

Second, a deviant label limits a person's interpersonal relations. Thus, an ex-convict may find few chances for attachments with conventional people and thus be limited to attachments with others who also have been labeled as deviant.

Third, being labeled a deviant can affect self-conceptions. Sociological theories of interaction have long held that we see ourselves as others see us. If others see us as deviants, we may come to accept their judgments. Then when we act as we are "supposed" to act, we will be acting in deviant ways.

Labeling theories have made some important contributions to understanding deviance. Like subcultural theories, they have sensitized us to the fact that norms are not absolute but are created by humans. Therefore, it is useful to examine how a particular norm was established, by whom, for what reasons, and, perhaps, *against* whom. Many norms are born in conflict, and many laws are passed by close votes. According to labeling theorists, this demonstrates that norms are often arbitrary. Thirty years ago, a doctor who performed abortions risked a prison sentence and expulsion from the medical profession. Today abortions are routine medical procedures. Labeling theorists therefore suggest that the question to be asked is not why deviants behave as they do, but why we decide to prohibit certain actions.

Labeling theories also closely examine the process by which some people are labeled as deviant while others who do the same thing go unlabeled. Labeling theorists argue that the higher a person's status, the less chance that he or she will be labeled for deviant behavior.

Finally, labeling theory calls attention to how the reactions by society to primary deviance can produce continuing patterns of secondary deviance—that by attempting to stop deviant behavior, we may cause it.

However, over the past twenty years, many hypotheses drawn from labeling theory have not been confirmed by research. For example, many studies have failed to show that people labeled as delinquents as a result of arrest and conviction subsequently increase their level of illegal activity (Gibbons and Blake, 1976; Klein, 1976; Liska, 1981). In fact, some studies show that juveniles who are labeled and punished for an offense are less likely to commit subsequent offenses than those who escaped being labeled (McEachern, 1968; Thornberry, 1973). We shall consider this further in Chapter 8.

Nor has the view been sustained that primary deviance is usually insignificant and harmless. To the contrary, quirky, transient, and trival norm violation is almost always ignored (Gove, 1975); people usually get labeled as a deviant after committing a serious act. That is, people are labeled as rapists after they have raped someone, as robbers after they have robbed, as murderers after they have killed. Thus Liska asks, "Are these actions unimportant when committed by primary deviants?" That is, are they to be considered not serious if the person does not already have a deviant label?

This brings us to the major shortcoming of labeling theory. While it may help us to explain why ex-convicts often commit new offenses and go back to prison, it cannot explain the initial act of deviance by which people get labeled as deviants. Thus, to explain why an ex-convict commits new offenses does not explain why he or she became a convict in the first place. Why they *start* to do it lies beyond the scope of labeling theories.

Labeling theories emphasize ways in which the official process of reacting to offenders pushes them to play the role of deviant. Labeling theorists would argue that this young man having his mug shot taken following an arrest would be more likely to commit subsequent offenses than if he had never fallen into the hands of the police. These claims have not received consistent empirical support.

CONCLUSION

This chapter has reviewed a number of partial theories of deviance. I mentioned at the start that these theories were much more complementary than conflicting and that the next step for sociologists is to fit them into a general theory of deviance. An introductory textbook is hardly the place to undertake such a task. Nevertheless, as an effective summary of the chapter, some of the components of such a general theory can be described.

First, it is certain that any general theory of deviance must include elements of learning theory. Nearly all human behavior is learned, including deviant behavior.

Next, a general theory must specify the sources from which conformity and deviance are learned. Here it will be necessary to apply theories of early childhood socialization as well as theories of differential and adult socialization (see Chapter 6). For example, since males are much more prone than females to commit criminal and delinquent acts, aspects of *sex role* socialization must be part of a general theory on deviance. Furthermore, elements of differential association theory should prove useful. In learning to deviate or conform, it will matter what a person's friends reward.

We know, too, that some people seem to be more easily influenced by their friends than others are. Thus, a general theory of deviance may need to draw upon personality theories dealing with traits such as weak self-esteem. We must also keep in mind the distinction between intentional and impulsive deviance, relying on psychology to help explain the latter.

To account for the existence of deviant groups that can provide differential association, elements of subcultural theory must be included. Although much deviance is not supported by subcultures, clearly some forms are, and some forms of deviance are stabilized by association with deviant subcultures.

All of the above elements help to clarify and extend control theories. Consider attachments—the bonds of affection between people. Clearly, learning provides the mechanism by which attachments form and influence our behavior. Differential association and subcultural theories help explain to whom we become attached. If we are attached to persons who reward conformity, we tend to conform. If we are attached to persons who reward deviance, we tend to deviate. And if we are unattached, we tend to do as we please. Other things being equal, it will probably please us to commit deviant acts, since most of them are inherently self-reinforcing. Here, too, psychological theories can help explain the inability of some people to form and maintain strong attachments.

The investment aspect of control theory incorporates the basic tenets of structural strain theory. If our investments in life are low, we are in a deprived condition: Life has rewarded us little and promises never to reward us very much. This does not drive us to break the norms as much as it frees us to do so. Moreover, because control theory examines all deviance in terms of relative gains and losses, it can explain the behavior of not only the unemployed burglar but also the wealthy embezzler.

Labeling theory can also contribute important insights to a general theory of deviance. To the extent that past acts of deviance stigmatize a person with a deviant label, his or her attachments to others may be severely limited. Conventional people may tend to avoid ex-convicts, prostitutes, or problem drinkers. This in turn frees the deviants of attachments that might cause them to conform. Moreover, lack of conventional attachments may prompt those who share a deviant label to associate with one another and thereby form a deviant subculture. Indeed, to the extent that deviant labels prevent people from building investments in conventional activities, they will also have greater freedom to deviate.

Finally, theories of social and moral integration place a general theory of deviance within the framework of large-scale social structures. That is, the overall condition of societies as whole systems can affect rates of internal deviance. For example, high rates of population instability hinder attachments, prompting deviance to rise. If there is a great decline in religious commitment, deviance ought to rise as moral integration weakens.

Clearly, this is no more than a sketch of obvious connections among current theories. It is meant to show you that despite the proliferation of partial theories, social scientists have been making progress in understanding deviance and conformity.

Review glossary

Deviance Behavior that violates norms. (p. 148)

Deviants People who are known to frequently break relatively important norms. (p. 149)

Born criminals Lombroso's term for people whose deviance he attributed to their more primitive biology. (p. 150)

XYY males Men with a rare genetic defect giving them two male chromosomes. (p. 151)

Differential association theory A theory that traces deviant behavior to association with other persons who also engage in this behavior. (p. 154)

Subcultural deviance Behavior through which a person deviates from the norms of the surrounding society by conforming to the norms of a subculture. (p. 156)

Structural strain Frustration or discontent caused by being in a disadvantaged position in the social structure. (p. 157)

Structural strain theories Theories that blame deviance on the frustrations of structural strain; for example, one such theory claims that people commit crimes because of their poverty. (p. 158)

Control theory A theory that stresses how weak bonds between the individual and society make people free to deviate, while strong bonds make deviance costly. (p. 158)

Social bonds Bonds that, as used in control theory, consist of the following:

1. **Attachments** Bonds to other people. (p. 159)

2. **Investments** The costs expended to construct a satisfactory life and the current and potential flow of rewards expected. (p. 160)

3. **Involvements** The amount of time and energy expended in nondeviant activities. (p. 161)

4. **Beliefs** Our notions about how we ought to act. (p. 161)

Internalization of norms The sociological synonym for conscience, refers to the tendency of people not simply to learn what the norms are, but to come to believe the norms are right. (p. 161)

Anomie A condition of normlessness in a group or even a whole society when people either no longer know what the norms are or have lost their belief in them. (p. 161)

Moral communities Groups within which there is very high agreement on the norms and strong bonds of attachment among members. (p. 162)

Social integration The degree to which persons in a group have many strong attachments to one another. (p. 162)

Moral integration The degree to which members of a group are united by shared beliefs. (p. 162)

Intentional deviance Norm violations that stem primarily from rational calculation and that persist for some significant period; for example, most burglaries are such norm violations. (p. 166)

Impulsive deviance Norm violations that occur suddenly without calculation and that do not persist for a significant period; for example, most homicides are such norm violations. (p. 166)

Labeling theory A theory that explains deviant behavior as a reaction to having been socially identified as a deviant. (p. 168)

Primary deviance Actions that cause others to label an individual as deviant. (p. 168)

Secondary deviance Actions carried out in response to having been labeled as deviant. (p. 168)

Suggested readings

Hindelang, Michael, Travis Hirschi, and Joseph G. Weis. *Measuring Delinquency*. Beverly Hills: Sage Publications, 1981.

Hirschi, Travis, and Michael Gottfredson, eds. *Understanding Crime: Current Theory and Research*. Beverly Hills: Sage Publications, 1980.

Kornhauser, Ruth. *Social Sources of Delinquency: An Appraisal of Analytic Models*. Chicago: University of Chicago Press, 1978.

Liska, Allen E. *Perspectives on Deviance*. Englewood Cliffs, N.J.: Prentice-Hall, 1981.

U.S. Department of Justice. *Sourcebook of Criminal Justice Statistics*. Washington, D.C.: U.S. Government Printing Office (issued annually).

Chapter

Eight

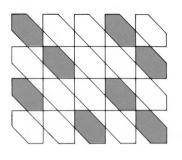

■ We have examined why people deviate. In this chapter we take a different point of view: How do groups attempt to prevent deviance? All collective efforts to ensure conformity to the norms are forms of **social control**.

The most common forms of social control occur during face-to-face interaction. Most of us conform most of the time to avoid offending those around us. Embarrassment results from mild norm violations in the presence of others and indicates our responsiveness to social control. Even when we are alone, we often limit our deviance for fear that someone might find out. Yet not everyone is equally responsive to social control. We all know people who are regarded as "outcasts," "misfits," or "jerks." Everyday speech includes a huge and colorful set of terms for people who lack the approval of those around them. The existence of these terms makes clear that while informal disapproval prevents much deviance, it doesn't prevent it all.

When informal methods of control fail and more serious acts of deviance occur, formal methods of social control are activated. A number of special roles and organizations exist in societies to enforce conformity to important norms: police, courts, psychiatrists, prisons, mental hospitals, even collection agencies.

These formal agencies of social control tend to operate as backup systems—they react to complaints. The police seldom try to discover that a crime has been committed; they go into action after a crime is reported to them. ■

Social
Control

CHAPTER PREVIEW

In this chapter we shall examine both informal and formal methods of social control. We already discussed informal social control when we repeatedly examined how attachments cause conformity to norms. Hence, this chapter will limit its examination of informal social control to classic experiments on the power of groups over member behavior and the responses of small groups to members who persist in deviance.

The bulk of the chapter is devoted to formal methods of social control. First, we shall examine programs and policies meant to prevent deviance. We shall examine a famous experiment that assessed a program for preventing young boys from becoming delinquents. We shall see why this program and other such programs have failed. Next, we shall examine whether punishment can deter deviance, that is, prevent some people from continuing to deviate and others from beginning to do so. Finally, we shall examine the criminal justice system—the police, the courts, and the prisons. How does the system operate? Can it serve to reform and resocialize deviants?

INFORMAL CONTROL

The culture in which we are socialized greatly shapes our behavior. Had we been born among the Arapesh studied by Margaret Mead, chances are we would

be gentle. Had we been born among the Mundugumor, we would probably be cruel headhunters. Through socialization, people learn what is expected of them, that is, to conform to group norms.

When very young, we require considerable coaching to conform, but as we mature we learn to take the role of the other, to see ourselves as others see us. We are able to evaluate our own actions from their point of view. For many of us, long exposure to a consistent set of norms, or **informal social control,** seems to create strong internal standards governing our behavior. That is, the norms become *internalized*: They become part of our own beliefs about how we should act. Sometimes norms are so firmly internalized that the person's conformity no longer seems to depend upon others being present to provide feedback. As mentioned in Chapter 2, nineteenth-century British adventurers and explorers dressed each evening for dinner, despite being in the wilderness amid natives who knew nothing of this norm. The code of manners governing how a gentleman behaved had become part of their self-esteem.

Chapter 2 introduced the concept of reference group, pointing out that people who ignore the norms around them may be conforming to the norms of an absent group whose standards they have adopted. The professor who ignores the good opinion of students and colleagues to devote his or her efforts entirely to research is often conforming to the norms of a reference group made up of specialists scattered over many universities.

Similarly, major portions of the previous chapter assumed the power of others to influence the individual. Control theory stressed how attachments to

For most of us, most of the time, our behavior is regulated by informal social pressures from those around us. These children playing in the sandbox do not need to constantly be told how to act. They know how they are supposed to behave, and an occasional glance in their direction by an adult is sufficient.

others limit an individual's deviance. Differential association attributed deviance to the influence of deviant friends upon an individual. Labeling theory assessed how others can stigmatize the individual for past deviance and thus cause further deviance.

Given the power of groups to affect the behavior of their members, it should be no surprise that for the past few decades social scientists have conducted many experiments to find out how effective groups are in creating conformity and to assess how groups react to member deviance. Closely examining several classic examples of this research can reveal much about informal means of social control.

Group pressure

 It is self-evident that people tend to conform to the expectations of others around them. But what are the limits of **group pressure**? Can group pressure cause us to deny obvious physical evidence?

The most famous experimental test of the power of group pressure to produce conformity was performed by Solomon Asch (1952) more than thirty years ago. Since then his study has been repeated many times, with many variations confirming his original results. Perhaps the best way to understand

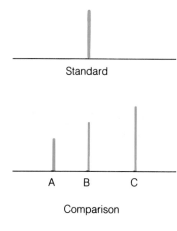

Standard

Comparison

Figure 8-1 / Asch's comparisons.

These two cards are one of the pairs used in the classic experiment by Solomon Asch to measure conformity to group pressure. Subjects were asked to pick which of the three lines on the second card matched the line on the first card. The correct choice is very easy to see. But many subjects would agree when everyone else said line 1 matched line A.

what Asch discovered is to pretend that you are a subject in his experiment.

You have agreed to take part in an experiment on visual perception. Upon arriving at the laboratory, you are given the seventh in a line of eight chairs. Other students taking part in the experiment sit in each of the other chairs. At the front of the room the experimenter stands by a covered easel. He explains that he wants you to judge the length of lines in a series of comparisons. He will place two decks of large cards upon the easel. One card will display a single vertical line. The other card will display three vertical lines, each of a different length. He wants each of you to decide which of the three lines on one card is the same length as the single line on the other card. To prepare you for the task, he displays a practice card. You see the correct line easily, for the other lines are noticeably different from the comparison line.

The experiment begins. The first comparison is just as easy as the practice comparison. One of the three lines is obviously the same length as the com-

parison line, while the other two are very different. Each of the eight persons answers in turn, with you answering seventh. Everyone answers correctly. On the second pair of cards, the right answer is just as easy to spot, and again all eight subjects are correct. You begin to suspect that the experiment is going to be a big bore.

Then comes the third pair (Figure 8-1). The judgment is just as easy as before. But the first person somehow picks a line that is obviously wrong. You smile. Then the second person also picks the same obviously wrong line. What's going on? Then the third, fourth, fifth, and sixth subjects answer the same way. It's your turn. You know without doubt that you are right, yet six people have confidently given the wrong answer. You are no longer bored. Instead, you are a bit confused, but you go ahead and choose the line you are sure is right. Then the last person picks the same wrong line everyone else has chosen.

A new pair is unveiled, and the same thing happens again. All the others pick an obviously wrong line. The experimenter remains matter-of-fact, not commenting on right or wrong answers but just marking down what people pick. Should you stick it out? Should you go along? Maybe something's wrong with the light or with your angle of vision. Your difficulty lasts for eighteen pairs of cards. On twelve of them, all the others picked a line you knew was incorrect.

When the experiment is over, the experimenter turns to you with a smile and begins to explain. You were the only subject in the experiment. The other seven people were stooges paid by Professor Asch to answer exactly the way they did. The aim of the experiment was to see if social pressure could cause you to reject the evidence of your own eyes and conform.

In his first experiment, Asch tested fifty people in this situation. Almost a third of them went along with the group and gave the wrong answer at least half of the time. Another 40 percent yielded to the group some of the time, but less than half of the time. Only 25 percent refused to yield at all. Those who yielded to group pressure were more likely to do so as the experiment progressed. Nearly everyone withstood the group the first several times, but as they continued to find themselves at odds with the group, most subjects began to weaken. Many shifted in their chairs, trying to get a different line of vision. Some blushed. Finally, 75 percent of them began to go along at least a few times.

The effects of group pressure were also revealed in the behavior of those who steadfastly refused to accept the group's misjudgments. Some of these people became increasingly uneasy and apologetic. One subject began to whisper to his neighbor, "Can't help it, that's the one," and later, "I always disagree—darn it!" Other subjects who refused to yield dealt with the stress of the situation by giving each nonconforming response in a progressively louder voice and by casting challenging looks at the others. In a recent replication of the Asch study, one subject loudly insulted the other seven students whenever they made a wrong choice. One retort was "What funny farm did you turkeys grow up on, huh?"

The Asch experiment demonstrates that a high proportion of people will conform even in a weak group situation. They were required merely to disagree with strangers, not with their friends, and the costs of deviance were limited to about half an hour of disapproval from people they hardly knew. Furthermore, subjects were not faced with a difficult judgment—they could easily perceive the correct response. Little wonder, then, that we are inclined to go along with our friends when the stakes are much higher and we cannot even be certain that we are right.

Cohesiveness

In a variation on his original experiment, Asch (1952) found that the influence of groups on conformity did not depend on the size of the group. Subjects were as likely to yield to the group when only three or four confederates were present as when seven or even fifteen confederates were used. However, yielding was influenced greatly by the degree to which the group stuck together. When just one of the confederates was instructed to give the correct answer, yielding to the others dropped dramatically. Only 5 percent of the subjects conformed as much as half the time. This is perhaps experimental evidence that misery loves company.

Other research has demonstrated that the social integration of a group determines how effective group

pressure will be. For example, Festinger and his colleagues (1950) found that housing units occupied by married college students differed in the degree to which the occupants were united by bonds of friendship. The higher the proportion of friendships, the smaller the proportion of occupants who deviated from the unit's norms. Similarly, the more that church congregations are united by bonds of personal friendship, the greater the consensus on religious doctrines (Stark and Glock, 1968). Thus we shall see that Durkheim's theory of integration, discussed at length in Chapter 7, applies not just to very large groups but to small ones as well.

Group responses to deviance

 It is evident that group pressure, even when imposed by very cohesive groups, does not produce conformity among all members. How do groups respond to a member who fails to conform?

In 1951 Stanley Schachter conducted an experiment that reversed Asch's approach. Instead of setting up a group of confederates who conspired against a single subject to cause conformity, Schachter recruited subjects to form a number of groups, and within each he placed one or two confederates whose job was to deviate.

Each group was read a story about a young man who had had a difficult childhood in a tough neighborhood and who now awaited execution on death row. Then each group discussed the case, with the experimenter acting as moderator. After a period of discussion, each member's position on what should have been done about this young man was assessed. Groups tended to agree closely on a scale of reactions ranging from love to punishment, with a strong bias toward the love end of the scale. The paid deviant, however, took a strong stand at the extreme punishment end of the scale. As discussion continued, clerks watching through one-way mirrors kept close track of what was said to whom. At the end of the experiment, each group member filled out a sheet indicating how much they liked or disliked the other group members.

The data yielded two clear patterns. First, as soon as the paid deviants expressed their views to the rest, they became the center of attention. More remarks were directed toward the deviants than toward any other group member. Second, when the paid deviants stuck to their position, they began to receive less attention. By the end of the experiment, few remarks were directed to them. When the rating sheets were examined, the deviants stood out clearly—others tended to like everyone else but the deviants.

These patterns are easily understood. The initial reaction of these groups to deviance was to try to squelch it. Group members ganged up on the deviant and tried to convince him or her to share their point of view. But when it became clear that the deviant member would not conform, they reacted by cutting the deviant out of the group and no longer talking to him or her. Judging from the ratings given the deviant, it is clear that had this been a real-life occurrence, group members would have avoided the deviant in the future.

Schachter then introduced a variation into some of these discussion groups. Using two confederates, he had both begin taking strong, deviant stands in favor of punishment. But while one kept resisting pressure from the group, the other gradually gave in. This confederate, called the "slider" because he or she slid from deviance to conformity, was not rejected by the group. Although the slider did not receive as high a liking score after the experiment as group members who had conformed from the beginning, his or her scores were noticeably better than those given the deviant.

Schachter's experiment also supports the importance of social integration to conformity. Schachter was able to distinguish groups on the basis of how much members indicated liking one another. In groups where average liking scores were high— indicating greater integration—the deviant was more strongly disliked, while groups whose members liked one another less also disliked the deviant less.

These studies reveal why most of us probably play by the rules most of the time. Even in the brief and artificial setting of a social science laboratory, groups exert considerable pressure to conform and react quite strongly to deviation from group norms. Yet these studies also reveal that group pressure does not guarantee conformity. Groups have long recognized that more drastic and formal measures of social control must often augment informal methods.

FORMAL CONTROL

When you invite friends to dinner, you can assume that they will use silverware and not eat with their fingers, that they will use their napkins and not wipe their chins on the tablecloth, and that they will not throw plates of food against the wall. You can also assume that when they leave, they won't take your stereo system or your car. Your friends will not act this way because they *are* your friends—they respond to informal pressures to conform. But not everyone does. When people do not, we often call upon formal agencies of social control to act on our behalf.

Formal social control is not applied to just any norm violation. The police won't come just because you happen to have friends who *do* eat with their hands or wipe their chins on the tablecloth. They might come if plates thrown against the wall are bothering your neighbors. And they definitely will come if people steal your belongings. This illustrates that formal means of social control are used only for acts of deviance that are also illegal or otherwise defined as providing legal grounds for intervention. Thus, even private collection agencies are limited to pursuing the payment of legal debts, rather than debts from illegal gambling or claims having no standing in common law.

Formal social control is attempted in three principal ways. The first is to *prevent* deviance by removing opportunities for it to occur or by eliminating its causes. The second is to *deter* deviance by the threat of punishment: to make people afraid to deviate or at least to deviate again. The third is to *reform* or *resocialize* people so they cease wanting to deviate. Let us see how each of these methods of social control functions in our society.

PREVENTION

For people to commit a deviant act, they must have the *opportunity* to do so. Thus, many approaches to formal social control are based on **prevention,** or the attempt to reduce opportunities. Campaigns encouraging people to lock their cars are meant to reduce the opportunity for auto theft, for example.

The prohibition of alcoholic beverages in the United States during the 1920s was intended to prevent alcohol abuse, as laws today against the sale of certain drugs are intended to prevent drug abuse.

Recent research by Lawrence E. Cohen and Marcus Felson (1979) has connected the increase in crime rates in the United States over the past several decades with the increase in the number of homes that are empty during the day. This increase, in turn, is due to the increased employment of married women, larger numbers of one-person households, and great increases in out-of-town travel. Unattended homes create greater opportunities for burglars (Cohen et al., 1980). Other research has related increased opportunities for crime to changes in the structural design of neighborhoods. New designs prevent people from easily observing one another's homes or businesses, and few people are on the street to come to the aid of persons being assaulted, robbed, or raped (Taylor et al., 1980).

In response to these conditions, such methods as block-watch programs have been initiated to increase observation. The recent boom in the sale of home security systems also reflects efforts to reduce opportunities for crime.

However, the major effort in preventing crime and deviance has been directed toward removing its causes. Here the emphasis has been placed on childhood *socialization*. It has long been an article of faith, not just among social scientists but among nearly everyone, that adult deviance is the result of a long journey down the "wrong road," a journey that begins in youth. The most persistently addressed question has been, What can be done to intervene soon enough? How can we get kids headed on the right road before it's too late?

The Cambridge-Somerville experiment

In the middle 1930s, a New England physician, Richard Clarke Cabot (a member of one of the oldest upper-class families in the East), decided that it was time to launch a major effort to help young

boys grow up to go straight. More importantly, he was determined to test the results of this effort rigorously. He thus initiated and funded a ten-year social experiment that even today is regarded as a model attempt at a delinquency prevention program and a model sociological experiment.

In essence, Cabot decided to give poor boys many of the same opportunities as boys from well-to-do homes. First, he tried to provide for their physical well-being. Second, he sought to enrich their experiences and broaden their horizons. Finally, he tried to provide close relationships with adults, who could give the boys good advice and serve as models of well-adjusted adults.

In 1937 Cabot launched his project by selecting two economically distressed industrial communities near Boston, Cambridge and Somerville. He hired a staff of counselors and researchers, who selected 650 boys (with an average age of about 11) as subjects for the delinquency prevention program. To know whether his program really did prevent delinquency, Cabot could not place all the boys in the program, for then there would have been no control group for comparing the delinquency rates. So he *randomly* divided the group into two groups of 325. One group was recruited to receive the experimental treatment. The other group was left alone, although their school and criminal records were examined periodically. Cabot had no difficulty getting all of his chosen 325 boys into the program. Little wonder, for during the Depression he offered these youths free health care, tutoring, attendance at summer camps, field trips, an elaborate recreational program, and individual counseling.

In May 1939 the program got under way. Unfortunately, Dr. Cabot died just as his ambitious undertaking began, but in his will he provided the needed funds, and his family supervised the project. Some aspects of the program had to be cut back during World War II—gas rationing cut into field trips, for example. Nevertheless, the project was carried through to its projected end (when the boys all reached 18).

What were the results of this massive project? To find out, the researchers compared the criminal records of boys in the control group with those of the boys in the experimental group. They found that 40 percent of the boys in the control group had been convicted of a crime. They also found that 40 per-

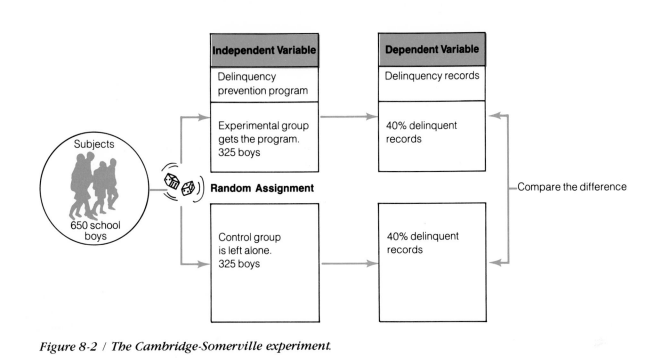

Figure 8-2 / The Cambridge-Somerville experiment.

Because the researchers were able to randomly decide whether boys took part in the delinquency prevention program or were placed in the control group, this is an experiment. Note the lack of difference in the proportion of boys in the experimental and control groups who got into trouble with the police.

cent of the boys in the program had been convicted of a crime! Moreover, boys in the experimental group had committed as many crimes as those in the control group (Powers and Witmer, 1951). Obviously, the program had had no effect on delinquency. Boys who were left on their own were no more likely to get into trouble than boys who were part of the elaborate program (Figure 8-2).

Those associated with the study were astounded by these results and in the end refused to accept them. This is understandable. You can spend a number of years trying to help young people stay out of trouble only if you believe your efforts can make a difference. Sure, you can't help them all, but daily you see some kids going straight and you take comfort in that fact. Of course, you lack similar intimate observations of those outside the program, and so you cannot notice that they are doing just as well (or as badly) without your care. Having built up years of personal "experience" with the effects of

your program, you will not readily accept research findings that your perceptions are biased and your effects negligible. Indeed, in their effort to show that the results of the experiment were wrong, the directors of the Cambridge-Somerville study simply discarded the control group altogether.

Instead, they engaged in a minute examination of the case records of each boy in the experimental group. For only these data could

satisfy the clinical worker, who, by the nature of his task, has little interest in averages. What such a person wants to know is whether there were any cases—even if only a few—in which the introduction of the [program] tipped the balance in a boy's favor (Powers and Witmer, 1951).

From this private reading of the files, Powers and Witmer concluded that there was clear evidence that fifty-one of the boys in the project had been helped. But if this was true, why did the experimental group not have a smaller proportion who were arrested? Did the program also push some boys into crime who otherwise would have gone straight? That seems unlikely. But that leaves us to ask what was helping the boys in the control group. As Cabot understood, the experimental results were the only reliable basis for judging the worth of the programs. Since random assignment made the two groups equally prone to commit crimes, the program could be termed successful only if the experimental group had fewer crimes. There is no better evaluation method available.

This can be underscored by a poignant example. In an effort to show that the experiment was insensitive to the real results of the prevention program, the directors wrote to former participants and asked if the participants believed they had benefited from taking part. Many said they had, including one young man who wrote this testimonial about how much his counselor had helped him:

He told me what to do—what's right and wrong—not to fool around with girls [emphasis added]. It gives a boy a good feeling to have an older person outside the family to tell you what's right and wrong—someone to take an interest in you (Powers and Witmer, 1951).

Several years later, this same young man began serving a five-year sentence for a serious sex offense (McCord and McCord, 1959).

Later, social scientists reopened this classic study, hoping that some evidence in favor of the program could still be found. William and Joan McCord had the useful hypothesis that perhaps the research had ended too soon, that possibly the effects of the program would not stabilize until later in life. So they reexamined the police records of the experimental and control groups for ten years after the original study had ended. But this hypothesis also turned out to be false; no difference could be found (McCord and McCord, 1959).

Thus ended the first experimentally evaluated attempt to prevent delinquency by trying to influence socialization of the young. But it did not end efforts to achieve this goal.

Other prevention programs

In the decades following the Cambridge-Somerville study, scores of delinquency prevention programs have been tried and evaluated. Until very recently, the result was an unbroken string of failures (Weis, 1977). During the 1950s and 1960s, immense effort was made to utilize forms of psychotherapy to reform delinquents. None succeeded (Toby, 1965). Prevention efforts were also taken into the streets by social workers attempting to reform juvenile gangs. These efforts were also judged failures (Miller, 1962). Toward the end of the 1970s, just as sociologists became convinced that nothing would work, the first evidence appeared that something might. A group of psychologists in Oregon began to have at least modest success with their efforts to train the parents of problem kids to more effectively control their children's behavior. We shall examine this project in depth in Chapter 12. But it now appears that many kids simply never outgrow the selfish, aggressive, antisocial behavior that is normal for two- and three-year olds. In fact, children don't cease such behavior unless their parents punish them for it. Studies of really misbehaved children show that their parents do not consistently punish them. Although the Oregon group has had some succcess in training parents to cope with their children, it remains to be seen how applicable the results are. For one thing, many parents (especially those of the worst-behaved kids) are unwilling or unable to improve their parental performance. Secondly, intervention must occur at a very early age in order to be effective. Finally, such intense levels of training seem needed that it may be economically impossible to make such training widely available.

Why did none of the other programs work? Because they failed to truly change the life circumstances of people. Training adults to be better parents may strengthen weak attachments within a family; simply providing a kid with a counselor will seldom have such an effect. A counselor is not an adequate substitute for parents or close friends, and a delinquency program fails to give kids a stake in conformity—it may even do the reverse. Kids who mess up do not risk being kicked out of a delinquency program.

Immense effort has been and continues to be invested in various therapeutic techniques aimed at correcting patterns of deviant behavior or preventing its recurrence. This group of young people is taking part in an encounter group led by an adult therapist. There is no research evidence to suggest that such therapy succeeds.

However, even if we can't set up programs to make kids want to conform, couldn't we make them afraid to be deviant?

DETERRENCE

As far back as written records go, humans have constructed legal codes that specify not only which acts are prohibited by law but also which punishments are to be given to offenders. The Code of Hammur-

abi, written about 4,200 years ago, tells us that if a man destroys another man's eye, the offender's eye should be taken out; if a son strikes his father, the son shall have his hand cut off. Early legal codes tried to achieve symmetry—to provide justice by matching the punishment with the offense. This is repeated in many places in the Old Testament. In the Book of Deuteronomy we read; "Life shall go for life, eye for eye, tooth for tooth, hand for hand, foot for foot."

However, even in these early philosophies of justice, punishment was not meant merely to serve as revenge for victims or their relatives. Instead, punishment has long been intended as a means of making life and property more secure by reducing the

This public beheading took place in China around 1860. For centuries it was believed that public executions served to deter the onlookers from committing similar crimes. But for most of this century, social scientists rejected this view. Only recently has support for deterrence theory reappeared in social science journals.

likelihood of a person committing a crime or a second offense.

This aspect of social control is called **deterrence**—the use of punishment to deter people from deviance. As Plato put it 2,300 years ago, "Punishment brings wisdom; it is the healing act of wickedness." This occurs, Plato explained, because the point of punishment is not to "retaliate for a past wrong," but to make sure that "the man who is punished, *and he who sees him punished* [emphasis added], may be deterred from doing wrong again."

As human societies evolved into complex states, governments increasingly sought to deter crime; hence punishments became increasingly severe as crimes continued to occur. **Capital punishment** (execution) became common; in England during the eighteenth century, more than two hundred different crimes carried the death penalty. Moreover, executions typically were conducted in public, often drawing large crowds, in an effort to deter those who witnessed the punishment from committing similar acts.

However, many began to speak out, calling capital punishment cruel and disgusting. In time the opponents of capital punishment succeeded in applying the death sentence to fewer and fewer offenses. By the twentieth century, some nations dispensed with it altogether. In 1972 the Supreme Court prohibited capital punishment in the United States on the grounds that it was being applied in a discriminatory fashion. Since then, however, many states have managed to redraft their capital punishment statutes in a way acceptable to the court, and in 1977 the first execution since the late 1960s took place.

It has been followed by several others. In April 1981, 794 persons were in prison under sentence of death.

While much of the debate over capital punishment has centered on moral issues, a major element has been the argument that it does not deter crimes (mainly homicide, but also rape) for which it has been used. Indeed, by the 1950s the accepted view among social scientists, which was presented in most introductory textbooks, was that the threat of punishment does not prevent deviant behavior, and the experience of having been punished does not cause people to cease their deviant behavior. Deterrence was dismissed as an obsolete notion, exposed as such by scientific research; in fact, very little research had ever been done. As we shall see, especially with regard to capital punishment, the little research that had been done was flawed by poor methods and the great difficulty in obtaining appropriate data.

By the early 1970s, however, a growing number of social scientists began to reconsider the deterrent effects of punishment. For many, it was simply a response to their realization that they attuned their own behavior on the basis of potential punishment. For example, on trips across the country, they drove faster or slower depending on a state's reputation for enforcing speed limits. Are these self-observations merely illusions? Can it really be that if penalties for crimes were repealed, the crime rate would not go up? The case for deterrence was reopened.

Jack Gibbs, a sociologist, led the way by reformulating the theoretical issues concerning deviance. Isaac Ehrlich, an economist, reopened research on the effects of capital punishment on homicide. Both men provoked angry reactions from many of their colleagues. Together, however, they have stimulated an immense amount of theoretical and research effort; deterrence is no longer a discarded concept.

Jack Gibbs: a theory of deterrence

 As Jack Gibbs examined the grounds on which deterrence had been dismissed from social science, he recognized that much of the reasoning and the evidence cited missed the mark. The case against deterrence came down to this. Many people are punished for committing crimes, including some who are executed for homicide. Nevertheless, the crime rate, including the homicide rate, remains high. Moreover, most people who serve a prison or jail sentence for a crime turn right around and commit new crimes when they are released. Clearly, then, punishment fails to deter.

Gibbs concluded that this argument is irrelevant to the fundamental issue. It claims, in effect, that if some people seem not to be deterred, no one is. When the issue is posed this way, it is impossible to demonstrate any deterrent effects of punishment unless it is 100 percent effective. This is the same as saying that aspirin has no effect on headaches unless it cures every headache for everyone. To see if punishments influence people to conform, Gibbs pointed out, we cannot look at just those who were not deterred; rather, we must look at everyone. That is, we need to know more than the fact that some people do risk punishment; we need to know if the fear of punishment influences those who do not commit offenses. This is, of course, a much more difficult research problem.

Although Gibbs was very concerned with improving research on deterrence, he recognized that he first had to formulate an adequate theory. Why and how should punishment produce conformity? Until such an explanation was proposed, we could not say what empirical observations would be predicted or prohibited and therefore what research ought to be undertaken.

Gibbs (1975) set out to formulate a clear theoretical statement of the effects of deterrence. Drawing on social learning and control theories of deviance, Gibbs proposed that it is not only the severity of punishment that matters but also the rapidity and certainty of punishment. Stated briefly, Gibbs's **deterrence theory** postulated that the more rapid, the more certain, and the more severe the punishment for a crime, the lower the rate at which such crime will occur.

Thus, Gibbs predicted that severe sentences will not effectively deter crimes if people realize that they have little chance of being caught or that their punishment will be long delayed if they are caught. On the other hand, not even quick and certain punishment will deter crime if the punishment is very

Jack Gibbs.

mild, for then the costs of detection often will be outweighed by the rewards of the crime. Here Gibbs's theory links with control theory to explain why the same punishment might be much less severe for some than for others. For example, two years in jail is a much greater cost to someone with a happy family and a good job than to an unemployed drifter. Deterrence thus fits into control theory as another of the costs to be considered by the potential deviant. The higher that cost and the swifter and more certain it is to be imposed, the greater the conformity.

It is important to recognize that Gibbs's theory of deterrence, like other sociological theories of deviance, does not apply to all deviant acts. Clearly, a person who acts on impulse or in a drunken rage is not likely to be deterred, since he or she is unable to consider the consequences of the crime (Geerken and Gove, 1977).

Even though what Gibbs's theory predicts and prohibits is very clear, proper testing has been difficult. As we shall see later in this chapter, punish-ment for crimes in the United States today is often far from certain or swift and often not very severe. This makes it difficult to test the theory against available statistics. Gibbs was able to show, however, that people are less likely to be convicted for an offense a second time when the police have a high rate of success in solving such cases. For example, the police can solve rape cases far more often than burglaries. Thus, the certainty of arrest is greater for rape. Examining prison statistics, Gibbs found that far fewer people are arrested a second time for rape than are arrested a second time for burglary: Only 16 percent of those in prison for rape were second offenders, compared with 51 percent for burglary.

Once Gibbs's theory was published, many social scientists began to design studies to test it more rigorously. The most important breakthrough was to recognize that what matters most is not the actual certainty, swiftness, or severity of punishment but the *perceptions* of these aspects of punishment. Suppose the actual odds of being caught for some offense were very high. A person who mistakenly thought that they were very low would act on this perception. Indeed, Gibbs's theory assumes a link between reality and perception, that the true conditions governing punishment will act as a deterrent because people will perceive these conditions. Thus, Gibbs's theory can be tested without encountering problems concerning the present operations of the criminal justice system. Instead, we can simply find out how people perceive the situation and see if that perception influences their rates of deviance and conformity.

In the past few years, many such studies have been done (see Anderson, 1979; Jensen et al., 1978). The findings strongly support deterrence theory. People who think that it is hard to get away with crimes, that justice is swift, and that present levels of punishment are severe are much less likely to commit such offenses than are people who think that the opposite conditions are true.

Later in this chapter, we shall see that people with actual experience with police, courts, and the prison system often perceive lower risks in crime; this can be a major factor in sustaining chronic criminal behavior. This has led many deterrence researchers to discuss the importance of naiveté in social control. Indeed, many have suggested that a primary way in which differential association (see Chapter 7) can influence deviance is by exposing a naive individual to a perception of much lower risks (G. Jensen, 1969; Parker and Grasmick, 1979; Minor and Harry, 1982).

At present, deterrence is one of the most active theoretical and research topics in the field of deviance and social control. Nevertheless, many sociologists have been reluctant to acknowledge this renewed interest. For example, the term *deterrence* does not appear in the index of the current editions of any leading introductory sociology textbooks. By not mentioning deterrence, a social scientist can escape moral criticism—charges that whether or not deterrence works, it is wrong. In fact, many social scientists have expressed outrage that colleagues would even study deterrence and thereby lend scientific respectability to an obviously immoral point of view.

However, careful reading of these criticisms suggests that the real issue is not deterrence in general but concern that the renewed interest in deterrence will reopen a much more sensitive question—whether capital punishment deters homicide. For many people, the idea of the legal system putting people to death is so repugnant that there can be no valid scientific purpose in researching the deterrent effects of capital punishment. For many others, including most American citizens (see Figure 8-3), some acts of murder are so repugnant that the killer has no right to life.

Here we can see the pressures that inevitably come to bear on social scientists. On the one hand, we are active participants in the world we study, and like all human beings, we must deal with moral issues. On the other hand, we have a responsibility to provide facts pertinent to many moral controversies. In this instance, a most pertinent fact is whether capital punishment deters homicide. If it does not, then there may be no reason to debate the morality of the matter. Of course, we cannot know the facts until adequate research has been done. Often it is difficult for sociologists to switch back and forth between the role of scientist and that of concerned citizen— to insulate our research procedures from our moral convictions. Keeping this in mind, let's observe the interplay of moral commitments and scientific research in this controversial area.

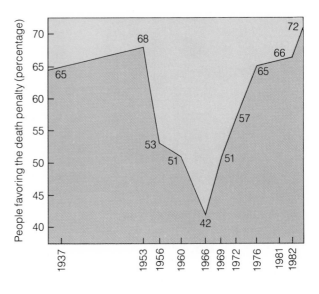

Figure 8-3 / Support for capital punishment.

The graph shows the percentage of American adults who favored use of the death penalty for murder during the past five decades. (Gallup, 1982.)

The capital punishment controversy

Capital punishment in the United States has been opposed for many reasons. Some have opposed it for religious reasons. In fact, we shall see later in this chapter that the Quakers were the first to institute prison sentences as punishment in an effort to eliminate torture and execution. Some have opposed it on grounds of racial discrimination, since blacks were executed more often than whites (53.5 percent of the persons executed in the United States between 1930 and 1967 were black). In fact, one basis for the Supreme Court decision against existing capital punishment laws was racial discrimination. Other opponents of capital punishment have even argued that executions actually increase homicides because capital punishment brutalizes public perceptions of the value of life (Bowers and Pierce, 1980).

However, a major aspect of the debate over capital punishment has been social scientific research

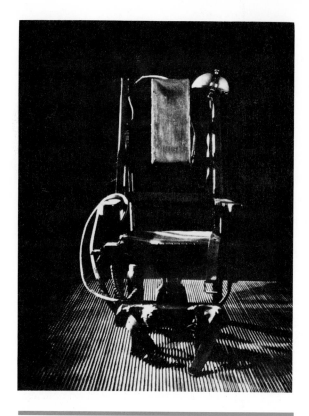

This is "Old Sparky," New York State's electric chair. It was the world's first, going into service in 1890. A total of 695 persons were put to death in this chair from 1890 through 1963.

that seemed to show that capital punishment does not deter homicides. If this is so, many have argued, then we should not risk executing an innocent person or risk other possible negative consequences of capital punishment, since nothing is gained. Unfortunately, this conclusion was based on uncritical acceptance of very deficient research.

The deficiencies in the research were partly due to the limited statistical techniques used by social scientists in the 1930s and 1940s, when the research was done. They also were due partly to problems in the data available for analysis. In effect, these early studies simply compared the homicide rates of states that used capital punishment with the rates of states that did not. These comparisons showed no correlation: States without capital punishment did not have

higher homicide rates than states with capital punishment.

Unfortunately, little or no concern was given to the problem of spuriousness, even though states differed in many ways besides the use of capital punishment. For example, New York, which used capital punishment, had a homicide rate as high or higher than North Dakota, which did not use capital punishment. However, to conclude that capital punishment did not deter homicide was to assume that these two states were identical in other ways. A much better test would have been to see what happened to the homicide rate in New York if capital punishment were repealed and what happened in North Dakota if capital punishment were reinstated. But, of course, such data are lacking.

Nevertheless, most social scientists in the 1950s and 1960s, few of whom had read the pertinent research studies, assumed that capital punishment had no deterrent effect. But then Isaac Ehrlich, an economist, challenged the accepted belief.

In an article in the *American Economic Review* of June 1975, Ehrlich used sophisticated statistical techniques to see if the homicide rate and execution rate for the United States from 1933 through 1969 were correlated. Ehrlich concluded that there is a negative correlation between the two and that the deterrent effects of capital punishment were huge. In fact, he concluded that each execution prevented eight additional homicides. That is, each time someone was executed for committing a murder, eight other people escaped becoming murder victims. Thus, Ehrlich concluded, by putting to death those who have taken a life, we save many additional lives.

Ehrlich's article provoked a storm of protest and moral condemnation. Many attempted to dismiss his findings as the result of improper statistical procedures (McGahey, 1980). Other scholars rose to Ehrlich's defense, including statistical experts who claimed his methods were superior to those used by his critics (Yunker, 1982). Moreover, when the data used by Ehrlich were extended to the 1980s, a period when the first executions since the court decision of 1972 occurred, the results were even stronger (Yunker, 1982).

The homicide rate has tended to fluctuate with the execution rate from 1930 through the late 1950s. Then, when executions became very rare and eventually ceased entirely, the homicide rate began a rapid ascent. However, as we saw in Chapter 3, correlation alone is not sufficient proof of causation. And it is difficult to conclude from these data alone whether executions really do deter homicide. A major problem is that the data are very crude and apply to the United States as a whole. However, many states did not have capital punishment during this period, and states differed greatly in their homicide rates. Perhaps these are meaningless averages that are accidentally correlated.

These difficulties showed the need for research able to detect subtler influences. So, let us watch how David Phillips found better ways to study the deterrent effects of capital punishment.

David Phillips: deterrence through the press

Recall that Plato believed we may be deterred from deviance by seeing someone punished for a crime. Plato was discussing punishments administered in public, where people actually saw a person tortured or executed. In modern times, executions are not held in public, and only a small number of people actually see an execution. Thus any deterrent effects of punishments do not result from actual observation. Rather, we "see" such punishment only to the extent that mass media make us aware of it.

This line of reasoning led David Phillips to formulate a new approach to detect the deterrent effects of capital punishment on the homicide rate (Phillips, 1980). He argued that deterrence does not depend upon how frequently people are executed for murder but on how much publicity is given to the executions. Moreover, Phillips argued that previous studies ignored the possibility that the impact of a given execution may not be long-lasting. Thus, while previous studies compared homicide rates for periods of a year or longer, it might be crucial to examine the possibility of marked but relatively brief changes. Unfortunately, virtually all known statistics on homicide are yearly.

After a long search, however, Phillips discovered that weekly homicide statistics had been published

for London from 1858 through 1921. Next, he consulted an encyclopedia of notorious murders to construct a list of the most heavily publicized English executions during this period. Finally, he consulted the *London Times* and counted the column inches of coverage given to each case. For each execution he computed the number of homicides that occurred for several weeks before the execution, during the week of the execution, and for several weeks following the execution. His hypothesis was that the homicide rate would be lower for several weeks after a well-publicized execution than for the weeks just before.

His results supported the hypothesis. A very significant drop in homicides consistently occurred immediately after a well-publicized execution. Indeed, the week after one of these executions averaged more than a third fewer homicides than a normal week. Moreover, the greater the number of inches the newspaper devoted to the story, the greater the drop in homicides. However, as Phillip had suspected, the impact of executions seemed to be short, lasting only about two weeks. After that the homicide rate climbed back to the level prevailing during the weeks before the execution.

However, this does not mean that executions simply caused some people to delay a homicide, thus adding only several weeks to the lives of potential victims. Had that been true, then when the "delayed" homicides occurred, the homicide rate should have been higher than normal until the delays had been made up. This was not the case. Therefore, it seems clear that some homicides were not merely delayed but prevented. The fact that most homicides are not premeditated but are done in the heat of the moment further corroborates the finding that even a brief deterrent effect can have lasting consequences.

Phillips's research provided social science with the most persuasive evidence that capital punishment—when it is publicized—does deter homicides. But he, too, has drawn considerable criticism. In particular, critics have objected that a two-week deterrent effect, even if it occurs, is too brief to matter. Phillips replies that people who survive because of these short lulls might believe otherwise.

Clearly, many knotty research problems still surround the topic of deterrence. Common sense tells us that punishment often does restrain us. Yet as we have seen, it is difficult to show that deviant acts that do not happen were deterred. And it is very easy to show that some people are not deterred—the prisons are full of them. Thus, we must return to the argument against deterrence that Gibbs dismissed as irrelevant: Why are the prisons filled with people, most of whom have served previous sentences, if punishment deters crime? To answer this question, we must examine the operations of the American system of criminal justice.

THE WHEELS OF JUSTICE

Let's imagine a young man who is contemplating a career of crime in the United States today. He will need to take into account three vital facts: It's far from certain that he will be punished for committing a crime; if he is punished, it will likely be long after the crime; and it is quite likely that the punishment will not be very severe, at least not the first few times he is caught. To see why the situation is this way, we must look at the police and the courts.

The police

Except for traffic officers, American police spend little time looking for violations of the law. Instead, the police respond primarily when offenses are reported to them; only then can they attempt to solve a case. A major reason why the odds of getting caught for a crime are so low is that a large proportion of the crimes that occur are never reported to the police.

Table 8-1 is based on a huge national survey designed to measure the true incidence of major crimes. Every several years, the Justice Department sends interviewers to 60,000 randomly selected American households to ask detailed questions about crime victimization. For each crime that respondents say has been committed against them during the past year, the question is asked, "Was this incident reported to the police?"

The data in Table 8-1 show that about half of the time the answer was no. Larceny is the least fre-

quently reported crime (25 percent), while auto theft is the most frequently reported (68 percent). The latter reflects the fact that victims may not collect their auto insurance unless the theft is reported; in addition, people realize that there is a very good chance that the police will find their car. Still, a third of auto theft victims did not report the crime. When the police don't even know about a crime, they are obviously unlikely to catch the criminal. Thus, about half the time one can expect to get away with a crime simply because the victim fails to report it.

Of course, even when a crime is reported, the police are often unable to find the criminal. Table 8-2 shows the proportion of various reported offenses that led to an arrest in 1982, according to nationwide statistics collected annually by the FBI. Most murders are solved; 72 percent of the cases reported in 1981 resulted in an arrest. This reflects the fact that most homicides are sudden acts of passion committed by a friend or relative of the victim, so often the murderer is apprehended at the scene of the crime. Reported assaults and rapes result in arrests about half of the time, whereas only a quarter of reported robberies result in arrests. Notice that in each of these latter three offenses, the police are aided by the fact that the victim sees the person who commits the crime. Without this advantage, the police do poorly in solving larcenies, burglaries, and auto thefts.

Clearly, the odds of being caught seem low. Yet Table 8-2 overstates the odds of being caught, since it gives the percentages of *reported* cases that led to an arrest. Since about twice as many crimes are committed as are reported, the proportion of cases that are solved by arrest is only about half of what is shown in the table. For example, 3.7 million burglaries were reported to the police in 1981, 14 percent of which led to an arrest. However, based on the victimization survey for that year, an estimated 7.7 million burglaries actually occurred. If we base the computation on the actual number of burglaries, then slightly less than 7 percent were solved by the police. That means that the odds against getting caught for committing an act of burglary are nearly 20 to 1.

Of course, that does not mean that only one burglar in twenty gets caught. Burglars tend to commit a series of crimes, so eventually the odds catch up with them. Yet they have such a good chance of

Table 8-1 / Proportion of crimes reported to the police.

Offense	Percent Reported
Larceny	25%
Assault	42%
Burglary	48%
Rape	51%
Robbery	55%
Purse snatching	59%
Auto theft	68%

Source: U.S. Department of Justice, 1982.

Table 8-2 / Reported crimes cleared by arrest.

Offense	Percent Cleared
Murder	72%
Assault	58%
Rape	48%
Robbery	24%
Larceny	19%
Burglary	14%
Auto theft	14%

Source: Federal Bureau of Investigation, 1982.

One of the most common court room scenes: A defendant in a criminal case, the prosecutor, and the defense lawyer approach the bench to discuss a plea bargain. Because of the load of pending cases, the courts will usually seek to avoid a lengthy trial by permitting defendants to plead guilty to an offense less serious than the one with which they have been charged.

avoiding arrest that they tend to explain getting caught as simply "bad luck" or a "silly mistake" (Irwin, 1970). Similarly, studies find that juveniles who have had contact with the police by being arrested or stopped and questioned have a lower, not a higher, expectation of being caught for an offense (Piliavin and Briar, 1964; G. Jensen, 1969). Of course, this expectation is further depressed for crimes such as burglary, for which the actual odds of being caught are low anyway. Recall that Gibbs found that of people serving prison sentences for burglary, 51 percent had served a prior sentence for the same offense.

Clearly, then, the threat of jail fails to deter burglars in part because they do not see punishment as certain—in fact, they see it as unlikely. Other offenders have similar feelings.

The courts

What about people who are arrested for a crime? It is still not certain that they will be punished, and even if they are, punishment is likely to be long delayed. Many arrests do not lead to trial or sentencing. Some cases are dismissed because of faulty arrest procedures, some are dropped when witnesses refuse to testify or are unable to appear at a scheduled hearing or trial, some defendants are permitted to plead guilty to a less serious offense, and some people are found not guilty.

We lack good data on the outcome of most arrests made by local and state police. The data available include only persons charged under federal laws and faced with prosecution in U.S. district courts. Federal courts deal with a different mix of offenders than do state and local courts. Fewer offenders are charged with rape, homicide, petty burglaries, and property offenses. Nevertheless, of 36,560 defendants in U.S. district courts in 1980, the charges against nearly 7,000 were dropped without trial. Nearly 2,000 others were acquitted by the judge or jury. More than 80 percent of the remaining number—23,000—pled guilty, usually to a less serious crime.

But even the guilty were not necessarily punished. More than half were not sent to jail, most being placed on probation. Of those who were jailed, only 20 percent received a sentence as long as five years. And few of these will serve their full sentence, since most prisoners are paroled well before their time is up. Moreover, even when finally sentenced to prison, people often remain free for a long time while awaiting appeals.

Criminologists believe that the federal courts are tougher and more efficient than most state and local courts. If this is true, an even higher proportion of those arrested for offenses escape trial and punishment than these federal data suggest.

One major difference between federal and nonfederal courts can be demonstrated. Only a small proportion of the defendants brought before federal officials are juveniles and thus eligible for lenient treatment as minors. However, a third of the persons arrested for serious crimes by state and local police in 1981 were juveniles. Indeed, of the more than 400,000 people arrested for burglary, 43 percent were under age 18, and the same proportion of arsonists were also juveniles. Juveniles are rarely tried for their crimes; instead they are usually released to juvenile authorities, who are reluctant to place them in detention.

In sum, for those who commit crimes in the United States, punishment is very uncertain, not often swift,

and usually not very severe. Consequently, crime is not highly deterred, and those convicted of crimes are very likely to commit subsequent offenses: A recent survey of all persons being held in state correctional facilities showed that 64 percent had served a previous sentence (U.S. Department of Justice, 1982).

REFORM AND RESOCIALIZATION

Few people today realize that prisons as places where people serve sentences for crimes are quite new. For centuries, prisons and jails were merely places where people were held while awaiting trial or until they received their sentences. Punishment did not involve spending time in prison but took the form of execution, mutilation, branding, or flogging. Authorities regarded it as unthinkably expensive to confine and feed able-bodied offenders for an extended period. Not until the late seventeenth century was confinement in prison used as an alternative to physical punishment.

The first serious experiments with prisons began in Pennsylvania under the direction of William Penn, whose Quaker beliefs caused him to oppose physical punishment. Penn directed that prisoners spend their sentences at hard labor in order to pay for their own upkeep and to pay damages to their victims. Penn's prisons became notorious for vice. Men, women, and juveniles were locked together, and the guards profited from the sale of liquor. So, in 1790 the Quakers of Pennsylvania tried a new approach—the penitentiary.

The new name reflected a whole new philosophy for dealing with criminal offenders. They were to be placed in circumstances much like monasteries, where they would be forced to contemplate their sins and become penitent (hence the name). Each prisoner was placed alone in an 8-by-6-foot cell and lived under a rule of silence. This Quaker example was copied by other states. Soon prisoners were required to work in order to pay the costs of their support, although the rule of silence prevailed.

This engraving of a prison in Rome, made by Giovanni Piranesi in about 1760, reveals a great vaulted structure with the prisoners wandering around. Even in this period prisons were not used primarily as places where people served sentences, but as places where people were held until the government decided what to do with them. Punishment usually consisted of torture or execution.

Problems continued, however. Convicts learned to get around the rule of silence and continued to cause problems of disorder and frequent escape. Then, in 1816 a new prison was built in Auburn, New York. This prison was novel both architecturally and in operating principles. Cells were built in tiers five floors high, making it possible for a few guards to observe the interiors of cells from strategically placed viewing points. Prisoners were divided into three groups. Dangerous troublemakers were placed in solitary confinement. A second group was allowed out of their cells for work only. The third and by far the largest group worked and ate together during the day and went into seclusion in their cells only at night. Internal discipline was maintained by adopting military procedures. Prisoners were marched from their cells to their places of work or the mess hall.

Texas is one of the few states that still sends prisoners out to perform labor on work gangs. These young men are hard at work under the watchful eye of a mounted guard. Prison reformers in the 1930s ended the use of such prison work gangs in most states and also brought an end to prison industries. As often happens, the reform measures may not have improved prison conditions. For, as is shown in the picture on the right, in most contemporary prisons convicts have little or nothing to do and must suffer through days of tedium.

Modern prisons are typically modeled on the Auburn design. However, a major change occurred during the 1930 and 1940s, when finding work to keep most inmates busy was no longer possible. In state after state, political opposition, especially from labor unions, to the sale of prison-made goods and the use of prisoner labor to construct roads and bridges resulted in the termination of prison work projects. This left wardens with very few jobs to occupy inmate time and, of course, it increased the cost of prisons, which were once virtually self-supporting, immensely. At the same time, efforts to reform the prisons by making them more humane and turning them into therapeutic institutions also made them much more expensive to staff. At present, it costs more than $20,000 a year to keep a person in prison.

Encouraged by the social sciences, especially psychology, many prisons have discarded their punish-

ment philosophy in recent years and adopted a therapeutic philosophy of reform and resocialization. Since the Quakers had meant prisons as places where criminals regained their moral judgment through solitary meditation, the therapeutic prison has sought to use psychological therapists and social workers to help inmates gain the necessary insights and to make the needed personality adjustments so they do not return to crime. But just as counselors proved ineffective with juveniles in the Cambridge-Somerville project, so too have they failed to find a method for making adult prison inmates conform to patterns of nondeviant behavior. The **recidivism rate**, the proportion of those released from prison who are sentenced to prison again, is as high among the new, therapeutic prisons as among the older, punitive prisons: about 60 percent.

While the threat of going to prison probably causes many people to obey the law, clearly it does not deter some, even after they have served a prison sentence. Nor do the prisons seem able to achieve the **resocialization** of inmates so they will not want to continue in crime. If we take seriously the theories of deviance discussed in Chapter 7, it should be no surprise that prisons fail to create conformity. If a lack of attachments tends to lead to deviance, then taking people who already have inadequate attachments out of the community will weaken these attachments even more.

Moreover, labeling theory suggests that, upon release from prison, the stigma of being an ex-convict will further limit the ability of offenders to form attachments with conventional people. In fact, prison may well foster new attachments to other deviants. In this fashion, tiny subcultures of deviants form in prison and survive as members are released.

Furthermore, whatever investments the person had prior to prison (which failed to be a sufficient

Table 8-3 / Public opinion of prison policies.

Proposal	Percent U.S. Adults Approving
1. Build more prisons in this state	57%
2. Convert unneeded army bases into prisons	76%
3. Require prisoners to learn a trade	94%
4. Require prisoners to learn to read and write	89%
5. Use prisoners to work on public construction projects and to make products needed by state	83%
6. Pay prisoners for work, but make them give two-thirds to victims and to pay for their own upkeep	81%
7. Have separate prisons for serious offenders	88%
8. No parole for those who have been paroled before for a serious crime	80%
9. Permit prisoners' wives or husbands to make private weekend visits	61%
10. Raise taxes to build more prisons	49%

Source: Gallup Poll, 1982.

reason to conform) must diminish while a person is in prison. Most people leave prison with little money, no job, and no promising career. Ex-convicts thus have very little to lose by subsequent deviance. And in prison they may gain an exaggerated view of how much can be gained by deviance and how low the odds of being caught are. In this way the prison system contributes to career deviance, especially as inmates return again and again.

Many efforts have been made to break this vicious cycle and prevent ex-convicts from committing new crimes. One of the most ambitious of these programs, and one that was subjected to the most careful evaluation by research, recently involved paying convicts salaries during their first months back in society. By watching carefully as this study was conducted, we can gain a better understanding of the problems faced by the criminal justice system.

SALARIES FOR EX-CONVICTS: THE TARP EXPERIMENT

Critics of the criminal justice system have stressed the economic plight of persons just released from prison. Lacking jobs, ex-convicts may be forced to commit new crimes to get money to live. Thus, these critics argued that recidivism could be reduced substantially if the government provided economic support to tide people over during their transition from prison back into society. In 1976 Kenneth J. Lenihan persuaded the U.S. Department of Labor to support an experimental program to test this hypothesis. Lenihan also recruited his colleagues Peter H. Rossi and Richard A. Berk to direct research to study the effects of the program.

The study was designed as an experiment, thus allowing the most accurate evaluation possible. Arrangements were made with authorities in Texas and Georgia to identify all persons serving time in state prisons who were scheduled to be released soon; approximately 2,000 adult men and women were listed. These inmates were randomly assigned to two groups. One group was given a weekly paycheck ($70 in Georgia and $63 in Texas). These payments continued for about six months. The other group received no checks and left prison in the usual manner and condition.

The study is referred to as the TARP study (for Transitional Aid Research Project). It was carried out with the strictest experimental controls. Since prisoners were randomly assigned to receive or to not receive payments, and since a large number of subjects were involved, the group that was paid should not have been different from the group that was not paid.

The dependent variable was also clearly defined. Since the goal was to see if payments eased the way back to a conventional life, people were judged successful in doing so if they managed to avoid arrest for one year after release from prison. Thus, the experimenters kept track of each person in the experimental and control groups and recorded when anyone was arrested.

What were the results? Among those who had not received TARP checks, 49 percent had been rearrested within a year of their release—a pretty dismal

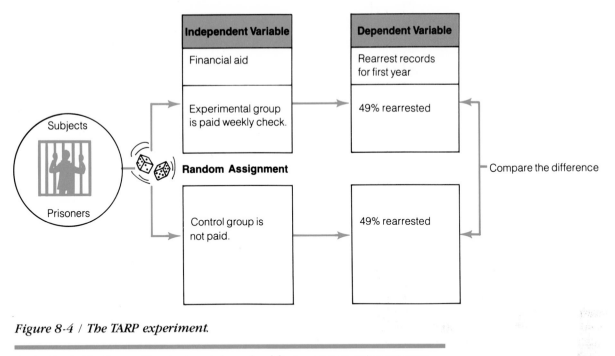

Figure 8-4 / The TARP experiment.

As the Cambridge-Somerville experiment showed a delinquency prevention program failed, this experiment showed that an effort to help ex-convicts stay out of jail by giving them financial aid while they reestablished their lives had no effects either. Because of random assignment of ex-convicts to experimental and control groups, the possibility of spuriousness is eliminated.

picture. But then the sociologists found that 49 percent of those who had been given financial aid had been rearrested during the first year. The payments had made no difference at all (Figure 8-4). Keep in mind that this was only the proportion who got into trouble within the first year. Others undoubtedly got arrested in later years.

Like delinquency prevention programs, the attempt to prevent recidivism by giving released convicts financial aid totally failed. But just like those who conducted the Cambridge-Somerville delinquency prevention study, the social scientists who conducted the TARP project also refused to accept the clear results of their own research. They, too, have ransacked the files on those in the experimental group and offered arguments that the program really did help some of them (Rossi, Berk, and Lenihan, 1980, 1982; Berk, Lenihan, and Rossi, 1980). Other scholars with no emotional stake in the study, however, regard the results as clear—the program failed (Zeisel, 1982).

It would be comforting to argue that the failures of the prison system to reform convicts are caused by a lack of effort, investment, and public enlightenment—and people untrained in criminology often make such charges. But the facts are that legions of dedicated men and women have worked hard to provide effective therapies and programs to reform convicts and that immense energy and many resources have gone into the prison system. There has been no shortage of new ideas, and every few years new programs and styles of prisons are introduced. The problem is that nothing has worked. The most modern therapeutic treatment centers have achieved no better results than did the Quaker penitentiaries: The majority of those who leave the prisons commit new offenses.

But if prisons are unable to reform, they do serve to isolate from society for the duration of their stay persons who have been judged dangerous to life and property. The policy of locking up serious offenders is more acceptable in our culture than

As the results of the TARP experiment showed, a very high proportion of people who are sent to prison commit new offenses when they get out. In this New York City precinct station, this man is beginning his trip to prison, where he will join a majority of prisoners who have served previous sentences. High recidivism rates have caused some to argue that it is useless to send people to prison. That is true if the only purpose of prisons is to reform criminals. But so long as we don't know how to reform people, prisons serve a second important function. As James Q. Wilson put it, "Wicked people exist. Nothing avails except to set them apart from innocent people."

physical torture or frequent resort to execution. That is, while we attempt to restructure prisons so that inmates are reformed or to discover other means of doing so, it is worthwhile to remember why prisons were invented in the first place—as a more humane form of punishment.

CONCLUSION

It is easy to draw overly pessimistic conclusions from this chapter and to assume that social control doesn't work. Granted, social control doesn't prevent some people from committing acts of serious deviance— more than 13 million crimes are reported to the police each year, and the actual number of crimes committed is probably about twice that number. Keep in mind, however, that even if each of these crimes were committed by a different person, then only about one person in ten engaged in a criminal act each year. And since we know that some people commit many crimes, only a tiny fraction of Americans are responsible for our crime rate.

Viewed this way, social control usually seems to work—most of us usually conform to the law. And, to a great extent our conformity is rooted in informal social control. Long before we wonder if the police will catch us or the courts jail us for committing a crime, we restrain such impulses because we know how our families and friends would react. Thus, as pointed out at the beginning of the chapter, formal methods of social control are activated only when informal methods fail. In an important sense, the police, the courts, and the prisons must assume responsibility for the people whom we—all of us in society—have failed to bind to the moral order. If the justice system typically fails to reform these people, this failure must be evaluated in light of the kinds of people they confront. To keep even 40 percent of such people from committing new offenses might be judged a substantial achievement.

Clearly, however, formal social control could be more effective. Improving the reporting of crimes should be possible. In fact, recent police efforts to educate the public and to treat victims more sensitively have greatly increased the reports of rape. Better coordination between the police, prosecutors, and the courts could probably prevent the dismissal of so many cases on technical grounds. And many proposals exist for speeding up court procedures and preventing serious offenders from getting off lightly.

But if crime can be reduced somewhat by overhauling the criminal justice system, it would be unrealistic to expect truly dramatic changes. For the fact remains that in every human group known, some people break the norms—not just in small ways, but in very serious ways. Even in tiny, isolated, utopian religious communities, where each person has voluntarily chosen to join the group in its retreat from a "wicked" world, some people commit grave crimes. Surely, then, we shouldn't be surprised that some people commit crimes in a much less socially and morally integrated society such as ours.

As we have seen in the past two chapters, sociologists can explain much about why people deviate and conform. But to know why deviance occurs often does not provide the knowledge for preventing it. Moreover, social scientists do not know how to reform many people who exhibit chronic patterns of serious deviance.

Review glossary

Social control All collective efforts to ensure conformity to the norms. (p. 172)

Informal social control Direct social pressure from those around us. (p. 173)

Group pressure The impact of group expectations and reactions on the behavior of the individual. (p. 174)

Formal social control Actions by organizations and groups that exist to uphold the norms. (p. 177)

Prevention As a form of social control, all efforts to remove the opportunity for deviance or to deactivate its causes. *When acts of deviance occurs* (p. 177)

Deterrence The use of punishment (or the threat of punishment) in order to make people unwilling to risk deviance. (p. 182)

Capital punishment The death penalty. (p. 182)

Deterrence theory The proposition that the more rapid, the more certain, and the more severe the punishment for a crime, the lower the rate at which that crime will occur. (p. 183)

Recidivism rate The proportion of persons convicted for a criminal offense who are later convicted for committing another crime. Sometimes this rate is computed as the proportion of those freed from prison who are sentenced to prison again. (p. 193)

Resocialization Efforts to change a person's socialization, that is, to socialize a person over again in hopes of getting him or her to conform to the norms. (p. 193)

Suggested readings

Geerken, Michael R., and Walter R. Gove. "Deterrence, Overload and Incapacitation: An Empirical Evaluation." *Social Forces* (1977) 56:424–447.

Gibbs, Jack. *Crime, Punishment, and Deterrence*. New York: Elsevier, 1975.

Phillips, David P. "The Deterrent Effect of Capital Punishment: New Evidence of an Old Controversy." *American Journal of Sociology*. (1980) 86:139–148.

Yunker, James A. "The Relevance of the Identification Problem to Statistical Research on Capital Punishment." *Crime and Delinquency* (1982) 28:96–124.

Zeisel, Hans. "Disagreement over the Evaluation of a Controlled Experiment." *American Journal of Sociology*. (1982) 88:378–389.

Percentage of the labor force belonging to unions (excluding farm workers), 1980. National = 25.2 percent.

Unions have played a major role in reducing income differences among Americans, particularly by greatly raising the relative salaries of people employed in major manufacturing industries such as steel and automobiles. However, today the great majority of employed Americans are not union members—and union strength varies greatly across the country. Unions are strongest in the heavily industrial regions: the East North Central, Middle Atlantic, and East South Central areas. They are weakest in parts of the South lacking heavy industries. New York (38.8 percent), Michigan (37.3 percent), and West Virginia (34.4 percent) are the most unionized states. South Carolina (7.8 percent), North Carolina (9.6 percent), and Texas (11.4 percent) are least unionized.

Pacific 28.0

Mountain 18.9

West North Central 23.0

East North Central 31.8

Middle Atlantic 34.8

New England 23.7

West South Central 13.1

East South Central 31.0

South Atlantic 15.0

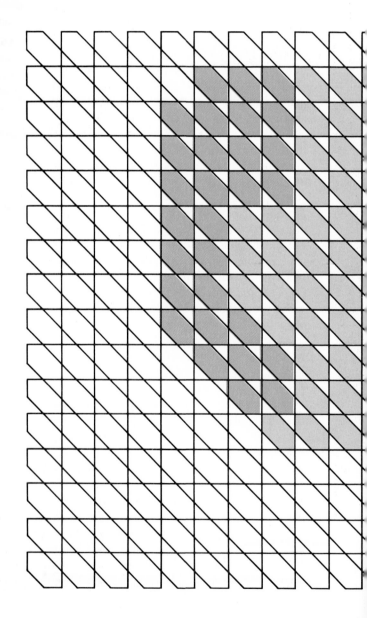

Stratification
and Conflict

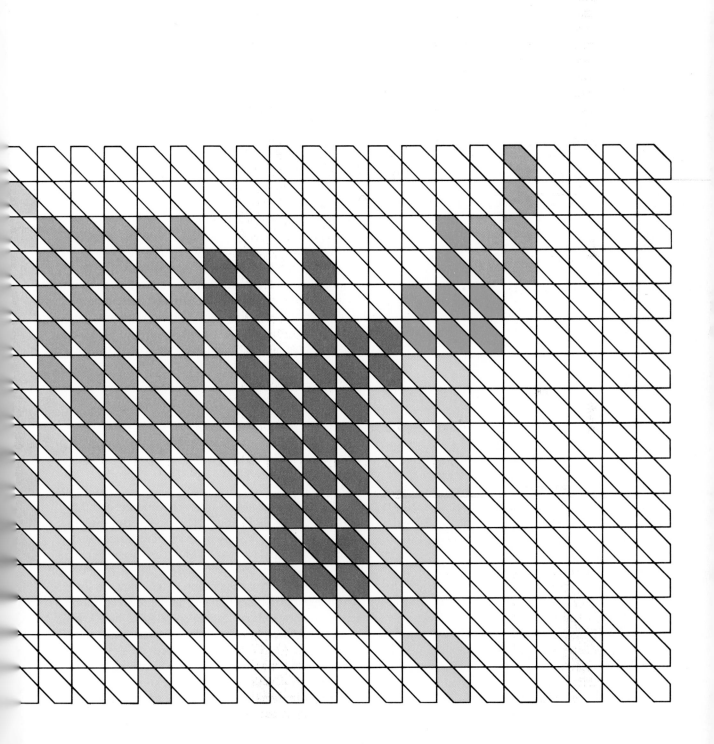

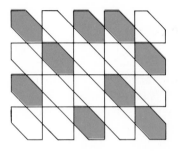

■ Stratification—the organization of society whereby some members have more and others have less—has been a constant theme in moral, political, and philosophical writing through the ages. Millions of words have been written to denounce inequalities in wealth and power. Millions have also been written to justify these inequalities. From the point of view of modern sociology, this is an irresolvable conflict based on two stubborn facts. First, stratification has many undesirable consequences. People at the bottom of stratification systems often suffer greatly, both physically and emotionally. Second, some degree of stratification seems to be absolutely necessary—an unavoidable feature of social structure. ■

CHAPTER PREVIEW

This chapter examines the basic concepts and theories used by sociologists to describe and explain stratification. It begins by examining various concepts of social class. In Chapter 2, classes were defined as groups of people who share a similar position, or level, within a stratification system. Now we shall pursue this definition in greater depth and explore differences in how leading sociologists have conceived of classes. We will also analyze the phenomenon of social mobility: upward or downward movement by individuals or groups within a stratification system. Armed with these conceptual tools, we shall then examine theories of stratification. Why

Concepts and Theories
of Stratification

RPK

are societies stratified? To what extent can stratification be minimized? In Chapter 10 we shall apply these principles by examining stratification and mobility in different societies.

CONCEPTIONS OF SOCIAL CLASS

Many different schemes have been used to identify *social classes,* or divisions of rank and wealth, within societies. Some schemes have used broad distinctions and others have used narrow ones in deciding which people occupy similar positions in a stratification system. Are classes large and few in number, or are they small and numerous?

Aristotle divided ancient Greek society into three broad classes: a rapacious upper class, a servile lower class, and a worthy middle class that, having all virtues and all failings in moderation, could be trusted to see after the common good of all. Plato saw only two classes in Greek society, the rich and the poor, and he believed them to be locked into eternal conflict. The word *class* comes to us from the Romans, who used the term *classis* to divide the population into a number of groups for the purpose of taxation. At the top were the *assidui* (from which the word *assiduous* comes), who were the richest Romans. On the bottom were the *proletarii,* who possessed nothing but children.

However, not until the mid-nineteenth century was the concept of class given significant meaning for modern social theorists. The person who first did this was Karl Marx (1818–1883).

MARX'S CONCEPT OF CLASS

Marx aimed to explain social change and produce a theory of history: Why and how do societies change, and what will they be like in the future? He believed that the answer lay in class conflict. The whole of human history, Marx and Engels wrote in *The Communist Manifesto* in 1848, has been "the history of class struggles." These struggles are the engines that pull societies into new forms, and the history of human societies is a history of one ruling class being overthrown by a new one.

Marx saw that there is no single answer to the question of how many classes to identify in societies. Instead, the answer depends upon which society and when. Thus, he identified four classes in ancient Rome—patricians, knights, plebians, and slaves—and a larger number in Europe during the Middle Ages.

The bourgeoisie and the proletariat

According to Marx, the development of capitalist societies had caused (or would eventually cause) a great simplification of the stratification system into two fundamental classes: "Society as a whole is more and more splitting up into two great hostile camps, into two great classes directly facing each other: Bourgeoisie and Proletariat" (*The Communist Manifesto*).

Class conflicts within industrial societies often take the form of strikes. Indeed, the right to have unions and to strike were major concessions won by employees in the late nineteenth and early twentieth centuries. This young textile worker was arrested in Lawrence, Massachusetts, in 1912. She and hundreds of other strikers had demonstrated in the streets in violation of a court injunction.

Marx defined these two classes in terms of their different relationship to the means of production. The **means of production** are everything besides human labor that goes into producing wealth. Chief among these are land (on which crops grow, cattle feed, and buildings stand), machines and tools, and investment capital. One class, the **bourgeoisie** owns these means of production. The other class, according to Marx, is everyone who does not own such means and therefore must sell his or her labor to the bourgeoisie. Marx called this class the **proletariat,** employing the name used by the Romans to identify the poor. These terms essentially refer to owners (or employers) and workers (or employees).

Marx realized that all capitalist societies in his time had many people who did not fit into his two-class scheme, but he believed that these groups would not significantly affect history. One such group was the middle class, including small merchants and self-employed professionals, such as doctors and lawyers. Marx believed that as the capitalist system evolved, the middle class would eventually be crushed and forced into the proletariat. He also dismissed a large number of people who were marginal to the economy—vagrants, migrant workers, beggars, criminals, gypsies, and the like. He classi-

Karl Marx.

fied such persons as members of the **Lumpenproletariat** (literally, the "ragamuffin proletariat"). Such people had so little social purpose and self-respect, Marx believed, that they would have no effect on the impending revolutionary struggle. Finally, Marx excluded farmers and peasants from his conception of class because he believed that the drama of historical change would occur in the urban, industrial sector of capitalist societies; rural people would play little or no part in shaping social change. The fact that communist revolutions have come in backward, rural nations rather than advanced, industrial countries is an embarrassment to Marxist theorists. Also, the omission of peasants from his class conceptions was probably a serious flaw in Marx's work.

Class consciousness and conflict

In addition to *material* position in society, Marx also added an important *psychological* component to his notion of class. To be considered a real class, people must be similarly placed in society and share similar prospects, but they must also be aware of their circumstances, their common interests, and their common class enemy. Marx called this awareness **class consciousness.** Much of his theory about the coming of the communist revolution concerns how the proletariat will achieve class consciousness, at which point their superior numbers will ensure their success. Marx also worried about the tendency for workers to believe they had common interests with the ruling class and called this **false consciousness.**

By incorporating assumptions about class consciousness into his definition of social class, Marx inserted portions of his *theory* of revolution into his *concept* of class. This made key portions of his theory true by definition and thus untestable. By Marx's definition, if a group of people with a common economic position in society does not recognize their common interests and organize to pursue them, they are not a class. To say that classes will be self-conscious and organized, then, is to predict nothing about the course of history; it is simply stating a definition. Indeed, Marx denied that classes could exist without class struggle, again by definition. He wrote, "Individuals form a class only in so far as they are engaged in a common struggle with another class." Hence, when Marx said class struggle is inevitable, he had already made that statement necessarily true by his definition of the word *class*.

Economic dimension of class

The most important feature of Marx's definition of class is that it is determined only by the *economic* dimension. Property ownership is the only factor for ranking people, and then they are divided into only two groups: those who own the means of production and those who do not.

When Marx rested his distinction between the bourgeoisie and the proletariat entirely on this single criterion, he necessarily implied that all other differences in position among people in society are wholly the result of property ownership. Thus, if some people are more powerful than others, or if

The Sandinista regime in Nicaragua illustrates Marx's miscalculations about where and why communist revolutions would occur. He thought the most industrialized capitalist nations such as Germany, Great Britain, and the United States would be the first to have revolutions. Instead, Marxist revolutions have been restricted to less industrialized societies and have been based mainly on peasant support.

some people are more admired or respected than others, it is entirely due to the underlying economic differences between them. For, Marx claimed, the relationship to the means of production is "the final secret, the hidden basis for the whole construction of society." The rest of the culture of a society results from the underlying economic arrangements. Indeed, for Marx culture was a "superstructure of various and peculiarly formed sentiments, illusions, modes of thought, and conceptions of life" that arises from economic relations.

Marx nowhere gave empirical evidence that eco-nomic differences were the sole basis of other social differences such as power and respect (Dahrendorf, 1959). His claim, however, was an empirical one that could be tested by other social scientists. If power or prestige can be shown to vary independently of property, then Marx's statement is at least excessive and perhaps false. Indeed, the likelihood that the economic dimension of property does not govern all aspects of stratification made many sociologists who came after Marx very uneasy with his single-factor conception of class. Among them was Max Weber.

WEBER'S THREE DIMENSIONS

Max Weber (1864–1920) is one of the great names in the history of sociology. We shall assess his work on religion and social change in Chapter 16, and his work on bureaucracy in Chapter 19. In Weber's lifetime, as in ours, the influence of Marx on social theory was immense. And some of Weber's major works were attempts to modify Marxist positions.

Weber believed that Marx's wholly economic view of stratification could not capture primary features of modern industrial stratification systems. Looking around in Germany, Weber noticed that social position did not always seem to be simply a matter of property ownership. Many Germans who belonged to the nobility lacked wealth yet possessed immense political power; for example, only they could be officers in the army. On the other hand, Weber noted that some German families possessing very great wealth, who owned factories and other great companies, lacked political power and social standing because they were Jewish.

Strictly applying Marx's conception of class would classify these Jewish families as bourgeoisie, while many powerful *Junkers* (aristocrats) would belong to the proletariat. Thus, Weber thought Marx's scheme was too simple. He proposed that stratification is also based on other, independent factors. He suggested three such factors: *class, status,* and *power.*

Modern social scientists have found several of Weber's terms somewhat confusing; therefore they have renamed them to constitute the "three P's" of stratification: *property* (what Weber called "class"), *prestige* (what Weber called "status") and *power* (as Weber defined it).

Max Weber.

Class or property

By *class* Weber meant groups of people with similar "life chances" as determined by their economic position in society—the goods they possess and their opportunities for income. This is what modern social scientists refer to as **property.** Weber stressed class membership based on *objective* economic position. Unlike Marx, he did not reserve the word *class* only for groups that had developed class consciousness and had organized for class conflict. Instead, Weber regarded the banding together by persons with the same economic position as merely possible or potential. Thus, a key question for Weber was when and why class conflicts occur. Making class conflict part of the definition of class would not answer the question.

Furthermore, Weber did not stress ownership of property but realized that in some circumstances *control* of property might be independent of ownership. If a person can control property to his or her personal benefit, it matters little whether the person legally owns the property. Thus, Weber was able to recognize the high class position of managers (whether of capitalist corporations or socialized industries) who control firms they do not own. Marx had placed such persons in the proletariat.

Status or prestige

Weber recognized that economic position can rest on control without ownership because he saw that

All of these senior officers of the German General Staff in 1871 could claim member-ship in the nobility. Yet, some of them had no private wealth and had to depend mainly on their army pay. Weber conceptualized stratification as multidimensional and there-fore could take into account the power and prestige of these commanders while also recognizing their relative lack of property.

prestige (or "status" in his terms) and power were not wholly the consequence of property relations. Instead, they could be the source of property relations. To use a trivial example, when famous sports stars or military heroes endorse a commercial product, they are exchanging their **prestige,** or social honor, for economic advantage. Indeed, people often enjoy high prestige in a society while having little or no property. For example, poets and saints may have immense influence in a society while remaining virtually penniless.

Power

The case for power as being independent of wealth is even more obvious. Weber defined **power** as the ability to get one's way despite the resistance of others. People may be very powerful without acquiring much property. For example, a corporation president may wield great power within the corporation and even in the political process of a society without person-ally owning any part of the corporation. The same is often true of senior civil servants who run such powerful agencies as the CIA, the FBI, or the Federal Reserve while receiving relatively modest salaries. Furthermore, power is often traded for economic advancement. Many politicians manage to retire rich even though they were paid only modest salaries while in office. The whole notion of influence peddling assumes the sale of power, while Marx seemed to believe that power can only be bought.

STATUS INCONSISTENCY

In Chapter 2, *status* was defined as any position within the stratification system. (This is not what Weber meant by the term, and that is one reason why sociologists often use the term *prestige* for Weber's concept.) This definition says nothing about the *basis* for status in a stratification system. Thus, a particular status or position can be high or low on the basis of the property, prestige, or power (or all three) associated with that position. We can also refer to *status characteristics*—certain individual or group traits that determine status. For example, various ethnic or racial minorities may be confined to a low status in society. Therefore, ethnicity and race are status characteristics: Variations in them influence position in society.

Because the term *status* denotes any particular position in the stratification system, it is a more general concept than class, which is just one measure of status. As Weber pointed out, there is more to stratification than simple economic differences.

If there are at least three basic dimensions of stratification in society, and if these can vary independently of one another, then individuals or groups can hold different ranks (or different status levels) on each of the three dimensions. For example, a person could be rich but have low prestige and little power. This state of affairs is called **status inconsistency.**

Status inconsistency theories predict that people whose status is inconsistent, or higher on one dimension than on another, will be more frustrated and dissatisfied than people with consistent statuses. A major proponent of status inconsistency theory, Gerhard Lenski (1954, 1956, 1966), explains the process this way: When people rank higher on one status dimension than on another, they will emphasize their highest claim to rank and deemphasize their lowest. Thus, in presenting themselves to others, they will expect to be judged according to their highest status. Others, however will tend to respond to them according to their lowest status, for others will seek to maximize their own position.

Consider the case of black physicians in America. They will seek to be treated by others on the basis of their high-prestige occupation and advanced education. But some whites will ignore this claim and treat them as of low social position because of their race. Women physicians often experience a similar denial of status. Likewise, the uneducated, self-made oil millionaire trying to participate in high society may find that others discount his high status in terms of property and respond instead to his low status as an unpolished person. The phrase "the vulgar rich" expresses the status inconsistency of many wealthy people.

Lenski argued that persons who are denied the social rank that they believe they deserve become antagonistic toward the rules governing status in their society. Consequently, persons suffering from status inconsistency will be favorable toward political actions aimed against upper status groups; that is, they will support liberal and radical parties and proposals. This very important theoretical conclusion helped explain why persons of considerable social standing often seemed to turn their backs on their own class interests and support the claims of the less privileged, a phenomenon that Marx found very difficult to explain.

Early efforts to test status inconsistency theory were not very successful because they failed to see that it applied *only* to people with some claim to *upper* status and not to everyone with one status higher than his or her other statuses. That is, status inconsistency causes people to become antagonistic to the rules of stratification primarily when they are denied *high* status. Working from this revised point of view, Gary Marx reasoned that, in the 1960s, all wealthy, famous, or highly educated black Americans suffered from status inconsistency. Therefore, according to the theory, upper status blacks ought to be *more* militant about changing racial conditions than were blacks with consistent low statuses. So, Gary Marx predicted that black bankers and physicians, for example, would be more radical than black janitors and housekeepers. Research based on large national samples confirmed his hypothesis (G. Marx, 1967).

By the same token, Jewish bankers and industrialists in the United States and Europe ought to have a record of support for liberal and radical parties, and they do (Cohn, 1958). The theory also explains the strong preference of wealthy and powerful American Catholics for the Democratic Party (Baltzell, 1964).

The notion of status inconsistency is possible *only* if we accept Weber's view that there are multiple bases for rank in societies. If we follow Marx and accept only one basis for rank, then, of course, it is impossible to conceive of inconsistency. However, no matter how we conceptualize stratification systems, questions arise about how *people gain* their positions. And this brings us to the topic of social mobility.

SOCIAL MOBILITY

Societies differ greatly in the amount of upward and downward movement that goes on within their stratification systems. In some societies few people rise above or fall below their position at birth. In other societies there is a great deal of mobility. The amount of mobility in societies depends on two things. First, the *rules* governing how people gain or keep their positions may make mobility difficult or easy. Second, whatever the rules, mobility can be influenced by *structural* changes in societies.

Rules of status: ascription and achievement

Chapter 2 introduced the two primary rules by which societies determine status. *Achieved* status is a position gained on the basis of merit, or achievement. *Ascribed* status is a position based on who you are, not what you can do. When a society uses ascriptive status rules, people are placed in status positions because of certain traits beyond their control, such as family background, race, sex, or place of birth.

In all known societies, both achievement and ascription operate, but societies differ in which rule dominates. In medieval Europe, for example, one's status was predominantly based on ascription. Persons born of the nobility were very likely to remain in high positions; persons born of peasants were very likely to remain in low positions.

When ascription is the overwhelming basis for status, we often speak of *caste* systems. Traditional society in India was composed of dozens of castes. Each person's caste group was defined by the caste he or she was born into, and each group was restricted to certain occupations. All the filthy and demeaning jobs, such as garbage collecting, were reserved for one caste, whose members were permitted to hold no other occupations. Similarly, highly skilled occupations such as goldsmithing were the exclusive right of another caste. However, even in caste systems, some people managed through luck and talent to rise above their origins—great prowess as a soldier, in particular, was often a ticket to higher status. And some high-born persons managed to fall to low positions because of misbehavior or incompetence.

Achievement is the primary basis of status in the United States and other advanced industrial nations. The majority of Americans are socially mobile; they rise above or fall below the positions of their parents. Nevertheless, ascription plays a significant role in our society, too. Although blacks and women are not wholly excluded from upper status positions, they are underrepresented in such positions and overrepresented in lower ones. One reason for this is discrimination based on race and sex.

It will be clear that social mobility is much more frequent when achievement rather than ascription is the primary basis for status. But societies also differ in the amount of social mobility that occurs because of the direction of structural change in their overall status systems.

Structural and exchange mobility

When the proportion of upper status positions in a society increases, some upward mobility is inevitable. Because more openings exist at the top for the present generation than existed for the previous

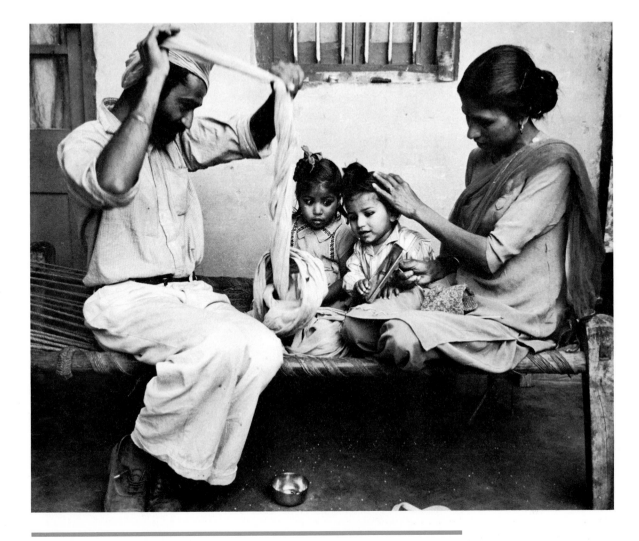

Fifty years ago the adult status of these Indian children would almost certainly have been exactly the same as that of their parents. Today, India's caste system is not as strictly observed as it used to be. However, it is still very likely that these children will inherit their parent's caste position when they grow up.

generation, some children of lower status parents must be placed in high positions in order to fill them.

A simple example will make this clear (see Figure 9-1). Suppose that in 1940 a society had 100 jobs, 25 of which were high-prestige, high-paying jobs and 75 low-prestige, low-paying jobs. However, the economy changed. As machines replaced humans on the job, there was less need for people to do unskilled work and a greater need for people to do highly skilled work (such as designing and maintaining the machines that replaced unskilled laborers). Thus, in 1980, this society still contained 100 jobs, but 50 were high-status positions.

Suppose that in 1940 each of the 100 people holding the 100 jobs had one child who replaced him or her in the economy. Then by 1980, 25 children of persons who held low positions would have

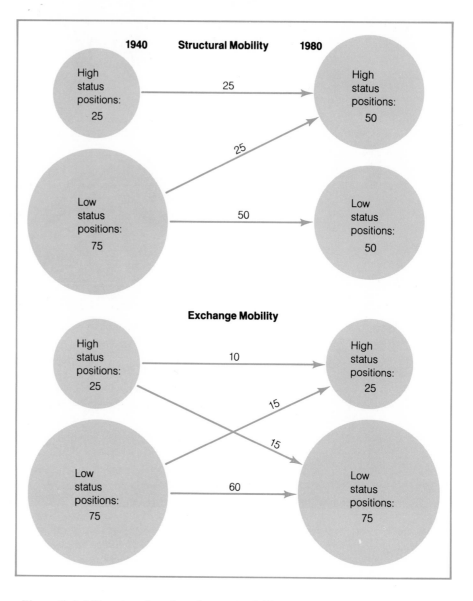

Figure 9-1 / Structural and exchange mobility.

Structural mobility occurs because of changes in the ratio of upper to lower positions. When there is an increase in positions at the top, some people will have to be upwardly mobile in order to fill them; when such positions decrease, some people are forced downward. Exchange mobility occurs when some people create openings at the top by being downwardly mobile, thus allowing others to rise.

entered high positions, simply because 25 low positions had been eliminated from the status system and 25 high positions had been created. Thus, a third of the offspring of low-status people in 1940 become upwardly mobile simply as a result of changes in the status system. The reverse would have occurred if the proportion of high positions had decreased rather than increased.

Social mobility that results from changes in the distribution of statuses in society is called **structural mobility.** Also note that structural mobility occurs *regardless of the rules governing status.* Had our hypothetical society been based on ascriptive status rules, the outcome would have been the same. For example, if the demands of a particular occupation exceeded the capacity of the appropriate caste group, members of other castes would have filled the openings. Therefore, we can learn little about the rules governing status in a society merely by knowing the degree of mobility. We must also know whether that mobility is structural or exchange mobility.

Mobility that is not structural is called **exchange mobility.** The word *exchange* indicates a trade-off. In exchange mobility, some people rise to fill positions made available because other people have fallen in the status system. Let us reconsider our simple illustration in Figure 9-1. Suppose that the proportion of upper status positions did not increase between 1940 and 1980. Thus, in 1980 there are still 25 upper status positions and 75 lower positions. The only way that the offspring of persons in lower positions can gain an upper position is if someone born of upper status persons moves to a lower status, thus making room at the top.

There is very little exchange mobility when the ascriptive status rule operates, but if status is through achievement, there is a fair amount of such movement. Many children of talented and ambitious parents do not inherit the talent or ambition that earned their parents high rank. Conversely, many children of low-status parents are more talented and ambitious than their parents. Hence, if the status system is truly based on achievement, we can expect a good deal of reshuffling each generation. In Chapter 10, we shall examine mobility in the United States and other industrial nations.

THEORIES OF STRATIFICATION

Thus far we have examined concepts of stratification, but now we must confront the basic theoretical issues: Why are societies stratified and can stratification be eliminated? As was pointed out at the beginning of this chapter, these issues have been debated for centuries. In the remainder of this chapter, we shall see that the debate continues among contemporary sociologists. However, before examining the three principal sociological theories of stratification, it will be useful to relate the contemporary debate to its roots in the Nineteenth century.

MARX AND THE CLASSLESS SOCIETY

Karl Marx lived and wrote during a period of extremely rapid social change, which produced a great deal of social displacement and individual suffering. Across Europe the Industrial Revolution was in full swing. Great factories dotted the countryside, belching forth noxious smoke as well as an unprecedented volume of production. Until that time, most human beings had lived on farms or in tiny villages. But soon most people were to be living in cities, and it seemed that most would end up sweating over machines in factories.

To many, trading a life in a cow barn for a life in a factory was not real progress. The successful rise of industrial unions was yet to come. Many people, including Marx, found existing conditions intolerable, and out of their anger and frustration came an immense burst of utopian social thought.

A **utopian** constructs plans for an ideal society. Thousands of utopian schemes have been proposed over the past two centuries alone. Indeed, many have been tried. During the nineteenth century, for example, scores of groups in the United States set up their own separate communities, where they attempted to enact a utopian living plan (Nordhoff, 1875; Noyes, 1870). Some of these groups, such as Oneida and Amana, were based on a common set

One of the most famous efforts at a utopian community in the United States was the Oneida Colony in upper New York State. Founded in 1848 under the leadership of John Humphrey Noyes, the group experimented not only with life styles but with economic activities—here members can be seen busy making bags. In time, the Oneida community was so successful in manufacturing lace and silver plate that they gave up their communal experiment and became an ordinary corporation.

of religious beliefs. Some, such as New Harmony, embraced socialism. The religious commune groups tended to last much longer, but they all broke up in the end. Nevertheless, whether religious or socialist or both, these groups reflected a deep discontent with the quality of life in nineteenth-century industrial societies (Kanter, 1972).

Within this context of rapid social change, widespread social unrest, and rampant utopian thought, Marx set out to create a scientific theory of history. The aim of his theory was to show how the inevitable forces of history would produce a revolution of the proletariat, which in turn would produce socialism and a communist society. After years of writing, Marx concluded that the coming revolutionary societies would be "classless"; that is, everyone would belong to a single social class.

Marx's conclusions, which were joyfully received by many, sharply contrasted with the predictions of **anarchists,** who were a major force in radical thought and politics at the time. The anarchists had reached a conclusion similar to that held by modern sociology: Stratification is an inescapable feature of human societies. Unlike most modern sociologists, the anarchists reacted to this conclusion by proposing to dispense with society. Indeed, they earned their name by proposing to "smash the state" and to live without social organization. However, since anarchists failed to explain convincingly how humans could live apart from society without also living in constant fear, danger, and disorder, most people found their solution worse than the problem. Then, in a few sentences, Marx claimed to prove the anarchists incorrect by showing how both society and equality were possible.

To see how he arrived at this conclusion, we must recall how he defined social class. As stated earlier in the chapter, Marx conceived of only two classes in modern industrial societies, and these classes differed on the basis of the ownership (or nonownership) of the means of production. Thus, by Marxist definition, classes exist only because privately owned property exists. This alone separates people into the bourgeoisie and proletariat. Thus, to achieve a classless society, the *private ownership of the means of production* must be abolished. Then, the bourgeoisie ceases to exist and everyone becomes a proletarian.

But how can this be done? If the state seizes ownership of the means of production, no person will own these means. Moreover, since everybody will belong to the same class, there will be no class conflict.

Following Marx, communist regimes that have come to power have proclaimed their societies to be classless, since they have placed ownership of the means of production in the hands of the state. These claims have long caused heated debate among people in noncommunist nations, because it has been evident that communist societies have remained very noticeably *stratified.* How could they be classless?

DAHRENDORF'S CRITIQUE

The most penetrating analysis of Marx's claims about the creation of classless societies was written by Ralf Dahrendorf (1959). Dahrendorf is a leading conflict theorist of stratification, and we shall examine elements of his work later in his chapter. Here we shall concentrate on his argument that Marx's claim about classless societies was a "magic trick" that didn't mean what it appeared to mean.

Dahrendorf pointed out that everything Marx said about communist societies being classless was true, *but only true by definition.* Marx defined *class* according to the ownership of the means of production. If the state owns all means of production, everyone falls into one class *as Marx defines class.*

But, Dahrendorf continued, notice that Marx never said this would produce *unstratified* societies. Indeed, communist societies have one class only in the limited sense expressed by Marx, but Marx did not say that everyone would have equal power or equal prestige. Moreover, it does not even follow that people in communist societies would be equal economically. For, Dahrendorf asked, *who is the state?* Is it really all of the people? Or is the state in fact controlled by political specialists?

Here Dahrendorf turned to Weber. What would happen to Marx's prediction of a classless society if he had based his definition not simply on the ownership of the means of production but on its *control?* People do not have equal control over the means of production, even if private ownership is outlawed. Human affairs still require organization and direction. Someone still must manage each factory, for example. Since Weber argued that variations in the control of the means of production are often more significant than technical ownership, the socialization of industry clearly does not create classless societies as Weber used the term. Instead, people still differ greatly in their *control* over the means of production. Those who run the government in effect "own" the means of production.

Indeed, Dahrendorf argued, Marx did not escape the anarchist's conclusion at all. He only resorted to a solution by definition that did not alter the brute reality of stratification. As Weber himself noted, Marx was only proposing to replace the capitalist boss with a communist boss, and there is no reason to suppose that this would reduce stratification.

Interestingly enough, Dahrendorf's critique of Marx had been anticipated in 1896 by a young Italian sociologist, who also anticipated major elements of both modern functionalist and conflict theories of stratification.

MOSCA: STRATIFICATION IS INEVITABLE

In his book *The Ruling Class* (1896), Gaetano Mosca (1858–1941) laid out a three-step "proof" that societies must be stratified. His first proposition was that human societies cannot exist without political organization. Mosca used the term *political organization* in the very broadest sense to mean all forms of coordination and decision making in human activities. This proposition simply recognizes that human society is impossible if everyone runs around helter-skelter. Instead, in order for there to be group life there must be mutual undertakings and the actions of individuals must be directed and coordinated. Put another way, in order to have societies, humans must take collective actions.

Mosca's second proposition resembles the conclusion reached by the anarchists: Whenever there is political organization (or society), there must be inequalities in power. Here Mosca simply recognized that coordination requires leaders, and leaders, by definition, have greater power than their followers—to lead, a person must be able to give orders and have them obeyed. Thus, according to Mosca, differences in power are built into the basic social roles by which societies are created and maintained—an insight that anticipated modern functionalist theories.

By themselves these two propositions establish that societies will always be stratified in terms of power. But Mosca carried his reasoning one step further and anticipated modern conflict theories of stratification. He argued that since human nature is inherently self-seeking, people with greater power will use it to exploit others and therefore to gain material advantages. Thus, given the existence of power inequalities, material inequalities will always exist too. Thus Mosca concluded that stratification is not something that human societies can avoid, but an inescapable feature of collective life. For advancing this view, many of Mosca's contemporaries dismissed him as a cynic and a reactionary. But today, a century later, his ideas have become part of the sociological mainstream. Indeed, as we now examine in detail modern theories of stratification, it will be obvious how fully they were anticipated by Mosca.

FUNCTIONALISM AND STRATIFICATION

The modern functionalist view of stratification is most closely identified with the work of Kingsley Davis and Wilbert E. Moore (1945, 1953). The key to their **functionalist theory of stratification** is in seeing society as a system of roles or positions. Inequality or stratification exists in societies because it is built into these roles and into the problem of filling them adequately.

Davis and Moore began by arguing that positions in society differ in the degree to which they are functionally important. That is, poor performance in some roles is more damaging to the society than is poor performance in some other positions. For example, while it is true that a society engaged in a war requires both soldiers and generals, a general is in position to make more devastating errors than is any given soldier. Remember that for every famous general who won a battle that seemed unwinnable there was a general on the other side who lost a battle that seemed unlosable. History has a tendency to be unkind to societies that appoint generals who snatch defeat out of the jaws of victory (Fair, 1971).

Not only are some positions inherently more important to the system, Davis and Moore argued that some are inherently more difficult to fill adequately. This is because these positions require qualities that are naturally in short supply or that require a considerable preliminary investment in time, training, and effort. For example, some positions in a society require occupants with very high intelligence or great tact or other characteristics that are always in short supply in any population. Others—surgery, for example—also require many years of training. Extensive training is always potentially in short supply, for new people constantly must begin training in order to fill future needs.

Thus, all societies face a general problem of motivation—"to instill in the proper individual the desire to fill certain positions, and, once in these positions, the desire to perform the roles attached to them" (Davis and Moore, 1945). How can this be accomplished? Davis and Moore argue that the only way to produce this kind of motivation is to adjust the reward system. Theirs is a supply-and-demand argument. To ensure an adequate supply of the right people, it is necessary to attach higher rewards to the positions that are most important and hardest to fill. Why would anyone want to become a general if the rewards were the same as those of a private?

Furthermore, it isn't enough to find some people who want to be generals—it is important to attract the right kind of people to the position of general. Stratification, therefore, exists because the positions in society differ in their importance to the system and because it is necessary to ensure that the most important positions are filled by competent people. Indeed, people also vary in their ability to perform important positions. Hence, as Davis and Moore (1945) put it, stratification or social inequality

is an unconsciously evolved device by which societies insure that the most important positions are conscientiously filled by the most qualified persons. . . . Those positions convey the best reward, and hence have the highest rank, which a) have the greatest importance for the society and b) require the greatest training or talent.

Differential rewards, according to Davis and Moore, prevent less essential or less important positions in society from competing with the more important for scarce talents.

Replaceability

Many have attacked Davis and Moore for attempting to justify social inequalities—for arguing that people get pretty much what they deserve in life. Davis and Moore rightfully respond that they are not trying to justify stratification, merely to explain it. They no more chose to make stratification an inevitable part of society than physicists chose to make gravitation a part of the physical universe. Nevertheless, the Davis and Moore explanation of stratification has been criticized justifiably because it comes dangerously close to being circular (Stinchcombe, 1968). The trouble stems from their inability to define the notion of functional importance adequately.

Davis and Moore based their analysis on the proposition that positions or roles in society differ in functional importance, that is, in their consequences for the continued operation of society. This is vital to their argument that stratification results from the need to motivate the most qualified people to take these positions. Unfortunately, they found it difficult to establish that one position is more important than another except on the basis of how hard it is to fill that position. That is an inadequate standard.

Today it is very hard to fill the position of housekeeper; to ensure an ample supply would require wages to be set at a level most potential employers are unwilling to pay. Clearly, it does not follow that this position is extremely important. But should we then count it as of low functional importance because we are not willing to pay much to fill the position? To rate the importance of a position on the basis of how much people are paid for filling it leads into a trap. Then one must argue that rewards differ because of functional importance, but that is to say that rewards differ because rewards differ, since functional importance has been defined as a difference in rewards. This is a tautology, or circular argument.

Fortunately, positions can be ranked according to functional importance without leading to contradiction or tautology. A position is of high functional importance to a society depending on its **replaceability,** that is, to the degree that *either the position itself or its occupants are hard to replace*. Let us return to the example of housekeepers. The salary paid people to clean other people's houses is very low, even when those willing to take such jobs are in short supply, because the position of housekeeper is very replaceable. That is, their employers are fully able to take over the functions of the housekeeper, and when they are sufficiently motivated to

The principle of replaceability is evident in this shot of a Lakers–Celtics game being played in the Boston Garden several years ago. The highest-paid player in the picture was the man with the ball. The reason is that, while everyone on the floor was a superb player, Wilt Chamberlain is the only one of them who is seven feet tall. It is easier to find good 6'7" power forwards than it is to find good 7' centers. Thus, centers have the highest average pay of any position in the National Basketball Association.

do so (by the financial savings involved), they will tend to do so.

A *position* is highly replaceable when its functions can be performed by people in many other positions. Thus, hospital janitors are highly replaceable because their job could be performed by all other hospital workers. Orderlies are next most replaceable, since doctors and nurses could perform their functions. Doctors are least replaceable because, presumably, not even nurses could fully take on their hospital duties.

People are highly replaceable when little skill is needed to perform their particular roles. Little training or skill is required to mop floors, for example, and thus people who hold such positions are always potentially in competition with all other workers to hold their own positions. On the other hand, very few people have the talent and the years of training needed to be surgeons, and so few people can compete for these positions. Thus, positional replaceability is the dominant basis of functional importance. People in highly replaceable positions also tend to be individually highly replaceable. Given the replaceability notion, the functionalist theory can easily be shown as a supply-and-demand argument about the existence of stratification.

A toy society

People who study the operation of systems often employ models in order to try out different arrangements to see what happens. Sometimes these models are small replicas of the actual system, but often they are very simplified versions of the system. The latter models omit many components of the original system in order to study a few features of the system more closely. In a sense, such a simplified model is an educational toy, for, as George Homans (1974) has aptly put it, such a toy "should be taken lightly like the serious thing it is. . . . At the very least the toy may show how inadequate our assumptions and formulations are."

To help explain stratification systems, we can learn much by closely inspecting a very simplified toy society. Imagine a spaceship on a long voyage that is suddenly forced to crash-land on a tiny asteroid. Four people live through the crash. Let's call them Ay, Bee, Cee, and Dee. To survive, they will need four things: food, air, water, and heat. The survivors differ greatly in their technical skills. Ay is able to produce all four critical products, as shown in Table 9-1. Bee can produce everything but air; Cee can produce food and heat; and Dee can produce only heat.

It is clear that Ay is irreplaceable. If Ay dies or stops making air, everyone will die. Moreover, if Ay stops *sharing* air with the other three, they will die. Yet Ay can live without any of the others. To an exaggerated degree, Ay is like a doctor in relation to the rest of a hospital staff—he or she can do all the jobs.

Conversely, consider the situation of Dee. Everyone can get along without Dee, while he or she can't live without aid from the others. Clearly, Ay can make the most favorable exchanges with the other survivors. Ay has a monopoly on air and needs nothing from anyone else. He or she may decide not to bother making heat and let Dee provide heat in exchange for air. But Ay will not trade air for heat if the effort to make air for Dee is equal to or greater than the effort Ay would have to expend to make his or her own heat. Similarly, Ay may bargain with Bee and Cee, perhaps to get water from Bee and food from Cee, in return for air. As a result of this bargaining process, Ay will always end up with more food, water, and heat than the others. This is because Ay will supply his or her own food, water, and heat and refuse to trade air, whenever the terms of exchange do not favor Ay.

Now let's introduce time into this model. Like all humans, these marooned travelers will eventually die. Let's assume, however, that they have children and therefore our toy society has a future. If the next generation is to survive, these children must be prepared to take over the vital productive functions. Clearly, it is imperative to find a replacement for Ay. Without an air maker, all will die. But suppose that air making requires a very rare talent or a very long period of difficult training. Someone with the talent must be motivated to become an air maker or to invest the time and effort needed to learn air making. How can this best be assured? The most efficient way is to make every child desire to be an air maker. Thus, the only person with the potential for air making will not be wasted by becoming a heat maker. The way to do this is to greatly reward air making so that people will aspire to this occupation. Indeed, we have already seen that air making will be highly rewarded so long as it is the least replaceable skill.

This toy society reveals the essential points of the

Table 9-1 / Abilities of space survivors to provide needs.

Survivor	Ability to Produce			
	Air	Water	Food	Heat
Ay	X	X	X	X
Bee		X	X	X
Cee			X	X
Dee				X

functionalist theory of stratification. We can see how specialization and exchanges between specialists result in stratification. Of course, many aspects of real societies have been omitted from this toy society. Among these are forces that limit the potential exploitation of Cee and Dee by Ay and Bee. These will be discussed in the section on the conflict theory of stratification.

SOCIAL EVOLUTION AND STRATIFICATION

Chapter 4 pointed out that all functionalist theories depend upon an evolutionary premise. Indeed, recall that Davis and Moore referred to stratification as "an unconsciously evolved device." Therefore, no functionalist theory completely explains any phenomenon unless it is connected to an evolutionary theory. Thus, we need to know how social stratification evolves.

The fundamental premise of all social evolutionary theories is that humans will retain that culture which they believe is rewarding. Humans persist in efforts to find ways to gain rewards—to find procedures and implements that will achieve the desired results. Those that don't seem to work will be discarded; those that appear to work best will be preserved. If humans preserve culture, then as time passes culture will accumulate—that is, over time humans will possess a more complex culture (Lenski, 1966, 1976).

As culture becomes more elaborate, something important happens—any given individual can master less of it. Why? The human mind can learn a limited amount of information. Thus, as culture becomes more complex, it very soon exceeds the capacity of any individual to master all of it.

According to the **evolutionary theory of stratification**, when no single individual can master all aspects of a culture, specialization must occur. That is, individuals will master parts of their culture and enter into exchanges with others who have mastered other parts. In this way the accumulation of culture inevitably leads to a division of labor and therefore to stratification.

Some aspects of culture are more valued than others. That is, people desire or need certain things more than they do other things. As people and groups within a society specialize, some will be able to command higher prices for their goods and services than others. The existence of such inequalities is what is meant by stratification.

Therefore, the accumulation of culture, because it results in cultural specialization, also results in stratification. The notion of replaceability is pertinent in determining the relative advantage of one specialty over another. Indeed, at this point a social evolutionary theory must draw upon functionalism in order to assess how specialties will be valued in the stratification system. Furthermore, as we shall now see, a full understanding of stratification must also incorporate the important insights of conflict theory.

CONFLICT AND STRATIFICATION

Modern conflict theory provides a needed corrective to functionalist theory. Like the functionalists, most conflict theorists accept that stratification is unavoidable (Harris, 1979; Ossowski, 1963; Lenski, 1966). But the **conflict theory of stratification** adds several key insights about how stratification systems are subject to distortion. The first of these concerns how persons high in the stratification system will take advantage of their position to exploit others. This makes societies more stratified than can be accounted for by functionalist theory alone. The second of these insights concerns how the political process can be used to influence the stratification system, particularly by limiting replaceability.

Exploitation

Modern conflict theorists build upon Mosca's third proposition: Humans pursue their own self-interests (Dahrendorf, 1968). It therefore follows that people who are in a position to exploit others will tend to do so. Thus, if societies must be stratified, those on top will use their position to increase their rewards even more. As a result, societies are always more stratified than they need to be (Lenski, 1966).

Let's reexamine our toy society. Ay is functionally irreplaceable, being the only air maker. While Ay alone can provide others with air, he or she can do without the others because Ay can also make water, food, and heat. According to the functionalist theory, inequality occurs in this toy society because it is vital to reward Ay highly in order to ensure that someone will always be able and willing to make air. But conflict theorists point out that Ay is also a monopolist and therefore has immense power. Ay can set a very high price for air, limited only by the fact that if the price is too high, the others will die for lack of food, water, or heat (having given too much to Ay) and therefore will be unable to pay Ay anything at all for air. It follows that Ay can set a higher price on air than would be needed simply to motivate air making. In fact, Ay can get more for air than the minimum price at which he or she would be willing to make air. The difference between the price that Ay actually gets and the minimum price at which Ay would sell air, is **exploitation.**

When we look around at real societies, we frequently see examples of exploitation of this sort. The OPEC nations, for example, banded together to monopolize oil supplies in order to inflate the price of oil far beyond the level needed to motivate people to drill, refine, and sell oil. Similarly, the earnings of physicians would probably have to decline substantially before the number and qualifications of students seeking entry to medical school would also fall. The functionalist theory can explain why doctors earn more than orderlies, but it requires conflict theory to explain why the actual income gap between these two occupations is as large as it is.

The politics of replaceability

Looking once more at our toy society, we can discover another major omission. A monopoly like Ay's is unlikely to occur naturally. Such monopolies usually cannot exist unless power is being exerted to prevent others from competing. Members of the medieval nobility, for example, were able to monopolize the ownership of all land and therefore set the rents that peasants had to pay only because the nobility also monopolized military force. Their monopoly of military force did not occur because they were the only able-bodied men in medieval societies or because they were so much stronger and braver than all other men. It arose because they were the only ones able to possess the most advanced military technology—armor, war horses, and weapons—against which other men were helpless. The nobility prevented other men from receiving military training. Indeed, when the crossbow was invented, it was outlawed because it enabled people with little training and no expensive equipment to attack the noble knights. Thus, coercion was the basis of the knighthood's monopoly. And coercion underlies most (if not all) forms of monopoly.

The implications of this fact are important because they suggest that the principle of replaceability, so central to the functionalist theory, is also subject to distortion—that power may be used to control and manipulate replaceability artificially. This means that political power may be used to exaggerate or minimize the degree of stratification in societies. To examine this possibility, consider two examples of how groups can use power to decrease a position's replaceability artificially: professions and unions.

Professions **Professions** first attempt to establish their positions as irreplaceable and then make their members irreplaceable in the position (Freidson, 1973). The claim to irreplaceability is based on some form of expertise that no other position can per-

form. This tendency to monopoly is a natural outgrowth of the proficiency a position develops (or is thought to have developed).

Consider the medical profession. In the nineteenth century, medical doctors were not very proficient. Not until about the turn of the century were people better off to go to a doctor than not to go, by some estimates. Most treatments and medicines used in the nineteenth century were useless, and some were quite harmful. During this period of limited proficiency, the position of doctor faced serious competition from other positions in performing the function of healing. Other healing practitioners such as osteopaths, homeopaths, food faddists, faith healers, patent medicine sellers, and the like claimed to be able to perform the needed medical function as well as or better than medical doctors. Eventually physicians could demonstrate that their ability to heal was greater than that of people in these other positions. Demands for consumer protection against health frauds intensified, and in the end medical doctors were given a monopoly on the right to prescribe drugs and perform surgery (later the osteopaths joined with the medical doctors).

Once they have a monopoly on expertise and are thus highly irreplaceable, professions tend to seek control over who can fill their positions. In part this is because only they possess the essential knowledge and skills of the position, so they alone can pass them on to others. This, of course, makes it possible for professions to control who and how many enter the professions—and thus to control supply and increase their rewards beyond what successful recruitment would require. That is, doctors can limit the supply of doctors. They can also limit the freedom of nondoctors to perform medical tasks. To the extent that they are successful in limiting supply and preventing competition, doctors increase their irreplaceability, and like Ay, they can force others to pay higher prices for their services.

Unlike the medieval knights, however, professions such as medicine do not possess the means to force other people to do as they are told. Therefore, the monopolies created by professions are always subject to external checks. The government, which possesses a monopoly on the means of force, may refuse to protect a medical monopoly on prescriptions, for example. Or political power may be used to standardize or reduce fees charged by a profession. Or political power may force an increase in the supply of trained members admitted to the profession. If the rewards for being a doctor get too low, the quality and supply of physicians will decline. But if the rewards rise too high, they may be reduced by political decisions that the profession cannot control.

Unions **Unions** are also efforts to create monopolies—to use power to decrease replaceability. To see how unions do this, let us return to our toy society. Suppose our simple four-person society were greatly enlarged and that there were many more Cees and Dees than Ays and Bees. Let us also assume a democratic political process so that the wishes of the Cees and Dees count. It is easy to see that these "lower class" persons might use their collective political power (or even coercive force) to make better bargains with the Ays and Bees. Again, the key to an improved bargaining position depends on how positions can be made less replaceable.

The standard union tactic is to use contracts and laws to prevent other positions from performing the main function of their own position. That is, if Dee can prevent the other three members of our four-person society from producing heat, despite the fact that they could produce it, then his or her position is equal to Ay's.

Craft union rules have precisely this effect. In construction work, for example, union contracts clearly specify what tasks belong to which position, and other positions are barred from performing such tasks. In extreme instances, a crew of carpenters and a crew of plasterers may wait all day for an electrician to come and turn on a switch that any normal adult could have managed. In this way, the actual high replaceability of a position is converted into an artificial state of very low replaceability.

As with professions, the second goal of unions is to control the conditions for entering positions. This is accomplished by mandatory union membership—the closed shop—and entrance and apprenticeship procedures governing membership.

As we shall see in Chapter 10, unionization has been a major force in reducing the exploitive tendencies of stratification in industrialized democracies. For example, the difference in average pay between blue-collar and white-collar workers has been drastically reduced. Thus, the politics of replaceability work not only for business monopolies and the professions but also for factory workers. Indeed, the business monopoly has been subjected to the strictest regulation.

CONCLUSION

In Chapter 4, I suggested that although there are a number of distinctive theoretical schools in macro sociology, to me they seem quite compatible. Here we have seen that each of these theoretical approaches explains something important about stratification that is left unexplained by the others. Functionalist theory explains why various occupational specialties are differentially rewarded—because some workers are much less replaceable than others. Evolutionary theory explains how specialization arises in societies and thus supplements the functionalist theory. Conflict theory adds a vital point—that power will be exploited to increase or decrease stratification, and thus stratification will reflect the outcome of conflicts among groups in a society.

Since the aim of this chapter is to present the conceptual and theoretical tools used by sociologists to analyze stratification, it has necessarily been quite abstract. To apply this material to concrete issues, Chapter 10 examines how stratification systems operate in a variety of human societies.

Review glossary

Means of production Everything, except human labor, that is used to produce wealth. (p. 202)

Bourgeoisie Marx's name for the class made up of those who own the means of production; the employer or owner class. (p. 202)

Proletariat The name that Marx applied to the class made up of those who do not own the means of production; the employee or working class. (p. 202)

Lumpenproletariat Literally, the ragamuffin proletariat; the people on the very bottom of society whom Marx labeled "social scum." (p. 203)

[handwritten note: No one individual master all aspects of culture → specialization occurs]

Class consciousness The concept used by Marx to identify the awareness of members of a class of their class interests and enemies. (p. 203)

False consciousness A term that Marx applied to members of one class who think they have common interests with members of another class. (p. 203)

Property The term used by many sociologists to identify what Weber called *class*. Property includes all economic resources and opportunities owned or controlled by an individual or a group. (p. 205)

Prestige Social honor or respect; synonymous with Weber's term *status*. (p. 206)

Power The ability to get one's way despite the opposition of others. (p. 206)

Status inconsistency A condition in which a person holds a higher position (or status) on one dimension of stratification than on another. For example, an uneducated millionaire displays status inconsistency. (p. 207)

Status inconsistency theories Theories built on the proposition that persons who experience status inconsistency will be frustrated and will, therefore, support political movements aimed at changing the stratification system. (p. 207)

Structural mobility Mobility that occurs because of changes in the relative distribution of upper and lower statuses in a society. (p. 211)

Exchange mobility Mobility that occurs because some people fall, thereby making room for others to rise in the stratification system. (p. 211)

Utopian One who tries to design a perfect society. (p. 211)

Anarchists Followers of a political philosophy that regards the state as inevitably repressive and unjust and who, therefore, propose to destroy the state and live without laws or government. (p. 213)

Functionalist theory of stratification A theory that holds that inequality is built into the roles of any society because some roles are more important and harder to fill, and in order to ensure that the most qualified people will seek to fill the most important positions, it is necessary to reward these positions more highly than others. (p. 214)

Replaceability A measure of the functional importance of a role based on the extent to which other roles can substitute for or take on the duties

[handwritten note: Either the position or occupants are hard to replace]

of that particular role. For example, a doctor can easily substitute for an orderly, but the reverse is not so. (p. 215)

Evolutionary theory of stratification A theory that holds that because culture accumulates in human societies, eventually it happens that no one can master the whole of a group's culture. At that point, cultural specialization, or a division of labor, occurs. Since some specialties will be more valued than others, inequality, or stratification, will exist. (p. 218)

Conflict theory of stratification A theory that holds that individuals and groups will always exploit their positions in an effort to gain a larger share of the rewards in a society, and therefore societies will often be much more stratified than functionalism can explain. Put another way, this theory holds that the stratification system of any society is the result of conflicts and compromises between contending groups. (p. 218)

Exploitation All profit in an exchange in excess of the minimum amount needed to cause an exchange to occur. (p. 218)

Professions Occupational organizations that can prevent their functions from being performed by those not certified as adequately trained and qualified in an extensive body of knowledge and technique. (p. 219)

Unions Occupational organizations that can prevent their functions from being performed by others on the basis of contractual rights. (p. 220)

Suggested readings

Bell, Daniel. *The Coming of Post-Industrial Society.* New York: Basic Books, 1973 (especially Chapter 1).

Bendix, Reinhard, and Seymour Martin Lipset, eds. *Class, Status, and Power,* 2nd ed. New York: Free Press, 1966.

Dahrendorf, Ralf. *Class and Class Conflict in Industrial Society.* Palo Alto: Stanford University Press, 1959.

Freidson, Eliot, ed. *The Professions and Their Prospects.* Beverly Hills: Sage Publications, 1973.

Lenski, Gerhard. *Power and Privilege.* New York: McGraw-Hill, 1966.

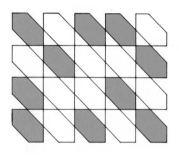

In an old comedy routine, one man asks another, "How's life?" "Compared to what?" is the reply. This piece of foolery reveals the basis of all scientific investigations. Virtually every important question asked by sociologists requires comparisons.

Suppose we ask, "How stratified is the United States?" The first reply must be, "Compared to what?" To answer that question requires us either to compare the United States as it was at several points in its history (thus permitting an answer such as "less stratified than it used to be") or to compare several societies (thus permitting an answer such as "much less stratified than India").

This chapter examines stratification systems by comparing different kinds of societies. In this way, the concepts and theories of stratification covered in the previous chapter can be applied and illustrated.

CHAPTER PREVIEW

We shall examine stratification and social mobility in three major types of societies. First, we shall examine the simplest form of human society: the small band of hunter-gatherers. Next, we shall examine the more complex agrarian societies and see why they are so much more stratified than simple societies. Finally, we shall examine stratification in modern industrial societies. Here we shall focus on the United States.

The way societies are ordered in this chapter—from the least to the most modern—implies social evolution. It is true that agrarian societies developed out of simple hunting and gathering societies and thus appeared later. It is also true that industrial societies grew out of earlier agrarian societies. However, such an evolutionary process is neither inevitable nor uniform. Many, probably most, simple societies did not evolve into agrarian societies—indeed, hunting and gathering societies still exist. Most agrarian societies did not become industrialized—indeed, some began to industrialize and then lapsed back into agrarianism (Chirot, 1976; Wallerstein, 1974). In Part Five we shall examine social change and consider why and how societies evolve or fail to do so. For now, simply keep in mind that the concept of social evolution is surrounded by uncertainties.

SIMPLE SOCIETIES

Societies covering large areas and containing large populations are relatively recent. For most of human history, societies were very small—usually having only about fifty members (Murdock, 1949). Indeed, the largest simple societies rarely exceeded several hundred members, and then only in extremely favorable environments (Kroeber, 1925). These simple societies often wandered over large areas, but the territory they inhabited at any given moment was small.

There were several kinds of simple societies, if we classify them by how they made their living. (I shall use the past tense in describing these societies, but keep in mind that they still exist). The majority were **hunting and gathering societies.** Rather than living in a fixed spot, they moved in search of game and edible plants. Slightly more advanced simple societies lived by herding animals. They, too, moved about as their animals required new grazing areas. Other simple societies mastered elementary gardening, and thus tended to be less nomadic than the herders or the hunter-gatherers. Nevertheless, they tended to stay in one spot only long enough to grow one crop and then moved on. Only about 10 percent of simple societies managed to live in a fixed location (Lenski, 1966).

Both the herding and gardening societies were wealthier than the hunter-gatherers and had a slightly more complex division of labor. Therefore, they also tended to be more stratified. However, because the hunter-gatherer societies represent the most primitive level of human existence, they reveal the most elementary forms of stratification. For this reason, we shall look at them closely.

The major fact of life in hunting and gathering societies was the threat of death. These societies had few members because they could not support more. Traveling on foot, they could not cover much distance in a day. Hence they could only feed the number of members who could survive on the food found within so restricted a range.

They were not very deadly hunters. Most of them probably lacked weapons even as primitive as the bow and arrow and relied instead on stones, clubs, spears, and traps. In part this was because they lacked enough production to support specialists who could develop better weapons (Lenski, 1966). Furthermore, edible vegetation is usually seasonal and in most places not abundant. Because they could not preserve food very well, if at all, they experienced chronic famines and only occasional feasts. Even when meat was abundant, it spoiled quickly, leaving

Eskimos on the move to a new camp site along Coronation Gulf in northern Canada, during the winter of 1911. All hunting and gathering societies are very small, but environmental conditions caused Eskimo societies to be tiny. Danish explorer Knud Rasmussen explained: "It took a large stretch of ground to provide the single individual with the necessities of life; the fewer the hunters the better were the chances, so they migrated along the coasts in little flocks."

the group again without food. Colin Turnbull (1965) has reported that Pygmies in the dense jungle of the Congo deplete an area of fruit and game (scaring more away than they catch) within about a month and then move on.

These simple societies frequently lost the battle to survive. This is evident when we consider how slowly the population of humans on earth grew until historical times. Recent archeological discoveries in Africa indicate that humans existed more than 3 million years ago. Yet only 10,000 years ago, after at least 3 million years of reproduction, it is estimated that there were fewer people on earth than live in New York City today (Davis, 1971; Harris, 1979). Ten thousand years ago the human population was still growing so slowly that it would have taken another

60,000 years to double in size. Today the world's population is doubling about every thirty-seven years, and our problem is not too few but too many people. Population growth was the result of increased food production, which widened the margin of survival enough to insure against constant crises and an appalling death rate. For most of our time on earth, however, the constant problem was simply to survive.

Under such circumstances human societies were not very stratified in terms of property. (Harris, 1979). Possessions were limited to what could be carried from place to place. Since there was never much more than enough wealth to go around, the wealthiest could accumulate very little more than the poorest. Furthermore, with very little role specialization—no full-time leaders, for example—power was also greatly equalized (Fried, 1967; Harris, 1979). Indeed, the ability to coerce others was quite limited and thus provided little basis for power. If, for example, some hunters began forcing others to give them their game, there was little to prevent those being exploited from deserting the band. Nor could the strongest hope to live merely by taking from others because unless everyone worked hard at getting food, survival was jeopardized. If you cannot produce more than enough for yourself, you cannot be exploited easily.

However, hunting and gathering societies were nevertheless stratified to a significant degree. Usually the primary bases for stratification were age and sex (van den Berghe, 1973). Adults held power over children, and men dominated women. Biology forced women into subordinate positions in premodern societies, for women were physically smaller and were pregnant or nursing much of the time. Men did the hunting and fighting and therefore dominated the political decision making of the group because the major decisions tended to involve male specialties: when and where to move in pursuit of game and how to respond to danger from predators, both animal and human (Harris, 1979; Leacock, 1978).

However, within age and sex groups, simple societies were not very stratified. Men were essentially equal in terms of possessions and political power, as were women. Stratification within each sex was based mainly on achievement. Some men dominated others because they were bigger or smarter, better hunters or braver fighters, or more persuasive in group decision making. These distinctions showed up as differences in prestige and power rather than in material inequalities. Similarly, among women, prestige differences on the basis of skill at domestic tasks, wisdom, persuasiveness, fertility, and perhaps physical appearance undoubtedly existed.

The rule seems to be that the smaller, poorer, and less secure a human society is, the less it is stratified. Universal poverty was the basis of equality among hunters and gatherers. But as soon as humans became more productive and better organized, their societies became more unequal. Herding societies and simple horticultural (gardening) societies were more stratified than hunter-gatherer societies. When humans finally settled in one place and began to grow crops, inequality increased enormously (Har-

ris, 1979; Cohen, 1977). Suddenly gaps in status appeared as great as those between slaves laboring in a field and emperors living opulently in palaces.

AGRARIAN SOCIETIES

The development of agriculture changed the world (Pfeiffer, 1977). No longer did humans wander the earth eking out a hand-to-mouth existence. They were able to settle in permanent locations and therefore could construct better shelters and accumulate possessions. More importantly, life ceased to be a constant struggle to find food.

As time passed, the technology of agriculture improved. With each improvement, human society became more complex. The basis for this growing complexity was surplus food production. When a family could produce enough food to feed others as well as themselves, two new social phenomena became possible: *specialization* and *cities*.

So long as everyone had to take part in the quest for food, no one could devote full time to other pursuits. Thus, during most of human existence, there were no full-time priests, political leaders, or other specialists. But when farmers could produce some surplus, others could be supported who made their shoes, forged their tools, conducted their religious ceremonies, and guided their political affairs. Furthermore, people not needed for food production could congregate in a central place and thus create cities.

Production, surplus, and specialization

With the invention of plows and effective animal harnesses, agricultural productivity became so great that some people were freed from farming. At that point **agrarian societies** appeared, some of which became great empires and perhaps the first real human civilizations. However, the number of persons who didn't farm, even in the most advanced

Nomadic societies lack possessions because of the constant need to move on. If you cannot own more than you can carry with you, you will never have very much. Here we see the women and children of a nomadic African society moving across a barren waste. They own nothing but what they are wearing on their backs or balancing on their heads.

agrarian societies, was not really that large. Gideon Sjoberg (1960) estimates that no agrarian society had fewer than 90 percent of its members engaged in farming, and usually 95 percent were needed. Still, even by freeing one in twenty from farming, people could pursue a great variety of specialized tasks and produce an elaborate social structure.

It is important to realize that the famous cities of historical agrarian societies were not very big by modern standards (see Chapter 18). In fact, even by 1800, when industrialization was already well under way, fewer than fifty cities in the world had more than 100,000 residents (Davis, 1955). Nevertheless, they were cities, not farming villages, because the residents did not grow their own food. Until agriculture became relatively efficient, there were no cities at all.

Improved agriculture produced something else new in human affairs: warfare. Hunter-gatherers sometimes chased others off their hunting territory or raided another band for wives, but such conflicts were infrequent because nobody had anything worth taking. Even the fighting that did occur was usually very stylized and had only limited goals, such as causing the other side to run away. The number of fighters involved was small, and casualties were light. Many groups placed more importance on "counting coup"—touching an enemy during battle—than on killing.

With the rise of agrarian societies, all this changed. Such societies were worth raiding after harvest time to steal their crops, and many nomadic bands adopted a way of life based on raiding agricultural societies. Agricultural societies were also worth raiding to take their land or to seize control of the surplus produced by their peasants.

Agrarian societies lived in a chronic state of warfare. In a historical survey of eleven European nations during their centuries as agrarian societies, Pitirim Sorokin (1937) computed that they had been at war 46 percent of the time. Lenski (1966) reports that Sorokin's figures are probably too low because he ignored many minor conflicts. Marc Bloch (1962) characterized agrarian European history as "the state of perpetual war." As we shall see, constant warfare contributed to the extreme stratification of agrarian societies.

In the agrarian society we can first apply Marx's notions about the ownership of the means of production. In simple societies the means of production were primarily physical and therefore personal. But when the means of production are material things, they can be conceived of as property. Fields are different from land that is simply out there to travel over in search of game; fields must be cleared, planted, cultivated, and harvested. Thus, the question arises: Whose field? The answer to that question determines who is rich and who is not. In addition to land, many other forms of potential property existed, such as farming tools, livestock, seed, permanent houses, and the food stored up from the last harvest. Because wealth was substantial, some people became much wealthier than others (Harris, 1979).

The increased wealth of agrarian societies combined with (and permitted) a complex division of labor that produced even greater stratification. We have seen that it is hard for one hunter to be much wealthier than another. But, as Chapter 9 demonstrated, persons in a particular occupation can have bargaining advantages over persons in other occupations. Since durable wealth existed in agrarian societies, bargaining advantages could be stored up to produce increasingly greater inequalities.

Indeed, because human labor in agrarian societies was so productive, other humans could be exploited. When people can barely produce enough to feed and clothe themselves, others cannot live off their labor. But in agrarian societies, a few could live off the labor of many. This capacity for labor to produce surplus—that is, for peasants to grow more food than they required to live—was the basis for the marked inequalities found in such societies.

Indeed, the ability to produce a surplus raises the possibility of *humans becoming property*. When labor produces little or no surplus, there is no profit in owning another person. But when labor produces surplus, then by owning another person one can possess all of the surplus that the other person can produce. In fact, when people are sufficiently productive, they can support those whose task it is to keep them enslaved. With the emergence of slavery, the human being became a means of production.

Even very primitive agriculture made human societies incredibly richer than before. Here we see people in Senegal grinding wheat in a way little different from that used thousands of years ago by the earliest agrarians. In addition to giving them a reliable food supply, agriculture makes it possible for them to have the large houses that can be seen in the background and a great many possessions beyond the means of hunting and gathering societies.

The production of surplus also makes government possible. Full-time specialists who coordinate the activities of societies can be supported. Thus, at the apex of every agrarian society was a ruling elite whose members "neither spin nor reap" but who lived by extracting surplus production in the form of taxes and tributes from the peasants.

Soon agrarian societies produced sufficient wealth so that ruling elites could live in immense splendor. In medieval society feasting was a major social activity for the wealthy, and the amounts sometimes consumed seem extraordinary. For example, when a new Prior of Canterbury was installed in 1309, his guests consumed 36 oxen, 100 hogs, 200 piglets, 200 sheep, 1,000 geese, 793 chickens, 24 swans, 600 rabbits, 9,600 eggs, and huge amounts of bread and wine. Needless to say, the Prior's peasants had to tighten their belts that winter while their flocks and herds recovered.

Military domination

In agrarian societies, the elite held power by dominating the military force. The production of surplus also made this possible by enabling some members of society to become soldiers and to specialize in developing and using military technology. As these specialists began to appear, a gap opened between the military capacity of the average man and that of the specialist soldier. Marc Bloch (1962) pointed out that so long as the average male citizen is a potential soldier who lacks nothing "essential in his equip-ment," he can resist being exploited. In simple societies, the weapons of war were much like those used for hunting, and all able-bodied adult males were therefore armed and capable of battle.

But with surplus production the means of warfare became specialized and differed from hunting weapons. Soon a special group of men existed who had been trained from childhood in the tactics and techniques of fighting and who possessed superior weapons and equipment for fighting. The medieval peasant, armed with a hayhook, an axe, or a knife, was simply no match for the heavily armored knight.

A great deal of wealth was needed to equip one knight with armor, lance, long sword, and an adequate horse (see Special Topic 3). Thus, surplus provides the conditions necessary for a ruling class to monopolize military capacity (Lenski, 1966).

Because agrarian societies were based on military rule, they also tended to be expansionist. Armies are expensive to maintain, even when they are not fighting. Rulers therefore often paid for their armies by having them seize or plunder neighboring peoples—hence the chronic warfare found in such societies. Moreover, chronic warfare also centralized power within the ruling elite, who surrendered power to a king or an emperor (Lenski, 1966).

Culture and ascription

Often ruling elites did not evolve within agrarian societies but were imposed from without. Frequently a group of nomadic raiders, who lived by repeatedly plundering a farming region, would decide to settle down and become permanent exploiters of the region by ruling over it and gathering taxes. For this reason, ruling elites in agrarian societies were often of a different ethnic background and occasionally spoke a different language than their subjects. Thus, cultural differences reinforced stratification: Those on the bottom had to cross a cultural as well as an economic barrier to rise in the system.

Moreover, even if the ruling elite was not a different ethnic group, cultural differences between them and their subjects soon appeared. A major difference between any elite and the masses is leisure. The rise of civilization—the development of an elaborate culture—is rooted in the existence of a leisure class (Veblen, 1899).

People who tilled the fields or dug in mines from dawn until dusk had little time to study the heavens, compose poems, pursue theology, or invent new tools. Such activities require spare time, which can only be provided by surplus production that frees people from labor. The elite alone had leisure and were therefore the primary creators of culture. Because they created culture, the ruling elites developed a culture much more elaborate than the culture of those whom they ruled.

The most visible cultural differences between the elite and the masses involved speech, etiquette, protocol, and even body language (Braudel, 1981). Thus, the leisure of the elite was translated into a huge array of interaction cues that strongly influenced how prestige was displayed, protected, and passed on. A peasant who donned fine clothes and attempted to impersonate a gentleman had little chance of succeeding. He would talk wrong, walk wrong, and act wrong. The cultural barrier between the elite and the masses made it virtually impossible for a person not born and raised in the elite to fit in, even if she or he somehow managed to achieve high rank. This cultural wall not only severely limited upward mobility but also restricted contact between the elite and the masses, thus widening the gap between them. Indeed, in agrarian societies the elite often came to believe that it belonged to a superior human species.

As a result of these factors, agrarian societies were extraordinarily stratified. The overwhelming majority toiled endlessly and had but the barest necessities of life. Braudel (1981) reported that in agrarian societies around the world the peasants were (and are) physically stunted by their meager diets. These usually consisted of nothing but boiled grain (rice, wheat, oats, or corn) or bread and vegetables in season. Meat and dairy products were the rarest luxuries. Indeed, the dramatic change in diet resulting from industrialization was the primary reason for the marked changes in the size and age of maturation of humans, discussed in Chapter 5. Peasants in agrarian societies had to work very hard and received very little, and their lives were restricted. Sometimes they were slaves. Usually they were bound by law and custom to remain on the land where they were born and accept their lot.

Above the huge mass of peasants in agrarian societies were artisans and merchants, who were well-off by comparison but who had little power, property, or prestige compared with the nobility—the actual ruling elite. The elite was a tiny proportion of the overall population, rarely more than 2 percent and usually much less (Lenski, 1966). At the apex of the elite was a king or an emperor, surrounded by a splendid court, who possessed

The productivity gains made possible by the invention of agriculture had the ironic consequence of making possible extreme levels of exploitation, including slavery. Egyptian slaves like these depicted in a pharaoh's tomb, could be held in bondage because they could produce an economic surplus—a surplus that made it possible and worthwhile to enslave them.

immense power and incredible wealth. The ruler took as much as one-fourth of the society's production, and the ruling elite as a whole may have had as much as half (Lenski, 1966). Thus, while poor people in industrial societies are far richer than average people in agrarian societies, the most powerful people in agrarian societies are far wealthier than the richest members of industrial societies. No person in the United States has the wealth that an average Egyptian pharaoh took with him to his tomb, to say nothing of the many palaces staffed by thousands of servants he left behind. And Catherine the Great of Russia personally owned about 27 million serfs—peasants held in virtual slavery who farmed her immense estates. The most successful agrarian societies of history—ancient Egypt, Rome, Byzan- tium, Persia, China, the Inca and Aztec empires, and the nations of medieval Europe—were the most highly stratified societies in the history of the world.

INDUSTRIAL SOCIETIES

The historical succession of human societies clearly shows that whenever human beings are able to produce more, their societies became more unequal. The hunting and gathering nomads had almost nothing and were relatively egalitarian. Simple gardening technology increased the degree of stratification. As fields grew larger and life became more secure, the gap between those on the bottom and those on top became immense. Undoubtedly the conditions of life of the average person improved as societies became more complex; even though most of their crop was taken from them, medieval peasants ate and lived better than hunter-gatherers (Braudel, 1981). But the life of the average person became progressively inferior to the life of the powerful. Ironically, the more productive human labor became, the more that laborers could "pay" someone to oppress and exploit them.

Thus, it is not surprising that nineteenth-century scholars expected that the staggering increases in productivity made possible by industrialization would make societies even more stratified. Marx, for one, predicted that the ruling class would become ever smaller and ever richer, while everyone else was crushed into the proletariat. He believed that wages would fall to the lowest possible level and lead to industrial slavery: masses of workers forced to toil at their machines in return for but the barest essentials. But it didn't turn out that way.

The trend toward greater stratification in response to greater productivity suddenly reversed itself. Instead of all but a few being crushed into the lowest working class, the middle classes expanded rapidly and unskilled labor jobs began to disappear. The gap in the standard of living between the top and bottom levels of society narrowed. Welfare programs were instituted to place a "safety net" under society to prevent privation. Social mobility greatly increased. Thus, status was based much less on ascription than on achievement.

Why did these changes occur? And what does the stratification system look like in modern industrial societies? To answer these questions, we shall examine the American stratification system, partly because it has been the most exhaustively studied and partly because the basic aspects of stratification in democratic nations are quite similar.

Industrialization and stratification

To explain why industrialization led to less stratification, we must combine insights from functionalist and conflict theories of stratification, as summarized

in Chapter 9. Industrialization caused two major social changes that reduced stratification.

The first is that industrialization raised the level of skill and training required to perform the average job (Lipset and Bendix, 1959; Wallerstein, 1974). Or, as Peter Drucker (1969) put it, **industrial societies** are not based on getting people to work harder, but to "work smarter." Men with picks and shovels undoubtedly work much harder to build a road than men who drive bulldozers, but by working smarter rather than harder, one bulldozer driver does the work of hundreds of hand laborers. This in fact is what the term **industrialization** means: using technology to make work much more productive.

However, industrialization changed more than tools and work techniques. It also changed the skills needed to do the work. For example, illiterates can do an excellent job of shoveling dirt. Nor do shovelers need to know any arithmetic. They also need no special training to use their tools or maintain them. This is not true for bulldozer operators. They need to be able to read and follow directions on how much dirt to remove and where to put it. They need training to operate their machines skillfully and to maintain and repair them.

To the extent that occupational positions require education and training they are *less replaceable*. Men employed to shovel dirt can easily be substituted for men employed to hoe fields, but a bulldozer driver cannot be replaced so easily by operators of modern farm machines. It follows from the functionalist theory of stratification that as positions become less replaceable, their relative rewards increase.

In the long run, industrialization has made the average worker less replaceable. Compared with workers in agrarian societies, a much greater investment of time and money must be expended to prepare the average industrial worker for his or her job. Not until industrialization changed the nature of work did any society attempt to teach everyone to read, write, and do arithmetic. Indeed, technological societies like the United States can exist only with an educated labor force. As a result, the average worker can produce much more than before. More importantly, the training necessary to do most jobs has enabled workers to demand a higher level of reward.

*In modern industrial societies there has been a rapid trend toward more complex and skilled jobs, while unskilled jobs have been disappearing. The result has been to make the average worker **less replaceable** and therefore to decrease the wage differentials across jobs.*

This leads to a second consequence of industrialization: The average worker is more powerful and thus more able to resist coercion. As a result, wages and profits are determined by bargaining rather than by force. In agrarian societies, force or the threat of force could be used to get people to work hard. For example, overseers with whips could keep slaves busy digging ditches. But it is much more difficult to force people to work smarter—slaves did not seek ways to be more productive. Moreover, as members of a society are educated and trained, it becomes increasingly costly to coerce them, because education inevitably increases awareness and raises

aspirations (Lipset and Bendix, 1959). For this reason, it was illegal to educate blacks in many parts of the South before the Civil War (Sowell, 1978).

Industrialization has gone hand in hand with the rise of democracy. As we shall see in Chapter 16, some social theorists argue that economic exploitation by the ruling elite had to be curtailed for industrialization to occur; thus, democratization caused the Industrial Revolution. Even if this argument is not valid, industrialization clearly caused the proliferation of democracy—for example, it greatly expanded the proportion of the population allowed to vote. As the gap in skill and training required of average jobs and the most demanding jobs has decreased, so have the differences in power between the members of these occupations.

According to conflict theory, people exploit their power to influence their rewards. Thus, as large sectors of the population in industrialized societies became more powerful, they demanded a larger share of the economic pie. Let us recall the toy society discussed in Chapter 9. There we saw that under conditions of political freedom, the Cees and the Dees could use their numbers to obtain a better bargain with the Ays and the Bees. Thus, the decrease in stratification in industrialized societies can be seen as the outcome of ongoing conflict over who will get what. For example, automobile factory workers receive a lower wage than they would like but higher than management would like to pay. Both sides compromise on the basis of the relative costs of a strike.

To sum up, industrialization could yield incredible levels of production only by changing the nature of work. Thus, it not only led to an immense rise in the possible level of living for the average person, it also made such a rise necessary. Because in order for the average worker to become so much more productive, he or she had to receive far more education and training. This, in turn, made the average worker much less replaceable and hence more powerful. Thus it became necessary to satisfy workers' demands for a larger share.

Keep in mind that this does *not* mean that industrialized societies are unstratified. The rich and the poor, the powerful and the weak, the famous and the unknown exist in all societies. What distinguishes industrialized from agrarian societies are two things: first, industrialized societies are less stratified—there is a smaller gap between the top and the bottom; second even the poor in industrialized societies are better off than even rather well-off people in agrarian societies. Thus, with the rise of industrial societies, for the first time since humans settled down and began to build complex civiliations, the trend toward increased social inequality was reversed.

Industrialization did more than simply reduce stratification; it also dramatically changed the *rules* governing stratification. Status was no longer primarily ascriptive but came to depend more on achievement. This change stimulated (and was stimulated by) social mobility. Indeed, to really understand stratification systems in industrial nations, the best thing to study is social mobility: How common is it for people to rise or fall in the stratification system and why and how do they do so?

Social mobility in industrialized nations

Historically, America has been regarded as the land of opportunity, where hard work could lead to success regardless of family background. Alexis de Tocqueville, a French aristocrat who visited the United States during the 1830s and wrote the classic study *Democracy in America* (1835), was surprised not only that Americans frequently achieved great wealth and power despite humble beginnings, but also that they were proud to have done so. In Europe, Tocqueville noted, people who had been upwardly mobile tried to hide their humble origins. Tocqueville, like nearly all other observers, assumed that upward mobility was unusually common in the United States compared with other industrializing nations.

During the 1930s and 1940s, American sociologists began research on social mobility and found that indeed many Americans did rise above their social origins, while others were downwardly mobile. But was this a high rate of mobility? Any answer required a *comparison,* and studies comparing social mobility in America with that in other countries were lacking. Let us watch as two sociologists pioneered comparative studies of social mobility, thereby opening issues to which an immense amount of research has been directed ever since.

Lipset and Bendix: comparative social mobility

 In the 1950s Seymour Martin Lipset and Reinhard Bendix, two sociologists at the University of California at Berkeley, set out to see how much social mobility there really was in the United States compared with other industrial nations. Such a study had only just become possible because of the spread of public opinion polling to many industrial nations after World War II. Often these studies asked respondents their occupation and sometimes the question "What was your father's occupation?" (Until very recently, because so many women did not work or held only short-term employment, mobility studies covered only males.)

Thus, Lipset and Bendix (1959) collected opinion poll studies from a number of industrialized nations and calculated for each nation the proportion of sons whose occupations were of higher status than the occupations of their fathers and vice versa. This allowed them to compare the rates of upward and downward mobility for these nations.

They found a great amount of social mobility in *all* the industrialized democracies studied. In fact, the total amount of social mobility was virtually identical (see Figure 10-1). These findings seemed to refute the widespread belief that the United States has an unusually open stratification system. Thus, Lipset and Bendix concluded that the interesting question was not why there was so much social mobility in the United States but why there was so much mobility in all of these societies despite great differences in their cultures and social histories.

Lipset and Bendix argued that status based on individual achievement is inherent in the technological demands of industrial societies. Efficiency is the dominant concern in these societies, and therefore inept offspring of successful parents are necessarily displaced downward by more talented people moving up from below.

Also, a great deal of the upward mobility Bendix and Lipset observed in these societies is *structural mobility*. That is, industrialization has caused a great increase in the proportion of higher-status occupations and a corresponding decrease in lower-status occupations. As we saw in Chapter 9, when this occurs, many people must be upwardly mobile just to fill the demand. Figure 10-1 reveals that in the societies studied by Lipset and Bendix, a much larger proportion of people has risen than has fallen in occupational status.

When structural change forces a great deal of upward mobility, people's attitudes are likely to change. That is, when upward mobility is common

Alexis de Tocqueville.

and not at the expense of people born into high-status families, it is hard to oppose it or to discriminate against those who have risen.

But if America does not have an unusual amount of mobility, Lipset and Bendix did find that industrial nations do differ in the amount of exchange mobility. Recall that exchange mobility occurs when someone born to high status falls and thus makes a place into which someone of low status can rise. The United States has considerably more exchange mobility than many other nations. While structural mobility may only reflect industrialization, exchange mobility reflects openness of opportunity. That is, not only can people rise through merit, but they can also fall for lack of merit. By this standard, the United States has a relatively open stratification system.

As pioneers, Lipset and Bendix had to conduct their research with serious limitations. Lacking large samples, they were limited to very crude measures of social mobility. They were forced to define mobility as movement between only two general levels of

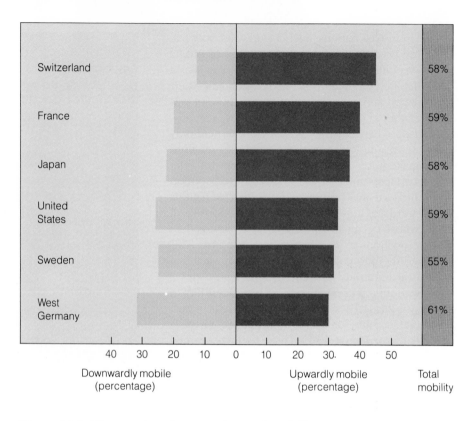

Figure 10-1 / International comparisons of mobility.

These data, gathered and published by Lipset and Bendix (1958), show why they concluded that high rates of mobility are characteristic of industrialized nations in general, not just the United States. There is little difference in the total amount of mobility they found in these six nations, but there are significant differences in the amount of downward mobility, with Germany being higher than others and Switzerland being lower. Later research showed, however, that the United States does differ from other industrial nations in its rate of long-range (rags-to-riches) upward mobility.

occupations: persons holding white-collar (or non-manual) jobs and those holding blue-collar (or manual) jobs. A man was scored as upwardly mobile if his father had been a factory worker and he was an office clerk. Thus, small differences between the occupations of a father and his son could register as upward mobility. These crude measures also prevented Lipset and Bendix from assessing dramatic changes in status.

Lipset and Bendix also stimulated renewed research on why and how people achieve their occupational status in the United States. A number of ambitious studies were launched, including a massive effort by William H. Sewell to follow a sample of more than 10,000 Wisconsin high school students over the course of their working lives (Sewell, 1964; Sewell, Hauser, and Wolf, 1980). This research has found that education is the major determinant of occupational status, while, as we shall see, family background is of only modest importance. However, many sociologists continue to be interested in comparative mobility, especially in whether the United States might differ from most other nations in terms of "long distance," rags-to-riches mobility.

Blau and Duncan: long distance mobility

 In time, more precise data on mobility in industrial nations became available. By the late 1960s, it was possible to examine movement across more detailed occupational categories, such as unskilled laborer to manager, than Lipset and Bendix had been able to study.

Thus, Peter M. Blau and Otis Dudley Duncan (1967) were able to test the hypothesis that the United States has an unusually open stratification system in terms of great changes in occupational status. **Long distance mobility** is not moving from the lower rungs of the occupational structure to the middle, as when a ditch digger's son becomes a store clerk. Instead, it is going all the way from the bottom to the top in one generation, as when the son of a janitor becomes head of the New York Stock Exchange.

Blau and Duncan confirmed the hypothesis that Americans do have a *very* unusually high rate of long distance mobility. In fact, they found that in the United States, 1 out of every 10 sons of manual laborers ends up in an elite managerial professional occupation. By comparison, only 1 Italian in 300 makes such an upward leap, 1 Dane in 100, 1 Frenchman in 67, and 1 Swede in 30. Thus, it is not upward mobility per se but the possibility of going all the way to the top that separates Americans of humble origins from their European counterparts. Only Japan, where 1 person in 14 rises from bottom to top, approaches the American pattern.

This also helps to explain what Tocqueville observed more than a century ago. A substantial proportion of the most successful people in America have made the leap from the bottom to the top of the occupational ladder. Since many more people are in humble positions than in elite ones, if 10 percent of these people achieve elite positions, they will constitute much more than 10 percent of all those holding such positions.

A recent study of the American business elite—presidents, board chairmen, and senior vice presidents of the 600 largest industrial corporations—confirmed Blau and Duncan's findings on long distance mobility. Only one of ten of these top executives came from a wealthy home, while more than a third had risen from very humble families (Lipset, 1976). Since so few of the most successful Americans claim high status origins, there should be little wonder that no effort is made to hide humble origins. Indeed, the most obvious basis for bragging is to emphasize how far one has come—a common American trait that Tocqueville found so unusual.

Jencks: family and mobility

 Whereas most research on social mobility has examined fathers and sons, a particularly interesting variation involved comparisons of brothers. Christopher Jencks and his colleagues (1972) reasoned that if family background is an important factor in where people end up in the stratification system, then brothers ought to have much more similar incomes and occupational achievement than pairs of men selected at random from the U.S. population. That is, sons of the same parents, raised in the same home, ought to gain equal advantage or disadvantage in life. Most sociologists, in fact most Americans, probably expected that Jencks would find considerable similarity among brothers in this regard.

But that is not what Jencks found. Instead, his results showed:

There is nearly as much economic inequality among brothers raised in the same homes as in the general population. This means that inequality is recreated anew in each generation, even among people who start life in essentially identical circumstances.

Using a measure of occupational prestige developed by Blau and Duncan (1967), Jencks found that the prestige of randomly selected pairs of men differed by an average of 28 points (on a 97-point scale). In comparison, the occupational prestige scores of brothers differed by an average of 23 points. The difference between the two averages is slight. Furthermore, using data collected in 1968, Jencks selected groups of two men at random and compared their incomes, finding that the average difference was $6,200 a year. He then compared the incomes of his sample of brothers and found an average difference of $5,600 a year. Again, the differences between brothers is close to that for random pairs of men. Thus, brothers who grow up in the same home end up nearly as different in terms of their occupations and incomes as unrelated men who grow up in different homes.

Thus, family background does not seem very important in determining success. Not only is there a great deal of upward and downward mobility, but brothers end up about as unequal as people in the population generally. What small influence family background does have on success appears limited to how much education people complete. Blau and Duncan (1967) found that people with the same amount of education have similar levels of success, regardless of their father's occupation. In Chapter 15 we shall pursue at length the immense role of education in determining occupational success and therefore income. Here it is worth noting that two major factors in the extensive social mobility found in industrial nations are easy access to schools and colleges and the reliance on education to place people in the occupational structure.

But if the occupational achievements of brothers are not much alike, the same does not apply to husbands and wives. Michael Hout (1982) found that couples who both work full-time are very likely to hold jobs of a quite similar prestige level. That is, men who work in factories tend to have wives who do also, while professionals also tend to marry one another.

That couples tend to hold similar jobs is not surprising. The two most usual places for married couples to have met are in school or at work. Hence married couples tend to be similar in education, and people who meet at work tend to hold similar jobs. In addition, when one partner in a marriage is much more successful than the other, the probability of divorce is increased.

However, we must qualify the image of America as a society where status rests on individual achievement. Not all Americans have been free of ascribed status roles. Until very recently, discrimination excluded blacks from most of the better jobs. In the next chapter we shall examine this matter in depth.

In a somewhat different fashion, women were long excluded from many occupations. In Special Topic 2 we examined how sex-role socialization discouraged women from seeking careers and from pursuing "male" activities and encouraged men to exclude women from many occupations.

CONCLUSION

Chapter 9 presented the basic concepts and theories used by sociologists to understand stratification. In this chapter we have used these concepts and theories to examine how stratification systems work in different societies. Thus, we have seen that the relative lack of stratification among primitive hunter-gatherers was an equality of poverty. The rise of civilization and the rise of social inequalities went hand in hand. As societies became more productive and complex, the masses of humanity were increasingly exploited by a tiny elite. But this trend was reversed with the advent of modern industrial societies, despite expectations that these would become the most stratified societies in history.

We have also seen that industrialization increased the skills required for most occupations and therefore decreased the replaceability of the average worker. This improved the bargaining position of the average worker and led to a reduction in inequalities. Moreover, the development of democracy in industrial societies has severely limited the ability of the elites to use force to exploit others. In this way, status based on ascription has given way to status based on achievement in industrial societies.

But these changes have not affected everyone in these societies, at least not at the same time. Thus, while some people can achieve high status, others continue to be ascribed a low status, especially those who belonged to certain racial or ethnic groups. Therefore, in the next chapter we shall apply principles of stratification and an understanding of stratification systems in modern industrial nations to analyze ethnic and racial conflict.

Review glossary

Hunting and gathering societies The most primitive human societies; their rather small numbers of members (often less than 50) live by wandering in pursuit of animal and plant food. (p. 223)

Agrarian societies Societies that live by farming. Although these were the first societies able to support cities, they usually require that about 95 percent of the population be engaged in agriculture. (p. 225)

Industrial societies Societies with economies based on manufacturing in which machines perform most of the heavy labor. (p. 232)

Industrialization The process by which technology is substituted for manual labor as the basis of production. (p. 232)

Long distance mobility Mobility that occurs when an individual or group rises from the bottom to the top of the stratification system. (p. 237)

Suggested readings

Blau, Peter M., and Otis Dudley Duncan. *The American Occupational Structure*. New York: Wiley, 1967.

Bloch, Marc. *Feudal Society*. Chicago: University of Chicago Press, 1962.

Giddens, Anthony. *The Class Structure of Advanced Societies*. New York: Harper and Row, 1975.

Jencks, Christopher, et al. *Inequality: A Reassessment of the Effects of Family and Schooling in America*. New York: Basic Books, 1972.

Pfeiffer, John E. *The Emergence of Society*. New York: McGraw-Hill, 1977.

work smarter not harder
are less stratified
→ smaller gap between
top & bottom

Stirrups and Feudal Domination

Stratification in agrarian societies arose from the ability of the elite to monopolize military capabilities. As Chapter 10 explained, when the weapons of war are like those for hunting, and when the average man has both the training and the essential equipment for going to war, the ability of the elite to coerce him is very limited. The immense inequalities of agrarian societies arose as a group of specialists in waging war emerged. In medieval European societies, this military monopoly arose as the unexpected consequence of a very small technical innovation—the stirrup.

After the fall of the Roman Empire, western Europe was a collection of tribal kingdoms that were not very stratified. One such tribe was the Franks, whose territory included most of modern France. Like the other tribal kingdoms, Frankish society was composed largely of free and independent farmers. When war came, all able-bodied men took their shields, swords, and spears and formed a huge host of infantry (Figure 1). They wore no armor and depended on their number and high morale to gain victory. They were part-time farmer-soldiers. As such, they could resist not only invaders but also their king.

Then came the stirrup. Until the seventh century, horse saddles did not have stirrups. Without stirrups, a mounted soldier is handicapped; he can use only the strength of his arm, not the full weight of rider and horse, to deliver a blow. Thus cavalry was little used. The Romans, for example, used mounted soldiers only for scouting duties and the pursuit of fleeing enemies (see Figure 2). With stirrups, however, a rider is much more securely seated and can smash a lance into a target with the full force of a galloping horse.

Late in the sixth century, the stirrup reached

Figure 1 / The Frankish host.

As depicted here in the Utrecht Psalter, the Frankish host was formed of all able-bodied males. The host was a mass of lightly armed infantry. Agathias, an historian who wrote during the middle of the sixth century, gave this description of the Frankish host:

> The arms of the Franks are very rude; they wear neither mail-shirt nor greaves, and their legs are only protected by strips of linen or leather. They have hardly any horsemen, but their foot-soldiery are bold and well practised in war. They bear swords and shields, but never use ... the bow. Their missiles are axes and barbed javelins. These last are not very long, they can be used either to cast or to stab.

Europe from China (White, 1962). Soon a few mounted Franks began to show up for battle armed with long lances. As these mounted tactics evolved, defenses also evolved. For protection against the lances, riders began to wear heavier armor. This required them to ride very big, strong horses. Soon the knight in armor had come into being, but only in very small numbers.

During the seventh century, a few of the very richest Franks began to report for military duty wearing armor and mounted on horses. The rest came on foot as always. Possibly the first charge by knights took place in a battle between the Franks and the Saxons in 626 (Montgomery, 1968). But it was another century before the real military supe-

riority of the knights was recognized. In 733 Charles Martel led the Frankish host against the invading Saracens, Moslems who had conquered Spain and sought to push their rule north. At the Battle of Tours, the Franks routed the Saracens and pushed them back across the mountains into Spain. The turning point in the battle came when the Saracen ranks collapsed under the weight of a thundering charge by mounted knights. Lacking stirrups, the mounted Saracens could not withstand the lance attack (Figure 3). Victory convinced Charles Martel that knights held the key to military supremacy. He began to transform the Frankist host from an army of foot soldiers to an army of armored cavalry.

This ended the importance of farmer-soldiers in

Figure 2 / Roman cavalry.

As can be seen in this classic statue, the Roman cavalry had no stirrups. A mounted soldier like this one could strike only with the strength of his arm. Had he tried to charge with a lance, he would have been vaulted off his horse because he could not brace his feet.

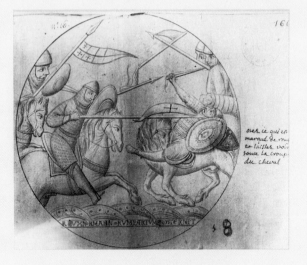

Figure 3 / Frankish knights.

Here Frankish knights, braced in their new stirrups and wearing protective chain mail armor, sweep over Saracen horsemen, as shown in the stained glass choir windows of St. Denis Abbey. The Saracen rider on the right has no stirrups; his sword and shield are useless against the long lance of the Frankish knight.

Frankish military operations. They could not afford to arm as knights. History records that in 761 a Frank named Isanhard "sold his ancestral lands and a slave for a horse and a sword" (White, 1962). To buy weapons and a suit of armor in the eighth century cost the equivalent of twenty oxen, enough for ten plow teams, at a time when only well-to-do farmers owned such a team. Moreover, a knight needed an unusually big, fast, well-trained horse—a horse, as Field Marshal Montgomery (1968) put it,

strong enough to carry him when fully-armed, sufficiently trained not to bolt or panic in battles, and fast enough to take part in a charge at full gallop. Such a horse had to be specially bred and trained.

The famous breeds of huge horses that appear today in ads pulling beer wagons were not developed to pull loads but to carry knights wearing armor so heavy that they had to be hoisted up by a derrick and lowered onto the saddle (Figure 4). Moreover, a knight could not go off to war with only one horse; he needed spare mounts. He also needed someone to hold his spare mounts during the battle, to help him get into his armor, to hoist him onto his horse, and to transport his supplies. Thus, each knight needed a retinue of aides and servants. These people also had to have mounts and some weapons. Furthermore, horses must be fed grain, not just grass. It required the grain crop of several peasant farms to feed one war-horse for a year. Finally, it took years of training to learn to fight as a mounted knight. Knights had to be free to dedicate their lives to military training from early childhood, freedom only a few could have (White, 1962).

To have an army of knights required the transformation of Frankish society. Few could afford to be knights, and even a king could not afford to equip

Figure 4 / Knighthood in full flower.

Both horse and rider wear heavy, elaborate armor in this display of authentic equipment used in the late Middle Ages. Some military historians regard such horses and riders as forerunners of the modern tank. They were virtually immune to spears and arrows, and they could overtake infantry and literally run over them.

and support more than a few. But the peasants could. So each knight was given title to a tract of land and the authority to tax all who lived on it in return for his service as a knight when called upon. This is the political system known as *feudalism.*

In feudal societies, land ownership is based on military obligations. The ruler grants title to large areas in return for the fulfillment of a military quota. A great lord, for example, might have been obligated to provide several hundred knights when called upon. To do so, he assigned portions of his estate to lesser nobles in return for promises to provide some portion of this force. They, in turn, could assign land to others for a pledge of service. The result is that the great mass of society was taxed to support a relatively small number of knights who ruled the people. The people could be greatly exploited because they did not possess the essential equipment and training necessary to resist the knights. With the rise of the knight, the average Frank became a heavily taxed peasant, subject to coercion. Knights held their control of land as a hereditary right, but only so long as they fulfilled their military obligations, for knighthood was not a ceremonial title. War was chronic, and woe unto him who failed to fulfill his obligations to his lord when ordered to duty. Excerpts from a summons sent by Charlemagne, the great emperor of the Franks, to his nobles in 806 suggests how Frankish society had changed since the days of the infantry host and hints at the seriousness of the feudal system of obligations:

You shall come to Stasfurt on the Boda, by May 20th, with your 'men' prepared to go on warlike service to any part of our realm that we may point out; that is, you shall come with arms and gear and all warlike equipment of clothing and victuals. Every horseman shall have shield, lance, sword, dagger, a bow and a quiver. On your carts you shall have ready spades, axes, picks and iron-pointed stakes, and all other things needed for the host. The rations shall be for three months. . . . On your way you shall do no damage to our subjects, and touch nothing but water, wood, and grass. . . . See that there be no neglect, as you prize our good grace (quoted in Montgomery, 1968).

Of course, as the Franks used their knights to extend their rule over new territory, their neighbors soon followed their example. For centuries, all Europe was held in thrall by feudalism.

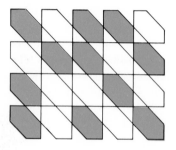

■ The year is 1862. The scene is the outback of Australia. Two tiny bands of natives have crossed paths. No one sees familiar faces in the other group, and everyone is tense. Then spokesmen for each group begin to discuss their ancestry, examining the family trees of both groups minutely. This is not a ritual form of greeting; its outcome may decide the fate of all present. Everyone hopes desperately that some mutual relatives will turn up in the examination, for only if the groups are related can they be friends. If they are not relatives, they are strangers. Their language does not distinguish between the word for stranger and the word for enemy: Strangers *are* enemies. If the bands are strangers, there is nothing to be done but to flee or to fight. The only good stranger is a dead one.

Fear and loathing of strangers are not peculiar to the culture of Australian aborigines. It is almost a universal human trait. The outsider, the foreigner, the stranger has always provoked anxiety, suspicion, hatred, and dread in human beings (Williams, 1947). Such responses are especially likely when the strangers are noticeably different because of cultural or physical differences. Inventing social and cultural means to neutralize conflict between groups with noticeable differences has been one of the major tasks faced by modern societies (Lofland, 1973).

Let's return to 1862, to the Great Plains of the United States. Many Indian tribes still move across their ancestral hunting grounds in pursuit of the great buffalo herds. Each tribe is quite small, often having no more than 1,000 members. Each small tribe holds strongly negative beliefs about the other

Intergroup Conflict:
Racial and Ethnic Inequality

tribes, and conflicts among tribes are frequent. However, all of the Plains tribes reserve their greatest contempt and hatred for the Utes, who live in the foothills of the Rockies. The Utes have darker skins than the other tribes, and they are universally loathed and described as ugly. Everyone thinks it natural to kill Utes whenever possible. Meanwhile, white settlers are moving onto the plains. They cannot tell one tribe from another, and to them all Indians are savages, thieves, drunkards, and dangerous killers. In time they begin to say that the only good Indian is a dead Indian.

Also in 1862, the Chinese and the Japanese are just beginning to have extensive contact with Europeans. They find this contact unpleasant. European customs seem barbaric, and, to make matters worse, Europeans are very ugly. (Asians also complain that Europeans smell extremely bad. Asians bathed regularly, while Europeans almost never did so.) Because of large, protruding noses and long, narrow faces, Europeans are called "dogfaces." Europeans, in turn, find the faces of Asians oddly flat, and they describe the Asians as "slant-eyed."

Nor is 1862 a banner year for brotherhood elsewhere in the world. East of the Mississippi the Civil War rages, which will kill nearly 400,000 Yankees and Confederates, and the list of atrocities will be long. In part, this war is fought to determine whether blacks will continue to be held in slavery. Yet even if the majority of Northerners want to free the slaves, they do not intend to accept blacks into their society. Free blacks are not permitted to vote or to testify in court in most Northern states, and schemes to ship all blacks back to Africa or to relocate them in Indian territory are popular.

In Europe it is much the same. The Austrians hate the Slavs. The French hate the Germans. The Germans look down on the Poles. And the English look down on everyone, treating even the Scots and the Welsh as inferior foreigners. The Irish flee to America to escape the harsh conditions of life imposed on them by the English, but the Irish find they are not too welcome in America, either.

In 1862 Charles Darwin's new theory of evolution arouses the greatest intellectual excitement. It argues that complex biological species evolved from simple, primitive forms of life. The horse, for example, was once the size of the jackrabbit (and about as numerous), and apes and humans are cousins. The theory of evolution seems to answer a problem that has long vexed Europeans. Over the previous three centuries, Europeans explored the globe, and they now are poking into the last uncharted regions. Everywhere they go they find human societies with a lower level of technology than theirs. Indeed, they find society after society still living in the Stone Age. Why is ignorance so widespread? Why are Europeans so much more advanced? Evolutionary theory is used to support supremacist notions: The white race is at a higher stage of human evolution, and nonwhites are more primitive species of humans. Europeans have long believed in their racial superiority; now they think they have a scientific basis for it. And if whites are more advanced biologically, should they not be careful to preserve their heritage and not dilute it by crossbreeding? ▉

On July 8, 1853, Commodore Matthew Perry led a squadron of four American warships into Tokyo Bay in defiance of Japan's laws excluding foreign contacts. After a period of negotiations, Japan agreed to treaties opening its ports to western shipping. These portraits were drawn of Perry (far right) and his senior officers by a Japanese artist. The Asian reaction to the facial features of Westerners is clearly displayed in this set of drawings: The "dog face"—the protruding face with a large nose—is evident in each. Moreover, other than for minor details such as glasses and whiskers and variations in age, all Westerners looked alike! Notice, however, that the Japanese artist depicted all of them with eyelids of typical Asian shape.

CHAPTER PREVIEW

This chapter examines the causes of intergroup conflicts due to noticeable cultural or physical differences, particularly conflicts within rather than between societies. Specifically, it explores racial and ethnic differences as the basis for ascribed low status—how factors such as race, religion, language, and customs generate inequalities among members of a society. Indeed, this chapter will argue that inequalities in property, power, and prestige among different racial and ethnic groups in a society are the basis of intergroup conflict. We shall see how such inequalities make particular groups into strangers, thereby provoking the unreasoned reactions typical of humans confronting strangers. We shall also see that as status inequalities between groups disappear, so do prejudice and hatred.

INTERGROUP CONFLICT

Chapter 2 introduced the basic concepts that sociologists use to examine intergroup conflicts, but some additional comments will prove useful here. This chapter discusses *intergroup* conflict rather than *interracial* conflict, since much of the hatred, prejudice, and discrimination among groups is not based on race. Conflicts between Protestants and Catholics in the United States during the nineteenth and twentieth centuries were not interracial, nor is the deadly and festering conflict in Northern Ireland today. The recent bloody civil war in Nigeria was also not a matter of race. All of these conflicts were between groups of the same race, but with different *cultures*.

The term **intergroup conflict** encompasses all such disputes, whether they are over culture or over skin color. However, this chapter is not concerned with intergroup conflict between two groups with an identical culture and racial heritage, who may battle over politics or wealth. Our concern is only with intergroup conflicts based on noticeable physical or cultural differences.

Race

A **race** is a human group with some observable, common biological features. The most prominent of these is skin color, but racial groups also differ in other observable ways such as eyelid shape and the color and texture of hair. They also differ in

subtle ways that are not visible, such as blood type. Although race is a biological concept, racial differences are important for intergroup relations only to the extent that people attach cultural meaning to them (van den Berghe, 1967). Only when people believe that racial identity is associated with other traits such as character, ability, and behavior do racial differences affect human affairs. Historically, racial differences have typically been associated with cultural differences as well, because persons of different races were usually members of different societies. Race, then, has usually been an accurate indicator of who is and who is not a stranger.

Major trouble arises when different racial groups exist within the same society and people still assign cultural meanings to these physical differences. For one thing, members of one racial group usually cannot escape prejudice by "passing" as members of another racial group, although many light-skinned blacks can and do pass as whites. While an Italian could change his name to Robert Davis, join the Episcopal Church, and deny his true ancestry, people cannot as easily renounce their biology.

This does not mean, however, that racial differences must always produce intergroup conflict. Biological differences may be unchangeable, but by themselves they are not important. It is what we *believe* about these differences that matters. And what

we believe can change. The notion of a society that is color blind simply refers to a society in which no cultural meanings are attached to human biological variations.

Ethnic groups

Ethnic groups are groups whose cultural heritages differ. We usually reserve the term for different cultural groups within the same society. By themselves, cultural differences are not enough to make a group an ethnic group. The differences must be noticed, and they must bind a group together and separate it from others. As Michael Hechter (1974) put it, an ethnic group exists on the basis of "sentiments which bind individuals into solidarity groups on some cultural basis."

For example, nearly 9 million Americans today are the descendants of persons who came here from Italy. Some of them can speak Italian, many cannot. Some like Italian food, some do not. Some are Roman Catholic, some are not. But the existence of an Italian-American ethnic group does not simply depend on such cultural factors. What is important is that some of these people think of themselves as sharing special bonds of history, culture, and kinship with others of Italian ancestry. This makes them members of an ethnic group.

Cultural pluralism

For a long time, it was believed that intergroup conflicts in the United States would be resolved through *assimilation*. As time passed, a given ethnic group would surrender its distinctive cultural features and disappear into the dominant American culture. At that point, people would no longer think of themselves as ethnic, nor would others continue to do so.

Today many once formidable intergroup conflicts have been resolved in our society. Yet the ethnic groups in question, mostly Europeans, did not disappear. True enough, their ethnic identity differs from that of their forebears. Typically, they have lost their native language and their bonds with the old country. Their present culture retains some elements of the old—religious affiliation, for example—plus a new heritage based on the special experiences of the group in the United States (Glazer and Moynihan, 1970). The important point is that conflict disappeared without the disappearance of noticeable differences; conflict ended because the differences became unimportant. Such conflict resolutions are called accommodation, not assimilation. The growth of mutual interests between conflicting groups enables them to emphasize similarities and deemphasize differences.

When intergroup conflict ends through accommodation, the result is ethnic or cultural pluralism—the existence of diverse cultures within the same society. That the United States is no longer a Protestant nation, but a nation of Protestant, Catholics, and Jews, as well as followers of other faiths (plus nonbelievers), demonstrates cultural pluralism.

Obviously, accommodation and assimilation are not the inevitable outcomes of intergroup conflict. Conflict has sometimes been resolved by the *extermination* of the weaker group, as happened with the Jews in Nazi Germany, Catholics in Elizabethan England, Indians in the Caribbean and on the American frontier, Armenians in Turkey, and various tribal minorities in black Africa today. Intergroup conflicts have also led to the *expulsion* of the weaker group.

Jews have often been expelled from nations, and Europeans were expelled from Japan in the sixteenth century. Following World War II, Pakistan expelled Hindus, India expelled Muslims, and Uganda recently expelled both Pakistanis and Indians, while Vietnam has driven out several hundred thousand Chinese. Intergroup conflicts have also been stabilized by the imposition of a **caste system**, whereby weaker groups are prevented from competing with the stronger, and through *segregation,* whereby a group is inhibited from having contact with others.

The history of the United States contains all of these methods of resolution: Groups have been assimilated, accommodated, exterminated, expelled, and placed in a low-status caste. This variety, plus the persistence of intense intergroup conflicts, makes the United States extremely important in the study of intergroup relations. The United States is a huge natural laboratory for examining the dynamics of such conflicts and useful means for overcoming them.

Such an examination inevitably arouses our emotions. When we examine the history of prejudice and discrimination in America, we cannot—nor should we—avoid anger and frustration. However, it would be tragic if we let these feelings prevent us from appreciating the extent to which hatred has been overcome, for the erosion of bigotry is also a prominent feature of American history. The study of this erosion can teach us much about how present problems may be resolved.

PREOCCUPATION WITH PREJUDICE

Until very recently, social scientists regarded prejudice as the *cause* of intergroup conflict. Hostile actions against some racial or ethnic minority were believed to reflect the underlying hostile beliefs or prejudices groups had about one another. Therefore, the urgent questions were Why do people become prejudiced? and What can be done to cure them of their prejudice? Little attention was paid to social and economic relations among groups that might give rise to mutual hostility. Instead, prejudice was blamed on personality defects or ignorance. For a long time, social scientists searched the heads and hearts of people to discover what was wrong with them that caused them to be prejudiced. This search culminated in the mid-1960s.

An immense number of theories have been advanced to explain why people develop prejudices toward people of different racial or ethnic backgrounds. For several decades the most influential of these was the theory of the *authoritarian personality* (Adorno et al., 1950). Its proponents argued that some people are, in effect, oversocialized, so that they accept the norms and values only of their own group and reject any variations. When such people are confronted with others whose norms and values differ from theirs, they become very anxious. To resolve this anxiety, they adopt the belief that all who differ from them are inferior, sinful, inhuman, or otherwise objectionable. Prejudice, then, was seen as a defense mechanism against having to question one's own cultural heritage. In addition, another theory blamed prejudice on feelings of personal inadequacy or low self-esteem; that is, people adopted prejudices in order to have someone else to look down on (Ackerman and Jahoda, 1950).

Many sociologists, myself included, reacted against the notion that prejudice was entirely in the head. Consequently, an immense number of studies were done to link prejudice to social influences on the individual, especially to channels by which prejudice might be learned or unlearned. Again and again, it was found that the more educated a person and the higher one's income, the less likely a person is to be prejudiced against other racial and ethnic groups (Selznick and Steinberg, 1969; Quinley and Glock, 1979). Other studies found that the more religious a person is, the more likely that person is to be prejudiced against members of other faiths; however, religion had no effect on prejudice against persons of other races or ethnic groups of the same religion (Glock and Stark, 1966: Stark et al., 1971).

Yet despite immense effort over several decades, prejudice researchers failed to explain compellingly why people are prejudiced. Moreover, it began to seem likely that prejudice was not the fundamental cause of intergroup conflict. Instead, it became increasingly evident that intergroup conflict causes prejudice. Thus, the proposition that curing prejudice will relieve conflicts reverses cause and effect. To the contrary, sociologists became convinced that only by resolving conflicts will prejudices subside.

In the remainder of this chapter, we shall examine why sociologists came to accept the proposition that racial and ethnic conflicts are rooted in status inequalities between groups and generate prejudice. As we shall see, this approach contradicts many popular beliefs about intergroup relations. For example, if prejudice were the result of ignorance and a lack of understanding, an obvious solution would be to break down the barriers that isolate one group from another. According to this view, strangers need to get to know one another. Thus, intergroup relations are improved by more frequent intergroup contact.

For decades that sounded like very good advice, and innumerable programs were instituted to "bring people together."

Today sociologists think that such efforts are doomed so long as real grievances between groups exist. In fact, increased contacts between groups can increase conflict, hostility, and prejudice. To see why, let's watch as several social scientists first began to develop this new theoretical approach.

Allport's theory of contact

Research on prejudice in the 1940s and 1950s seemed to support the popular belief that prejudice thrives in isolation and thus getting people together will overcome prejudice. However, some social scientists began to doubt this conception of the problem. Foremost among them was Gordon W. Allport of Harvard, one of the world's most distinguished social psychologists at the time.

If contact is the answer to the problems of prejudice, Allport reasoned, then why didn't racial prejudice in the South disappear long ago? One might argue that northern racists have simply never had a chance to get to know black people, but in the South blacks and whites have long been in close contact. Many white southerners, for example, grew up having much closer relations with a black servant than with their own parents. In small southern towns, blacks and whites had been in close, regular, daily contact for generations. Yet antiblack prejudice was as strong in these towns as anywhere in America. Why?

In 1958 Allport proposed his answers in a classic

Contact between groups will decrease prejudice when it occurs under conditions of equal status and cooperation as illustrated by these U.S. Marines. Thus, full integration of the armed forces, ordered by President Eisenhower, was a significant step toward interracial harmony.

ity, in which one group is dominant and the other subordinate. This accounts for the failure of race relations to improve in the South until recently. White merchants did not have contact with black merchants, but only with black customers. White children did not have contact with black teachers or black fellow students, but primarily with black servants. White people's views of themselves as superior were thus reinforced by such contacts. The inequality of the situation forced blacks to submit and caused whites to perceive blacks as submissive.

This view of the effects of contact was supported by studies of the U.S. Merchant Marine. The prejudice of white seamen against blacks did not decrease as a result of repeated voyages with black cooks and mess stewards aboard. But it changed significantly after President Harry S Truman ordered the merchant marine to become integrated and white seamen voyaged with black seamen of equal rank (Brophy, 1945).

However, even contact between groups of equal status does not always improve relations, Allport pointed out. Prejudice will intensify if the groups are engaged in competition (poor whites competing with poor blacks for unskilled jobs, for example), but decline if the groups cooperate to pursue common goals. Thus, when white policemen work with black policemen, their prejudice decreases (Kephart, 1957).

Since Allport's work was published, considerable research has supported his views (Ford, 1973). Contact overcomes prejudice only when people meet on equal terms to cooperate in pursuing common goals. Contact accompanied by inequality and competition breeds contempt. In fact, it can even turn former friends into strangers.

book, *The Nature of Prejudice.* Contact won't necessarily make relations between two groups better, he argued; often it will make relations worse, depending on the conditions under which the contact occurs.

According to **Allport's theory of contact**, prejudice will decrease if two groups with equal status have contact. But prejudice will increase or remain high if it occurs under conditions of *status inequal-*

The Sherif studies

 In the 1950s, Muzafer and Carolyn Sherif of the University of Oklahoma conducted a series of studies of young boys at summer camp. Their results vividly demonstrate how easily prejudice arises among groups. The Sherifs assigned young boys to living groups when they arrived for a 2-week stay at summer camp and then manipulated their activities to test how prejudice arose and declined between groups. Posing as the camp janitor, Muzafer Sherif was able to wander about the camp at will in a nearly invisible role and eavesdrop on the boys.

In one experiment, the Sherifs (1953) broke up existing friendships by assigning boys who were friends to different living groups. Living groups were then made the basic camp units for activities, and each living group was treated as a separate team in sports competition. During activities requiring frequent competition among living groups, the Sherifs found that hostile stereotypes characteristic of intergroup prejudices arose within several days. For example, one group soon labeled another as "crybabies," another as "cheats," and another as "sissies." These harsh feelings arose even when many boys in one group had close friends in another. When the Sherifs altered the contact so that the groups performed cooperative tasks, the negative stereotypes quickly subsided.

If such hostilities can be produced in a few days among young boys of similar background and with long-standing friendships, is it any wonder that antagonism arises so easily in the real world between groups of strangers who are separated by truly noticeable differences and different life experiences?

Based on the important theoretical work by Allport and the amazing experimental results obtained by the Sherifs, a new approach to intergroup conflict began to spread among social scientists. Sociologists were especially attracted by the ways that Allport's theory could be applied to large social structures. For example, since prejudice among groups of unequal status is likely, most groups of new immigrants coming into contact with the established groups in a society are likely to encounter prejudice.

As sociologists began to make these theoretical applications, many widely accepted beliefs were called into question. For example, it had long been assumed that racist attitudes led to slavery in the United States. Now it suddenly seemed more likely that slavery was the cause of the unusually virulent racist beliefs that had flourished in the American South. Before we discuss how economic inequalities or status differences cause prejudice, let us briefly examine the institution of slavery.

SLAVERY AND THE AMERICAN DILEMMA

Two hundred years ago, the American Founding Fathers risked their lives and fortunes by signing the Declaration of Independence from British rule. The second paragraph of that document begins, "We hold these Truths to be self-evident, that all Men are created equal." It is beyond dispute that these American patriots meant this line. It is also beyond dispute that many of them, including Thomas Jefferson,* who wrote these words, also owned slaves.

The doctrine of equal opportunity and the sanctity of individual freedom have long been fundamental American values. Yet these beliefs were maintained in the face of continuing slavery and later through decades of harsh discrimination against blacks. How could Americans square their ideals with their practices?

In 1944 Gunnar Myrdal, a Swedish economist, published the results of a monumental study of American race relations. In it he focused on the stunning contradiction between our democratic ideals and our racist practices. The title of his famous book termed this contradiction as *An American Dilemma*.

It is clear that many Americans dealt with **the American dilemma** between democratic values and racism by rejecting racism. The Puritan descendants of New England were as opposed to slavery as they were to English colonialism, and they provided the grass roots support for the Abolitionist movement that culminated in the Civil War and Lincoln's Emancipation Proclamation. But most Americans found another way out of this contradiction. They did not regard human slavery as proper, but they did not consider blacks fully human. If black people are not fully human, then the ideal that "all men are created equal" does not apply. (The humanity of black *men* was at issue. That *women* were omitted from this phrase was not then embarrassing.) As

---

*Jefferson made many efforts to outlaw slavery and once nearly succeeded in doing so in Virginia. However, he felt it irresponsible to free his slaves within a slave society because he believed that they would only suffer worse fates.

Black slaves plant sweet potatoes on a plantation on Edisto Island, South Carolina, in April 1862. The picture was taken during a period of occupation by the Union Army (which explains why some of the men wear parts of U.S. Army uniforms). It would be eight more months before the Emancipation Proclamation went into effect, and by then the Union troops had withdrawn.

a result, slavery in America was perhaps as much a *cause* of prejudice as a consequence of it.

But how could seemingly intelligent people become convinced that just because people have a dark skin they are not fully human? It wasn't just skin color. Nor was it just that blacks came from exotic, primitive cultures. It was the nature of the institution of slavery and the contact between slave and master that enabled whites to see slaves as inhuman: Blacks were required to behave as if they were, in fact, not fully human (Genovese, 1974).

Recall the conditions under which Allport believed contact would worsen prejudice, and then consider slavery. There is no greater status inequality than that between master and slave. No group can be more dominant over another than slave owners over slaves. Slaves were not educated, and they rarely had been anywhere except on the plantation where they were born. They were traded and sold like prize livestock, and because they were black, they could not easily run away and blend into the free population. They were required to be subservient to whites, who dealt with their resistance severely. Because blacks had no choice but to be wholly dependent, most blacks appeared to be childlike to their masters. Whites denied them experience, knowledge, and literacy, thus keeping them ignorant.

If you regard people as livestock, raise them to act in such a fashion, and prevent them from acting in other ways, it is no surprise that they then reinforce your belief that they are livestock. Centuries of slavery had made blacks and whites complete strangers. And the harsh racist prejudice employed to justify slavery has lived on to infect black-white relations in our own time.

STATUS INEQUALITY AND PREJUDICE

As mentioned, sociologists currently view status inequality as the cause, not the result, of prejudice and discrimination. Now we shall examine this line of reasoning in depth.

When two groups obviously differ on some cultural or physical characteristic (religion or race, for example) and encounter one another, their initial perceptions will be dominated by these differences. Each group will tend to magnify the differences and to attribute unflattering traits to the other. However, whether these initial reactions subside or intensify depends upon the conditions under which their contact continues.

If both groups live in the same society, contact is hard to avoid. According to Allport's theory, future relations between the two groups depend on whether the two groups are of equal status and whether the benefits of cooperation outweigh those of competition. When such groups are (or come to be) of equal status and when they benefit from cooperation, relations ought to improve rapidly, regardless of initial negative reactions. But if their status is unequal (and so long as it remains unequal), contact between these groups will worsen feelings. Moreover, when two such groups are of unequal status, economic competition between them is virtually unavoidable.

From this line of reasoning, several conclusions follow. First, contact between culturally and racially distinctive groups of unequal status will increase prejudice and probably discrimination as well. Second, this prejudice will not subside until after the status inequality and economic competition have been eliminated. Finally, within any society, noticeable physical and cultural differences will produce prejudice only if they are associated with status inequality or with competition.

If these conclusions are correct, then efforts to overcome prejudice before overcoming status inequality are bound to fail. Instead, effort should be directed at eliminating the inequality; then prejudice should subside.

To see how these processes work, it is useful to examine the relations between Catholics and Protestants over the past century in the United States. For contrast, we shall also examine relations between Protestant and Catholics in Northern Ireland today.

As discussed in Chapter 2, the arrival of large numbers of Catholic immigrants into the United States during the latter part of the nineteenth century provoked bitter reactions among American Protestants.

Like most immigrants, the Catholics arrived with little money or education and took unskilled labor jobs. For several generations, Catholics were at or near the bottom of the American stratification system. Indeed, the average income of Catholic families lagged considerably behind that of Protestants until well into this century. This inequality fueled the bitter prejudices held by Catholics and Protestants toward one another.

Economic inequality and discrimination placed Catholics in direct conflict with the Protestant majority. For Protestants, Catholic efforts to achieve economic parity represented a threat of loss, for Catholic gains would come at the expense of Protestant privilege. Indeed, as we shall see later in this chapter, the exclusionary immigration laws adopted by the United States in the early 1920s were imposed by the Protestant majority in an effort to protect their relatively high wages from being undercut by Catholic immigrants willing to work for less.

Eventually, Catholics did gain economic parity with Protestants (Greeley, 1974). When that happened, the basis for conflict subsided. Catholics were no longer of lower status than Protestants; the competition over privilege had ended in a draw. It was then, not before, that bitter anti-Catholic and anti-Protestant prejudices began to subside. Indeed, they subsided so rapidly that few college-age Protestants and Catholics today even know of them, although they were still widespread when their parents were young. As recently as the 1950s, books attacking Catholics as pagans and the enemies of democracy became best-sellers. Nonetheless, in 1960 a Catholic was elected President of the United States.

During the days of Catholic-Protestant conflicts in the United States, observers were convinced that these conflicts were caused by cultural differences—specifically, by differences in religion. Since these differences were unlikely to disappear, it was thought that prejudice would remain as well. However, since these religious differences do not provoke prejudice today, they must not have been the cause. Rather, the religious differences were used as indicators, or "**markers**," of underlying conflicts over status. With the conflict resolved, these markers lost their ability to inflame antagonisms.

In his recent major work on intergroup relations,

Young Catholics in Belfast, Northern Ireland, taunt British troops. The soldiers are on patrol to prevent riots and terrorism between Catholics and Protestants. This intergroup conflict illustrates that cultural differences can produce as much bitterness and prejudice as can racial differences.

Stanley Lieberson (1980) explained how cultural and racial markers are made potent by status conflict:

I am suggesting a general process that occurs when racial and ethnic groups have an inherent conflict [competition over status between unequal groups]. Under the circumstances, there is a tendency for the competitors to focus on differences between themselves. The observers (in this case the sociologists) may then assume that these differences are the sources of the conflict. In point of fact, the rhetoric involving such differences may

indeed inflame them, but we can be reasonably certain that the conflict would have occurred in their absence.

He then suggested a "thought experiment." Since Protestants in Northern Ireland refer to themselves as "Orangemen," while Irish Catholics identify with the color green, let's suppose that the Protestants in Northern Ireland had orange skins and the Catholics green skins. Clearly these marked physical differences would become part of the rhetoric of hatred and prejudice in Northern Ireland, serving as additional markers of difference. Lieberson even suggested that such physical differences would play a secondary role in fueling conflict. However, it would be silly to credit the orange and green, "racial" differences as the real cause of the conflict, because a bitter, murderous conflict over economic opportunity and status already exists without such differences. In similar fashion, Lieberson argues, physical differences between blacks and whites, both real and imagined, enter into the rhetoric of interracial conflict in the United States, but they are not the cause.

Lieberson (1980) concluded that fear of blacks as economic competitors is the real cause of racial stereotypes. This means

that were the present-day [economic] conflict between blacks and dominant white groups to be resolved, then the race issue could rapidly disintegrate as a crucial barrier between the groups just as a very profound and deep distaste for Roman Catholics on the part of the dominant Protestants has diminished rather substantially.

Keeping in mind this overview of how economic inequality generates prejudice, let us now examine these matters in detail.

ECONOMIC CONFLICT AND PREJUDICE

 The roots of ethnic and racial antagonism usually lie in economic inequality and conflict. This is primarily because subordinate racial and ethnic minorities represent an economic threat to many members of the dominant majority. That is, the presence of a disadvantaged racial or ethnic group in a society makes available a supply of persons who can be hired for wages lower than those paid majority group workers for the same job. Such persons will work for less—either because they lack the power to demand wages as high as those of the dominant group or because they have different economic motives for working.

Edna Bonacich (1972, 1975, 1976) has examined the relationship between labor market conflict and racial and ethnic antagonism in considerable detail. She has identified four factors that often cause or require members of subordinate racial and ethnic groups to work for substandard wages.

The first of these is a very *low standard of living.* Often enough, such groups migrate from a region with so low a standard of living that wages considered substandard by members of the dominant group are very attractive to them. Illegal Mexican workers in the West and Southwest work for much less than the going wage paid to American citizens, but they earn far more than they could in Mexico. Similarly, blacks who migrated from the rural South in the 1930s and 1940s improved their standard of living even though they were paid well below union wages (and often were employed as strikebreakers) in northern mines, mills, and factories. The same was true of Chinese and Japanese workers arriving on the West Coast at the turn of the century. Indeed, white, Protestant "Okies," who fled the farms of the Southwest for California in the 1930s, during the days of the Dust Bowl and the Great Depression, found substandard wages in California to be a great improvement over the abject poverty they faced when they lost their land.

A second impediment to high wages pointed out by Bonacich is a *lack of information.* Immigrants from a very poor country may be recruited without knowing that they are being exploited. Or members of a subordinate group may not know about minimum wage laws, legal recourses for unpaid wages, and the like, often because they do not speak the language.

A third factor that limits the ability of ethnic and racial minorities to secure high wages is their *lack of political power.* They may lack citizenship and thus have no voting power or be too few in number to force favorable reforms. In contrast, workers of the dominant group may have substantial political power and strong unions that enable them to demand high wages, which in turn makes them vulnerable to wage competition from groups unable to unionize or to wield political power. This is especially true for unskilled jobs. As we saw in Chapter 9, unskilled positions have high replaceability, which always depresses wages unless political power can be used to create artificial conditions that lower replaceability. Because most immigrant workers in America were not skilled, they had little power, and their ability to strike was limited by the ease with which they could be replaced.

A contrasting case makes the point. Some of the first successful unions in the United States were founded by Jewish workers in the late nineteenth century. They rapidly won contracts for better pay and shorter hours, conditions not enjoyed by most industrial workers at that time (Howe, 1976). The key to the power of the Jewish trade union movement lay in the special skills of the Jewish workers, especially those in the garment industry. An alternative supply of skilled tailors and seamstresses was not available to factory owners. Interestingly enough, the employers from whom Jewish unions won their settlements also tended to be Jews. This success in one industry shows that Jews arrived in the United States already possessing the skills needed to make rapid economic progress.

The *economic motives* of subordinate racial and ethnic groups are also a factor in their low wages, according to Bonacich. Often they only intend to be temporary workers. As a result, they often accept low wages and poor working conditions, knowing they need not endure them forever. In addition, temporary workers have little to gain and much to lose by strikes or by refusing bad jobs in hopes of getting better ones. For workers with short-term economic goals, lost wages often outweigh the prospects of better wages.

Many Italian immigrants came as sojourners to America. They were young men who came to earn and save a certain amount of money and then to return to rural Italy, where the much lower standard of living made their American-earned money worth much more. For them to participate in a long strike over an unpleasant work environment or to go unemployed while searching for a higher-paying job conflicted with their goal: to save money as fast as possible and return home.

Similarly, Millis (1915) reported that Japanese workers in California displaced other workers not only because they accepted low wages but also because they worked twelve to fourteen hours a day and on weekends. They did this so that they could save money faster and return to Japan sooner. In

Africa, workers from the villages will often work very cheaply because they plan to work just long enough to afford the price of a bride, a rifle, or a bicycle (Berg, 1966). Furthermore, as Bonacich pointed out, it is against the interests of management to pay high wages to sojourners, lest the workers achieve their short-term goals faster and leave that much sooner.

Clearly, then, the existence of racial and ethnic groups willing to work for substandard wages threatens the economic well-being of other workers and is likely to cause strong antagonism toward the subordinate group. Cheap labor threatens to make *all* labor cheap. Workers belonging to the dominant group must either work for less or lose their jobs to members of the subordinate racial or ethnic group, unless such economic competition can be prevented.

Two strategies have commonly been employed to prevent a subordinate group from competing with the dominant group by providing cheap labor (Bonacich, 1972). The first is *exclusion*. Members of the subordinate group are denied entry into the society or driven out if they have already entered. The second is to establish a *caste system* that limits the subordinate group to certain occupations, often the most menial and undesirable ones.

Exclusion

The influx of cultural and racial groups who are perceived as a threat to the wages of the dominant group often causes a nativistic reaction: a demand that foreigners be kept out. As already mentioned, massive immigration of Catholics during the latter part of the nineteenth century led to nativistic policies in American politics, often justified by vicious racial and ethnic prejudice. Italians and eastern Europeans were seriously discussed as "inferior racial stocks" whose immigration threatened the "racial purity and superiority" of Americans (Grant, 1916). Following World War I, Protestant opposition to the resumption of immigration led to immigration quotas designed to prevent Catholics and Asians from entering the country in significant numbers. American workers won these tight quotas over the opposition of big business, which wanted to keep its historic supply of cheap labor.

258 / Three: Stratification and Conflict

Similarly, it was a workingman's party that spearheaded the drive to exclude Asians from the West Coast. As the socialist Cameron H. King, Jr., wrote in 1908, this party swept California "with the campaign cry of 'The Chinese must go.' Then the two old parties woke up and have since realized that to hold the labor vote they must stand for Asiatic exclusion" (in Bonacich, 1972).

Laborers and farmers patrolled California and tried by illegal means to prevent Okies from entering the state during the 1930s (McWilliams, 1945). And it has almost always been white workers who have tried to drive out blacks moving into the industrial regions of the North from the rural South.

Caste systems

Total exclusion has often not been possible. Under such circumstances, dominant-group members have often tried to create a caste system that would restrict minorities to certain occupations, thus preventing them from competing for places in other occupations (Hechter, 1978). As previously discussed, stratification in caste systems is based on heredity, and status is determined by ascription. Each caste group has exclusive access to certain occupations and positions in the society. Only those born to the highest caste are permitted to perform the most important occupations and hold the most powerful positions. Those born to the lowest caste are required to perform the most unattractive and servile work.

India is a classic instance of a very elaborate caste society. However, elements of a caste system can exist in a society in which status is generally based on achievement rather than ascription. Within the dominant group of such societies, status may be based primarily on achievement, but one or more racial or ethnic group may be ascribed a uniformly low status and thereby constitute a lower caste.

A low-caste status prevents a racial or ethnic group from competing with the dominant group for wages. A caste system may be created directly by strict rules about which positions a subordinate group may or may not hold or indirectly by excluding the subordinate group from entering unions or schools or from performing certain activities required to obtain better positions. For example, taboos against using drinking fountains or restrooms used by an upper caste may confine lower-caste members to a few limited physical locations and thereby to a narrow range of jobs. These subtle caste systems—long typical of race relations in the United States—constitute what Michael Hechter (1974) has called a **cultural division of labor**, whereby cultural or racial differences among members of a society are used as the basis for occupational placement.

Middleman minorities

It is important to realize that a cultural division of labor need not place an ethnic or racial minority on the bottom of a stratification system. Often minorities have been used as "middlemen" in societies, serving as both links and buffers between the upper and lower classes. As Blalock (1967) and Bonacich (1973) have pointed out, **middleman minorities** often defuse potential class conflicts by becoming the focus of frustration and anger. In times of stress or unrest, Blalock noted, elites and the lower class often form a coalition against the middleman minority and vent their frustration on it. For example, many nations in feudal Europe permitted Jews to perform only certain middleman roles, such as moneylender, tax collector, and merchant. Thus, they were always potentially in conflict with both the nobility and the peasants. In hard times, the nobility blamed Jewish tax collectors for decreased revenues but let them be the targets of peasant anger about high taxes. And in hard times, both the nobility and the peasants were in debt to the Jewish moneylender or the Jewish merchant. Often enough, killing or expelling the Jews proved a most attractive way for both nobles and peasants to cancel their debts.

Chinese and Indian minorities have often formed middleman minorities in societies in Africa and Southeast Asia. They, too, have often been used as scapegoats for social conflicts within the dominant group (Blalock, 1967).

IDENTIFIABILITY

Status conflicts always cause bitterness. For example, it is common in American high schools for groups to be quite clearly distinguished on the basis of school performance, popularity, and, often, athletic skill, and for there to be strong negative feelings between higher and lower status groups (Coleman, 1961). This is true even when the groups are of precisely the *same* race, ethnic background, and religion—in Irish Catholic high schools in Boston, for example. Indeed, we have seen how rapidly such barriers arise among little boys at summer camp.

When the conflicts truly affect one's life, and when conflicts occur between easily identifiable groups, they are even more bitter. For example, when people lose their jobs to strikebreakers or to those willing to work for lower wages, they are, of course, bitter. When the offending group is not set apart by cultural or racial differences, the anger must focus on the offending group as individuals, and their behavior is explained as the result of personal flaws. However, when the offending group has a clear group identification, bitterness can be directed toward *the group as a whole*. Then it is not a case of Harry, Marty, Mary, or Beth taking jobs, but of those "dirty Swedes" taking them. In this manner, racial and cultural differences are infused with the passionate hatreds generated by status competition and conflict—what is merely different is made contemptible, and strangers are transformed into enemies.

Racially and culturally identifiable "enemies" frequently acquire derogatory names reflecting prejudice, hatred, and contempt directed toward them. In America, these names have included such terms as Wops, Hunkies, Micks, Krauts, Dagos, Gringos, Prots, Frogs, Breeds, Polacks, Rednecks, Kikes, Greasers, Wogs, Mackerel Snappers, Japs, Chinks, Chukes, and Niggers.* Indeed, as discussed above,

*Many readers will be unable to connect some of these names with the ethnic or religious group to which they were applied. Good. You are living evidence of how rapidly prejudice can subside once status conflicts have been resolved. Most people over 50 could easily recognize these group epithets; they did not pass some of these words on to their children. Perhaps you will let your children be ignorant of the rest.

one such group was known as Okies—people who moved west to California from the Oklahoma Dust Bowl during the 1930s. The prejudices against Okies were no different from those typically held against other racial and ethnic minorities (McWilliams, 1945). They were said to be dirty, to breed like rabbits, and to be superstitious, shiftless, sly, and ignorant. Yet, the Okies were all white Anglo-Saxon Protestants, most of whom could trace their ancestry back to early colonial settlers. What made these people Okies? First, economic conflict did, because they would take any job at any wage to feed their hungry families. Second, they had easily identifiable cultural traits: a rural southern dialect and country ways.

EQUALITY AND THE DECLINE OF PREJUDICE

Today, many of the richest farms in California are owned by people who arrived as Okies during the 1930s. Nobody calls these people Okies anymore, although they sometimes call themselves Okies as a way of taking pride in how successful they have become.

If status competition and conflict fuel prejudice, status equality causes the tank to run dry. With status equality, there is no longer anything to fight about. Once a subordinate group has achieved economic equality, for example, it no longer threatens as a source of cheap labor. And it no longer makes inroads into skilled occupations or into upper status professional and managerial fields. The inroads have already been made.

Contact rapidly reduces prejudice under status equality, since it occurs among equals with a mutual interest in improving society—in cooperating to make the economy more productive or the environment more pleasant. Under these conditions, old hatreds and fears dissolve. This process is accelerated as younger generations with no experience of past conflicts become adults. Let us examine a recent example in detail.

This photo of a country store, taken in Gordonton, North Carolina, by Dorothea Lange in 1939, reveals the poverty and isolation of the rural South, which, in comparison with other parts of the country, made the South like a foreign land. Here we can glimpse some of the complexities and contradictions of southern race relations at that time. The white store owner, standing in the doorway, seems to be on friendly terms with the black men sitting on his front porch. Yet, while these men are free to enter the store and buy whatever they like, they may not sit down and relax inside: They can buy soda pop inside but must return to the porch to drink it, because both whites and blacks shop at this store. Had the store been for blacks only, then they could have sat down inside. The poverty of the black customers (several wear no socks) is evident, but so is that of the white owner of this dilapidated store. While whites enjoyed many social privileges denied blacks, most whites as well as blacks suffered from the economic and social deprivations that marked life in the rural South until recent times. Some of these young black men may have migrated North. If so, their journey was more like that of immigrants coming through Ellis Island than like that of people moving from one northern state to another.

Farm families from Oklahoma, bankrupted by the Dust Bowl and the Great Depression, loaded their remaining belongings onto old cars and pickups and set out for California. Despite being white, Anglo-Saxon Protestants, they were greeted in the Golden West as undesirable foreigners—as "dirty Okies"—and many Californians tried to keep them out or drive them away.

The case of Japanese-Americans

The experience of Japanese immigrants and their descendants in the United States is of special interest because both cultural and racial differences set them apart from the majority. Moreover, the Japanese immigrants were primarily farm laborers, literate but lacking education when they arrived here, and for decades they were the targets of intense prejudice and discrimination, especially on the West Coast. How the Japanese overcame these barriers and achieved greater economic success than that achieved by many older groups of European origin provides an excellent foundation for the remainder of this chapter.

The Japanese never made up more than a tiny portion of the great tide of immigration to America. In 1907, their peak year of entry, only 30,000 arrived, making up only 3 percent of all immigrants for that year. However, the Japanese immigrants located

Japanese-Americans picking berries near Los Angeles before World War II. Because of laws hindering them from owning land, this field has been leased. At this time the majority of Japanese-Americans were farmers.

mainly in Hawaii and California, causing great local upset about a "yellow peril."

In California, an alien land law was passed to prohibit Japanese from owning land. For a time, the Japanese easily evaded this law by putting the land in the name of white neighbors or their American-born children. In 1920 a referendum was placed before California voters that attempted to close these loopholes and to exclude all aliens who were ineligible for citizenship from owning land. At that time

only Asian aliens living in the United States were ineligible to become citizens. The law passed by a three-to-one margin, indicating the degree of public hostility to the Japanese. In time, court decisions and new evasion tactics defeated the intent of the law.

Meanwhile, in 1924 immigration from Japan and other Asian nations was prohibited by federal law—an action that caused great offense in Japan and played a role in decisions leading to World War II. The immediate consequences of this Asian exclusion

Table 11-1 / Race and educational achievement of males in America (1940–1980).

	Median Number of Years of Schooling			
	1940	1960	1970	1980
White	8.7	10.7	12.2	12.5*
Black	5.4	7.7	9.9	12.0*
Japanese (U.S. born)	12.2	12.4	12.5	†
Chinese (U.S. born)	6.2	12.3	12.4	†

*Among white and black males aged 25 through 29, the figures were 12.9 and 12.6, respectively.
†Data not available.
Source: U.S. Bureau of the Census and Stanley Lieberson (1973).

policy were a halt to immigration and a rapid transformation of the Japanese-American population from being primarily foreign born to being primarily American born. This, in turn, led to rapid upward mobility by the Japanese, since no new, poor, unskilled immigrants arrived to depress the average status of the group.

Rapid Japanese economic success was not limited to farming, although that was the usual occupation of the first generation. Early on, the Japanese discovered a great demand for their gardening skills, a form of self-employment requiring little more capital investment than a truck, mowers, and various hand tools. As early as 1928, there were 1,300 self-employed Japanese gardeners in southern California (Kitano, 1969). The Japanese also set up produce markets in the cities to sell their vegetables and fruits, and in 1929 there were more than 700 such markets in Los Angeles alone (Light, 1972). As late as 1940, the majority of Japanese men in America were farmers. That same year about one-third of all commercial truck farm crops grown in California were produced by Japanese-American farmers (Kitano, 1969; Petersen, 1971, 1978; Sowell, 1981). The Japanese also excelled in running other small businesses where unskilled labor, especially the labor of children, could be most productive. For example, by 1919 almost

half of the hotels and a fourth of the grocery stores in Seattle were owned by Japanese-Americans (Light, 1972).

The first generation of Japanese-Americans worked hard to establish their own farms and small businesses. They were aided in this by the creation of their own credit associations, in which they pooled their savings and used them to finance one another in starting businesses or buying property (Miyamoto, 1939). But the first generation did something else equally important: They sent their children to school.

By 1940, native-born Japanese-Americans had attained a much higher average education than had native-born white Americans. Indeed, the average Japanese-American male had gone slightly beyond high school, while the average white American male had gone only slightly past the eighth grade (see Table 11-1)! Later this would pay huge occupational dividends.

But first we must consider the war. On December 7, 1941, carrier aircraft of the Japanese Imperial Fleet made a massive surprise attack on the American fleet lying at anchor in Pearl Harbor. At the same time, Japan launched invasions of many parts of Southeast Asia and many Pacific islands. The war inflamed public emotions. Most Americans at that time agreed with President Franklin D. Roosevelt that December 7, 1941, was a "day that will live in infamy."

In the immediate aftermath of Pearl Harbor, concern mounted about the allegiance of the Japanese-American population. Many American leaders expressed the belief that they remained loyal to Japan and posed a threat as saboteurs and spies. Initially, 1,500 Japanese who had been outspoken supporters of Japan were arrested as potential security risks. Building upon the already substantial public prejudice against the Japanese, war hysteria led to the rounding up of 100,000 Japanese-Americans living on the West Coast—men, women, and children. They were relocated in a number of internment camps, to the applause of political leaders and writers across the political spectrum. All seemed united in the belief, expressed by General J. L. DeWitt, who directed the roundup, that "a Jap's a Jap, and it makes no difference whether he's a citizen or not." The blind prejudice of such views was later exposed by the tens of thousands of Japanese-Americans who fought in Europe during World War II, including the legendary 442 Regimental Combat Unit, whose heroics made them the most decorated unit in the U.S. Army.

Internment brought economic disaster to the Japanese living on the American mainland (oddly enough, only they were interned, while the 150,000 Japanese-Americans in Hawaii, living close to Pearl Harbor, were not). Thousands of farms and small businesses were lost forever, while many others were sold for next to nothing by desperate people forced to leave for a camp. And bigotry flourished. A Gallup Poll conducted on the West Coast in December 1942, a year after Pearl Harbor, found that an overwhelming majority of white Americans in that region said they would never again hire Japanese or shop in stores owned by Japanese after the war was over.

At war's end, the Japanese resumed their efforts to find a place for themselves in American life. Once again many turned to gardening. But now the huge educational advantages made before the war enabled them to make rapid gains in the booming postwar economy with its increasing demand for highly educated people. Japanese-Americans were much more likely to have college degrees than were other racial and ethnic groups. Moreover, their degrees were

Japanese-American children in California in about 1910 with their book bags suspended from a carrying pole. Although Japanese immigrants were not well educated and primarily worked in agriculture, from the very start they sent their children to school. Within a few decades they far surpassed the average level of education of other Americans.

primarily in fields such as engineering, the professions, and business administration (Sowell, 1981)—degrees that led to high-paying technical, professional, and managerial positions. By 1959, seventeen years after their internment and terrible financial losses, the family income of Japanese-Americans had caught up with that of the white population

(Petersen, 1971). Ten years after that, the average family income of Japanese-Americans was 32 percent higher than that white Americans! Part of this was due to the concentration of the Japanese-American population on the West Coast, where wages were higher. But even among the population there, the average income of Japanese-Americans was higher.

As the Japanese-Americans overcame economic inequality, attitudes toward them shifted rapidly. This can be demonstrated in several ways. The first is intermarriage. Perhaps nothing emphasizes the stress in relations between a majority and a disliked minority more than the question, Would you want your son or daughter to marry one? The answer is always a resounding no. In the 1920s, only about 2 percent of all Japanese-American marriages involved a non-Japanese spouse. By the 1950s this had climbed to about 20 percent (Levine and Montero, 1973), and now is about 50 percent (Kihumura and Kitano, 1973; Heer, 1980). High rates of intermarriage dramatically show that attitudes on both sides have changed.

Direct evidence on attitudes can be seen in Table 11-2. These data were collected in the San Francisco Bay Area in 1963, once a hotbed of anti-Japanese prejudice and discrimination. While the survey did not, unfortunately, ask about the Japanese specifically, it did include responses to "an Oriental." Note the high level of acceptance of Orientals only slightly more than twenty years after Pearl Harbor. These data also reflect the rapid economic and educational progress of the Chinese over the past forty years (see Table 11-1). Indeed, by 1970 the average family income of Chinese-Americans was 12 percent higher than that of the average white American family (Sowell, 1981). Here, too, West Coast residence is partly responsible for the higher average income of Chinese-Americans.

Thus, we see that despite deep prejudice, despite clear racial and cultural markers, despite the added hysteria caused by war with Japan, Japanese-Americans suddenly ceased to be strangers as they achieved status equality.

Let us now analyze how groups succeed in America. How did Italians, Poles, Irish, Japanese, and the other immigrant groups rise from poverty to equality and acceptance?

MECHANISMS OF ETHNIC AND RACIAL MOBILITY

In the course of American history, a great many different ethnic and racial groups have been on the bottom of the stratification system. Nearly without exception, while each was on the bottom, it was widely believed that their future was hopeless and that they would always be on the bottom. For example, at the time of the American Revolution, Benjamin Franklin wrote that the Germans who had recently settled in Pennsylvania would never fit in or make a contribution to our society.

But, time and again these prophesies have been wrong, as group after group has escaped an ascribed low status to achieve equality and thereby eliminate prejudice. The proper Bostonians "knew" that the "drunken, lazy, superstitious Irish" would never amount to anything. But today their average income is slightly higher than that of Protestants of English origins (Greeley, 1974).

The waves of immigrants from southern and eastern Europe who began arriving after 1880 caused one of America's leading sociologists of the time, E. A. Ross, to write in 1914 that they were so racially inferior that they would drag the nation down, intellectually and morally:

It is fair to say that the blood now being injected into the veins of our people is "sub-common," [Many of these new kinds of immigrants] are hirsute, low-browed, big-faced persons of obviously low mentality. . . . Clearly they belong in skins, in wattled huts at the close of the Great Ice Age.

That the mediterranean peoples are morally below the races of northern Europe is as certain as any social fact. Even when they were dirty, ferocious barbarians, these blonds [northern Europeans] were truthtellers.

The Northerners seem to surpass southern Europeans in innate ethical endowment . . . but they will lose these traits in proportion as they absorb excitable mercurial blood from southern Europe.

The year Ross published this book, he served as president of the American Sociological Society and as professor of sociology at the University of Wisconsin. Ironically, in 1959 Ross's pioneering essays on social control were rescued from obscurity, edited, and republished by two leading American sociologists, Edgar F. Borgatta and Henry J. Meyer—an Italian and a Jew! Presumably, eastern and southern Europeans had biologically evolved an incredible amount in only fifty years, if one were to take Ross's 1914 judgments seriously.

If many groups have made it in America, how have they done so? Through what tactics or mechanisms have groups achieved their upward mobility? Three basic elements seem crucial. First is geographic concentration. The second is internal economic development and occupational specialization. The third is development of a middle class (Wirth, 1928; Glazer and Moynihan, 1970; Sowell, 1981).

Geographic concentration

Subordinate ethnic, racial, and religious minorities have often been forced by discrimination to live in enclaves segregated from the surrounding dominant group. However, in addition to discrimination, the tendency for racial and ethnic minorities to concentrate in certain neighborhoods has been encouraged by the needs and desires of subordinate groups: to band together for self-help, to maintain familiar features of their native culture (such as churches, festivals, and traditional foods), and to use their own language in daily life (see Chapter 18).

Geographic, or neighborhood, concentration is often denounced as a barrier to better intergroup relations. Yet Allport's theory suggests that, at least in the early days of a subordinate group's American experience, concentration may help to minimize the negative consequences of contact. But geographic concentration may have additional benefits as well: When a group is concentrated in a few locations its economic and political power is maximized.

Consider the Irish. Today they make up about 8 percent of the U.S. population. Suppose that when they had arrived in this country, they had scattered across the landscape. If they had spread out evenly, then everywhere they would have constituted 8 per-

Table 11-2 / Relative acceptance of racial and ethnic groups in northern California (1963).

"It sometimes happens when we first meet a person that we know only *one* thing about him. We may know what he does for a living, or what his religion is, or where he comes from, and so on. We all tend to form a first impression of this person on the basis of this one thing we know about him. Now, would you put yourself in the situation of having just met a person and the *only* thing you know about him is that he is a _____ . Knowing only this *one* thing about him, what would your immediate reaction tend to be?" (Glock and Stark, 1966).

Descriptor	Percent Responding Favorably*
Englishman	79%
Irishman	79%
Italian	74%
German	71%
Oriental	67%
Pole	67%
Jew	65%
Puerto Rican	58%
Negro	57%
Russian	46%
Average	66%
Other selected traits	
Episcopalian	77%
Roman Catholic	72%
Baptist	63%
Jehovah's Witness	28%
Atheist	24%
Alcoholic	16%
Communist	4%

*Percentage who said, "Friendly and at ease."

cent of the population, and nowhere would they have been more numerous. But the Irish congregated in a few major cities and in particular neighborhoods within those cities. As a result, they soon were a majority or a sizable minority of the local population. Hence they soon exerted maximum pressure on local affairs affecting their interests. The Irish soon ran the governments of many cities and used their power to further their economic and social interests.

In similar fashion, the Japanese and Chinese congregated on the West Coast, where their numbers mattered. Indeed, from 1976 through 1980, three U.S. senators were Japanese-Americans, although Japanese make up less than 0.4 percent of the U.S. population. Jews have also achieved political influence beyond their numbers because they are geographically concentrated.

Internal economic development and specialization

Geographic concentration also facilitates a group's ability to develop its own economic resources and institutions, which can then be used to finance further upward mobility. In the beginning, most subordinate groups have difficulty getting credit to finance business or agricultural enterprises, and they desperately need financial resources not subject to outside control. To meet this need, the typical first step of immigrant groups is to pool their funds to provide start-up capital for purchasing or starting small stores and businesses within their own neighborhoods. Then, by buying within their own community and by reinvesting the profits, they gain economic freedom.

Here geographic concentration can be vital. If a group is not concentrated in particular neighborhoods, then it will be difficult to shop only in stores run by group members. But when a group is concentrated, then economic self-interest is reinforced by the convenience of shopping close to home.

Here, too, language may play a role. Unlike most groups, the Irish did not start their rise to equality by first acquiring neighborhood businesses. This may have been because the Irish spoke English. Polish or Japanese housewives were often willing to pay higher prices at small groceries run by Poles or Japanese, because they wanted to shop where clerks understood their language. However, Irish housewives lacked this inducement to patronize Irish grocers.

This factor may also pose a major difficulty for blacks attempting to run small shops in black neighborhoods. Unlike Puerto Ricans and other Spanish-speaking groups in America, blacks, like the Irish, have not tended to run small businesses. Although Spanish-speaking consumers may be reluctant to shop in larger stores where clerks do not speak Spanish, black consumers have no language barrier hindering them from going where prices are lowest (Glazer, 1971).

A major step forward for most subordinate groups has been the founding of their own financial institutions. We have seen that the Japanese-American created small credit associations and eventually founded their own banks. In Chapter 2 we traced the history of a small neighborhood bank that began as a source of loans for the Italians in San Francisco and eventually grew into the Bank of America. The small, local savings bank was also a typical feature of Irish communities. In fact, Joseph Kennedy, father of President Kennedy, began his remarkable financial empire by opening such a small savings bank.

In addition to seeking economic development and independence, many racial and ethnic minorities have taken advantage of the particular occupational opportunities existing at the time they arrived. As a result, they have often been (and continue to be) very overrepresented in certain specialized occupations. We have already seen how the Japanese-Americans specialized in a few occupations: truck farming, gardening, and running small hotels and grocery stores. Today they are greatly overrepresented in engineering, optometry, medicine, and dentistry (Lieberson, 1980; Sowell, 1981). Such specialization maximizes the ability of self-help: People already in an occupation can aid friends and relatives by showing them how to gain entry to the occupation (and perhaps even hiring them); in fact, such people can be the primary source of training for that occupation (Hechter, 1978).

Such occupational specialization has been typical of American subordinate groups. For example, the Irish used their control of city governments to enter civil service occupations. As late as 1950, the Irish were 3 times more likely than other whites to be policemen and firemen. In similar fashion, in 1950 Italians were 8 times overrepresented among barbers, Swedes were 4 times overrepresented among carpenters, Greeks were 29 times overrepresented among restaurant operators, Jews were 17 times overrepresented among tailors, and nearly all diamond cutters were Jewish (Lieberson, 1980).

The dragon is an essential part of Chinese New Year celebrations such as the one shown here in New York City's "Chinatown." The existence of separate racial and ethnic communities within cities often reflects segregation. But these communities also help groups build up their internal economic resources.

Development of a middle class

Progress by subordinate groups requires leadership and expertise. To create financial institutions requires group members who know how to run them. To use a concentrated population to influence local politics requires political leadership.

We saw in Chapter 2 that some immigrant groups arrived with a large middle-class contingent—Jews and, later, Cubans are examples. Both groups made extremely rapid economic progress because they already had the skills needed for effective community building. Moreover, both groups used higher education to provide their children with a rapid route for entering upper-income occupations not requiring much capital investment. Unlike buying a store or starting a bank, no initial investment is required for a person to earn a high salary as a scientist, physician, engineer, or accountant. The person need only obtain the appropriate education. That the Jews rapidly became the most highly educated group in America accounts for the fact that they also have the highest average family income of any racial, religious, or ethnic group (Greeley, 1974). As we have seen, the Japanese also used higher education to improve their status quickly.

When a racial or ethnic group lacks a substantial middle class, its upward mobility is slowed until a middle class develops. Hence, Italians made much slower progress at first than Jews.

What can this analysis of how various immigrant groups succeeded in America tell us about the prospects for today's subordinate groups? At first glance, our analysis might seem of little relevance. Although many of these groups are not recent immigrants, they remain in low status positions and are the targets of prejudice. Thus, they must face problems unlike those faced by the immigrant groups just discussed. As we shall see, blacks, for example, may have special barriers to overcome, but it still is useful to consider blacks as *recent immigrants* and to analyze their recent, rapid upward mobility in terms of this same model.

TODAY'S MINORITIES AS "IMMIGRANTS"

Although some racial and ethnic minorities arrived in North America only recently, many others are not recent immigrants. For what it's worth, "native" Americans immigrated to this country about 25,000 years ago. And most American blacks have been in this country for more generations than any white group. As early as 1680, most blacks in North America were native born, and by 1776 nearly all of them were (Fogel and Engerman, 1974). Similarly, Hispanics have lived in the American West and Southwest for centuries; in fact, these regions belonged to Spain and then to Mexico until the middle of the last century.

Thus, it may seem silly to apply to these groups our model of how new immigrants succeeded in this country in only two or three generations, since these groups remain disadvantaged after many generations. However, a number of sociologists (Lieberson, 1973, 1980; Sowell, 1981) have recently rejected this conclusion. They argue instead that, in the ways that count, blacks, Hispanics, and American Indians have, until recently, been nearly as isolated from the mainstream of American society as they would have been had they lived in another country. In analyzing their recent history, therefore, it makes

more sense to regard these groups as recent immigrants. To illustrate why this view is useful, let's examine black history more closely.

GOING NORTH: BLACK "IMMIGRATION"

Even today, about half of the black population in the United States lives in the South. Until the 1940s, the overwhelming majority of blacks lived in the South. In addition, the black population was not merely Southern, it was also very heavily rural.

World War II propelled a great wave of black migration north. Recruiters for northern industries toured the South, sending trainloads of blacks north to work in the defense industries. After the war, the movement north continued, eventually involving millions of people. As a result, while only a few decades ago most blacks lived in rural areas, today most live in cities. More blacks now live in Chicago than in the whole state of Mississippi, and more live in New York City than in any southern state.

Admittedly, blacks crossed no national border when they journeyed from Tupelo to Chicago or from Macon to New York. But because of the conditions of life in the South until very recently, going north for blacks was more like a journey from rural, southern Italy to America than a journey from Chicago to Detroit.

Recent industrial development and population growth have transformed the American South so greatly that even many younger southerners are unaware that only a few years ago this region was mired in grinding poverty and backwardness. Indeed, while the legacy of slavery lived on in the discrimination against blacks (they could not attend schools with whites or even drink from the same public water fountains as whites), it is important to recognize that the most severe deficiencies of southern life affected both blacks and whites. For example, southern agriculture was not organized into the large, prosperous, high-technology family farms typical of the North, but consisted primarily of tiny tenant farms (sharecropping) and of subsistence farms, on which people raised only enough food to feed themselves. Indeed, the poverty of the South meant poor education for both whites and blacks. In 1900, for example, southern black and white children were equally likely to be enrolled in school but were much less likely to be in school than children outside the South (Guest and Tolnay, forthcoming). However, black students in the South attended lower-quality schools than white students (Lieberson, 1980). Yet the differences were not so great as might be expected in view of the racial prejudice of white southerners at the time, since white schools were also very inferior to those outside the South. The South simply could not afford schools like those of other states. Horace Bond (1934) pointed out that Alabama in the 1930s would have had to impose school taxes 6 times higher than California's in order to spend the same amount per student. He computed that Mississippi would have had to

devote from 20 to 30 percent of its total income from all purposes to education, and the other Southern states would have to do the same in but slightly smaller proportions [in order to match the schools of most Northern states]. Not even our most advanced educational systems have found citizens willing to levy such an immense tax upon their resources.

Thus, only if every individual and business in the South had been willing to give twenty to thirty cents from every dollar they earned to the schools could the South have matched the educational outlays of the North. People in the North could afford such schools because their incomes were so much higher that education cost them less than one cent out of each dollar earned.

Blacks who headed north had known only subsistence farming or field labor and had little schooling (which was of low quality), no technical training or job skills, and no experience with the complexities of city life. In this important respect they were going to a new country. Only their ability to speak English set them apart from other immigrant groups.

All packed and waiting for her transportation to arrive, this young black woman is fleeing the poverty of the rural South in 1940 to begin a new life in the North. Although technically she was not an immigrant, her journey crossed cultural gaps as great as those crossed by people who came from overseas.

Black progress

Stanley Lieberson (1973, 1980) has severely criticized sociologists assessing black progress for failing to take into account the fact that blacks are so newly arrived from the South. When sociologists analyze the progress of other racial and ethnic groups, they automatically control for the number of generations in this country. For example, when we compare the educational achievement or the income of Italian-Americans with German-Americans, we first sort the data to eliminate differences resulting from

To truly understand the American experience of blacks, it is necessary also to under-stand the economic and social history of the American South—to know that until recently most southern whites as well as blacks lived in rural poverty, received inferior educations, and suffered from poor nutrition. When white southerners like this little girl grew up, many of them also went North. And there, they too resembled immigrants and encountered many of the problems faced by blacks from the South.

the fact that one group has been in America longer. Thus, we try to compare first-generation Italians with first-generation Germans, and so on.

Until recently, sociologists compared northern blacks with northern whites without such generational controls. In fact, only in recent years have a substantial number of blacks been born in the North, and relatively few blacks are the children of parents born in the North. When such generational controls are taken into account, many black-white differ-

ences are greatly reduced. The more generations that blacks have lived in the North, the higher their education and the better their jobs (Lieberson, 1973, 1980; Sowell, 1981).

The fact that most blacks lived in the South for so long has been a major impediment to their success. That many southern whites have recently followed the blacks north emphasizes this point, for these white migrants have displayed many of the same disadvantages. Recall from Chapter 5 that

Table 11-3 / Median black and white family income (1939–1979).

	1939	1950	1960	1970	1979*	
					All Families	**Family Head Under Age 35**
Whites	$1,325	$3,390	$5,424	$9,284	$21,821	$20,256
Blacks	$489	$1,671	$3,058	$6,073	$16,887	$17,278
Percentage of Black Income to White Income	37%	49%	56%	65%	78%	85%

*Data include only families having two adult members.

southern whites have scored equally poorly on IQ tests. Thus a great deal that has been attributed to racial differences and racial problems might be explained much more adequately as a more common phenomenon: the problems faced by new immigrants from less developed societies.

A second important matter in assessing recent black progress is age. Because blacks have had a higher birth rate than whites in recent decades, the black population is somewhat younger than the white population. For this reason, comparing the average family income of blacks and whites is also comparing the average income of younger and older families. Since people usually earn more as they get older, such comparisons can misleadingly suggest racial and ethnic differences in success that are merely due to age differences (Sowell, 1981).

All these matters aside, blacks have been making rapid progress in education and income. Table 11-1 shows how rapidly blacks have gained on whites in average education. In 1960 the average American black had not completed the eighth grade and was three years behind the level of education of the average white. In the next decade both blacks and whites increased their average education, but blacks increased more rapidly, closing the gap to 2.3 years of schooling. In 1980, blacks had closed the gap to only half a year. Moreover, the average American black aged 25 to 29 in 1980 had 12.6 years of schooling, compared with 12.9 years for whites.

Table 11-3 shows a rapid closing of the gap in the average family income of blacks and whites. In 1939, just before the start of the great black migration north, black families had only slightly more than one-third the income of white families. By 1950 this had risen to 49 percent. Over the next decade it rose to 56 percent, and over the next to 65 percent. In 1979, the average black family had 78 percent of the income of the average white family.

But even this pattern understates black progress, since the black population tends to be younger and older blacks have much less education than both younger blacks and whites. Thus, among families in which the household head was under age 35 in 1979, blacks earned 85 percent of the income of white families. In these younger families where both husband and wife worked, the average black income was 91 percent that of the white income. The gap was even smaller when we compare only northern families.

This portrait of rapid black economic gains must be qualified, however, due to a sharp rise in the proportion of black families lacking an adult male. In 1950 only about a tenth of black families with children below the age of 18 were headed by a woman. In 1980, 47 percent of these black families lacked a father. Families headed by a female, black or white, are much more likely to be poor than are families headed by a male. Because of the dramatic increase in female-headed black families (only 14 percent of white families with children below 18 were headed by females in 1980), a substantially

Between 1960 and 1980, the proportion of American blacks with professional occupations more than doubled from 4.8 percent to 12.7 percent, while the proportion of whites in the professions increased only from 12.1 percent to 16.5 percent. Meanwhile the proportion of blacks in managerial positions also rose rapidly from 2.6 percent to 5.2 percent.

higher proportion of black than white families are poor. Little or nothing has been done to explain why this change has occurred.

But even with the poverty experienced by female-headed families, the economic situation of black Americans has improved greatly in recent decades. If we accept the notion of blacks as immigrants, then they began to arrive in large number only forty years ago, and many came much more recently. Viewed this way, their record of achievement compares very favorably with that of most earlier ethnic and racial groups. This observation is in no way intended to minimize the centuries of black suffering in North America or the continuing poverty of many black citizens. But it does demonstrate the immense achievements of millions of black Americans, achievements that are overlooked by the news media, which tend to portray recent black history as marked by unrelieved poverty, frustration, and helplessness.

Indeed, Thomas Sowell (1981) has bitterly attacked the common political rhetoric that racism prevents black progress and that only a massive reformation of society can enable blacks to gain equality as propaganda that dishonors and demeans blacks. To accept such a position, he wrote, means that "some of the longest and hardest struggles for self-improvement must be denied—which is to say, history itself must be denied."

However, an accurate portrait of the situation of black Americans must also consider the many impoverished black families and the special barriers that blacks must overcome.

Barriers to black progress

Every racial and ethnic minority that began at the bottom of the American status structure had unique features that influenced how rapidly and easily it was able to rise. While the general model of how groups make it in America applies to each, we have also paid attention to these special features. Although blacks have been making considerable progress, it is important to consider their special handicaps.

The legacies of slavery Earlier in this chapter, we saw how the existence of slavery in America and the American ideal of individual freedom created a special American dilemma that gave rise to ardent racial prejudice. While all disadvantaged minorities in America were hampered by prejudice, none has faced such harsh prejudice and discrimination as have blacks. That antiblack prejudice has waned so substantially in the past twenty years reflects rapid black economic and educational achievement. But prejudice and discrimination have also placed much greater burdens on blacks than on other groups.

Moreover, centuries of slavery severed blacks from all but traces of their traditional cultures and limited their sense of common identity. To a very important extent, in recent decades blacks have had to rediscover their cultural roots and construct a cohesive group sense to give them a common cause (Carmichael and Hamilton, 1967).

No homeland American blacks also lack a homeland, in the sense of having a specific nation or society of origin. This is because blacks came from many different parts of Africa; moreover, until recently these areas were not independent nations but colonies ruled by European powers. This has had major practical as well as symbolic consequences.

Most immigrants to the United States based their decisions about when and whether to immigrate on calculations about opportunities here versus opportunities in their homeland. Thus, immigration into the United States fluctuated sharply in response to economic conditions, rising when our economy boomed and jobs were plentiful and falling during times of recession. Blacks never chose to come to America, nor did they choose when to become free and thus when and where to start to earn a living. In fact, blacks had to scrape for their first jobs in the aftermath of the Civil War, in a South ravaged by defeat. While their migration north often reflected the desire for greater opportunity, here, too, blacks were less able than other immigrants to respond to fluctuations in opportunity.

As pointed out in Chapter 2, ethnic and racial immigrants could go back to their homelands if things did not turn out well for them here. During the Great Depression of the 1930s, about 500,000 immigrants went back to Europe (Handlin, 1957). Blacks lacked this option.

Finally, the homeland governments often aided many immigrants after they were here. For example, many governments provided clergy to staff churches in America for immigrants from their nations. Other governments officially intervened with the U.S. government to influence the treatment of immigrants from their countries. Nothing of the sort was available for blacks in America (Lieberson, 1980).

Visibility Although the stereotypes of prejudice associated distinctive physical traits with many ethnic groups (that Jews could easily be recognized by their noses, for example), most members of these groups lacked such traits. For example, a study of Jewish men in New York revealed that only 14 percent had what was regarded as a "Jewish nose" (Fishberg, 1911). Moreover, while many immigrant groups had a distinctive culture and quite distinctive names, these traits could easily be changed, thus concealing one's ethnic origins and diminishing **visibility**. That Tony Curtis, Karl Malden, Judy Garland, Hal Linden, and Kirk Douglas, were once known as Bernard Schwartz, Malden Sekulovich, Frances Gumm, Hal Lipshitz, and Issur Danielovitch demonstrates the point. A Pole or an Italian could learn to speak unaccented English, change his or her name, join a Protestant church, and claim to be a WASP. Most blacks are native speakers of English, have Anglo-Saxon names, and are Protestant, but they're still black.

Racially different groups cannot pass as members of the majority, which may present a more difficult barrier. However, Japanese and Chinese have achieved equality despite being racially different, and most eastern and southern European immigrants did not discard their names, religions, or many of their distinctive cultural patterns en route to acceptance and equality.

Numbers Perhaps one of the greatest problems faced by blacks is simply that they greatly outnumber all other previously disadvantaged racial and ethnic minorities. Thus, while several hundred thousand

Japanese and Chinese sufficed to cause a "yellow peril" on the West Coast, black migration north has involved millions of people. Moreover, sheer numbers prevent blacks from adopting some of the tactics used by other groups. Occupational specialization is one of these. As Lieberson (1980) put it, "Imagine more than 22 million Japanese-Americans trying to carve out initial niches [in the U.S. economy] through truck farming!"

Thus, given that economic conflict is the primary factor in prejudice and discrimination, the large size of the black population has made them a greater threat to whites, especially in earlier times when blacks constituted a huge source of cheap labor. When changes in the immigration laws stemmed the tide of cheap labor from abroad in the 1920s, blacks became the only significant competitive threat to whites, especially whites holding unskilled labor jobs. Thus, the antagonism that once was spread across many groups—Italians, Poles, Japanese, as well as blacks—focused primarily on blacks; race, not religion or ethnicity, became the burning concern of organized hate groups.

Of course, the size of the black population also presents opportunities. Once barriers to black voting were removed, for example, they became a potent political bloc, which, in recent years, has been reflected by a sharp increase in the number of blacks holding elected office.

None of these barriers to black progress seems so effective as to limit blacks to economic and social inequality. Indeed, each has been substantially overcome, if with great pain and difficulty. Yet it is important to see how each has made the road upward unusually difficult.

Of course, blacks are not the only group still suffering inequality in America; they are simply the largest of these groups, and the one whose American experience constitutes the most shameful and painful chapter in our history. Thus, it is instructive to see the extent to which blacks have fulfilled the dream expressed in the anthem of the Civil Rights Movement, "We Shall Overcome." If blacks can retrace the steps taken by so many other disadvantaged groups in American history, there should be no doubt that Puerto Ricans, Chicanos, and Native Americans will also succeed, as well as other racial and ethnic minorities.

CONCLUSION

The primary purpose of this chapter was to show that prejudice, discrimination, and conflict caused by racial and cultural differences are not recent phenomena or limited primarily to the United States. These problems are best understood not on the basis of peculiar historical circumstances or even white bigotry, but on the basis of sociological theories having universal application. Intergroup conflict fueled by racial and cultural markers is as old as human existence. So are the processes by which these conflicts are overcome.

That these conflicts cause such agony is reflected by the intensity with which social scientists have sought to understand and prevent them. In my judgment, the contents of this chapter demonstrate that this search has been fairly successful. Current sociological theories of intergroup conflict have dispelled much of the fog shrouding these hostilities. We can now say with some certainty why and how strangers become enemies and how and why these antagonisms will pass.

As we have seen, the key to intergroup conflict is status inequality. Contact between groups who are unequal in status and competing for status produces prejudice. Prejudice does not subside until status equality has been achieved. Keep in mind that two groups being of equal status does not mean that all members of each group must be of the same status. Italians have not achieved status equality with WASPs as a result of all Italians becoming rich. Rather, groups are of equal status when the distribution of their members in the status structure is the same. Thus, when a person's race does not reliably indicate his or her status, then racial equality has been achieved. At that point, members of different races are equally likely to be rich or poor.

Review glossary

Intergroup conflict Conflict between groups that are racially or culturally different. (p. 246)

Race A human group having some biological features that set it off from other human groups. (p. 246)

Ethnic groups Groups that think of themselves as sharing special bonds of history and culture that set them apart from others. (p. 247)

Caste system A stratification system wherein cultural or racial differences are used as the basis for ascribing status. (p. 248)

Allport's theory of contact A theory holding that contact between groups will improve relations only if the groups are of equal status and do not compete with one another. (p. 250)

The American dilemma Term used by Myrdal to describe the contradiction of a society committed to democratic ideals but sustaining racial segregation. (p. 251)

Markers (cultural or racial) Noticeable differences between two or more groups that become associated with status conflicts between the groups. (p. 254)

Cultural division of labor A situation in which racial or ethnic groups tend to specialize in a limited number of occupations. (p. 258)

Middlemen minorities Racial or ethnic groups restricted to a limited range of occupations in the middle, rather than lower, level of the stratification system. (p. 258)

Visibility The degree to which a racial or ethnic group can be recognized—how easily those in such a group can pass as members of the majority. (p. 275)

Suggested readings

Bonacich, Edna. "A Theory of Ethnic Antagonism: The Split Labor Market." *American Sociological Review,* (1972) 37:547–549.

Bonacich, Edna. "Abolition, the Extension of Slavery, and the Position of Free Blacks." *American Journal of Sociology* (1975) 81:601–628.

Greeley, Andrew J. *Ethnicity in the United States.* New York: Wiley, 1974.

Lieberson, Stanley. *A Piece of the Pie: Blacks and White Immigrants Since 1880.* Berkeley: University of California Press, 1980.

Petersen, William. *Japanese Americans: Oppression and Success.* New York: Random House, 1971.

Sowell, Thomas. *Ethnic America: A History.* New York: Basic Books, 1981.

Minorities
and Stardom

The majority of players on every team in the National Basketball Association are black. White boxing champions are rare. A far greater proportion of professional football players is black than would be expected on the basis of the size of the black population. Furthermore, blacks began to excel in sports long before the Civil Rights Movement broke down barriers barring them from many other occupations. This has led many Americans, both black and white, to conclude that blacks are born with a natural talent for athletics. How else could they have come to dominate the ranks of superstars?

The trouble with this biological explanation of blacks in sports is that it ignores a very obvious historical fact: It is typical for minorities in the United States to make their first substantial progress in sports (and, for similar reasons, in entertainment). Who today would suggest that Jews have a biological advantage in athletics? Yet at the turn of the century, the number of Jews who excelled in sports far exceeded their proportion in the population. And late in the nineteenth century, the Irish dominated sports to almost the same extent as blacks have done in recent decades.

By examining an encyclopedia of boxing, for example, it is possible to draw accurate conclusions about patterns of immigration and at what period which ethnic groups were on the bottom of the stratification system. The Irish domination of boxing in the latter half of the nineteenth century is obvious from the names of heavyweight champions, beginning with bareknuckle champ Ned O'Baldwin in 1867 and including Mike McCoole in 1869, Paddy Ryan in 1880, John L. Sullivan in 1889, and Jim Corbett in 1892. The list of champions in lower weight divisions during the same era is dominated by fighters named Ryan, Murphy, Delaney, Lynch, O'Brien, and McCoy.

Early in the twentieth century, Irish names became much less common among boxing champions, even though many fighters who were not Irish took Irish ring names. Suddenly, champions had names like Battling Levinsky, Maxie Rosenbloom, Benny Leonard, Abe Goldstein, Kid Kaplan, and Izzy Schwartz. This was the Jewish era in boxing. Then, Jewish names dropped out of the lists, and Italian and eastern European names came to the fore: Canzoneri, Battalino, LaMotta, Graziano, and Basilio; Yarosz, Lesnevich, Zale, Risko, Hostak, and Servo. By the 1940s, fighters were disproportionately black. Today, black domination of boxing has already peaked, and Hispanic names have begun to prevail.

The same patterns can be found in other sports. Once the Irish dominated baseball—Babe Ruth was one of the last of the Irish superstars. In the 1940s, Hank Greenberg, the Detroit Tiger's slugger, and Sid Luckman of the Chicago Bears, pro football's first star quarterback, were among the last of the Jewish superstars.

The current overrepresentation of blacks in sports reflects two things: first, a lack of other avenues to wealth and fame, and second, the fact that minority groups can overcome discrimination most easily in occupations where the quality of individual performance is most easily and accurately assessed (Blalock, 1967). These are the same factors that led to the overrepresentation of other ethnic groups in sports earlier in American history.

It is often difficult to know which applicants to a law school or a pilot training school are the most capable. But it is very easy to tell who can box or hit a baseball. As we shall see, the demonstration of talent, especially in sports and entertainment, tends to break down barriers of discrimination. As these fall, opportunities in these areas for wealth and fame open up, while other opportunities are still closed. Thus, minority groups will aspire to those areas in which the opportunities are open and tend to overachieve in these areas.

In an important theoretical contribution to racial and ethnic relations, H. M. Blalock (1967) was one of the first to explain why minorities more rapidly

Yankee Sullivan was the first great Irish-American prize fighter. In 1853 he lost the American heavyweight championship in a bareknuckle bout lasting 37 rounds. The first American to win the world heavyweight championship was also named Sullivan (John L.) and held the title from 1882 until 1892 when he lost it to another Irish-American named James J. Corbett, who, in turn was succeeded by an Irish-American named Bob Fitzsimmons. In the late nineteenth century nearly every famous boxer in every weight class was an Irish-American.

overcome discrimination in sports. Let's consider several of his propositions.

First, Blalock argued, work groups differ in the extent to which an outstanding individual can bring success to the whole group. A worker on an assembly line, for example, does not increase the earnings of other workers by working faster. But a great quarterback or a great hitter can transform an average team into champions. Thus, Blalock theorized, the more an individual can increase the benefits of all work group members, the less that group will discriminate against minority members. This will be particularly so when it is easy to judge how much a person could add to the group's success.

To illustrate Blalock's point, consider a baseball team. All the players are white, and many of them are prejudiced against blacks. However, they also want to win the pennant and the World Series, but they need a better power hitter to do so. Such a team will be inclined to ignore their prejudice against blacks if they have a chance to get a star hitter who is black.

Blalock also suggested that when employers compete intensely for talented people, they will be much less likely to discriminate. Since such competition is the essence of management in sports, highly talented minority players will be an irresistible temptation for owners and managers. Thus, discrimination should cease in sports long before it does in most other high status occupations. Blalock's proposition also implies that less successful teams would take the lead in ending discrimination, while the most successful teams would resist it. In fact, during the many years when they routinely won the pennant and the World Series, the New York Yankees were the least integrated team in baseball.

Thus, the overrepresentation of an ethnic or racial minority in sports is often a sign of that group's early progress in struggling up from the bottom of society. However, the real signal that a group is making it comes when their overrepresentation in sports begins to decline, for it means that young people of this racial or ethnic background have other possible roads to success. This is not to suggest that it is better for people to become lawyers or dentists than to become linebackers. (I much prefer to watch a linebacker fill a hole than a dentist.) But it is to suggest that no group should face such limited opportunities that playing sports is their only escape from poverty and prejudice. Thus, the overrepresentation of a racial or ethnic minority in sports does not reflect inborn athletic talent any more than their underrepresentation in science reflects an inborn lack of academic talent. Instead, both reflect limited opportunities.

These same principles apply to overrepresentation in the entertainment world. The early success of blacks in music, for example, led to the belief that they were born with a "natural sense of rhythm." Again, when opportunities are few, people will concentrate their efforts. Blacks who could play musical instruments, dance, sing, or write music dedicated themselves to perfecting their skills, as did other ethnic groups when their opportunities were limited. Like athletic talent, entertainment skills are very visible and easily demonstrated. Bill "Bojangles" Robinson could have become a star just by dancing on a street corner (which he often did even after he was world famous). Louis Armstrong's trumpet playing was as obviously inspired as Julius Erving's dunk shots. To claim that Fats Waller couldn't play the piano would have been as silly as to say Joe Louis couldn't punch. Thus, as in sports, barriers of discrimination tend to fall early in the entertainment industry.

Number of live births per 1,000 population, 1980. National = 15.9.

Back in 1820 when the first nationwide fertility statistics were computed, the U.S. birth rate was 55.2 births for every 1,000 persons. By 1900 it had fallen to 32.3. In 1980 it was only 15.9. Such a low level of fertility helps explain why the size of the average American household has fallen to only 2.7 people. Despite the great decline in fertility, there still is substantial variation in the birth rate among states and regions—differences that would surprise many people. Fertility is lowest in the Northeast and South, and substantially higher in the western regions. Connecticut (12.5), Massachusetts (12.7), and Rhode Island (12.9) have the lowest rates among the 50 states despite their large proportion of Roman Catholic citizens. Utah (28.6) has the highest rate, followed by Alaska (23.7) and Wyoming (22.5).

Pacific 17.0

Mountain 19.9

West North Central 16.8

East North Central 16.0

Middle Atlantic 13.4

New England 13.1

West South Central 18.7

East South Central 16.4

South Atlantic 14.8

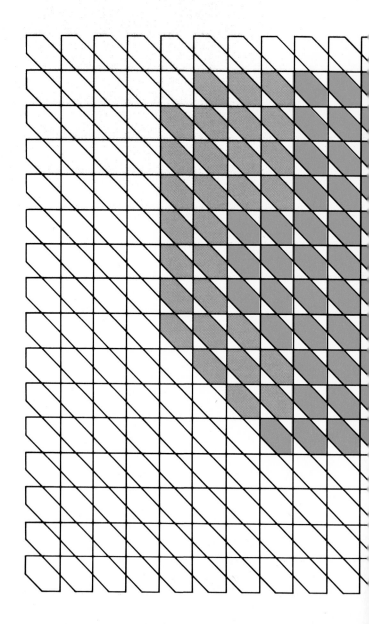

Social Institutions

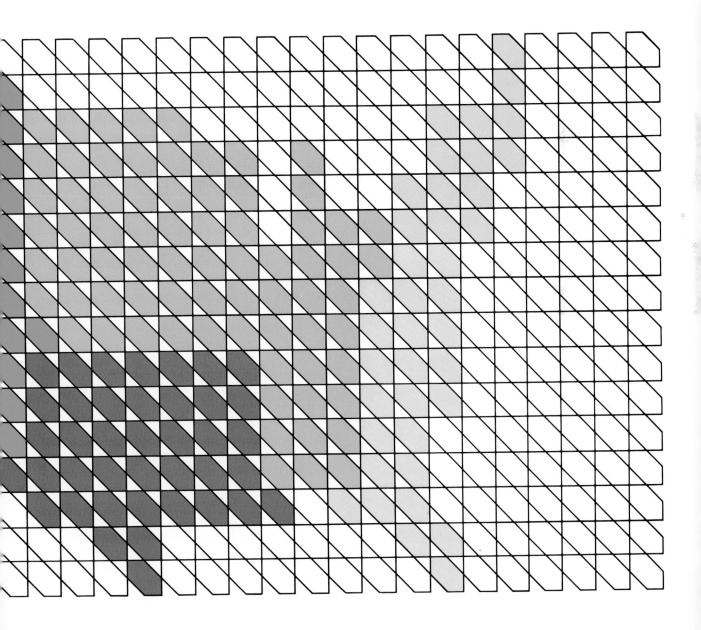

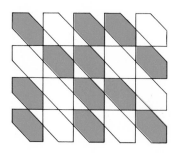

■ Sociological writing on the family has long been dominated by two themes: *universality* and *decline.*

The theme of universality asserts that the family exists in all human societies. For a number of compelling reasons, humans cannot live as solitary creatures, nor can human females raise their young by themselves as mother cats do. Hence, humans always live in groups containing adults of both sexes as well as children. Moreover, within any society, humans form small clusters, called **families**, containing males and females, adults and children. Membership in these clusters is determined by common ancestry and sexual unions.

This must seem like a very vague definition of the word *family.* However, sociologists and anthropologists have failed to discover a more specific definition that can apply to the amazing variety of social forms called families in different societies. Wherever social scientists have looked at social life, they have discovered families. But who belongs to the same family differs greatly from one society to another. In some societies, for example, the biological father is not a member of the same family as his children, the social role of father being fulfilled by the wife's brother. Among the Nuer of East Africa, some families contain no adult males—an older woman can adopt a younger woman and her children (Murdock, 1949; Levi-Strauss, 1956; Gough, 1974).

Faced with this difficulty, sociologists have quit trying to formulate a general definition based on who belongs to families and have concentrated instead on examining what the family does, that is, its social functions. These functions make the family a universal feature of human societies. There-

The Family

fore, early in this chapter we shall assess the basic functions of the family.

The second theme in modern sociological writing on the family is that, despite the universality of the family, in modern societies the family is in *decline.* It is claimed that modernization has dangerously eroded the family: Families are now shrunken and unstable, and the modern family is increasingly unable to provide for the well-being of its members. Indeed, recent textbooks typically end discussions of the family with the question: Will the family survive? The answer usually given is maybe.

The theme of universality is supported by a great deal of historical, anthropological, and cross-cultural evidence. The family *is* a fundamental social institution occurring in all societies, although its particular forms differ substantially from place to place. Even the radical utopian communes of the nineteenth century did not succeed in eliminating the family as the basic unit of social relations (Nordhoff, 1875).

The theme of decline has seemed equally well supported by evidence. Statistics show that in all of the most modernized nations, the divorce rate has risen rapidly. This would seem to reflect the weakness of fundamental family bonds today. However, to know whether the modern family is really less able to fulfill its functions, we need to know whether the family in traditional societies fulfilled them better. For a long time, social scientists thought it self-evident that the traditional family did function better, and so they didn't bother to seek pertinent evidence.

Recently, however, much has been learned about families in the "good old days." This evidence seriously challenges the theme of decline. In fact, it can be argued that the family has become more important than ever during the past century and much better able to provide strong emotional attachments between its members than did families in traditional societies. ■

CHAPTER PREVIEW

In this chapter, we shall first examine the functions of the family—what a family does that makes the family a universal social institution. We shall then see how the family has changed in response to modernization and thus deal with the theme of decline. To do this, we shall examine what the family was like in Europe several hundred years ago. How did families live? How did they treat one another? How did they feel about one another? How distinct was the family unit from the larger community? Against this benchmark, we shall assess the modern family. Is family life better or worse than it used to be?

FUNCTIONS OF THE FAMILY

If the family is a universal social institution, it must do something vital for human beings, something that is not done as well or as easily in other ways. Sociologists and anthropologists identify three basic functions of the family: (1) reproduction and child rearing, (2) economic support, and (3) emotional support. Examination of each of these functions provides a basis for assessing families in different times and places.

Reproduction and child rearing

The facts of human reproduction and maturation virtually assure the existence of families. First of all, humans rarely give birth to more than one infant at a time. Therefore, rather than having all their children in a single litter, many human females experience a number of pregnancies, during which they are somewhat physically limited. Moreover, since human infants take many years to mature and require close supervision when they are young, pregnant females must often care for growing children. Consequently, human females need help to feed and care for their young.

In addition, children require lengthy and elaborate socialization. This, too, requires the presence of several adults with long-term commitments to each child. Because of the very high mortality rates and short life-expectancies of humans before modern times, one or both biological parents frequently died before their children were grown. This encouraged the formation of families containing more than one adult couple.

Extended and nuclear families When Americans think of the family, they think of an adult couple and their children. This is called the **nuclear family**. In many societies, however, nuclear families do not live apart from other relatives. Rather, the basic family unit includes several nuclear families; these are called **extended families**. Extended families can be composed in many different ways. For example, they can consist of an adult couple (the grandparents), their children, and the spouses and children of their children. Since people in some cultures often die before they become grandparents, the extended family often consists of several brothers, their wives and children, and sometimes unmarried siblings.

Regardless of its composition, the extended family is larger than the nuclear family and always contains more than one adult couple. Extended families would seem able to provide more effective and attentive child care and socialization than nuclear families simply because more adults are available for these tasks. For example, one woman can watch the infants while the others go out to pick fruit or gather eggs. Consequently, sociologists have long believed that the extended family fulfills its basic functions better than the nuclear family, which accounts for the prevalence of this family form in preindustrial societies.

Sexual unions In all societies, norms restrict sexual relations. That is, sexual relations are limited to certain pairs. In all societies, moreover, sexual relations are prohibited between some family members. Virtually every society prohibits sexual relations between parents and their children and between brothers and sisters. This kind of prohibition is called the **incest taboo**. In many societies, the incest taboo also applies to sexual relations between cousins.

Incest taboos have several benefits. First of all, they prevent the frequently harmful biological results of inbreeding. Second, they force children to marry outside the family and thus to create bonds between families (Cohen, 1978). But perhaps the most important benefit is to protect families from sexual disputes and jealousy. Family members must depend upon one another, and such disputes would undermine these relationships.

Typically, societies restrict sexual relations to marriage partners. Although rules against extramarital sex are often broken, they also exist to protect the family. For one thing, rules against extramarital sex spare family bonds from the stress of external attachments. They also establish a sense of responsibility toward one's children—only by knowing who a child's father is can an unambiguous claim for responsibility toward the child be established.

Economic support

Families serve as the primary economic units of societies. This is because families contain **dependents**—such as children, the elderly, and the disabled—who cannot support themselves. Other fam-

This little girl is finding out about where babies come from. She is learning more than the physiology of reproduction, however. She also is learning the essential sociological truth that **people come from families.** *Around the world families function not simply for reproduction but for child rearing, for the economic support of dependents, and for the emotional fulfillment of adults as well as children.*

ily members care for their dependents. In primitive societies, adult males hunt and adult females gather food; together they feed the rest of the family. In modern societies, some family members earn money to support the others. Furthermore, the distribution of resources within a family is determined by the family.

Emotional support

Families serve as primary groups for their members. From our families, we gain our earliest sense of emotional security, our sense of belonging and of personal worth. If our parents, our spouses, and our children don't love us, who will? Indeed, the family,

as the primary locus of sexual relations, includes the most intimate human attachments.

These three basic functions of the family are, of course, intertwined. Sexual unions and the rearing of children both cause and reflect emotional attachments. Similarly, these attachments underlie economic relations within societies: Some family members work to support others at least partly because of their feelings toward them. Moreover, parents often rear large families because of the economic security children provide when they become adults.

However, not all families are equally able or willing to fulfill these primary functions. Children can be neglected, incest can occur, family members can be brutal to one another, and families can fail to support their dependents. Usually only a few families in a society function poorly, in most cases because of defects of particular members. Sometimes families in a society fulfill basic functions relatively poorly because of social forces. Indeed, the theme of family decline asserts that conditions of modern life have forced families to function less well than they used to. To assess this claim, we shall examine how well the family functioned in Europe a few centuries ago.

LIFE IN THE TRADITIONAL EUROPEAN FAMILY

 Not until quite recently did social historians and sociologists of the family begin to dig out reliable data on family life in times past, and not until the early 1970s did substantial reports on these efforts begin to appear (Rosenberg, 1975). Up to that time, our notions about family life in, for example, seventeenth-century Europe came from novels, letters, diaries, and autobiographies written at the time. The trouble with these sources is that they reflect a narrow stratum of society—the wealthy and literate. Although they may shed light on how the privileged few lived and felt, they tell us very little about the lives of the vast majority.

Europe's peasants and urban laborers left no literary traces. To discover what the life of an average family was like in past times and places, scholars have had to laboriously reconstruct the period from tax records; lawsuits; parish records of baptisms, weddings, and funerals; and even information on gravestones. These labors proved to be worthwhile. The picture of traditional family life is far from the warm, intimate, loving, caring extended family that we have long celebrated.

For sociologists, the first real fruits of these historical searches came with the publication of Edward Shorter's *The Making of the Modern Family* in 1975. In it Shorter combined the research of many scholars to depict the traditional family and contrast it with the modern family. Shorter's book has changed the views of sociologists about the family. Let's see what Shorter found out about the traditional European family.

Household composition

The first step in assessing family life is to know who is living with whom; that is, what the usual composition of a household is. From many studies of different parts of Europe, Shorter discovered that the extended family living in a single household was not typical except for the wealthy, both urban and rural. As we shall see, the typical household did include more than a nuclear family, but the additional members were often only temporary members, such as lodgers and hired hands. Moreover, the traditional household was much smaller than had been assumed. While wealthy households often included ten or more people, most households had only five or six members.

How could this be? We know that in those days women gave birth to many children, often as many as eight or ten. How, then, could the normal household be so small? One reason was high infant and child mortality. One of every three infants died before the age of one, and another third died before reaching adulthood. Another reason is that children typically left the household to take full-time employment at ages that seem incredibly young to us.

In the eighteenth century, for example, children in western France left home to work as servants, shepherds, cowherds, or apprentices, at the age of 7 or 8! By the age of 10, virtually all children had gone off on their own. In England at this same time, children did not begin to leave home until the age of 10, but by age 15 nearly all of them had left. Keep in mind that people physically matured much later in this period (see Chapter 5). These were little kids who were having to go it alone.

Of course, not all the children left. Eldest sons stayed home or returned home after a period of working elsewhere, and one day took over the farm. In some places, daughters remained home until they married. Nevertheless, the traditional household is remarkable for the small number of children living in it, especially given the large number who were born.

In addition, the traditional household contained fewer adults than one might expect. High mortality meant that there were few elderly in the households, and many homes lacked either a father or a

New historical research has found that preindustrial households contained many fewer children than had been supposed because children were sent off on their own at so young an age. Three centuries ago in France, for example, children began to leave home to work as shepherds, servants, and apprentices at age 7 or 8 and by 10 nearly all children had left home.

mother. In fact, female-headed households were as common in the past as they are today. The primary cause of such households today is divorce, and thus the father often continues to see the children and to send financial aid. Back then, the cause was death. The average married couple had only about ten years together before one died. As a result, many people remarried; therefore, many children grew up with a stepparent and with half sisters and half brothers.

Thus, the image of the large extended families of preindustrial societies is based on wealthy households. These households were large because their rate of mortality was lower (the rich were much more likely to live to see their grandchildren, and more grandchildren survived), because their children were not pushed out to fend for themselves at

There was no privacy in preindustrial households; most dwellings had but a single room in which all activities took place. Often more than one family shared a one-room home. Imagine yourself growing up in this Flemish household painted by Pieter Bruegel (1525–1569).

young ages, and because many servants were part of the household.

Crowding

Although the average household was not large, even compared with modern households, it was crowded. The overwhelming majority of traditional European families lived in one room, where all indoor family activities took place. Rural families usually shared their one-room houses with livestock and poultry, while urban families frequently had a lodger or some other nonfamily member sharing their living space. Usually the one room wasn't even very large. At night,

beds were arranged on the floor, and when people had mattresses, the beds were often crowded: Adults and children, males and females, family members and outsiders huddled together for warmth.

As late as the 1880s, when good census data were first recorded, half of the people in Berlin and Dresden still lived in one-room households. This situation seemed to be much more common throughout Europe earlier in the century. In Chapter 18, we shall see that far less crowding in households can cause serious strains among family members. When American families have more than one person per room, husband-wife and parent-child relations become strained. With whole families crowded into one room, family relations in preindustrial times were simply terrible, as we shall see.

"Outsiders"

Though much smaller than had been believed, many traditional households contained nonfamily members. Many rural households contained male and female teenagers who served as hired hands. Such outsiders were particularly common during the peak of the farming season. Urban households frequently included lodgers who paid to eat and live with a family. Often, one-room urban homes were shared by several unrelated families, forced into a common residence by poverty. Moreover, there was a considerable coming and going by these live-in outsiders. Thus, families tended to have people they did not know well living temporarily in their midst.

Clearly, the traditional family lacked privacy and a well-defined boundary. Family members ate, slept, gave birth, engaged in sex, and argued not only in full view of one another, but in full view of a changing audience of outsiders. Moreover, the traditional family was under close observation by neighbors, too. Even rural families did not live far apart, each on their own farm as in the United States, but in cramped farming villages. As we shall see, these crowded living conditions undermined feelings of family unity.

Child care

We have seen that the traditional family was quick to send kids out on their own. This reflected more than mere economic necessity or the fact that unskilled children could perform productive labor in preindustrial economies. It also reflected an indifference toward children and neglectful child care practices. Shorter put it bluntly: "Good mothering is an invention of modernization."

A good index of neglect and indifference is found in examinations of journals kept by local doctors. All of these doctors complained about parents leaving their infants and young children alone and untended for much of the day. Rashes and sores from unchanged swaddling clothes afflicted nearly all infants. Repeated accounts tell of children burning to death by having been left too close to an open hearth, and reports of unattended infants being eaten by barnyard pigs are frequent. In the part of France where silkworms were raised, a peasant proverb acknowledged that children were neglected during the busy season: "When the silkworms rise, the kids go to paradise." Indeed, throughout Europe, rural infants were most likely to die during the harvest season, when they were most neglected.

Even when parents were around their infants, they ignored them. Mothers rarely sang or talked to their infants when they tended them, nor did they play games with them as the children grew older. In fact, mothers didn't even refer to children by name, calling a child "it" or, in France, "the creature."

Mothers frequently were unsure of their children's age (Shorter reports a mother who said her son was either 11 or maybe 14), failed to recall how many children they had given birth to, and often gave the name of a child who died to the next one born.

Because of the high rates of infant mortality, it might be understandable that parents were somewhat reluctant to form intense emotional bonds with their babies. But in some parts of France, it seems to have been typical for parents not to attend funerals for children younger than 5, and there is widespread evidence that infant deaths caused little if any regret or sorrow. Instead, parents often expressed relief at the deaths of children, and many proverbs reflected this attitude. Moreover, dead and even dying infants were often simply discarded like refuse and were frequently noticed "lying in the gutters or rotting on the dung-heaps."

Indeed, large numbers of legitimate infants whose parents were still living were abandoned outside churches or foundling homes. Some scholars suggest that as many as half of the children abandoned in parts of France during the eighteenth century were abandoned by intact families. Additional evidence of indifference and neglect can be seen in the large numbers of infants sent off to wet nurses, despite the well-known fact that such children faced much higher probabilities of death. Indeed, wet-nursing became a high cottage industry outside of major cities in the eighteenth and nineteenth centuries, as families, especially the poor, sent away infants so that the mother would not be tied down by nursing and child care responsibilities. It is estimated that at least one-sixth of all babies born in Paris in 1777 were shipped out to wet nurses.

Once at the wet nurse's, infants were often not

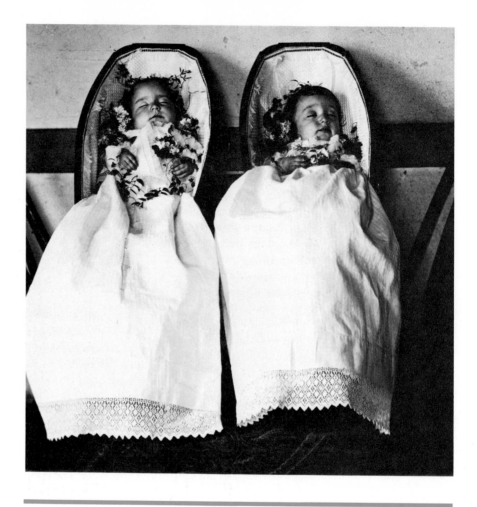

This poignant photograph of twins in their coffins, taken in Wisconsin in the 1890s, stands in dramatic contrast to the attitudes toward children typical in preindustrial families. Funeral portraits like this showed the determination of grieving parents to remember their lost children. In preindustrial times parents were little interested in the death of a child—often simply reusing its name for a later one.

nursed at all but fed a paste of grain and water and given little attention. In truth, these homes were baby barns, crowded with infants. Parents seldom, if ever, visited. Deaths were often covered up so that payments could still be collected. But staggering numbers of these babies were never seen again. Nor, it seems, were they missed.

The extraordinary infant death rates in preindustrial Europe now become easier to understand. The general conditions of life and public health practices alone would have produced high rates. But the actual rates were pushed even higher because of neglect and indifference. Indeed, as late as the 1920s, a government study in Austria attributed about 20 percent of infant deaths to "poor care."

Obviously, infants gained little emotional support from the preindustrial family. But what about other family members? What Shorter found seems as alien to us today as the idea of parents engaging in sex while sharing their bed with children and a lodger.

Relations between husbands and wives

Only in modern times have people married for love. In the good old days, they married for money and labor—marriage was an economic arrangement between families. How much land or wealth did the man have? How large a dowry would the bride bring to her spouse? Emotional attachments were of no importance to parents in arranging marriages, and neither the bride nor the groom expected emotional fulfillment from marriage.

Shorter noted an absence of emotional expression between couples and doubted that more than a few actually felt affection. The most common sentiments seem to have been resentment and anger. Not only was wife-beating commonplace, but so was husband-beating. And when wives beat their husbands, it was the husband, not the wife, who was likely to be punished by the community. In France, a husband beaten by his wife was often made to ride backward through the village on a donkey, holding the donkey's tail. He had shamed the village by not controlling his wife properly. The same practice of punishing the husband was frequently employed when wives were sexually unfaithful.

The most devastating evidence of poor husband-wife relations was the reaction to death and dying. Just as the deaths of children caused no sorrow, the death of a spouse often prompted no regret. Some public expression of grief was expected, especially by widows, but popular culture abounded with contrary beliefs. The following proverbs are reported by Shorter:

The two sweetest days of a fellow in life,
Are the marriage and burial of his wife.

Rich is the man whose wife is dead and horse alive.

Indeed, peasants who rushed for medical help whenever a horse or cow took sick often resisted suggestions by neighbors to get a doctor for a sick wife. The loss of a cow or a horse cost money, but a wife was easily replaced by remarriage to a younger woman who would bring a new dowry.

Bonds between parents and children

We have already seen the lack of emotional ties to infants and young children. But emotional bonds between parents and older children were also weak. First, most of the children left the household at an early age. Second, when they did so, it was largely a case of "out of sight, out of mind." If a child ventured from the village, he or she was soon forgotten, not just by the neighbors but by the parents. All traces were lost of those who moved away. According to Shorter, a French village doctor wrote in his diary in 1710 that he had heard about one of his brothers being hanged but that he had completely lost track of the others.

Finally, even the children who stayed in the village did not come to love their parents. Instead, they fought constantly with their parents about inheritance rights and about when their parents would retire, and they openly awaited their parents' deaths. Shorter concluded that dislike and hatred were the typical feelings between family members.

Peer group bonds

Surely people in traditional societies must have liked someone. Unfortunately for our image of traditional family life, the primary unit of sociability and attachment was not the family but the peer group. The family provided for reproduction, child rearing (such as it was), and economic support (often grudgingly), but emotional attachments were primarily to persons of the same age and sex *outside* the family.

Wives had close attachments to other wives, and husbands to other husbands. Social life was highly segregated by sex and was based on childhood friendships and associations. For example, a group of neighborhood boys would become close friends

In preindustrial times the primary adult attachments were not between husbands and wives, but between persons of similar age and sex, peer groups made up of people who had grown up together. The host in **Meal of The Peasants** *(painted by the Nain brothers about 1645), probably shared his inner feelings much more fully with his two guests than with his wife. And she probably shared her confidences with other women her age.*

while still very young, and these friendships remained the primary ties of these people all their lives. The same occurred among women. While this no doubt provided people with a source of intimacy and self-esteem, it hindered the formation of close emotional bonds within the family.

Thus, a woman would enter marriage expecting to share her feelings not with her husband but with her peers. Men reserved intimate feelings for their peers, too. In this way the weak boundaries defining the household were perforated by primary relations beyond the family. Thus, much that went on within a household was determined by outsiders. Husbands and wives often acted to please their peers, not one another.

Of course, sometimes people loved their children, and some couples undoubtedly fell in love. But most evidence indicates life in the preindustrial

Had photography existed three hundred years ago there would have been very few pictures like this one. Only in modern times has it become typical for parents to be deeply attached to their children.

household was the opposite of the popular, nostalgic image of quiet, rural villages where people happily lived and died, secure and loved, amidst their large families and lifelong friends. It was instead a nasty, spiteful, loveless life that no modern person would willingly endure. Indeed, as modernization made other options possible, the family changed radically because no one was willing to endure the old ways any longer.

MODERNIZATION AND ROMANCE

In Part Five we shall examine the why and how of the immense social changes that have resulted from modernization. Here we shall point out that life in modern societies is not simply better than in preindustrial societies, *it is different*.

Nowhere is this clearer than in the transformations in family life. Where once a "happy couple" meant an absence of mutual antagonism, today that phrase is reserved for people who feel strong positive sentiments. We do not hope for a tolerable marriage; we seek love. Nor do we think it enough that parents do not hate, abuse, or neglect their children; we expect parents to love, nourish, and encourage them. We expect people to grieve when their parents die, not to be relieved that they are out of the way. In short, we assume that families foster deeply felt emotional attachments. How did this transformation come about?

Quite simply, modernization radically changed the conditions of life, giving people the opportunity to seek individual happiness. Shorter has sketched a number of these changes. First of all, industrialization freed individuals from depending on inheritance for their livelihoods. Eldest sons no longer had to wait for their father's land; daughters no longer had to wait for a husband with land. Both sons and daughters could seek wage-paying work, especially in the rapidly expanding urban industries. Soon young people were heading off to the cities in droves.

This allowed people to make their own marital choices, free from both parental approval and concern about keeping property in the family. People no longer had to delay marriage until their parents died or retired, nor did property concerns any longer dominate the choice of a spouse. As these matters became less important, other concerns emerged. And as men and women began to select their marriage partners, they began not surprisingly to seek people who appealed to them. Romantic attraction rapidly became the basis for marriage. "I love you" became the precondition for asking, "Will you marry me?"

Notions of romantic love were not first expressed in modern times. But until then they had not been regarded as a significant, let along primary, consideration in marriage. In fact, the Puritans were the first to give common expression to romantic sentiments between husbands and wives. And the Puritans represented the emergence of a well-to-do middle class in England who could afford to marry for love.

In fact, affluence explains much of modern family life. The average modern family is wealthy beyond the dreams of preindustrial families. One of the first fruits of this affluence was space and privacy. As rapidly as economic circumstances permitted, families sought sufficient household space to gain privacy from one another and to shield themselves from outsiders. While married couples today routinely and openly express affection in ways unthinkable in the past, they are able to keep their most intimate relations private.

Moreover, the rise of romantic love in marriage redirected the primary attachments of the individual to within the household. Husbands and wives now expect their relationship to take priority over attachments to peers. A song that was popular at the turn of the century proclaimed, "Those wedding bells are breaking up that old gang of mine." For with modernization it came to be expected that husbands would not remain "one of the boys."

This redirection of primary attachments to family members was facilitated by mobility. People now seldom remain in the same place throughout their lives. As people become adults, they move away and break ties to their peers. Even if an individual does not go away, most of the peer group does. A common observation today is that if you want a lifelong friend, you had better marry one. Husbands and wives have become the only consistent, permanent emotional attachments.

Romantic love between spouses has also affected parent-child relationships. It is now a common belief that children must be wanted or they should not be engendered. By the late nineteenth century, books on child care and good parenting became a major topic in publishing (Zuckerman, 1975). Attitudes toward children have changed so dramatically that it is now against the law to treat children in ways that were once customary.

Indeed, family life has become so important to modern life that marriages have become unstable. It is perhaps ironic that in days when couples lacked emotional ties, they seldom divorced; now, when couples marry for love, they often divorce in anger and disappointment. Let us explore why divorce in modern societies occurs and what it implies for family life.

MODERNIZATION AND DIVORCE

The divorce rate has been rising rapidly in the United States and other modern nations for a long time. Until recently, however, no one knew exactly what the rates really were. The usual figure given is inaccurate: the number of divorces in a given year divided by the number of marriages in that year. Nearly all of the divorces in any year terminate marriages that occurred in previous years. If the population is growing, this procedure underestimates the divorce rate. An accurate divorce rate should be based on the eventual outcomes of all marriages that took place in a given year. Of course, such a rate cannot be fully computed until every marriage that year has ended, either through divorce or through death (see Table 12-1).

It turns out, however, that an accurate divorce rate can be estimated in other ways (Preston, 1975). Such rates reveal a dramatic rise in divorces over the past fifty years. Of all American couples wed in 1923, 19 percent of their marriages ended in divorce. For couples who married in 1950, 27 percent got a divorce. For 1960 the divorce rate is projected at 34 percent, and for 1975 at 50 percent. Since then, however, the rate may have stabilized (Weed, 1980). No one can yet say if this is a momentary pause or an end to the increase in divorce. In any event, when half of all marriages end in divorce, it seems reasonable to call that a very high rate.

Divorce means the end of a marriage, but it does not necessarily mean the end of a family, because two-thirds of the divorces occur between people who have children. One parent (usually the father) leaves the household, but a family remains. Moreover, divorce does not mean that many people experiment with marriage and then opt for a single life. Fewer than 5 percent of American adults at any given moment report their current marital status as divorced; more than 90 percent who divorce remarry. Thus, millions of couples give up on their marriages but not on marriage. This offers an important insight into *why* people get divorced.

Most people who get divorced report that their marriage ceased to provide adequate emotional satisfaction—that is, their relationship was no longer

Romantic love is essentially an invention of the industrial age. Of course, people in earlier centuries sometimes fell in love, but it was not typical, and certainly rarely was love the basis for deciding whom to marry. Although modern people are determined to fall in love, they also have discovered the pains of falling out of love.

happy. That might mean that the current high divorce rate indicates a lot of unhappy marriages, but it could also mean that at any given moment the great majority of marriages are happy ones. How is this possible?

Over the past eighty years, divorce laws have been made much less restrictive. The intention behind this legislation was to strengthen the family by permitting intolerable marriages to dissolve. The rationale was that if the bad marriages are ended by divorce, most marriages will be good ones. Today,

Table 12-1 / Length of marriage at time of divorce in the United States.

	Percentage	Cumulative Percentage
Under one year	4.4%	4.4%
One year	8.1%	12.5%
Two years	9.0%	21.5%
Three years	9.2%	30.7%
Four years	8.4%	39.1%
Five years	7.2%	46.3%
Six years	6.2%	52.5%
Seven years	5.7%	58.2%
Eight years	4.7%	62.9%
Nine years	4.1%	67.0%
10–14 years	13.5%	80.5%
15–19 years	8.0%	88.5%
20–24 years	5.4%	93.9%
25–29 years	3.3%	97.2%
30 or more years	2.8%	100.0%
	100.0%	
Median (1979)	6.8 years	

Source: U.S. Census, 1981.

when half of all marriages end in divorce, it seems unlikely that people are enduring bad marriages to the same extent as when only 10 percent got divorced. Indeed, it seems likely that people today become dissatisfied with marriages that would have seemed acceptable to people fifty years ago.

Marital satisfaction is partly a matter of comparison. In days when few people divorced, a couple comparing themselves with their friends might have rated their marriage as quite good. Today the same couple might find theirs to be a poor marriage by comparison since the standard has risen: Marriages must be better to qualify as satisfactory when more unsatisfactory marriages are eliminated by divorce. Thus, as divorce rises, the average level of satisfaction in existing marriages should rise also. There is reason to suspect, however, that a substantial part of this perceived satisfaction is simply a "newness" or "variety" effect. That is, as people divorce and remarry, many may not actually find someone who suits them better but simply a replacement for a partner who had become too familiar.

In any event, sociologists attribute high modern divorce rates to two general causes: (1) the fact that romance is a highly perishable commodity and (2) the increased opportunities to get divorced.

When romance fades

We have seen that romance has become the basis for marriage in modern times. People now expect deep romantic sentiments to lead them into marriage and to sustain their marriages. Unfortunately, these feelings can fade and be difficult to revive. Since so many adults rely on their spouses for their deepest emotional ties, immense weight is placed on these romantic feelings. Even small tensions are easily magnified, for any discontent or threat to this primary attachment provokes anxiety. Indeed, romantic sentiments may suffer from too frequent assessment, and the slightest doubts can easily shatter that "special feeling." So, too, can the simple passage of time. This may be especially true when sexual attraction is the focal point of romance.

Studies suggest that sexual attraction, in and of itself, is based partly on novelty and tends to decline with time (Pineo, 1961). If this is an intrinsic feature of sexual attraction and not just a temporary aspect of current sexual patterns, then a decline in sexual attraction and satisfaction will permanently threaten marriages based on sexual attraction. That is, if sexuality is a primary basis for emotional attachment between husbands and wives, then marriages will tend to weaken as familiarity causes a loss of fervor. In this sense, a good deal of divorce may reflect a form of swapping sexual partners.

Clearly, however, most people do not equate love with sexual thrills. Thus, while a decline in sexual novelty may be at the root of many divorces, many other couples find that their relationships improve the longer they live together. That is, research shows that marital satisfaction is higher the longer a couple has been married (Campbell, 1975). Once again, this could partly reflect a bias of selection. As time passes, more of the less satisfied couples get divorced. However, many couples report that their marriages have gotten more satisfying over time and that they are happier now than when they were just married.

Increased opportunities for divorce

In contrast with preindustrial societies, modern societies make it much easier for people to get divorced. The geographic mobility of modern societies allows people who get divorced to do so in relative privacy. During or following a divorce, many couples do not have to face all of their relatives and old friends or even one another. They have long since moved away from where they grew up, and after a divorce they often move to new places and make new friends.

Female employment and small families also make divorce more likely in modern societies. A major impact of the massive entry of women into the labor force has been to decrease the dependence of wives on their husbands for economic support. This has had many beneficial effects. For example, a woman need no longer cling to a brutal or drunken husband merely because she has nowhere else to turn. But it also encourages some women to give up on a relationship more quickly. Similarly, husbands have greater economic freedom to divorce wives who work, since substantial alimony is seldom granted to working wives. Thus, the conditions that have enabled people to seek marriages based on romance have also enabled them to continue that search if a marriage fails to satisfy.

In addition, the increase in the number of women who work increases the opportunities for extramarital affairs. Wives who work have a much greater opportunity than housewives for regular contact with men other than their husbands. Similarly, with so many women at work, husbands have more contact with other women than did their fathers or grandfathers.

As we saw in Special Topic 2, the huge, recent influx of women into the labor force both reflects and contributes to a low birth rate. Since young women today bear only two children on the average, they are not tied to the home by long years of childbearing or child care. In fact, the average American woman today gives birth to her last child by age 25, which means that by age 30 her children are all in school. This also facilitates divorce by reducing the financial burden of child support. Indeed, even if couples decide to remain together until their chil-

dren are grown up, they will only be in their early 40s by that time and can expect another thirty years of life.

The one-parent family

The primary concern raised by high divorce rates is not broken marriages but broken families: How does divorce affect children? In recent years, a good deal of research has been devoted to this question. The results are somewhat inconsistent, but in general they indicate that divorce usually has little impact on children if they are not subsequently raised in a one-parent home (Rosenberg, 1965; Landis, 1965). It is important to see, however, that many one-parent homes are not the result of a divorce. Some are caused by the death of one parent, and a rapidly growing number occur when single women become mothers.

For several decades, social scientists have been awaiting a rapid decline in the number of unwed mothers because of the very rapid rise in the abortion rate and in the use of birth control. However, instead of experiencing a decline, the rate at which children are born out of wedlock has continued its upward path. In 1960, only 5.3 percent of births were to unwed mothers. Today the rate is nearly 20 percent, and among blacks it exceeds 50 percent.

The combined effects of divorce and births to unwed mothers have led to a substantial increase in the number of families with only one parent. In 1982, 22 percent of households with children were one-parent families (see Table 12-2). In addition, more than 90 percent of one-parent families are headed by a woman—they are fatherless families, at least to the extent that no adult male lives in the household. Thus, at present approximately 18 percent of all children live only with their mother, 13.5 percent of all white children and 43.8 of all black children.

A major problem faced by the female-headed family is lack of income. The median income in 1980 for female-headed households was only $10,408.00, while the median income for married couples was $21,023.00. One reason for the lower income is that there can be only one employed adult in a female-headed family, while among the majority of married

Modern life has liberated most people from the stifling confinement of one-room homes, from loveless marriages, and from indifferent parents. But it also has produced an era of unstable families, in which marriages frequently end in divorce, often leaving mothers as the primary parent.

couples, both husband and wife work. But even when compared with families in which only the man works (median income of $18,972.00), the average female-headed family suffers from a much lower income. A second reason for lower incomes in female-headed families is that nearly two-thirds of women heading such families do not work at full-time jobs. Yet, even when a woman is employed full time, her family has a median income of $15,947.00, or two-thirds as much as that of male-headed families in which the wives do not work. A third reason for the lower income of female-headed families (and also for their low rate of employment) is that women who head families are likely to have less education than the average American woman. Thus, while only about 16

percent of American women aged 25 to 44 have not graduated from high school, more than 40 percent of the women who head families did not complete high school (much of this lack of education can be attributed to becoming a mother at a young age). The fact that blacks have lower incomes than whites also helps explain the lower income of female-headed families, since such families are disproportionately black. Finally, of course, women remain less likely to hold high-paying jobs than men do; thus sex bias depresses the incomes of families lacking a male wage earner.

Lack of income can, of course, have many negative effects on family life. But sociologists have long feared that the major shortage experienced by the

Table 12-2 / Households with children: 1970, 1982.

American Children Under Age 18	1970	1982
Living with both parents	85%	75%
Living with one parent	12%	22%
With mother	11%	20%
With father	1%	2%
Living with other relatives	2%	2.5%
Living with nonrelatives	0.7%	0.6%

Source: U.S. Census, 1983.

one-parent family is not money but *time*. When there is only one parent rather than two, supervision of children may be reduced greatly. In the case of divorce, when children must split their loyalties between parents, the result may be weaker attachments to each in comparison to attachments in two-parent families.

From Chapter 7 it should be clear that if one-parent families cannot sustain the same level of supervision and the same strength of attachments as can two-parent families, then research ought to find that the one-parent family is in greater risk of having delinquent children. Research on this hypothesis has produced mixed results over the years. The most recent studies suggest that children in one-parent families are more prone to various forms of delinquency, but that the differences are not great (Wilkinson, 1980).

What research does find is that *poor parenting, regardless of the structure of the family, is a primary cause of deviant behavior among children*. Put another way, it isn't how many parents a child has in his or her home that matters, it's how effective they are at being parents that is of primary importance in how a child turns out. Because this line of research is so new and so important, it seems worthwhile to watch over the shoulder of Gerald Patterson as he demonstrated the link between poor parenting and childhood deviance and as he made progress in training parents to become more effective at parenting.

Gerald Patterson: incompetent parents and problem kids

 Since the early 1970s, Gerald Patterson and his colleagues at the Oregon Social Learning Center have studied and attempted to treat young children (many not yet of school age) who frequently engage in acts of deviant and antisocial behavior. These are not just kids who throw tantrums and act up; many of them are already serious offenders—kids who constantly steal and even child arsonists.

Initially, Patterson and his colleagues adhered to the standard approach recommended by behavior modification psychology: The way to get rid of undesirable behavior is to not reward it and to instead make sure to reward desirable behavior. As time passed, however, Patterson noticed that much undesirable behavior simply did not disappear no matter how much others ignored it. Indeed, by studying very young children of 2 and 3 Patterson discovered that little kids engage in a great deal of antisocial behavior, such as pushing and shoving and yelling. Moreover, they have no understanding of property rules and simply take anything they want if they can reach it, whether it might be a cookie, their sister's doll, or their father's car keys. Having established "normal" rates for these forms of antisocial behavior for 2- and 3-year-olds, Patterson soon discovered that his problem children were simply continuing to behave in a way that was normal for much younger children. This discovery led to an important conclusion: Kids will not cease these forms of misbehavior unless they are forced to. In effect, kids continue to act in such ways unless parents effectively use punishment to teach them not to.

Thus, Patterson and his group learned that there is solid scientific evidence for what our grandmothers always believed: Parents are to blame when their children misbehave. By the late 1970s, Patterson and his group had turned their fullest attention to the parents of problem kids. What did they fail to do, or do wrong? Could they be trained to do better?

Eventually, Patterson (1980) described adequate parenting skills in terms of seven tactics:

1. Notice what the child is doing.

2. Keep track of the child's behavior over long periods.

3. Act in ways you want the child to act (and don't act in ways you do not want the child to act).

4. Clearly state the rules the child is expected to obey.

5. Consistently apply sane punishments for violations of the rules.

6. Consistently reward conformity.

7. Negotiate disagreements so that they get settled rather than escalate.

Patterson himself has described these procedures for dealing with children as obvious and mundane. But, he pointed out, increasing numbers of parents have not had the kind of experiences with younger brothers and sisters that helped people in the past learn how to parent. Moreover, there seem to be a number of reasons why some parents simply are unwilling or unable to use these procedures.

One major problem is lack of attachment. Throughout this book, we have seen the power of attachments to shape behavior, and Chapter 7 gave emphasis to how attachments to parents resulted in young people's conforming to the norms. But Patterson has drawn attention to the other side of that coin—the attachment of parents to their children. He found that many of the parents of the problem children treated by his center didn't really like their kids, feel obligations toward them, or even want to be parents. It was very hard, and often impossible, to teach such people to be adequate parents. And it surely is no surprise that kids are not strongly attached to parents who reject them.

A second major impediment to good parenting is that people often refuse to "see" what their children are doing. Many of the parents of children who were chronic stealers simply denied all charges of theft unless they had personally seen the child steal. Indeed, many of these parents applied the word *steal* only when an act of theft could be proven, as if it weren't stealing if you could get away with it. Pursuing this insight, Patterson and his colleagues found that the parents of chronic stealers had deviant views of misbehavior; in fact, they had attitudes most

similar to those of delinquent adolescents. Thus, while these parents probably seldom went so far as to reward stealing behavior in their children, they often did not punish it because it did not really offend them.

Parents of problem children often fail to punish them for failing to obey. Such parents frequently will ignore everything the child does until or unless it irritates them sufficiently to take action. As a result, even when they do punish an offense the punishment often fails to cause the misbehavior to diminish. First, the child has learned that he or she can often get away with the misbehavior; second, the punishment is often without any lasting consequences. As Patterson put it, "These parents yell, scold, threaten, and occasionally physically assault the child." The adequate parent, on the other hand, backs up threats and scoldings, and even spankings, with the withdrawal of privileges or the assigning of extra household chores.

Having concluded that parents are the primary cause of problem children (that when an 8-year-old child steals or hits other kids, he or she has been allowed to do so), Patterson and his group have set out to attempt to treat problem kids by training their parents how to control their children's behavior. The results so far are promising. While some parents simply will not or cannot be helped, many others have been helped to improve the behavior of their children.

The Oregon project is the first delinquency prevention program that has produced some signs of success. For this reason, Patterson and his colleagues can claim to have made a truly major scientific breakthrough. That does not mean, however, that this program can be put into practice across the country with major benefit. For one thing, it has proven to be extremely time consuming (and thereby expensive) to teach parents to deal more adequately with their children. Moreover, even when parents have learned to manage their kids, they will often slide back into their old neglectful ways, especially if they encounter difficulties in their own lives. It will require a great deal more experimentation and study to see whether lasting improvements can be achieved in a large enough number of cases to justify the immense expense needed to apply Patterson's techniques nationally.

CONCLUSION

The modern family has many imperfections. Many families abuse or neglect their children. Arrest statistics show that family fights are common and that homicides frequently occur within families (see Chapter 7). Perhaps half of today's marriages will end in divorce. Yet these problems do not demonstrate that family life is deteriorating or that the family is less able to fulfill its functions. We have seen what the good old days were like, and as far as family life is concerned, they should be called the "miserable old days."

I have emphasized an historical view in this chapter not to minimize concern about current family problems, but to put them in perspective. It's not helpful to run in search of answers to why the world is going to pot if that is not really what's happening. Here the decades of sociological concern about the decline of the family seem instructive. For example, for years sociologists asked why marriage no longer worked without asking if a high divorce rate might reflect unceasing efforts by individuals to find marriages that do work. Preindustrial marriages may have lasted, but did they work? If we rate them by current standards, they seldom did.

Review glossary

Families Small groups including adults and children wherein membership is determined by common ancestry and sexual unions. (p. 284)

Nuclear family A family made up of only one adult couple and their children. (p. 286)

Extended families Families made up of at least two adult couples. (p. 286)

Incest taboo Prohibition against sexual relations between certain members of the same family. (p. 286)

Dependents Family members unable to support themselves. (p. 286)

Suggested readings

Erlanger, Howard S. "Social Class and the Use of Corporal Punishment in Childrearing: A Reassessment." *American Sociological Review* (1974) 39:68–85.

Patterson, G. R. "Children Who Steal." In Travis Hirschi and Michael Gottfredson, eds., *Understanding Crime: Current Theory and Research*. Beverly Hills: Sage Publications, 1980.

Rosenberg, Charles E., ed. *The Family in History*. Philadelphia: University of Pennsylvania Press, 1975.

Shorter, Edward. *The Making of the Modern Family*. New York: Basic Books, 1975.

College Couples

Marriage in America is based on romantic relationships; people fall in love and get married. Yet despite a mountain of studies of the family, there has been very little research on why people fall in love and how dating leads to marriage. Until recently, the little that was known on these matters came from surveys of people already married. These people were asked to recall such things as how they met, what attracted them to one another, and how long they had dated before they wed. But no research had been done on people while they were actually in the process of becoming couples.

In the 1970s, Charles Hill, Zick Rubin, and Letitia Anne Peplau at Harvard University began a study of dating couples. They recruited 231 couples from the student bodies of four colleges in the Boston area. Some of these couples had just begun to date, others had dated for a year or longer, and some couples were living together. The researchers interviewed each person several times over a two-year period. They wanted to find out what brought the couples together, what caused them to stay together or break up, and what factors led to marriage.

At the end of the two years, 103 couples (45 percent) had broken up. Of the rest, 65 were still dating, 9 had become engaged, 43 were married, one person had died, and 10 couples could not be found.

The accepted view in the social sciences of romantic relationships is not that opposites attract but that like attracts like—people fall in love with others who share their interests and preferences and who have similar personalities. Hill, Rubin, and Peplau (1976) found only modest support for this view. On a great many characteristics, there was no evidence of similarity between couples. On others,

The library date is common among college couples because of their need to fit their time together into their academic schedules. For similar reasons college couples time their "breakups" to coincide with breaks in the school year.

couples did tend to be somewhat alike, but the correlations were modest. Couples did tend to be about the same age, to be equally physically attractive, to have similar IQ scores, to be of the same religion, and to want the same number of children. But on each of these characteristics, a substantial minority of couples differed markedly from one another. In fact, on only one question was there very high agreement: on whether they were "in love."

Although the initial interviews failed to find that similarity was very important in bringing couples together, the follow-up interviews found that similarities played a much more important role in keep-

ing couples together. Those who were together after two years were much more closely matched than couples who broke up, especially in terms of age, IQ, educational plans, and physical attractiveness. Thus, couples were much more likely to break up if one person was a lot smarter, more attractive, or older. It is easy to imagine why these differences would matter. If one person is much more intelligent or mature than the other, this could cause conflicts. If one person is much more attractive, he or she will have more opportunities for other relationships.

Yet other characteristics that would seem of equal

importance in relationships turned out not to matter. Those who stayed together differed not at all from those who broke up in their degree of similarity on religion, sex role attitudes, attitudes about sex, idealism or the number of children they wanted. Surely, one might suppose that marked differences in sex role attitudes would cause friction or that religious differences might lead to breakups. But there was no evidence of this.

In fact, conflict was not one of the important reasons people gave for breaking up. The overwhelming majority said they broke up because they got bored with the other person. Often this resulted in one of the pair becoming interested in someone else, thus prompting the split. Perhaps surprisingly, the woman got involved with someone else far more often than the man. Moreover, women were much more likely to initiate a breakup than men, regardless of the grounds. However, people were more likely to remain friends after the breakup if the man initiated the split. This suggests that the male ego is more sensitive to rejection.

The researchers became very interested in why women took the lead in ending relationships. They found two important reasons. The first is that a woman's economic position depends more on her husband's success than his position depends on her success. Thus, a poor choice of mate is much costlier to a woman than to a man. A woman, therefore, can't "afford to stay in love too long with the wrong person" (Hill et al., 1976). A second reason why women often take the lead in breakups is that they are often socialized to have greater emotional sensitivity. Thus, some women reported they had noticed that the man was losing interest in the relationship before he was willing to acknowledge that fact.

Perhaps the single most fascinating result of the study pertained to the timing of breakups. One might suppose that couples break up whenever they feel like it. But this sample of college couples did not. Breakups were not scattered randomly over the year but were clustered during breaks in the school year!

The biggest breakup month was June, when school ended. The next highest was September, just before school started. The third highest period was during the holidays from late December to early January. Why do people break up at these times? Breaking up takes time and energy (especially for those couples living together, where one must move out). So students wait for a convenient time to end relationships.

These breakup patterns among college students resemble those for divorce in the general population. People tend to get divorced just after they complete college or graduate school, after they find a satisfactory job, after the children have grown up and left home, or when one person is taking a job in another city—that is, when it is more convenient to undergo the practical difficulties involved in ending a marriage. The difference in student breakups is that they are seldom as costly or as difficult as is divorce. In fact, many students looked back on a breakup as fortunate because it prevented a probable divorce. This prompted Hill, Rubin, and Peplau to end their research article with the line, "The best divorce is the one you get before you get married."

Chapter

Thirteen

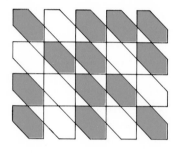

■ Nobody knows when humans first possessed religion. Unlike tools chipped from stone, cultural ideas do not lie secure for millions of years, awaiting the archeologist's pick. So, while we know that humans living over a million years ago made tools, we can only guess about their religion. However, there can be no doubt that our Neanderthal ancestors had religion at least 100,000 years ago, because evidence of their faith has been unearthed. The Neanderthal buried their dead with great care and provided them with gifts and food for use in the next world. And deep in their caves, the Neanderthal built small altars out of bear bones. These relics make it clear that the Neanderthal believed in life after death and conducted ceremonies to seek the aid of supernatural beings. Such beliefs and practices are properly called religion, and all human societies since the days of the Neanderthal have had religion. ■

CHAPTER PREVIEW

In this chapter we shall try to understand why religion is a vital part of human societies. What does religion do for people? How does it influence social life? Then we will explore the concept of a **religious economy**—the marketplace of competing faiths within a society. Although societies often claim to have only one faith (and sometimes use military force to keep competing faiths out), this is never really true. We shall see why not, why "underground" faiths exist even in the most repressive

Religion

nations, and why these sometimes erupt into significant movements whenever repression eases. Viewing the religious sector of societies as economies of faith permits us to examine how religious organizations influence one another. We shall see that in time the most successful religious organizations become increasingly worldly, a process called **secularization**. As this occurs, conditions become favorable for new organizations to break away and restore a less worldly form of the conventional faith, a process called **revival**. We shall also see how wholly new religions can arise in societies, a process called **religious innovation** or cult formation.

We shall use our model of religious economies to examine current conditions and trends in the United States. Then we shall apply the model to Canada and the nations of Western Europe.

THE NATURE OF RELIGION

A most difficult problem facing sociologists of religion has been to define their subject matter. An adequate definition must include the vast array of faiths found in the world without including too much. As Georg Simmel urged in 1905, a general definition of religion must apply "alike to the religion of Christians and South Sea Islanders." It must isolate the common elements in Buddhism, Islam, and other faiths of modern times, as well as the faiths of our primitive ancestors, such as the Neanderthal.

For a few decades, this problem was solved by recognizing that all religions had one feature in common: They always involve answers to **questions about ultimate meaning**, such as, Does life have a purpose? Why are we here? Is death the end? Why do we suffer? Does justice exist?

It is characteristic of humans to ask such questions. Indeed, these questions must have troubled the Neanderthal, for they had accepted answers to some of these questions. Hence, religion has been defined as socially organized beliefs and activities offering solutions to questions of ultimate meaning. But that definition turned out to be too broad. It applies to communism as well as Catholicism. And it applies to a philosophical system that denies that there can be answers to questions of ultimate meaning. It is inconvenient to have a sociological concept that ignores differences between what are widely regarded as religious and antireligious positions.

In the end, most sociologists agreed that the term *religion* ought to be applied to only particular kinds of answers to questions of ultimate meaning—those that posit the existence of the **supernatural**. Defined this way, religion possesses a capacity that nonreligious philosophies lack: to invoke the power, wisdom, authority, and aid of the gods (Spiro, 1966; Berger, 1967; Stark, 1981; Stark and Bainbridge, 1985).

The gods

If we closely examine the ultimate questions that humans keep asking, it is clear that many of them require a very special kind of answer. Humans do not usually ask if life has meaning; they ask what is the meaning of life. Why does the universe exist?

Why do I exist? For life to have meaning, in this sense, history must be guided by intention. For this to be true, a consciousness capable of imposing intention on history must exist. In other words, if the universe is to have purpose, it must have been created and directed by a conscious agent—a being capable of making plans and having intentions. Such a being has to be of such power, duration, and scale as to be beyond the natural world. That is, such a being must be supernatural.

Many questions of ultimate meaning, therefore, can only be answered by referring to the supernatural—to beings or forces beyond nature who are able to suspend, alter, ignore, and create physical forces. To believe, for example, that there is life beyond death is to accept the supernatural. To believe that earthly suffering is compensated in the world to come also requires belief in the supernatural. Some things that humans greatly desire cannot possibly be attained in this world but can come only from the gods.

By defining **religion** as socially organized patterns of beliefs and practices concerning ultimate meaning and that assume the existence of the supernatural, sociologists can isolate the essential element that sets religion apart from other aspects of social life and that accounts for its universal appeal.

Systems of thought that reject the supernatural cannot satisfy the concerns of most people. Atheists can search for explanations of how the universe functions, but they cannot say that these functions have underlying purpose. Communists can promise to reduce poverty, but they cannot offer an escape from death. In any society, some people can accept the beliefs that the universe has no purpose, that what we gain in this life is all we shall receive, and that death is final. But, as we shall see throughout this chapter, for most people this is not enough—only religion can fulfill their needs, their hopes, their dreams.

Legitimization of norms

Religions do more for humans than supply them with answers to questions of ultimate meaning. The assumption that the supernatural exists raises a new

Thousands of years ago our ancestors created sacred chambers by painting superb animal figures like this on the walls of natural caverns. Even modern visitors are awed within these exotic confines and immediately sense the sacred intentions of those who used to come here at times of special religious significance.

These Roman Catholic children are taking part in the sacrament of Holy Communion—a ritual that illustrates the unique capacity of religions to answer questions of ultimate meaning. Communion, also known as the Lord's Supper among many Protestants, symbolizes that all may be saved in Christ and gain everlasting life.

question. <u>What does the supernatural want or expect from us?</u>

Let us return to the Neanderthal. They believed that life has purpose and that the individual survives death. They also believed that the supernatural controls events in this world. How should they prepare for the next life? How could they enlist the aid of the supernatural in this world? The Neanderthal were greatly concerned about escaping the anger of the supernatural. All around them were signs of the terrible wrath of the gods: lightning bolts, violent winds and storms, deadly forest fires, floods, droughts, sickness, and injury. As demonstrated by their altars and their burial customs, the Neanderthal had beliefs about what the gods required. Like other primitive peoples, they undoubtedly observed elaborate codes

of behavior meant to please the unseen spiritual forces that surrounded them.

By specifying what the gods require of humans, <u>religions</u> in effect <u>regulate human behavior by formulating rules about how we must and must not act.</u> Such rules of behavior, of course, are social norms. Religions explain why certain norms exist and why they should be obeyed.

For norms to be obeyed, most members of a society must believe that the norms are proper and right. Sociologists have long recognized the important role of religion in legitimizing norms. Why shouldn't we steal? Because the gods forbid it. Why should we obey our parents? Because the gods demand it. Why should we obey the king? Because he was chosen by the gods to rule over us.

Thus, religious institutions can be a major force in holding societies together, giving legitimacy and reason to the norms, and giving divine sanction to other social institutions, such as the family or the state. Indeed, as we have already seen in Chapter 4, religion fosters conformity to the norms primarily by creating moral communities, not simply by influencing the beliefs and practices of individuals. Recall that religious teenagers were less delinquent than nonreligious teenagers only in communities where the majority belonged to a church. The power of religion to create moral communities is also demonstrated by research showing that cities with high church membership rates have considerably lower rates of crime, suicide, venereal disease, and alcoholism than cities with low church membership rates (Stark, et al., 1983; Stark, Doyle, and Rushing, 1983).

Of course, religion is not the only reason why people observe norms. In Chapter 3 we saw that norms also arise from interaction. Many people who lack religious beliefs accept social norms and obey them (Hirschi and Stark, 1969). For many people in all societies, however, religion has served as the ultimate justification for norms.

RELIGIOUS ECONOMIES

Early religions were local affairs. A tribe or very small society and its religion were one. A person was born into a religion as part of being born a member of his or her group. Although religion constantly changed even in small, primitive societies, the idea of choosing a religion was as alien as the idea of choosing one's tribe or family.

As societies became more complex, they began to include several cultures and religions. Larger cities of ancient Greece, Egypt, and the Roman Empire contained a variety of different religions (Johnson, 1979; Meeks, 1983). In such cities, people could compare religions, worry about which one was best, and regard religion as a matter of choice. Such a religious situation is best described as a *religious economy*. Just as commercial economies consist of a market in which different firms compete, religious economies consist of a market (the aggregate demand for religion) and firms (different religious organizations) seeking to attract and hold a clientele.

The notion of religious economies underscores the dynamic interplay of religions within a society. This interplay accounts for the religious makeup of societies at any given time and explains why and how religions change.

As with commercial economies, a key issue is the degree to which a religious economy is regulated by the state. To what extent do free market conditions prevail and to what extent is the religious economy distorted toward monopoly by coercion? For reasons explained below, the natural state of a religious economy is **religious pluralism**, wherein many "firms" exist because of their special appeal to certain segments of the market (or population). However, it is always in the interest of any particular religious organization (as it is for a commercial organization) to secure a monopoly. This can only be achieved, and even then to just a limited extent, if the state forcibly excludes competing faiths.

In medieval Europe, states used coercion to create a monopoly for Catholicism. However, even at its most powerful moments, the medieval Catholic Church was beset by dissent and heresy from all sides and never achieved full monopoly. Whenever and wherever state coercion wavered, competing faiths burst forth and prospered (Johnson, 1979). Nevertheless, regulation often made it difficult and dangerous for competing faiths, thus greatly reducing religious choice. However, even medieval society is best understood in terms of its religious economy.

To understand why religious economies incline toward pluralism, it is necessary to understand the major processes at work within them. We shall explore these processes by first explaining why a virtually endless supply of new and competing organizations exists in any religious economy.

CHURCH-SECT THEORY

In 1929 H. Richard Niebuhr published a book called *The Social Sources of Denominationalism*. In it he tried to explain why Christianity was fractured into so many competing denominations. Why weren't Christians content with one church? Why did they constantly form new ones?

The answer he proposed combined two concepts developed by Max Weber with elements of conflict theory. Weber had distinguished two kinds of religious organizations: churches and sects. **Churches** intellectualize religious teachings and restrain emotionalism in their services. They offer an image of the gods as somewhat remote from daily life and the individual. **Sects** stress emotionalism and individual mystical experiences, and tend toward fundamentalism, rather than intellectualism, in their teachings. They present the gods as close at hand, taking an active interest and role in the lives of individuals.

Perhaps the issue of prayer provides the best contrast between church and sect. Churches favor the use of formalized prayers, often recited from memory or read from prayer books. Sects favor extemporaneous, informal prayers. Church prayers imply gods who are very far away: "Our Father, who art in Heaven." Sect prayers imply gods who are nearby: "Yes, Lord, we feel you present. Bless this poor sinner kneeling here before you now."

Niebuhr argued that churches and sects differ greatly in their ability to satisfy different human needs. Sects provide for the religious needs of persons low in the stratification system—the masses. Churches provide for the religious needs of the middle and upper classes (McKinney and Roof, 1982). Class conflict, according to Niebuhr, underlies the religious conflicts that split Christianity into many different denominations.

Niebuhr stressed the unique ability of religion to make life bearable, even for those in misery. This is achieved by turning one's thoughts away from this world and stressing the primacy of the spiritual world. The more we believe that this life is only a brief prelude to afterlife and that we shall find relief from our pains in the more perfect world to come, the more easily we can bear life's burdens. Indeed, religions commonly teach that if you spurn material pleasures in this life, you will increase your rewards in the everlasting life to come—that the social order will be turned upside down in the next life, where "the first shall be last, and the last, first."

When members of a congregation actively participate in the services as this woman is doing—when members seem to be really enjoying themselves—chances are that the group is one that sociologists would classify as a sect. Groups with more formal and sedate services usually are classified as churches.

To make these views convincing, however, religions must resist the pleasures of the material world. A religious organization filled with members, especially its leaders, enjoying material pleasures is hampered in its efforts to serve the religious needs of the deprived.

The key to Niebuhr's theory is the proposition that <u>successful religious organizations always shift their emphasis toward this world and away from the</u>

Church-sect theory stresses the need of the poor and dispossessed for an intensely other-worldly religion, as illustrated by this Peruvian family saying their prayers. People who are better off, on the other hand, tend to prefer a more worldly religion. Out of this tension comes a succession of new sect movements.

next. He argued that as religious organizations grow and become more popular, the proportion of middle- and upper-class members will increase. These members have much less need than the deprived to reject this world in favor of the next. Indeed, they will want to harmonize their religious beliefs with their own worldly success. In time, these members will prevail, and the religious organization will cease to preach that material success in this life will be punished in the next. Indeed, these faiths will cease to emphasize the spiritual and will portray the supernatural in ever more remote and less vivid terms. That is, the religion will become progressively worldly.

However, such a shift will erode the ability of the religious organization to satisfy the religious needs of the lower classes. This will lead to growing discontent. Eventually the masses will defect to form a

Degree of Tension with Sociocultural Environment

Low   Medium   High

Figure 13-1 / Degrees of tension between religions and society.

The clergyman who "fits right in" illustrates that some religious groups are wholly accommodated to their social environment. Clergy who demonstrate in protest against pornography or abortion reflect that some degree of tension exists between their religious group and the social environment. Clergy who are jailed for refusing to submit to state regulation of church-sponsored grade schools show that religious bodies can exist in a state of high tension with their environment. The higher the tension between a group and its environment, the more sectlike it is.

new religious organization, a sect, wherein the otherworldliness of the former organization is emphasized.

Thus, Niebuhr proposed a dynamic cycle. Religions originate as sects designed to serve the needs of the deprived. If they grow and flourish, these sects increasingly serve the interests of the middle and upper classes and are transformed into churches, thereby making them less effective in satisfying the needs of the poor. Thus, the conditions that prompted the original **sect formation** are re-created, a split occurs, and a new sect is formed. In time this sect, too, is transformed into a church, whereupon a new sect is born—thus, there is an endless cycle of the birth, transformation, and rebirth of new religious organizations. Niebuhr explained the existence of the huge array of Christian denominations as the result of countless cycles of this church-sect process.

In the fifty years since Niebuhr first sketched his **church-sect theory**, it has been much refined and elaborated (Wilson, 1959, 1961, 1970; Wallis, 1975). Niebuhr's definitions of church and sect were not clear or efficient. Thus, in 1963 Benton Johnson proposed better ones. He suggested that church and sect are opposite poles on an axis representing the degree of tension between religious organizations and their sociocultural environment (see Figure 13-1). Tension, as Johnson defined it, is a manifestation of deviance. To the degree that a religious organization sustains norms and values different from those of the surrounding culture, it is deviant and tension will exist between its members and the outside world. In the extreme case, tension is so high that the group is hunted down by outsiders. Religious groups whose norms and values resemble those of the larger society have no tension. *Churches* are religious bodies with relatively low tension; *sects* are religious bodies with relatively high tension.

Niebuhr tended to limit this application of church-sect theory to religious organizations. But the theory is even more useful when it is applied to whole societies. Let's see how church-sect theory has recently been linked with the concept of religious economies.

SECULARIZATION AND REVIVAL

Social scientists and modern intellectuals have generally paid close attention to only one aspect of church-sect theory: They have noted the movement away from traditional Christian teachings by many of the largest and most respected denominations. Projecting these trends into the future, they have predicted that religion is in its last days, that soon religion will disappear. Noting that these denominations continue to retreat from a vivid, active conception of the supernatural, many social scientists have concluded that this is because supernatural beliefs cannot be maintained in an increasingly scientific age, and therefore human societies will soon, to paraphrase Freud (1927), be cured of the infantile "illusion" of religion.

The process by which religion will disappear has been called *secularization* to indicate a turning away from religious to secular explanations of life. This process is regarded as far along and irreversible. Indeed, the distinguished anthropologist Anthony F. C. Wallace (1966) spoke for the majority of modern social scientists when he wrote:

The evolutionary future of religion is extinction. Belief in supernatural beings . . . will become only an interesting historical memory. To be sure, this event is not likely to occur in the next generation; the process will very likely take several hundred years. . . . But as a cultural trait, belief in supernatural powers is doomed to die out, all over the world, as a result of the increasing adequacy and diffusion of scientific knowledge.

Besides overwhelming religion, many scholars have thought that science might provide a substitute for religion—people might perform solemn rituals patterned on those of religion but with an explicitly antisupernatural thrust (see the photo on p. 318). In fact the French philosopher August Comte, who coined the term *sociology,* intended that sociology serve as the scientific substitute for religion. Thus, the assumption that religion is both false and doomed has been widespread among social scientists from the start. This assumption has led them to discover terminal symptoms in every sign of decline in religion, but to ignore or be perplexed by every sign of vigor. Thus, for 150 years or more, social scientists have predicted the triumph of secularization. Whenever they have confronted broad-based religious revivals, they have dismissed them as dying spasms.

I must confess that as a young sociologist I largely shared these views. But as I did research on religious groups, from Moonies to major denominations, I found it very difficult to square these views with what I saw. For millions of people, faith was alive and well. Many sophisticated scholars appeared to have no problem in reconciling science with a belief in the supernatural. Could the secularization thesis be flawed? By 1980, I had concluded that it was—that secularization was but one aspect of religious change (Stark, 1981; Stark and Bainbridge, 1980, 1985). Other sociologists began to express similar views (Bell, 1980; Martin, 1981). Together, we began to apply church-sect theory to religious economies and to argue that the secularization thesis rested on a misperception—that social scientists had mistaken the obvious decline of once powerful religious organizations for a general decline of religion. In this sense, they had seen only the transformation of some religious organizations into states of ever lower tension but had failed to note the reactions to this trend elsewhere in religious economies. A more comprehensive view of religious economies suggests that secularization is a self-limiting process that does not lead to irreligion but to a shift in the sources of religion. One of the ways this occurs was already implicit in church-sect theory.

Church-sect theory suggests that many religious bodies are always in the process of becoming very worldly. That is, secularization should occur in all religious economies. But we must also expect the trend toward secularization to produce religious reactions: the formation of sects. We can call this process *revival.* As secularization weakens some organizations, new ones split off to revive less worldly versions of the faith. This not only helps to explain why some religious bodies have declined as the secularization thesis predicts they should, but also why religion refuses to fade away: why, for example, a religious body like the Southern Baptist Convention

A Russian couple is married in a "socialist wedding palace" in Kiev, complete with an altar and a bust of Lenin. This is part of the latest effort in a seventy-year government campaign to eradicate religion in the USSR. But according to the Soviet press, vast numbers of the Soviet people remain committed to religious organizations (many of them illegal). Sociologists of religion argue that religion without the supernatural is no religion at all, and therefore that efforts like this cannot succeed.

can grow at an extraordinary rate in contradiction of the secularization thesis. The Southern Baptists have moved into the market vacuum created by the secularization of once dominant Protestant bodies. The result is a change in the source of religion—in what religious group people turn to—not the demise of religion.

But there is a second response to secularization besides revival. Sometimes people do not revive the conventional faith by embodying it in new organizations, such as the Southern Baptists did. Sometimes they turn to new faiths altogether.

INNOVATION: CULT FORMATION

Sects are not new religions, they are new organizations reviving an old religion. They claim to have returned to a more authentic version of the traditional faith from which its parent organization has strayed. Thus, a set of churches and sects will form a single religious tradition. For example, most churches and sects in the United States and Europe are part of the conventional Christian religious tradition.

Sometimes, however, organizations appear that are based on religions outside the conventional religious tradition. This may occur by importing a faith from another society—Hinduism in the United States and Christianity in India are examples. New faiths also appear through cultural innovation. Someone may have new religious insights and then succeed in attracting followers. New religions, whether imported or the result of innovation, are deviant and thus elicit unfavorable reactions from others. Thus, like sects, they are in a high state of tension with surrounding society. But unlike sects, new religions cannot claim cultural continuity with conventional religious beliefs and practices.

The hostility usually directed at new religions is reflected in the name applied to them: cults. Sociologists use this term without prejudice to distinguish new religions from sects arising out of old religions. Thus, **cults** are religious movements that represent a new or different religious tradition, while churches and sects represent the prevailing tradition in a society. The negative connotations of the word *cult* reflect the unusually high tension between these movements and their social environment.

All religions begin as cult movements. All of today's great world faiths once were tiny groups whose members were regarded as weird, crazy, foolish, and sinful. How Roman intellectuals in the first century would have laughed at the notion that a messiah and his tiny flock in Palestine, an obscure corner of the empire, posed a threat to the mighty pagan temples. But from obscure cult movements have risen not only Christianity, but also Islam, Buddhism, and other faiths that today inspire hundreds of millions of faithful.

Given their current rate of growth, the Church of Jesus Christ of Latter-day Saints, the Mormons, may be repeating this pattern of a meteoric rise from obscurity to world significance. In 1830 this faith began with six members: the three Smith brothers, the two Whitmer brothers, and Oliver Cowdry. Today there are more than 5 million Mormons, and even if they continue to grow at a somewhat slower rate, there will be at least 265 million Mormons worldwide a century from now (Stark, 1984).

New religions appear constantly in all societies (Stark and Bainbridge, 1985). Nearly all of them fail. To succeed, many things are required, but the primary necessity involves *opportunity.* That is, for new firms to make their way against large, long-established firms in a religious economy, the older firms must be failing to serve the needs of a significant number of people. People do not abandon a faith that satisfies them to embrace a new faith; new faiths prosper only from the weaknesses of old faiths.

Sometimes new faiths find opportunity because of great social crises that overwhelm conventional faiths. For example, plagues or natural disasters may cause a sudden loss of confidence in conventional faiths (Wallace, 1956). Wars can have the same effect, especially on the losing side. For example, new faiths repeatedly swept through the Indian tribes of North America as their efforts to resist white encroachments failed (Mooney, 1896), and a great number of new religions have flourished in Japan since World War II (McFarland, 1967; Morioka, 1975).

But a major opportunity for new faiths results from the excessive secularization of the old. That is, after many cycles of the church-sect process, an entire religious tradition may lose its ability to provide a plausible faith for a substantial portion of the population. Such moments are rare, but when they occur, new faiths quickly rise in influence, just as Christianity overwhelmed a highly secularized and complacent paganism.

Thus, secularization prompts two reactions that restore religion: revival and innovation (**cult formation**). Rather than being a symptom of the death of religion, secularization provides the impetus for religious change.

CHARISMA

We saw in Chapter 3 that people join new religious movements primarily because of their attachments to members of those movements; when a sufficient proportion of a person's attachments are to members of some religious group, the person is likely to accept that religion. That tells us something not only about how religious movements recruit and grow but also about *how they begin.*

Suppose a young electrical engineer in Korea

believes he has received a revelation from God. He then believes he has a divine mission to launch a new religious movement that will create an era of great religious vigor and purity and unite the many religions of the world into One True Faith. Is this the birth of a cult movement? Not yet.

As long as only one person accepts a new religious message, no religious movement exists. To launch a social movement, this engineer must convince other people to share his beliefs and join him. Many people each year believe they have discovered a new faith, but only a few of them can convince others to join. What characterizes those who can attract followers? What was it about a Korean electrical engineer, famous today as Reverend Sun Myung Moon, that enabled him to attract ardent followers and to found a major cult movement (the Unification Church, known as the Moonies)?

Pondering the special gifts of religious founders, Max Weber credited them with charisma. **Charisma** is a Greek word meaning "divine gift." Weber used it to indicate the ability of some people to inspire faith in others, to get others to believe their message. For contemporary sociologists of religion, the basis of this gift is an unusual ability to form attachments with others. Just as people join religions out of attachments to members, in the beginning people accept the claim of a founder of a new faith because they develop very strong attachments to the founder. All studies of new religions report that the founders possessed remarkable gifts for interpersonal relations (Wallis, 1982).

Moreover, founders of new faiths typically turn first to those with whom they already have strong attachments in their quest for converts. Joseph Smith, the founder of the Mormon Church, first converted his two brothers and three close friends. Jesus, likewise, numbered his own brothers among his early followers. In founding Islam, Mohammed's first convert was his wife Khadîjah, the second was his cousin Ali, the third was his servant Zeyd, and then his old friend Abû Bakr joined and brought his family and his slaves into the new faith.

Having outlined the dynamic character of religious economies and the processes by which sects and cults form, we can now analyze religion in the United States. Then we shall see how the same dynamic patterns occur in a variety of other nations.

THE AMERICAN RELIGIOUS ECONOMY

Since well before the American Revolution, observers have marveled at both the diversity of religions and the high levels of participation in religious activities found here. Max Weber, for example, noted that Americans gladly contributed sums of money to their churches that would shock people in Europe. Others wondered how so many faiths could exist side by side.

It is true that the American religious economy is very diverse. Over 1,200 religious denominations exist in this country (Melton, 1978). Church attendance is high—in any given week, about 40 percent of Americans attend services. Moreover, almost two-thirds of Americans (62 percent) are official members of a local congregation (Stark, forthcoming).

However, there is nothing really unique about the American religious economy other than that it is an exceptionally free market with little regulation. Within this economy, the three major processes of secularization, revival, and innovation are well developed and related.

Secularization and revival

Many major religious bodies in the United States have become highly secularized in the sense that they no longer present traditional versions of their faith or emphasize the supernatural. This can easily be seen in Table 13-1, which is based on a nationwide survey of the American public. At the top of the table are some of the oldest and most prominent American Protestant bodies: Unitarians, Congregationalists, Presbyterians, and Episcopalians. Toward the bottom are major denominations that arose as sects in the United States: the Missouri Lutherans, Baptists, and an array of smaller groups (including the Nazarenes, Assemblies of God, and Seventh-Day Adventists), who have been combined under the heading of "Other Sects."

Note the immense differences in commitment to traditional Christian beliefs concerning the supernatural among members of these various groups. In the denominations at the top, only small minorities express faith in major Christian doctrines. Toward the bottom, the overwhelming majorities believe in them. There is virtually no difference between Roman Catholics and Protestants as a group, but the huge differences among the Protestant denominations suggests that the term *Protestant* is of very limited use.

If secularization weakens faiths, then those denominations at the top of Table 13-1 ought to display symptoms of decline, for they have greatly deemphasized other-worldliness. In fact, these denominations are exhibiting great weakness. Their members attend church less frequently and contribute relatively less money to their churches, despite having higher average incomes than other Protestants (Stark and Glock, 1968). Moreover, their membership has long been declining and has recently begun to fall rapidly (Kelley, 1972). The less secularized religious bodies, meanwhile, enjoy high levels of member support and rapid rates of growth. Thus, we see evidence that secularization of some religious bodies prompts revival: Sects break away to revive the religious tradition.

Sect formation is very common in the United States. At least 417 American-born sect movements currently exist, and probably hundreds of others have existed in times past (Stark and Bainbridge, 1981). Most sects are very small: 28 percent have fewer than 500 members today. However, some are very large: the Southern Baptists, with more than 13 million members, are the largest Protestant body in the nation.

Sect formation revives the conventional religious *tradition* and reflects efforts by church members to remain church members: Those committed to the religious tradition but who find their church has become too worldly form sects to restore the other-worldliness of that tradition.

This analysis suggests that membership in conventional religious groups will be highest where sects are most active. This is precisely what contemporary data show. Sect movements are clustered in those states where membership in Christian churches is highest. Sects are very underrepresented in parts of the country where overall church membership and attendance are low (Stark and Bainbridge, 1980). That is, sects do not move into the market openings

Table 13-1 / American denominations and orthodoxy (national sample).

Protestant Denomination	Percent Scoring High on Orthodox Beliefs
Unitarian	0%
Congregational*	28%
United Presbyterian	38%
Episcopal	41%
Christian Church (Disciples of Christ)	46%
Methodist	49%
Presbyterian Church, U.S.A.	50%
American Lutheran	50%
Evangelical and Reformed	50%
Lutheran Church—Missouri Synod	52%
American Baptist	55%
Other Baptist bodies	63%
Southern Baptist	75%
Other sects	76%
All Protestants	55%
Roman Catholics	54%

Source: Stark and Glock, 1968.
Note: Beliefs measured include a belief in God (a personal one), belief in life after death, and belief in Satan.
*Now the United Church of Christ.

where there is general religious inactivity, but only into those where people are active but dissatisfied. I shall expand on this point as we examine the contrasting patterns of cult success.

Secularization and innovation

If sects represent efforts by the churched to *stay* churched, then cult movements represent efforts by the unchurched to *become* churched. That is, cult movements arise where both sects and churches fail to satisfy the religious market. To see this more fully, it will be helpful to examine the geography of religion in contemporary America.

The "unchurched" belt The American South is frequently called the "Bible belt," where religion, especially evangelical Protestantism, is unusually strong. In many of our recent studies, however,

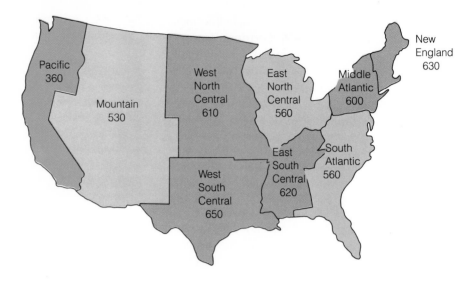

Figure 13-2 / Church membership rates per 1,000 population.

Bainbridge and I have failed to find evidence of such a belt (Stark and Bainbridge, 1985). The South does not differ from most other regions of the nation in terms of church membership rates, church attendance rates, belief in God, or belief in life after death. These regional patterns can be seen in Figures 13-2 through 13-5.

Although the South may not be a Bible belt, the Far West is certainly an "unchurched" belt. As is clear in Figure 13-2, church membership is far lower in the Pacific region that in any other region. Moreover, Table 13-2 shows that church membership is uniformly low among Far Western states: Washington, Oregon, California, Alaska, and Hawaii are the bottom five states in terms of church membership.*

Figure 13-3 shows that the Far West also has low rates of church attendance. Clearly, the conventional churches have failed to take root along the shores of the Pacific. However, Figures 13-4 and 13-5 show that it is church membership, and not religious belief, that is missing in the Far West. Westerners are nearly as likely to have faith in God and believe in life after death as people elsewhere in the country. Thus, the average westerner believes in the supernatural but lacks a church affiliation that gives form and expression to his or her beliefs. This should provide an ideal market opportunity for cult movements able to form attachments with unchurched West Coast "believers."

The geography of cult movements It should be no surprise that religious innovation is far more common and successful in the Far West than elsewhere in the nation. Figure 13-6 shows the distribution of the headquarters of 501 cult movements active in the United States today. The Pacific region towers over the rest (with the Mountain region, second lowest in church membership, standing second). These patterns are the same as those examined in Chapter 1. Recall that the Far West is also where the

*The rates used in Figure 13-2 and Table 13-2 underestimate church membership. They have been corrected so that they accurately reflect regional differences in church membership, but the figures are somewhat depressed because of omissions in reporting. If these rates were summed, they would produce a national church membership rate of 56 percent, whereas the correct rate for the United States is about 62 percent.

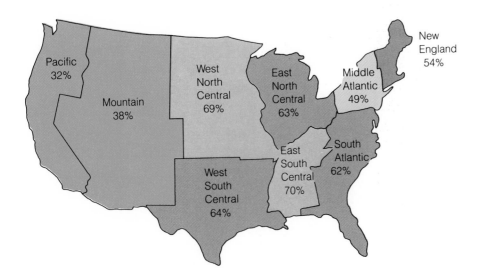

Figure 13-3 / Percentage of population attending church more than once a month.

The figure for the Mountain region includes only Colorado, Arizona, and Montana. The national rate is 54 percent.

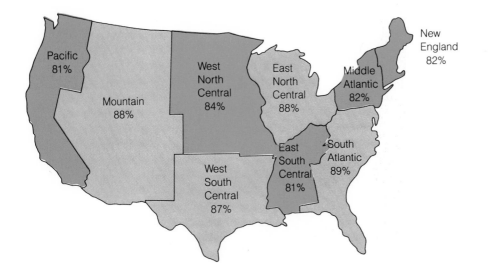

Figure 13-4 / Percentage of population who "believe in the existence of God as I define Him."

The figure for the Mountain region includes only Colorado, Arizona, and Montana. The national rate is 84 percent.

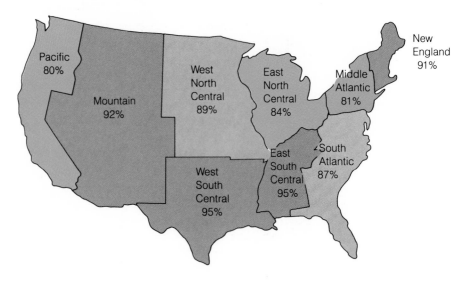

Figure 13-5 / Percentage of population who are sure that "There is life beyond death."

The figure for the Mountain region includes only Utah, Arizona, and Montana. The national rate is 86 percent.

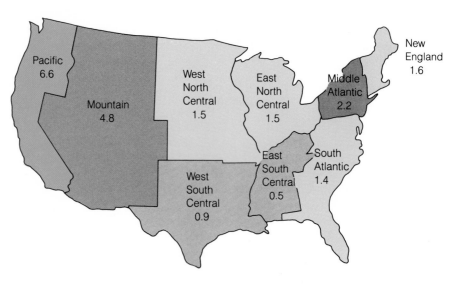

Figure 13-6 / Cults per million residents.

The national rate is 2.3 cults per million residents.

subscription rate for *Fate* magazine and the rate of *Yellow Pages* ads for astrologers are highest.

Nor is this a recent development. Data collected in a special 1926 U.S. Census tally of religious groups showed that even then church membership was comparatively very low in the Far West and cult membership very high. This was true even as long ago as 1890 (Stark and Bainbridge, 1985).

A major cause of low church membership rates on the West Coast is constant and rapid population movement (Welch, 1983). When people move frequently, as has always been common in the West, they abandon attachments to all social organizations—not just churches, but also fraternal clubs, hobby groups, veterans organizations, PTAs, political groups, and the like. Arriving in a new place, they also find it difficult to reestablish such connections in communities where many others are also newcomers and transients. Instead, they are likely to form attachments to people who are not attached to such organizations. Recall from Chapter 3 that after moving to San Francisco, the Moonies only began to grow again when they discovered how to locate and build attachments with other newcomers to the city. In places where unattached newcomers abound, new movements have a much greater opportunity to grow than in places where the population is settled and attached. And unlike most of the conventional churches in the Far West, cults go out in search of members.

In a sense, the disorganization of the Far West caused by population instability is somewhat like that created in times of crisis, when religious changes are likely to occur. Wars and natural disasters result in dramatic social disorganization. Constant population movement provides a less obvious but persistent form of the same thing.

However, the fact that cults attract members in all parts of the nation shows that secularization itself, even when not assisted by disorganization, produces a market for new faiths. Indeed, this is demonstrated by data on who joins cult movements.

Who joins cults? The belief that secularization is leading to the demise of religion assumes that people who discard conventional faiths have embraced rationalism and no longer find supernatural beliefs plausible. Thus, sociologists have interpreted in-

Table 13-2 / Church membership per 1,000 population by state.

Rank	State	Membership per 1,000 population
1	Utah	836
2	Louisiana	814
3	Rhode Island	768
4	North Dakota	766
5	Mississippi	762
6	South Carolina	719
7	South Dakota	692
8	Wisconsin	689
9	Minnesota	667
10	Massachusetts	666
11	Pennsylvania	656
12	New Mexico	640
13	Connecticut	638
14	Illinois	634
15	North Carolina	631
16	Texas	630
17	Iowa	629
18	Alabama	623
19	Nebraska	617
20	Georgia	598
21	New Jersey	590
22	Oklahoma	584
23	Kentucky	583
24	Tennessee	581
25	New York	577
26	Missouri	562
27	Kansas	550
28	Idaho	537
29	Maryland	529
30	Vermont	521
31	Virginia	518
32	Ohio	515
33	Michigan	508
34	Arkansas	505
35	New Hampshire	503
36	Florida	500
37	Delaware	493
38	Arizona	481
39	Wyoming	477
40	Indiana	475
41	Montana	466
42	Maine	448
43	Colorado	424
44	West Virginia	418
45	Nevada	394
46	Hawaii	380
47	Alaska	376
48	California	364
49	Oregon	332
50	Washington	331

Contrary to conventional wisdom, those who join new religious movements (or what sociologists call cult movements) are not mostly a bunch of maladjusted or deprived people from an intensely religious family. If this Hare Krishna member is typical, he is well educated and from an affluent background. It also is very likely that his parents are irreligious or at least religiously inactive and that he grew up without participating in any religious group.

creases in the proportion of people who say "none" when asked their religious affiliation as very significant evidence of the trend to irreligion.

I also long assumed that people who claimed no religious affiliation were primarily nonbelievers. I was extremely surprised, therefore, when one of my studies showed that far from being secular humanists or rationalists, people who say they have no religion are those most likely to express faith in unconventional supernatural beliefs (Bainbridge and Stark, 1980, 1981a). These people were many times more likely to accept astrology, reincarnation, and various psychic phenomena and to value Eastern mysticism.

Subsequently, my colleagues and I obtained the results of surveys of members of a number of contemporary cult movements: the Moonies, Hare Krishnas, Scientologists, witches, and several groups studying yoga. In each case, we found extraordinary overrepresentation of persons who had grown up with parents claiming no religious affiliation. Most of the rest of these members had parents who were not active members of any faith although they had a nominal affiliation (Stark and Bainbridge, 1985).

Thus, to the extent that large numbers of people grow up in irreligious homes (that is, in times and places where large numbers have drifted away from the conventional faiths), large numbers of potential converts to cult movements will exist.

SECULARIZATION, REVIVAL, AND INNOVATION IN EUROPE

Although the thesis that secularization is a self-limiting process that prompts revival and cult formation fits very well with data for the United States, many scholars have denied that the thesis has general applicability. Instead, they have tended to dismiss it as true only of the United States.

This prompted a series of studies to see whether the thesis applied in other places. The first of these studies was carried out in Canada. There we found that cults abound in places where the proportion of people reporting no religious affiliation is highest and church attendance is lowest. As in the United States, this area in Canada also borders the Pacific; the rate of people with no religious affiliation in British Columbia is more than three times the national average. In addition, British Columbia towers over the rest of Canada in terms of cult movements, *Fate* subscribers, and other such measures of religious innovation. We repeated the analysis for Quebec province separately and found that cults are strongest in those Quebec cities and towns with the high-

Table 13-3 / Indian and Eastern cult centers per million population.

Country or Area	Centers per Million Population
Denmark	3.1
United Kingdom	3.0
Finland	2.8
Sweden	2.5
France	2.5
Austria	2.1
Netherlands	2.0
Federal Republic of Germany	1.4
Belgium	1.0
Italy	0.7
Spain	0.6
Europe*	1.8
United States	1.3
Canada	1.5

Source: Stark and Bainbridge, 1985.
*Figure based only on nations listed above.

The spread of religious movements imported from Asia, such as this Zen Buddhist Center in San Francisco, permits an unbiased assessment of the comparative receptivity of European and North American nations to new religions. In computing rates for these nations, congregations of Asian immigrants were not counted. Instead, the rates were based only on congregations made up primarily of Westerners—as the picture shows this group to be.

est concentrations of people with no religious affiliation (Bainbridge and Stark, 1982).

At this point, Europe became the crucial test case. In many European nations, church membership and attendance are extremely low. In Denmark, only 3 percent attend church weekly, in Finland 5 percent, in Sweden 9 percent, and in Great Britain 15 percent. If secularization leads to innovation, then these nations should be awash with new religions. Yet most observers agreed that cults did not abound in Europe, but only in America, where conventional religion is still strong. Thus, they argued that secularization in Europe is real—the decline in religious participation represents a turn from *all* forms of religion (Wilson, 1975, 1979, 1982).

As it turns out, however, Europe is not lacking in cults, only in scholarly interest in them. Contrary to popular wisdom, the United States is not the land of cults. Cults are much more plentiful and successful in most of northern Europe and Great Britain than in the United States or Canada. Indeed, this is even true of groups that originated in the United States (Stark and Bainbridge, 1985).

The most telling comparison is based on groups that did not originate in either North America or Europe, but which have attempted to gain converts on both continents. The success of these groups reveals the receptivity of some nations to the same alien faiths. Table 13-3 shows the rates of Indian and Eastern cult centers for the United States, Canada, and the nations of western Europe (Norway, Ireland, and Portugal are omitted for lack of data). These

Since religion serves to answer questions of ultimate meaning, its appeal is not limited primarily to the poor, as many sociologists long have believed. For the fact is that all humans are subject to some of life's greatest tragedies and mysteries. Thus rich and poor, young and old, male and female are found in the ranks of pilgrims such as these at Fatima, Portugal.

centers represent various Eastern faiths, from Hinduism to Zen Buddhism, that have recently been brought to Western nations and whose followers are largely Western converts. The statistics do not include Indian and Eastern faiths sustained by congregations of Indian and Eastern immigrants. The results are very revealing.

Overall, the rate of cult centers per million people is higher for Europe than for the United States or Canada. But even this is misleading, because the European figure includes the populations of Italy and Spain, large nations that are not greatly secularized and that should not have many cults. (The weekly church attendance rates for Italy [53 percent] and Spain [78 percent] exceed that of the United States.) Thus, the truly interesting comparisons are between nations. These reveal that most European nations shown in the table have considerably higher rates of Indian and Eastern cult centers than the United States. And what nations are these? Primarily those with the lowest church attendance rates.

Clearly, secularization is producing religious innovation in Europe as well as in the United States and Canada. Moreover, areas where Indian and Eastern religions are having the greatest success in Europe have also been receptive to Scientologists, Hare Krishnas, and Mormons. But this pattern is reversed for sect movements, as predicted by our theory.

Initially, it seemed impossible to find good data on sect movements for the nations of Europe. It turns out, however, that hundreds of American and Canadian Protestant sects maintain very active missionary programs in Europe. These groups periodically submit reports on their work, which are collated and published in the *Mission Handbook*. These data show that American sects have had no impact in the most secularized nations of Europe. Thus, while Sweden has three Hare Krishna Temples and well over 100 full-time Scientology staff members, it has only one congregation founded by Protestant missionaries from North America. This is not for lack of effort—in 1979, there were 55 such missionaries stationed in Sweden. On the other hand, in Italy, where no Scientology staff members are stationed and where Indian and Eastern cult centers are scarce, there are 1,624 Protestant mission congregations. Thus, sects do best where they tap into a strong religious tradition. Cults abound where the conventional religious tradition is weak.

THE UNIVERSAL APPEAL OF FAITH

At the start of this chapter, we examined the unique ability of religion to satisfy basic human needs.

So long as humans want to know what existence means, so long as they are prone to disappointment, suffering, and death, the religious impulse will not be stilled. Only religions, only systems of thought that include belief in the supernatural, can address problems of this magnitude.

From this line of analysis, we can see that Niebuhr left a vital element out of his church-sect theory. In stressing the needs of the deprived and the lower classes for an other-worldly faith, he failed to note that in the face of some of life's greatest questions, all human beings are deprived. No one, neither the rich nor the poor, can achieve immortality in the natural world. And both rich and poor seek to find meaning in existence. Thus, the rich as well as the poor join religions. Granted, the rich tend to prefer more worldly churches, but there comes a point at which a religion can become too worldly, too emptied of supernaturalism, to serve either rich or poor. Thus, rising, vigorous, other-worldly religions attract the rich as well as the poor. Although well-educated and successful people tend not to join sects that are in a very high state of tension with the environment, they are often overrepresented among cult converts. In fact, the average cult convert in the United States these days is not a social outcast lacking education and good job prospects. The average convert is unusually well educated with excellent career potential (Stark and Bainbridge, 1985).

CONCLUSION

For more than a century, social scientists have confidently predicted the end of religion. Each new generation of social scientists has expected that their children, or surely their grandchildren, would live in an irrreligious society.

But religion has not gone away. Granted, many of the great religious organizations of today may be fated to slide into oblivion. But to notice only their decline and to ignore the vigor of new religious organizations and of new religions in general is to look only at sunsets and never at the dawn. In the long course of human experience, many religions have come and gone, but religion has remained.

Oddly enough, while social scientists have awaited the end of religion, they have been content to teach that religion has been a universal social institution, found in all societies. They attribute this universality to the ability of religion to serve universal human needs. Thus, to expect religion to vanish meant that such needs would vanish or at least that a new institution such as science would replace religion.

However, this implication ignores the unique aspect of religion and the fundamental differences between religion and science. As discussed early in this chapter, some things that humans seem to desire can come only from the gods. So long as such desires exist, religion will exist to satisfy them. Moreover, the supernatural claims of religion are, in their purest form, immune to scientific disproof. Scientists can send cameras and detection equipment through space to inspect the planets for signs of life, but they cannot send probes to test for life after death.

Review glossary

Religious economy The set of competing faiths, and their adherents, within a given society or geographic area of a society. (p. 308)

Secularization The process by which particular religious organizations become more worldly and offer a less vivid and less active conception of the supernatural. (p. 309)

Revival Movements within religious organizations, or the breaking away of new organizations, to reaffirm less secularized versions of a faith (see *Sect formation*). (p. 309)

Religious innovation The appearance of new religions in a society either by the founding of a new faith (see *Cult formation*) or by the importation of a new faith from another society. (p. 309)

Ultimate meaning, questions about Questions about the very meaning of life, the universe, reality; for example, Does life have purpose? Is death the end? Why do we suffer? (p. 309)

Supernatural That which is beyond natural laws and limits. (p. 309)

Religion Any socially organized pattern of beliefs

and practices concerning ultimate meaning that assumes the existence of the supernatural. (p. 310)

Religious pluralism The existence of several religions in the same society. (p. 313)

Churches Religious bodies in a relatively low state of tension with their environment. (p. 314)

Sects Religious bodies in a relatively high state of tension with their environment but which remain within the conventional religious tradition(s) of their society. (p. 314)

Sect formation The breaking off of a group from a conventional religion in order to move into a higher degree of tension with the environment. (p. 316)

Church-sect theory The proposition that, in time, successful sects will be transformed into churches, thereby creating the conditions for the eruption of new sects. (p. 316)

Cult A religious movement that represents a faith that is new and unconventional in a society. (p. 319)

Cult formation The process by which a person or persons with new revelations succeed in gathering a group of followers. (p. 319)

Charisma The unusual ability of some religious leaders to influence others. (p. 320)

Suggested readings

Chalfant, H. Paul, Robert E. Beckley, and C. Eddie Palmer. *Religion in Contemporary Society.* Sherman Oaks, Calif.: Alfred, 1981.

Hadden, Jeffrey K., and Theodore E. Long, eds. *Religion and Religiosity in America.* New York: Crossroad, 1983.

Meeks, Wayne A. *The First Urban Christians: The Social World of the Apostle Paul.* New Haven: Yale University Press, 1983.

Melton, J. Gordon. *The Encyclopedia of American Religions.* Wilmington, N.C.: McGrath, 1978.

Stark, Rodney, and William Sims Bainbridge. *The Future of Religion: Secularization, Revival and Cult Formation.* Berkeley: University of California Press, 1985.

Wilson, Bryan. *Magic and the Millennium.* Frogmore: Paladin, 1975.

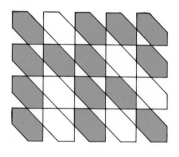

Why must human beings institute governments? Since ancient civilizations, the answer to that question has been the same: to provide for the common or collective good. Many things that humans need and want can be obtained only by coordinated, collective actions. Human survival is possible only in groups; in order to live in groups, certain conditions must be met.

First, humans must be secure against harm from other members of the group; that is, internal order must be maintained. We cannot risk living together if we constantly fear that others, for whatever private reason, might kill us, take our food and shelter, or abandon us. Security for each group member requires that others observe norms prohibiting certain behavior. Enforcing these norms requires social control.

Second, for a group to survive, it must be secure against external dangers—harm from other groups. Human history is littered with accounts of groups that fell to enemy attack. Thus, defense also requires collective action. Warriors must band together and fight in a coordinated way, and they must not desert at the first sign of trouble.

Third, certain beneficial activities or projects for the general welfare—often called **public goods**—are necessary for group life. Such goods can be provided only if group members act on behalf of group, rather than private, interests. For example, public works such as an irrigation system can be created only if large numbers of people work together to dig irrigation ditches.

Why do these three social needs require the creation of a government or state? Couldn't people live in anarchy, or without government, and simply cooperate out of their own self-interest or their

Politics
and the State

sense of responsibility toward others? That possibility has been debated by political philosophers for centuries. Some have concluded that governments are avoidable evils—a source of repression and exploitation that humans would be better off without. Indeed, 100 years ago the French philosopher Proudhon wrote that to be governed

is to be watched, inspected, spied upon, directed, law-driven, numbered, regulated, enrolled, indoctrinated, preached at, controlled, checked, estimated, valued, censured, commanded by creatures who have neither the right nor the wisdom nor the virtue to do so.

Proudhon argued that people ought to destroy their governments and live under anarchy. Although many other social thinkers accept Proudhon's view of government, they dismiss the idea of anarchy as impossible. They conclude that the state—a politically organized body of people—is an unavoidable evil. Many reasons have been given for the necessity of government, but all can be reduced to a single point: The only way human groups can maintain internal order, remain secure against external dangers, and promote the general welfare is by taking the risk of creating governments. ■

CHAPTER PREVIEW

To see why humans are driven to create government, we shall first examine the nature of collective goods and how they can be obtained. Then we shall see that the state is not only necessary but also dangerous. The state through most of history has been an institution of repression and the cause of great human suffering. Thus, we confront one of the oldest dilemmas of political philosophy: how to have the state and keep it tame. As we examine theories of limiting the state's power to repress, we discover two fundamental types of state: the elitist state, which tends to be tyrannical, and the pluralist state, which tends to permit considerable individual freedom.

In the second half of the chapter we shall shift from a macro analysis of how states function to a more micro assessment of political democracy. Paying close attention to the wealth of poll data on American political opinion and behavior, we shall examine who votes, who doesn't vote, and why; party affiliation; and the lack of major ideological differences among voters and between the major parties.

COERCION AND THE STATE

Mancur Olsen (1965) has argued that governments are unavoidable features of human societies. His conclusion rests on a simple point: In order to provide for collective or public goods, coercion (the use of force) is necessary. This is so because in creating public goods, the interests of the individual and the interests of the group collide.

Public goods can be created only if members of the group contribute wealth, time, and energy, or obedience, to create these goods. Although everyone gains from public goods, any given individual may be better off by avoiding making a contribution. Because of the nature of public goods, they usually

This memorial to those who died when the Battleship Arizona *was sunk during the Japanese attack on Pearl Harbor illustrates that the burden of providing national defense in World War II fell more heavily on some Americans than on others. Any individual American would have been better off if he had evaded military service (and kept his name off memorials like this), so long as others went out and won the war. To prevent such inequalities and to provide the public good of national security, the government required all qualified men to serve.*

cannot be withheld selectively. For example, if an enemy is driven off, all group members benefit, whether or not they took part in the fighting. Therefore, any given warrior profits more by staying home than by going off to battle. If individuals can avoid the risk of death or injury and still benefit from the group's survival, most individuals will avoid the risk.

By the same token, all members of a group benefit if members are prevented from stealing from one another. However, any individual benefits more if, while others are prevented from stealing, he or she is able to steal. Or consider the example of the irrigation ditch. All farmers benefit from having water for their fields, but any given farmer profits more by spending his or her time tending crops while others go out and dig the ditch.

Olsen concluded that because it is against the self-interest of any individual to contribute to the

The great dilemma of human societies is the need to create a state and the frequency with which the state then turns upon its citizens—most states in most human history have exploited and repressed their citizens. These citizens of Prague, Czechoslovakia, watch as troops roll into the city bringing to an end their nation's brief experiment with a less repressive regime.

public good, there will be no public goods unless means exist to force each individual to contribute. Often this force need not be used, but its use must always be a credible threat.

Governments arise because of the need to provide such a threat, and the threat cannot be made without organizing and monopolizing the use of coercion. Indeed, that is the definition of the state in sociological terms. As Max Weber put it, "Ultimately, one can define the ... state sociologically only in terms of the specific *means* peculiar to it ... namely the use of physical force." (Weber, trans. 1946)

Thus, only through organized coercion can humans assure themselves of public goods. And therein lies the greatest of all social dilemmas. We must have certain kinds of public goods in order to exist. To get them, we must create organizations capable of coercing us. By doing that, however, we set up the possibility, even the probability, that those who control the means of coercion will act in their own interest rather than for the public good. As a result, political leaders may use the government monopoly on coercive force for their personal benefit. Thus, peasants driven to create a government capable of defending them from bandits have often found themselves victims of a ruling elite. The members of this elite turn the coercive powers of the state against the peasants and tax them severely so that the elite can live in luxury.

FUNCTIONS OF THE STATE

As we have seen, Max Weber argued that the essence of a **state** or government is that it "claims the monopoly of the legitimate use of physical force" within its boundaries. Robert Nozick (1974) has developed this definition more fully:

A state claims a monopoly on deciding who may use force when; it says that only it may decide who may use force and under what conditions; it reserves to itself the sole right to pass on the legitimacy and permissibility of any use of force within its boundaries; furthermore it claims the right to punish all those who violate its claimed monopoly.

To understand why the state's monopoly on force arises, it is helpful to see how the state uses this monopoly to secure certain public goods. In some cases, the government must use coercion in order to prevent coercion by individuals. For example, one primary collective good is security against being the victim of coercion by other individuals, such as robbers.

Indeed, it is precisely here that anarchist proposals to dispense with the state break down. Without a collective good such as security against harmful actions by other group members, people would not be able to remain within the group. That is, without organized coercion to prevent private coercion, humans would live in a condition that Thomas Hobbes described as "the war of all against all." In his book *Leviathan,* published in 1651, Hobbes tried to describe what life would be like in a condition of anarchy:

Hereby it is manifest, that during the time men live without a common power to keep them all in awe, they are in that condition which is called war . . . where every man is enemy to every man. . . . In such condition, there is no place for industry; because the fruit thereof is uncertain: and consequently no [agri]culture . . . no society; and which is worst of all, continual fear, and danger of violent death; and the life of man, solitary, poor, nasty, brutish, and short.

Hobbes argued that there could be no freedom where there was no security of person or property.

An individual's freedom to live and to benefit from his or her efforts requires that limits be placed on the freedom of others. I am not free to live unless you are not free to kill me. I am not free to create unless you are not free to take my creations from me. When the attempts of individuals to coerce each other are not held in check, the possibility of preserving group life is destroyed.

Thus, a primary function of the state is to preserve internal order, to make life predictable and secure. However, the state also exists to provide the collective good of external security. In fact, the state serves to provide all **collective goods**—things its members could not individually provide for themselves, from irrigation ditches to armies to legal codes.

These functions of the state were clearly understood by those who wrote the preamble to the Constitution:

We the People of the United States, in Order to form a more perfect Union, establish Justice, insure domestic Tranquility, provide for the common defense, promote the general Welfare, and secure the Blessings of Liberty to ourselves and our Posterity, do ordain and establish this Constitution for the United States of America.

Rise of the repressive state

As we have defined it, all societies, even the tiniest and most primitive hunting and gathering societies, have a state. However, in small, simple societies, the state is loosely organized. Some persons hold authority in the group for settling disputes and overseeing the creation of public goods. There are no full-time leaders. Indeed, simple societies are organized much like families and often contain no more than several extended families. If an individual commits an act of serious deviance, adults who head the group administer punishment, usually by physical force. The offender may even be driven from the group or killed. Relations between the individual and the state in such societies are direct and personal.

As societies become more complex, however, the machinery of state becomes more elaborate and specialized. With the development of agriculture and the availability of surplus food, specialists began to appear in societies. Among the first of these specialists were political rulers and full-time military commanders. Specialization has implications for internal relations in agrarian societies: Military specialists can give political rulers a very effective monopoly on force. For the majority of citizens in agrarian societies, the state is an irresistible force that is often used against them. A king, for example, uses his soldiers not merely to provide for the common defense and to ensure public order, but to exploit his subjects. It is this feature of the state that has long driven people to despair. How can the state be made bearable?

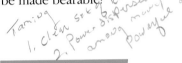

TAMING THE STATE

For more than 2,000 years, a dominant question in political thought has been how to limit the powers of the state. The nature of the problem seems clear enough. The state must exist. This means that the state will always have the potential to use its coercive powers to exploit and repress its citizens. How can the abuse of these coercive powers be limited without weakening the ability of the state to fulfill its necessary functions?

The Greek philosopher Plato thought the solution was creating a special class of philosopher-kings—persons trained to be fair and restrained in their use of state power. However, it seems too much to expect people placed in positions of immense power to practice self-restraint. Indeed, as Lord Acton claimed in a widely quoted maxim, "Power corrupts, and absolute power corrupts absolutely."

Rejecting hopes that the state could be tamed by putting people of high character in power, political theorists searched for social arrangements that would limit the power of leadership positions, regardless of the character of the leaders. By the eighteenth century, political thinkers had concluded that two things were necessary to tame the state. First, a clear set of rules (procedures and laws) had to be established that defined the limits of state power and the manner in which that power could and could not be exercised. But rules by themselves mean nothing. Some of the most repressive regimes on earth have model constitutions that guarantee all sorts of

The most famous contemporary symbol of the repressive state is the Berlin Wall, built to prevent people from leaving East Germany. The more repressive a state, the more effort required to keep people from fleeing.

rights and freedoms to citizens. Such guarantees do not mean anything unless they are embodied in a structure designed to ensure that the rules are observed. What kind of a structure can have this effect?

This leads to the second requirement for taming the state: a structure in which power is widely dispersed among many powerful groups. In this way, no one group can pursue its own interests without regulation; every group is checked by the other powerful groups acting to preserve their own interests.

We shall now examine how England and then the United States attempted to develop a structure for a tamed state.

England

English democracy evolved from a single principle, the right to private property. The English believed that the essential feature of state repression was the use of coercion to deprive people of their property. If this could be prevented, the state could be brought under control. In particular, if the king could be prohibited from taking any person's property without that person's permission, then the king could not squeeze all the economic surplus out of the people to provide for his luxuries. Nor could the king afford to go to war unless he had the support of the people, for he would lack the needed funds. Thus, the English believed that the state could be tamed if taxes could not be imposed or collected without the approval of those being taxed.

This view is in direct conflict with the Marxist theory of the state, which holds that private property is the root of all repression and exploitation by the ruling class. Marxists argue that the right to private property and the state's use of coercion to protect private property are the means by which the ruling class becomes and remains rich and exploits the masses. Thus, Marx claimed that only if property rights are abolished can the masses be liberated (see Chapter 9). Yet the fact remains that in Marxist states there is very little individual freedom, while in all nations with free elections and substantial individual liberty, the property rights of individuals are guaranteed by the state.

This contrast between capitalist and Marxist states would not surprise those who helped to create democracy in England or those who wrote the American Constitution. Long observation of European feudalism had convinced them that when property rights are not secure, it is the masses, not the rich, who suffer most. They recognized that the repressive state mainly confiscates the property of the powerless—the peasants, small merchants, and artisans—because the wealthy rule the state and receive the wealth seized by the state. To guarantee the property rights of everyone, therefore, would primarily protect those with the least property.

But the pressing question was How could property rights be protected from the state? The solution was not discovered by a political philosopher, but by a slow process of trial and error and some unplanned circumstances. The solution is not simply a law or a constitution, but a particular kind of social structure in which a number of powerful factions, or elites, restrict one another's ability to use the state's coercive power. The state can be tamed only when political power is dispersed among groups with diverse interests.

Such a dispersal of power developed in England partly by accident. In 1215 King John found himself unable to control the nobility. To remain on the throne, he was forced to sign the Magna Carta, a contract in which he agreed to impose no taxes on the nobility except when they freely agreed to be taxed. This led to the creation of the House of Lords, wherein the nobility gathered periodically to vote on tax requests from the king.

In time, the right to have one's property secure against seizure by the king was extended to property owners who were not members of the nobility. They began to send elected representatives to the House of Commons, where they, too, gave or withheld approval of the king's tax requests. The power to control the king's revenues proved to be the power to control the government. If the House of Lords or the House of Commons did not like a policy, they could withhold funds until it was changed.

Moreover, neither house of Parliament was dominated by a single group with identical interests. Policies favorable to some nobles often affected others adversely; policies good for merchants were often bad for shipowners or farmers. Thus, besides English kings having to depend upon the two houses for their revenues, decisions within each house required a coalition of groups and therefore a compromise of competing interests. Thus, governmental decision-making processes involved increasingly diverse groups and interests.

Of course, English rulers occasionally attempted to destroy these limits on their power and restore the absolute power of the throne. However, these efforts were always thwarted because too many people had too much to lose should the king regain

The unhappy Sufferers were Mess[rs]. Sam[l] Gray Sam[l] Maverick, Jam[s] Caldwell, Crispus Attucks & Pat[k] Carr
Killed Six wounded; two of them (Christ[r] Monk & John Clark) Mortally

The Boston Massacre, March 5, 1770: English soldiers fired on a crowd demonstrating against new tax measures, as depicted in this engraving by Paul Revere. Five Americans were killed, and their funerals became occasions for massive protest.

control. Therefore, if one faction of nobles wanted to restore an unlimited monarchy, others combined to block them. In fact, when King Charles I attempted to reassert absolute rule, he was overthrown and beheaded. When his family was restored to the throne, they were careful not to repeat his errors.

The United States

The American Revolution occurred primarily because the English failed to extend their principle of no taxation without representation to their North American colonies. The English tried to levy taxes on the colonies, but they did not grant the colonies representation in the House of Commons, where they could influence tax policies.

Once free of English rule, the Americans had to create their own system of government. By this time, however, political philosophers, especially the Scottish rationalists, had analyzed why and how the English system worked. Thus, the men who wrote the American Constitution did so with considerable understanding of the essential issues.

James Madison, the principal designer of the American Constitution, believed that democracy always faces two threats. The first is a tyranny of the minority—the historic danger that a privileged few would capture the state and use its coercive powers to repress and exploit the many. This classic problem of taming the state had given rise to the English form of democracy. But Madison was also concerned about the tyranny of the majority—the danger that a majority of citizens would use the machinery of representative government to exploit and abuse minorities. Here, Madison was mindful that even the English democracy persecuted religious dissenters and that coalitions of interest groups sometimes exploited weaker groups. Indeed, Madison was concerned that people who achieved great wealth be as secure in their property rights as anyone else, and he feared that the mass of citizens might use their superior numbers to impose discriminatory taxes on the rich and thereby escape paying taxes themselves.

To block both kinds of tyranny, Madison developed a system of government in which powers were widely distributed and procedures made somewhat cumbersome. Three branches of government—the executive, legislative, and judicial—each had the power to nullify actions taken by the other two. This system is called the system of checks and balances in government. Madison hoped to make it possible for minorities to block actions against them, at least for a long period, and for substantial majorities to be required to take any action, thereby blocking minorities from controlling the government.

The system of checks and balances has dominated the American political process for more than 200 years. It has not always produced ideal results, and sometimes the United States has been less democratic than Madison had hoped. Despite these defects, the state has remained relatively tame.

Moreover, many of the worst violations of individual liberty have been corrected within the system.

The important point, however, is that our Constitution, like all constitutions, is simply a piece of paper. Some of the most repressive regimes on earth have model constitutions that guarantee personal liberties. For example, while our Constitution simply guarantees freedom of the press, the constitution of the Soviet Union guarantees that the government will provide free printing presses and paper to the people so that they can express their views. However, since the Communist Party claims the sole right to speak for the people of the Soviet Union, Russians who print criticisms of the government are sent to labor camps. Clearly, freedom from state repression depends on social structures, not on legal documents.

By examining the rise of democracy in England, we could glimpse the social structures needed to tame the state. This served as a basis for sociological assessment of these structures.

ELITIST AND PLURALIST STATES

States are of two essential types: elitist and pluralist. In an **elitist state**, a single elite group rules. Sometimes power struggles go on within this elite, for example, when there is a dispute over who is to be the new king or the new party leader. But power resides almost totally with this single elite. They control the state and can therefore use its coercive powers as they see fit.

The elitist state is the most common type. The agrarian societies examined in Chapter 10 were elitist states, and most societies today are elitist states, regardless of what their constitutions say. Whenever only a single political party is permitted and rule is passed on by power struggles within the one-party elite, that state is elitist, even if it calls itself a democracy or a people's republic.

It is almost impossible for an elitist state to avoid being tyrannical. Plato's hypothetical unselfish philosopher-kings have not appeared. In short, the elitist state is an untamed state wherein the coercive powers of the state are used to repress and exploit people.

The Soviet Union is an example of an elitist state, ruled by a small circle of Communist Party officials. The party has attempted to eliminate all other power centers in Russian society—centers that might give rise to competing elites.

In a **pluralist state**, rules governing state power are maintained by the existence of many competing elites. The pluralist state has been tamed. That does not mean that all persons living in such a state have an equal amount of power in decision making. No such society exists. Indeed, the word *pluralist* refers to several (plural) elites. The state is tamed because power is dispersed among many contending minorities, or elites, each of which can secure some, but not all, of its desires.

The elitist state is ruled by a single minority; the pluralist state is ruled by shifting coalitions of many minorities. Robert Dahl (1956) explains the difference this way:

If there is anything to be said for the processes that actually distinguish democracy from dictatorship, it is not discoverable in the clear-cut distinction between government by a majority and government by a minority. The distinction comes much closer to being one between government by a minority and government by minorities.

Thus, Dahl conceded that in no states do majorities rule directly. Rather, in democratic states numerous minorities or interest groups represent the interests of most citizens: business interests, labor interests, religious interests, racial and ethnic interests, regional interests, and so on. It is the constant struggles and shifting coalitions among these groups that prevent any one from imposing its will on the others. Thus, should business become too powerful, labor unions and consumer groups may unite to hold it in check. Or should labor become too powerful, consumer groups may side with business. If the eastern states seek to exploit other regions, these regions will unite to protect themselves. And so it goes.

However, democracy is not the cause of pluralism. Rather, pluralism is the mechanism that sustains democracy as each of many political blocs acts to preserve its right to influence decision making. Indeed, in some nations that do not claim to be democracies, the existence of pluralism limits the power of the state—a pattern often found in Latin American countries ruled by military governments. In some nations that do claim to be democracies, the absence of pluralism results in little freedom for the individual; nations in the Soviet bloc are examples.

TOTALITARIAN AND AUTHORITARIAN STATES

Most societies, both past and present, have been undemocratic. Political power is not gained by open and free elections; instead, it is monopolized by a political elite. Members of the elite determine who governs, sometimes peacefully, sometimes by violent upheaval. Often we refer to such states as dictatorships, because the leaders dictate to the people rather than consult with them. However, even dictatorships differ in their degree of internal pluralism. In some, several elites exist and jointly influence decisions. In others, a single elite dominates all aspects of society. Contrasts between the two help show how pluralism limits the power of the state even in the absence of democracy.

The **authoritarian state** is undemocratic but is not dominated by a single ruling elite. Instead, power rests in a coalition of several elites, and thus decisions require agreement among elites having somewhat different interests. The political rulers must retain the support of other elites in order to act. For example, military leaders in Latin America have often seized power and installed a ruling junta. Usually, however, the junta cannot eliminate other powerful

elites. Thus, despite seizing the government, the military must negotiate government policies with other powerful factions such as business, religion, sectional or ethnic groups, and often even trade unions. So long as these other elites influence political decisions, the state will be somewhat responsive to a range of public interests.

In fact, in authoritarian states, it is primarily opposition to the authority of the state that is suppressed. The state tends to be very strict about the activities that are outlawed but often pays little attention to those activities that are permitted. For example, the authoritarian state may severely restrict political expression that challenges its right to rule but permit unlimited debate on other political issues, such as tax policies. Or the authoritarian state may outlaw political meetings but pay no attention to religious or cultural meetings. Typically, authoritarian states are strict about who enters the country but little interested in who leaves.

Authoritarian states are dictatorships and do not offer nearly as much individual freedom as democracies. However, they do not attempt to monitor and control all aspects of social life. Moreover, to the extent that they are pluralistic, there is a chance that they will become more democratic.

Indeed, this is what took place in England. A few centuries ago, England was an authoritarian rather than a democratic nation. In fact, democracy developed so gradually in England that it is not possible to say just when it became democratic. From the thirteenth century on, England evolved into an increasingly pluralistic and democratic nation.

Recently other authoritarian nations have become democracies very rapidly. For example, Spain under Franco, Portugal under Salazar, and Greece under a military junta were all authoritarian states with considerable internal pluralism. Each shifted abruptly to a democracy.

Thus even in dictatorships, pluralism holds the key to limiting the power of the state. It succeeds in doing so not by depending upon the virtue, conscience, or wisdom of political leaders, but by playing off the selfish interests of factions against each other.

In contrast, **totalitarian states** are dictatorships that lack pluralism. The political elite is the only organized power bloc. Unrestrained by competing elites, they are free to impose their will on their

The President of Bolivia and other high government officials on the reviewing stand during a parade in 1982. Bolivia at this time was an authoritarian state providing much less individual freedom than Canada, for example. However, to hold power in Bolivia, the political leaders must satisfy demands of many other elites including the military, business, and the church. Thus some degree of pluralism prevents Bolivia from being a totalitarian regime.

people. Of course, such policies are widely resented, since most people are getting a "raw deal." Thus, the totalitarian state must rely on terror and repression to hold power. Since grievances against the state are nearly universal, the elite cannot permit any activities that might permit the opposition to organize. In this sense, totalitarian governments must suspect everyone (Arendt, 1958).

In the declining days of the Roman Empire, the Caesars spent much of their revenues on spies and police in order to prevent rebellion. The same patterns occur in totalitarian societies today. Because

the elite fear the people, they make sure that the people fear them even more (Johnson, 1977).

Dictatorships of this sort are called totalitarian because they attempt total control of society. For example, the Nazis seized control of all German clubs and organizations; even the village chess clubs were disbanded and replaced by official Nazi Party chess clubs. In similar fashion, the Communist Party in the Soviet Union seized control of the Russian Orthodox Church, appointing all bishops, limiting and supervising the training of priests, and attempting to outlaw and eliminate all other religious groups

In Poland, as in other Communist bloc nations, all newspapers are strictly controlled by the government. Oddly, the government also makes it hard for citizens to get these papers. This long line of people in the main market square in Krakow, Poland, waits to buy a morning paper from the vending truck.

(Kowalewski, 1980). That the Communist Party failed to crush religion is a testament to religion's importance to people: That the party has tried to hard to crush religion displays the total control to which it aspires.

DEMOCRACY AND THE PEOPLE

The essence of popular democratic political theory is that government should be of the people, by the people, and for the people. But how can this be accomplished, and would it really be in the public interest? Clearly, it is impossible to run even a modest-sized city along the lines of the New England town meeting, where citizens gather to speak their piece and, by majority vote, make all town government decisions. Such a direct democracy requires tiny populations. Moreover, a substantial number of citizens do not take part in town meetings, and thus government is not by all the people. Even if those who fail to attend were rounded up and forced to take part, it is not clear that government would be conducted more wisely or even with greater concern for the interests of all. Many people seem too

Direct democracy is possible only for very small groups, such as this group of New Englanders gathered for a town meeting. For larger groups, representative democracy is required.

little interested in politics or too uninformed to make any responsible contributions to decision making.

For both of these reasons, practicality and indifference, democracies rest on the principle of representative government. Free elections are held to select persons to govern on behalf of the rest. Should these elected official stray too far from the public will, they can be turned out of office at the next election. But even this solution is not perfect if the concern is to represent everyone, since many citizens do not vote or otherwise participate in the political process. As a result, they give disproportionate political influence to those who do partici-

pate. Moreover, many who take part appear to have only the vaguest impression of what is going on and therefore may be better served politically by doing nothing.

In the remainder of this chapter, we shall explore political participation and political opinion in the United States to see how democratic political processes shape the state. However, before turning to these matters, it will be useful to see how the recent development of public opinion polls made it possible to determine how the American people feel about major issues and to discover who takes part in the political process.

GEORGE GALLUP: THE RISE OF OPINION POLLING

 Modern democracies are founded on the belief that those elected to represent the people will actually do so. This does not mean that they ought to be rubber stamps for popular opinion. In fact, political leaders often earn great respect when they risk popularity to abide by their principles. Nevertheless, in a representative government, elected representatives should at least know the people's feelings on various issues. Obtaining this knowledge does not seem very difficult today, when it is hard to open a newspaper or watch the nightly news on TV without learning the results of the latest opinion poll.

Nevertheless, until recently most elected officials could only guess about public opinion, even on major issues, and often their guesses were wrong. Those representing a minority viewpoint can often instigate massive letter-writing campaigns, public demonstrations, and editorial support so that they appear to be representing the majority. Before public opinion polling, it was very difficult to see the contrivance of such campaigns. In fact, some of the earliest polls were as misleading as publicity campaigns in support of particular points of view.

In 1936 Franklin Delano Roosevelt ran for his second term as President of the United States. His opponent was Alfred Landon, the Republican Governor of Kansas. In order to have advance knowledge of the election results, the *Literary Digest,* one of the leading magazines of the time, conducted a huge poll of public opinion. They sent postcards (which could then be mailed for a penny) to millions of Americans, asking them how they planned to vote. Based on more than 5 million responses, they confidently predicted that Landon would win in a landslide with more than 60 percent of the vote. In fact, it was Roosevelt who won with more than 60 percent of the vote.

Where had the *Literary Digest* gone wrong? By not selecting a random sample of the population (see Special Topic 1). Having no national list of the American public, the *Digest* editors used telephone books and automobile registration lists to get names and addresses for their poll. Unfortunately, people having telephones and automobiles in the depths of the Great Depression were much wealthier than the millions without such luxuries.

As we shall see later in this chapter, social class has considerable effect on voting choices. The *Literary Digest's* poll was biased, reflecting the voting intentions of a wealthy minority, not those of the public as a whole. As a result of this polling fiasco, the magazine was ridiculed and condemned, and it soon went bankrupt.

Meanwhile, in 1936 another poll on the election appeared in a number of newspapers. Unlike the *Literary Digest's* poll, it was not based on millions of respondents, but on fewer than 2,000; yet it correctly predicted an easy Roosevelt victory. This poll was conducted by the American Institute of Public Opinion (AIPO). AIPO had begun in 1935, and on October 20 of that year its first weekly report on public opinion about current issues appeared in a number of newspapers. It proved a very popular feature, and soon it was carried by scores of leading papers across the country. A year later, AIPO's correct prediction of the election made it an authoritative source of information on public opinion. The name of the president and founder of the American Institute of Public Opinion soon became well known: George Gallup.

George Gallup received a doctorate from Northwestern University in 1928 and was head of the department of journalism at Drake University from 1929 to 1931. He returned to Northwestern for a year as professor of journalism and advertising, but then went to New York to become director of research for Young and Rubicam, one of the nation's top advertising agencies. In 1935 he founded the polling organization that has come to be known as the Gallup Poll.

Gallup's aim was to provide frequent reports of public opinion on major political, social, and moral issues. As he put it in his first newspaper report in 1935, his was a "nonpartisan fact-finding organization which will report the trend of public opinion on one major issue each week.... The results of these polls are being published for the first time today in leading newspapers—representing every shade of political preference."

Gallup's first report demonstrated the difficulties of gauging public opinion without conducting a poll. In 1935 America was in the midst of the Great Depression. Millions were out of work, many banks

During the Great Depression of the 1930s the government hired large numbers of people in an effort to reduce unemployment. One such program put large numbers of artists on the federal payroll. The intent was to support the arts and to beautify federal buildings. This painting by Mitchell Siporin is one of the many bitter critiques of American society produced by these artists.

had failed, factories were closed or running at very reduced levels, and thousands of homeless people had taken to the highways in search of a livelihood. After three years in office, Franklin Delano Roosevelt's "New Deal" had made little progress toward economic recovery. As a result, a widespread campaign was begun to greatly increase government spending to feed and clothe the needy and to stimulate the economy. Countless public speakers claiming to represent the public demanded that Roosevelt increase federal spending. Many members of Congress joined in these demands, and press

accounts frequently echoed the cry that "the people demand action now."

Along came the Gallup Poll. The first Gallup Poll ever published reported national responses to the question: "Do you think the expenditures by the Government for relief and recovery are too little, too great, or just about right?" Only 9 percent of Americans thought the government was spending too little. Sixty percent thought it was spending too much. Thirty-one percent thought the current level of spending was about right. Whether or not increased public spending would have helped recovery, clearly those who supported it as representing the will of the people were incorrect.

This was only the first of many instances in which Gallup findings revealed widespread misperception and misrepresentation of public opinion. Two months later, Gallup reported that despite the fact that most members of Congress, encouraged again by many organized political groups, wanted to decrease military appropriations, the public overwhelmingly wanted them increased. For example, 7 percent of the American public wanted a smaller budget for the Army Air Force, while 74 percent wanted a larger budget. Apparently, the public was more concerned about the massive armaments programs then under way in Nazi Germany than were members of Congress.

In time, political leaders and the mass media learned how hard it was to judge public opinion without taking a poll, and polling became a major industry. But the Gallup Poll, which now has affiliates in more than fifty nations, remains the most influential source of information on political and social issues. Later in this chapter, we shall see that one reason for this is the outstanding record of the Gallup Poll in predicting elections. We shall also see why this is an extraordinarily difficult thing to do. But a second reason for the high regard toward the Gallup organization is its contribution to social science.

Through the years, the Gallup Poll has developed many survey research techniques now used by social scientists. However, these are not the main reasons why George Gallup (1901–1984) is so admired by sociologists, political scientists, and modern historians. Gallup's greatest contribution to knowledge was to provide invaluable data for researchers. He took great pains and incurred considerable costs to ensure that every Gallup study since 1935 is freely available through public archives so that scholars can reanalyze the data to test significant social scientific hypotheses. This has made countless studies possible without the need for major research grants; an entire Gallup survey can be acquired for a few dollars. Moreover, many of these studies could not have been done at any price, because time machines don't exist.

It is now too late to go back and conduct a survey to test a hypothesis about who supported Father Charles Coughlin, a right-wing political figure dur-

ing the 1930s. But in the early 1960s, when Seymour Martin Lipset (1963) wanted to test such an hypothesis, he could do so by using old Gallup studies. Contrary to the widespread belief that Coughlin's supporters were mainly middle- and upper-income opponents of President Roosevelt, Lipset showed that Coughlin's support came primarily from lower-income Americans who also supported Roosevelt.

Because Gallup often asked questions on the same issue from time to time, trends in public opinion on many issues over a period of four decades can be analyzed. The changing attitude on capital punishment, reported in Figure 8-3, is but one example.

The remainder of this chapter shall demonstrate the value of polling and especially of George Gallup's contribution to social science. As we examine features of political participation and opinion in the United States, it will be evident that much of what is known is from Gallup Polls.

POLITICAL BEHAVIOR

Because of the development of public opinion polling, it became possible to find out much more than how many Americans favored or opposed some policy. Hypotheses can be tested about what kinds of people take which positions and why and about who engages in what kinds of political activity and why. The Gallup Poll never asks Americans only one or two opinion questions. A Gallup interviewer asks many questions on a great variety of topics. Moreover, the interviewer also obtains basic biographical information on each respondent, such as age, sex, race, income, education, occupation, religion, marital status, and number of children. In addition, Gallup data also include where each respondent lives; this information allows the examination of regional differences, differences between rural and urban residents, and differences between people who live in large and small cities.

Nor do opinion polls restrict themselves to opinion. They can also ask people what they do. Through the years, Gallup and other polling organizations have asked people if they fish, if they play cards, and if they go to movies, operas, plays, football games, and prize fights. And they frequently ask people about their political activities: whether they are registered, whether they voted, whom they voted for, and the like. As a result of many analyses of poll data, we now know a great deal about the political behavior of the American public.

Political participation

People participate in the political process in many ways. One way is to contribute to political campaigns. However, fewer than one American adult in ten reports making any campaign contributions. Moreover, it is primarily people in upper-income brackets who make such contributions. Obviously, one would expect large donations to come only from those able to afford it. But there are many opportunities to give small amounts that nearly everyone could afford, but most Americans do not do so. Even fewer Americans report more active forms of participation, such as passing out leaflets or performing other campaign work. Once again, persons with better education and higher incomes dominate such activities (Berelson and Steiner, 1964; Gallup, 1972).

For the average American, political participation takes the form of voting, if it takes any form at all. In most elections, far less than half the voting-age population casts ballots. Even in presidential elections, only slightly more than half of all eligible Americans vote. In 1980, only 53 percent of the American citizens over the age of 18 went to the polls to determine who would lead the nation.

A major factor in low voter turnout is a low rate of registration. In 1980, only 71 percent of eligible Americans told the Gallup Poll they were registered to vote (and this figure might be inflated by those not wanting to admit they were not). Who is registered and who isn't? Table 14-1 provides a number of interesting comparisons. Men are very slightly more likely than women to be registered. Whites are somewhat more likely than blacks. There are very substantial differences by education and age, with the college educated and persons over 30 reporting much higher rates of registration. Finally, Republicans are somewhat more likely than Democrats or Independents to be registered. Not only are some kinds of people more likely to be registered, but these same kinds of people are more likely

Table 14-1 / Voting-age Americans registered to vote (1980).

Group	Percentage Registered to Vote
National	71%
Sex	
Male	72%
Female	70%
Race	
White	72%
Black	65%
Education	
College	79%
High school	68%
Grade school	65%
Age	
Under 30	50%
30–49	74%
50 and over	83%
Party	
Republican	79%
Democrat	74%
Independent	63%
Other	31%

Source: Gallup Poll, 1980.

to vote on election day. It is an axiom among campaign managers that Republican candidates are helped when voter turnout is low (on stormy days, for example), because Republican voters make a greater effort to vote.

As a result of these voting patterns, election day results often do not mirror public opinion. That is, the results are different from what they would have been had everyone who was eligible voted and different from preferences revealed by public opinion surveys. In fact, this is what makes it so difficult for pollsters to predict elections accurately. To call an election, pollsters must impose corrections to try to reflect the opinions of those who will actually vote, not simply the opinions of the whole public. These corrective procedures necessarily involve an element of risk. For example, they must rely on long-range weather forecasts, since a storm reduces turnout and changes the degree of correction needed.

It is a tribute to the art of opinion polling that the preelection poll predictions are as good as they are, and that they have gotten better since the first

Table 14-2 / Gallup Poll predictions for and actual results of presidential elections, 1936–1980.

Year	Gallup Prediction		Actual Results	
	Winner	Percentage of Vote	Winner	Percentage of Vote
1980	Reagan	47.0%	Reagan	50.8%
1976	Carter	48.0%	Carter	50.0%
1972	Nixon	62.0%	Nixon	61.8%
1968	Nixon	43.0%	Nixon	43.5%*
1964	Johnson	64.0%	Johnson	61.3%
1960	Kennedy	51.0%	Kennedy	50.1%
1956	Eisenhower	59.5%	Eisenhower	57.8%
1952	Eisenhower	51.0%	Eisenhower	55.4%
1948	Dewey	49.5%	Truman	49.9%*
1944	Roosevelt	51.5%	Roosevelt	53.3%
1940	Roosevelt	52.0%	Roosevelt	55.0%
1936	Roosevelt	55.7%	Roosevelt	62.5%

*Because of third-party candidates, a winner sometimes does not receive a majority of the votes cast.

scientific polls were taken in 1936. Table 14-2 shows how the Gallup Poll predicted every presidential election from 1936 through 1980. Only once, in 1948 when the Gallup Poll predicted Thomas Dewey would defeat Harry Truman, did the Gallup Poll fail to pick the winner.

Political interest and awareness

Why don't more people register to vote, and why don't more registered voters bother to cast their ballots? One reason is that many people have very little interest in or awareness of politics.

In 1972 the Gallup Poll reported that well over a third of American adults said they had "little or no interest in politics." That same year Gallup also asked a sample of the 44 million adults who had not voted in the 1972 presidential election why they hadn't voted. (Richard Nixon won by a landslide over George McGovern, getting 47 million votes, only slightly more than the nonvoting total.) In all, 57 percent, or the equivalent of 25 million voters, said they just weren't interested.

These nonvoters should probably be taken at their word. For a lack of interest is complemented by an amazing lack of awareness by the American public of elementary political knowledge. The following quiz is made up of questions that the Gallup Poll has asked national samples of the American public in recent years. Following each is the percentage who gave the wrong answer or who said they didn't know the answer.

1. What are the three branches of the federal government called? (Eighty-one percent missed.)

2. What is meant by the term "electoral college"? (Sixty-eight percent missed.)

3. Can you recall the name of your state's U.S. senators? (Seventy-two percent missed.)

4. Can you tell me the name of your congressman? (Forty-seven percent missed.)

5. Do you happen to know when [your congressman] comes up for election next? (Seventy percent missed.)

6. Is [your congressman] a Democrat or a Republican? (Forty-one percent missed.)

Millions of Americans usually ignore current events, and especially political conflicts. It takes a dramatic event like the Iranian takeover of the U.S. Embassy to attract the attention of the entire country.

Keep in mind that some of those who answered correctly were probably guessing. Clearly, then, the majority of Americans are not very concerned about politics. Indeed, political polls typically find large numbers of citizens who say they haven't heard of political questions that are currently being debated. However, this pattern shifts dramatically when events and issues arouse people's private interests. When the Iranians seized the American embassy and held U.S. diplomatic staff members hostage, public interest and awareness was virtually universal. The same happened during the British military expedition to recover the Falkland Islands and after the assassination attempts of Pope John Paul II and President Reagan.

Lack of political interest is not peculiar to the

American public, by any means. It is typical of citizens in most industrialized democracies. For example, polls reveal that the great majority of citizens in Great Britain, West Germany, and Italy pay little attention to news about political activities and governmental affairs (Almond and Verba, 1963).

To a considerable extent, this lack of interest reflects the fact that people in industrialized democracies are quite satisfied with the quality of their lives and therefore do not harbor political grievances that would prompt greater involvement. For example, in 1982 Gallup found that only 3 percent of Americans were "extremely dissatisfied" with their family income, and only 17 percent expressed any degree of dissatisfaction with their income. Similarly, only 9 percent expressed any degree of dissatisfaction with their job, while the majority were very satisfied. Yet there is a darker side to the lack of political participation.

Political discontent

For many Americans, politics seems irrelevant to the issues that concern them—their family life, their health, their jobs, their recreational activities, and their personal finances (Cantril and Roll, 1971). Indeed, a substantial number feel that when these matters are influenced by government at all, it is for the worse, not the better. In the past several years, these attitudes have been displayed on many automobile bumpers by stickers reading "Don't vote—it just encourages them."

For other Americans, the political scene does not provide the kind of politics they desire. Table 14-1 shows that slightly less than a third of the citizens who favor third parties (who give their party preference as "Other") said they were registered to vote. Since almost all successful candidates in American elections are either Democratic or Republican, those favoring parties to the far Left or far Right see little point in voting. In contrast to those who dismiss politics as irrelevant or harmful, these people tend to be politically involved, rejecting only the conventional political system, not politics per se.

It is hard to gauge just how much political inactivity is rooted in discontent rather than in a lack of interest and awareness. However, one thing is certain. Americans do not hold political officeholders in high esteem. In 1965 the Gallup Poll asked Americans "If you had a son, would you like to see him go into politics as a life's work?" Only 36 percent said yes. Since then, public respect for politicians seems to have declined even further. Table 14-3 shows various American institutions and the proportions of the public who expressed confidence in each in 1978. Organized religion is at the top, with a 60 percent confidence rating, followed by the banks, the military, and the public schools. Congress is at the bottom with an 18 percent confidence rating, just behind labor unions and television.

Party affiliation

Most Americans will state a party preference when asked. In 1980, at the time of the presidential election in which Ronald Reagan beat incumbent Jimmy Carter, 28 percent of Americans gave their political affiliation as Republicans, 41 percent as Democrats, and 31 percent as Independents. This division among the parties has not changed substantially for more than twenty years, except for a slight decline in the proportion of Democrats and a corresponding increase in the proportion of Independents.

How could a Republican have won the presidency in 1980, 1972, and 1968? For two reasons. First, many Americans who state a party affiliation do not always vote for that party's candidates. Thus, 26 percent of the Democrats in 1980 voted for the Republican Reagan, and 33 percent of the Democrats voted for Richard Nixon in 1972. Only 8 percent of Republicans in 1980 and 5 percent in 1972 crossed over to vote for Carter and McGovern, respectively. This enabled the Republican candidates to make up for their smaller party enrollment.

Second, Independent voters tend to vote for Republicans more than for Democrats. Thus, Reagan gained the votes of 55 percent of the Independents in 1980, while Nixon gained the votes of 69 percent in 1972. In fact, in only one presidential election from 1952 through 1980 have the majority of Independents voted for the Democratic candidate: 56 percent favored Lyndon Johnson over Barry Goldwater in 1964.

Given that party affiliation is only moderately

Table 14-3 / Percentage of American public expressing confidence in various American institutions.

Institution	Percentage Expressing Much Confidence
Organized religion	60%
Banks and banking	55%
The military	48%
Public schools	45%
Supreme Court	39%
Big business	27%
Television	21%
Labor unions	21%
Congress	18%

Source: Gallup Poll, 1978.

Table 14-4 / Party affiliations of American voters in 1981.

Group	Percentage		
	Republican	Democrat	Independent
National	28%	41%	31%
Sex			
Male	28%	38%	34%
Female	28%	44%	28%
Race			
White	30%	37%	33%
Black	8%	75%	17%
Education			
College	35%	32%	33%
High school	27%	41%	32%
Grade school	19%	59%	22%
Age			
Under 30	24%	36%	40%
30–49	27%	40%	33%
50 and over	31%	47%	22%

Source: Gallup Poll, 1981.

related to actual voting, Table 14-4 shows what kinds of people favor the various parties. Women are more apt to choose the Democrats, while men are more apt to be Independents. Blacks are overwhelmingly Democrats and support Democrats running for President even more overwhelmingly, while the Democratic margin over Republicans among whites is modest. Republicans outnumber Democrats among the college educated, but Democrats greatly outnumber Republicans among those who did not attend high school. Both parties have more supporters among persons over 50, while Independents are the largest group among persons under 30.

POLITICAL OPINION: ISSUES OR IDEOLOGIES?

Radicals, both on the Right and on the Left, often dismiss American politics as pointless and our democracy as an illusion because it offers no sharply differentiated choices. Both major parties adopt moderate positions based on compromises among the range of views represented in each. Therefore, voters do not get to select between two extremely different political approaches, but only between two quite similar parties that differ only on particular issues. Put another way, American parties are not committed to strict political *ideologies.*

An ideology is, in effect, a theory, and **political ideologies** are theories about how societies ought to be run. A political ideology consists of a few abstract premises about how societies operate and how they ought to operate. When faced with specific issues, persons committed to a political ideology do not attempt to assess the merits of various solutions. Instead, they base their responses on their ideological premises.

Ideologies are not really like scientific theories, however, in that they are often immune to all empirical evidence. Indeed, political ideologies require commitment based on faith in just the same way that religions are based on faith—as Christians are asked to accept the authority of the Bible, Communists are asked to accept the authority of Marxist-Leninist social theories.

As pointed out in Chapter 13, however, there is a crucial difference between religious and purely political ideologies. Religions are primarily concerned with the nonempirical world—the world of the spirit beyond all empirical assessment. So long as religions restrict themselves to statements about the other world—to saying, for example, that after death we go to another life beyond—they are immune from empirical failure. Political ideologies, on the other hand, must concern themselves primarily with the empirical world. They tell us that certain social arrangements, will produce certain results. Potentially, then, political ideologies can be as subject to empirical disproof as are real scientific theories. However, that political movements so often hold fast to their ideologies regardless of empirical contradictions indicates that faith, not science, is their real basis.

Moreover, since political ideologies are blueprints for political action, they must be expressed in rather simple terms in order to inspire a mass movement. This virtually ensures that an ideology will not be an adequate model of society and that members must frequently perform acts of faith—that constant failures of predicted outcomes must be ignored or explained away.

The appeal of ideology, of course, is this profound simplicity: The doctrine explains everything and does away with the constant need to assess the pros and cons of specific issues. Instead, as Daniel Bell (1961) put it:

Ideology makes it unnecessary for people to confront individual issues on their individual merits. One simply turns to the ideological vending machine, and out comes the prepared [solution].

Compared with Europe, politics in the United States is not very ideological. European voters can typically choose from many political parties, from the extreme Right to the extreme Left, many of which are based on a firm ideology. For example, in most European nations, voters can even select parties opposed to democratic rule on the grounds that their ideology is the truth and democracy merely permits erroneous political views to prosper. These are not only parties of the far Left, such as various communist parties, but also of the far Right—groups seeking to restore monarchies or authoritarian states.

People committed to political ideologies find the Republican and Democratic parties frustrating. Neither is based on a firm ideology. Both adopt platforms by assessing each issue separately, not by applying ideological tests. Moreover, repeated attempts by more ideological parties to challenge the two major parties have proved fruitless. Indeed, whenever either major party has drifted toward a more ideological stance, it has suffered a resounding defeat. For example, the Republican Barry Goldwater (in 1964) and the Democrat George McGovern (in 1972) were the two most ideologically oriented candidates nominated by either major party in decades. Each suffered a terrific beating and brought defeat to many other party candidates as well. In the aftermath of these fiascos, the defeated party returned to a more moderate, less ideological position.

One reason for the lack of significant ideological parties in the United States is that our political system is based on geographic representation. To be represented in Congress, for example, a party must win an election in a congressional district. Third parties have rarely been able to do this. In Europe, however, representation in parliaments is often proportional rather than geographic. Thus, if a party gets 5 percent of the vote, it gets 5 percent of the seats, even though it did not attract substantial support anywhere in the nation.

But perhaps the major reason for the failure of ideological parties and candidates in the United States is the American public. Barry Goldwater was badly defeated because large numbers of Republicans refused to vote for him. In similar fashion, large numbers of Democrats refused to vote for George McGovern. Americans overwhelmingly approve of the fundamental social and economic arrangements of their society and do not seek any radical changes. Therefore, they regard politics as the means to resolve specific issues, and they support candidates who take an issue-oriented approach. Countless poll results show widespread distaste for political ideology.

Indeed, Americans are reluctant to adopt even mild ideological labels. For example, in 1970 the Gallup Poll asked Americans whether they thought of themselves as "conservatives" or "liberals." In response, 38 percent said they were conservatives and 25 percent said they were liberals. Another 14 percent said they were neither, and 27 percent didn't know what the words meant. Moreover, it is clear

Many Americans are deeply committed to particular moral and political issues—as these anti-abortion demonstrators illustrate. But many other Americans have little interest in these issues and display no consistency in their responses during survey interviews.

Table 14-5 / Public attitudes on significant political issues, 1982.

Issue	Favor	Oppose
Ban on abortion	29%	69%*
Tougher pornography laws	77%	21%*
Mandatory death penalty for murder	56%	41%*
Equal Rights Amendment	59%*	36%
Prayer in public schools	53%	44%*
Increased government spending for social programs	48%*	48%

Source: Gallup Poll, 1982.
*Indicates the liberal position.

that many who said liberal or conservative don't really know what these words mean. When asked to choose the conservative or the liberal positions on many issues, such as increased welfare spending or reduced government control of business, a majority of Americans usually say they don't know or choose incorrectly (Robinson, Rusk, and Head, 1968; Harris, 1971). Thus, William Flanigan (1972) concluded, "As with other political ideas in the minds of Americans, the political ideologies are vague, superficial labels applied rather indifferently."

Perhaps the best evidence of the nonideological character of American political opinion is revealed by how the public defies ideological positions in their attitudes toward various issues.

Table 14-5 presents a series of significant public issues mentioned in a 1982 Gallup Poll on which there is a well-defined and publicized liberal and conservative position. Thus, persons with firm liberal or conservative ideologies would display a consistent voting pattern.

But notice that the majority opinion follows no such ideological pattern. A vast majority supports the liberal position against banning abortion, although a slight majority opposes legal abortion for a healthy, married woman (not shown in the table). Yet the majority support the conservative position for tougher antipornography laws even more strongly. A majority also rejects the liberal position by supporting a mandatory death penalty for murder, but the public favors the liberal position supporting the Equal Rights

Amendment. The public also sides with conservatives by supporting prayer in the schools. Finally, public opinion is evenly split on support for increased government spending for social programs.

Clearly, the major political parties understand this characteristic of the American public. Nominating candidates who are highly ideological and take a consistent position on controversial social issues is to select candidates with whom the public will disagree as often as agree. Clearly, most Americans see no reason why a candidate who supports abortion must also support pornography or oppose the death penalty. Americans tend to reject ideological candidates as extremists. Thus, both parties tend to choose moderates, people open to a variety of points of view, willing to compromise, and thus having a serious chance of being elected.

CONCLUSION

This chapter began with a macro assessment of the state. We saw that certain public goods can be provided only if the society forces members to conform and to contribute. As societies become more complex, the power to impose coercion on members of a society is vested in specialists who organize and control the state. However, throughout history the powers of the state have been used to provide luxury for those specialists.

This presents the inescapable human dilemma: It is not possible to dispense with the state, but the state itself is a danger to individuals—a constant threat to repress and exploit most citizens. We have examined political conditions that make it possible to tame the state and limit its power over the individual. Democracy appears to require the existence of many contending elites that constantly form temporary coalitions to limit one another's power. This is called pluralism.

In the latter half of the chapter, we made a more micro examination of the American political system. We have seen that many Americans do not take part in politics even by voting. Some groups are more likely than others to be active, and this gives them extra influence in setting policies. Much political inactivity is rooted in a lack of interest and lack of political awareness. Some reflects rejection of the conventional political system.

Finally, we have seen that the great majority of Americans do not embrace political ideologies, but approach issues pragmatically and in a spirit of compromise. This encourages the major parties to adopt political stances that are similar to one another and similar to the moderate positions supported by most Americans.

Review glossary

Public goods Things necessary for group life. (p. 332)

State The organized monopoly on the use of force (or coercion) within a society; synonymous with government. (p. 336)

Collective goods Things individual members of a society cannot provide for themselves and which require cooperative actions by many members; often synonymous with public goods. (p. 336)

Elitist state A society ruled by a single elite group; such states repress and exploit nonelite members. (p. 340)

Pluralist state A society in which power is dispersed among many competing elites who act to limit one another's power and therefore minimize the repression and exploitation of members. (p. 341)

Authoritarian state An undemocratic society that has a significant amount of pluralism. (p. 342)

Totalitarian states Undemocratic societies having little or no pluralism. (p. 342)

Political ideologies Abstract doctrines about how societies operate and ought to operate that are unresponsive to contrary evidence. (p. 353)

Suggested readings

Dahl, Robert. *A Preface to Democratic Theory.* Chicago: University of Chicago Press, 1956.

Gallup, George H. *The Gallup Poll: Public Opinion 1935–1971* (3 vols.). New York: Random House, 1972.

Gallup, George H. *The Gallup Poll: Public Opinion 1972–1984.* New York: Random House.

Nozick, Robert. *Anarchy, State and Utopia.* New York: Basic Books, 1974.

Olsen, Mancur. *The Logic of Collective Action.* Cambridge: Harvard University Press, 1965.

Renshon, Stanley A. *Handbook of Political Socialization: Theory of Research.* New York: Free Press, 1977.

In simple societies, children don't go off to school in the morning and their parents don't go off to jobs. Yet children still get educated and work gets done. As with the family, religion, and politics, educational and economic institutions are found in all human societies. The forms often differ, but the basic functions are always performed in an organized way. In hunting and gathering societies, children are educated by their parents and older siblings. Also, by tagging after their fathers and uncles, the boys slowly learn to perform the work expected of adult males, such as hunting. The girls learn their adult tasks from helping their mothers. Yet even in such primitive circumstances, the link between education and occupation is direct and powerful. Until people are sufficiently educated, they cannot fulfill their economic responsibilities.

In modern societies, the link between education and occupation is so obvious and important that we can often guess a person's education from knowing his or her occupation, and vice versa. We can be sure that lawyers and doctors spent many years in school and that unskilled laborers probably had minimal educations. Generally, the more education people have, the more they earn and the higher their occupational status. In fact, if we know people's education and occupation, we can often deduce many other things about them: how they vote, what kind of TV shows they watch, what kind of neighborhood they live in, and their tastes in food, clothing, art, automobiles, magazines, and music.

The Interplay Between
Education and Occupation

CHAPTER PREVIEW

Because of the interdependence of education and occupation, this chapter examines the *interplay* between these two social institutions. We shall begin by examining the dramatic shifts in the number and kinds of occupations produced by modernization. In Chapters 9 and 10, we saw that these changes resulted in a great deal of structural mobility. They also prompted major changes in the educational system, and these, in turn, led to more changes in the occupational structure. While the general connection between education and occupation is obvious, many of the links are rather subtle.

OCCUPATIONAL PRESTIGE

Because our occupations play a central role in our lives, we have very clear and sensitive notions about which jobs are "better" and which are "worse." This has been demonstrated by a long series of studies of **occupational prestige**.

Back in 1947, Paul Hatt and Cecil North presented a national sample of American adults with a list of ninety occupational titles (Reiss, 1961). Each respondent was asked to rate the "general standing" of each job as excellent (a rating of 5), good (4), average (3), somewhat below average (2), or poor (1). From the numerical weights indicated above, an average score was computed for each occupation. Because of the computational method used,

each occupation received a score between 20 and 100.

Table 15-1 shows the list of occupations and their scores. U.S. Supreme Court justice heads the list, followed by physician, nuclear physicist, scientist, government scientist, state governor, U.S. cabinet member, college professor, and U.S. congressman. At the bottom are garbage collector, street sweeper, and shoe shiner. This list of occupations has been rated many times both by the American public and by the public in other nations, and the results are very stable over time and place. Notice how many of the higher prestige positions require a college education or even postgraduate study.

It is hardly surprising that people give jobs different ratings. What is surprising is how consistent these ratings are over time and around the world. The original Hatt and North study has been replicated many times in the United States (Hodge et al., 1964), and the results have been virtually the same in each study. In addition, sociologists have conducted similar studies in other nations. In 1956, Inkeles and Rossi reported that studies done in Germany, Great Britain, Japan, New Zealand, and the Soviet Union had produced results very similar to American findings. Other sociologists conducted similar studies in less industrialized nations such as Ghana, Guam, India, Indonesia, the Ivory Coast, and the Philippines (Hodge et al., 1966). Again, virtually identical results were obtained.

Because of these similarities, sociologists suspect that people of all nations are familiar with the occupations found in industrial societies and the relative importance of these occupations.

Further research has determined why people rate

Table 15-1 / Occupational prestige scores.

Score	Occupation	Score	Occupation
94	U.S. Supreme Court justice	72	Policeman
93	Physician	71	AVERAGE
92	Nuclear physicist	71	Reporter on a daily newspaper
92	Scientist	70	Bookkeeper
91	Government scientist	70	Radio announcer
91	State governor	69	Insurance agent
90	Cabinet member	69	Tenant farmer who owns
90	College professor		livestock and machinery and
90	U.S. congressman		manages the farm
89	Chemist	67	Local labor union official
89	U.S. Foreign Service diplomat	67	Manager of a small store in a
89	Lawyer		city
88	Architect	66	Mail carrier
88	County judge	66	Railroad conductor
88	Dentist	66	Traveling salesman for a
87	Mayor of a large city		wholesale concern
87	Board member of a large	65	Plumber
	corporation	63	Barber
87	Minister	63	Machine operator in a factory
87	Psychologist	63	Owner-operator of a lunch
86	Airline pilot		stand
86	Civil engineer	63	Playground director
86	State government department	62	U.S. Army corporal
	head	62	Garage mechanic
86	Priest	59	Truck driver
85	Banker	58	Fisherman who owns his own
85	Biologist		boat
83	Sociologist	56	Clerk in a store
82	U.S. Army captain	56	Milk route man
81	Accountant for a large business	56	Streetcar motorman
81	Public school teacher	55	Lumberjack
80	Building contractor	55	Restaurant cook
80	Owner of a factory that	54	Nightclub singer
	employs about 100 people	51	Filling station attendant
78	Artist whose paintings are	50	Coal miner
	exhibited in galleries	50	Dock worker
78	Novelist	50	Night watchman
78	Economist	50	Railroad section head
78	Symphony orchestra musician	49	Restaurant waiter
77	International labor union	49	Taxi driver
	official	48	Bartender
76	County agricultural agent	48	Farmhand
76	Electrician	48	Janitor
76	Railroad engineer	45	Clothes presser in a laundry
75	Owner-operator of a printing	44	Soda fountain clerk
	shop	42	Sharecropper who owns no
75	Trained machinist		livestock or equipment and
74	Farm owner and operator		does not manage farm
74	Undertaker	39	Garbage collector
74	City welfare worker	36	Street sweeper
73	Newspaper columnist	34	Shoe shiner

Source: Hodge et al., 1964

various occupations high or low. Blau and Duncan (1967) found that if they took the average education of persons in a particular occupation and combined that with the average income of those persons, they could accurately predict the occupational prestige score that people would give that occupation. In other words, the more training an occupation requires and the more pay it offers, the greater its public prestige. This suggests that people rate a job by its importance. They seem to assume that no one will put in many years to prepare for a job that is unimportant and that society will not pay high salaries to get people to do unimportant work.

That prestige ratings reflect education and training indicates that the process of obtaining a particular occupational status begins when we are quite young. How much and what kind of education we receive is the primary factor determining our occupational opportunities. This touches on the matter of differential socialization discussed in Chapter 6. There we saw that much of socialization is geared to the specific roles a person is expected to play. One of the most important roles is the child's future occupation. Thus, from an early age, children tend to receive socialization appropriate to certain occupations. Children who display little academic aptitude tend to be placed in educational tracks that end with high school and lead to manual occupations. More academically talented children are tracked into college preparatory courses and groomed for technical and professional occupations. Education and occupation are thus intimately associated, and the interplay between them begins early in life.

THE TRANSFORMATION OF WORK

Peter F. Drucker (1969) examined how changes in work dramatically increased productivity to make modern standards of living possible. He pointed out that such achievements are not the result of harder work. Surely, modern workers do not work harder than their grandparents and probably they do not work as hard. They get better results from their work because, as Drucker put it, "they work smarter."

Technological innovations have made it possible to work smarter. In times past, ten laborers may have worked a week to dig a foundation for a new house. Today, one operator with an earth mover digs the same foundation in a few hours. This operator is obviously not working harder than those who dug with shovels. Having a machine and the technical knowledge to use it, one modern worker possesses the strength of many manual laborers.

However, not only machines let us work smarter. Applying any knowledge to work produces smarter work. Consider the accomplishments of Frederick W. Taylor, who originated time and motion studies of work. Taylor applied scientific principles to increase the efficiency of even very unskilled tasks.

One of Taylor's most famous experiments, conducted in 1899, involved teaching a group of unskilled laborers to shovel sand efficiently. He selected a man named Schmidt and began to work on increasing the rate at which Schmidt could shovel sand. The first thing Taylor did was to experiment with shovels of different sizes. He argued that the shovel should not be too big, or else workers would tire rapidly; then the amount of rest time they would need would offset the extra amounts they shoveled while they worked. On the other hand, if the shovel was too small, the work would be inefficient. Through trial and error, Taylor selected the right-sized shovel for Schmidt. Taylor then experimented with Schmidt to find the best technique for using it—the goal was to find the technique maximizing the sand shoveled and minimizing the energy expended. Finally, Taylor determined the most efficient intervals for rest periods. He found that it was better for men to rest frequently for short periods than to rest occasionally for long periods.

In a short time, Schmidt was able to shovel more sand per shift than the combined amount shoveled by the two strongest men not prepared by Taylor. As a result of his increased production, Schmidt earned more than twice as much as the other workers. Soon the whole shoveling team was on the new method, and each laborer earned a much higher salary than before. Not only did they shovel much more sand, but they were much less tired at the end of the day. All of this resulted not from using machinery but from what came to be known as **scientific management**—the application of scientific techniques to improve work efficiency.

Although Taylor's approach to the study of work

These Kansas farmers were already working smarter back in the 1890s. Using horse-drawn wagons and a newly invented shucking machine, this crew had picked and piled 10,000 bushels of corn. Today one farmer driving a modern harvester could out-work several crews this size.

is still being carried on today by a host of experts, his attempts to revolutionize manual labor were short-lived. Unskilled manual work has practically been taken over entirely by machines. As machines have replaced people in the most repetitive, dirty, and sweaty jobs, people have turned more and more to "knowledge" work—including using knowledge to design, maintain, and operate these machines.

Consequently, the kind of work people are most likely to perform in industrial nations has changed remarkably. In 1900, only 17 percent of Americans had white-collar jobs; most people did manual labor on farms and in factories. Today there are more white-collar than blue-collar workers, and fewer jobs involving manual labor are available each year.

Whereas manual workers manipulate "things" for a living, white-collar workers manipulate information. Therefore, in Drucker's judgment, we are changing from a primarily industrial economy to a "knowledge" economy. In fact, the most rapidly expanding job categories over the past century have been at the top—professional, technical, and managerial occupations. Today, one out of four working

Americans holds a job of this type. We are working smarter all the time, and this has changed who is working and why they work.

THE TRANSFORMATION OF THE LABOR FORCE

In highly industrialized economies, not only has what people do for a living changed, but the proportion of people who are employed has dramatically altered. In 1870, only 44 percent of Americans over the age of 16 were in the **labor force**. In 1980, 64 percent were in the labor force. This expansion of the proportion of Americans in the labor force occurred despite the fact that much smaller proportions of both young people and old people are working today. Today most Americans finish high school or college before entering the labor force, and most people must retire at age 70 (most retire before then). In 1870, few went to high school or college, and there-

Spring housecleaning at the turn of the century included hanging all of the bedding out to air. This housewife in Seattle is pumping a pail of water for scrubbing. If she wants it to be hot she will have to heat it on her kitchen range. On laundry day she will have to carry many pails of water into the house and heat them. After scrubbing the laundry by hand, she will carry it out to hang on the lines to dry. It will take her most of the next day to do the ironing.

fore most started work young; people rarely retired so long as they could continue to work. How did an enormous expansion of the work force occur despite these changes? Women joined the labor force.

Women in the labor force

In 1900, few women worked outside the home. Indeed, women made up only 18 percent of the American labor force. In 1981, women made up 42 percent. Much of this increase has been quite recent. For example, between 1970 and 1980, the male labor force grew by 15.3 percent, while the female labor force grew by 45.1 percent. This increase of women in the labor force is likely to continue until there are as many women as men who are working.

Why have so many women gone to work? There are probably many reasons. The feminist movement may have played a role. However, dramatic increases of women in the labor force preceded the feminist movement and may even have prompted its development. That is, the women's movement may have had more to do with getting women better jobs and pay than with getting women to seek employment in the first place.

A second reason women went to work is reduced fertility. Freedom from long years of pregnancy and child rearing has given women more opportunity to pursue a career. A third reason is increased freedom from housework. Women in 1900 made their own soap, spent Monday washing clothes, and needed most of Tuesday to iron them. The modern home has a washer and drier and commercial detergents, and clothes need little or no ironing. Reduced demands in the home have enabled women to take outside jobs.

However, another very important reason for the massive entry of women into the labor force has been a change in the kinds of work available. The shift to knowledge work has lured many women out of the home. Modernization has eliminated muscle power as a major source of energy; many jobs today are entirely "mental." In Chapter 18 we shall examine how technology revolutionized farming. Here we need only note that farming today requires a great deal of sophistication but only a modest amount of strength. In fact, very few jobs today require more strength than is possessed by the average woman.

A final reason should be obvious. The old cliché "Two can live as cheaply as one" was probably never true. But it surely is true that two can live better when they both have jobs. Today, in most upper-income families, both adults are employed. In fact, the average two-wage family in 1982 had an income 40 percent higher than the average family in which only the husband worked. Of families with incomes in the top 20 percent, only one in four depended on only one salary. This may give new meaning to the old suggestion about marrying for money.

However, the rapid entry of women into the labor force has placed an even greater premium on education for getting and holding jobs. With millions of talented and well-educated women in the labor force, it is increasingly difficult for less educated people to find employment. This has especially affected minority groups with relatively high rates of dropping out of school.

Unemployment

The term **unemployed** is not applied to everyone who is not employed, but only to those 16 years and older who are without jobs and seeking work. There are several ironies about unemployment that are often overlooked in news reports. Unemployment sometimes rises when jobs are more plentiful and declines when jobs are more scarce. This is because people often decide to look for work when they believe they are more likely to find a job.

When many jobs are available, people are drawn into the labor force. Rapid increases in the number seeking jobs but who have not yet found them cause the unemployment rate to rise. Conversely, when jobs are thought to be scarce, many people cease looking and thus are not counted in the unemployment rate. Some of this volatility in the supply of persons seeking work is due to married women and young people who are still living at home; both groups tend not to look for jobs when jobs are hard to get.

An important component of unemployment bears little connection to the health of the economy—several percent of the population are always seeking their first job or in the process of switching jobs. If people spend several weeks or more to get a first job, or find a new one, they will contribute to the unemployment rate. In addition, some of the unemployed are people who routinely cease working so that they can collect unemployment benefits. That is, some workers take periods of unemployment as planned vacations.

These kinds of unemployment do not cause much social concern, since the time without a job is brief and often voluntary. It is the long-term, chronic unemployment of many Americans that causes concern, because it results in poverty. Moreover, this unemployment is concentrated in certain areas, such as Appalachia, and in certain segments of the population, especially minority groups. For example, unemployment afflicts a higher proportion of blacks than whites, and urban black teenagers often have shockingly high rates of unemployment—sometimes running as high as 40 percent.

Why are rates of unemployment higher among blacks? Undoubtedly, discrimination plays a role, especially in skilled manual occupations (Lieberson, 1980). But a major cause is the dwindling supply of unskilled labor jobs. This is particularly evident in teenage unemployment, for only teenagers who are high school dropouts can be counted as unemployed—people enrolled in school are not counted as unemployed no matter how hard they seek work. Unfortunately, school dropouts are not qualified for most available jobs.

In Chapter 11 we examined the remarkable increases in black education over the past several

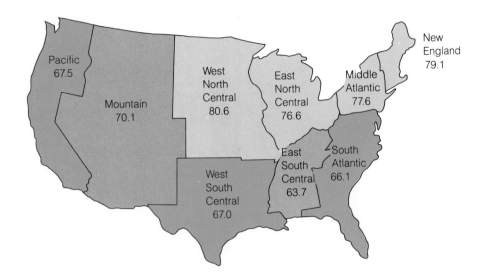

Figure 15-1 / Rates of high school completion, 1980.

According to a study released by the National Center for Educational Statistics in 1983, only 72 percent of Americans who were potential members of the high school graduating class of 1980 finished school. The top five states were: (1) Minnesota, 85.6; (2) Nebraska, 85.1; (3) Iowa, 84.6; (4) (tied) Hawaii, 83.1, and Montana, 83.1; and (5) North Dakota, 82.5. The bottom five were: (46) Nevada, 63.3; (47) Georgia, 63.1; (48) Arizona, 61.3; (49) Florida, 60.3; and (50) Mississippi, 60.1. Washington, D.C., with 56.9, was well below any state.

decades. In fact, blacks today are about as likely as whites to enter college. But they remain more likely than whites to drop out of high school.

In 1980, 72 percent of young Americans of the eligible age group actually graduated from high school (see Figure 15-1). As we shall see, this would have been considered a spectacular achievement 40 years ago. But changes in the nature of work today make it likely that most of the more than 1 million young people who dropped out of the class of 1980 will have trouble finding and holding jobs in the years ahead. There simply are fewer jobs for people with little education. Thus, while in the past newly arrived immigrants could get started in America by doing unskilled labor, immigrants today have far fewer opportunities of this kind. This imposes a special burden on blacks and other minority groups and an unusual need to seek education (see Chapter 11).

THE TRANSFORMATION OF EDUCATION

Clearly, no society can shift from an economy based on manual labor to one based on knowledge unless its people are educated—information cannot be processed by illiterates. The transformation of work in the United States was based on vast changes in its educational system.

When the United States was founded, nowhere in the world did many people get a chance to go to school. School was reserved for an elite few. However, from the very beginning, Americans were deeply concerned with education. They considered themselves part of one of the greatest social experiments in history: an attempt to establish a nation governed by the people through democratic procedures. But for people to participate in political decisions, they

In colonial days leadership and higher education went hand in hand. This page is from a notebook kept by James Madison during his junior year at Princeton. In it he recorded the fundamental principles of logic. Here he diagrammed the relationship between degrees of latitude and time zones.

Table 15-2 / Percentage of young people graduating from high school.

Year	Percent Who Graduated	Percentage of Males Among High School Graduates
1870	2.0%	44.0%
1880	2.5%	46.1%
1900	6.3%	40.4%
1920	16.3%	39.7%
1940	49.0%	47.3%
1950	57.4%	47.5%
1960	63.4%	48.1%
1970	75.6%	49.5%
1980	72.0%	49.0%

Source: U.S. Bureau of the Census.

must be informed; to be informed, a person must be able to read. Thomas Jefferson and many other leading spokesmen for the American Revolution feared that kings and tyrants would soon supplant democracy "if we leave the people in ignorance." Out of these concerns came the first efforts at mass education. Throughout the nation, local communities organized free elementary schools. In order to achieve universal schooling, local and state governments soon passed laws making it compulsory for children to attend school. By the late nineteenth century, laws in most states required children to attend school until age 16 or the completion of eighth grade.

Today we take universal elementary education for granted, although it is not much more than 100 years old in the United States and was achieved only through an enormous public effort and investment. By the end of the Civil War, little red schoolhouses dotted the nation, and for the first time in history anywhere, virtually all mentally competent children went to school to learn reading, writing, and arithmetic. This was thought to be an incredible achievement and a very desirable one—soon most other industrial nations followed suit.

Universal education not only sustained democratic political institutions in the United States but also provided the basis for rapid industrial and scientific development. As industry and commerce became more technical and specialized, the demand

for educated employees rose rapidly. However, although a large supply of people with eight years of education was a vital resource, soon there was a growing demand for persons with even more education.

More is better

Nearly all Americans attended elementary school during the nineteenth century, but very few went on to high school. In 1870, only 2 percent of Americans aged 17 or 18 finished high school (and it was very unusual for people to go back to finish once they left school). Thus, to be a high school graduate in 1870 was to be one of a tiny elite of very highly educated people (only 1.4 percent of the population went to college). In fact, most students in 1870 who did go to high school attended private schools (Trow, 1973).

However, having succeeded in the century-long effort to send everyone to elementary school, Americans began to consider raising their educational goals. If eight years of education was providing such a good investment, more years ought to be even better. And so, in the early part of this century, the campaign to send everyone to high school began. Table 15-2 traces the success of this campaign.

By 1920, 16.3 percent of young people completed high school, and more than 90 percent of them attended public institutions. Over the next twenty years, the proponents of a full high school education won major victories. In 1940 virtually half (49 percent) of American youth received high school diplomas. Soon a new phrase appeared in our language: "high school dropout." Back when very few people graduated from high school, such a phrase would have been nonsensical. But once a majority was completing high school, the term became meaningful, and it implied the serious economic consequences of failing to finish school. As we have seen, today more than 70 percent of young people complete high school. And nearly all who do not finish attend high school for a time.

During the 1940s, when more than half of American young people were completing high school, political and educational leaders once again raised their educational targets. It became the goal to send

Table 15-3 / The expansion of higher education, 1870–1980.

Year	Total Number of Colleges and Universities	Number of Students	Number of Faculty
1870	563	52,000	5,553
1920	1,041	598,000	48,615
1950	1,863	2,281,000	246,722
1970	2,556	8,580,900	474,000
1980	3,231	12,114,900	659,000

Source: U.S. Bureau of the Census.

high school graduates on to college. In the economic boom following World War II, there was massive construction of junior colleges, and existing colleges and universities were expanded immensely.

Table 15-3 depicts the recent explosion of higher education. In 1870 there were 563 institutions of higher education in the United States. These schools enrolled 52,000 students nationwide and employed 5,553 faculty members. By 1920 the number of institutions of higher education had almost doubled, and student enrollment was more than ten times what it had been fifty years before. But only recently has higher education literally exploded. In 1950 more than 2 million Americans were in college. Twenty years later, more than 8.5 million were enrolled! By 1980, enrollment was over 12 million, despite a decline in the number of persons of college age.

Today the majority of Americans enter college, and nearly a third of them graduate. Moreover, a higher proportion of Americans now enters graduate school than entered college in 1940.

Who goes to school?

Race used to be a primary determinant of who went to school in the United States. In 1850, 56.2 percent of whites between the ages of 5 and 19 were enrolled in school. Among nonwhites (nearly all of whom were black), only 1.8 percent were in school. Following the Civil War, this picture improved. In 1880,

These children pledging allegiance to the flag in Hampton, Virginia, around 1890 were among the minority of black children in the South enrolled in school at that time.

Table 15-4 / Declines in male dominance of college degrees.

| Year | Percent Males | | |
	All Degrees	Master's Degrees	Doctorates
1950	75.6%	70.7%	90.9%
1960	65.8%	67.1%	89.7%
1970	59.6%	60.2%	86.6%
1980	52.5%	50.5%	70.4%

Source: U.S. Bureau of the Census.

62 percent of white youth and 33.8 percent of nonwhite youth were in school. During the twentieth century, blacks closed the gap. Race is no longer a predictor of overall school enrollment, and since 1950 whites and nonwhites have been equally likely to be enrolled. In Chapter 11, data were presented showing how rapidly blacks have caught up in the mean years of education in recent decades. However, blacks remain more likely than whites to become high school dropouts.

Just as race has long played an important role in who goes to school, so has sex. The trends are rather interesting. In the last century, when few people attended high school, more women than men did so. Indeed, as recently as 1920, women earned 60.3 percent of the high school diplomas awarded. Since then, however, men have closed the gap; since 1970, males and females have completed high school in about equal numbers.

Historically, however, women have been less likely than men to go to college, and much less likely to graduate or to obtain advanced degrees. As can be seen in Table 15-4, as recently as 1950 men earned three-fourths of the degrees awarded. Since then there has been a rapid shift; in 1980, men earned only slightly more than half of the college degrees. Moreover, in 1980 women passed men in college enrollment, making up 51.4 percent of students that year.

Women have also caught up to men in earning master's degrees. In 1950, men received seven of every ten master's degrees awarded. In 1980, master's degrees were equally split between men and women. However, women still lag in earning doctorates. In 1980, men received 70.4 percent of the doctorates awarded. Still, this is a remarkable change from 1950, when more than 90 percent of the doctorates went to men.

The decline in quality

As increasingly large proportions of young people attend schools at all levels, concern has grown that the quality of education has been declining. Many people believe that students today learn less in school than students used to. It is very difficult to prove or disprove such claims. The available evidence suggests that these claims are part truth and part illusion. Let's explore the illusion first.

The average high school graduate of 1900 probably would have scored much higher on academic proficiency tests than the average high school graduate today. In fact, it would be astounding if that were not the case. Why? Recall from Table 15-2 that in 1900 only 6.3 percent of young Americans graduated from high school. Today more than 70 percent graduate. Since it was unusual to graduate from high school in 1900, the schools could impose very strict standards, and students who lacked the talent or motivation to meet these standards could be flunked out without being condemned to a life of poorly paid jobs. Therefore, those who graduated in 1900 were probably a very select academic group.

As the mission of high school shifted from educating a small, motivated, and talented elite to educating virtually everyone, average achievement had to decline. Thus, it is both unfair and unrealistic to expect the achievements of students in a mass system to equal the achievements of students in an elite system.

It would be much more reasonable to compare the top 6 percent of high school graduates today with the graduates of 1900, although we will never know what that comparison would show. But it is quite possible that even today's top graduates would fall below the levels of achievement attained by high school students in 1900. Schools providing mass education must also teach slow students. Since schools in 1900 could gear their curricula to their uniformly gifted students, the average high school graduate in the top 6 percent today is probably not as well educated as the average graduate of 1900.

But at the same time, the average American is probably much better educated today than the average American in 1900, when most people quit school before the end of the eighth grade.

A similar line of reasoning can be applied at the college level. Because colleges formerly trained only a tiny intellectual elite, the average graduate in those days would have tested higher than the average graduate today, when colleges train a much higher proportion of young people. When a much larger proportion of people attend college, their average aptitude will be lower, just as the average height of police officers would decline if the minimum height were reduced.

However, not all of the concerns about a decline in the quality of American education can be dismissed as the result of increased enrollments. Many studies have revealed substantial declines in student achievement over the past twenty years. For example, in 1963 the average American high school senior scored 490 on the **Scholastic Aptitude Test (SAT)**; by 1980 the average score had dropped to 445 (College Entrance Examination Board, 1981). The verbal aptitude scores on the SAT have dropped more than have the math aptitude scores, but both have dropped substantially. A national commission appointed to assess why the scores had dropped found that the decline was not the result of changes in who was taking the tests, but the result of an overall decline in what students were learning in school. Interestingly enough, SAT scores of black seniors have risen while those of other students have declined.

Some critics have dismissed the decline in student achievement scores as relatively unimportant, as merely reflecting a decreased emphasis on purely academic knowledge. But even scores on tests measuring simple, practical skills have fallen. For example, a 1975 study by the U.S. Office of Education found that 22 percent of Americans over age 17 are essentially illiterate, and another third have only a very limited ability to read and write. Such people are not prepared to participate in a knowledge economy—many of them cannot even fill out simple job applications. In a sense, then, the school dropout rate may be substantially higher than the statistics on enrollment indicate. Some students have effectively quit school while remaining in class. They can claim a diploma when they apply for a job, but

if they can't figure out how to fill out the application form, it won't matter.

In response to these developments, many school systems have reestablished more rigorous standards. In many places, standard examinations are being used to determine who passes to the next grade. The aim is to stop the widespread practice of passing students no matter how little they have learned. New emphasis is being given to such basic subjects as reading and arithmetic, and less to "self-expression."

A major impetus for school reform has come from international economic competition. American student test scores do not compare well with those of students of many industrialized nations to whom American industry has lost some of it share of world trade. Hence, current discussion of educational issues has focused on the need for a more competitive work force; if we are to recover sales lost to Japanese firms, for example, we must educate our children as well as the Japanese do theirs. In Japan, the school day is longer, as is the school year. In fact, most European students attend school more months per year than students in America. Suggestions that we ought to reform education in order to compete in international trade underscore the intimate connections between education and occupation.

DO SCHOOLS REALLY MATTER?

Current concern over the declining quality of American education reflects the assumption that schools play an important role in what students learn. It might seem self-evident that schools are critical to the educational process. However, beginning in the 1960s, many critics, including many prominent social scientists, began to argue that schools had little effect on what people learned or on preparing people for jobs.

Some critics pointed out that a great majority of people in colonial times could read, write, and do arithmetic even though few attended school, even grade school. Others pointed out that schools seem unable to overcome differences in background—students from privileged homes do well in school, while those from disadvantaged backgrounds do poorly. The conclusion was that schools simply certify the educational advantages or disadvantages that students bring to school (Jencks et al., 1972).

These views of the ineffectiveness of schools were lent some support by a huge study conducted by James Coleman and his associates (1966). Coleman had been commissioned by Congress to assess the nation's schools and determine which aspects of schooling were the most valuable. As he began his research, Coleman expected to find that blacks suffered from attending poor-quality schools, and hoped to prompt massive federal aid to correct the inequity (in Silberman, 1971).

What he found was startling. First, there was little difference in the quality of schools attended by blacks and whites in terms of expenditures per student, age and quality of the buildings, libraries, class size, and teacher training. Second, these aspects of school quality had no detectable impact on student achievement scores. Thus, lavish expenditures during the 1950s and early 1960s to upgrade schools had accomplished nothing in terms of actual education. Whether students went to school in ramshackle buildings or nice ones, attended large classes or small ones, or had fancy labs or makeshift equipment didn't matter. Nor did it matter if their teachers had advanced degrees or only two-year teacher's college certificates.

Coleman could only conclude that school was simply a place where students learned in proportion to the educational qualities of their homes, neighborhoods, and peer environment. Still, Coleman's report contained one finding often overlooked in subsequent discussions. How well students from any background did in school was correlated with the scores that their teachers made on a vocabulary test. As discussed in the conclusion to this chapter, this may suggest a link between declines in student achievement scores and a corresponding decline in the quality of teachers as measured by test scores.

In the wake of the Coleman study, many radical proposals thrived. Ivan Illich (1970) argued that the educational system was doing more harm than good by simply increasing the advantages of children from privileged homes, and he therefore proposed to "deschool society." Others began to seek the "real" goals of education, since imparting knowledge and preparing students for adult careers did not seem

to be what schools did. Marxists such as Samuel Bowles and Herbert Gintis (1976) charged that the true aim of the school system was to socialize students to accept the capitalist system and to be docile workers.

Randall Collins (1971) argued that education was not meant to prepare people for careers but to protect various class interests. For example, he argued that the expansion of higher education was meant not to prepare people for more sophisticated jobs but to exclude the lower classes from middle- and upper-class jobs.

Collins's conclusion contradicts the evidence presented in Chapter 10 that education is the primary avenue to upward mobility in the United States. That is, people from poor families rise to professional and managerial jobs by going to college. Therefore, it seems contrary to the class interests of privileged Americans to have backed educational policies that created more than 3,000 institutions of higher education in America, which now enroll the majority of young people. Surely they could have ensured the future of their children more easily by denying the masses access to higher education.

Even if we reject the claim that the educational system is a device to protect upper-class interests, the question persists, Do the schools actually accomplish anything? Do kids actually learn in school? For most social scientists, it seemed evident that people do learn in school, for even children from the most privileged homes are usually not taught to read, write, or do arithmetic at home. Most kids must be learning these things in school, if they learn them at all. Yet good evidence of the effectiveness of schools was lacking.

BARBARA HEYNS:
THE EFFECTS OF SUMMER

How can we see if schools have a real impact on learning? The most obvious way would be to randomly assign some children to attend school and others to stay home and then to compare the results. But that would be both illegal and immoral. Since schooling at the elementary level is universal in the United

A very noticeable change in American schools has been the increasing number of male teachers at the grade school level. Until recently, men rarely taught below the junior high level.

States, we can't seek out students who do not go to school and compare their achievements with those who do. Faced with this problem, Barbara Heyns (1978) came up with a brilliant solution.

Kids don't go to school all year. Why not compare the learning that occurs during the school year with that occurring during the summer vacation? In this way, summer learning can serve as a basis for esti-

mating what children might learn if they did not go to school. In effect, during each summer Ivan Illich's "deschooled society" exists. How well does it work?

Heyns gave verbal achievement tests to 2,978 students enrolled in Atlanta schools. The tests were given at the start of the fifth grade, at the end of the fifth grade, at the start of the sixth grade, and again at the end of the sixth grade.

Recent research suggests that these girls will make as much educational progress during their summer vacation as they would during a similar period of attending school—because they are reading books while school is out. Children who don't read fall behind during the summer.

Heyns's results gave strong evidence that school matters, but that it matters much more to some kinds of children than to others. On the average, children in Atlanta learned much less during the summer vacation than they did in an equivalent time period during the school year. Their verbal achievement scores rose much more rapidly on a monthly basis over the school year than over the vacation. However, children from higher-income families learned about as much during vacation as during the school year. Children from the most deprived backgrounds actually lost ground during the summer—their scores were not as high in the fall as they had been the spring before vacation began.

What Heyns found means that, rather than merely maintaining differences children bring to school, schools greatly improve the situations of poor children. Differences in the rates of learning between blacks and whites and between higher- and lower-income children were very small while school was in session; but when school was out, the kids from privileged backgrounds sprinted ahead. Schools therefore minimize initial background advantages by enabling the disadvantaged to keep up. However, schools can only accomplish this during the school year. The long summer vacations characteristic of most American schools undo much that is accomplished with underprivileged children during the winter. In the summer, the academic effects of students' backgrounds reassert themselves. Moreover, these summer effects accumulate, so that as children advance through the grades, the children of more advantaged families get further and further ahead of the others.

Surprisingly, Heyns found that attending summer school did not prevent summer learning losses. Atlanta has a massive summer school program (a fourth of the students enroll), and children from disadvantaged backgrounds are especially likely to enroll. However, attendance at summer school had no influence on summer learning. Heyns concluded that this was because the summer school programs were oriented toward recreation rather than the regular curriculum. Students overwhelmingly said they went to summer school because it was fun.

What did the kids from the more advantaged homes do during the summer that caused them to continue to learn? Heyns examined many possibilities, including vacation trips and participation in organized summer activities such as sports or camps. But only one activity had real impact: reading. As Heyns (1978) put it:

The single summer activity that is most strongly and consistently related to summer learning is reading. Whether measured by the number of books read, by the time spent reading, or by the regularity of library usage, reading during the summer systematically increases the vocabulary test scores of children.

In fact, Heyns estimated that every four books read over the summer produced an additional right answer on verbal achievement tests.

Heyns also discovered that a major factor affecting reading, independent of a student's background, was the distance from the student's home to the nearest public library. Eighty percent of the students who lived within seven blocks of a library used it regularly. Among children living more than seven blocks from a library, library visits fell rapidly. Thus, in showing that schools matter, Heyns showed that libraries do, too.

Heyns's findings also suggest that schools might be much more effective if the school year were extended. The long summer vacation was instituted back when most kids were needed to help on the farm, and it has persisted long after this need has vanished. Indeed, children in Japan and many other industrial nations attend school throughout the year with short breaks.

Heyns's study was a major breakthrough. First, it showed how to study school effects. Second, it showed conclusively that school does affect how well-educated students become. But does education really matter in gaining economic success? Some, including Randall Collins, suggest it does not.

DOES EDUCATION PAY?

Many historical analyses of the American educational system stress idealism—that Americans built, support, and attend our massive school and college system in search of learning and wisdom because we value education in and of itself, aside from material benefits. Clearly, most Americans do think education is good, and probably many have attended school primarily out of intellectual curiosity. But equally clearly, the educational system has been primarily based on more pragmatic concerns. Business and industry support education as a vital source of trained personnel. People pay for the educational system in hopes that it will increase their children's chances for success. And people go to school to qualify for better jobs.

Career preparation has been regarded as the pri-

Table 15-5 / Education and average income, U.S. adults, 1980.

Years of Schooling	Average Annual Income
Less than 8 years	$5,900
8 years	$7,900
9 to 11 years	$9,100
High school graduate	$13,300
1 to 3 years of college	$13,900
College graduate	$19,100
Postgraduate	$22,800

Source: U.S. Bureau of the Census.

mary educational function. Moreover, this view of education is not mistaken. We already saw in Chapter 10 that education virtually nullifies the effects of family background on occupational attainment. Among people with similar amounts of education, those who have grown up in high status homes are only slightly more likely to end up in top jobs than persons who grew up in low status homes. Industrial societies have long known this fact, which helps account for the rapid and continuing expansion of education.

And education does pay. Table 15-5 shows the average incomes of American adults in 1980 according to their education. People who attended graduate school earn almost four times as much as those who did not complete eighth grade, and people who graduated from high school earn more than twice as much as those who dropped out before the eighth grade. People who attended college but did not graduate enjoy little advantage over those who only finished high school, but college graduates enjoy a very marked advantage: Four years of college increase the average American's income by 44 percent over that of high school graduates.

Nevertheless, many critics have recently argued that college educations probably don't pay off for most people. Caroline Bird (1975), for example, has pointed out that many of the highest-income people in the United States achieved their success without having gone to college. They are entrepreneurs, people of driving ambition who develop a new idea or product that is of value to many others. Bird suggests that colleges cannot help cultivate such people. Bird fails to note, however, that very few people achieve extraordinary success (otherwise it would be ordinary) and that, for the rest of the population, those who attend college tend to be far more successful.

Indeed, education is mandatory for top occupations. Table 15-1 indicates that it is impossible to enter most of the highest-prestige positions without attending college and often graduate school. Going to law school does not guarantee that one will become a Supreme Court justice, of course, but it is unthinkable that a nonlawyer would be appointed or confirmed to such a position. Thus, although education is not a sufficient condition for success, it is usually a necessary one. Without it, many opportunities are closed.

Why, then, have some people begun to question the economic importance of education, especially college? One reason is the rapid rise in the relative earnings of skilled blue-collar workers, such as plumbers, electricians, long-distance truckers, and tool and die makers. Many college graduates end up in lower-paying occupations than these, and college is of no advantage for entry into these skilled trades. In fact, going to college would be a waste of earning years for people planning to enter these occupations. But perhaps the primary reason why people question the economic importance of education is simply that a college degree is not worth as much as it used to be.

When relatively few people earned college degrees, they possessed a scarce occupational qualification. Now many people earn degrees, and therefore a degree is not a certain ticket to success. When 5 percent of all Americans graduated from college, then only 5 out of 100 people could compete for a job requiring a college degree. But now, when a third of Americans earn degrees, 33 people out of 100 compete for those jobs requiring degrees. Hence, the decline in the value of a college education is the result not of colleges ceasing to prepare people for careers, but of colleges preparing so many people for careers.

Thus, as the level of education has risen in the United States and other industrial nations, the rel-

ative advantage of completing a given level of education has declined. If people today want to have the same educational advantage that their parents had, they must stay in school longer than their parents did.

The French sociologist Raymond Boudon (1974) has created elegant mathematical models of this process of educational "deflation." As he pointed out, however, it is important to realize that such deflation applies to all educational levels, not just the top. That is, not only is a college degree of less value than it used to be, but so is an eighth grade education. The child of a school dropout who also drops out of school will have a harder time finding and holding a job than the dropout parent did.

MEYER'S THEORY OF EDUCATIONAL FUNCTIONS

Most sociological writing and research on education has stressed the role of schools in socializing students to perform adult roles, especially occupational roles. The aim of education is seen as equipping students with the appropriate knowledge, self-discipline, and technical training to fulfill adult roles. Thus far in this chapter, we have examined the ability of schools to fulfill these tasks.

We have also mentioned social scientists, especially Marxists, who challenge this view of what schools do. They argue that the primary aim of the schools is not to educate but to *allocate,* to place people in a particular social status. From this point of view, increased educational requirements for most occupations have little, if anything, to do with what people actually learn in school. Instead, they are artificial barriers used to prevent certain people from entering these occupations (Collins, 1971).

A fact that supports this position is that a college education seems to be of little special use to a person performing one of the many jobs that typically require a college degree (newspaper reporter, for example). In fact, Collins (1971) has argued that if college training is relevant to a job, this training

Like most children, this boy probably wonders from time to time whether homework is worth it. Getting a lot of education won't guarantee him a good job, but lack of education would exclude him from most of the better-paid occupations.

could have taken place more rapidly and effectively on the job. If this is true, then questions arise about why so many jobs require college degrees. Attention must be paid to Collins's answer: These requirements are meant to screen out those lacking the opportunity to attend college or who rebel against the prevailing rules governing status allocation.

Because these allocation theories of education have typically taken the form of polemics against American society, many sociologists have tended to ignore them. In the late 1970s, however, John W. Meyer, a sociologist at Stanford, drew upon allocation ideas to formulate a general theory of the functions of education as a social institution. (Meyer, 1977)

Meyer began by accepting the traditional view of educational socialization—that, through schooling, people increase their knowledge and competence, which in turn increases their abilities to perform adult roles. But he then added the insight that <u>levels of education, in and of themselves, are social statuses</u>. That is, aside from any other status held by individuals, they have a distinct status based on their amount of formal education: high school graduate, college graduate, Ph.D., and the like. Schools, then, can be seen as institutions empowered, or chartered, by society to grant statuses to individuals.

Moreover, a major aspect of schools as socializing agents is to encourage individuals "to adopt personal and social qualities appropriate to the positions [or statuses] to which their schools are chartered to assign them." As with all positions in society, educational statuses come equipped with roles. A major effect of education, then, is that <u>people learn to play the role appropriate to the status that their school confers on them.</u>

This proposition allowed Meyer to explain why variations in school quality seem of little or no importance in the attitudes, values, opinions, and behavior of graduates. Research shows that the amount of formal schooling a person completes has a great effect on a wide variety of personal qualities and characteristics: from the way people vote to their religious commitment. If this is a consequence of the content of actual instruction, then people who attended very high quality schools ought to differ from those who attended low-quality schools. However, research has failed to turn up such differences (or they are extremely small). Instead, graduates of elite colleges resemble graduates of obscure schools much more closely than they resemble people who did not graduate from college.

According to Meyer's theory, this is to be expected if the real impact of schools is to admit people to a particular educational status. For then, all schools chartered to convey that status ought to have similar socializing effects. Indeed, Meyer pointed out that school quality is seldom of much importance in assessing a person's claim to a given status. Graduates of all American high schools, for example, have the occupational rights reserved for high school graduates—no one asks if their high school was a good one. By the same token, a college degree satisfies the requirements to claim the status of college graduate, whether the degree was from Harvard or North Dakota State College in Valley City.

Thus, Meyer argued that the most powerful socializing property of schools is the ability to confer statuses that are recognized in society at large, and that people who acquire a given status tend to perform the role attached to it in similar fashion. Indeed, Meyer cited research showing that people adopt personal qualities appropriate to a given educational role upon admission to a school chartered to grant that status; in fact, they often begin to do so upon acceptance to such a school, before they have even attended (Benitez, 1973; W. L. Wallace, 1966).

Moreover, Meyer argued that socialization into these roles does not stop when people leave school. Instead, people continue to act out the roles attached to their educational statuses throughout their adult lives, regardless of their occupation. Occupational success often varies over time, as do family relations and even geographic location, but a "college graduate" or "high school dropout" is an unchanging status once school is done. People continue to respond to an individual's educational status, and the individual continues to perform the role appropriate to that status. Indeed, John Irwin (1970) found that educational statuses even count among inmates in prison, where people with college degrees or postgraduate training are frequently sought out for advice and information.

Unlike Collins (1971), Meyer was not content to view educational institutions as allocating status only to the degree allowed by the occupational system. Collins argued that educational institutions simply allocate people into positions determined by the occupational system—for example, medical schools are chartered to produce doctors only insofar as the occupational structure has recognized this occupation and the occupational group (doctors) has granted this power to schools.

Meyer argued instead that the educational system has the power to create new occupations, even elite occupations, and to control the placement of these occupations in the occupational structure. This is possible because educational institutions, especially universities, play a leading role in defining new knowledge, developing new techniques and technologies, and giving these techniques legitimate occupational standing.

In other words, many of the most highly paid, highest status occupations found in contemporary society exist because universities invented them, defined their occupational worth, and determined the conditions under which people could enter these occupations. There were no economists until universities established the science of economics and legitimized its claim to special competence. Nor were there sociologists, geneticists, or even football coaches until universities created a special body of knowledge and began training people to use it.

In this way, Meyer undercut the narrow view of allocation theories—that education is a passive servant of the stratification system. Instead, "education helps *create* new classes of knowledge and personnel which then come to be incorporated in society." That is, the expansion of the education system increases the "number of specialized and elite positions in society."

In fact, as educational achievement has risen in the United States, the occupational structure has rapidly expanded at the top (more professional, managerial, and technical positions) and contracted at the bottom (fewer unskilled labor jobs). Meyer's theory, therefore, helps explain how we have increasingly become a "knowledge" economy.

Finally, Meyer argued that the rising level of mass education has expanded the proportion of the population regarded as having the citizenship responsibilities, capacities, and rights. The larger the proportion of the population who are educated, the harder it is for elites to exclude them from decision making or to ignore their economic demands. Here Meyer parted company with the allocation theorists, who argue that education serves only elite interests. Instead, Meyer noted, the primary emphasis in modern education is on mass education—on providing the maximum number of people with the opportunity to be educated and to gain entry to elite occupations.

Meyer's theory offers a more comprehensive and intelligible view of the way in which educational institutions fit into society. Because schooling is largely confined to childhood and very early adulthood, sociologists have tended to view educational institutions as only having early socialization effects, in much the same way that the cultural determinists (see Chapter 6) attempted to attribute adult personality wholly to child-rearing patterns. By recognizing how educational statuses continue to have socializing effects throughout a lifetime, Meyer was able to explain why these effects endure. It is not simply that what we learn in school lasts forever. Rather, we take with us from school an educational status that continues to influence our chances and experiences in life.

CONCLUSION

Education remains vital to occupational achievement, but as more people get more education, a given level of education becomes less valuable. This is because educational and occupational institutions remain somewhat independent. Although a shift to a knowledge economy can only occur with an increase in the supply of educated people, such an increase does not automatically create more knowledge jobs for them to fill. Nevertheless, as John Meyer

pointed out, schools can create new occupations, including new elite occupations. But the number of people aspiring to these occupations can still exceed the supply of positions available. A person may have the training and desire for a given occupation, but that alone does not create a position for that person to fill. On the other hand, as Boudon has pointed out, aptitude and motivation often suffice to gain an education. Thus, the supply of college-educated people, for example, may increase beyond the positions available in the economy, or at least beyond the level of upper positions.

In the nineteenth century, high school graduates qualified for most teaching jobs. Until the 1930s, a person who attended a teacher's college for two years was well qualified to teach. Today, most elementary and high school teaching jobs are reserved for people with master's degrees. The primary reason for this change has been an increase in the proportion of educated people.

Ironically, it is not clear that more years of education have increased the amount of education students receive. Clearly, as Barbara Heyns demonstrated, schools have a marked effect on how much children learn. But, equally clearly, how much people learn in school seems to have declined recently. Many factors have been cited for this decline, most of them involving school curricula, promotion practices, and classroom disorder. Yet Coleman's famous study found that only one aspect of schools was truly correlated with how well students learned—the educational achievement of their teachers as measured by a vocabulary test.

Keep in mind that the teachers' level of formal education was not correlated with how much their students learned. Nor was the formal education of teachers related to how well the teachers scored on the vocabulary test. Clearly, then, the increase in the level of formal education of teachers may have had no effect on their capacity to teach. Indeed, over the past twenty years, as the SAT scores of college seniors have declined, the SAT scores of those who become teachers have declined even more rapidly. In 1982, the SAT scores of those entering teacher-training programs were the lowest among all entrants to professional schools.

A major reason for the decline in the intellectual quality of teachers is changing sex roles. Not so long ago, women had few occupational choices; among these, school teaching was one of the most attractive. Thus, the teaching profession could tap a vast pool of very talented candidates. Today, women of high caliber have a great many more attractive options and are much less likely to become teachers. Indeed, this is reflected in the rapid decline in the proportion of teachers who are women. Not too many years ago, well over 90 percent of elementary and high school teachers were women. Today, a third are men.

The current debate over how to improve the schools (and the rapid growth of private and religious schools) may result in changes that once again attract more talented people into teaching. But, whatever happens, the vital link between education and occupation will be a major consideration in forming new policies.

Finally, we have seen that the connections between educational institutions and the rest of society are neither simple nor restricted to in-school instructional effects. Education has strong and lasting socialization effects because it creates permanent statuses. Consequently, people tend to perform roles appropriate to their educational status, even when they follow an occupation that is above or below the occupational status usually associated with their level of education. The school dropout millionaire never fully sheds that dropout status and is likely to continue to enact that role in some ways. Similarly, the person with a doctorate who drives a cab, will often be "Doc" to the other drivers. That people with the same amount of formal schooling hold the same educational status helps explain why variations in school quality have little or no effect on behavior—these people are equal in the way that continues to matter most in their lives.

The educational structure does not simply allocate people among occupational categories. It often creates new occupations and alters the occupational structure. In fact, the power of universities to determine the social significance of a body of knowledge is so great that John Meyer speculated about what might happen if universities began to offer accredited courses and degrees in astrology: Companies would soon begin to hire staff astrologers (perhaps placing them in the economic forecasting department), and government grants for research in astrology would

soon be forthcoming. Professional astrologers have failed to achieve high prestige despite their ability to attract large numbers of clients because they have been unable to convince universities that they possess a body of valid knowledge.

Clearly, then, educational institutions are not passive servants of elites and the occupational structure. Perhaps this is most easily illustrated by a norm among faculty at major research-oriented universities. They never list their occupation as "teacher," even though they teach. Instead, they call themselves chemists, economists, or sociologists—people who pursue a creative, technical profession. In this way, they claim an occupational status in the world beyond the classroom in the world of adults, not students. Because the modern university does not simply prepare people to perform various professions, but discovers and analyzes the knowledge on which these professions are based, faculty members feel justified in treating their teaching functions as secondary.

Review glossary

Occupational prestige The respect given persons on the basis of their job; often refers to a score on a standard system for rating occupations. (p. 359)

Scientific management The application of scientific techniques to increase efficiency. (p. 361)

Labor force Those persons who are employed or seeking employment. (p. 362)

Unemployed Persons 16 years old and older who are not enrolled in school, who do not have a job, and who are actively looking for one. (p. 364)

Scholastic Aptitude Test (SAT) A standardized test taken by many high school seniors planning to go to college. (p. 371)

Suggested readings

Boudon, Raymond. *Education, Opportunity, and Social Inequality: Changing Prospects in Western Society.* New York: Wiley, 1974.

Collins, Randall. *The Credential Society: An Historical Sociology of Education*. New York: Academic Press, 1979.

Heyns, Barbara. *Summer Learning and the Effects of Schooling*. New York: Academic Press, 1978.

Hodge, Robert W., Donald J. Treiman, and Peter H. Rossi. "A Comparative Study of Occupational Prestige." In Reinhard Bendix and Seymour Martin Lipset, eds., *Class, Status, and Power*. New York: Free Press, 1966.

Meyer, John W. "The Effects of Education as an Institution." *American Journal of Sociology* (1977) 83:55–77.

*Percentage of population growth, 1970–1980.
National = 11.4 percent.*

In this last part of the book we shall repeatedly see how
changes in population size can cause many other
changes in society. Overall, the American population
grew by 11.4 percent in the decade of the 1970s. But
some parts of the country grew much faster than that
and other parts grew by much less; the Middle Atlantic
region even lost population during that time. The
growth of the national population was caused by fertility and immigration. But the major cause of regional
shifts was migration. Large numbers of Americans move,
and these days many more move South and West than
move to the Midwest and Northeast. New York lost the
most (−3.7 percent), while Nevada (63.8 percent), Arizona (53.1 percent), and Florida (43.5 percent) grew
most. Good weather is often cited as the reason these
areas are growing so fast. Weather may well determine
where people move when they retire. But the rapid
growth of the Sunbelt states involves millions of people
far short of retirement age. Economic opportunity is
always the primary reason people move. The business
boom in the Sunbelt states is the reason so many people
move there, and by doing so, of course, they add to the
boom.

Pacific 19.8		New England 4.2
Mountain 37.2		West South Central 22.9
West North Central 5.2		East South Central 14.5
East North Central 3.5		South Atlantic 20.5
Middle Atlantic −1.1		

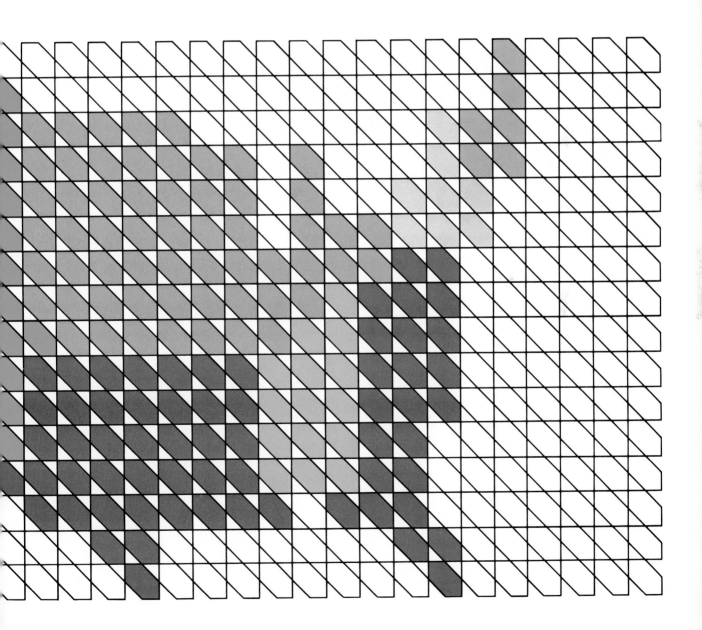

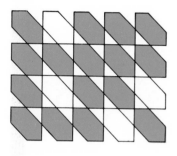

■ My father grew up in a world without airplanes, radios, or refrigerators. I grew up in a world without TV or polio vaccine—some of my classmates died and others were crippled by this dread disease that students today hardly know about. In your own lifetime, computers have shrunk from multimillion-dollar giants housed in air-conditioned, sealed environments to tiny, inexpensive gadgets found in millions of homes, and many of these microcomputers are much more powerful than the huge machines of a decade ago.

Once it was difficult to convince people that anything in life changed—for the pace of change was so slow that change was not apparent in one lifetime. Today, at least in modern societies, it is difficult to convince people that some things haven't changed and that some kinds of social change are not likely.

Yet many previous chapters have stressed continuity as well as change in social life, suggesting that some forms of societies are probably impossible. For example, Chapters 7 and 8 suggest that we shall never create societies without crime and other forms of deviance. Chapter 9 concluded that unstratified societies are impossible. Chapter 12 proposed that the family will persist and that the nuclear family has been made more important by the rise of urban, industrial societies. Chapter 13 examined the dynamics of religious change, which make it seem unlikely that religion will disappear from societies despite the periodic decline of some religious organizations.

Basic elements of social life limit the scope of social change—not all changes are equally likely or even possible. Moreover, social conditions influence the pace of change. For most of human his-

Social Change and Modernization

tory, change took place very slowly. In the past few centuries, change has been very rapid—but only in some parts of the world. While some societies launch space rockets, others have not yet learned to make tools from metal. These observations lead us to the central sociological questions about social change. Why does it occur? What factors stimulate or retard change? █

CHAPTER PREVIEW

In the first part of this chapter, we shall examine general principles of social change. First, we shall assess internal sources of change—things that go on inside societies that cause them to change. Then we shall see how external forces can produce change within societies.

These general principles will then be applied in examining the truly dramatic changes that have taken place in the world during the past several centuries—social and economic changes that are summed up by the term *modernization*. **Modernization** is the process by which agrarian societies (see Chapter 10) were transformed into industrial societies. Each of the remaining chapters in the book deals with particular aspects of modernization: the relationship between modernization and population trends, the rise of urban societies, new forms of organizations required to cope with and direct modernization, and the role of collective behavior and social movements in resisting and speeding modernization. In the latter half of this chapter, we shall try to see how modernization occurred. We will assess

four basic theories of what caused the rapid changes that transformed Europe and North America into modern societies. Why did so many other societies fail to modernize? What are the prospects that all societies will eventually be modernized?

INTERNAL SOURCES OF SOCIAL CHANGE

In Chapter 4, we examined societies as social systems. In a system, connections exist among the parts so that changes in one part cause reactions in other parts. Since social systems consist of self-conscious, active human beings, internal changes are always taking place, and often a particular change will have far-reaching consequences, many of which may not have been anticipated. Let us examine certain kinds of activities that often occur within social systems to see how they produce changes.

Innovations

The most obvious thing that happens inside societies is that people have new ideas and change how they do something. When the Quakers implemented the idea of using prisons as a substitute for physical punishment (see Chapter 8), many other aspects of society were affected, including the criminal justice system, which expanded greatly. Three basic kinds of new ideas, or innovations, frequently cause social change.

Plans to import modern technology often go astray. A rail line was laid near the village in which these women live. But so long as the rails serve only as a path and basket-carriers continue to serve as the primary means of transportaiton, no progress toward modernization has been made.

New technology New technology is a major source of social change. Chapter 10 traces the immense social changes produced by the invention of agriculture. Chapter 18 will explain how the invention of the automobile revolutionized the structure of cities and the character of urban life. Some historians suggest that the major revolutionary event in 1776 was not the rebellion of the American colonies against Great Britain but the perfection of the steam engine.

It is important to recognize that new technology does not change societies by itself. It is the response to the technology that causes change. Often, new technology appears and goes unused for a very long time. For example, the Romans fully understood how to use windmills and waterwheels to replace muscle

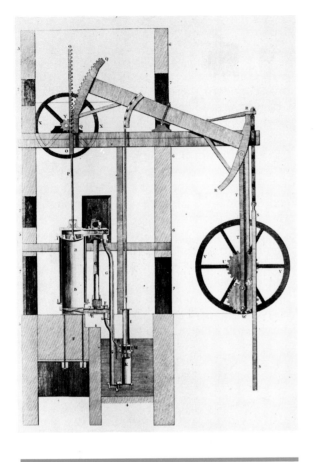

James Watt's steam engine revolutionized Western civilization. This drawing of his "double-acting" model incorporated the latest developments through 1791.

For a long time anthropologists wondered why civilizations as sophisticated as those of the Incas and the Aztecs had failed to discover the wheel. Then toys like this one were discovered in Aztec ruins in Mexico—little dogs on wheels so children could pull them. Suddenly the mystery deepened: Given that these civilizations did know about wheels, why did they use them only on toys and not to move heavy loads?

power for various kinds of work, but they made no use of this technology. Similarly, the Chinese had gunpowder centuries before Europe but did not exploit its military potential. And the Aztecs put wheels on many children's toys (see the photo above) but did not use the wheel for transportation; they carried goods on their backs rather than pulling them in wagons.

New culture Not only machines change the world. Beliefs and values can also produce dramatic social change. Indeed, many sociologists and historians have

argued that rapid technological changes in Western societies were stimulated by acceptance of the **idea of progress** (Nisbet, 1980). That is, unlike most societies that did not expect technological progress and often turned away from it, in Europe during the seventeenth and eighteenth centuries people widely accepted that such progress was not only possible but also certain. Such confidence inspired ever more determined efforts to achieve technological and scientific progress, and as these efforts bore fruit, they inspired even greater confidence and effort. To a considerable extent, Europe made progress because it believed in progress and underwent rapid social change because Europeans wanted change.

New social structures New forms of social structure can also be the result of invention. Chapter 19 is devoted to understanding the invention, application, and evolution of formal organizations as a new mode of social structure designed to cope with and direct modernization. Indeed, in the twentieth century, the search for technological innovation has been substantially directed by formal organizations such as the corporation, government, and the university.

Since roles are a very basic social structure, changes in roles and the creation of new roles often cause other social changes. Changing sex roles, discussed in Special Topic 2, have stimulated many changes in our society. For example, the fact that the majority of women now work has changed the family (see Chapter 12), and the fact that women can now choose from a wide range of occupations has greatly increased the proportion of men teaching the lower grades (see Chapter 15). Likewise, the development of full-time specialists in combat was a major factor in the repressive character of government in agrarian societies (see Chapter 10).

Conflicts

Innovation is not the only major internal source of change. Much change is produced by conflicts among groups within societies. Chapters 9, 10, and 11 discussed many such conflicts between classes, racial and ethnic groups, and residents of different regions. Thus, the Civil Rights Movement of the 1950s and 1960s not only removed many barriers to black participation in the mainstream of American society but also changed many other aspects of our society as well. Indeed, the end to official southern racism may have been essential to the rapid economic growth now taking place in the South. Or, in an earlier time, conflict among the many Protestant denominations seems to have been the basis for making separation of church and state part of the U.S. Constitution, with the consequence of creating a competitive religious economy that generates high rates of church membership.

Growth

As we shall see in the remaining chapters in this book, population growth has been a major engine driving modern social change. Large populations present new problems that demand new modes of social organization. For example, as pointed out in Chapter 14, small populations may permit direct democracy in which all citizens may participate in decision making. However, such procedures are impossible for large populations, which require new models of democracy such as representative government.

Similarly, large cities must be constructed very differently from small cities (see Chapter 18). Thus, the simple growth of cities has produced great social change. As we shall see in Chapters 17 and 18, the earliest stage of modernization, industrialization, caused rapid population growth, which in turn spurred even more rapid industrialization.

CHANGE AND CULTURAL LAG

Social change involves complex patterns of response, since a change in one part of society forces changes in other parts. For example, a sharp decline in the birth rate during the 1960s soon caused a crisis in the schools. Suddenly there were too many teachers and classrooms for the number of students. Thus, many teachers had to be let go, and many schools had to be closed. Ex-teachers had to find new occupations, and some use had to be found for unused school buildings. In addition, colleges reacted to the lower demand for teachers by cutting back their number of education majors. Thus, some students who had planned to become teachers had to rethink their career plans.

Beyond changing the schools, the reduced birth rate forced many readjustments elsewhere in our society. Industries and stores that specialized in products for infants and young children had to respond to rapidly declining sales. A leading baby food company launched new products designed for the elderly, for example; TV stations reduced the amount of children's programming. More recently, the lower birth rate has been reflected in smaller numbers of teenagers, with a corresponding decline in sales of records and tapes and of acne medications.

This is but a sketch of the most direct effects of the reduced birth rate (which resulted from changes in the family and in female employment). But none of these reactions was immediate. The schools did not readjust as soon as the number of births declined. In fact, they took no action until the number of elementary school students had seriously dropped. And the colleges did not reduce the number of new teachers they trained until massive unemployment confronted their graduates.

Thus, there can be considerable delay before a change in one part of a society produces a realignment of other parts. During such a period of delay, parts of a society can be badly out of harmony—such as when education departments continue to pump out waves of new graduates after there are no employment opportunities for them. William F. Ogburn (1932) described such periods as **cultural lags.** According to Ogburn, cultural lags are times of danger for societies because severe internal conflicts can result.

CULTURAL LAG AND THE IRANIAN REVOLUTION

The recent history of Iran illustrates the explosive potential of times of cultural lag. During the 1960s and 1970s, the Shah of Iran made an immense effort to rapidly modernize his country. Thousands of young people were sent to the West for advanced technical educations. Many new industries were founded, and many foreign experts were brought in to train Iranians to operate them. Indeed, the Shah encouraged the importation of Western culture generally—movies, music, books, clothing, and the like. For these reasons, most Western observers regarded Iran as the most modern and Western of Middle Eastern societies and a model of development for other nations in the region. Indeed, the Shah received unqualified praise for realizing that he had only a few years to modernize his country's economy before Iranian oil reserves were exhausted. Instead of spending the huge oil income of Iran on importing

luxury goods (as many other less developed nations have done), the Shah was using it to build a modern society, able to provide a high standard of living for Iranians after the oil wells were pumped dry (Halliday, 1979).

But the Shah fell victim to cultural lag. Beneath the gleaming surface of rapid modernization, which was all Westerners could see of this society, the majority of Iranians remained deeply committed to their traditional culture and to an unusually strict form of Islam. From this perspective, Western clothing and manners, especially for women, were intolerably evil. Since Islamic doctrine prohibits the making of images (which is why Islamic art excels in floral and geometric designs, but does not depict humans), movies and TV were regarded as blasphemous. In short, the mass of Iranian society was not readjusting to the rapid modernization fostered by the Shah and was instead increasingly scandalized and angry.

This anger led to constant opposition. Sometimes the opposition was mainly symbolic, such as shunning women in Western dress. At other times, acts of terrorism occurred—several times angry Muslim fundamentalists chained the doors of movie theaters during a movie and then burned down the buildings, killing those inside. Of course, the opposition produced countless conspiracies to overthrow the Shah. In response, the Shah resorted to repressive measures, using his growing secret police forces to uncover and punish his enemies. These measures aroused opposition among many of the most Westernized Iranians, who, educated in the United States, Canada, and Europe, aspired to greater democracy.

The Shah was caught between two irreconcilable forces, one reflecting cultural change and the other cultural lag. He could not democratize without the society exploding in civil war. But as protest in demand of increased democracy attracted support from Western governments, he was forced to try. Despite these efforts, civil unrest rapidly increased.

In hopes of regaining the support of the most Westernized citizens, the Shah appointed the opposition leader Shahpur Bakhtiar to the premiership on December 29, 1978. Still the public protests continued, and riots broke out between traditionalist and modernist factions. On January 16, 1979, the Shah and his family left the country on an extended

Here is graphic illustration of the cultural lag that developed in Iran as a woman in traditional Islamic dress passes a modern semi-trailer truck.

"vacation," hoping to give the new government a chance to gain support.

But then on February 1, 1979, the Ayatollah Khomeini, the most militant Muslim opponent of the Shah, returned from years of exile in France. The Ayatollah directed a civil war against the Shah's supporters and, in less than two weeks, seized the government.

Now the Westernized opponents of the Shah faced a day of reckoning. Music broadcasts were prohib-ited as "no different from opium." Women were commanded to don veils or at least the chador (a large head scarf). Swimming pools and movie thea-ters were shut down (Ismael and Ismael, 1980). Fir-ing squads began the bloody task of purging not only former supporters of the Shah but also all "blasphemers and servants of the devil" who opposed the Ayatollah.

In the midst of this terrible purge, the American embassy was stormed by a mob, and American cit-

Sharp contrasts between the modern and the traditional were greatly reduced in Iran after the Ayatollah Khomeini and his fundamentalist Muslim followers took over the government. Much Western culture was outlawed, including Western clothing styles for women.

izens were taken hostage. It took more than a year to secure their release and safe return. Meanwhile, war broke out between Iran and Iraq and has continued ever since. The oil has not run dry, but a breakdown of Iranian industry has reduced exports to a trickle.

Looking back, analysts now agree that the Shah failed because he tried to do too much too rapidly, creating intolerable internal strains. Iranian culture had no time to adjust to changes.

EXTERNAL SOURCES OF CHANGE

Unlike the solar system, social systems do not exist in a vacuum but within a social and physical environment. Interaction with that environment is a major cause of change within societies as well as a major factor limiting the kinds of changes that occur.

Assume that a number of small societies exist in close proximity, such as the many small societies of American Indians that once existed side by side. Assume that change is going on within each. Each change causes other parts within the societies to adjust in response to cultural lag.

But here internal changes can have external implications. That is, some cultural or social arrangements may weaken the ability of a society to withstand external threats, either from other societies or from the physical environment. Thus, some changes that may have been effective adaptations to internal social needs can be maladaptive to external demands. Societies that change in such directions are not likely to survive, as, indeed, many societies have not.

What has just been outlined is the process of *social evolution* (see Chapter 4). All theories of social change imply evolutionary mechanisms such as this. All social change is subject to external constraints, and external factors often produce internal changes.

Diffusion

We have seen that innovation is a major source of change. But innovations, whether in the form of new weapons, new customs, or new religions, are more often imported from other societies than developed independently within a society. As the famous anthropologist Ralph Linton (1936) put it:

The number of successful inventions originating within . . . any one . . . society . . . is always small. If every human group had been left to climb upward by its own unaided efforts, progress would have been so slow that it is doubtful whether any society by now would have advanced beyond the level of the Old Stone Age.

More rapid progress has been possible because societies borrow innovations from each other. This transfer of innovations is called **diffusion.** Anthropologists and many other scientists have specialized in tracing the routes by which innovations have spread, or diffused, from their point of origin to other societies. Special Topic 3 traced the diffusion of the stirrup from Asia to Europe and the role this played in the rise of feudalism. When Marco Polo returned to Italy from his journey to China, he brought back (among many other things) the noodle, which was the basis for the development of the many forms of pasta popular in Italy and the West today. The horse was brought to the Western Hemisphere by Spanish explorers and spurred immense changes in American Indian societies. Corn, tomatoes, turkeys, and peppers diffused from the Americas back to Europe and Asia. Gunpowder was invented in Asia and then spread around the world. And central to this chapter is the rapid diffusion of modern European culture and technology throughout the world and the impact of this diffusion.

Conflict

Threats from other societies are often sources of social change. The rapid evolution of firearms and artillery in Europe, once gunpowder reached there from Asia, occurred because Europe was divided into scores of feuding societies, each needing to match or exceed the military capacity of its neighbors. In contrast, the relative lack of conflict within the vast Chinese empire did not stimulate the development of similar innovations.

As we saw in Chapter 13, grave external threats often prompt religious innovation. For example, as repeated efforts by American Indian tribes to fend off westward development by European settlers failed, they often concluded that their difficulties stemmed from a faulty religion, from worshiping the wrong gods, or from worshiping them in the wrong way, and new religious movements flourished.

Ecological sources of change

Changes in the physical environment often produce social change. Concerns about depleting natural resources and polluting the environment have caused many recent changes in the United States. Droughts and natural disasters have often prompted massive social changes. Similarly, more favorable ecological changes have also prompted change.

The interplay between environment and society is well illustrated by the great Viking expansions that began about A.D. 900. The Vikings conquered or colonized Russia, large sections of northern Europe, Ireland, parts of England and Scotland, Iceland, and Greenland. This Viking "explosion" was probably caused primarily by several centuries of unusually warm weather (Mowat, 1965; Sawyer, 1982). Warm weather meant much more abundant crops in Norway and Sweden, and more food meant population growth. Soon this larger population lacked land, and younger sons who could expect no inheritance set out to seek their fortunes by raid and conquest. As it happened, they had the fighting skills and seamanship to succeed. Moreover, the good weather made it possible to voyage successfully in the North Atlantic to such places as Iceland, Greenland, and even North America.

In time, the weather turned cold once more and the population declined. The North Atlantic was once again shrouded in fog, battered by storms, and filled with icebergs. The Viking ships stopped going to Iceland and Greenland. The Vikings in Iceland adjusted to the new conditions and survived centuries of isolation, but the Viking settlements in Greenland slowly died out. By the time new explorers from Europe visited Greenland again, only ruins and graves remained. Yet the Greenland Eskimos, who had been there long before the Vikings came, survived the shifts in the climate and still live in Greenland today. Their culture was able to readjust to the frigid climate that made farming impossible for the Vikings.

In summary, both internal and external forces produce social change, and both can cause societies to break down. Europeans in the eighteenth century were probably correct when they came to believe that change was inherent in all societies. They were probably wrong, however, in their faith that change always means progress. Surely, the American Indians, despite gaining the horse, firearms, and other new technology from European settlers, did not find that change meant progress. In the end, change led to the destruction of their societies. Nor did north-

These Eskimo boys in northern Greenland (about 1900) demonstrate the survival advantages of hunter-gatherers in the frozen north. When a shift in the climate made it impossible for the Vikings in Greenland to farm, they perished. Meanwhile, the Eskimos continued to get their clothing from animal hides and their food from hunting and fishing.

ern and western Europe find that improved weather brought only progress, for it also brought fleets of Viking raiders down upon them.

Keeping in mind these principles of social change, we may now assess the causes of the dramatic set of social changes known as modernization.

THE RISE OF THE WEST

In the eighteenth and nineteenth centuries, European intellectuals found it easy to accept the idea of progress, because rapid economic and technological changes were transforming their societies. Looking back over their history, Europeans saw a long period, now called the Dark Ages, when change had been very slow. During that time, Europe had been technologically backward compared with the nations of the Middle East and Asia. Then, beginning in the sixteenth and seventeenth centuries, came an immense leap forward. Within a few centuries, European technology had raced far ahead of that of the rest of the world.

In the midst of this period of great progress, Europeans had set out to explore, colonize, and trade with the rest of the world. Everywhere they went they found themselves possessed of superior technology. Indeed, when Western fleets began to voyage to China, long known in the West for its advanced civilization, they found a backward nation unable to defend itself against a few ships armed with cannon (Mendelssohn, 1976; McNeill, 1982).

Thus, the questions arose: Why had China not kept pace? Why had social change been so rapid in Europe? Indeed, why was so much of the world so little advanced—why were some societies still huddled in the Stone Age, while in Europe machines were replacing human labor?

These were and continue to be the dominating questions in the study of social change. Moreover, new questions have arisen: Why has continued exposure to Western technology had so little effect in some parts of the world? Can all societies on earth become modernized? If not, why not? If so, how? You will recognize that these questions not only preoccupy sociologists interested in modernization and social change, but also are among the leading international political questions of our time.

There are four major bodies of theory about why the West suddenly produced the Industrial Revolution and sprinted ahead of the rest of the world. Since these theories range from Marxism to free market economic theories, they stand in vigorous, basic disagreement. Yet, perhaps surprisingly, they agree on their initial assumption. Each attributes modernization, the rise of industrialized Europe, to the same basic source: the development of a particular pattern of economic relations called *capitalism*. Indeed, no conservative economist has ever heaped more praise on capitalism as the source of modernization than did Karl Marx, even though he devoted his life to planning for the overthrow of capitalism.

It thus is fitting to begin our assessment of modernization by seeing why Marx thought it was the result of capitalism. Then we shall closely examine the nature of capitalism itself.

MARX ON CAPITALISM

Marx wanted a new world in which all people could enjoy a good life, where no one would be hungry or homeless, and where everyone would have freedom, dignity, and security. Throughout the ages, many people have longed for such a world. But in the mid-nineteenth century, Marx believed such a thing had become possible for the first time. In earlier times, equality could exist only as the equality of poverty. Humans simply were not sufficiently productive to provide themselves with comfort. But as Marx surveyed the immense flow of products from Europe's new and booming industries, he was convinced that societies were finally capable of providing everyone with a good life. The potential wealth was there; it had only to be shared.

Marx did not believe that the Industrial Revolution itself was the cause of Europe's new explosion of productivity. Instead, he thought that this new technology was the result of something more basic: a new mode of economic arrangements that unleashed the full productive potential of human beings. He called these economic arrangements *capitalism*.

Before the rise of capitalism, Marx wrote, humans had been victims of their own "slothful indolence." That is, people tried to get out of work and did not try to find ways to be more productive. In fact, many historians have been struck by the short work days of medieval society and the careless farming methods of medieval peasants (see Braudel, 1981; Thomas, 1979). Similarly, anthropologists have long noted the casual attitudes toward work among primitives, as compared with modern work norms. Marx believed that Europe's great leap forward occurred because people suddenly began to work harder and smarter as a result of the inducements of capitalism. Capitalist society, he wrote in *The Communist Manifesto* (1848), was

the first to show what man's activity can bring about. It has accomplished wonders far surpassing

Egyptian pyramids, Roman aqueducts, and Gothic cathedrals; it has conducted expeditions that put in the shade all former Exoduses of nations and crusades.

Moreover, capitalism cannot help but produce endless technological innovation: It must be "constantly revolutionising the instruments of production." This is because capitalism has stripped away the traditional bases of relationships among humans and left only one "nexus between man and man," that of "naked self-interest."

Here we encounter a great irony. Marx believed that the reason capitalism could be so productive was precisely the reason it ought to be destroyed. He believed that capitalist economies produced their economic miracles by degrading and alienating humans, both from one another and from themselves. By pursuing self-interest alone, humans ruthlessly exploit one another, according to Marx. Thus, he argued, capitalist societies not only were the first with the productive capacity to overcome poverty and exploitation, but also were incapable of doing so. Indeed, Marx believed that capitalist societies could only become increasingly unequal, eventually consisting of a tiny ruling elite (the bourgeoisie) possessed of incredible wealth and power, and a huge mass of "wage slaves" (the proletariat) sweating out their lives in dismal factories. Thus, Marx proposed communist revolutions, in which the masses would seize collective ownership of all means of production and turn the immense capacities of modern industrial societies to the benefit of all (see Chapters 9 and 10).

Although Marx believed capitalism had been the cause of modernization, he believed the benefits of modernization could be separated from this initial cause—that communism could replace capitalism, once modernization was sufficiently developed. But what is capitalism? What is the secret of its economic power?

Capitalism

Current dictionaries define **capitalism** as an economic system based on private ownership of the means of production and a system by which people compete to gain profits. Such a definition fails to reveal the feature of capitalism that differentiates it from other kinds of economies. For example, there was much private ownership of the means of production (farms, tools, and ships) in ancient Rome and medieval Europe, and there was competition for wealth. But these were not capitalist economies. What is unique about capitalism is its reliance on a free market.

In a free market, prices and wages are set by freely made choices of individuals. That is, people decide for themselves what price they will charge or pay. They cannot be forced to buy or to sell, to hire or to become employed. Each is free to make the best possible bargain.

Prices and wages are set by supply and demand. When many people sell some commodity, competition among them forces prices down. Competition among people wanting to buy something in limited supply forces prices up. Competition among people wanting to be employed forces wages down. Competition among persons wanting to hire forces wages up. The essence of the system is that everyone seeks to maximize personal gain and that such gains can be accumulated in the form of private property, secure from arbitrary seizure by the government.

In a free market, individuals benefit by being more productive. If one farmer works longer hours in his fields, at the end of the year he will have more wealth than his neighbors who worked less hard. Moreover, the free market rewards innovation and the reinvestment of wealth. A farmer who finds a way to plow better or faster will become richer. A farmer who saves some of his profits and uses them to buy more land, more cattle, or better machinery will become richer. In this way, capitalist economies motivate everyone to try to become wealthier, and these collective efforts increase production; when there is more to be had, standards of living rise. Indeed, Marx believed that capitalism had unleashed such productivity in Europe that it would soon be possible to eliminate all poverty.

Precapitalist command economies

Precapitalist societies do not rely on free market principles and individual economic self-interest. Instead, they are **command economies.** That is, some people decide what work is to be done and command others to do it. Thus, the lord of a medieval estate decided which fields were to be plowed, when, and what to plant and then ordered his peasants to do it. An emperor decided to build a road and ordered workers to be assembled and set to their tasks. The weakness of command economies is that those doing the work have nothing to gain by doing it well. A slave may avoid the overseer's whip by doing just enough, but a slave will not eat better or gain possessions by working harder or discovering ways to become more productive. Lack of worker motivation caused Marx to scorn the slothfulness of such economies.

The goal of command economies is consumption. Everyone tries to consume what they can before someone else takes it away from them. Thus, there is no motive to produce surplus. Indeed, as we saw in Chapter 10, when individuals lack secure property rights, their surplus production is simply taken from them—indeed, it will be used to support others who suppress and exploit them. The secret of capitalism is to reward surplus production: Permitting people to keep their wealth encourages them to seek wealth and to curb their consumption so that they can reinvest their wealth to create more wealth.

An episode from ancient China clearly reveals the productive superiority of capitalist over command economies. In the late tenth century, an iron smelting industry rapidly developed in the northern Chinese province of Hunan. By 1018, these iron smelters were producing more than 35,000 tons a year, an incredible achievement for the time. This iron industry was not the result of royal command. Instead, private individuals had recognized the great demand for iron and the good supplies of ore and coal in Hunan, and they realized that the smelted iron could easily be transported to distant markets over an existing network of canals and navigable rivers.

Having invested in foundries, these Chinese industrialists were soon reaping huge profits from their enterprises, much of which they reinvested to build more foundries. Production rose rapidly. The availability of large supplies of iron soon led to the introduction of iron agricultural tools, which in turn rapidly increased food production in China. Thus, China began to industrialize many centuries before Europe's great leap. Then, as suddenly as it had begun,

it all stopped. By the end of the century, only tiny amounts of iron came down the rivers from Hunan, and soon the foundries were forgotten ruins.

What happened? The imperial court had noticed that some commoners were getting rich by manufacturing iron and considered this undesirable. So the government taxed away their earnings, declared a monopoly on the sale of iron, and took over the smelters. Workers had flocked to work in the smelters, where they had earned more than they could as peasants, but now work was commanded of them. The motive for working died out, as did the fires in the smelters (McNeill, 1982).

If capitalism caused the rise of the West, what caused capitalism? Here Marx was relatively silent. He argued that it was invented by the bourgeoisie, who used it to overthrow the old medieval nobility. But he said very little about why and how the bourgeoisie developed capitalism. Thus, it was left to Max Weber to attempt the first general explanation of the rise of capitalism.

THE PROTESTANT ETHIC

The goal Weber set for himself was to explain why capitalism developed where and when it did and why it failed to appear (except in the brief instance cited in ancient China) in other societies that had achieved a stage of economic development similar to that of precapitalist Europe. In Weber's judgment, the essential question was, How had Europeans gained the self-discipline to cease unrestricted consumption while increasing production? Many societies have learned to curb consumption. Ascetic religions, for example, have led many people to spurn material things. But this has been accomplished by destroying their interest in creating material things. In Europe, however, people curbed their consumption while working all the harder to produce. How was this possible?

Weber believed the answer lay in the Protestant Reformation. In his famous book *The Protestant Ethic and the Spirit of Capitalism,* he argued that the religious ideas produced by Protestantism had motivated people both to limit their consumption and to pursue maximum wealth. This soon led to the discovery that reinvestment was the fastest road to wealth.

The **Protestant Reformation** began in Germany when Martin Luther (1483–1546) asserted that the church was not needed to mediate between a person and God. Rather, each person should seek his or her own salvation through direct relations with God. In Switzerland, John Calvin (1509–1564) carried this notion much further. He argued that God was entirely unknowable. Therefore, no person could achieve salvation by appealing to God or by obeying the commandments. Who would be saved and who would be damned had been decided by God at the beginning of time and could not be altered. This doctrine was called predestination: Our futures were predestined by God.

But then how could one be sure of being saved? Indeed, what motive was there not to sin? Calvin provided an answer that put extreme pressure on the individual to lead an exemplary life: You can never be certain you are saved, but there are clues that indicate who is elected by God for salvation— persons whose lives are above reproach and who succeed in life.

No longer was work merely a calling to be endured; now it was seen as a glorification of God and more of an end in itself. The successful worker was the successful servant [of God], and money became a metric for the measurement of grace (Demerath and Hammond, 1969).

In addition, Calvinist Protestants condemned the most conspicuous forms of consuming wealth as sinful. They believed that you could not show the world that you were rich by a great display of your wealth (and therefore you could not display that you were one of God's chosen). You could show your success only by visible productive activities. And since you could not consume much wealth, why not plow it back to gain even greater wealth and that much greater certainty that you would go to heaven?

Strict predestinarian views of salvation did not last long as a dominant theme in Protestantism, but the actions they set in motion did. It soon became popular Protestant doctrine that one could actually earn one's way into heaven. Economic zeal became the road to heaven.

From these cultural developments, Weber argued, capitalism blossomed. Soon the religious roots of

John Calvin.

capitalism were no longer needed, for capitalism became a secular ideology in its own right—**the spirit of capitalism.** This spirit then spread through both Protestants and Catholics and stimulated the Industrial Revolution. Weber quoted at length from Benjamin Franklin to show how deeply belief in the importance of saving and reinvestment had become imbedded in Western cultures.

Weber did not argue that the **Protestant Ethic** was the sole cause of the rise of capitalism. Nor did he ignore interaction between developing commercial activities and developing religious doctrines. He merely argued that the development of these religious and economic ideas gave rise to the Industrial Revolution. Today, many sociologists think that Weber emphasized religious values too much and economic changes too little. Nevertheless, a majority agrees that a shift in how people regarded wealth was an important part of the development of industrial capitalism.

THE STATE THEORY OF MODERNIZATION

A third line of social theory suggests that Marx and Weber were both correct, but both views are limited. Proponents of this perspective agree with Marx that capitalism led to the rapid modernization of Europe, but they agree with Weber that the rise of capitalism itself must be explained if we are to account for modernization. They disagree with Weber that Protestant theology led to the development of capitalism, arguing instead that both Protestantism and capitalism were produced by something more basic in European history: the taming of the state.

Building on classical economic theories, these social scientists propose that capitalism could develop only as the state became tamed; moreover, capitalism will always develop when the state is tame (North and Thomas, 1973; Nozick, 1974; Friedman and Friedman, 1980). Because of the centrality of the state in this explanation, it is called the **state theory of modernization.**

The state theorists argue that the critical event in European history was the limitation of the power of the state in several European nations, especially England and Holland. This resulted in capitalist economies, which in turn gave rise to the Industrial Revolution, or modernization.

The argument is very simple. When a repressive state exists, so will a command economy. Few persons in such societies benefit by being more productive, for the state supports itself by confiscating all surplus production, which is then consumed by the ruling elite. Under these conditions, as Marx recognized, it would be foolish to curb consumption or try to produce more because of the insatiable appetite of the state. Even the most powerful religious ideas could not cause people to act like capitalists in such societies. Even if some people do,

they will soon find their work is in vain, as did the Chinese iron makers.

However, if the powers of the state are limited so that private property is secure from seizure and people are free to pursue their economic self-interest, capitalism becomes attractive and possible. For then, the more that people work and save the better off they will be. Thus, whenever the state is prevented from seizing property, a free market, or capitalism, will develop. Rapid economic and technological progress then becomes very likely. When people are more productive, more wealth exists. In seeking to be more productive, huge numbers of people will seek more effective technology.

Marx was inclined to take technological progress for granted, seeing it as the natural result of human curiosity. The state theorists do not. They point to the historical fact that for long periods little, if any, technological progress occurred, while at other times new technology arose rapidly. Why is this? The answer they offer is that in some times and places, it is not worthwhile for people to develop new technology because they will not benefit from it. Why build a windmill so you can grind much more grain than you have been grinding by hand if your increased production will simply provide more flour for the nobility and no more for yourself?

Since patent records have been kept, inventions have not been developed at a steady rate; many more patents are applied for during economic booms than during recessions (Schmookler, 1966). This suggests that people tend to invent things when it is profitable to do so. In fact, historians of technology argue that it was the creation of patent laws that truly spurred invention during the Industrial Revolution (Jewkes, Sawers, and Stillerman, 1969). Patent laws protect an inventor's right to profit from his or her invention. Neither individuals nor firms would risk years of effort and the large investments needed to perfect many inventions if others could then simply steal their results.

Once the state had been tamed in parts of Europe, free markets sprang up, and, the state theorists argue, from then on the development of modern industrial societies was virtually certain (North and Thomas, 1973). Moreover, some state theorists claim that the taming of the state was the primary cause of the Protestant Reformation (Walzer, 1963).

In Chapter 13 we saw that religious pluralism is the natural state of religious economies—that different kinds of people have different religious needs, so that the market is served best by a variety of faiths. When the state does not try to create a monopoly for one faith, many faiths will exist. Thus, religious variety sprang forth in those European nations where the power of the state was restricted. However, state theorists go further than attributing religious pluralism to the taming of the state. They suggest that the rise of capitalism prompted specific Protestant doctrines, thus reversing Weber's argument. When people pursue their own economic self-interests, their sense of individualism is heightened. As a result, people want to deal with God directly rather than through a religious hierarchy. The stress in Protestantism that each person must seek his or her own understanding of God and his or her own salvation was thus compatible with daily economic activities.

DEPENDENCY AND WORLD SYSTEM THEORY

Each of the three explanations of modernization just examined seeks the causes of the Industrial Revolution within societies. That is, each points to social changes within a society. Marx believed that the development of capitalism within nations led to the Industrial Revolution. Indeed, Marx denied that nations could achieve communism without first passing though a capitalist phase. Similarly, Weber tried to show that capitalism arose only where the Protestant Reformation had first planted an ethic promoting hard work, saving, and reinvestment. State theorists argue that capitalism arose only in nations that had first tamed the state. But a fourth body of modernization theory looks not to changes within a nation but to changes in relationships among nations as the causative force. This is called **world system theory.**

Most advocates of world system theory claim to be Marxists, although the first extended statement of this view was not written by Marx, but by J. A. Hobson, an English economist. In 1902 he published a book called *Imperialism,* in which he charged

that industrial European nations looted their colonies by forcing them to sell their raw materials too cheaply and to buy manufactured goods at too high a price. In 1915 V. I. Lenin, who soon was to lead the Russian Revolution, borrowed Hobson's argument (as well as many of his statistics) and published them in a book called *Imperialism, the Highest State of Capitalism.* Ever since then, Communist writers have claimed that Western capitalist nations not only exploit the less developed nations of the world but actually prevent them from modernizing. A few years ago this approach gained serious advocates among American sociologists. The man most responsible for recruiting sociologists to world system theory is Immanuel Wallerstein.

Elements of a world system

In *The Modern World System* (1974), Wallerstein elaborated on the view that modernization of the West was paid for by its less fortunate neighbors. That is, the causes of the Industrial Revolution are to be found not within individual nations but in the relations among nations that unite them into a single social system. He therefore set out to examine in detail the world system existing in the sixteenth century, during which Europe began to develop capitalism and industrialize.

In Wallerstein's judgment, the crucial development in the sixteenth century was the growth of an international economy that was not politically united. Through this economy, some nations extracted wealth from other nations without having to resort to military force. Wallerstein argued that this was different from all previous forms of international relations. In the past, nations had extracted wealth from other nations by plunder or by forcing them to submit to political control as part of an empire. Thus, for a long period Rome and before it Egypt dominated huge empires from which taxes and tributes were extracted by the threat (and often the use) of coercion.

Such empires were not very efficient. They were command economies incurring great military and administrative costs. In fact, these costs probably were so great that they lowered the standard of living of all but the ruling elite. Any border troubles or internal rebellions raised the costs of maintaining an empire and strained available resources. When these costs could no longer be met, the empire became unstable and eventually collapsed.

What was unique about developments in Europe, according to Wallerstein, was that economic relations developed among nations whereby some could exploit others without paying the huge costs of running an empire. Thus, a few nations in western Europe were able to finance their rapid industrial development by extracting wealth from their neighbors without the need to plunder or dominate them through military force. Wallerstein called this international economy in sixteenth-century Europe the "modern world system," even though it was far from worldwide in scope. His usage emphasized that this was an international social system.

Within this world system, Wallerstein argued, stratification exists among nations. A few nations form an upper class, some a lower class, and a few a middle class. The class position of a nation is determined by its place in a geographic division of labor.

The dominant, or upper class, nations in a world system Wallerstein calls **core nations.** Core nations have very diversified economies and are the most modern and industrialized. Core nations have the strongest internal political structures marked by stable governments and little internal class conflict. As did Lenin, Wallerstein argues that this is because core nations can provide a very high standard of living for their workers and thus, in effect, buy their cooperation. Core nations also have a large middle class and permit considerable political freedom and individual liberty.

At the bottom of world systems are nations that Wallerstein identifies as **peripheral nations.** Many are located far from core nations. Typically, they have weak internal political structures and a low standard of living for workers. Because of their high potential for political instability and class conflict, they are ruled by repressive governments. Peripheral nations have highly specialized economies, typically relying on the sales of a narrow range of raw materials (such as food, ore, fiber, petroleum, or timber) to core nations.

A few nations in a world system may display features of both core and peripheral nations. Their economies are more diversified than those of peripheral nations, but more specialized than those of core nations. Wallerstein calls these **semiperipheral nations.**

Dominance and dependency

To explain the relations among nations in a world system, Wallerstein applied a Marxist analysis of class relations within nations. Thus, he argued, the core nations act as an upper class exploiting the peripheral nations, which are the lower class. Core nations are wealthy like upper classes because they extract all surplus production from the periphery. They do this by dominating trade relations with the peripheral nations, making them dependent and distorting their economies so that peripheral economies cannot develop into modern societies.

Wallerstein used this model to explain the unevenness of modernization and industrialization in Europe. He admitted that he could not explain why some nations in western Europe initially got the jump on others and became core nations. But once some had done so, he claimed, they forced the nations of eastern Europe to accept a peripheral position. In this fashion, he explained why nations such as Poland and Hungary began to industrialize, then stopped and regressed to agricultural nations that lived by exporting food to western Europe in return for manufactured goods. Because of their late start, Poland and Hungary could not successfully modernize against western European competition and thus became dependent upon the West.

Although Wallerstein's book dealt with Europe during the sixteenth century, his real interest (and the main interest of many other sociologists now using world system theory) is in current international relations. Thus the two primary questions are these: (1) Why is so much of the world so little modernized despite centuries of trade and contact with more advanced nations? (2) Can modernization ever become worldwide? The answers given by proponents of world system theory are that trade with advanced nations has prevented the less developed nations from developing and that unless these nations escape the control of advanced capitalist societies, they can never develop properly.

Proponents of world system theory argue that these Bulgarian peasant women must toil with old-fashioned methods because the developed nations prevent industrialization in the less developed nations.

Mechanisms of dependency

The world system theory specifies a number of mechanisms by which less developed nations are made dependent on and are dominated by the advanced nations (Frank, 1969; Galtung, 1971; Wallerstein, 1974; Chase-Dunn, 1975; Chirot, 1977).

The fundamental mechanism is that the less developed nations are dominated by foreign firms and investors that control their economies. This, in turn, has several consequences. First, profits flow back to the developed nations rather than being reinvested in the local economies. That is, foreign firms and investors spend or invest their profits back home. This denies the underdeveloped economies the capacity to grow.

Second, foreign firms and investors control what economic activities take place in underdeveloped nations. Developing manufacturing capacity is not in their interest; rather, they profit more by selling manufactured goods to underdeveloped nations and extracting raw materials from them. Therefore, for-

Harbor scenes like this in Cotonou, Dahomey, in West Africa, encourage belief in the dependency hypothesis—that when a nation is a primary exporter of unprocessed food and raw materials, its modernization is retarded. That nations lacking industry do not export manufactured goods is hardly surprising.

eign domination means that a peripheral nation remains a supplier of raw materials unable to become industrially self-sufficient.

Third, nations that specialize in exporting raw materials must remain poor. World demand for raw materials is relatively inelastic due to the small or negligible population growth in the advanced nations (so their need for raw materials does not increase). Therefore, a nation cannot increase its wealth by increasing the amount of raw materials it exports. Also, world prices for raw materials are subject to manipulation by speculators in the advanced nations

and often fall so low as to create economic depressions in supplier nations.

According to world system theory, nations that specialize in the export of raw materials also develop very distorted economies. Their development tends to be limited to small enclaves of workers employed in the export industries, while the rest of the nation remains undeveloped. The result is a dual economy that confines all modernization to the export sector, while providing neither incentives nor resources for modernizing the rest of the country (Frank, 1969; Paige, 1974; Chase-Dunn, 1975).

The dependency thesis is dealt a blow by scenes like this at the Port of Oakland, California. Huge numbers of containers like these, being loaded for export, contain food or unprocessed raw materials. Indeed, the United States not only is one of the most modernized nations, it is the major exporter of food, timber, and other raw materials.

DELACROIX: TESTING THE DEPENDENCY HYPOTHESIS

Intellectuals and many political leaders in the less developed nations find world system theory of great appeal. It tells them that the lack of progress in their nations is not their fault but is imposed upon them by the developed nations. These views have been rejected by many social scientists, however, especially those in the advanced nations.

Although world system theory offers an elegant model of international economic relations, many critics have argued that the real world is much more complex. The world system theory neatly divides the world into poor, underdeveloped nations that export raw materials and rich, modernized nations that export processed manufactured goods. However, critics point out that exceptions to this scheme abound. The United States and Canada are rich, modernized nations, yet they export more raw, unprocessed foodstuffs than the rest of the world combined. Taiwan's economy is dominated by foreign investors, yet rather than specializing in the export of raw materials, nearly 90 percent of its exports are manufactured goods (Barrett and Whyte, 1982). Moreover, research designed to support the dependency claims of world system theory was either unsuccessful or poorly designed and executed. Thus, a young graduate student at Stanford University in the mid-1970s saw an opportunity to do some important sociology.

Jacques Delacroix (1977) set out to test a major hypothesis about dependency: that specialization in the export of raw materials prevents modernization. More specifically, he hypothesized that nations that specialized in exporting raw materials would (1) experience relatively slow rates of economic growth and (2) have low enrollments in secondary education (high school).

Delacroix measured economic growth as gains in the per capita **gross national product (GNP)**— the total value of all economic activities in a society divided by the population. If the dependency hypothesis were correct, then the economic well-being of individuals in exporting nations should improve more slowly than that in nations that import raw materials and export manufactured goods. In effect, the advanced nations should be getting rich at the expense of the underdeveloped nations.

A nation's level of school enrollment, especially above the grade school level, represents both an investment in modernization and modernization itself. Only educated populations can deal with technology and modern culture. If the dependency hypothesis were correct, Delacroix argued, then dependent nations should lack the resources to expand their secondary educational systems. Any educational gains should be limited to people involved in exporting, leaving the rest of the society with little schooling.

Delacroix knew that the dependency hypothesis could not be tested properly at only one point in time. No one disputes that some nations are less developed than others. The issue is whether these nations are catching up in terms of modernization. Clearly, then, changes over time must be examined. So Delacroix obtained data for 1955 and 1970 for fifty-nine nations. He then examined changes in his dependent variables: changes in per capita GNP and changes in secondary school enrollment as these were related to his independent variable, the proportion of a nation's exports that are unprocessed raw materials.

What did he find? No relationships. Nations specializing in raw material exports showed as much increase in per capita GNP as nations specializing in the export of manufactured goods. Secondary school enrollment grew as greatly in the nations exporting raw materials as in those exporting manufactured goods. Thus, Delacroix found no support for the dependency hypothesis.

But he did find something else. Secondary school enrollments and increases in per capita GNP were strongly correlated. This led Delacroix to suggest that modernization is influenced primarily by internal processes rather than external processes of the world system. That is, nations that devoted substantial effort to educating their populations improved their standard of living, no matter what role they played in the world import-export system. Educational policy is decided within nations, not imposed upon them by their trading partners. Indeed, Delacroix concluded that even the least developed nations retain considerable "freedom to maneuver" in determining domestic policies and thus retain considerable opportunity, as well as responsibility, to establish their own patterns of modernization.

Since Delacroix's landmark study, a great deal of additional research has been done. These studies have also failed to support the dependency hypothesis, with the possible exception that there may come a point when further modernization in the most advanced developing nations may stop unless they adjust their economic specialties to the competition and opportunities in world trade (Delacroix and Ragin, 1981). Hence, an industrializing nation may find it difficult to develop automobile manufacturing because of too much existing competition in the world auto market. Such a nation would have to seek other export avenues. Nevertheless, even here we see that control rests primarily within individual societies, not with outside forces. Thus, most sociologists of social change and modernization today agree that "the central development problems of most developing nations are largely internal" (Diaz-Alejandro et al., 1978).

Delacroix's research showed that a major source of modernization is secondary school enrollment. To the degree that a nation invests in its young people by keeping them in school, its modernization is speeded up. These Ivory Coast children are their nation's primary asset.

CONCLUSION

However capitalism arose and modernization occurred, the fundamental fact remains that some nations are much more modernized than others and that the less developed nations desire the quality of life that modernization provides. In order to achieve this quality of life, they may have to develop "modern" values of thrift and reinvestment, as Weber proposed; develop capitalist economies, as Marx

believed; and tame their states, as state theorists argue. And they may have to pay close attention to their opportunities in the world trade economy, as world system theorists suggest.

Yet in all of this discussion of change and modernization, a primary element has been omitted. The first effect of modernization on the less developed nations has been an immense population explosion in recent decades. As rapidly as many of these nations have been increasing their wealth, they have been increasing their populations even faster. Thus, a pressing issue has been whether this rapid population growth can be halted before it results in catastrophe. The answers to this question have often been blurred by doomsday pronouncements based on distorted evidence and political rhetoric. Nevertheless, the answers remain vital for the future of the world. The next chapter is devoted to the sociology of population and thus will deal with many of the issues raised in this chapter.

Review glossary

Modernization The process by which societies develop advanced industrial technology and the political, cultural, and social arrangements appropriate to sustaining, directing, and utilizing that technology. (p. 385)

Idea of progress The philosophical doctrine that technological and social progress is inevitable. (p. 387)

Cultural lags Periods of delay following a change in one part of a society when other parts of the society have not yet readjusted. (p. 389)

Diffusion The process by which innovations spread from one society to another. (p. 392)

Capitalism An economic system based on free-market exchanges and individual property rights with the result that any individual can benefit from becoming more productive. (p. 395)

Command economies Economic systems wherein property rights are not secure and much productive activity is based on coerced labor. (p. 395)

Protestant Reformation The separation of Protestant Christians from the Roman Catholic Church during the sixteenth century; usually associated with the founding of the Lutheran Church in Germany. (p. 397)

Spirit of capitalism According to Weber, a non-religious version of the Protestant Ethic; values favoring hard work, thrift, and the importance of economic success. (p. 397)

Protestant Ethic According to Weber, doctrines holding that economic success reflects God's grace. (p. 397)

State theory of modernization Theory stating that wherever the power of the state to seize private property is curtailed, free markets will appear, capitalism will develop, and modernization will occur as a result of mass efforts to become more productive. (p. 398)

World system theory (or dependency theory) Theory stating that some nations became modernized by exploiting other nations and that their continuing exploitation prevents less developed nations from becoming fully modernized (p. 399)

Core nations According to Wallerstein, those most modernized nations, having diversified economies and stable internal politics, that dominate the world system. (p. 400)

Peripheral nations According to Wallerstein, those nations in the world system that are forced to specialize in the export of unprocessed raw materials and food to the core nations and that must import manufactured goods. This makes them dependent on the core nations, which in turn force them to adopt economic and social policies that prevent them from modernizing. (p. 400)

Semiperipheral nations According to Wallerstein, those nations that fall in between core and peripheral nations, being more industrialized than the latter and less industrialized than the former. (p. 400)

Gross national product (GNP) The total value of all economic activities within a society. When GNP is divided by the total population of a society, the result is per capita GNP. (p. 404)

Suggested readings

Chirot, Daniel. *Social Change in the Twentieth Century.* New York: Harcourt Brace Jovanovich, 1977.

McNeill, William H. *Plagues and Peoples.* New York: 1976.

North, Douglas C., and Robert Paul Thomas. *The Rise of the Western World: A New Economic History*. Cambridge: Cambridge University Press, 1973.

Wallerstein, Immanuel. *The Modern World System*. New York: Academic Press, 1974.

Weber, Max. *The Protestant Ethic and the Spirit of Capitalism*. New York: Scribner's, 1958.

White, Lynn, Jr. *Medieval Technology and Social Change*. London: Oxford University Press, 1963.

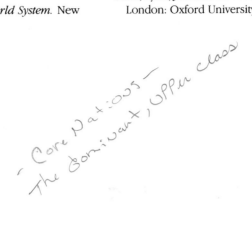

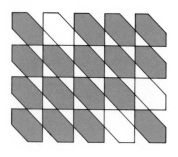

■ No sooner was he sitting upon the throne of England after winning the Battle of Hastings in A.D. 1066 than William the Conqueror sent his agents out to record how many people lived where and who owned what. The result was a massive document called the *Domesday Book* (pronounced "doomsday"). Today, historians consider the **Domesday Book** unsurpassed in medieval history for its thoroughness and for the speed at which it was assembled.

William was not the first ruler to count his population. The pharoahs of Egypt began doing so as early as 2500 B.C. The Old Testament records that once the Israelites were safely out of Egypt, "The LORD spoke to Moses, saying 'Take a census of all the congregation of the people of Israel, by families.'" The emperors of Rome also counted and assessed their subjects frequently—Augustus ordered a count of the entire empire in 28 B.C., in 8 B.C., and again in A.D. 14. Why all this interest in counting people? In order to estimate tax revenues and military manpower.

To know how much revenue a tax can produce, a government needs to know how many people will be paying it. Moreover, only by knowing how many people live in a particular district can the central government be sure that local officials are not embezzling. For example, a local tax official might report to the imperial government that there are 5,000 tax-paying families in his district when there are, in fact, 8,000, thus enabling him to pocket the taxes paid by 3,000 families.

By the same token, only by knowing the number of able-bodied males of military age can a ruler estimate how large an army he can raise. In the

Population
Changes

days of tiny hunting-and-gathering societies, it was easy to count noses and know that fourteen warriors were available for battle. But when societies grew to include tens of thousands of people, counting noses became a major task.

Thus, from ancient times, governments instituted a **census:** a population count, often broken down into useful categories such as sex, age, occupation, marital status, and the like. The *Domesday Book* was a census conducted to inform William the Conqueror what he had conquered—how many people there were in England and what levels of taxes they could afford to pay.

Even though William's agents conducted what was probably the most efficient census taken in medieval times, it took them two years to assemble the *Domesday Book,* and the cost of gathering the information was very great. Moreover, the *Domesday Book,* like any census, soon became outdated.

As we shall see, populations often change rapidly. Therefore, it may be necessary to redo a census frequently in order to have accurate information. However, because a census is very expensive, governments are reluctant to conduct them. Often that has meant muddling along with badly outdated information. Over time, however, ways have been found to gauge population changes between censuses. Moreover, because populations so often fluctuate in size, governments encouraged inquiry into why this occurs. Thus was born the science of *demography.* ■

CHAPTER PREVIEW

The word *demography* is formed from the Greek word *demos,* meaning "people," and *graphy,* meaning "description." Doing **demography** means describing the people. Whenever you read in the newspaper about such things as the marriage rate, the divorce rate, or population decline in the Northeast, you are reading about work done by demographers.

In this chapter we shall examine fundamentals of modern demography, a major area of specialization within sociology. We shall also see the important role of population shifts in prompting or impeding social change. The primary object of the chapter is to assess theories of population change.

Historically, human population trends have undergone four dramatic shifts, and a fifth major shift seems to have just begun. These shifts are the main subjects of the major theories of demography. Thus, we shall examine historical population patterns, while at the same time assessing the major theoretical achievements of demographers. Before we trace patterns of population change, however, we should understand a few basic technical tools used to monitor and describe human populations.

DEMOGRAPHIC TECHNIQUES

As a population changes, a census becomes out-of-date. For a long time, governments often lacked accurate information on the size and composition of their populations. Then one day some unremembered bureaucrat hit upon an ingenious way to keep track of what was going on. It became the law to record all births and all deaths with the government. This procedure became common among societies, and governments created bureaus of vital statistics to keep an accurate count of these registrations. These records made it possible to update the census each year. (In many countries, birth and death registration was facilitated by the clergy, who had kept local records for religious purposes.)

Let us consider a hypothetical nation that has just conducted a census showing that it has 10 million citizens. The next year 500,000 babies are born and 400,000 people die. By subtracting deaths from births, we determine that the population has undergone a net increase of 100,000. Adding this to 10 million, we know that this nation now has 10,100,000 citizens. Furthermore, by dividing the year's growth (100,000) by the total population of the year before (10 million), we can see that the population grew by 1 percent in one year. By making these computations each year, we can find out the size of the population and its rate and direction of change without taking a new census.

Suppose that each year 100,000 more people are added to this nation's population. Is this rate of growth the same year after year? No. As the population grows, each year 100,000 people constitute a smaller percentage of the existing population and thus represent a smaller percentage increase. We therefore know that population growth is slowing down. Because it is often vital to governments to know how fast their populations are growing, great attention is paid to the percentage of annual growth, or the **growth rate,** of the population.

Even what appear to be small growth rates can cause populations to grow at a breathless pace. For example, a population that is growing by 3 percent per year will double in size in twenty-three years and increase tenfold in only seventy-seven years. The growth rate is computed in this way:

$$\frac{\text{Net population gain (or loss)}}{\text{Size of population}} = \text{Growth rate}$$

For any given year, the net population gain (or loss) takes three variables into account: (1) the increase (or decrease) in births, (2) the increase (or decrease) in deaths, and (3) the increase (or decrease) due to migration.

A record of all births and deaths permits some crude insight into why a population changes in size. A population can grow because births are increasing, because deaths are decreasing, because people are migrating into a region, or all three reasons. Similarly, a population can shrink because of a decline in births, an increase in deaths, a loss of people who move away, or all these reasons. Assuming that migration is constant, suppose a government wants a larger population. It would need to know whether encouraging more births or combating disease is the more appropriate course.

Obviously, in answering this question, simply knowing the numbers of births and deaths over several years would not help very much. To compare, say, births for two years, we need to take into account the fact that the total population for these years is different, making a direct comparison between the number of births meaningless. Again the solution is to compute a percentage—the ratio of births to the population total for each year. Such percentages are called *rates*.

Rates

A **crude death rate** can be computed by dividing the total number of deaths for a year by the total population for that year. A **crude birth rate** can be computed by dividing the total number of births for a year by the total population for that year. By using rates, we can make meaningful comparisons between years in which the total population differed in size. For example, in 1910 there were 2,777,000 live births in the United States; in 1970 there were 3,731,000 live births. Despite the fact that there were almost a million more births in 1970, fertility was much higher in 1910—there were fewer than half as many people in 1910 as there were in 1970 to produce those births. Thus, newborns added only 1.8 percent to the total population in 1970, in contrast to 3 percent in 1910.

Crude birth and death rates give only limited information. They do not take into account some important factors: For example, not all members of a society can bear children. Males cannot, nor can prepubescent or postmenopausal females. What will happen if the proportion of fertile females in a population changes? A change in the crude birth rate will occur even if fertile women are reproducing at exactly the same rate as before. Therefore, demographers often do not use the total population as the basis for computing the **general fertility rate.** Instead, they divide the total number of births by the total number of females within a certain age span. (The U.S. Census bases its general fertility rate on women 15 to 44 years old.)

In order to have a handier number to work with, the result is multiplied by 1,000. Thus, we speak of the number of births in a population in a given year for each 1,000 women aged 15 to 44 years. By contrasting the fertility rates of 1800 (55 births per 1,000) and 1970 (18.4 births per 1,000), we see that the birth rate in the United States has declined sharply.

Another measure of fertility computes the number of live births to the average female in a society. In 1800, the average woman bore slightly more than seven children during her lifetime. The average woman in 1984 will bear fewer than two children (1.7) during her lifetime. (Of course, no mother ever really has 7.3 or 1.7 children. These are simply averages.)

Just as not all members of a society can reproduce, not all members of a society are equally likely to contribute to the death rate in a given year. It is very important to know who is and who is not contributing to the death rate. The *crude death rate* does not reflect these subtleties; it is simply the number of deaths per 1,000 in the general population. Demographers are mainly interested in **age-specific death rates.** These are computed by separating the population by age categories and computing the number of deaths per 1,000 of each age group.

Obviously, everyone dies. However, when people die greatly affects future population growth—and virtually every aspect of society. A comparison of crude death rates tells us that in 1900 nearly twice as many Americans per 1,000 (17.2) died as in 1970 (9.5). However, an examination of age-specific death rates reveals that a massive shift occurred in the age at which people died. In 1900, 162.4 infants (aged 1 year and younger) per 1,000 died. In 1970, only about an eighth as many infants (21.4 per 1,000)

In the eyes of his proud father, this baby boy is the newest member of the family. In the eyes of the neighbors, he is the newest resident of the village. In the eyes of the British census department, he is another member of the birth cohort made up of all infants born in Wales that year.

died. Furthermore, in 1900, 19.8 out of every 1,000 children age 1 to 4 died, whereas in 1970 less than one (0.8) per 1,000 of these children died. In 1900, the birth rate was much higher than in 1970; however, as we have seen, far fewer of those born grew up to reproduce. Therefore, the birth of 1,000 infants had less of a long-range impact on the population in 1900 than it does today.

Demographers concern themselves with a great many other rates. You have already seen a number of these in previous chapters. For example, we have discussed crime rates, marriage rates, divorce rates, disease rates, illegitimacy rates, and so on. All of these are constructed in the same way as fertility and death rates. Crude rates are based on units of 1,000 (or sometimes 10,000) persons in the total population. Other rates are specific to certain relevant groups within the population. For example, the crude rape victimization rate was 10.1 per 10,000 Americans in 1979. However, the specific rates for women 20 to 24 were 63.3 for whites and 99.2 for blacks.

Cohorts

One of the main uses of demographic data is to provide a basis for long-term planning. A government may project future conditions by saying, "If the present birth rate holds steady, then we will have a population twice as large thirty years from now. We must make provisions to house, employ, and feed these additional people." A very important unit in such planning is the birth cohort, or age cohort. A **birth cohort** consists of all of the persons born in a given time period, usually one year. The interesting feature of cohorts is that although they may get smaller as time passes, they never get any larger. At the end of 1984, there will be no more people born in that year. Therefore, if we know the number of persons included in the 1984 birth cohort, and if we have accurate age-specific death rates for our population, then we can predict the size of that cohort as it passes through all the stages of life, from infancy to old age. For example, by subtracting the figure based on mortality expected by age 6, we know the total number of children who will be entering first grade in 1990. Our society thus has some time to adjust the number of classrooms and teachers accordingly. Likewise, by subtracting the figure based on the probable mortality between birth and 18 years, we know how many 18-year-olds there will be in 2002. If we can predict what percentage of these people will choose to attend college, we can predict the size of the freshman class of 2002 at the end of 1984.

When fertility and mortality abruptly shift, governments often become obsessed with the future implications of a birth cohort. For example, the fact that the size of a cohort cannot be increased caused grave concern among French military planners. In 1870 France was totally defeated by Germany. For the next forty years, the French were determined to gain revenge. But while France and Germany had

French troops rushing to take part in the great battle at the Marne River where the German invasion was halted in 1914. Although the French eventually were on the winning side, their losses in World War I resulted in tiny birth cohorts for the next generation.

approximately the same-sized populations in 1870, Germany had 65 million to France's 40 million by 1914. In part this came about because Germany annexed new territory during this period. But in part it was because France had a lower—and declining—birth rate.

Thus, where it mattered, in the age cohorts of males suitable for military service, the Germans had nearly twice the number as France in 1914 (7.7 million to 4.5 million). According to Shirer (1969), "Gloomy prophets in Paris did not see how France could escape another military debacle if the Germans chose to attack again." In 1914 the Germans did attack and just failed to win the war in the first six weeks. Finally, in 1918, the Germans were

defeated, but only because millions of Russian, British, and American troops came to the support of France.

From a demographer's point of view, France's revenge on Germany for having been defeated in 1870 was gained at dire future cost. Of French men between 18 and 28, three of every ten died in the war and did not make their expected contribution to future fertility. More than a million more came home from war badly maimed and disabled and also did not reproduce to the extent they might have. In addition, there were at least 1,400,000 fewer births between 1915 and 1919 in France than there would have been had the young men not been off in the trenches. Thus in 1933, when the birth cohort of 1915 was old enough for military service, nearly half a million potential new soldiers came of age in Germany, while fewer than 190,000 did so in France. Worse yet, the depressed level of the number born during World War I led to a depressed number of women of child-bearing age in the 1930s. Thus, it was clear that Frenchmen of military age would be in even shorter relative supply by the late 1940s. Furthermore, the French fertility rate continued to drop throughout the 1920s and 1930s, while the German rate stayed high. In terms of potential manpower, France faced an ever-deteriorating military disadvantage with Germany.

In 1940 the Germans attacked again, and this time they did win in the first six weeks. The small French birth cohorts of 1915 to 1922 were overwhelmed as French military planners had long feared and as German military planners had anticipated for years.

Age and sex structures

Thus, small birth cohorts occurring in France had two major effects on population size. First, they were too small to replace their parents' cohorts, and the size of the population declined as older cohorts died. Second, when these smaller cohorts reached reproductive age they produced fewer children than a larger cohort would have.

Figure 17-1 / Population structures.

(a) Expansive population structure, with fertility of four children per couple. (b) Stationary population structure, with fertility of two children per couple. (c) Constrictive population structure, with fertility of one child per couple.

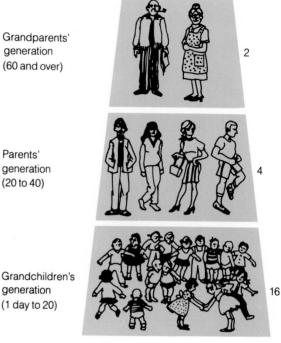

Grandparents' generation (60 and over)   2

Parents' generation (20 to 40)   4

Grandchildren's generation (1 day to 20)   16

a

This limit on population size directs our attention to another important demographic factor: the distribution of people of various ages and sexes within a population. Obviously, a population in which the majority are elderly or are males has a far lower potential for growth than a population in which the majority are females of reproductive age. Therefore, to predict future trends in a population, it is necessary to know not only fertility and mortality rates but also the **age structure** and **sex structure** (or distribution) of that population.

Normally, populations fall into one of three age and sex structures. These are depicted in Figure 17-1. The first structure is an **expansive population structure** and is characteristic of present populations in underdeveloped nations. The expansive structure is shaped like a pyramid—each younger cohort is progressively larger. Such a population grows very rapidly. At any given moment, there are many more people who have not yet begun to reproduce than there are who have. This situation has serious implications for growth, even if fertility suddenly falls. For even if couples suddenly limit

their families to only enough children to replace themselves, the population will continue to grow until each of the increasingly larger, younger cohorts has gone through the ages of reproduction.

That is what is causing population growth today in the United States and many other industrialized nations. Fertility in these nations has fallen to levels that will eventually cause a population decline, but the population continues to grow while the massive birth cohorts of the post–World War II "baby boom" pass through their reproductive years. Growth will not stop until the relatively smaller birth cohorts of the 1960s and 1970s take over reproduction. When that happens, the age and sex structure of the United States may resemble the **stationary population structure** shown in Figure 17-1. The base of this structure is in proportion to other cohorts. Thus, there are only enough infants and children to make up for early mortality, and each cohort entering the reproductive period is the same size as previous cohorts. Therefore, the population does not grow.

Finally, the third drawing depicts a **constrictive**

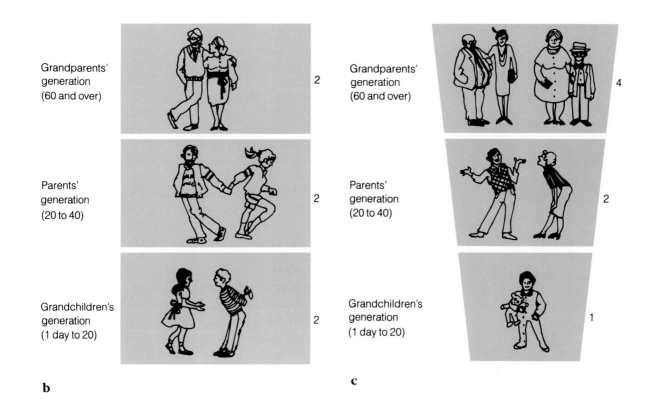

Grandparents' generation (60 and over)		2	Grandparents' generation (60 and over)		4
Parents' generation (20 to 40)		2	Parents' generation (20 to 40)		2
Grandchildren's generation (1 day to 20)		2	Grandchildren's generation (1 day to 20)		1

b

c

population structure. The bottom of this structure is smaller than the middle, indicating that in the future fewer people will enter reproductive ages. Such a structure reflects a declining population.

Armed with these elementary demographic concepts, we can now examine the history of human population trends.

PREINDUSTRIAL POPULATION TRENDS

Primitive societies often had a very difficult time maintaining their populations. Women had to bear many children in order to make sure that several would survive to have children of their own. Historians believe that, in primitive groups, about 50 percent of all children died before the age of 5 (Petersen, 1975). For over several million years, the human population of the earth grew so slowly that only a few more people were added every 100,000

years. Kingsley Davis (1976) estimates that only 10,000 years ago, after at least 3 million years of human reproduction, there were only about 5 million human beings on the face of the earth, a figure about equal to the population of Chicago. For most of human existence, we were an endangered species.

But then came the first great shift in human population trends: Beginning about 10,000 years ago we began to increase our numbers rapidly. This was caused by the development of agriculture. As humans ceased being nomadic hunters and gatherers and settled in one place to grow crops, life became more secure. There was a lot more food, and it was regularly available. With a better diet, we became healthier, and our reproductive rates finally began to outstrip death rates. More babies lived to maturity, and the population began to grow more rapidly. Davis (1976) estimates that 8,000 years later, by the year 1 A.D., the worldwide human population was about 300 million. That means 296 million more people (or 50 times as many) had been added in 8,000 years than had been amassed over the previous several million years. (In the past 2,000 years,

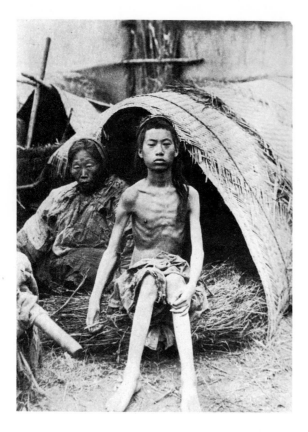

A famine victim in China's Honan Province at the turn of the century. Famine was a chronic cause of high mortality rates in China for more than 2,000 years and struck again in the 1960s when the Cultural Revolution disrupted farming and food distribution.

the population has increased by more than 1,300 times, to a world total of more than 4 billion.)

Nevertheless, although the human population began to grow rapidly, growth was not continuous. The population trends of agrarian societies fluctuated, as rapid growth was followed by rapid decline. By 1700, the world population was only about twice as large as it had been in the year 1 A.D. What caused these periodic declines in the population? A sudden increase in the death rate. Every so often, human populations were laid waste by famine, disease, or war.

Famine

Though the invention of agriculture permitted a rapid increase in the human population, agrarian societies were extremely vulnerable to crop failures caused by drought, storms, or blight (plant disease). Famine could cause an immense number of deaths directly through starvation and indirectly through undernourishment, making people more vulnerable to disease. Europe suffered from severe periodic famines through the last century. Often these famines were confined to one country or to one section of a country, but they sometimes affected most of the continent, as they did from 1315 to 1317, in the 1690s, and again from 1708 to 1709 (Petersen, 1975). Mortality rates soared and the population was seriously reduced. The last great famine in Europe took place when blight destroyed the potato crops in Ireland in 1845. As Chapter 2 pointed out, millions of Irish immigrants fled to the United States to escape starvation, but perhaps a million others, unable to flee, died as a result of the blight.

Nevertheless, Europe was much less vulnerable than Asia to this cause of widespread death. In part, this may have been because European agriculture was less productive. In good times, European agriculture could not support great population growth; therefore, in bad times there were fewer people in danger of starvation. Asian farming, on the other hand, was very efficient but was vulnerable to the highly variable and unpredictable monsoon rains. Asia suffered more than Europe from severe droughts but had more plentiful crops between droughts. Famine was chronic in Asia (Petersen, 1975), and Mallory (1926) found that a serious famine has been recorded in some part of China almost yearly for the past 2,000 years.

Petersen (1975) reported on one of China's more recent and severe famines:

One of the worst famines of modern China struck four northern provinces in 1877–78. Communications were so poor that almost a year passed before news of it reached the capital. Cannibalism was common, and local magistrates were ordered "to connive at the evasion of laws prohibiting the sale of children, so as to enable parents to buy a few days' food." The dead were buried in what are still today called "ten-thousand-men holes." From 9 to 13 million, according to the estimate of the Foreign Relief Committee, perished.

Similarly, Davis (1951) calculated an immense loss of life due to famine in India during the 1890s by contrasting the rates of population increase for several decades:

In the previous decade [India's population] grew 9.4 percent, and in the following decade 6.1 percent. If the 1891–1901 decade had experienced the average rate of growth shown by these two decades, it would have grown by 7.8 percent instead of 1 percent. The difference is a matter of some 19 million persons, which may be taken as a rough estimate of loss due to famines.

Davis also pointed out that a great deal of food was shipped to India to help overcome the famine. If this famine had occurred in premodern times, millions more would have died.

Disease

A second major cause of a sudden rise in mortality is the outbreak of deadly, contagious diseases. One of the worst was bubonic plague, known as the Black Death, which often thinned the populations of agrarian societies in Europe and Asia. The worst outbreak began in Constantinople (today known as Istanbul, Turkey) in A.D. 1334. In less than twenty years, the Black Death mowed down millions in Europe and Asia; some estimates of plague deaths run as high as 40 percent of the total population of Europe and Asia (see Figure 17-2). After the plague, thousands of villages in Europe and Asia stood completely uninhabited and were never resettled (McNeill, 1976).

Smallpox was another epidemic killer. In 1707, 31 percent of the population of Iceland died of smallpox. Shortly after the first Spanish expedition reached the New World, smallpox and measles epidemics wiped out as many as three-fourths of the inhabitants of Mexico and the West Indies (McNeill, 1976).

This drawing is from a manuscript published by Henri de Mondeville in 1314, the first book on human anatomy that was based on actual dissections. Lacking such research, physicians could make little progress in understanding disease, since they had virtually no knowledge of how the body functioned.

War

Throughout recorded history, innumerable societies have been ravaged and even destroyed by war. A case in point is the Thirty Years' War, which embroiled the nations of northern Europe from 1618 to 1648. The war was fought partly as a result of the Protestant Reformation, and religious antagonisms made it especially savage. By the end of the struggle, only 6,000 of 35,000 peasant villages survived in Germany, and an estimated 8 million Germans had perished (Montgomery, 1968). An even more dev-

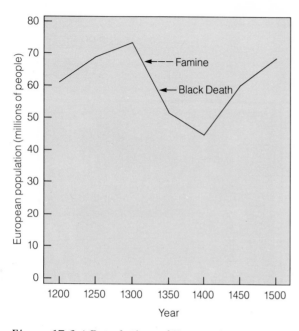

Figure 17-2 / Population of Europe, A.D. 1200–1500.

Famine and plague reduced Europe's population by nearly 40 percent from A.D. 1300 to 1400. (Source: M. K. Bennet, in Douglas C. North and Robert Paul Thomas, The Rise of the Western World: A New Economic History. *New York: Cambridge University Press, 1973.)*

Thomas Malthus.

astating war was the Taiping Rebellion in China (1851–1864), in which prisoners were slaughtered and farms were burned (Ho, 1959). In one area of 6,000 square miles, no trace of human life remained. Earlier estimates that 20 to 30 million people were killed are now considered too low! A century later the populations in the four provinces that fought the war were estimated to be still 14 percent below the number living there when the fighting began (Petersen, 1975).

MALTHUSIAN THEORY

At the end of the eighteenth century, modern social science was born with the publication in 1776 of

Adam Smith's economic treatise, *An Inquiry into the Nature and Causes of the Wealth of Nations*. This book not only was the start of economics but also led to the first demographic theory. In attempting to account for economic changes, Smith found it necessary to consider population patterns. This led him to a famous proposition: "Men, like all other animals, naturally multiply in proportion to the means of their subsistence." In other words, human populations grow or decline according to the availability of the necessities of life, especially food. A century later, Charles Darwin adopted this proposition of Smith's to help formulate the theory of evolution. Long before then, however, Smith's proposition prompted Thomas Robert Malthus to construct the first theory of population change.

Malthus was born in 1766, and, like Smith, he was a Scot educated in England. At 22, he became a clergyman in order to realize "the utmost of my wishes, a retired living in the country." However, he soon became fascinated with Smith's economic theories, especially in using them to explain the growth and decline of human populations. In 1798, he published a short book, *Essay on the Principle*

My grandfather may have been a member of this crew threshing wheat in North Dakota's Red River Valley in the 1880s. Although the crew is very large and the machinery antiquated compared with modern harvesting methods, these men were able to produce food at a level their own grandfathers would have found unbelievable. The result of the early industrialization of agriculture was a population explosion in Europe and North America.

activation of the positive checks of famine, disease, and war, just as Malthus had postulated. But even as Malthus was writing, the second great shift in population trends was under way, which seemed to defy Malthusian theory. The Industrial Revolution was taking place. It was accompanied by extraordinary population growth in Western nations without activating the positive checks predicted by Malthus. A new optimism grew. Most people began to believe that by mastering technology humans could overcome the forces of fertility and mortality. Soon many social scientists considered Malthus's views outdated and pessimistic.

MODERNIZATION AND POPULATION

To most people, the phrase "Industrial Revolution" suggests machines and factories. But the Industrial Revolution first affected agriculture. Indeed, the age of the factory and the growth of large, urban industrial cities were possible only because of the modernization of agriculture. Recall from Chapter 10 that in agrarian societies about 95 percent of the labor force is needed on the farms in order to grow enough food. Today, although fewer than 4 percent of Americans farm, they grow enough food not only to feed all the rest of us but also to make the United States by far the largest exporter of food in the world. As we shall examine in Chapter 18, the industrialization of agriculture caused this dramatic change. With machines replacing draft animals and hand labor, better plant and animal varieties, new techniques of crop rotation and field design, and the use of chemical fertilizers, food production soared. As Malthus would have predicted, so did the population.

In England, where the Industrial Revolution began, the population was three times larger by 1841 than it had been in 1700. As modernization spread across northwestern Europe, so did rapid population growth. In 1650, Europeans (including those living overseas) made up 18 percent of the world's population. In 1920, they made up 35 percent (Davis, 1971).

This growth was possible only because there was enough food. Indeed, the specter of famine suddenly disappeared from Europe: People began to eat far better despite there being millions more mouths to feed. This is demonstrated by the virtual disappearance of nutritional-deficiency diseases as causes of death in western Europe. Scurvy, a dread disease produced by a lack of vitamin C, was once a major cause of death. In less than a century, it became so rare that in 1830 a leading English physician failed to recognize its symptoms (Drummond and Wilbraham, 1957). Indeed, as we saw in Chapter 5, the improved diets resulting from modernized agriculture caused a revolution in the patterns of human growth and maturation in modern societies.

In addition to providing much more food, modernization resulted in more effective protection against disease. Public health measures caused the mortality rate to drop rapidly. Vaccination and inoculation campaigns prevented huge numbers of deaths, especially among children. For centuries, smallpox was a dreaded killer. In 1980 World Health Organization officials announced it no longer existed on earth. Of perhaps even greater importance were modern sanitation measures. Sewers, sewage treatment, and the availability of safe drinking water saved huge numbers of lives (as we shall see in Chapter 18).

Thus, the increase in food and sanitation measures greatly reduced mortality. As a result, during the eighteenth and nineteenth centuries, the population grew so large and so fast that we now speak of this as the first population explosion.

In the wake of these changes, many began to regard Malthusian theory as outdated. Modernization seemed to have given societies the capacity for unlimited growth, since food supplies could expand as quickly as population grew. However, others suspected that modernization had simply postponed the day of reckoning, when Malthus's positive checks would again strike. Before this proposition could be tested, however, a third great shift in human population trends occurred. And this shift seemed to discredit the Malthusian theory once and for all.

THE DEMOGRAPHIC TRANSITION

According to Malthus, population size is determined by fluctuations in mortality, since human fertility always remains high. This seemed to fit the patterns of population growth and decline observed up to Malthus's time. In the beginning, the Industrial Revolution affected mortality almost exclusively. Increased food supplies and the conquest of many diseases caused mortality to fall and therefore the population to grow. But then what Malthus said would not happen began to happen: Fertility began to decline in the more modernized nations.

We have seen that the population of England tripled between 1700 and 1841. Growth continued for a few more decades but at an increasingly slower rate, until by 1930 the population stabilized. However, growth was not halted by increased mortality. Instead, as mortality continued to decline, fertility also began to decline in the 1860s. Growth ceased by the 1930s because fertility no longer exceeded mortality.

Table 17-1 shows this fertility decline in the United States. As you can see from the table, fertility in the United States has been falling since 1820 and by 1940 was below replacement level. This pattern was briefly reversed by the post–World War II "baby boom," but by the mid 1960s fertility had dropped back to prewar levels. Like women in other modernized nations, the average American woman began in the 1820s to have fewer children each decade until replacement-level fertility (or less) had been reached. **Replacement-level fertility** occurs when the number of births each year equals the number of deaths. In the most modern societies, replacement fertility occurs when the average woman has only slightly more than two children—one to replace herself, one to replace her husband, and a slight excess to make up for infant mortality. Replacement-level fertility produces **zero population growth** as soon as the age structure has adjusted.

Most industrialized nations achieved replacement-level fertility rates by the 1930s. Then, after World War II, population stability was upset by a brief baby boom (see Special Topic 6). However, fertility soon began to drop once more, and by the late 1960s it was down to replacement level. The population will continue to grow for a few years more, as the baby boom goes through the reproductive age.

Nevertheless, modern nations have undergone a radical change in population patterns described as the **demographic transition.** This transition involves a change from the age-old pattern of high fertility and high but variable mortality to a new pattern of low mortality and fertility. The demographic transition seemed to prove that Malthus's theory of population was no longer valid: In the modern world people did control their fertility and thus averted the suffering that occurs when population size is determined wholly by mortality.

Table 17-1 / Crude annual birth rate per 1,000 population, United States, 1820–1980.

Year	Birth rate per 1,000	
1820	55.2	
1840	51.8	
1860	44.3	
1880	39.8	
1900	32.3	
1910	30.1	
1920	27.7	
1930	21.3	
1940	19.4	
1945	20.4	
1950	24.1	Baby boom
1955	25.0	
1960	23.7	
1965	19.4	
1970	18.4	
1980	15.8	

Source: U.S. Census.

KINGSLEY DAVIS: DEMOGRAPHIC TRANSITION THEORY

 Why had this happened? How had modernization led to a decline in fertility? In 1945, Kingsley Davis, one of the most important American sociologists (and my most formidable and stimulating teacher), proposed a theory of the demographic transition. Acknowledging that Malthus's theory still seemed applicable to less modern parts of the world, Davis attempted to isolate those aspects of modernization that Malthus had not anticipated.

Davis argued that modernization naturally leads to life conditions encouraging low fertility. People in modern societies had fewer children because they no longer wanted large families. One reason was that with mortality so greatly reduced, especially infant and childhood mortality, families no longer needed to have many children in order to ensure that some lived to adulthood. Second, the economic value of children had declined. In fact, children ceased to become an economic asset and became an economic burden.

On preindustrial farms and even in preindustrial crafts and manufacture, child labor is valuable. For example, even small children on preindustrial farms can more than earn their keep by feeding chickens, gathering eggs, herding animals, milking, pulling weeds, and helping with household chores. Under such circumstances, larger families tend to be wealthier than smaller families. But, as we shall examine in detail in the next chapter, a major aspect of modernization was a shift of population from farms to cities. In cities, the labor of children is of much

Children were an economic benefit on preindustrial farms: This New England farmer would have had a difficult time plowing with his ox team without his son to walk in front and goad the oxen. Although this picture was taken in 1899, long after the picture of harvesting in North Dakota, the farming methods in use are preindustrial. New technology was adopted much sooner in the frontier regions of the Great Plains than in the long-settled Northeast.

less value than on a farm. In fact, city kids are a financial drain.

Drawing on the choice premise that is basic to all social science, Davis argued that as large families became a cost rather than a benefit, people changed their conceptions about how many children they wanted. His stress on choice is important, because the great reduction in fertility in modern times occurred before most modern birth control devices were invented.

Indeed, anthropologists have found that tech-

niques for limiting fertility are known and often practiced in even very primitive societies (Ford, 1952; Harris, 1979). Moreover, historical demographers have learned that Malthus was simply wrong in his belief that humans never restricted their fertility. Throughout European history, long before the Industrial Revolution, fertility was greatly controlled whenever conditions made reduced fertility a reasonable course of action. For example, fertility often fell during economic depressions (Simon, 1981). Thus, the demographic transition did not reflect new contraceptive technology, but new conditions that influenced what people chose to do.

As outlined by Davis, the initial consequence of modernization is a sudden drop in mortality, which causes rapid population growth. This is because there is a delay before fertility begins to drop. The shifts from rural to urban living and from unskilled to skilled labor must also occur before the conditions that depress fertility prevail.

Davis's **demographic transition theory** has been subjected to a great deal of refinement and testing in the forty years since it was first published. In the current form of the theory, demographers have included a number of "thresholds" of modernization that must be crossed before fertility is substantially reduced.

A recent listing of these thresholds (Berelson, 1978) helps clarify the theory:

1. More than half of the labor force is not employed in agriculture.

2. More than half of the persons from age 5 to 19 are enrolled in school.

3. The average life expectancy reaches 60 years.

4. Infant mortality falls to 65 deaths per 1,000 infants.

5. Eighty percent of females from age 15 to 19 are not married.

6. Per capita gross national product reaches $450.

7. At least 70 percent of adults can read.

Berelson suggests that these are not precise rules and that each threshold need not be met for a nation to undergo the demographic transition. Rather, meeting any three or four of these criteria will cause a fertility reduction. Nevertheless, each threshold indicates a major aspect of modernization. Unfortunately, some nations on earth fall quite short of crossing these thresholds.

This fact has troubled demographers and produced doomsday predictions about a "population bomb." Many dire predictions have been highly publicized during the past twenty years, each claiming that a huge new population explosion may soon reactivate Malthus's positive checks. Although many nations have failed to become sufficiently modernized to reduce their fertility, they have become modernized enough to reduce their mortality. Indeed, just about the same time that Davis published his theory, the fourth great shift in population trends occurred: massive, unprecedented population growth in the less developed nations.

THE SECOND POPULATION EXPLOSION

As we have just seen, the first population explosion occurred in Europe and North America as a result of modernization. The industrialization of agriculture and advances in public health reduced mortality. Eventually, however, rapid population growth was halted by a decline in fertility. While the demographic transition changed basic population patterns in the modern nations, preindustrial population patterns persisted in the rest of the world: high fertility checked by high mortality. Then, suddenly, mortality quickly fell in less developed nations, thus initiating the greatest population explosion in history.

Shortly after the end of World War II, demographers noticed rapid population growth nearly everywhere on earth. Growth soon halted in the most modern nations, but elsewhere growth rates continued to rocket. Throughout the 1950s and 1960s, the population in most of the less developed nations grew by rates of from 2 to 3.5 percent a year. Such rates mean that populations double in size every twenty to thirty-five years. Thus, populations can increase enormously in a short time. For example, in the early 1970s, the world's population was growing at a rate that would double its size every thirty-seven years. If that rate were to hold for only 200 years, then instead of fewer than 5 billion people on earth, as there are now, there would be 157 billion!

Understandably, these population projections frightened demographers, as well as a lot of other people, and world population patterns received widespread publicity. For example, people were shocked when demographers pointed out that if Mexico continued to grow at the rate maintained during the thirty years following World War II, its population would increase from 63 million to 2 billion by the year 2080. Obviously, long before 2 billion people lived in Mexico, disaster would strike—if nothing else, massive starvation would set in.

In the wake of the second population explosion, predictions of world calamity received great publicity. Oddly enough, some of the most obviously faulty projections attracted the greatest attention and acceptance. For example, a small book called *The Limits to Growth* (Meadows et al., 1972), which predicted that the world would run out of most raw materials and food in only a few years, sold over 4 million copies, despite its arguments having been dismissed as incompetent in virtually every scientific periodical (see Simon, 1981).

Still, very competent demographers and economists were influenced by the widespread anxiety about rapid population growth and warned of impending calamity. I confess that I joined in this dismal chorus. In a textbook on social problems I published in 1975, I ended the chapter on population by telling students that they would be hearing of terrible famines in the underdeveloped nations for the rest of their lives. That will not be the message of this chapter. Apparently Western social scientists forgot something important: Populations do not have babies—only people have babies. And people turn out to be a lot smarter than we sometimes assume. So, let's examine the population explosion in the less developed nations to see why and how it occurred and how people have recently responded to it.

The sudden decline in mortality

Whereas the brief **baby boom** in Western nations after World War II was caused by a rise in fertility, the population explosion in the less developed nations was not. There, fertility had always been high. The population explosion was caused by a sudden and dramatic plunge in the mortality rate.

The most important feature of this decline in mortality is that it was not produced primarily by internal changes in these nations but by external forces. That is, low mortality resulted from a few elements of modern technology imported from developed nations. Thus, while the decline in mortality experienced in the West had developed slowly, in the less developed nations it came suddenly and often without significant changes in other parts of these societies. The result was a period of extreme cultural lag, as we shall see.

To grasp just how the second population explosion took place, consider the case of a single nation. At the end of World War II, Sri Lanka (then known as Ceylon) had a very high mortality rate typical of agrarian societies in warm latitudes. The average life expectancy was only 43 years, and the crude death rate in 1945 was about 22 deaths per 1,000.

Then, in 1946, the World Health Organization provided a small sum of money that Sri Lanka used to buy DDT from Switzerland and to hire some free-lance pilots with surplus U.S. Army planes to spray the country. Thus, in the most literal sense, a modern, low mortality rate fell upon Sri Lanka from the sky. Disease-carrying insects, especially the dreaded malaria-carrying mosquitoes, were nearly wiped out in a few days.

As a result, Sri Lanka's mortality rate fell by more than 40 percent within a few months. Understandably, everyone in Sri Lanka thought it was wonderful to have greatly increased life expectancy. Since this program could be continued simply and cheaply, it was continued. By 1954, Sri Lanka's crude death rate had fallen to about 10 per 1,000 per year. By 1975, it was down to 7.7—a rate lower than that of most modernized nations (partly due to its very young population). As a result of its reduced mortality, Sri Lanka's population began to grow very rapidly.

In other less developed nations, similar changes took place: Insects were sprayed, swamps and stagnant pools of water were drained where insects bred, populations were inoculated against dangerous communicable diseases such as smallpox, and safe drinking water was provided. Everywhere the mortality rate plunged. From 1940 to 1965, the mortality rate fell by 59 percent in Mexico, 63 percent in Puerto Rico, 44 percent in Egypt, and 72 percent in Taiwan.

But something besides imported public health technology was involved in the second population explosion: the modernization of agriculture. Modern chemistry provides not only insect killers, but also weed killers and fertilizers. Agricultural biologists have made rapid progress in breeding faster-

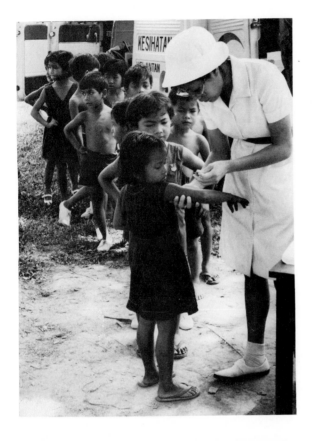

A generation ago many of these children would already have been dead and others would have died before reaching adulthood. The introduction of modern sanitation and public health measures into the less developed world, during and just after World War II, caused a dramatic decline in death rates—and produced the second great population explosion.

growing, disease-resistant, higher-yielding varieties of basic food plants. The less developed nations also imported these plants, along with farm machinery and modern irrigation techniques. Thus, the food supply increased in all parts of the world. Indeed, despite the rapid growth of population, food production increased even more rapidly; today people in most nations eat more and better food than they did twenty years ago (see Table 17-2). This, too, reduced mortality.

Table 17-2 / Index of world food production per capita (1948–1952 = 100).

Year	Index
1950	100
1955	109
1960	115
1965	116
1970	123
1975	126
1979	137

Source: United Nations data. Simon, 1981.

High fertility and cultural lag

The demographic transition theory suggests that the long-term effect of modernization is population stability: eventually fertility will balance out with mortality. The question posed about the population explosion in the less developed nations is whether they will have the time to pass through the demographic transition before their populations become so huge that mass starvation results.

The demographic transition in the West was gradual, based on broad internal social changes, and the first population explosion was slow compared with the second. In the West, infant mortality fell slowly for a number of generations, and people had a long time to adjust to the changed conditions. So a gradual downward trend in fertility was sufficient to prevent catastrophic rates of growth. Some people argue that mortality has fallen so fast in the less developed nations that people have had no time to adjust. Age-old customs favoring high fertility are necessarily slow to change, but unless they change very rapidly, runaway population growth will overwhelm these nations.

This resultant cultural lag has been the focus of the grave anxieties about the second population explosion. Indeed, hundreds of millions of dollars have been spent to popularize family planning and to reduce fertility in the less developed nations. However, for a long time, it looked as if these programs would fail and that fertility would not be

The cultural gap responsible for the population explosion in the less developed world is symbolized by these boats belonging to a remote tribe of Indians in Mexico. When modern levels of mortality were combined with preindustrial levels of fertility, the future of these societies was placed in jeopardy. When powerful modern outboard motors were combined with primitive wooden boats, the future of the passengers was placed in jeopardy.

checked in time. Indeed, this prompted not only projections of disaster but also the frequent depiction of people in the less developed nations as virtual animals, incapable of reasonable behavior. For example, William Vogt (1948), in the first best-selling book on the population explosion, blamed it on "untrammeled copulation" by people in the less developed nations, whom he characterized as the "backward billion." Many others asserted that fertility in these less developed nations was outside the realm of decision making (Simon, 1981).

Amidst all this hue and cry, people in many of the less developed countries began to respond reasonably to their new conditions of life. The cultural lag began to be reduced. As happened in the modernized nations, fertility began to decline in most of the less developed nations. Thus, the fifth great shift in population patterns began to develop.

THE POPULATION EXPLOSION WANES

By the early 1970s, leading demographers began to detect a fertility decline in the less developed nations. At first the downturns seemed slight, and for a while no one was willing to announce a significant new trend. Moreover, projections were difficult because population statistics for many of the less developed nations are unreliable.

However, as time passed and more statistics came in, it became clear that very substantial fertility declines were taking place in most of the less developed nations where population growth had been exploding. In fact, fertility began to go down in most of these countries at the very height of the population explosion scare in the West—in the latter part of the 1960s.

For example, between 1965 and 1975, India's crude birth rate fell by 16 percent, China's by 24 percent, South Korea's by 32 percent, Colombia's by 25 percent, Malaysia's by 26 percent, and Sri Lanka's by 18 percent. Declines at least as great are predicted for the period from 1975 to 1985, although the figures will probably not become available until around 1990 (Berelson, 1978).

The fertility rate has not yet fallen in every less developed nation, but substantial declines have occurred in most, particularly those with the largest populations. Countries where fertility has not fallen have only 16 percent of the total population of the less developed nations.

Keep in mind that populations that have been growing rapidly will still continue to grow even after their fertility has fallen to replacement level. This is because in quickly growing populations, each new birth cohort is larger than the one before it. Thus, even when fertility falls to replacement level, the largest age cohorts have yet to pass through their reproductive years, and even if they only replace themselves, the population will increase further.

Nevertheless, the sudden plunge in fertility that has already occurred invalidates the projections of huge world population totals that were considered nearly certain only a few years ago. We still cannot be sure how large the world's population will become or that overpopulation problems have been wholly averted. Indeed, some nations are likely to experience severe problems caused by overpopulation. Nonetheless, there has been a dramatic improvement in the overall picture. To conclude this chapter, let us examine this picture in greater detail.

BERNARD BERELSON: STABILITY BY THE YEAR 2000?

Perhaps no demographer has paid closer attention to population trends and efforts to reduce fertility in the less developed nations than Bernard Berelson, who for many years served as president of the Population Council, an organization of demographers devoted to international research. Berelson was one of the first to spot the sudden decline in fertility rates in the developing nations and played the major role in assessing just where and why it was taking place. In 1978, when many scholars were still warning that population catastrophe was at hand, Berelson published a major reassessment of future growth.

Berelson concentrated his analysis on the twenty-nine largest less developed nations, each having a population of more than 10 million. The goal of his study was to predict which of these nations would be likely to reduce their annual crude birth rate to 20 per 1,000 by the year 2000. A crude birth rate of 20 translates into approximately 2.5 births per adult female. Given the probable infant and child mortality in these nations, this birth rate would be close to replacement-level fertility; at most, this would produce very little population growth.

Berelson found that the population patterns and modernization rates divided these nations into four categories. First were three nations that seemed "certain" to achieve a crude birth rate of 20 by the year 2000 and probably much sooner: South Korea, Taiwan, and Chile. Next were ten nations for whom it seemed "probable" that the crude birth rate would fall to 20 by the end of the century: China, Brazil, Mexico, Philippines, Thailand, Turkey, Colombia, Sri Lanka, Venezuela, Malaysia.

Berelson rated India, Indonesia, Egypt, and Peru as "possible." Finally, twelve nations seemed "unlikely" to succeed in bringing their fertility that low by the year 2000: Bangladesh, Pakistan, Nigeria, Iran, Zaire, Afghanistan, Sudan, Morocco, Algeria, Tanzania, Kenya, and Nepal. Fortunately, these twelve nations make up only 16 percent of the total population of the 29 nations. Unfortunately, they are concentrated on the continent of Africa and thus lack close neighbors who could give them aid.

Why have some of these nations been so much more successful than others in reducing fertility? The answer lies in the demographic transition theory. Recall that the reduced fertility of the West is the result of modernization: Modern conditions of life discourage high levels of fertility.

We also saw that demographers (especially Berelson) had made the demographic transition theory more precise by stating a set of thresholds of modernization that marked when fertility would decline. By the late 1960s and early 1970s, many of these nations had crossed many of the thresholds of modernization, and their fertility suddenly declined as predicted. This further supported the demographic transition theory.

In rating the chances of each of the 29 larger developing nations to control their fertility by the year 2000, Berelson (1978) used the seven thresholds of modernization discussed earlier in this chapter. The nations he rated in the "certain" category have crossed nearly all of the thresholds, as have those in the probable category. Those rated as possible have crossed only a few thresholds but are moving closer to them. The nations rated as unlikely are still well below achieving these thresholds of modernization. Their fertility has not yet begun to decline because they have not yet become sufficiently modernized.

Because the doomsday forecasts of runaway population growth turned out to be wrong does not mean that all our population problems are over. Clearly, the twelve nations in the unlikely category, with a current population total of 383 million, may encounter serious problems. Still, their problems should not be insurmountable with assistance from other countries, since current projections do not indicate the imminent exhaustion of raw materials or food supplies. Indeed, even in many of the nations rated as unlikely to reduce fertility soon, the food

supply has greatly increased (Simon, 1981). Bangladesh, for example, the largest of the unlikely group, has recently increased its agricultural production significantly. And American agriculture remains severely hampered by overproduction despite elaborate government programs to limit planting.

CONCLUSION

There have been five major shifts in human population patterns during the past 10,000 years. The first of these occurred when the invention of agriculture permitted the population to begin to grow rapidly. This period of growth, however, was marked by cycles of growth and decline, as population was periodically cut back by sudden rises in mortality. This led Malthus to formulate a theory of population based entirely on fluctuations in mortality.

But no sooner had Malthus published his book when a second great shift occurred. Industrialization stimulated a long period of uninterrupted growth, sometimes referred to as the first population explosion. After several centuries of rapid population growth in the industrial countries, however, a third great shift occurred—one Malthus had believed impossible. Population was halted by a decline in fertility. This is called the demographic transition, which resulted in stable populations in which low mortality was balanced by low fertility.

In the aftermath of World War II, a fourth population change took place, a population explosion in the less developed nations caused by decreased mortality and increased food supplies. This growth was so rapid that many people predicted a return to Malthusian conditions, in which population growth would be halted by terrible famines. These predictions failed to anticipate the fifth major shift in population patterns: sharply falling fertility in most of the less developed nations as they, too, underwent the demographic transition.

This last shift in population patterns took most scholars, even expert demographers, by surprise. Perhaps the most influential book on population problems was *The Population Bomb,* published in 1968 by Paul Ehrlich, a biologist at Stanford. In it he wrote, "The battle to feed all of humanity is over.

In the 1970s the world will undergo famines—hundreds of millions are going to starve to death." In 1974 the famous novelist and scientist C. P. Snow told the *New York Times,* "Perhaps in ten years, millions of people in the poor countries are going to starve to death before our very eyes. . . . We shall see them doing so upon our television sets."

And in 1975 I wrote in a textbook for college students:

The population explosion is not just someone else's problem. It threatens every nation and every person. There will surely be global famines and mass starvation. . . . For the rest of your life, you will be hearing of terrible famines.

Despite such hysterical predictions, per capita food production continued to increase worldwide, as it had been doing for decades (Simon, 1981). We are now well into the 1980s, and millions have not dropped dead of hunger. Instead, the world has continued to eat even better than in the 1970s. Moreover, the hopeless fertility situation about which we all wrote with such absolute confidence and gloom has already begun to change.

Demographic and economic forecasting is extremely difficult and frequently very wrong. The possibility of error is maximized when current trends are projected into the future without an underlying theory about relationships among these trends. Here we see that much more attention should have been given to demographic transition theory and much less to simple projections of fertility. The less developed nations not only experienced a huge decline in mortality because of modernization but also increased their agricultural production, thus increasing food supplies. In time, modernization began to have the predicted effects on their fertility.

Reactions to the population explosion might have been more subdued had social scientists remembered that at many times in history humans have limited their fertility when necessary. If even primitive tribes have achieved low fertility when they wanted to, we should have suspected that people in nations already somewhat modernized might possess similar abilities. And, of course, they did.

In this chapter, I have tried to explain population trends. However, after all is said and done, the key to understanding population lies in the most basic premise of micro sociology, introduced in Chapter

1. Human behavior is based on choice, and humans choose to do what they believe to be in their own best interests. When mortality is high, the reasonable family will have many children. But when mortality is low and children are not an economic asset, the reasonable family will have fewer children. And that is the fundamental thesis Davis developed in his theory of the demographic transition.

Review glossary

Domesday Book Pronounced "doomsday" book, this was an outstanding medieval census conducted by William the Conqueror following his takeover of England in 1066. (p. 408)

Census A population count, often recorded in terms of categories such as age, sex, occupation, marital status, and the like. The United States Census is conducted during the first year of each decade. (p. 409)

Demography Literally, description of the people; the field of sociology devoted to the study of human populations with regard to how they grow, decline, or migrate. (p. 409)

Growth rate Population gains or losses computed by dividing the net gain or loss for a particular period by the population total at the start of that period. (p. 410)

Crude death rate The total number of deaths for a year (or similar period) divided by the total population that year. (p. 410)

Crude birth rate The total number of births for a year (or similar period) divided by the total population that year. (p. 410)

General fertility rate The total number of births for a year divided by the total number of women in their child-bearing years (the U.S. Census bases this rate on all women from age 15 to 44). (p. 411)

Age-specific death rates The number of deaths per year of persons within a given age range divided by the total number of persons within that age range. (p. 411)

Birth cohort All persons born within a given time period, usually one year. (p. 412)

Age structure The proportions of persons of various age groups making up a total population. (p. 414)

Sex structure The proportions of males and females in a population. (p. 414)

Expansive population structure An age structure in which each younger cohort is larger than the one before it; such a population is growing. (p. 414)

Stationary population structure An age structure in which younger birth cohorts are the same size as older ones were before mortality reduced them; such a population neither grows nor declines. (p. 414)

Constrictive population structure An age structure in which younger cohorts are smaller than the ones before them; such a population is shrinking. (p.414)

Arithmetic increase A constant rate of growth (or decline); the same number of units are added (or subtracted) each cycle, as in 1-2-3-4-5. (p. 419)

Exponential increase A rate of growth (or decline) that speeds up as an increasingly larger number of units is added (or subtracted) each cycle, as in 1-2-4-8-16. (p. 419)

Positive checks According to Malthus, famine, disease, and war—the primary factors that check or stop population growth. (p. 419)

Malthusian theory of population Theory stating that populations will always rise to, and then somewhat above, the limits of subsistence and then will be reduced by the positive checks, only to rise again and be checked again. (p. 420)

Replacement-level fertility (sometimes called **zero population growth**) Point at which the number of births each year equals the number of deaths. (p. 423)

Demographic transition A shift in population trends from high fertility, controlled by high mortality, to one of low mortality and low fertility. (p. 423)

Demographic transition theory Theory stating that the demographic transition was caused by modernization, which reduced the need for and the value of large numbers of children. (p. 425)

Baby boom A brief period of high fertility in many Western industrial nations immediately following World War II. (p. 426)

Suggested readings

Berelson, Bernard. "Prospects and Programs for Fertility Reduction: What? Where?" *Population and Development Review* (1978) 4:579–616.

Davis, Kingsley. "The World Demographic Transition." *Annals of the American Academy of Political and Social Sciences* (1945) 237:1–11.

Petersen, William. *Population.* New York: Macmillan, 1975.

Simon, Julian L. *The Ultimate Resource.* Princeton: Princeton University Press, 1981.

Wrigley, E. A. *Population and History.* New York: McGraw-Hill, 1969.

The Life Cycle
of the Baby Boom

In May 1946, nine months after the surrender of Japan brought World War II to an end, demographers noticed that the number of births in the United States was up that month by 10 percent. The next month fertility continued to rise. By October births were up 50 percent. And by the end of the year an all-time record of 3.4 million babies had been established—one baby had been born every nine seconds.

These statistics were widely publicized and prompted many jokes about returning war veterans. But no one took this surge in fertility very seriously. During 1946 the director of the U.S. Bureau of the Census explained that the U.S. population might climb as high as 163 million by the year 2000, but that the current spurt in the birth rate was a brief and freakish postwar event. Demographers agreed that the American population could never come close to the 200 million mark—for the demographic transition had already taken place, and it was final. Indeed, most of what was written about fertility in 1946 and 1947 was concerned with a fertility deficit that would cause the population to decline rapidly.

How little the experts knew. For the "baby boom" following World War II was not a brief event. The birth rate remained high for almost 20 years—not until 1965 did it drop back to the level of 1940. The unthinkable 200 million mark was passed in 1968.

The baby boom was much more than a set of birth statistics. The reality was that a nation with relatively few infants and children suddenly was filled with them. As high fertility persisted, these huge birth cohorts of infants and young children began to cause major changes in our society. In fact, the baby boom age cohorts, those born between the mid-1940s and the early 1960s (and who are now in their late 20s and 30s) continue to have immense impact on society simply because there are so many of them. Let's retrace the impact of the "baby boomers" on American society and then anticipate their influence on the future.

EARLY DAYS

If academic demographers took a while to grasp the meaning of the rapidly rising fertility rates in the aftermath of the war, American business was not slow to see that radical changes were being wrought in basic consumer market patterns.

Consider the following (Jones, 1980):

- Sales of baby food rose from 270 million cans in 1940 to 1.5 billion in 1953.
- Sales of toys grew from $84 million a year in 1940 to $1.25 billion by the early 1950s.
- Business boomed for companies that bronze-plated baby shoes.
- Diaper sales doubled and redoubled as did sales of washing machines.
- In June 1946, Pocket Books published *The Common Sense Book of Baby and Child Care,* by Benjamin Spock, M.D. Unadvertised, unpromoted, and unreviewed, the 35-cent book sold 4 million copies by 1952 and has now sold well over 30 million copies.

New parents were not only rushing to buy food, clothing, and toys for their infants but also were seeking a comfortable environment in which to raise them: The baby boom accompanied a massive expansion of the suburbs. Between 1950 and 1970 the population of America's suburbs doubled from 36 to 72 million: More than 80 percent of the population growth during this period was located in the suburbs, as were 85 percent of all the homes built then. Suburban life influenced other consumption patterns. It spurred automobile sales by necessitating the two-car family. Sales of lawn furniture and backyard barbecues zoomed, and hotdog sales tripled in the decade of the 1950s.

The average American family, now living in the suburbs with young children, changed its entertainment patterns. Mom and dad no longer went dancing, and the era of Big Bands and popular ballrooms came to a crashing end. Moreover, mom and dad stopped going to movie theaters (and during the 1950s large numbers of huge, luxurious, downtown movie palaces closed their doors). Instead, they loaded the whole family in the station wagon and went to the drive-in. In 1948 there were fewer than 500 drive-in movies in the nation. A decade later there were more than 4000, with everything from playgrounds to laundromats. When they weren't at the drive-in, the baby boom family was beginning to sit in front of a flickering little box in their living rooms and watch television.

The baby boom kids were the first to grow up with television, the first to sing "M-I-C-K-E-Y M-O-U-S-E," the first to, in effect, live in a movie theater. From the very start television has been shaped to an extraordinary extent by and for the baby boomers. Not only was early television inundated with programming for little kids, but the grown-up shows mirrored the lives of the suburban baby boom family: *Ozzie and Harriet, I Love Lucy, Father Knows Best,* and *Leave It to Beaver.*

Then one day the baby boom kids headed off for school. When they got there they found they were unexpected. In 1952–1953 the kids born in 1946–1947 turned six and began first grade—their group was 38 percent larger than the group a year ahead of them! As they passed through the school system, followed by even larger waves of students, they burst the seams of the system. By 1964 one of every four Americans was enrolled in the lower grades or in high school.

Since demographers had claimed, through the first years of this population explosion, that it would be brief and unimportant, provision had not been made to provide space and teachers for these throngs who suddenly showed up at the classroom door. Many schools went to double shift schedules, and

The baby boom cohorts were the first to grow up with television. In the 1950s the puppet Howdy Doody and his friends, Buffalo Bob and Clarabell the clown had the top-rated children's show.

everywhere class sizes were huge. Crash school construction programs began everywhere—during the 1950s, California opened a new school every week. Because they were in such demand, teachers found their salaries rising rapidly.

Looking back, it appears that the schools were not able to cope with the baby boom and that the quality of education that members of these cohorts received probably was seriously inferior to that of people slightly older. In 1964 the first crop of baby boomers graduated from high school and took the Scholastic Aptitude Test (SAT). Their average score was lower than that of the year before. And every year since then the nation's average SAT score has declined.

The growing baby boom kids had a major impact after school too. Their tastes registered in a series of fads (see Chapter 20). For example, in 1955 kids reacted to an episode on the Disneyland TV show, starring Fess Parker as Davy Crockett, and went out to spend more than $100 million in seven months, buying imitation coonskin caps (real coonskin prices jumped up by 3200 percent), toy muzzle-loading rifles, T-shirts, and thousands of other items with a Crockett motif. In 1958 they rushed to buy more than 20 million Hula Hoops in a few months.

THE TEEN BOOM

The baby boom eventually produced crops of teen-agers who continued to cause dislocations and re-arrangements in the world around them. The sales of skin medications skyrocketed. So did record sales: from $182 million in 1954 to $521 million in 1960. With these sales came a dramatic shift in what music was popular and in the range of music performed. Although the baby boomers did not invent rock and roll, they turned it into what was, for over a decade, the *only* popular music—the maturing baby boom-ers had ears for only "their" songs. An immense repertoire of popular songs suddenly disappeared. (This music began to reappear in the early 1980s, often revived by country performers such as Willie Nelson.)

Of course, the baby boomers soon did to col-leges and universities what they had done to the public schools. Never before had so many people attended college. More important, never before had so high a proportion of people attended. Of people 25–34 in 1980, 45 percent had completed at least a year of college, while only a fourth of the people 35 and older had done so. The consequence was a massive increase in the number and the size of col-leges and universities and in the number of faculty members (see Table 15-3).

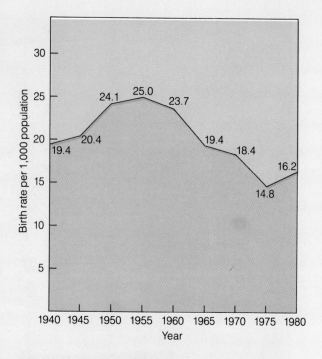

Figure 1 / The baby boom.

The baby boom in the United States is shown in the rise in the crude birth rate—the number of babies per 1,000 population. In 1940, just before World War II, the rate was 19.4. During the war the birth rate rose slightly to 20.4 in 1945. But then it shot upward and stayed high until about 1963. By 1965 it was back at the level of 1940. Throughout the 1970s the birth rate continued to fall, but then it turned upward modestly in 1980 as the baby boom cohorts began to have children.

MOVING ON

Thus far we have looked only at the impact of the front end of the baby boom, but they left important consequences behind them as well. For example, the boom in elementary education turned to a bust in the 1970s as the small birth cohorts behind the baby boom left the nation with far too many schools and teachers. A similar, but less sharp, depression also has hit higher education as large cohorts have been followed by smaller ones. Moreover, since the baby boom, fertility rates have fallen to all-time lows (Figure 1), and baby product manufacturers have struggled to survive in shrunken markets. The amount of children's television programming has declined.

In June 1984 perhaps the most symbolic event in the baby boom's passage through the life cycle came in the announcement by Levi Strauss & Co., that it was shutting eleven manufacturing plants in the United States, laying off 3,200 workers. This brought to twenty-seven the number of plants the company had closed in less than two years. What did these

Table 1 / The baby boomers work out.

	Baby Boomers	People Older Than Baby Boomers
Belong to a health club	17%	8%
Currently in an exercise class	18%	9%
Do garden and lawn work	49%	61%
Take regular walks	56%	56%
Go hunting	14%	10%
Go fishing	29%	26%
Jog regularly	26%	10%
Swim regularly	46%	23%
Bicycle regularly	29%	11%

Adapted from: Brown, 1984.

plants make? The famous Levi's blue jeans. Why did the plants close? Because the baby boomers outgrew the age for wearing blue jeans, according to company officials, and there was a sudden drop in the size of the population 18 to 24 years old, the primary jeans consumers. In the 1960s and early 1970s, the baby boomers had made Levi Strauss one of America's most successful companies. Now they have left Levi Strauss with far too much production capacity.

Now other companies enjoy a huge upsurge in sales. The hot new products suddenly are those associated with anxieties about getting old—many of the baby boomers are nearly 40. The runaway sales figures for *Jane Fonda's Workout Book* reflect the sudden new markets for fitness. Creams to keep the skin soft and youthful have taken over the markets once dominated by acne remedies. Table 1 shows that the baby boomers are twice as likely as older Americans to belong to a health club and to be currently taking part in an exercise class. However, they are much less likely to get exercise by doing garden or lawn work, they are no more likely to go for regular walks, and not much more likely to hunt or fish. But they are much more likely than older Americans to jog, swim, and ride bicycles.

In other aspects of leisure-time pursuits, the baby boomers often have distinctive patterns too. Table 2 shows that they are not more likely to attend plays, eat out, read, or watch TV. But they are much more likely to go to movies and concerts, to attend parties, to listen to records, and to play video games. And the baby boomers, with a reputation as a self-centered generation, are less likely to perform volunteer work. Given the disproportionate size of the baby boomer age cohorts, these preferences continued to shape our leisure economy.

THE FUTURE

Of course, the wrinkle creams and the fitness programs will not work in the long run: the baby boomers will get old. When they do they will continue to shape society. Businesses and products directed at the elderly ought to thrive. But perhaps the major impact will be an overload on the economy as we find that the retired population outnumbers those who are working. How will today's cohorts of college freshmen manage to provide adequate goods

Table 2 / The baby boomers play.

	Baby Boomers	People Older Than Baby Boomers
Attend plays	18%	19%
Eat out	68%	67%
Read	63%	65%
Watch television	80%	85%
Go to movies	66%	35%
Attend concerts	33%	16%
Go to parties	66%	49%
Listen to records	71%	46%
Play video games	25%	8%
Do volunteer work	12%	19%

Adapted from: Brown, 1984.

and services for so huge a number of dependents? It seems likely that many of the baby boomers won't retire or won't retire as young as most people do today. For as the baby boomers begin to reach these ages a labor shortage will develop (unless increased immigration is utilized to greatly expand the population younger than the baby boomers). Such a labor shortage will give many baby boomers a chance to stay in their jobs beyond the age of 65 or 70. But will they want to? And can the Social Security system survive if they do retire?

In future years you will hear much discussion of these issues and of what policies and programs ought to be pursued. But the reason for all these problems remains a simple one: For a few years following World War II young American couples turned their backs on the demographic transition and produced relatively large families in a short period of time. This resulted in some immense age cohorts and, ever since, they have formed a disproportionate population bubble moving through the life cycle, distorting the system as it goes.

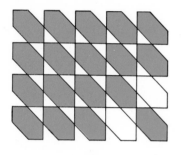

■ Until very recently, the vast majority of human beings lived and died without ever seeing a city. The first city was probably founded no more than 5,500 years ago. But even 200 years ago, only a few people could live in cities; nearly everyone lived on farms or in tiny rural villages. In fact, it was not until this century that Great Britain became the first **urban society** in history—a society in which the majority of people live in cities and do not farm for a living.

Britain was only the beginning. Soon many other industrial nations became urban societies. The process of *urbanization*—the migration of people from the countryside to the city—was the result of modernization. Thus, modernization has rapidly transformed not only how people live, but also where they live. In 1900, less than 40 percent of Americans lived in urban areas. Today more than 70 percent are urban residents, and less than 4 percent live on farms (the remaining 26 percent live in small towns and villages).

Large cities were impossible until agriculture became industrialized. Recall from Chapter 10 that even in advanced agrarian societies, it took about ninety-five people on farms to feed five people in cities. That kept cities very small. Until modern times, cities were inhabited mainly by the ruling elite and the servants, laborers, craftsmen, and professionals who served them. Cities survived by taxing farmers and were limited in size by the amount of surplus food produced by the rural population and by the ability to move this surplus from farm to city.

Over the past two centuries, the Industrial Revolution has shattered this balance between the city and the country. Modernization drew people to the

Urbanization

cities and freed them to come by making farmers incredibly productive. Today, instead of our needing ninety-five farmers to feed five city people, one American farmer is able to feed nearly fifty non-farmers. ■

CHAPTER PREVIEW

This chapter examines the urbanization of industrial societies. It explores in detail why and how the shift to urban life occurred. We shall also examine the structure of cities: why and how cities have grown and changed. Finally, we shall examine the impact of urban living on people. Have big cities really worsened the quality of life, destroyed the intimacy of social relations, and undermined the health and sanity of human beings?

Before turning to these questions, it is important to have a basis for comparison. Let us therefore go back into history and examine what life was like in the famous cities of preindustrial times. What was it really like in ancient Athens and Rome? What was it like in London and Paris when they had only 40,000 to 50,000 residents and before they had factories or freeways, subways or suburbs?

PREINDUSTRIAL CITIES

Until very recently, cities were small, filthy, disease-ridden, densely packed with people, and disorderly, and they were dark and very dangerous at night. If that description is unlike your image of Athens during the Golden Age of Greek civilization, that is because history is so often told with the mud, manure, garbage, and misery left out.

Typically, preindustrial cities contained no more than 5,000 to 10,000 inhabitants. Large national capitals were usually smaller than 40,000 and rarely larger than 60,000. Only very few preindustrial cities, such as ancient Rome, grew as large as 500,000, and then only under very special circumstances. Moreover, these cities rapidly shrank back to a much smaller size as slight changes in circumstance made it impossible to support them.

Limits on city size

A major reason why cities remained small was poor transportation; food had to be brought to feed a city. With only animal and human power to bring it, however, food could not be transported very far. Therefore, cities were limited to the population that could be fed by farmers nearby. The few large cities of preindustrial times appeared only where food could be brought long distances by water transport. Ancient Rome, for example, was able to reach the size of present-day Denver (and only briefly) because it controlled the whole Mediterranean area. Surplus food from this vast region was shipped by sea to feed the city's masses.

However, as the power of the empire weakened, Rome's population declined as the sources of food supplies dwindled. By the ninth century, the seapower of Islam had driven nearly all European shipping from the Mediterranean, and the cities of

The Dutch artist Pieter Bruegel demonstrated in this painting his awareness that the rise of the city was dependent upon increased agricultural productivity. The city in the background could exist only because farmers like this plowman could produce enough surplus food to feed city people. When European peasants began to plow with horses rather than oxen, they could farm twice as much land and so cities got larger.

southern Europe, including Rome, were virtually abandoned. In fact, Europe had practically no cities during the ninth and tenth centuries (Pirenne, 1925).

The size of cities was also checked by disease. Even early in the twentieth century, cities had such high mortality rates that they required a large and constant influx of newcomers from the countryside just to maintain their populations. As recently as 1900, the death rate in English cities was 33 percent higher than that in rural areas (David, 1965). A major reason for the high mortality in cities was the high incidence of infectious diseases. These diseases are spread by physical contact or by breathing in germs emitted by coughs and sneezes. Disease spreads much more slowly among less dense rural populations (McNeill, 1976).

Disease in cities was also caused by filth, especially by the contamination of water and food. Kingsley Davis (1965) pointed out that even as late as the 1850s, London's water "came mainly from wells and rivers that drained cesspools, graveyards, and tidal areas. The city was regularly ravaged by cholera."

Sewage treatment was unknown in preindustrial cities. Even sewers were not very common, and what sewers there were consisted of open trenches running along the streets into which sewage, including

Nobody worried much about littering in cities where horse-drawn wagons were the pri-
mary means of transportation. The preindustrial city suffered from much worse prob-
lems of pollution than does the modern industrial city.

human waste, was poured from buckets and chamber pots. Indeed, sewage was often poured out of
second-story windows without any warning to
pedestrians below.

Garbage was not collected and was strewn everywhere. It was hailed as a major step forward when
cities began to keep a municipal herd of pigs, who
were guided through the streets at night to eat the
garbage dumped during the day. Of course, the pigs
did considerable recycling as they went. Still, major
cities in the eastern United States depended on pigs
for their sanitation services until the end of the nineteenth century.

Today we are greatly concerned about pollution,
especially that produced by automobile exhausts and
factories. But the car and the factory cannot match
the horse and the home fireplace when it comes to
pollution. It is estimated that in 1900 horses depos-
ited 26 million pounds of manure and 10 million
gallons of urine on the streets of New York City
every week.

London's famous and deadly "fogs" of previous
centuries were actually smogs caused by thousands
of smoking home chimneys during atmospheric
inversions, which trapped the polluted air. Indeed,
the first known air-quality law was decreed in 1273

Herds of municipal pigs such as these were used as street-cleaning crews in many nine-teenth century cities and even in small towns. These "road hogs" did remove some gar-bage, but they left more.

by England's King Edward I. It forbade the use of a particularly smoky coal. The poet Shelley wrote early in the nineteenth century that "Hell is a city much like London, a populous and smokey city." In 1911, coal smoke during an atmospheric inversion killed more than a thousand people in London, and this incident led to the coining of the word *smog* (Miller, 1982).

Pedestrians in preindustrial cities often held per-fume-soaked handkerchiefs over their noses because the streets stank so. They kept alert for garbage and sewage droppings from above. They wore high boots because they had to wade through muck, manure, and garbage. And the people themselves were dirty, since they seldom bathed. Not surprisingly, they died at a rapid rate.

Population density also contributed to the un-healthiness of preindustrial cities. People were packed closely together. As we saw in Chapter 12, whole families lived in one small room. The houses stood wall to wall, and few streets were more than 10 to 12 feet wide.

Why was there such density when the population was so small? First of all, for most of its history, the city was also a fortress surrounded by massive walls for defense. Once the walls were up, the area of the city was fixed (at least until the walls were rebuilt), and if the population grew, people had to crowd ever closer. Even cities without walls were confined. Travel was by foot or by hoof. Cities did not spread beyond the radius that could be covered by these slow means of transportation, and thus the city limit

This engraving by William Hogarth (1697–1764) depicts the many perils of the London streets at night, including the chamber pot being emptied from second-story window, splattering two drunken Free Masons on their way home from a lodge meeting. The "wickedness" of cities has been a theme in literature and art through the centuries.

was usually no more than 3 miles from the center (Blumenfeld, 1971).

Second, preindustrial cities could not expand upward. Not until the nineteenth century, when structural steel and reinforced concrete were devel-

oped, could very tall structures be erected. Moreover, until elevators were invented, it was not practical to build very high. By expanding upward, people could have much greater living and working space in a building taking up no greater area at ground level. This could, of course, have meant that cities would become even more crowded at street level. They did not, however, because even modern high-rise cities have much more open space than did preindustrial cities, and, as we shall see, newer cities have expanded primarily outward rather than upward.

As already stated, preindustrial cities were not only dirty, disease-ridden, and dense, but also dark and dangerous. Today we sometimes say people move to the city because they are attracted by the bright lights, and we joke about small towns where they "roll up the sidewalks by 9 P.M." The preindustrial city had no sidewalks to roll up, and no electricity to light up the night. If lighted at all, homes were badly and expensively illuminated by candles and oil lamps. Until the introduction of gas lamps in the nineteenth century, streets were not lighted at all. Out in the dark, dangerous people lurked, waiting for victims. To venture forth at night in many of these cities was so dangerous that people did so only in groups accompanied by armed men bearing torches. Many people today fear to walk in cities at night. Still, it is much safer to do so now than it used to be.

Why live in such cities?

Knowing what preindustrial cities were like, one must ask why anyone willingly lived there and why a large number of newcomers were attracted to cities each year from rural areas.

One reason was economic incentive. Cities offered many people a chance to increase their incomes. For example, the development of an extensive division of labor, of occupational specialization, virtually required cities. Specialists must depend upon one another for the many goods and services they do not provide for themselves. Such exchanges are hard to manage when people live far apart. Thus, skilled craftsmen, merchants, physicians, and the like gathered in cities. Indeed, cities are vital to trade and commerce, and most early cities developed at intersections of major trade routes.

In addition to economic attractions, cities drew people because they offered the prospect of a more interesting and stimulating life. As Sjoberg (1965)

noted, "new ideas and innovations flowed into [cities] quite naturally," as travelers along the trade routes brought ideas as well as goods from afar. Moreover, simply by concentrating specialists in an area, cities stimulated innovation not just in technology, but also in religion, philosophy, science, and the arts. Moreover, the density of cities encouraged public performances, from plays and concerts to organized sporting events.

Cities undoubtedly also enticed some to migrate from rural areas in pursuit of "vice." The earliest writing we have about cities includes complaints about rampant wickedness and sin, and through the centuries cities have maintained the reputation for condoning behavior that would not be tolerated in rural communities (Fischer, 1975). In part, this may be due to the fact that from the beginning cities have been relatively anonymous places. In fact, preindustrial cities may have been even more anonymous, given their size, than modern cities.

Consider that cities relied on large numbers of newcomers each year just to replace the population lost through mortality. As a result, cities tended to abound in people who were recent arrivals and who had not known one another previously. Before modern identification systems, many people in cities were not even who they claimed to be—runaway sons and daughters of peasants could claim more exalted social origins. The possibility of escaping one's past and starting anew must have drawn many to the cities. But this also meant that cities then were even less integrated by long-standing interpersonal attachments than modern cities.

In any event, it was primarily adventuresome, single, young adults who constantly replenished city populations. E. A. Wrigley (1969) has computed that in the years from 1650 to 1750, London needed 8,000 newcomers each year in order to maintain its population. The newcomers averaged 20 years of age, were unmarried, and came from farms. Most of these newcomers came from more than 50 miles away—at least a two-day trip at that time.

For all our complaints about modern cities, industrialization did not ruin city life. Preindustrial cities were horrid. Yet for many young people on farms, the prospect of heading off to one of these miserable cities seemed far superior to a life of dull toil. Then, as the Industrial Revolution began, the idea of going off to the city suddenly appealed not

This view of Siena, Italy in the fourteenth century shows the density and the cultural variety of the medieval city. In those days, travelers were the only source of news, the only ones able to tell of what lay beyond the horizon, the ones who brought new ideas as well as new fashions and tools from afar.

Table 18-1 / The emptying out of the countryside; decline in U.S. farm population, 1820–1980.

Year	Farm Population	Percentage of Total Population
1820	6,924,000	72.0%*
1920	31,974,000	30.0%
1930	30,529,000	24.9%
1940	30,547,000	23.2%
1950	23,048,000	15.3%
1960	15,635,000	8.7%
1970	9,712,000	4.8%
1980	7,241,000	3.3%

*Computed by Kingsley Davis (1976).
Source: U.S. Census, 1975, 1981.

Table 18-2 / The agricultural revolution.

Year	Number of Persons Supplied with Farm Products by One U.S. Farm Worker
1820	4.1
1900	7.0
1940	10.7
1950	15.5
1960	25.8
1970	47.1

Source: U.S. Census, *Historical Statistics of the United States* (1975).

just to restless young people but to whole families. Soon the countryside virtually emptied, as people flocked to town (see Table 18-1).

INDUSTRIALIZATION AND URBANIZATION

Industrialization and urbanization are inseparable processes; neither could have occurred without the other. Industrialization made it possible for most people to live in cities. It also made it necessary: Industrialization requires the concentration of highly specialized workers. To understand how industrialization both caused and depended upon urbanization, let us first examine how the effects of the Industrial Revolution on agriculture made urbanization possible.

The agricultural revolution

Preindustrial farmers could support only a very small urban population, and only by accepting a very low standard of living. Cities could live only by coercing peasants to surrender their crops and livestock. Industrial technology changed all that. Suddenly, farm productivity soared to undreamed of heights, and farmers became eager to sell their crops to the cities. Let us chart this change as it took place in the United States, since good records exist and since American agriculture has become the most industrialized and productive in the world (see Table 18-2).

In 1820, when very little modern technology had yet appeared on the farms, a full-time farm worker could produce only enough food to feed 4.1 persons (including the farm worker). That left very little to send to the cities after farm families had fed themselves. But by 1900, the average American farm worker could feed 7.0 people. At the turn of the century, the average American farmer was feeding 5.3 Americans and 1.7 persons abroad. This was only the beginning, for by the middle of the twentieth century, farm productivity began to accelerate at an incredible pace. In 1960, the average American farmer was feeding 22.3 Americans and 3.5 persons living in other nations. By 1970, one farmer fed 39.9 Americans and 7.2 foreigners. In addition, the farmer in 1970 was feeding each person more food than had the nineteenth-century farmer, despite the fact that the government, through various subsidy programs, was preventing modern American farmers from growing nearly as much as they could. Perhaps even more surprising is the fact that the modern farmer accomplishes these wonders by working far fewer hours and with much less physical exertion than did preindustrial farmers.

Back in 1800, American farmers worked 56 hours

Modern self-propelled combines harvesting wheat near Pullman, Washington. With such a machine a single farmer can harvest more land in several hours than huge threshing crews at the turn of the century could do in a week. At present it is estimated that there are enough of these giant combines at work in the United States so that together they could harvest an area the size of the state of Kansas in a single day.

for every acre of wheat they raised (see Table 18-3). In return, they harvested an average of 15 bushels from each hard-worked acre. Today American farmers farm their wheat fields while riding in the air-conditioned cabs of huge diesel tractors and self-propelled combines. It takes them an average of 2.8 hours a year to farm an acre of wheat. And they average 31.4 bushels from each acre: twice as much wheat for only 5 percent as many hours of work.

Similarly, corn yields have more than tripled, while only 4 percent as much labor is required. Modern farmers give less than one-third the hours of atten-

tion to each of their milk cows as their grandparents did in 1910, but the cows now give three times as much milk. In 1910, it took ranchers 4.6 hours of labor to raise 100 pounds of beef. Today, ranchers work 1.3 hours to raise that much.

Many things have gone into this agricultural miracle: new machines, new animal breeds, new varieties of plants, weed sprays, fertilizers, crop rotation, drainage and irrigation systems—in short, the application of science and engineering to farming. But the major effect was the huge reduction in labor. Only because fewer farmers could feed greater

Table 18-3 / Changes in agricultural productivity, 1800–1980.

Product	1800	1900	1980	Product	1910	1980
WHEAT				MILK		
Hours of labor per acre (yearly)	56.0	15.0	2.8	Hours of labor per cow (yearly)	146.0	45
Hours of labor per 100 bushels	373	108	9	Hours of labor per 100 pounds of milk	3.8	0.4
Yield per acre (in bushels)	15	13.9	31.4	Milk per cow (in pounds) yearly	3,842.0	11,000
CORN				BEEF		
Hours of labor per acre (yearly)	86.0	38.0	3.6	Hours of labor per 100 pounds of meat	4.6	1.3
Hours of labor per 100 bushels	344	147	4	PORK		
Yield per acre (in bushels)	25.0	25.9	95.2	Hours of labor per 100 pounds of meat	3.6	0.5
				CHICKEN		
				Hours of labor per 100 pounds of meat	9.5	2.9

Source: U.S. Census, 1975, 1981.

numbers of people did it become possible for people to move to the cities and staff the great urban industries.

Recall from the previous chapter that the percentage of the population engaged in agriculture is one of the critical thresholds of modernization used by demographers. Only when people are released from field work can they live in cities and pursue industrial occupations (and, as a result, begin to reduce their fertility).

If city people today were asked to name the machines vital for the existence of cities, they would probably mention automobiles, typewriters, telephones, and the great machines used in heavy industry. In fact, modern cities depend upon machines few city people ever see: the tractors, plows, cultivators, pickers, and harvesters of the farms. Without these, our cities would be small, and most of us would spend our lives following horses across grain fields or riding them to round up herds.

Specialization and urban growth

Industrialization requires urbanization because it depends upon the coordinated activities of large numbers of specialized workers who must perform their tasks in a few central locations.

Industrialization depends on specialization—an elaborate division of labor—to simplify production. As an example, let us consider the industrialization of shoemaking. The preindustrial shoemaker was a skilled craftsman who took a number of years to learn the various steps in the process of making a pair of shoes. In a modern shoe factory, a worker need only learn to perform one simple task in this process in order to be productive. By the use of machines to perform some tasks and by the concentration of labor in the most time-consuming aspects of shoemaking, many more shoes can be made for the same amount of labor expended by traditional shoemakers.

One consequence of this is that shoes became

much cheaper to consumers. A second consequence is that while the traditional shoemaker could locate his shop anywhere he could find customers, industrialized shoemakers must gather in one place where each can make his or her contribution to the complex manufacturing process.

Industrialization also depends upon bringing together many highly trained specialists in order to achieve goals beyond the ability of single individuals. It takes many people with a variety of sophisticated skills to make computers or jet planes or to construct oil refineries. This, too, requires people to gather.

But industrialization also produces an elaborate division of labor, not just within organizations but among them. Plant A gets parts from plant B, and supplies its production to plant C. It is often efficient if these plants are close together. Indeed, in the early stages of industrialization, limited transportation made proximity vital.

If people must gather in large numbers to work, they will also concentrate in that same area to live. This was especially true in days when most people walked to work. When people congregate in one place in large numbers and do not farm for a living, we call that place a city. Thus, urbanization and industrialization are inseparable.

METROPOLIS

Suppose a young man left his father's farm and moved to Silo, North Dakota, population forty-three, where he got a job in a cafe. Is this an example of urbanization? Most people wouldn't think so. Even though the folks in Silo are not farmers, their way of life would not seem very urban to people used to large cities (in small North Dakota towns, people still do not lock their doors, and many leave their ignition keys in their cars). It seems we have some notion that to be urban a place must be larger than Silo. But how much larger?

There can be no "true" answer to that question; it is simply a matter of judgment. American demographers classify a locale as an **urban place** if it has a population of more than 2,500 people. Thus, the statement that nearly three out of four Americans today live in urban places means that they live in communities larger than 2,500.

This makes it obvious that many urban places are not cities, at least not in the sense that the term is normally used. In fact, the U.S. Census does not classify a community as a **city** unless it has at least 50,000 residents, but that standard can be very confusing. Many large communities are crisscrossed by political boundaries that separate them into many independent units—often a major city is surrounded by dozens of smaller independent communities. Suppose one of these has fewer than 2,500 people. Should we classify its residents as part of the rural population? What if most of the adults in this community commute to jobs in the heart of the major city? The political boundaries that divide large communities often have no relation to the actual social and economic boundaries. In fact, the notion of a city as a legal entity is faulty.

The word *city* once had a rather clear meaning, and a person either lived in a particular city or not. But today, two strangers meeting on a plane may say they live in Chicago and Dallas when they are not legal residents of either city. Instead, each lives in a **suburb**, a smaller community in the immediate vicinity of a city. Yet these travelers were truthful in the real, if not the legal, sense. Cities do not simply stop at their legal boundaries but extend socially and economically into many adjacent communities. That's why we often speak of Greater Chicago or Greater Dallas—to identify this larger aspect of cities.

Back in 1910, the U.S. Census tried to find a more suitable definition of city than is provided by legal boundaries. Recognizing that many surrounding areas are functionally part of a central city, they substituted the term *metropolitan area* for city and began to lump suburbs with their central city as a single unit: the **metropolis**.

The first metropolitan areas had 200,000 or more residents, including the settled areas around a city. In 1940 this was again revised. To be a metropolitan area, the central city had to have 50,000 people, no matter how many more lived in surrounding areas.

Still, problems persisted. As Roderick McKenzie (1933) had pointed out, still "only a part of the area that is economically and socially tributary to each of these central cities was included." What was needed was a way to identify the **sphere of influence** of a city—the area whose inhabitants depend on the central city for jobs, recreation, newspapers, television, and a sense of common community.

Therefore, in 1950 the **Standard Metropolitan Statistical Area (SMSA)** was created. Around central cities with 50,000 or more people, counties are included in the SMSA if at least 75 percent of those working in the county do not hold agricultural jobs and if the county serves either as the residence or place of employment for at least 10,000 nonagricultural workers. Furthermore, at least 15 percent of the workers living in a county must commute to the central city or at least 25 percent of those working in the county must commute from the city.

Thus, sociologists no longer use the term *city* in their technical vocabulary but speak instead of a metropolis or metropolitan area. Thus, we agree with people from Oak Park, Illinois, when they tell strangers they are from Chicago. The industrialized city is no longer a tight, tidy, compact entity, contained within defensive walls. It sprawls hither and yon across the landscape—a reality better expressed by the term *metropolis*.

But even the modern metropolis isn't completely formless. Cities exist as places to work and to live. Given these fundamental purposes, the shape and organization of cities has been determined primarily by transportation. Two basic forms of modern metropolises exist, depending on the dominant forms of transportation when the metropolises grew. These are the **fixed-rail metropolis** and the **freeway metropolis**.

Much concern about cities and urban policies has been generated recently because many people think cities must be like those built before cars and trucks took over transportation from fixed-rail systems. These critics dislike the new form of the metropolitan area, especially the way the older form is changing to be more like the new. Since this dispute helps reveal basic aspects of urban sociology, we shall examine and compare these two basic urban forms.

The fixed-rail metropolis

The preindustrial city was small and dense because people relied primarily on walking for transportation. Although industrialization caused cities to expand, the continued reliance on foot transportation still caused the cities to be cramped and workers to be housed close to their factories. The development of rail transportation made it possible for cities to expand greatly in area.

First came horse-drawn trolleys running on rails. Then came electric- and steam-powered trolleys running on the same rails. These new modes of transportation were much faster than walking (or even than riding on a horse) and were cheap enough so people could afford to live farther from work. Thus, cities began to expand outward, but they did not expand evenly. They expanded only along the rail lines. People could travel only where the rails led and could live or work only out from the center of the city along the rail lines.

Riding on these fixed-rail mass transit systems was quite unpleasant. The cars were usually overcrowded and dirty. Still, it beat walking. Moreover, it enabled large numbers of city dwellers to escape apartments close to huge, noisy, dirty factories and to move out where real estate was cheaper and life less hectic. As soon as railroads appeared in the 1840s, many wealthy people fled the cities and commuted from country estates or distant, luxurious communities.

As industrializing cities began to sprawl, they began to resemble spiders. From a dense center in which business and industry were concentrated, the metropolitan area expanded along narrow corridors, where the fixed-rail lines extended (Ward, 1971). Fixed-rail transportation requires many riders going from and to a small number of stops. Thus, rail lines were extended from the city center only as the population grew at the end of the line. People were not as cramped as before, but they still had to crowd together.

Moreover, fixed-rail transportation made the center of the city the focal point. Offices and stores were concentrated here since everyone could most easily travel to the center. Industry was also concentrated in the heart of the city, usually adjacent to the business section. Factories relied on rail transportation to bring in supplies and to carry out the finished goods to market. Thus, factory locations were also close to rail routes.

The metropolis that was built to suit fixed-rail transportation fits our image of the old industrial

New technology often requires new skills: These girls in a Brooklyn high school in about 1900 used time in gym class to develop their skills in boarding trolley cars. Their practice apparatus allows them to learn to grab a bar and swing aboard the high side step.

Here a fashionable New York woman boards a real trolley. Since these vehicles had no center aisle, people just slide into the seat from either side. At rush hour the outside of the car was lined with riders unable to find a seat. The route of trolley lines determined the corridors along which cities grew during this era before the automobile.

cities of the eastern United States and Europe: dense cities where, in the very center, the streets are jammed with people going to shop by day and to restaurants, theaters, nightclubs, concert halls, and sports arenas by night. Whether the citizens called it the Great White Way, the Loop, or the Hub, this was the heart and soul of what everyone found exciting and sophisticated about the city.

Today the central core of most such cities is in decay, abandoned by shoppers, by offices, by industry, and by nightlife. Billions have been spent to renovate and renew these central cores in hopes of luring department stores, offices, and nightclubs to return. Yet they do not recapture their old glory. And many newer cities never had such centers at all. Why?

The freeway metropolis

Compared with rail lines, streets and roads are inexpensive to build and maintain. With the mass production of automobiles and trucks, the metropolis no longer was forced to resemble a spider. The empty areas between the rail lines became easy to reach. Moreover, people could settle in sparsely populated areas where no rail line could afford to run but where anyone with a car could easily go. The metropolis began to spread outward evenly, shaped more by geographic barriers (such as rivers, harbors, hills, and ravines) than by rail routes. And just as the car freed people to live where they liked, the truck freed industry to decentralize.

The center of a city had always been a constrictive

Fixed rail transportation, such as the Elevated Railroad running down New York City's Third Avenue, created cities with densely packed central areas. The coal-burning engines also made a considerable contribution to air pollution.

location for industry and business. There was always a shortage of space for expansion and considerable congestion from the dense concentration of plants. These shortcomings were offset by the urgent need to be located on a fixed-rail line and to be able to send material from one local plant to another by slow horse-drawn wagons. But the truck ended the dependence of industry on rail transport. Today, more than 80 percent of all commercial transportation is by truck.

Meanwhile, new technology forced industry to seek low-density locations in the suburbs. Assembly-line methods of manufacturing require long, low buildings and therefore considerable space. Machines for handling and stockpiling materials, such as forklifts, work best in one-story buildings. Thus, plants have shifted to outlying areas where land is plentiful and cheap. Indeed, with workers now commuting mainly by car (and 87 percent of American workers do so), business and industry often require parking lots that cover considerably more area than their plants and office buildings.

And so the metropolis has become decentralized. Business has moved to outlying locations, as have many residents. Not surprisingly, so have many stores and shops—the shopping center has replaced the old central core as the dominant retail locale.

Although decentralization has caused substantial changes in cities that grew large during the era of fixed-rail transportation, it has not caused similar upheavals in many cities west of the Mississippi. These cities grew up after the automobile and the truck had already displaced the trolley and the train. They were never high-density cities revolving around a cramped but thriving central core. They were never shaped like spiders.

For decades, literary Easterners have scoffed at the decentralized cities of the West for not being "real" cities at all. Los Angeles, for example, has been described as a dozen towns in search of a city. Why in the world, they complain, don't Westerners get their cities put together so that one need not travel 20 miles down a freeway to get from the office to the theater or from one department store to another?

This charge is accurate enough. Los Angeles does not have a "downtown"; instead, it has at least eight downtowns. Indeed, as many people in decentralized cities have discovered that the time it takes to get somewhere matters more than the actual distance traveled. By avoiding the congestion of shopping in dense, central cores, millions of Americans have demonstrated that they would rather zip along a freeway and find easy parking at a shopping center than take much longer to go a few blocks in heavy traffic. That brings us to the fundamental point in the dispute over what a real city is. Most people want cities to be decentralized.

Preferring a decentralized metropolis

A number of signs show that people find life better in sprawling, decentralized cities than in the older, centralized cities. First of all, when the chance came to move out of the central city and to the outskirts, millions did so as fast as they could. Although the dense central core offers an exciting urban life, it also causes vast numbers of people to live in cramped, unattractive housing and their children to play in the streets.

A second sign is that people running large industrial and business firms have joined in the move to less dense areas, taking their plants and offices with them. Surely the rich can maintain luxury and privacy even in dense central cores, but they were among the first to leave. As early as 1848, approximately 20 percent of the leading businessmen of Boston were commuting to their downtown offices by train from the suburbs (Ward, 1971).

Third, large numbers of people have been migrating from the old, high-density cities to the new decentralized metropolitan areas of the South and West.

Fourth, people avoid public transportation whenever possible. Indeed, almost as many Americans walk to work (5.5 percent) as ride mass transit (6.3 percent). No public mass transit system in the nation can attract enough riders at a high enough fare to break even. People seem willing to commute long distances, but they seem to want the freedom of driving their own vehicles. Hence, they prefer a metropolis constructed with auto transportation in mind—freeway cities.

But we need not rely on these indirect signs. The Gallup Poll (1972) asked Americans: "If you could live anywhere you wanted to, would you prefer a city, a suburban area, a small town, or a farm?" Only 13 percent chose to live in a city. In contrast, a third picked the suburbs, another third said a small town, and one-fifth said they would like to live on a farm. Indeed, of people who were living in cities, only one person in five preferred living there.

This might suggest that Americans long to undo urbanization and return to the good old days of living in small towns and on farms. But that isn't true. Gallup asked those who said they would like to live on a farm or in a small town how far from a major urban area they would like to be. Three out of four said no more than 30 miles (Fuguitt and Zuiches, 1973). Thirty miles is little more than a half-hour drive from the city. That is not a retreat to the sticks. Indeed, as Claude Fischer (1976) remarked about these findings, anyplace "within thirty miles of a large city is essentially a suburb. That seems to be what most Americans want." But not everyone who wants this has been able to get it.

URBAN NEIGHBORHOODS

The ethnic or racial neighborhood has always been a feature of the city. In the cities of the Roman Empire, various sections of cities were named according to the ethnicity of persons living there—for members of a minority group lived in the same neighborhood. In addition to racial and ethnic divisions, city neighborhoods have always been differentiated by class or status, with neighborhoods ranging from the very wealthy to the very poor.

Of course, cities are constantly changing. Thus even in ancient times, what was a Jewish or a Greek neighborhood in one generation might be something else a generation or two later. And rich neighborhoods sometimes turn into slums, and vice versa.

In America, the rapid growth of cities and the huge waves of immigration produced complex neighborhood patterns. Our cities have abounded with neighborhoods occupied by a single racial or ethnic group—many cities have (or have had) a "little Italy," a "Germantown," or a "Chinatown."

The fixed-rail city required that large numbers of residents live in crowded, expensive housing. Whenever people have had the opportunity, most have abandoned such areas for life in the suburbs. Despite complaints that the suburbs are dull, the people who live there usually seem to be having too good a time to notice.

And all cities have their wealthy areas (New York's "Silk Stocking district," Chicago's "Gold Coast," and Seattle's "Highlands") and their slums.

Observers of the nineteenth-century American city noticed the remarkable turnover in the ethnic identity of neighborhoods. A slum area occupied by the Irish or the Germans would suddenly change as these groups moved out and newer immigrants such as the Italians or the Jews moved in. In time, these groups also were replaced, often by blacks, Asians, or Hispanics.

Minority ethnic and racial groups concentrate in particular neighborhoods for several reasons Members of a group are lured to the same neighborhoods in which their relatives and friends live—a

place where their native language, their customs, their food, and their religion predominate. They are also pulled toward these neighborhoods because they can afford to live there. Higher housing costs in other neighborhoods and discrimination act to keep members of ethnic groups out of these other neighborhoods. Thus, discrimination has long produced segregated neighborhoods by preventing certain groups from buying or renting outside certain districts.

Recently, of course, discriminatory laws and real estate deeds have been repealed and nullified. In fact, informal methods of discrimination have been outlawed: It is illegal to refuse to rent or sell housing to a person because of race, religion, or national origin. However, long before these legal measures took force, many groups that once were the targets of discrimination in housing escaped their segregated neighborhoods and became integrated. In the 1920s, two of America's most famous early sociologists proposed an explanation of this process.

Park and Burgess: ethnic succession

Robert E. Park (1864–1944) and Ernest Burgess (1886–1966) proposed that ethnic and racial segregation in cities was based primarily on economic and status differences. In their famous book *The City* (Park and Burgess, 1925), they proposed a **theory of ethnic succession** that closely resembles the economic explanation of prejudice and discrimination outlined in Chapter 11. Park and Burgess argued that new immigrant groups huddle together in segregated neighborhoods upon arriving in America. However, as these groups begin to rise in the stratification system, these changes "tend to be registered in changes of location." That is, as new groups succeed in America, they move out of ethnic neighborhoods. This occurs, first, because they can afford to live in better neighborhoods; second, because they no longer are so tied to their traditional culture; and third, because they have shed the stigma of low status: They are no longer regarded as undesirable neighbors.

Park and Burgess also accounted for the process of *succession,* whereby slum neighborhoods are successively occupied by the lowest-status groups of the time. For a long time, the Park and Burgess viewpoint dominated sociology. Moreover, a number of later empirical studies seemed to confirm it. Lieberson (1961, 1963) found that from 1910 through 1950, older European ethnic groups (such as the Germans) and newer ones (such as the Italians) increasingly lived together in the same neighborhoods. Taeuber and Taeuber (1964) found similar trends.

However, in the wake of the racial confrontations of the 1960s, other sociologists suggested that the Park and Burgess model was inadequate, that it glossed over continuing ethnic inequalities, and that

it did not apply to racial, as opposed to ethnic, neighborhood integration. Working with data for Toronto, Darroch and Marston (1971) reported that individuals belonging to different ethnic groups still tended not to live in the same neighborhoods in Toronto, even when they were of equal status. Kantrowitz (1973) drew similar conclusions from New York City data, suggesting that even when ethnic groups escape the city, they tend to form segregated suburbs.

Once again, prejudice was judged the primary barrier to integration. Yet this did not square with the deemphasis on prejudice as being a major factor in race and ethnic relations, as we saw in Chapter 11. This was a serious discrepancy, and something was clearly wrong with one of these positions.

Guest and Weed: economics and integration

In 1976, Avery M. Guest and his student James A. Weed attempted to resolve this contradiction. First, they carefully reexamined what Park and Burgess had actually argued. They discovered that Park and Burgess were discussing group, not individual, upward mobility. That is, Park and Burgess did not suggest that as soon as a few members of a low status economic group manage to become wealthy, they are welcomed in the best neighborhoods. Rather, they argued that when a particular group, such as the Italians, achieves economic parity with the majority, at that point their ethnicity will not be a barrier in choosing where to live.

This is a critical distinction. Darroch and Marston had shown only that higher-income members of a low status group do not live in integrated neighborhoods, not what would happen when groups achieve status equality. But Guest and Weed, following Park and Burgess, argued that so long as a group's overall status is low, it will reflect on all members, including the more successful ones. As an example, they suggested that, in evaluating a neighborhood in which many Poles are living, a person of German descent will not ask, "Do *these* Poles earn as much as I do?" but "Are Poles as a *group* similar in status to Germans as a group?" If the answer is yes, the German will move into the neighborhood. If the answer is no, the German will choose to live elsewhere. Group inequality, not individual comparisons, lies at the heart of prejudice and discrimination, Guest and Weed argued.

To test this view, Guest and Weed assembled data for the Cleveland, Boston, and Seattle SMSAs. They chose these three cities because of their different histories and ethnic makeup, a choice that proved to be wise. Their first step was to determine the extent to which various racial and ethnic groups live in integrated neighborhoods.

The degree of segregation or integration of a neighborhood is measured by an **index of dissimilarity** (Taeuber and Taeuber, 1969). This index contrasts the racial and ethnic makeup of a neighborhood with the racial and ethnic makeup of the whole metropolitan area. If the racial and ethnic composition of a neighborhood is the same as that of the metropolitan area, the neighborhood scores zero on the index—it is fully integrated. On the other hand, if a single racial or ethnic group lives in a neighborhood, while other racial and ethnic groups live in the metropolitan area, the neighborhood scores 100—it is wholly segregated. To measure the degree to which a particular racial or ethnic group is integrated or segregated in a city, sociologists compute the average dissimilarity scores for the neighborhoods in which this group lives. Guest and Weed's findings substantially supported the Park and Burgess theory and the status inequality approach to prejudice and discrimination.

Group neighborhoods differed as would be predicted from current status differences among them. Persons of British origin, the people often known as WASPs, live in the most integrated neighborhoods. Others of northern and western European descent (such as Swedes, Germans, and Irish) are virtually as integrated. Groups arriving later from eastern and southern Europe (Czechs, Poles, Hungarians, and Italians) live in only slightly less integrated neighborhoods. Persons of Mexican descent live in quite unintegrated neighborhoods in Cleveland and Boston but in neighborhoods as integrated as those of eastern and southern Europeans in Seattle. Blacks and Puerto Ricans live in the least integrated neighborhoods, but again the differences are

smaller in Seattle. Finally, and importantly, Asians live in neighborhoods as integrated as those of most people of European origin.

By comparing 1960 and 1970 data, Guest and Weed found that all neighborhoods had generally become more integrated. Asians had made the greatest gains, but black neighborhoods had also become less solidly black.

These data appear to support the group mobility interpretation of Park and Burgess. Asians have recently made striking status gains, and they have become quite well integrated. Earlier status gains of eastern and southern European ethnic groups also show up in the breakup of the once solidly Italian, Polish, Hungarian, and Czech neighborhoods. Between 1960 and 1970, blacks made substantial status gains, and their neighborhoods began to reflect these gains.

However, Guest and Weed were able to test the Park and Burgess model more rigorously. Using sophisticated statistical regression techniques, they found that when the effects of income differences among racial and ethnic groups are removed, relatively little neighborhood segregation based on race or ethnicity remains. That is, status inequality between groups seems to be the primary neighborhood barrier. As status inequalities disappear, so do racial and ethnic neighborhoods. At that point, neighborhoods are identified only on the basis of class.

However, Guest and Weed also found evidence that neighborhood patterns tend to persist. Seattle is simply a more integrated city than Boston or Cleveland, no matter which racial or ethnic group is examined. Guest and Weed suggested that since Seattle is a much younger city, various ethnic enclaves never existed in Seattle because these groups had already achieved status equality by the time the city developed. Thus, whereas the Irish, the Poles, the Italians, and other ethnic groups had to abandon their traditional enclaves in Boston and Cleveland, a process that may have been delayed by many factors other than discrimination, this process was skipped in the newer cities of the West.

Thus, Guest and Weed showed that racial and ethnic succession, from ghetto to integration, continues in accordance with current theories of intergroup conflict.

Recent studies show American cities are becoming much less segregated on the basis of race and ethnicity. A generation ago it would have been hard to find a scene like this to photograph. Today such scenes don't attract special notice.

Karl Taeuber: segregation declines

In 1983, Karl Taeuber, who originated the index of dissimilarity, announced that American cities had become less segregated between 1970 and 1980. This confirmed the results of Guest and Weed's study. Taeuber's research was based on the twenty-eight American cities having more than 100,000 black residents. Using data from the 1970 and the 1980 censuses, Taeuber examined each city block by block and computed dissimilarity scores. Oakland, California, ranked as the most integrated of these cities; only 2 percent of blacks in Oakland lived on an all-black block. Surprisingly, Chicago, where a black mayor won election in 1983, was the most segregated city. Nearby Detroit, on the other hand, was one of the least segregated cities (see Table 18-4). While nearly all cities showed a decline in black neighborhood segregation, segregation in Philadelphia and Cleveland increased. Southern cities, on the other hand, showed marked declines.

Taeuber pointed out that integration was occurring primarily as blacks moved into the suburbs or into white neighborhoods. Little reverse integration was taking place—that is, whites moving into heavily black neighborhoods.

Table 18-4 / Index of dissimilarity scores for twenty-eight U.S. cities with more than 100,000 black residents (the higher the score, the more segregated blacks are from whites).

City	1970	1980
Chicago	93	92
Cleveland	90	91
St. Louis	90	90
Philadelphia	84	88
Baltimore	89	86
Atlanta	92	86
Kansas City	90	86
Memphis	92	85
Birmingham, Ala.	92	85
Dallas	96	83
Pittsburgh	86	83
Indianapolis	90	83
Jacksonville, Fla.	94	82
Houston	93	81
Los Angeles	90	81
Nashville, Tenn.	90	80
Boston	84	80
Milwaukee	88	80
Washington, D.C.	79	79
Richmond, Va.	91	79
Cincinnati	84	79
Newark, N.J.	76	76
New Orleans	84	76
New York City	77	75
Columbus, Ohio	86	75
Detroit	82	73
Gary, Ind.	84	68
Oakland, Calif.	70	59

Source: Taeuber, 1983.

This seems an appropriate place to explain why a chapter devoted to urban sociology appears in the section of the book that is devoted to social change. A city is not an enduring physical structure, despite its permanent appearance. Instead, a city is as much a process as a structure: it is constantly changing. The great fixed-rail metropolis, for example, which still dominates our conception of the city, existed in all its glory for less than a century. Millions of Americans have nostalgic memories of the ethnic neighborhood in which they grew up but which has completely disappeared.

In 1959, when I became a reporter for the *Oakland Tribune,* Oakland was a very segregated city where editors did not regard a story of a black murdering another black as worth printing. Today, Oakland is the least segregated of cities with substantial black populations, the mayor is black, and the *Tribune* now has black owners. So, the next time you look around in a city, keep in mind the impermanence of what you see.

To conclude this chapter, we must return to a basic question about city life raised in Chapter 1. Has urbanization harmed social relations and dulled our sensibilities?

THEORIES OF URBAN IMPACT

By the middle of the nineteenth century, educated people in Europe and the United States recognized that rapid urbanization was under way—and they didn't like it. Cities were still unhealthy, squalid places. In 1841, the average life expectancy of men in London was five years less than in the rest of England. In the United States, the life expectancy of urban dwellers did not equal that of rural folk until after 1940 (Simon, 1981). As cities grew, it seemed that their problems could only grow worse. So, many asked at what price people were being uprooted from their intimate, healthy, traditional lives in rural areas and crowded into impersonal, unhealthy, chaotic cities. Most people who raised this question were sure that the costs of urbanization would be devastating, even though they could see no way to stop the great migration to the cities.

One of the first social scientists to write in detail about the dangers of urbanization was Ferdinand Tönnies. In the mid-1880s, he introduced the concepts of *Gemeinschaft* (community) and *Gesellschaft* (society or association) to capture the different qualities of life in preindustrial and industrial societies.

Gemeinschaft identifies the qualities of life Tönnies thought were being lost because of urbanization. It describes small, cohesive communities such as the farming village. People know one another

Street scenes like this abound in all modern cities in defiance of nineteenth-century urban sociologists, who predicted that city growth would create massive anomie, that people would become estranged from one another and thus lose their moral bearings. Most people in cities are not alone but are firmly attached to others.

well and are connected by bonds of friendship, kinship, and daily interaction. In such places, people agree on the norms, and few people fail to conform. In fact, such communities serve as primary groups for most of their members.

Gesellschaft is the exact opposite. People tend to be strangers, and they are united only by self-interest, not by any sense of common purpose or identity. There is little agreement about norms and much deviance. Human relationships are fleeting and manipulative rather than warm and intimate.

If we think of people as marbles, then in the *Gemeinschaft* the marbles are glued together into a solid piece, while in the *Gesellschaft* the marbles

are constantly being tossed about in a revolving drum.

Following Tönnies, a long line of social scientists characterized urban life in such terms. Émile Durkheim wrote in 1897 that a primary consequence of urbanization was the breakdown of order: Urbanites live in a situation in which norms lack definition and force, a state he called **anomie**. In losing their attachments to others, people lose their primary source of moral judgment. As an early control theorist (see Chapter 7), Durkheim believed that conformity to the norms is caused by attachments, and thus urbanization, by destroying attachments, destroys the normative order. He therefore described the modern urbanite as adrift in a sea of normlessness (or anomie). He thus attempted to show that cities had much higher deviance rates than rural areas.

Anomie theories

Early American sociologists found Durkheim's theory of urban anomie very compelling. Perhaps this was partly because the great majority of them were raised on farms and in small towns, and Durkheim's position agreed with their own personal reactions to city life. In any event, sociologists have long believed that cities are inimical to human relations and thus to the very basis of social life.

A major contribution to this position was made by Louis Wirth (1938) in a paper called "Urbanism as a Way of Life." In it he argued that city life forces the individual to become withdrawn from others. This occurs, first of all, because city people so often interact with complete strangers. Such interactions are necessarily impersonal, and this impersonality becomes a habit. Second, cities threaten to overload the senses of human beings, forcing them to shut out and ignore most of what is going on around them. We walk down streets filled with strangers, traffic flows past, store windows beckon, signs seek our attention, sirens and car horns blare, phones ring: The sights and sounds of the city would overwhelm us if we did not set up sensory buffers to filter out most of these stimuli. But in so doing, we become insensitive and unresponsive.

In the aftermath of World War II, Wirth's assertions about city life were incorporated into mass society theories to help explain why people responded to mass movements such as Nazism and Communism. Mass society theorists argued that as isolated, unattached individuals, city people were easily attracted to mass movements, especially those that promised to restore order and provide followers with a clear sense of belonging.

In Chapter 1, we examined the fate of mass society or anomie theories when they were subjected to sociological research. These theories were correct in arguing that a lack of attachments results in deviance and anomie (see Chapter 7). Where they went wrong was in the claim that anomie was characteristic of urbanites. Research found that people typically maintain close attachments even in the largest cities. Human relations turn out to be much more durable than the early sociologists had supposed. Indeed, as we saw in Chapter 3 and will examine again in Chapter 20, people do not join social movements because they are loose marbles bouncing randomly in normless cities, but because they are attached to persons who already belong to the movement.

This is not to say there are no lonely, isolated people in cities. There are, and many display the symptoms predicted by Durkheim and others: alcoholism, suicide, criminal behavior, and mental illness. But most urbanites do not lack attachments, and the city does not have the destructive effects that earlier sociologists believed it did.

Effects of crowding

What about the problem of "psychic overload"? This supposed effect of urban living was first identified by Louis Wirth, but it gained widespread attention in the 1960s as a potential hazard caused by population growth (Calhoun, 1962; Hall, 1966). Many critics of modern urban life have proposed that the population density of cities causes serious physical and mental pathologies. Noting that when rats are crowded into cages they become extremely abnormal, many sociologists have issued doomsday predictions—Hall (1966) warned that increased urban density is an impending disaster "more lethal than the hydrogen bomb." Once again sociologists turned to empirical research.

Macro studies of crowding

The initial studies attempted to see whether neighborhoods with greater population density had higher rates of pathology than less dense neighborhoods. The results did not support the psychic overload theory. People in dense neighborhoods were not more prone to alcoholism, mental illness, suicide, and other such problems than were people in less dense neighborhoods—in fact, city people were no more prone to these problems than rural people (Fischer, 1975; Galle and Gove, 1978).

Sometimes the studies did find differences indicating crowding effects, but these proved to be spurious. That is, the kinds of people most likely to live in the most crowded places tend to have higher rates of pathologies wherever they live. That is, those who live in the most crowded neighborhoods also tend to be poor, without families, or elderly or to have been mentally ill before they arrived in the neighborhood. When these characteristics of residents were taken into account, no crowding effects could be detected. Thus density, viewed at the macro level, has no effect on people.

Micro studies of crowding

 Although these studies disproved the wild assertions of impending doom from urban density, several sociologists thought that a more modest proposition—that excessive crowding of a person's immediate environment has negative effects—might still be valid. That is, the density of a neighborhood might not matter, but the degree to which people have privacy or "personal space" might matter a good deal.

Walter Gove, Michael Hughes, and Omer Galle (1979) designed a study to see if it mattered that some people live in very crowded homes. Thus, they set out to discover whether crowding at the micro sociological level mattered. They reasoned that when a family lives in a home where there are several people to each room, it will be difficult for them to have privacy and to limit interaction with others. Therefore, people in crowded homes ought to experience a lack of privacy and an overload of demands on them from others. This might cause them to withdraw, both by staying away from home and by being unresponsive to other members of the household. Such withdrawal ought to have negative consequences for attachments and for mental health.

Gove and his colleagues selected more than 2,000 homes that varied in the number of persons per room. Analysis of the data, which were obtained by interviews with members of these households, supported their expectations. They found the following:

1. The more persons per room, the more that people complained of a lack of privacy and of too great demands on them by others.

2. People responded to crowding by withdrawing, both physically and emotionally.

3. People in crowded homes had poorer mental health.

4. Members of crowded homes had poor social relations with each other. There were more family fights, and husbands and wives were less satisfied with their marriages.

5. Child care in crowded homes was poor. Parents expressed relief at getting the kids out of the home and were much less aware of where their children were and what they were doing when they were out.

6. The effects of crowding began to show up when there was more than one person per room in a household.

Thus, we see that crowding can have negative effects. Although it doesn't seem to matter how many people live in a neighborhood or even in a single home, it does matter how much room people have to find peace and quiet. When ten family members live in a ten-room home, they will be happier and healthier than when they live in a four-room home.

Thus, Gove and his colleagues found support for micro effects of crowding. However, these are of little import for the more general fears about urban crowding. Few urban families live in crowded conditions, that is, with more than one person per room. In 1970 only 8.2 percent of households in America had more than 1.01 persons per room. The median household had almost two rooms per member. Moreover, crowding is declining, not increasing. In 1950, 15.7 percent of American households had more than 1.01 persons per room, and the median household had only about 1.5 rooms per member.

These changes partly reflect a decline in the average family size. But they primarily reflect the decentralization of cities and the decreased density that results. The preindustrial city was extremely crowded. The early fixed-rail industrial city was less crowded, but much more crowded than the freeway city. Transportation has always been the key to density.

New York City's St. Patrick's Cathedral nestles among its towering neighbors—a scene to remind us why people persist in moving from rural areas to the city. There is a compelling sense of excitement and of human possibilities inherent in the physical structure of cities. Unlike Niagra Falls, the Grand Canyon, or the other natural wonders, we made this place.

As transportation changes enabled people to escape crowded, centralized cities to get some elbow room, they rushed to do so. They did not wait for sociological research to tell them that it was desirable to have a large enough home so that family members could find privacy.

CONCLUSION

We have seen that until very recently cities were small, unhealthy, filthy, dangerous, and crowded. Little wonder, then, that when rapid urbanization began in the nineteenth century, so many regarded it as tragic. However, the very processes of industrialization that prompted migration to the cities also transformed city life itself. Granted, many mistakes have been made in the design and administration of modern cities—such errors are inevitable when experience is lacking. Nevertheless, if gloomy prophets such as Tönnies and Durkheim could visit a modern city, they would be dumbfounded—not by the errors in planning or the problems that persist, but by the comfort, cleanliness, beauty, and tranquility of our cities.

Of course, our cities have ugly, dirty, and dangerous neighborhoods. But even the worst parts of modern cities are an improvement on large sections of cities during the early days of the Industrial Revolution, to say nothing of the squalor and misery of preindustrial cities. On a walk through the most horrid urban neighborhood today, no one will see dead or dying infants lying on dung heaps—or even any dung heaps. This is hardly to suggest that there are no urgent urban problems. It is merely to give historical perspective to current concerns.

Perhaps the most important sociological lesson in this chapter is that the future is not always a simple extension of the past. Modern cities are not simply big versions of older cities. As cities grew, they were greatly transformed. Indeed, in the next chapter we shall see that growth alone is often enough to revolutionize social structures and organizations.

Review glossary

Urban society A society in which the majority of people do not live in rural areas. (p. 440)

Urban place According to the U.S. Census, a community having at least 2,500 inhabitants, the majority of whom do not farm. (p. 451)

City According to the U.S. Census, a community having at least 50,000 inhabitants. (p. 451)

Suburb An urban place in the immediate vicinity of a city. (p. 451)

Metropolis A city and its sphere of influence. (p. 451)

Sphere of influence (of a city) The area whose inhabitants depend on a city for jobs, recreation, newspapers, television, and a sense of common community. (p. 452)

Standard Metropolitan Statistical Area (SMSA) According to the U.S. Census, a central city (with at least 50,000 residents) and all surrounding counties where 75 percent of the labor force is not in agriculture and where either 15 percent of the workers commute to the city or 25 percent of the workers commute from the city. (p. 452)

Fixed-rail metropolis A city whose form and size are determined by the routes of rail transit systems (trains and trolleys). (p. 452)

Freeway metropolis A city that developed after the widespread use of autos and trucks freed city structures from rail dependency. (p. 452)

Theory of ethnic succession Theory stating that ethnic and racial groups will be the targets of neighborhood segregation only until they achieve economic parity and that slum neighborhoods will therefore house a succession of ethnic and racial groups. (p. 458)

Index of dissimilarity A measure of the degree to which a given ethnic or racial group lives in integrated or segregated neighborhoods; it compares the ethnic makeup of city blocks with the ethnic makeup of the city as a whole. (p. 459)

Gemeinschaft A German word meaning community and used to describe the intimacy of life in small villages. (p. 461)

Gesellschaft A German word meaning society or association and used to describe the impersonality of life in cities. (p. 462)

Anomie A state in which norms lack definition and force, that is, in which people aren't sure what the norms are and don't greatly care. (p. 462)

Suggested readings

Bourne, L. S., ed. *Internal Structure of the City.* New York: Oxford, 1971.

Fischer, Claude S. *The Urban Experience*. New York: Harcourt Brace Jovanovich, 1976.

Gove, Walter, Michael Hughes, and Omar Galle. "Overcrowding in the Home." *American Sociological Review* (1979) 44:59–80.

Pirenne, Henri. *Medieval Cities*. Princeton: Princeton University Press, 1925.

Sjoberg, Gideon. *The Preindustrial City*. New York: Free Press, 1960.

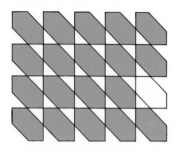

Napoleon Bonaparte was the last great captain to exercise direct command of his army, but, by the end of his career, even he failed at the task. Armies had simply become too big, and the area of the battlefield too vast. Even by standing on a hill and using a telescope, Napoleon could not keep track of everything that was going on. His orders to various units began to arrive too late and often they were wrong (Chandler, 1966).

Napoleon's problems were neither unique nor limited to the command of armies. During the nineteenth century, many human activities grew in size and complexity to the point that no single leader could orchestrate them. When he was President, George Washington personally evaluated every government employee: There were fewer than 700 of them! Today the U.S. government has more than 3 million employees, not including members of the armed forces. In fact, today General Motors employs more people than the total able-bodied adult population of the United States in 1776.

When organized human activities reached the scale of Napoleon's Grand Army of 1812 (about 600,000 troops), a crisis developed. Traditional principles of leadership and organization failed. When one of the greatest leaders in history could no longer master affairs on this scale, it was obvious that new methods were needed for directing and coordinating large-scale activities. If no one individual could manage large organizations, somehow several persons had to share the management. But how? How could leadership and decision making be shared among people without a breakdown in coordination? When Napoleon relied on his subordinates to act on their own, the result was often chaos, as different units marched off in different directions and to defeat.

The Organizational Age

The answer was the creation of a new kind of group, the **formal organization**. Because such an organization was produced by applying reason to the problems of management, and because the key to its success lies in operations based on logical rules, it is often called a *rational organization*.

A formal organization has a few characteristics that distinguish it from older forms of organization. First of all, it depends on a clear statement of goals. What is it meant to do? Second, a formal organization requires suitable operating principles and procedures for pursuing these goals. Third, leaders must be selected and trained in the use of these operating principles. Fourth, clear lines of authority and communication must be established along which instructions can be issued, information transmitted, and activities of different groups coordinated. Finally, to avoid misunderstanding and error, written records and communications must be used.

These five elements of the formal organization seem familiar and obvious to us today, for we live in an age dominated by such organizations. Yet formal organizations are very new human creations—so new that we still do not fully understand how to make them work effectively. Moreover, our understanding of formal organizations has been painfully gained by trial and error and in the face of urgent necessity. ■

CHAPTER PREVIEW

When you complain about the government, your employer, or your college or university, chances are that your complaint is not really about shortcomings of individuals. More likely, your complaints are about typical features of large, formal organizations. Everywhere you turn, you find that some aspect of your life is governed by and occurs within such organizations. That makes it important to know something about how such organizations operate and the theoretical principles behind their structure and performance. In this chapter, you will see that although organizations are created by and for humans, we are not free to create them in just any way we like.

Because large formal organizations are so new— very large organizations have existed for little more than 100 years—and because how they are created and operated has such far-reaching effects, they have been the object of intense study. From the beginning, theories of organization have influenced the structure and operations of organizations, and changes in theory and in organizations have gone hand in hand. We can therefore trace the development of both organizations and theories of organizations at the same time.

THE CRISIS OF GROWTH: INVENTING FORMAL ORGANIZATIONS

During the nineteenth century, the first large formal organizations were created, and the first social scientific attempts were made to figure out how to create and control them. These developments went forward in three somewhat independent sectors of industrializing societies: the military, business, and government. It is instructive to examine developments in each of these sectors before we focus on the work of the first great sociologist of formal organizations, Max Weber.

The case of the Prussian General Staff

After Napoleon's defeat at Waterloo in 1815, Europe entered a long period of peace. Armies were cut back to small professional corps, and interest in military science waned in most nations. Only in Prussia (later to become Germany) did they study the crises of command that emerged during the last stages of the Napoleonic Wars, when mass armies took to the battlefields. In Prussia the question was addressed head-on: What would happen if war broke out again and huge armies—made possible by the recent European population explosion and the mass production of arms—once again engaged in battle? Napoleon's failure had shown that such armies could not be led in the traditional way. The Prussians concluded that military command and organization had to be completely revised (Ropp, 1959).

If Napoleon was the last Great Captain of history, Helmuth von Moltke was the first Great Manager of the modern military era. Moltke took command of the Prussian army in 1857 and rapidly built up a new system based on the principle of using highly trained and interchangeable staff officers. These elite officers were trained in a war academy. Each year 120 young officers were selected from the whole officer corps on the basis of competitive examinations. Of these, only about 40 finished the intensive scholastic course of the academy. And of these graduates, Moltke selected only the best 12 to be trained for the General Staff (Howard, 1962).

In peacetime, officers cannot get real experience in their profession, so Moltke arranged for the academy to provide the next best thing: making battle plans for a great variety of hypothetical campaigns and analyses of past battles. By fighting battles on paper, young officers were trained in Prussian strategic and tactical theories. After their academic studies, officers chosen for the General Staff spent several years with Moltke at his headquarters and rode with him through a series of field maneuvers in which real troops participated. Then these officers were assigned a period of duty with a regiment. After that, they rotated between assignments on Moltke's staff and regimental duty (Ropp, 1959).

The point of all this training was to overcome the inability of a single commander to direct a war fought with mass armies. Since the supreme commander could not be everywhere at once, the next best thing was to try to create many "duplicates" trained to act as he would act. The decision of one leader could then be carried out

through the reflexes which he had already inculcated in his subordinates through previous training: so that, even when deprived of his guidance, they should react to unexpected situations as he would wish. . . . Thus the Prussian General Staff acted as a nervous system animating the lumbering body of the army, making possible the articulation and flexibility which alone rendered it an effective military force (Howard, 1962).

Between wars, the Prussian General Staff spent time looking ahead, planning in minute detail for future wars, and agreeing on proper tactics and strategies for various circumstances. When war came, each military problem was solved according to the overall plan and the approved methods. Thus, Moltke dealt with the overwhelming scale of modern warfare by training corps of subordinate managers he could count on to be not only his eyes and ears on the battlefield but also his brain.

While Moltke was creating an interchangeable set of military managers, he also perfected another military system that gave these managers standardized units to work with. This was the **divisional system**. Before the Napoleonic Wars, European armies were organized by armament and function. The cavalry, the infantry, and the artillery were separate branches of service and appeared on the battlefield as separate units under separate commanders. Coordinating these units was the task of the supreme commander of the army, who arrayed these forces into a battle formation and then told infantry units where to march, cavalry units where to charge, and artillery units where to fire.

However, as armies grew, this system proved cumbersome. Under Napoleon, the French army began to break up into smaller units, each of which was an independent mini-army consisting of infantry, cavalry, and artillery and capable of doing battle on its own.

These French formations were of varying size, and their makeup was never standardized. However, Napoleon's British archrival, the Duke of Wellington (who in his long career never lost a battle), adopted this idea of mini-armies and created a standardized unit called the division. British divisions, being complete units, could be detached to fight as self-sufficient units, combined to form larger units, and interchanged. For example, a rested reserve division could replace a fatigued division in combat.

Moltke carried the standardization of Prussian divisions to the point that commanders could easily move from unit to unit. Each division was similar to the others in makeup, training, size, and structure. Indeed, Moltke's divisional system was so detailed that each division had an exact number of spoons and cooking pots.

In 1871, Moltke tested his new military managers and his divisional structure in the Franco-Prussian War. During a lightning campaign, the Prussians utterly routed the much more experienced French Army. The Prussians did not win because they were better armed, had more soldiers, or were braver in battle. The French Army was their equal in all these ways. But the French General Staff was only a group of messengers and clerks serving the commander, and the French commander could not control his far-flung armies.

Noting Moltke's success over the French, all major nations soon copied his methods. Later, with the advent of telephones and radios, commanders could better guide their subordinates in the field. But the principle of delegating command to officers on the spot, who are highly trained in a common military theory and in the command of standardized military units, has remained the only workable solution to the problem that overwhelmed Napoleon.

The cases of Daniel McCallum and Gustavus Swift

It seems fitting that while the key to managing huge military organizations was first found in Prussia, the key to managing huge business organizations was

Field Marshal Helmuth von Moltke.

first discovered in the United States. For business, the rapid growth of railroads in the 1850s was the equivalent of Napoleon's Grand Army—the railroads revealed the inability of traditional organizational principles to cope with large-scale enterprises. The crisis appeared in dramatic fashion: Small railroads made profits while the big railroads lost money.

In 1855 Daniel C. McCallum, general superintendent of the Erie Railroad, pointed out that the reason his line and other large lines such as the New York Central, the Pennsylvania, and the Baltimore & Ohio were in financial distress was a problem of management. He wrote:

A Superintendent of a road fifty miles in length can give its business his personal attention and may be constantly on the line engaged in the direction of its details; each person is personally known to him, and all questions in relation to its business are at once presented and acted upon; and any system however imperfect may under such circumstances prove comparatively successful (Chandler, 1962).

A train crossing the Niagara Suspension Bridge in 1859. When trains were new, people often went out to watch them go by, as these gentlemen are doing. Notice the horse and buggy on the lower level. In those days, people knew a lot more about building and operating trains than they did about managing the railroad business.

Collection, The Museum of Modern Art, New York

These comments recall the spectacular ease with which Napoleon dealt with grave military disadvantages when he had only seventy to eighty thousand troops to maneuver on a single, compact battlefield. But, McCallum continued, when one attempts to manage a railroad "five hundred miles in length a very different state exists. Any system which might be applicable to the business and extent of a short

road would be found entirely inadequate to the wants of a long one." It was for want of an adequate organizational system, McCallum argued, that the large railroads faced financial failure.

McCallum quickly moved to install a management system to replace the overloaded manager. He broke his railroad into **geographical divisions** of manageable size. Each was headed by a superintendent responsible for the operations within his division. Each divisional superintendent was required to submit detailed reports to central headquarters, from where McCallum and his aides coordinated and gave general direction to the operations of the separate divisions. Lines of authority between each superintendent and his subordinates and between each superintendent and headquarters were clearly laid out. In sketching these lines of authority on paper, McCallum created what might have been the first organizational chart for an American business (Chandler, 1962). Soon the other great railroads copied the Erie's system, enabling the big railroads to function as effectively as small ones. As a result, railroads rapidly became the largest industrial companies of that time.

The railroads had two direct effects on other industrial firms. First, they made it possible for other firms to grow by using rail shipments to reach national rather than just local markets. Rail shipments could carry goods across the nation and bring needed supplies from far away. Second, the railroads provided a first crude organizational model for operating large firms. As other kinds of firms grew, they adopted the idea of divisions, but as we shall see, these were based on functions rather than geography. As they grew, new industrial firms created **functional divisions** that controlled each step in production through a process called **vertical integration**. These two features of industrial firms came to dominate organizational theory for many decades.

The story of Gustavus Swift, who built a huge meat-packing firm in the 1870s and 1880s, reveals how the new industrial organizations came into being.

Swift was a wholesale butcher in New England who moved west to Chicago in the 1870s. At that time a major problem was that the population was concentrated in the East, while the herds of livestock were concentrated on the Great Plains. Getting the meat to market was a cumbersome and inefficient process that depended on the uncoordinated services of small, specialized, local firms. Swift was determined to bring order and efficiency to the process by creating a firm that controlled each step from ranch to retail store. In 1878 he made an experimental shipment of meat from Chicago to the East, using the newly invented refrigerator car. The success of this experiment encouraged Swift and his brother Edwin to found Swift & Co. But they still faced vast problems. Shipping refrigerated meat east required refrigerated storage facilities at the other end; so Swift built them. Then the meat had to be sold; so Swift hired a sales crew and set up a distribution system in each major city. Local butchers tried to prevent the sale of his western meat in eastern markets, even claiming that it was unhealthy to eat "meat killed more than a thousand miles away and many weeks earlier" (Chandler, 1962). Massive advertising was required to convince consumers that Swift meat was safe. Soon Swift built additional packing plants in Omaha, St. Louis, St. Joseph, St. Paul, and Fort Worth.

Then Swift turned his attention to making supplies of meat dependable. He organized stockyards to purchase large numbers of animals on a regular and orderly basis. Finally, he branched out to make use of animal by-products by entering the leather, glue, fertilizer, and soap businesses.

Swift & Co. became a vertically integrated company: It controlled each step in the process of bringing meat products to the consumer. Although Swift did not raise cattle, the company took over at the point of sale and conducted each step thereafter: buying, packing, shipping, and marketing. Furthermore, each of these steps was the province of a different division of the company. That is, rather than creating geographic divisions, as the giant railroads had done, Swift based its divisions on different functions. In fact, Swift broke its organizational divisions up in the same way that the Industrial Revolution had divided the labor of workers into a few specific production steps. Just as each worker on an assembly line performed only one or a few specialized functions, each division of large industrial firms handled only one aspect of the industry.

Swift had a marketing division, a meat-packing division, a purchasing or stockyards division, a shipping division, a sales division, and an advertising division. Each of these divisions was headed by a manager to whom subordinate managers reported; each manager reported to and received directions from corporate headquarters. As Moltke's General Staff mastered large armies, vertical integration and functional divisions under centralized command made it possible to create and operate huge business firms.

The huge stockyards founded by Gustavus Swift in Chicago, the first of many operated by his company. In Swift's new organizational scheme, stockyards not only made up a functional division of the company but also were the initial level in the vertical integration of the company—control of each step in the process of bringing beef from the range to the meat counter.

The case of civil service

Armies and corporations were not the only organizations that grew to immense size in the modern world. Governments also got very large because of the rapid expansion in size and complexity of the societies they governed. As governments got big,

they, too, found that they could no longer function with outdated practices.

In traditional agrarian societies, the government was nothing more than the king's household and court. Such needed functionaries as clerks, accountants, and tax collectors were servants of the king, equal in status to his cooks, grooms, and butlers.

When the king needed a general, an advisor, a chief justice, or an administrator of the treasury, he asked one of the noblemen in his court to do the job. These noblemen did not regard a government post as an occupation or even as a full-time activity. Often they had no special training and little aptitude for their government duties beyond their noble birth and their social graces.

Such a system worked because governments did little governing. Beyond extracting taxes from the populace, maintaining some semblance of public order, and defending the realm against invaders, there was little to do. After all, more than 90 percent of the population were peasants leading quiet lives of rural toil. No complex laws, no large regulatory agencies, and no swarms of government experts were needed. Indeed, if the central government had disappeared, it would have taken a long while for people in outlying districts to have noticed.

With the growth of population and of cities, the complex divisions of labor, and the development of technology, it became increasingly difficult for agrarian governments to control their societies. Indeed, modern societies require more control than agrarian societies.

Governments adopted much the same solutions as did armies and industries. Government functions were carried out by organizations created specifically to perform them in an orderly and efficient manner, and these organizations were staffed by persons specially trained to perform their duties. In fact, the question of staffing governmental positions caused the greatest conflict.

Kings were accustomed to rewarding their loyal and valued friends with government positions. Early democratic governments continued this practice—the party or political faction in control of the government appointed its favorites to office. When the government changed hands, government officeholders were also changed. Thus, when Thomas Jefferson became President of the United States in 1801, he dismissed hundreds of Federalists appointed by Presidents Washington and Adams and replaced them with his supporters. This practice is known as the **spoils system**—the spoils, or benefits, of public office go to the supporters of winning politicians. The spoils system probably reached its height in the United States during the presidency of Andrew Jack-

A Dutch tax collector in about 1500. His filing system consists of several spikes on the wall and a ledger. If asked who he was, he would not say a government employee or a tax collector. Instead, no doubt he would say, "a gentleman." He would find modern Civil Service practices as strange as computerized accounting systems.

son in 1828, when thousands of officeholders were replaced.

A major problem with government based on the spoils system is not simply that disorganization arises from so much turnover but that people are prevented from making a career of government service. The administration of government organizations is forever left in the hands of untrained novices. To combat this problem the U.S. government adopted a practice in 1882 that was by then widespread in Europe: civil service.

The Pendleton Act, passed in 1882, established a government commission to choose federal employees on the basis of merit. Persons entered the civil service on the basis of their educational and occupational qualifications and by successfully competing with others on a written examination. When the government wanted accountants, it hired trained accountants with the highest scores on the civil service examination rather than the brother-in-law of the Governor of New Mexico. What Moltke learned was needed for modern war and what Gustavus Swift had discovered about business, modern government also put into practice: a carefully designed organizational system operated by specially selected and trained people.

WEBER'S RATIONAL BUREAUCRACY

At the turn of the century, Max Weber began to study the new forms of organization being developed for managing large numbers of people engaged in far-flung and complex activities. As a German, he was very familiar with Moltke's development of the General Staff. Furthermore, Germany had been an early leader in developing a civil service. And, in Weber's day, German industry was rapidly adopting the organizational methods developed in the United States. Surveying this scene, Weber attempted to isolate the elements common to all of these new organizations.

Weber concluded that all these new large-scale organizations were similar. Each was a **bureaucracy**. Today many of us regard *bureaucracy* as a dirty word suggesting red tape, inefficiency, and officiousness. As we shall see, bureaucracies can develop these features, especially if authority is highly centralized. Weber's purpose, however, was to define the essential features of new organizations and to indicate why these organizations worked so much better than traditional ones. Let us examine the features that Weber found in bureaucracies.

Above all, Weber emphasized that bureaucratic organizations were an attempt to subdue human affairs to the rule of reason—to make it possible to conduct the business of the organization "according to calculable rules." For people who developed modern organizations, the purpose was to find rational solutions to the new problems of size. Weber saw bureaucracy as the rational product of social

engineering, just as the machines of the Industrial Revolution were the rational products of mechanical engineering. He wrote:

The decisive reason for the advance of bureaucratic organization has always been its purely technical superiority over any former organization. The fully developed bureaucratic mechanism compares with other organizations exactly as does the machine with nonmechanical modes of production. (Trans. 1946).

Thus, for Weber, the term *bureaucracy* was inseparable from the term *rationality*. And we may speak of his concept as a "rational bureaucracy."

But what were the features developed to make bureaucracies rational? We have already met them: (1) functional specialization, (2) clear lines of hierarchical authority, (3) expert training of managers, and (4) decision making based on rules and tactics developed to guarantee consistent and effective pursuit of organizational goals. Weber noted additional features of rational bureaucracies that are simple extensions of the four outlined above. To ensure expert management, appointment and promotion are based on merit rather than favoritism, and those appointed treat their positions as full-time, primary careers. To ensure order in decision making, business is conducted primarily through written rules, records, and communications.

Weber's idea of functional specialization applies both to persons within an organization and to relations between larger units or divisions of the organization. We have already seen how this applied to Swift & Co. Within a Swift packing plant, work was broken down into many special tasks, and employees were assigned to one or a few such tasks, including the tasks involved in coordinating the work of others. (Such coordination is called administration or **management**.) Furthermore, Swift was separated into a number of divisions, each specializing in one of the tasks in the elaborate process of bringing meat from the ranch to the consumer. Weber argued that such specialization is essential to a rational bureaucracy and that the specific boundaries separating one functional division from another must be fixed by explicit rules, regulations, and procedures.

For Weber, it was self-evident that coordinating the divisions of large organizations requires clear lines of authority organized in a hierarchy. That means

Records are the basis of bureaucratic organizations. If organizations are to run on the basis of rational procedures, exact records must be kept of each transaction—for only then can the operation of the system be reviewed and improved.

that there are clear "levels of graded authority." All employees in the organization must know who their boss is, and each person should always respect the chain of command; that is, people should give orders only to their own subordinates and receive orders only through their own immediate superior. Only in this way can the people at the top be sure that directives arrive where they are meant to go and know where responsibilities lie.

Furthermore, hierarchical authority is required in bureaucracies so that highly trained experts can be properly used as managers. It does little good to train someone to operate a stockyard, for example, and then have that manager receive orders from

someone whose training is in advertising. Rational bureaucracies can be operated, Weber argued, only by deploying managers at all levels who have been selected and trained for their specific jobs. Persons ticketed for top positions in bureaucracies are often rotated through many divisions of an organization in order to gain first-hand experience of the many problems that their future subordinates must face (recall how Moltke rotated his General Staff officers through various regiments).

Finally, Weber stressed that rational bureaucracies must be managed in accordance with carefully developed rules and principles that can be learned and applied, and that transactions and decisions must be recorded so that rules can be reviewed. Only with such rules and principles can the activities of hundreds of managers at different levels in the organization be predicted and coordinated. If we cannot predict what others will do, we cannot count on them.

Moltke had to be sure that staff officers faced with an unexpected crisis would solve it as he would. To ensure that, officers had to be trained in Moltke's tactical principles and rules. Similarly, Gustavus Swift had to know that his stockyards would not buy meat faster than his packing plants could process it or that more meat would not be shipped than his eastern refrigerators could accommodate. Of course, it is impossible to spell out detailed rules to fit all contingencies. Therefore, it is important that decision makers be highly trained and that they report their decisions promptly and accurately to their superiors.

For a long time, Weber's rational bureaucracy model dominated social science thinking about large, modern organizations. If organizations did not operate quite as Weber had said a bureaucracy should, then the solution was to bring them in line with the ideal bureaucratic procedures. However, by World War II, sharp criticism of Weber's ideas began to surface. Particularly in the United States, social scientists began to argue that Weber had ignored much of what really went on in organizations—the conflicts, the cliques, and the sidestepping of rules and the chain of command. The problem, according to Philip Selznick (1948, 1957), lay in the fact that bureaucracies were not and could not be like machines because they consisted of human beings. In the final analysis, people will simply not imitate machines.

RATIONAL VERSUS NATURAL SYSTEMS

Weber stressed the rationality of bureaucratic organizations; that is, organizations are created and maintained to pursue clearly defined goals, and the structure and operation of organizations are the result of reasoned, conscious efforts to attain these goals.

This approach to studying organizations is called the **rational system approach**.

Alvin Gouldner (1959) described the rational system viewpoint as one in which

the organization is conceived as an "instrument"—that is, as a rationally conceived means to the realization of expressly announced group goals. Its structures are understood as tools deliberately established for the efficient realization of these group purposes. . . . changes in organizational patterns are viewed as planned devices to improve the level of efficiency. . . . the focus is, therefore, on . . . the formally "blueprinted" patterns.

From this viewpoint, organizations that make poor choices and fail to achieve stated goals are assumed to be guilty of ignorance and miscalculation.

However, many sociologists have criticized the rational approach as too limited. They argue that many important goals of organizations are not the "announced goals" and that often not all members of an organization pursue the same goals. Critics further argue that the real lines of communication and authority in organizations are not always the same as those laid out on the organizational chart. In fact, the real lines may violate the formal structure.

Persons approaching organizations in this way focus on the natural system. They argue that the general principles of the natural behavior of people and groups apply to the behavior of bureaucratic organizations; thus, these principles, not the rational system, reveal what is really going on in the system. A fundamental principle of the **natural system approach** is that the rarely stated but overriding goal of organizations is simply to survive. The living, breathing human beings who staff an organization develop a personal stake in the life of that organization, regardless of the stated goals of the organization. For its members, the existence of an organization means the continuation of jobs, careers, and friendships. When an organization folds, its members are cast adrift. Thus, people can be expected to resist such a fate even at the expense of the formal goals of the organization. Therefore, features of an organization that appear as miscalculations from the rational perspective may in fact be reflections of people's efforts to keep the organization alive.

Goal displacement

The importance of survival over other goals is well illustrated by an organization created during the 1930s to combat the dread disease of polio. The National Foundation for the March of Dimes created a huge network of volunteers in each American community who, guided by the professional staff, conducted an extremely successful annual fund drive. The funds were used to support the treatment of polio victims and research for a way to cure or prevent the disease. The March of Dimes was an extremely successful and well-run organization. Then, one day, it was too successful. In the 1950s, research supported by March of Dimes funds led to the discovery of effective vaccines. A massive vaccination drive soon resulted in the virtual elimination of polio. The March of Dimes had achieved its goals.

Yet this achievement was not met with an office party of gleeful people toasting to victory and going off happily to pursue new careers. Instead, there was something closer to panic as the March of Dimes staff searched for a new goal to sustain the organization. Quickly they declared war on birth defects and, as the National Foundation, continue still to raise funds and to conduct business as usual (Sills, 1957).

Organizations often change, or displace, their goals in the pursuit of survival, but not often as dramatically as did the National Foundation. Philip Selznick (1949) has documented substantial **goal displacement** by the Tennessee Valley Authority (TVA). When created during the 1930s, TVA announced broad goals to transform the whole social structure of the rural farming region served by its hydroelectric power and flood control projects. Many found these goals too radical, and opposition to the TVA grew. In reaction to threats to disband the agency, these far-reaching social goals were replaced by the more limited goals of rural electrification and resource management.

These examples illustrate the truth of a principle: When the formal goals of an organization threaten its existence, the goals will be changed.

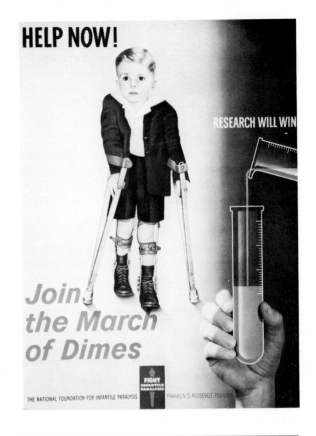

Posters like this were on display everywhere when I was growing up. Some of my playmates died of polio (often called infantile paralysis); many more were badly crippled. The line "Research will win" turned out not to be an empty slogan. Research paid for by March of Dimes contributions funded the discovery of the polio vaccine.

Goal conflict

Natural system theorists also argue that different groups within an organization tend to pursue different goals, which often have nothing to do with (and may even conflict with) the goals of the larger organization. This situation is called **goal conflict**.

The official goal of corporations is to earn profits for stockholders, but the managerial revolution—whereby owners have been separated from the control of corporations—resulted in the displacement of the profit goal as the overriding goal of modern corporations. Managers as a group have goals that may *conflict* with the profit goal of a company. For example, managers may approve lavish expenses—sales meetings in posh resorts, elegant business entertainment, and company-owned jets and limousines—that cut into potential profits. They do this to reward themselves rather than a mass of anonymous, disorganized owners (stockholders).

A second reason why managers may deemphasize profit seeking is because other groups in the corporation effectively pursue goals that also conflict with the profit goal. Consider the case of labor. Maximum profits depend upon getting the greatest amount of production from workers for the lowest possible wage. While all managers seek to raise worker productivity and to hold down labor costs, modern corporation executives do not do so without regard for their own welfare. Unions often resist changes in work procedures and the introduction of new technology and press for the highest possible wages. Therefore, management often does not seek the most profitable labor contracts, settling instead for a compromise that involves the least disruption and stress.

Management and labor are the most obvious examples of groups who strike bargains that affect the structure and operations of an organization. Many such compromises are not designed to make the organization more effective in pursuing its stated goals. Organizations often develop many competing interest groups. Thus, various divisions of a company may strike bargains with one another over who is responsible for what. Such bargains may reflect desires for enhanced status or lesser workloads, but they may lower efficiency.

Informal relations

Formal organizations are based on clear lines of authority and responsibility. Each member is supposed to know to whom to give orders and from whom to take them. However, natural system theorists point out that people often do not adhere to the formal chain of command. They constantly construct social relations that serve as bases for authority, influence, and communication that often bear little resemblance to relations set out in the formal blueprint.

Suppose Jack in division A needs assistance from division B. He could go to his supervisor, who would then request the assistance from the supervisor of division B. He could also call his friend Sally in division B and get what he needs without either supervisor knowing what is going on. Indeed, Jack and Sally could call on each other all the time. They could thus get around the formal procedures for interdivision cooperation and override the formal system. It is well known in many organizations that you must see certain people in order to get certain things done, despite the fact that these people do not hold the formal position that is supposed to control these activities. In addition, friendships and enmities may also lead to the overriding of formal operations.

But if the rational system approach overemphasizes the organizational blueprint, the natural system approach tends to forget that there is one. Although organizations are filled with informal channels of authority, influence, and communication—informal networks of social relations and groups pursuing goals other than the corporate goals—most of what people do most of the time can be predicted from the corporate blueprint. Persons who are hired to work on an automobile assembly line, for example, may cooperate to keep production at the level that they think is best for them and get around their supervisors to alter procedures, but they do not work in the accounting office sorting invoices, in the design division drawing new models, or in the showrooms selling cars. When we know the official duties and responsibilities of a particular job, we can predict a great deal about what people hired to fill that job will spend their time doing.

Consequently, neither the rational nor the natural system approach can fully explain formal organizational activities. They are complementary views. The long conflict over which approach better explains organizations is probably nothing more than an academic dispute between college departments. Those who have given the most time to study of the rational system are usually employed in the department of business administration. Those who opt for the natural system are mainly employed in sociology

A clear organizational chart could easily be created of this newspaper staff. Everyone has a distinct job title with specific responsibilities, and clear lines of authority state who is supposed to report to whom. But observation would reveal great differences between the chart and what really goes on.

and psychology departments. In the competition for customers (in this case, students), each firm (or department) stresses the merits of its product. But the wise customer knows that making a choice is unnecessary; one need not choose between cereal or fruit for breakfast, but may benefit from mixing both in the same bowl.

The important point is that when people design or evaluate an organization, they must pay attention not only to what people are supposed to do but also to what they are apt to do.

THE CRISIS OF DIVERSIFICATION

In the case studies examined at the beginning of this chapter, we saw some basic solutions to problems in managing large organizations. Thus we saw that Gustavus Swift was among the first to organize a large business firm on the basis of vertical integration of functional divisions. Moltke was one of the first to recognize the need for highly trained, interchangeable commanding officers steeped in a common military doctrine. And civil service arose to ensure experienced and competent managers in government.

As time passed, however, the solutions of Swift, Moltke, and others to the problems of operating large organizations began to fail. As organizations continued to grow and become more complex, a need arose for even better organizing and managing of principles. In part, this new crisis occurred because the rational system approach created some organizational problems that exceeded the natural human capacities of managers. There are limits to how much any one person can know and do. These new problems, and the principles they spawned, can best be understood by examining one of the first organizations in which such problems became evident and were solved.

Du Pont is one of the oldest and most successful firms in the United States. It began in 1802 when Éleuthère Irénée Du Pont, an immigrant from France, built a gunpowder factory on the banks of historic Brandywine Creek near Wilmington, Delaware. The factory grew and prospered. Throughout the nineteenth century, Du Pont sons attended West Point or M.I.T., the best engineering schools in the country at that time, and then went into the family business. The firm grew larger and larger. Although the product line expanded to include blasting powder and dynamite as well as gunpowder, the firm manufactured explosives almost exclusively.

Functional divisions

By the turn of the century, Du Pont displayed the same problems of bigness that many other organizations faced at that time. With many factories requiring massive amounts of raw materials, supplies had to come in regularly and at predictable prices, and the production flowing out of these plants had to be directed to customers in an orderly and efficient manner. When the operations of Du Pont became bogged down, the directors responded, as Gustavus Swift had done, by reorganizing the firm into functional divisions.

All personnel and facilities involved in manufacturing explosives were grouped into a single admin-istrative unit under a general manager. All purchasing was centralized into a single unit, rather than having factories buy on their own. Sales were coordinated within a single unit, as were engineering, research and development, finance, and legal services. An effective reporting system was instituted so that a steady flow of information kept managers aware of the operations for which each was responsible. This information flowed upward to provide an accurate picture of operations on which the president and directors could base major policy decisions.

Once reorganized, the firm functioned extremely well. In 1914, World War I broke out in Europe and created a sudden, nearly inexhaustible demand for gunpowder and high explosives. To meet this demand, Du Pont undertook one of the largest expansions the world of business had ever seen. At the start of the war, Du Pont plants had a maximum capacity of slightly more than 8 million pounds of smokeless gunpowder a year. In little more than twelve months, they had expanded their factories by nearly twenty-five times to 200 million pounds a year. By 1917 they had increased production by more than fifty times, to 455 million pounds a year. Expansion of production capacities for high explosives grew almost as dramatically. Similarly, the company's payroll expanded enormously. In the fall of 1914, Du Pont employed 5,300 people. In 1918, they employed more than 85,000. And the company's investment in plants and equipment grew from $83 million to $309 million.

The new organization based on functional divisions coped very well with these terrific demands. Efficiency did not suffer, and the firm earned excellent profits on its investment. But the enormous growth presented the company with both an opportunity and a challenge. What would they do when the war ended? The demand for gunpowder and explosives would then return to low prewar levels. Should they plan to close down the huge new plants they had built and lay off most of their employees? Or should they try to find a way to convert these new assets into peacetime production?

The Du Ponts decided to diversify by entering the growing market for chemical products, a market for which their mastery of explosives manufacture was ideally suited. Demand for early synthetics such as patent leather, synthetic silks, and plastics was growing, and Du Pont prepared during the war to enter these new markets when peace returned.

In 1919 these plans were put into operation on a huge scale. The company became a large manufacturer of paint, dyes, plastics, chemicals, fertilizers, and the host of products associated with the chemical industry today. Du Pont had immense amounts of money from its wartime profits to invest in these new activities. It had the plants, skilled labor, and highly skilled managers. The quality of its products was excellent, and sales rose rapidly. But the company almost went broke.

What happened? The principle of functional divisions, a hugely successful arrangement for organizations engaged in a relatively narrow set of activities, turned out to be a disastrous arrangement for organizations engaged in a broad range of activities.

Autonomous divisions

Before diversifying into its many new activities, Du Pont resembled Swift & Co. The company was organized to govern each step in the manufacture of explosives from the acquisition of the needed raw materials to their delivery to customers. But now they were engaged in many parallel operations. For example, before diversification, the sales division had dealt with only a few very large customers— primarily governments and manufacturing firms (for example, ammunition manufacturers). To sell paint, however, they had to deal with thousands of small retail merchants and create a demand for Du Pont paint among consumers. The same was true of their soap, glue, and finished plastic products. The sales department found itself overwhelmed by an immense array of products that had to be sold in different ways to many different kinds of customers.

The same thing was happening in the manufacturing division. Instead of having a number of similar factories, each engaged in similar production processes and thus facing similar difficulties, Du Pont now had factories that were not much alike at all. The paint factories bore little resemblance to the plastics factories, the fertilizer factories, and so on. Similarly, the purchasing department no longer

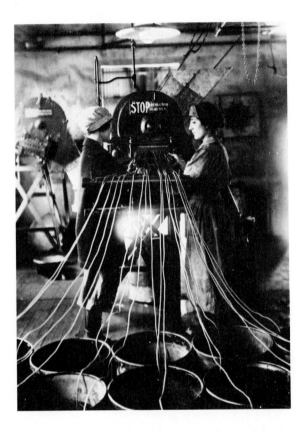

Women at work in a Du Pont factory making smokeless gunpowder during World War I. Frantic pleas from England and France for powder prompted Du Pont to undertake one of the most rapid industrial expansions in history.

searched for a few raw materials but for a huge variety from many different sources.

With diversification of the firm into many businesses, executives faced demands that exceeded their capabilities. Executives in the manufacturing division could not grasp the major technical problems of so many different manufacturing processes. Nor could the sales force master knowledge about so many different products or the appropriate sales techniques for every market. In addition, as the firm diversified, upper management had too many people to supervise.

Considerable research has demonstrated that there are limits on the number of people a given person can supervise effectively. This limit is called the **span** of control. Research suggests that no executive should have more than seven subordinates who report directly to him or her. Beyond that number, confusion begins to set in, and the executive has neither the time nor the memory to serve each subordinate adequately (Drucker, 1967). But in Du Pont, the span of control imposed on senior executives was far more than seven, many having direct responsibility for thirty to forty subordinate managers.

Faced with operations of such magnitude, the organizational system began to creak and split open. Just as the large railroads had once lost money while the small railroads were highly profitable, Du Pont began to lose money while small, specialized competitors flourished. Worse yet, the more Du Pont sold of its new products, the more money it lost! Thus, when sales of paint and varnish rose from $1 million to $4 million over three years, annual losses on these products rose from $100,000 to $500,000. Even this giant company with its huge wartime cash reserves couldn't endure such losses, which came to $2.5 million in the first six months of 1921 alone.

Unlike government agencies, business firms get very nervous when their profits fall, because unlike government agencies, they can go broke. The top managers at Du Pont sat down and carefully rethought their entire organization. They knew that they were engaged in the right business, because their products sold well. But they also knew that they were not conducting their business properly. As one of their directors put it in a memo to his fellow board members: "The trouble with the Company is right here in Wilmington, and the failure is the failure of administration for which we, as directors, are responsible" (Chandler, 1962).

After careful consideration, Du Pont management realized that the failure of their administration lay in current theories of organization: The functional division system was wrecking them. This system is fine for a firm that produces a narrow line of products or performs a narrow line of services. It is an excellent system for an explosives company or a meat company. But it is an unworkable system for a **diversified organization** that manufactures many different kinds of things.

Indeed, what the Du Pont managers suddenly realized was that they should no longer think of themselves as a single firm. They had grown so large and were in so many different businesses that they needed to reorganize themselves into divisions organized around each business, not around each function. Functional divisions could be retained but at a lower level of management: only within **autonomous divisions** constituted as independent firms. The larger company of Du Pont would consist of a number of divisions, each fully organized to conduct its own business.

What Du Pont had done was to discover the business version of the military divisions created by the Duke of Wellington and perfected by Moltke. As a military division included all essential components of an army, a Du Pont division included all components of a manufacturing company. It would purchase its raw materials (and pay the market price, even if they were purchased from another Du Pont division), supervise its own manufacturing, conduct its own research and development, and operate its own marketing and sales organization.

Each division would be run by a general manager who had the authority to make business decisions for the division and who would answer to top management, who were primarily interested only in the success or failure of the overall operation. The top management at Du Pont stepped back from the details of the operations of its divisions. Instead, it appointed or fired top division managers, decided which divisions to keep and which to dispose of, and made plans for creating and acquiring new divisions. Like Moltke, the Du Pont management planned and communicated the grand strategy of the firm but delegated the tactical decisions to commanders on the spot.

Soon most major American firms faced problems similar to Du Pont's, and they, too, solved them by establishing autonomous divisions. In this way, Alfred Sloan remodeled sprawling General Motors into the Chevrolet, Pontiac, Oldsmobile, Buick, and Cadillac divisions. With their separate assembly plants, their own systems of exclusive dealerships, their own advertising budgets, and their own financial resources, they competed with one another almost as fully as they did with Ford, Chrysler, and other competitors.

These autonomous divisions transformed single firms that had become too big and too complex to manage into a cluster of smaller, coordinated firms. This was the second step taken in a new approach to managing big organizations: **decentralization**.

BLAU'S THEORY OF ADMINISTRATIVE GROWTH

 We have seen that the solution for managing large corporations lies in creating a division of labor among executives—parceling out administrative responsibilities so that several people perform duties too numerous for any one person to handle. A direct consequence of the growth of organizations has therefore been an even more rapid growth in the number of persons required to manage them. Peter M. Blau (1970, 1972) considered the rapid expansion of managerial positions and formulated a theory of organization. Two of his major propositions were:

1. Organizational growth causes differentiation. This is precisely what we have seen throughout this chapter. As organizations get larger, they must be broken down into units so that their activities can be controlled.

2. As organizations become more differentiated, the size of the administrative component increases relative to the size of other components. Blau argued that the difficulties of coordinating and communicating across differentiated units are much greater than *within* units. Therefore, the greater the number of units, the greater the effort required to coordinate them, and the greater the number of supervisors and managers needed.

From these two propositions it follows logically that the larger the organization, the greater the proportion of total resources that must be devoted to management functions.

By now there is considerable empirical support for **Blau's administrative theory**. Its most obvious implication is that organizations are less costly to run when they are kept smaller and that efficiency may be lost rather than gained when several organizations are combined into one huge organization. The reason for creating larger organizations has always been to achieve savings. For example, a grocery chain can undersell an independent grocer because of the great savings made possible by large-scale purchasing and marketing. However, at some point such savings must be weighed against the greater resources needed to manage the organization. These accelerating management costs are an overhead—they add to the costs of the goods and services offered by an organization. Some organizations are too small and some are too large to be efficient.

It is impossible to give a general answer to the question, How big is too big? For any given organization, that can only be answered by weighing administrative costs against savings and then determining when bigness offsets efficiency. But organizational theorists now believe that any organization can get too big.

Blau's theory, therefore, once again leads to the principle of decentralization. When organizations got too big for one person to control, means had to be found to place the control in the hands of many people, that is, to decentralize authority. The various ways to cope with great size that we have examined were all meant to decentralize organizations without letting them become uncoordinated. It turns out, however, that efforts to decentralize organizations tend to run into resistance from the natural system within organizations.

RATIONAL AND NATURAL FACTORS IN DECENTRALIZATION

The goal of top executives in most business organizations has long been to get decisions off their desks and place them on the desks of subordinates. Thus, McCallum ceased making operating decisions for the Erie Railroad and instead asked his division superintendents to make them. Ever since, business has sought ways to push this process of decentralization further. Indeed, maximum decentralization is the main principle of current management science.

Business theorists such as Peter F. Drucker (1946, 1967, 1974) preach that companies ought to create the smallest possible operating units in order to give maximum flexibility to the person on the spot.

Drucker argues that it is impossible for higher management to have firsthand experience of the specific conditions in a remote department. Let the people in charge of those departments make the decisions, because they will usually make the right ones. As long as the overall performance of a department is satisfactory, leave it alone. If performance falls, appoint new people. But never try to run it from upstairs.

This doctrine is often called **management by objectives**, because managers and their subordinates negotiate the objectives to be reached by the subordinates. Then managers give subordinates maximum freedom to decide how to achieve the objectives and later judge the subordinates by how well they succeed. In this way, decision making is delegated to those in the best position to make particular decisions quickly and correctly.

The key element in the decentralization of organizations is *discretion,* the freedom to make choices and decisions. Decentralization consists of giving the maximum number of subordinates in an organization discretion in running their part of the operation. But discretion involves two closely linked elements: (1) the *responsibility* for making decisions and (2) the *authority* to carry them out. Giving people responsibility is futile unless they are also given the power to meet their responsibilities. This is more than a truism, however. Often it is very difficult to give members of organizations enough authority to allow the decentralization of decision making to be effective.

Limits on the power to implement decisions come from both within and without organizations. Internal limits come from the necessary interdependence of the many subunits of an organization. Limits can also come from having to deal with external factors, such as suppliers, markets, competitors, and regulatory agencies, which organizational members cannot control. For example, a decision to increase efforts to market a particular item may be thwarted when suppliers cannot increase their production, when competitors cut their prices or introduce an improved model, when the market fails to respond, or when the government imposes new requirements.

Reflecting on these aspects of decentralization, James D. Thompson (1967) developed a number of theoretical propositions. Several of these pertain to the conditions under which members of an organization will accept discretion. Thompson proposed that when individuals in an organization believe that they cannot adequately control conditions affecting decisions, they will try to evade discretion—they will try to pass responsibility on to someone else (usually someone higher in the organization). Thus, the more a particular position in an organization depends on other positions in the organization, the less willing people in that position will be to exercise discretion. Similarly, the more that a decision involves forces outside the organization, the less willing people will be to make that decision.

Second, the more serious the potential consequences of an error are perceived to be, the less willing people will be to assume discretion. People want to share responsibility for a decision with all who will be affected by the decision if it turns out to be wrong. A variant on this is that the more discretion assigned to a position in an organization, the more a person holding that position will seek power over those affected by his or her decisions. This also minimizes the negative consequences of poor decisions by limiting the power of others to retaliate.

Thus, we see that despite efforts to impose decentralization on the formal system, forces generated within the natural system tend toward recentralization. People often seek to regain dispersed power in order to control the conditions affecting their decisions more fully. Or people seek to disperse responsibility for decisions that the organization meant to place in their hands alone.

From the point of view of formal organizational models, decentralization has many benefits. It places decisions in the hands of those closest to the scene. Although decentralization disperses power widely, thus diluting the power of top management, it limits an organization's dependence on any given decision maker. That is, decentralized organizations are like ships with many separate, watertight compartments. If such a ship strikes an iceberg, flooding is limited to a few compartments and the ship remains afloat. Similarly, decentralized organizations suffer only limited damage from bad choices made by any given person, for each makes only a few decisions. However, Thompson's theory suggests that the natural system within an organization often thwarts these formal arrangements and cuts holes in the watertight compartments.

We have seen why Thompson stated that the natural system of organizations tends to be less decentralized than the formal system. Moreover, coalitions tend to form within an organization (see Chapter 1). Thompson postulated that whenever an individual given discretion has insufficient power to control conditions governing his or her decisions, that individual will seek added power by forming a coalition with other decision makers. For instance, consider someone empowered to decide how much of a product to produce and someone else empowered to decide how to market that product. The marketing decisions depend upon supply, and production decisions depend upon sales. No matter how the company is organized, the production and marketing managers are likely to get together and act jointly—to form a coalition.

Perhaps the most interesting of Thompson's propositions about coalitions pertains to attempts to control external threats to decisions. When these threats are very great, persons given substantial discretion will seek to form coalitions with people outside the organization. For example, marketing managers for competing firms may secretly agree to split up the potential market and thereby limit their vulnerability. Or a production manager may make secret agreements with suppliers in order to reduce uncertainties. Indeed, newspaper editors have noted that reporters assigned to cover the police form coalitions with police commanders, trading favorable coverage for special access to information. A reporter assigned to cover the police risks his or her job if the police favor competing reporters with inside information, and police commanders fear unsympathetic reports will provoke public criticism. Coalitions therefore serve the interests of both commanders and reporters but undercut the interests of both organizations (Stark, 1962, 1972).

But if the natural system of organizations often circumvents decentralization, the fact remains that many organizations, especially business organizations, are much more decentralized than they used to be. Indeed, this has been the major trend for formal organizations generally. The Napoleonic problem of managing large armies was solved by delegating authority. The problem of managing big railroads was solved by breaking them up into functional units, each the size of a small railroad. And the problems of managing a huge, diversified company like Du Pont were solved by treating parts of the organization as independent companies. The adoption of management by objectives, in which authority is delegated to ever smaller internal organizational units, is simply an extension of this same trend. But it would be misleading to end this chapter without noting that not all organizations have followed this decentralizing trend. Thus, while decentralization has dominated organizations in the private sector, government organizations have tended toward ever greater centralization.

Governments have grown rapidly in the twentieth century. In most modern societies, including the United States, the government is by far the largest employer, and government spending makes up a very substantial proportion of all monetary transactions—today the government spends about $25 out of every $100 earned or spent in the United States.

But as governments have grown huge, they have become ever more centralized. Thus, many government activities that were left wholly to local jurisdictions even twenty years ago are centralized today in Washington. For example, schools were entirely the responsibility of local governments until recently. Now much of the funding comes from state and federal governments, and many aspects of local schools are initiated, directed, and controlled from Washington.

In Europe, government is even more centralized than in the United States. In most nations, local government is nearly nonexistent—local mayors are appointed and controlled by the central government. Many colleges and universities are run by a ministry of education in the capital. The ministry not only determines how money is spent but also makes all faculty appointments, chooses textbooks, and even controls student admissions.

Governments in communist nations are even more centralized. In fact, the government in these nations attempts to administer the whole economy—industry, retailing, farming, and so on—from a central bureaucracy. The results have been detailed in dozens of studies of inefficiency and waste caused by

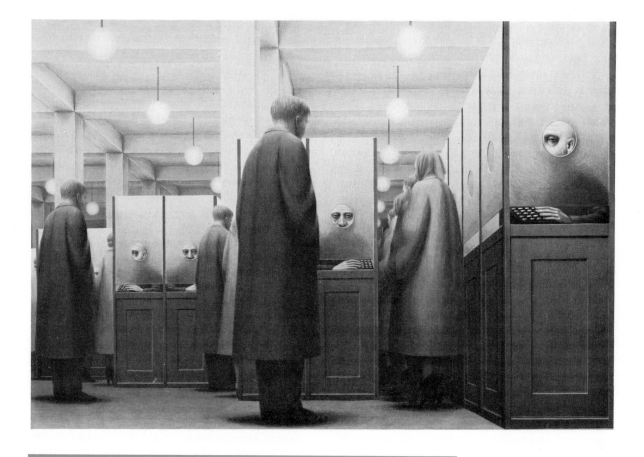

After spending weeks in city offices trying to get a building permit in Brooklyn, artist George Tooker painted Government Bureau, *which now hangs in New York's Metropolitan Museum of Art. We catch but glimpses of the bureaucrats hiding behind their rules and regulations.*

decision makers buried in a sea of detail (Kaiser, 1976; Smith, 1976).

If so many other organizations have found that they became too big and too centralized to work, why haven't governments, democratic and communist alike, learned this lesson too?

BUREAUCRACY AND THE BOTTOM LINE

In everyday speech the words *bureaucracy* and *bureaucrat* are often used negatively. They suggest meddlesome people and muddled organizations. Yet as Weber noted, all modern organizations, public or private, are bureaucracies. The reason we often think of government agencies and personnel when we hear the terms *bureaucracy* and *bureaucrat* is because government agencies generally do not work as well as private organizations. The reason they don't is because they do not face the same pressures to reexamine and improve their organizational methods.

The strength of private bureaucracies is their vulnerability. They can and often do go broke. This means that they are under constant pressure to earn the right to exist, to achieve their goals, and to adapt to changing circumstances. The Du Pont executives stayed late at night in 1921 trying to figure out how to put their organization right, not because they were more conscientious than government executives, but because their time was rapidly running out. If they had not found immediate effective solutions to their organizational problems, they soon would have had to inform their creditors that Du Pont was bankrupt.

Business organizations, therefore, have a very clear standard by which to judge their performance—profit and loss. While profit is not the only goal of corporation executives, it is the ultimate one. Day in and day out, profit and loss provide a gauge indicating which operations are working better and which are working worse, which managers are doing better and which are doing worse. The bottom line is always evident. Thus, Du Pont executives could not take comfort in the great popularity of their new paint products or in their high quality, for to do so meant bankruptcy.

Government bureaucracies do not have so clear a gauge of their success or failure. They do not go broke, they do not count profits, and they can claim great credit when their actions are popular without asking if their actions are effective or efficient. This does not mean that the effectiveness of government bureaucracies cannot be measured. But often it just simply isn't measured.

Recently many political scientists have proposed that measures of government effectiveness be required. Of course, they do not suggest that government agencies should operate on the basis of profit and loss. They do suggest that government agencies should measure their results objectively so that their performance can be evaluated. Such measures are not hard to devise if the goals of an organization are clearly identified.

Imagine that we are going to reorganize a welfare agency. First, we would need to set its goals. One goal might be to provide jobs for the maximum number of welfare workers. While some suspect that this is often the goal of public agencies, it would not be acceptable as an official goal. Suppose that we set the goal as getting the maximum amount of welfare money into the hands of poor people. Then we might want to close the welfare agency and send all its administrative funds to poor people. That is precisely what proposals such as a guaranteed income or a negative income tax intend to accomplish.

However, we might choose as our goal to minimize the time people spend on welfare by returning a maximum number to economic self-sufficiency as soon as possible. Then we could evaluate the agency by keeping track of the proportion of persons leaving the welfare rolls and the average length of time people were on welfare. With these measures one program could be compared with another. Then we could see if a cheaper program worked as well as or better than a more expensive one, whether some welfare workers were more effective than others, and whether different programs were needed in different places. If decentralization theory is correct, we would expect a program to work better when local welfare offices were given maximum authority and responsibility to achieve the stated goal.

CONCLUSION

The fundamental theme of this chapter is that organizations are human inventions intended to serve human needs. The rational, or formal, organization based on bureaucratic principles was a major social invention necessitated by the great increase in the scale and complexity of human activities in modern times. Perhaps the primary lesson we have learned from our brief experience with formal organizations is that there is no such thing as a perfect organization. Instead, organizational forms and principles that serve extremely well under some conditions can be inadequate or even harmful under others.

Effective organizations are therefore the momentary results of constant reassessment and redesign. When the effectiveness of organizations is not tested, they rapidly tend to become unresponsive and inefficient, taking on the negative features associated with the term *bureaucracy*. In the final analysis, we get the kinds of organizations we deserve. We create them; we run them. If they make our lives unpleasant, only we can change them. The fundamental truth about organizations is this: Organizations never do anything; only people do things. While much of what people do is the result of their positions in formal organizations, the fact remains that organizations never make decisions, pursue goals, assess means, or adopt new policies. Only people, acting in the name of organizations, do such things.

By the same token, societies don't change. Society didn't invent the steam engine; James Watt did. Societies don't have babies, women do. And societies become urban only as people move to town. Thus, it is time to shift the focus of this introduction to sociology away from large social structures and back once more to human behavior. To conclude this book, we shall examine how people cause and resist social change.

Review glossary

Formal organization Synonymous with rational organization, a group created to pursue definite goals wherein tactics and procedures are designed and evaluated in terms of effectiveness in achieving goals, members are selected and trained to fulfill their roles, and overall operations are based on written records and rules. (p. 469)

Divisional system As initially used in armies, the organization of troops into small, identical units, each containing all military elements (infantry, artillery, and cavalry). (p. 470)

Geographical divisions Divisions resulting from breaking an organization into smaller units on the basis of geography and making each division relatively independent. (p. 472)

Functional divisions Divisions resulting from breaking an organization into smaller units on the basis of specialized activities or functions, such as when a corporation has separate divisions for manufacturing, purchasing, marketing, and the like. (p. 473)

Vertical integration The inclusion within an organization of the divisions that control every step in the production and distribution of some product or service. (p. 473)

Spoils system System in which government jobs are taken over by the winners after each election. (p. 475)

Bureaucracy A formal organization that, according to Weber, is based on (1) functional specialization, (2) clear, hierarchical lines of authority, (3) expert training of managers, (4) decision making based on rational rules aimed at effective pursuit of goals, (5) appointment and promotion of managers on their merit, and (6) the conducting of activities by written communications and records. (p. 476)

Management Coordination of the work of others. (p. 476)

Rational system approach Emphasis on the official and intended characteristics of organizations. (p. 478)

Natural system approach Emphasis on the informal and unintended characteristics of organizations. (p. 478)

Goal displacement That which occurs when the official goals of an organization are ignored or changed. (p. 479)

Goal conflict Situation in which one goal of an organization limits the ability of that organization to achieve other goals; for example, the desire to avoid losses due to strikes will conflict with an organization's goal to minimize labor costs. (p. 479)

Span of control The number of subordinates one manager can adequately supervise, often estimated as seven. (p. 483)

Diversified organization An organization that is not very specialized but instead pursues a wide range of goals. (p. 484)

Autonomous divisions Parts of an organization, each of which includes a full set of functional divisions. (p. 484)

Decentralization Dispersing of authority from a few central administrators to persons directly engaged in activities. (p. 484)

Blau's administrative theory Theory stating that the larger the organization, the greater the proportion of total resources that must be devoted to management functions. (p. 485)

Management by objectives Situation in which managers and subordinates agree on goals that subordinates will try to achieve; subordinates then have maximum freedom in how they will try to reach their objectives. (p. 486)

Suggested readings

Chandler, Alfred D., Jr. *Strategy and Structure: Chapters in the History of the American Industrial Revolution.* Cambridge: M.I.T. Press, 1962.

Drucker, Peter F. *Management.* New York: Harper and Row, 1974.

Perrow, Charles. *Complex Organizations,* 2nd ed. Glenview, Ill.: Scott, Foresman, 1979.

Peters, Thomas J., and Robert H. Waterman, Jr. *In Search of Excellence: Lessons from America's Best-Run Companies.* New York: Harper and Row, 1982.

Selznick, Philip. *Leadership in Administration.* New York: Harper and Row, 1957.

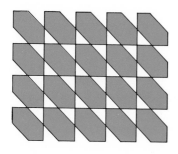

Author's note Although the topics covered in this chapter are of great importance to sociology and are definitely related, the field has lacked a clear conceptual scheme that integrates them. This has posed great difficulties for textbook authors. As I grappled with the problem of how to fit together such diverse topics as the spread of Hula Hoops, riots, economic panics, and the rise of new political movements, I discovered that my friend William Sims Bainbridge had developed a very effective conceptual framework. However, he had not published it, having used it only in his courses. If I had adopted his ideas, I could not cite any published work, and thus I urged him to publish his new ideas quickly so that I could draw on them in good conscience. As we talked, it became obvious that the best solution was simply to have Bill write this chapter. So he did. Since he and I have often written together, our styles are much the same. My only contributions to this chapter have been some minor touches to integrate it with the rest of the book.

Rodney Stark

William Sims Bainbridge

Collective Behavior and Social Movements

By William Sims Bainbridge

Harvard University

Alvin "Shipwreck" Kelly sat high atop the flagpole on the Steel Pier at Atlantic City for 49 days and 1 hour back in 1930. Who would want to do anything so crazy? Several people, apparently. Soon after Shipwreck invented this stunt, "Hold 'em" Joe Powers spent 16 days at an altitude of 647 feet on the flagpole of the Morrison Hotel in Chicago. Elsewhere other daredevils sat on flagpoles, and the news media began calling this phenomenon a *craze* or *fad* .

Since the early days of Shipwreck and Hold 'em Joe, this craze has reappeared several times in the United States. In 1976 Frank Powers set a new record by perching for 400 days on a flagpole in San Jose, California, coming down to earth on the nation's bicentennial. Several news stories at that time stressed that a person has to be "a little bit nuts" to do something like this.

In New York in 1970, during a march staged to protest the Vietnam war, one group of demonstrators carried a Viet Cong flag and chanted Communist slogans. As they passed a building site, a group of construction workers became angry about what they regarded as anti-American behavior. The workers rushed into the street, seized the flag, destroyed it, and beat up some of the demonstrators. The press called their behavior a *riot.* Many people believe that rioting is crazy behavior—that rioters have temporarily lost their sanity and have been swept away by "mob psychology."

On July 20, 1969, Edwin "Buzz" Aldrin saluted the U.S. flag as it flew from the "highest" flagpole ever—on the moon, a quarter of a million miles from Earth. To some people this seemed like a glorious thing to do. To others it seemed as crazy as sitting on a flagpole or tearing up a Viet Cong flag.

CHAPTER PREVIEW

This chapter is not about flags or flagpoles, nor is it about crazy behavior, although it is about behavior that is sometimes called crazy by people who do not understand the reasons behind it. The kind of behavior this chapter is about often is misunderstood because it is *novel*—people are acting in unusual ways, outside of conventional channels. However, this chapter is not about just any kind of unusual behavior. It is not, in other words, a chapter on deviance. Rather, the unconventional behavior discussed here is limited to *actions related to social change*.

Actions may be related to social change in four ways:

1. The action itself may be a social change. It may be an activity that is new in a society, such as sitting on flagpoles or going to the moon.

2. The action may be undertaken in order to cause social change, such as staging a peace march.

3. The action may be aimed at preventing social change, such as attacking those who mock patriotism.

4. The action may be caused by social change, such as when rapid economic changes prompt people to act in new ways.

However, we shall not concern ourselves with the individual actions of isolated individuals, even if these are related to social change. Instead, we shall only examine actions involving a number of people who influence one another. When these people form an organization and therefore attempt to coordinate their actions according to a plan, we may refer to them as a *social movement*. Often, however, group activities related to social change lack organization and planning. Such actions are called *collective behavior*. In both instances, people are acting together, but differences in the amount of organization and planning involved often prove critical, as we shall see. We shall also see that collective behavior sometimes develops into social movements; hence the need to consider these two patterns of activity together.

Thus, the theme of the chapter is how individuals can get together to cause, prevent, or otherwise respond to social change and why their efforts so often fail. To pursue this theme, we must focus on the behavior of people in particular circumstances. By doing so, we can assess two of the most vital tasks of sociology. In fact, these may be the two primary reasons for doing sociology.

The first of these tasks is to understand the interplay between the individual and society—or, in other words, between us and our history. Some sociologists argue that we are almost entirely the creations of our society and that our history determines our destiny. Other sociologists disagree. They believe that we have considerable freedom to make our own history, and that societies are created and changed by human beings according to their desires, capacities, and actions. As you read this chapter, you may want to examine the actions of the people involved in each case and ask how much impact they had on their history, or to what extent they simply were puppets dancing to social forces beyond their control.

The second primary task of sociology is to make social life less mysterious—to uncover the reasons behind events so that the strange and alarming become understandable and ordinary. At first glance, the behavior of the people described in the introduction to this chapter may have seemed crazy to you. But social behavior is seldom really crazy. If we look carefully, we usually find that there is rhyme and reason to what groups of people do. So long as we fail to recognize why they are acting as they are and dismiss them as nuts or fools, we are the ones who don't understand what is going on. Remember, too, that behavior can be reasonable without being "good" or even acceptable. Indeed, we often seek the reasons behind behavior in order to put a stop to it.

With these points in mind, we shall examine the flag-related activities described earlier and clarify some essential concepts.

A FRAMEWORK FOR ANALYSIS

Crazes or fads, such as flagpole sitting, are instances of what sociologists call **collective behavior**. For a behavior to be classified as collective, each of the following elements must be present:

1. The act must be unusual.

2. The action must be taken by a group of people, not by lone individuals.

3. The people involved must influence one another in some way.

4. This influence must occur with little or no planning, and there must be little or no organization of the group.

Shipwreck Kelly was an out-of-work sailor and movie stuntman. One day in 1924 he hit upon flagpole sitting as a scheme for making money. It worked like this: When he sat on a flagpole, crowds gathered and the news media gave him publicity. Therefore, sponsors would pay him to publicize a product, a new building, a fair—anything that could profit from a publicity gimmick. Soon he was able to earn $100 a day, a huge sum at that time. In his best year, 1929, he spent a total of 145 days on top of flagpoles and earned about $29,000. He wasn't really so crazy. It was the lure of money, too, that drew Hold 'em Joe and others to copy Shipwreck's novel actions.

Let's see how flagpole sitting fits the definition of collective behavior. First, the actions of flagpole sitters are unusual. That's why they attract so much public attention. If thousands of Americans celebrated every Fourth of July by sitting on their flagpoles, flagpole sitting would not be unusual. Instead of collective behavior, it would merely be behavior governed by custom and tradition. Second, Shipwreck was not the only person who sat on flagpoles; a number of people did so. Third, the flagpole sitters influenced one another. Hold 'em Joe and the others took up flagpole sitting when they saw that Shipwreck was on to a good thing. Soon they competed with one another for records of height and duration. Finally, the flagpole sitters never did get together to plan future activities, and they never formed a flagpole sitters' organization. Thus, all four characteristics of collective behavior apply to flagpole sitting.

The construction workers who rioted against demonstrators carrying a Viet Cong flag also engaged in collective behavior. The workers' action was unusual: running around beating up people and destroying flags are not normal occupational or recreational activities. In addition, the men influenced one another, but they acted on the spur of the moment, without planning or organization.

However, the demonstrators who carried the Viet Cong flag were not engaged in collective behavior. They were members of a political organization, and their actions had been well planned. However, the demonstrators' behavior was related to social change; they were trying to end a war and promote radical politics. When people get together in an organized way to cause or prevent social change, we identify them and their actions as a **social movement**. Had the construction workers been members of an organization that arranged for them to attack the marchers in order to prevent the changes that the marchers wanted, then the workers, too, would have represented a social movement.

Social movements consist of organized groups dedicated to causing or preventing social change. Social movments may be concerned with many kinds of social changes, including changes in religion, politics, economics, technology, art, morals, or ethics. However, not every group devoted to causing or preventing social change constitutes a social movement. Only an organized group acting in unconventional or unusual ways or acting outside of conventional channels to promote or prevent change constitutes a social movement. When police are ordered to halt a riot, even though the officers and their actions may promote or prevent change, they are not a social movement because they are acting in a typical fashion and within conventional channels. However, sometimes social movements are so successful or skillful that they transform themselves into conventional social institutions or enlist such institutions to pursue their goals.

Alvin "Shipwreck" Kelly poses for an aerial photographer while sitting on a flagpole. The rapid spread of flagpole sitting during the 1920s can be classified as a craze. But there was nothing crazy about this behavior—Shipwreck and the others earned huge fees for doing it.

Let's look again at Buzz Aldrin standing on the moon. How did he get there? His action was the result of a massive engineering project, directed by the government, staffed by thousands of scientists and engineers, and costing $24 billion. What could be more within conventional channels? But when we look closely, as we shall at the end of this chapter, we see that the astronauts did not reach the moon because of conventional government actions (although much social change is the result of conventional actions). They reached the moon because an intensely dedicated international social movement promoted and sustained government investments in rocket flight, first in Germany and then in the United States and the Soviet Union.

Obviously, to argue that spaceflight was the work

of a social movement is not to suggest that the space program was therefore "bad" or that the money was misspent. Nor are marchers waving a Viet Cong flag conspirators simply because they are behaving as members of a social movement. How one feels about the activities that give life to social movements depends upon how one feels about their methods and goals. The question for sociologists is not whether social movements are good or bad, but why and how they arise and function. You must keep that in mind throughout this chapter, for as you read on you will undoubtedly find you are for some of the movements described in the chapter and against others. That is as it should be, for the chapter reveals that social movements can be dedicated to good or to evil—and often enough to both. However, good and evil are not sociological judgments; they are moral judgments that must be made independently of sociology. Sociological tools work as well on good movements as on bad ones.

In this spirit, we will devote considerable attention to the Nazi Party in this chapter. By examining the Nazis' rise to power, we can learn something about how social movements may be transformed into social institutions. For a bloody period of modern history, the Nazi Party did in fact become virtually identical with German society as a whole.

To sum up, collective behavior and social movements differ in their degree of planning and organization. They also differ in their duration. Collective behavior tends to be brief (like a riot), episodic (something that occurs periodically, like flagpole sitting), and unorganized. Social movements are sustained by organization and planning, and they often endure for a long period of time (like the Nazi Party or the space program).

This chapter begins with the least organized instances of collective behavior. It then examines increasingly more complex and organized activities, culminating in an extended study of two social movements. What these activities have in common is more than the fact that they are all related to social change. Indeed, the difference between them is really a matter of degree. Social movements are more organized than collective behavior is, but there is not a sharp dividing line. Social organization can gradually grow until collective behavior evolves into a social movement.

Furthermore, all our examples illustrate an important fact sometimes overlooked even by social scientists: Collective behavior and social movements are always connected to other parts of the society in which they arise. Social change can only take place in relation to a particular set of historical and social conditions. Even the least organized cases of collective behavior are greatly influenced by the traditional customs and institutions of the society around them. Social movements often try to change or even take over the government. And some of the most radical collective behavior and social movements arise inside the most powerful and respected institutions. To clarify how actions related to social change evolve, it seems useful to consider a hypothetical case.

FROM THIEVERY TO BUREAUCRACY: A CASE STUDY

Our particular interest in collective behavior and social movements is to see how they work as social enterprises: What are their internal structures and dynamics? How do they gain and hold members? How do they interact with their social environments? However, before examining particular kinds of change-related human actions, it is useful to understand that they have a common root. For this purpose, we will consider a hypothetical example.

Imagine a town in a country ravaged by famine. Some citizens have food; others do not. At night, starving individuals sneak into their neighbors' houses to steal a crust of bread or a scrap of meat. They have not conspired together to plan these raids, and some are not even aware that many other people are also nocturnal thieves. Each person is doing the same thing for the same reason, but each is doing it alone. This is called **parallel behavior**. Although it takes place in a social context, it is not socially organized.

Now suppose that a number of hungry people collect in the town square and mill about in front of the food warehouse. After a few have gathered, word spreads: "There's a hungry crowd in the town square!" Others come to see what all the fuss is about. Folks urge each other, "Come to the square!" They argue excitedly about the famine for a while, then they start demanding that somebody give them bread. Finally, they break down the doors of the warehouse and take everything that is inside. An unplanned gathering of hungry people has turned into a riot for food. People facing a common problem or opportunity tend to communicate informally and influence each other's actions so that they end up doing similar things in a somewhat unified way. Interaction among people reveals to them their common concerns and turns parallel behavior into collective behavior.

Now that the famine has become a public issue and starving people have shared a social experience (breaking into the warehouse), they start discussing their mutual problem at length in order to find a solution. First in little groups and then in mass meetings, they plan and organize. After several meetings, they set up an organization called "Food for All," dedicated to making the town government solve the crisis. The organization is now a social movement: Many people are working together toward a specific goal through coordinated action. Continued, focused interaction has transformed collective behavior into a social movement.

In response to the growing strength of the movement, the town council appoints the leaders of Food for All to head a new government agency, the Department of Food. New laws empower the Secretary of Food to distribute bread to the needy and to set up a grain reserve to be ready for the next famine. Social agitation in this crisis has led to the establishment of a social institution in which bureaucrats occupy set positions in a hierarchy, perform standard roles, and work together according to established procedures.

Social institutions derive their identity from the fact that they are recognized by other social institutions. The Department of Food meets this criterion because it is integrated into the established government. Through legitimate, formal procedures, a social movement has become a social institution.

In everyday life, parallel behavior sometimes becomes collective behavior, which becomes a social movement, which leads to the establishment of a social institution. This is a success story. However, individuals often remain caught in unproductive parallel behavior and never succeed in getting together. A particular collective behavior may arise again and again without ever producing an effective movement. And movements themselves frequently disappear after they have had a slight impact on society. Failure can break the evolutionary sequence at any point. In this chapter, we shall look at several different kinds of collective behavior and social movements, keeping in mind the question: How do people get together to do something new?

COLLECTIVE BEHAVIOR

We shall first examine three types of collective behavior: crazes, panics, and riots.

Although these forms of collective behavior are not formally organized, as social movements and institutions are, they do show a degree of order. People act together, even though they do not follow a plan. The task of sociology is to uncover the orderly aspects of collective behavior and to explain them. We shall begin with crazes, because they are the simplest type and also because they provide a good introduction to panics and riots.

Crazes

Webster defines a **craze** as a "transient infatuation," meaning a quick and fleeting love affair with a fashion or style. Other words having a similar meaning are *mania* and *fad*. Crazes are not really crazy. There is nothing insane about enjoying novelty, and nothing loony about becoming bored with an activity once it is no longer novel. Crazes provide antidotes to the high degree of order imposed on people by modern institutions. However, crazes themselves are in many cases direct products of those very institutions.

Crazes have been big business for decades. Corporations and churches, periodicals and political

Break dancing is a recent example of a craze. Begun by young dancers (inspired by the dancing in several popular movies), this form of collective behavior quickly was transformed by organized competitions just as had the Frisbee craze.

parties have consciously hunted for attractive new products, images, and ideas to sell to the general public. Usually a craze fails to get off the ground. Sometimes one grips public fancy for a few months and then fades away. Occasionally a novelty starts as a craze but then establishes itself as a beloved and permanent part of the culture. A good example is the Frisbee Flying Saucer, a favorite toy of college students and the terror of campus airspace.

The Frisbee Frisbee is the traditional name for the game of skimming paper plates through the air. A former air force pilot came up with the idea of a plastic, aerodynamic plate that could boomerang and

hover. He gave the idea to the Wham-O Company of San Gabriel, California. It sold like any other fad at first, but the demand for it continued and it now seems destined to become a permanent part of our recreational culture. Today there are organized Frisbee competitions.

Wham-O is an American corporation. It had its first great success with the Hula Hoop, which burst upon the American scene in 1957 and peaked in sales in the spring of 1958. By the end of the first year, 20 million hoops had been sold, many of them imitations put out by competitors. Not all Wham-O products became crazes, but it takes only one or two to make a company successful.

Tulipomania When we think of Holland, romantic images of windmills, wooden shoes, and tulips come to mind. In actuality, the Netherlands, which has been one of the most advanced countries of Europe for hundreds of years, is not the quaint land of our imagination. There is, however, a valid reason for associating tulips with that country. In the early 1600s, the Netherlands experienced great economic growth and came to be a major trading and financial power. The Dutch built a colonial empire overseas, and at home great artists like Vermeer and Rembrandt flourished. During this prosperous period, the Dutch were gripped by a craze known as *tulipomania*. This "disease" apparently addled the brains of many Dutch speculators and caused them to invest great sums in tulips. Several scholarly writers have delighted in calling this the craziest of crazes.

The tulip had entered Europe in the 1550s. Before then it had not been found west of Constantinople (now Istanbul). Soon after 1600, tulips became well known and highly desired for their beauty. Florists began not only to sell tulips but to cultivate them and create new varieties. Prices rose above those for other flowers. In a book on tulips, Joseph Jacob (1912) wrote:

In addition to the impetus which arose from the legitimate needs and rivalry of the florists, there seems to have grown up in Paris a fashion for ladies of the higher classes to wear flowers, especially tulips, in their low-cut dresses, so that competition of the wealthy beaux to obtain the rarest and most novel to present to their lady friends drove prices still higher.

Rare tulips had become status symbols, indicators that the owner was a person of high social status. In this way, tulips gained a social value. Historian Charles Mackay wrote that in Holland in the early 1630s, "it was deemed a proof of bad taste in any man of fortune to be without a collection of them." Prices shot through the ceiling.

In 1634, the rage among the Dutch to possess them was so great that the ordinary industry of the country was neglected, and the population, even to its lowest dregs, embarked in the tulip trade. As the mania increased, prices augmented, until, in the year 1635, many persons were known to

invest a fortune in the purchase of forty roots (Mackay, 1852).

A single bulb of the rare Viceroy variety sold for 2,500 florins, enough money at the time to buy twenty oxen! A price like this certainly encourages the interpretation that tulipomania was insane.

The sad story is told of a sailor, home in Holland after a long voyage, who was sitting in a warehouse about to eat a herring for his breakfast. He noticed what looked like an onion sitting on a counter and picked it up to have with his fish. The sailor sat down on a pile of ropes and began munching on alternate pieces of herring and onion. Suddenly a merchant rushed up and shrieked that the sailor was eating his prize tulip worth 3,000 florins! Horrors! For his mistake, the sailor spent several months in jail.

In fact, of course, the financial side of tulipomania was nothing more than a particularly colorful example of an entirely normal economic phenomenon: speculation on rising prices in a well-organized market. So long as the price of tulips went up, it was to the advantage of investors to buy them, even if they personally detested tulips. The classic way to make a quick profit is to buy something for a low price and sell it for a high price. When many people decided to invest in tulips for this reason, the price was driven up even faster. So long as the price continued upward, it was completely rational for each individual investor to buy more.

Soon the collective behavior of tulipomania had been partly institutionalized. Stock exchanges in several Dutch cities began trading in tulips, just as the exchanges had done in other investment arenas. Then the tulip market acted very much like the American stock market just before the great crash of 1929. As George Edmundson (1922) commented:

Perfectly inordinate sums were offered in advance for growing crops or for particular bulbs; most of the transactions being purely paper speculations, a gambling in futures. Millions of guilders were risked, and hundreds of thousands lost or won. In 1637 the crash came, and many thousands of people in Amsterdam, Haarlem, Leyden, Alkmaar and other towns in Holland, were brought to ruin.

The craze ended in a crash once people saw that tulip prices were dropping. Realizing that the longer they held on to their tulips, the more they stood to lose, investors quite rationally tried to sell out as quickly as possible. Since everyone else was also unloading tulips, prices were driven down even more quickly. Many investors lost their shirts, and tulip-omania—which had been based more on greed than craziness—died out.

Panics

Financial crashes like the one that ended tulipo-mania are sometimes called **panics**, a word also used to describe situations in which terrified people attempt to flee danger. Crazes and panics are mirror images of each other. In a craze, a group of people rushes toward something they all desire. In a panic, people rush away from something they all fear. Panic can be inspired by a real danger, particularly one that is immediate and difficult to avoid (such as a fire in a crowded theater), but panic can also be caused by imaginary dangers and rumors of danger.

Although panics seldom spawn formal social organizations, panics do have a strong social aspect in that individuals often react to the panic of others in a way that spreads the panic further. Frequently panics contribute to social change by fueling the growth of social movements. As we shall see later in this chapter, the German Nazi Party gained much popular support during the financial panics of 1923 and 1929. Another case we shall discuss is the American panic reaction to the first Russian space satel-lites, a collective response that did much to promote the later Apollo missions to the moon. Therefore, panic is an important form of collective behavior.

Crowd behavior It remains a widespread belief that crowd behavior is crude and almost mindless. Gus-tave Le Bon's little book *The Crowd* (1895) is the classic statement of this point of view. Le Bon said that crowds are guided by primitive, subconscious motives and that the crowd is stupid, impulsive, and frequently rendered mad by fantastic images. "Like a savage, it is not prepared to admit that anything can come between its desire and the realization of its desire . . . . Its acts are far more under the influ-ence of the spinal cord than of the brain." Le Bon believed that the individual member of a crowd "is

no longer himself, but has become an automaton who has ceased to be guided by his will."

Moreover, by the mere fact that he forms part of an organized crowd, a man descends several rungs in the ladder of civilization. Isolated, he may be a cultivated individual; in a crowd, he is a barbarian—that is, a creature acting by instinct. He possesses the spontaneity, the violence, the ferocity, and also the enthusiasm and heroism of primitive beings, whom he further tends to resem-ble by the facility with which he allows himself to be impressed by words and images—which would be entirely without action on each of the isolated individuals composing the crowd—and to be induced to commit acts contrary to his most obvious interests and his best-known habits. An individual in a crowd is a grain of sand amid other grains of sand, which the wind stirs up at will.

Despite the fact that most people agree with this view of crowds, it is entirely false. Le Bon despised the common people and had no sympathy for the masses, their problems, or their attempts to solve those problems. The behavior of individuals in a crowd should be regarded as rational, and research can be conducted to determine the factors that are at work.

War of the Worlds In 1897, crowds went wild with terror in London when malevolent and powerful invaders from Mars launched a devastating attack. Of course, this happened only in H. G. Wells's sci-ence fiction novel *War of the Worlds*. (Although the book was pure fantasy, its description of people's reactions fits our definition of panic behavior.) The Martians had landed and were killing everyone with ray guns and poison gas. The transportation system could not get everyone out of London in time. People fought with each other for places on the trains. A mob looted a bicycle store.

Although motivated by extreme fear, this panic was quite reasonable behavior. People were sud-denly thrown into a life-or-death competition for scarce resources, and there were a limited number of chances to escape doom. On those rare occasions when people have panicked in a burning nightclub or theater and blocked the exit in their struggle, it is clear that a better coordinated, less violent evacuation might have saved more lives. But there was no chance to organize one.

One evening in 1938, thousands of Americans believed they had heard a radio news broadcast informing them that real Martians were actually invading the country and killing everyone in sight. Legend has it that the roads were immediately choked with panicked families, and thousands ran about hysterically. "The Martian invasion panic" was widely reported in the newspapers and was regarded as a striking example of mass craziness.

What actually happened was that CBS Radio had broadcast a dramatization, produced by actor Orson Welles and his Mercury Theatre company, of the *The War of the Worlds*. According to one estimate, 6 million people heard the broadcast; about 1.7 million mistakenly thought the realistic play was a news event, and about 1.2 million were frightened by it. In his social psychological book on the incident, Hadley Cantril (1941) says, "Thousands of Americans became panic-stricken. . . . Probably never before have so many people in all walks of life and in all parts of the country become so suddenly and so intensely disturbed as they did on this night."

Public expression of fear over a specific danger may often be magnified if people have other worries that they can do nothing about. The fictitious Martian invasion came at a time when people all over the world were anxious about the possibility of a real invasion. Hitler had begun his march toward war and was just about to seize a big chunk of Czechoslovakia. War fear had been constantly stimulated by all the papers. It is possible, therefore, that the Martian invasion gave people the opportunity to express their anxiety by focusing on a specific disaster. It could be called a *summary event*—a concrete representation of a vague but intense social and emotional situation.

In their issues for November 7, 1938, both *Time* and *Newsweek* made this point. *Newsweek* explained that on many people "already made danger-conscious by the recent war scare the effect of Wells-Welles realism was galvanic." *Time* was surprised that so many people had failed to understand that the program was pure fiction and concluded:

The only explanation for the badly panicked thousands—who evidently had neither given themselves the pleasure of familiarizing themselves with

According to Life, *Bill Dock, a New Jersey farmer, was prepared to shoot it out with the Martian invaders. Here he reenacts his behavior on the night of the famous radio broadcast. Today, sociologists tend to think there was no widespread panic that night, despite press reports.*

Wells's famous book nor had the wit to confirm or deny the catastrophe by dialing another station— is that recent concern over a possible European Armageddon has badly spooked the U.S. public.

The original H. G. Wells novel was set in England. When a Boston newspaper carried it in serialized episodes, it renamed the story "The War of the World—In and Around Boston." The Mercury Theatre broadcast had the Martians land in New Jersey, just a few miles from its New York studio. When

Hollywood produced a movie version in the early 1950s, the scene was shifted to California.

These moves illustrate the principle that panic is most likely when an ambiguous threat is seen as immediate—when its potential victims are suddenly endangered right where they are. If you were to hear that Martians had landed on the other side of the world or that they had just left Mars and were not expected to land on us for a few weeks, then you would have time for a leisurely response—time to discuss the situation at length, to gather the best possible information, and to make careful plans for concerted action. But when the Martians suddenly land in your backyard and disintegrate your neighbor, the only sensible thing to do is drop everything and run.

Of course, the Martians didn't land in anybody's backyard. Perhaps the most interesting question Cantril's study asked was why some people misunderstood the radio broadcast and thought it was news instead of a play. The format of the show did indeed imitate radio news journalism, but at the beginning and at intermission it was clearly stated that the program was fictitious. Not surprisingly, one of the factors that made listeners mistake the show for a news item was tuning in late and missing the disclaiming announcement. Another finding (based on an analysis of a poll conducted by CBS) was that better-educated listeners were less likely to believe that the dramatization was real. However, the most striking impression conveyed by Cantril's book was a false one—that real mass panic followed the broadcast. By quoting the stories of a few people who claimed to have been very frightened, Cantril implies that there was widespread panic. There wasn't. A few people did drive like maniacs along the roads or went in terror for help, but a few isolated incidents of fearful behavior do not make a panic.

Remember that 1.2 million people were frightened to some extent by the show. Out of such a large number, we would expect at least a thousand to be out doing loony things that night anyway! Afterwards, they could have attributed their actions to the Martian invasion. Many of them found that news reporters delighted in hearing extreme tales of fear or valor. Old Bill Dock, a New Jersey farmer, reenacted his brave defense of America from the Martians for *Life* photographer by taking cover behind a pile of grain sacks with his shotgun. The whole affair was more a news media craze than a mass panic. Cantril, whether intentionally or not, reinforced the popular misconception that insane panic is the common response of normal people to real or imagined danger. Since the 1930s, sociologists have continued to study how people react—whether they do in fact follow the maxim: "When in danger or in doubt, run around and scream and shout!"

The Barsebäck incident On November 13, 1973, sociologists in Sweden were presented with a golden opportunity to use scientific methods to study a similar panic. To dramatize concerns about the dangers of atomic power, Swedish Radio broadcast a short play about a fictional accident said to have taken place at the Barsebäck nuclear power station. Quantities of deadly radioactive substances had supposedly been ejected into the air, where they were spreading out and threatening the lives of people for miles around. In fact, the real Barsebäck station had not even been completed yet. Sociologists Rosengren, Arvidson, and Sturesson of the University of Lund were waiting to study the effects of the broadcast. "Within an hour the broadcast media reported widespread panic reactions in southern Sweden, and the next day the morning and afternoon newspapers followed suit, carrying page-wide headlines on the panic" (Rosengren, Arvidson, and Sturesson, 1975).

Using a random sample of more than a thousand adult residents drawn from area population registers, the researchers conducted telephone interviews and mailed questionnaires. They also interviewed police and other authorities. The researchers discovered that, in fact, no panic had occurred at all. Although 7 or 8 percent of the population had taken the program seriously and had been frightened by it, only 2 percent had taken action of any kind. These actions, far from constituting mass panic, had been reasoned responses to danger. Some folk contacted family members; others closed their windows to keep radiation out; a few made plans to evacuate the area.

Whereas Cantril had found that education and a few other variables were linked to whether persons had misunderstood the Martian invasion broadcast, the Swedish researchers found no variables (in personality or social status) that seemed to relate to the mistake of believing the Barsebäck disaster. Table 20-1 shows what the sociologists did find. Those people who happened to know that the Barsebäck reactor was not finished and those who had tuned in at the beginning and heard that the program was a play were not fooled. These two factors were the only ones that seemed to make a difference: There were no variables indicating propensities to public craziness.

How, then, did a panic get reported when none had occurred? For one thing, the police and news reporters received a number of telephone calls from worried citizens. These calls, which came from a tiny minority of the population, were nearly all rational attempts to find out what was really happening. But they were misinterpreted as indicative of widespread terror. A news reporter at the Malmö radio station thought that there might be a panic in progress, and phone calls to two police departments seemed to support his idea. With no other information and an approaching deadline for a regularly scheduled news broadcast, he apparently decided to gamble and announce a panic in order to scoop other reporters.

Panic was the main theme of his message, panic in a whole county, perhaps two. The telephone exchanges of the police stations, fire stations and mass media in two counties were reported to be jammed. People queueing up before the civil shelters. Large crowds in the communities around Barsebäck taking to the roads. People in Malmö collecting their valuables and heading southward in their cars (Rosengren et al., 1975).

Although this story was almost completely fabricated, it was widely broadcast by other reporters. Newspeople sometimes invent something exciting to report. Soon opponents of nuclear power had climbed on the bandwagon and were recounting the fable of the great panic that had never happened. The phenomenon was nothing but a media craze. It sprang not from disorganized mobs but from two standard institutions of Swedish society—the police and the press. Real panics do occur—when a financial market crashes, when an army is routed, or when a theater catches fire. But crazy panics in which people act in unreasonable ways are very rare.

Table 20-1 / The Barsebäck atomic disaster panic.

		Percent of Listeners Who Misunderstood the Show as Factual News		
		Tuned in from the beginning	Tuned in after the beginning	Total
Knew the power station was not running yet	No	38%	82%	72%
	Yes	20%	39%	34%
	Total	26%	55%	48%

Source: Rosengren et al. (1975).

Riots

The term **riot** is often used very broadly. Here we will use it in a restricted sense as referring to a hostile outburst of collective behavior in which a crowd of people threatens or attacks other persons or property. As we have seen, mistakes in reporting can happen, and sometimes what seems to be riots are not really so. In some cases, police may attack a crowd of peaceful demonstrators and it may be reported that the crowd rioted (Stark, 1972). In general, true riots or hostile outbursts are political actions in which a group of people (called a mob by their opponents) seeks changes in their social and economic positions. Sometimes terms like prepolitical or primitive "rebels" are used to describe rioters. Both of these terms imply that the issue behind the outburst is a political one (as indeed it is) but that the rioters have not yet built a coherent enough movement to work effectively through conventional political channels. Often these conventional channels are closed to the persons who resort to riot. If the political establishment refuses to deal with their grievances, riot may be the most effective political action open to the group. It has been frequently suggested that the riots in American ghettos in the 1960s were the only possible reponse by ghetto residents to their dismal situations. White resistance to reform and a stalling of the Civil Rights Movement prevented ghetto residents from obtaining effective action through conventional political channels (Howard, 1974).

Blues and Greens Once upon a time (from A.D. 527 to 565, to be exact), the Imperior Justinian ruled over the Byzantine Empire. From his capital at Constantinople (now Istanbul), he sent his generals out to conquer Italy and North Africa until much of the old, broken Roman Empire was in his grasp. Justinian was actually a Roman himself, a Christian who wanted to rule the Roman world in the name of his God. He built great buildings and had scholars codify laws. Superficially, everything was grand.

However, beneath the surface were intense conflicts and terrible grievances. The government was exceedingly corrupt. All of Justinian's great enterprises were paid for by heavy taxation squeezed out of the common people. Government officials committed many hideous crimes without being punished. The great laws of Justinian protected no one—his goodness was a lie and his greatness an illusion.

The Byzantine people had no legitimate mechanisms by which they could work to improve their system. Although personal politics abounded within the imperial court, there was no political structure, in the modern sense, to which the people could turn. Justinian and his wicked wife Theodora made the decisions, and it was the duty of everyone else to do as they were told. There was only one way to remove an emperor—to kill him.

The empire was ready to explode at any moment, like a pressure cooker with no safety valve and no way to turn off the heat. Hundreds of thousands of people were intensely unhappy and angry. However, these people were not organized in any kind of political movement that allowed concerted action toward solving their common problems. How could enough people get together to make a powerful political force since political parties were outlawed?

The answer, surprisingly enough, was at horse races. Like ancient Rome before it, Byzantium loved chariot races. For a time there had been four major teams of charioteers, named after the colors of their decorations: white, red, blue and green. Over the years the Whites and the Reds disappeared, leaving two teams, the Blues and the Greens. Informal fan clubs sprang up, and racing enthusiasts divided themselves into rabid factions behind the Blues and the Greens. Constantinople's immense outdoor stadium, the Hippodrome, had room for many thousands of spectators. It was the scene of exciting races, at which the two factions would cheer, boo, and sometimes resort to violence when their team lost. Other cities throughout the empire also held races, and much of the urban population divided into the two fan factions.

The Blues and the Greens developed into highly partisan, aggressive associations, the nearest thing to political parties within the system. Emperors themselves supported one or the other group. Justinian supported the Blues, who in turn supported him, while the Greens were attached to the relatives of an earlier emperor, Anastasius. The favored Blues persecuted the Greens, often robbing or beating them with little fear of punishment. However, both groups were victims of Justinian's tyranny; the Blues were simply a little better off than the Greens.

In January 532, Justinian presided over the races in the Hippodrome, and the Greens used this opportunity to express their grievances to him. Throughout the first twenty-two races, they shouted their discontent, getting angrier and more disrespectful with each race. When he reprimanded them, they argued back. The Blues were finally so enraged that they chased the Greens out into the city, where they spread riot and disorder. Had a modern political system existed, these events might have taken the form of a peaceful election, with Blues and Greens as rival parties.

Right in the middle of chaos, one of those random events that frequently spark rebellion occurred. A group of seven assassins from both factions were dragged through the city by guards. Four were beheaded, a fifth hung, but the remaining two, a Blue and a Green, escaped to the sanctuary of a church. The Blues, who had been suffering almost as much as the Greens under Justinian, now turned their anger against the emperor, too. The two factions stopped fighting each other and joined forces against the government. They massacred palace guards. For five days they battled Justinian's unprepared forces, until the sly Empress Theodora was able to revive the loyalty of the Blues and again set them against the Greens. These riots are called the Nika uprising, because the rioters shouted "Nika" ("Victory") as they ran through the streets.

The Emperor Justinian and his entourage are depicted in this mosaic. Justinian under-took a major codification of Roman law, yet his disregard for legality and his repres-sive practices caused riots that nearly toppled his government.

Like all historical events, the Nika uprising had complex motives behind it. However, some socio-logical principles are clearly applicable. Major riots are not random, insane outbursts. Participants are motivated by feelings of resentment, injustice, frus-tration, and outrage. Some social mechanisms are necessary to coordinate the behavior of the many people involved, and there is always a triggering event. In this case, the sports factions were the organizing structures, and the races that day pro-vided the sparks that ignited the riot. The result was a five-day coalition that rivaled Justinian's govern-ment in strength. Only the collapse of that coalition allowed him to survive.

The Luddites Anyone who is opposed to techno-logical progress, who fights to block it, or who actually breaks machinery is called a **Luddite**. The original Luddites were English textile workers who smashed machines in a series of riots from 1811 to 1816. Their legendary leader, Ned Ludd, gave the uprising its name. Some English newspapers at the time believed Luddism was a sinister conspiracy to over-throw society, and frightened members of the upper classes urged harsh action. There was in fact no conspiracy, and the rioters concentrated their attacks on the little textile factories in their own areas, often on their very places of employment. Luddism was an instance of collective behavior in which groups of workers beset by the same problems act in an uncoordinated way to solve them, with only the most rudimentary communication about the best course of action.

The standard explanation of the Luddites' behavior is that they smashed the new machinery because it was so efficient that it threatened to take over many jobs. Earlier, it had taken thousands of workers weaving or knitting by hand to make woolen cloth; now machines did it all. Earlier, workers had used huge, 40-pound shears to cut the fuzz off the cloth; now machines were taking over that job. In order to hold their jobs, these "backward" textile workers were trying to stop progress. This theory pictures the Luddites as stubborn diehards caught up in an historical process entirely beyond their control.

The major problem with this theory is that the machinery had been in use long before 1811. Although mechanization had increased in some factories, the smashed machines were only a symbol of the real grievances. England was suffering a great loss of foreign markets for its textiles in this period, mostly because of the wars against Napoleon and the war from 1812 to 1816 against the United States. Food prices soared sky high, while wages dropped into the cellar. The unemployed had no bread, and many employed workers did not have enough to eat. Hunger, misery—what some sociologists dispassionately call *strain* or *deprivation*—drove desperate people to do something. The only question was, What?

In many cases of collective behavior, two sets of factors are at work: the factors that make people want to do something (general motivation) and the factors that narrow people's choices so that they do something specific (channeled motivation). The Luddites were motivated in a general way by their own deprivations, but the specific form that their action took was determined by social and cultural factors.

They could not act through the standard political process because, since they were not property owners, they were not allowd to vote. They could not demand help through labor unions, because unions were illegal at the time and their organization had been effectively suppressed. The workers must have been reluctant to kill their employers, nor did the rebels want to destroy the factories, because they needed jobs. But the Luddites had to get across the message that they needed higher wages, and they had to give employers some reason to grant them. So they smashed the machines. The machines were a relatively safe and available target, and attacks on them were not crazy orgies of anger but logical and rational actions. In his book on the Luddites, Malcom I. Thomis points out how near to modern labor union practices the uprising really was by describing it as "collective bargaining by riot" (Thomis, 1970).

Failure to organize The Blues and Greens and the Luddites were ultimately unable to organize effective movements to improve their living conditions. The Byzantine and British governments effectively blocked the rebels in each case with military force. However, government prohibition is not the only barrier to the organization of social and political movements. Obviously, some groups of people—infants, the very poor, the seriously mentally retarded, and the seriously mentally ill—may lack the resources to organize at all.

A very different kind of social barrier has been discussed by Mark Granovetter, a sociologist who has analyzed networks of human relationships and social ties. In a well-known article (1973), he refers back to Herbert Gans's book *Urban Villagers* (1962), which describes the failure of residents in Boston's West End section to organize in order to keep their neighborhood from being destroyed by urban renewal. The Boston city government, in which West Enders had little influence, decided that the neighborhood was a blight, and officials took the necessary steps to replace it with high-income housing. The West Enders were thrown out and dispersed to other parts of the city, where they found it hard to get cheap housing and where they missed the fellowship of their long-time neighbors. The city bulldozers came in and scraped away the West End to ground level.

Gans gives several plausible explanations for the feebleness of the efforts to stop the bulldozers, but Granovetter's explanation is particularly interesting.

He stresses the kinds of social relations that had linked West Enders, who were tightly bound into small groups or cliques with weak bonds between groups. Gans characterizes the West Ender of that time as first and foremost a member of a small peer group, and he says that

peer group society dominates [the West Ender's] entire life, and structures his relationship with the community and the outside world. . . . The West End, in effect, may be viewed as a large network of these peer groups, which are connected by the fact that some people may belong to more than one group (Gans, 1962).

Granovetter likes this idea, but argues that these groups were too isolated from each other to build a movement. Members of one group would not trust the leaders of other groups, and there was not enough time before the bulldozers arrived to develop the new relations necessary to form a successful movement. Both Gans and Granovetter are convinced that the neighborhood would have had a much better chance to survive if it had already been organized as a community.

Granovetter further emphasizes the fact that social relations are the primary means by which movements are built. Less personal means are rather ineffective:

Leafletting, radio announcements, or other methods could insure that everyone was aware of some nascent organization; but studies of diffusion and mass communication have shown that people rarely act *on mass-media information unless it is also transmitted through personal ties; otherwise one has no particular reason to think that an advertised product or an organization should be taken seriously. Enthusiasm for an organization in one clique, then, would not spread to others but would have to develop independently in* each one *to insure success* (Granovetter, 1973).

SOCIAL MOVEMENTS

Crazes, panics, and riots may all influence social change, but only when people are able to organize into an effective social movement can they have a good chance of achieving their goals. We have used the Blues and Greens, Luddites, and West Enders to indicate how collective behavior may evolve in the direction of a true movement and how the efforts of such groups may be thwarted, but it is time to look at a movement that really succeeded. You may have been sympathetic to the people we have just been discussing, but you will most likely deplore the mass movement now to be analyzed: Hitler's Nazi Party. Although it is essential for individuals to make judgments of good and evil, these are not scientific judgments. Sociologists approach an appalling phenomenon like Nazism with dispassionate spirit in order to conduct scientific research for determining the social factors behind the movement.

A successful mass movement: the Nazis

The Nazi Party was a political movement that began in complete obscurity after World War I. Yet from 1933 until 1945, Adolf Hitler's Nazi Party ruled Germany and terrorized the world. As the established government of a nation, it controlled a cluster of social institutions.

Faulty theories It has been long fashionable for anti-Nazi writers to explain the rise of Hitler's party as the natural result of certain aspects of "the German soul." The Germans were by nature barbarians, some have said. They had never really accepted civilization. Writers pointed to one another piece of German culture that had been adopted by the Nazis, and thus claimed that German philosophers and composers shared in the blame. But these cultural explanations tend to account mainly for the style of the Nazis or the specific cultural content of the movement. If Nazism had been an American movement, Nazis would have sung American marching songs, spoken English, and revered American history. It was not significant, therefore, that the Nazis sang German marching songs, spoke German, and revered German history. Some of these cultural explanations may simply be romantic literary fiction; most of them are at bottom racist, nationalist propaganda that is hardly more scientific than the Nazis' own propaganda was.

The Nazis cannot be explained in terms of some imagined German inferiority. The nation that invented the automobile and the jet plane was certainly not backward technologically. The nation that gave us Beethoven and half the philosophers of the nineteenth century was certainly not backward culturally. Nor can we explain the Nazis simply as the victims of some sorcery performed by Hitler. The Nazis were a social movement, and they can only be explained in terms of social factors.

Another common but feeble theory holds that movements succeed because they can transmit powerful ideologies (systems of beliefs and values) that arouse masses of people. Although ideology is not unimportant, it usually plays a passive role in the growth of a movement. As we saw in Chapter 3, it is attachments, not ideology, that play the major role in attracting people to join movements. Perhaps the most powerful function of an ideology is to control and direct the activities of people who are already members of the group.

This seems to have been the most effective role of ideology in the Nazi movement. In countless speeches and articles, Hitler and propagandists claimed that the Jews were corrupting Germany, accused the old German political parties of having betrayed the country, and promised that the Nazis would save Germany. Specific statements were usually vague and contradictory. However, in his book *Mein Kampf* (My Struggle), Hitler wrote at length about his ideas and plans, giving the full Nazi ideology, which had only been hinted at in his speeches. If ideology is important in recruiting new members, then we would expect sales of the book to have led the growth of the party. In fact, the opposite was true. Table 20-2 shows sales of the book and Nazi Party membership for the years 1925 to 1931. In 1932, when Hitler received more than 13 million votes in a national election, only 90 thousand copies of *Mein Kampf* were sold, or 1 for every 149 voters. After Hitler seized power in 1933 he was able to sell 1 million copies a year.

The Nazi constituency and its needs Two conditions are necessary for the growth of a mass movement: (1) a *natural constituency*—a segment of the population for the movement to represent that does not have effective representation, and (2) a vigorous

Table 20-2 / Sales of Hitler's book *Mein Kampf* and Nazi Party growth

Year	Sales of *Mein Kampf*		Nazi Party Membership
	Copies Sold in Each Year	Copies Sold to Date	
1925	9,473	9,473	27,000
1926	6,913	16,386	49,000
1927	5,607	21,993	72,000
1928	3,015	24,008	108,000
1929	7,664	34,672	178,000
1930	54,086	86,758	380,000
1931	50,808	137,566	800,000

Sources: Hale (1955), p. 837; Shirer (1960), pp. 169, 171; Carsten (1967), p. 143.

internal society—a cohesive network of social relationships within the movement capable of attracting and incorporating large numbers of new members. The Nazis had both. Individuals from the natural constituency were drawn in by the movement, whose internal society made sure they found membership rewarding.

In the chaos after the German defeat in World War I, literally hundreds of little movements sprang up. Some movement members seized power briefly in one city or another before being ousted by a larger movement or by the central government. These movements grew up in response to a wide range of public issues, and members proposed a great variety of solutions to the many serious problems facing German society. Social disorganization on a large scale often leads to increased social organization on a small scale. When a central government breaks down, smaller political units take over its functions. In the economic chaos of the early 1920s, many German towns printed emergency money, called *Notgeld*. Destruction of the national army produced many private armies, and the discrediting of old political parties produced many new ones.

Most of these new movements attracted only a few followers and soon died. But movements that addressed one of two major problems—German national weakness and economic disaster—tended to receive wide support: First of all, not only had

When it was printed, this bill was worth 100,000 German marks. If Germany issued such a bill today it would be worth about $40,000 in U.S. currency. However, when this bill was printed in the 1920s, 100,000 marks weren't worth forty cents. Runaway inflation had made German money virtually worthless—it took trillions of marks to equal $1.

the country been defeated in World War I, but Germany was still at the mercy of its enemies. When the nation was unable to pay the vast reparations demanded by its conquerors in 1923, the French moved in and took over the highly industrialized Ruhr district. German historians might well date the beginning of World War II from this French invasion of Germany, rather than from the later German invasion of Poland. Second, in 1923 and again in 1929 unemployment soared, leaving millions of people with neither the livelihood nor the self-respect that a job provides. Table 20-3 shows the cataclysmic inflation that rendered paper money valueless, liquidated savings and many investments, and reduced many middle-class citizens to poverty.

These two problems caused a lot of agony for the majority of the German people, making them a free-floating, natural constituency for any party that could organize them. But as a rule, parties dealt with only one of these issues, not both. With the support of the upper class and the army, the German Nationalist Party was able to capitalize on dissatisfaction over Germany's position as a nation, but it never appealed to the little people—either the workers or the members of the middle class—who suffered most from the economic dislocations. The Social Democratic Party (the Socialists) attempted to deal with the economic problems, but it was in the unhappy position of being forced to collaborate with Germany's French and British enemies. The Communists capitalized somewhat on the economic disaster, but they were unable to appeal to the large middle class; furthermore, because they were directed from Moscow, they could not express nationalist sentiments. However, the Nazi Party, with no history binding it to any one segment of the population and no ideological commitment to either one of the two issues, was able to take the broad approach necessary for a successful mass movement. The Nazis attacked both issues simultaneously

Table 20-3 / The catastrophic inflation in German money, 1923.

Date	Number of German Marks That Equaled One American Dollar
1921	75
1922	400
1923 (beginning)	7,000
January 1923	18,000
July 1, 1923	160,000
August 1, 1923	1,000,000
November 1923	4,000,000,000
After November 1923	trillions

Source: Shirer (1960), p. 95.

Table 20-4 / 1933 German occupational distributions.

Occupation	Nazi Party Members	Total Gainfully Employed
Manual workers	31.5%	46.3%
White-collar employees	21.1%	12.5%
Independents*	17.6%	9.6%
Officials	6.7%	4.6%
Peasants (farmers)	12.6%	21.1%
Others**	10.5%	5.9%
	100.0%	100.0%

*Skilled artisans, professional persons, merchants, etc., excluding independent peasants.
**Domestic servants and nonagricultural family helpers.

Source: Gerth (1940), p. 527.

and garnered membership from the widest possible natural constituency: Germans. *Nazi* is a slang word, a contraction of the first word of the official name of Hitler's party, *Nationalsozialistische Deutsche Arbeiterpartei* (the National Socialist German Workers' Party). The very name expresses the principle behind the party: Something for everyone—that is for all Germans.

Writers often suggest that the Jews became the scapegoats for German failure because of a more or less pathological refusal by Hitler and his followers to confront the real reasons for the Germans' defeat in World War I and the economic troubles that followed. However, a sociological explanation is also possible. Each of the other political parties supported the interests of some Germans against the interests of others. The Nazi Party claimed to support the interests of *all* Germans against the interests of non-Germans such as Jews and other "foreigners."

Several of the parties described German politics in terms of a war between socioeconomic classes, and such parties fought to make their class the winner. Hitler asserted that all classes could win under Nazism. Here ideology did play an important, though passive, role. Each of the other parties was hindered by its ideology—which was simply the expression of the special interests of its constituency—from

recruiting all of German society. Before Nazism, Germans faced each other as enemies fighting for a piece of the economic action. With Nazism, Germans stood shoulder to shoulder against Jews and foreign enemies. The incredible but logical consequences of this extremely effective political maneuver were the extermination camps and the war against the world.

The Nazis' greatest strength lay in the middle class. The economic disasters of the 1920s injured everyone, but none more than the millions struggling for middle-class respectibility. In 1925 there were 20 million Germans earning lower-class incomes while attempting to live according to middle-class standards they had known (Schoenbaum, 1966). Table 20-4 shows that the Nazis drew members from all occupational groups, but particularly from white-collar employees and independent members of the middle class, such as shopkeepers. Sociologist Hans Gerth (1940) noted the appeal Nazism had for "persons whose career expectations are frustrated or who suffer losses in status or income," and reported:

Such "unsuccessful" persons were to be found in every stratum of German society. Princes without thrones, indebted and subsidized landlords, indebted farmers, virtually bankrupt industrialists, impoverished shopkeepers and artisans, doctors

Table 20-5 / Age distribution in the county of Oschatz-Grimma in the German state of Saxony.

Age in Years	General Population (1933)	Social Democratic Party (1931)	Nazi Party (1931)
18–30	31.1%	19.3%	61.3%
31–40	22.0%	27.4%	22.4%
41–50	17.1%	26.5%	8.0%
51 and over	29.8%	26.8%	8.3%
	100.0%	100.0%	100.0%

Source: Schoenbaum (1966), p. 38.

without patients, lawyers without clients, writers without readers, unemployed teachers, and unemployed manual and white-collar workers joined the movement.

Youth and opportunity in the radical parties

Both the Nazis and the Communists strongly appealed to young adults. In times of high unemployment, youth suffers more than other age groups. Older people are in a better position to get jobs because of their experience and personal contacts, and they tend to hang on to whatever jobs they already have. Young people coming into the work force for the first time have a hard time finding work of any kind. Table 20-5 shows the age distribution in 1931 in one German county for members of the well-established Social Democratic Party and for members of the up-and-coming Nazi Party compared with the distribution in the population as a whole. The Social Democrats had a small proportion of young members, while the overwhelming majority of the Nazis were young.

Political parties offer a variety of job opportunities for able and loyal followers. Such positions in the older German parties were just about filled up, while the newer Communists and Nazis had a number of jobs open for active young adults. Table 20-6 shows the age distribution in 1930 Reichstag (German parliament), the equivalent of Congress. We see percentages in each age category for the Reichstag as a whole and for the three largest parties, the old-time Social Democrats, the Communists, and the Nazis. Notice that the young were represented in the two radical parties to a far greater degree than in the Social Democrats or all parties as a whole.

The Nazi movement and its competition

The political system of the German Republic was somewhat different from the American system, but the basic structure of German politics then still exists in a number of European nations today. Americans have only two parties holding power in government, but the Germans had many parties, simply because the election laws were very different. Whereas in the United States political contests are winner-take-all, the Germans had a system of proportional representation. Each party received the same proportion of seats in the Reichstag as the proportion of votes it received in the election. The American system works to the disadvantage of minor parties, but the German system favored such parties. This difference is one example of the ways societal institutions shape social movements: Election laws determine how power is divided and hence what groups have the potential to win a share. Figure 20-1 shows the percentage of representatives from the major parties in the Reichstag after nine different elections, from 1919, when Germany became a republic, until 1933, when it became a Nazi dictatorship.

A glance at Figure 20-7 shows that the seven major parties experienced marked changes in strength. The Nazis and the Communists rose from nowhere to become two of the strongest parties, while other groups lost strength. Germany's disastrous economic crises in 1923 and 1929 dramatically affected the voting. In the first election in 1924, the representation by Social Democrats (Socialists), the party that had been in power, dropped by nearly half; the two radical parties, the Nazis and the Communists, achieved their first great successes. The Socialists were blamed by many voters for the economic calamity of 1923, while the Nazis and Communists acted as lightning rods for voters' desperate hopes. When the economy improved again in the mid-1920s, the Nazis dropped back and the Socialists recovered somewhat. The 1929 crash of the American stock

Table 20-6 / Age distribution in the 1930 Reichstag and its three largest parties.

Age in Years	Total Reichstag	Nazis	Communists	Social Democrats
under 30	4%	11%	11%	0%
30–39	25%	55%	58%	12%
40–49	30%	22%	29%	34%
50–59	31%	10%	1%	38%
60 and over	10%	2%	1%	16%
	100%	100%	100%	100%
Number of Representatives	577	107	77	143

Source: Doblin and Pohly (1945), p. 43.

market touched off a worldwide economic depression and led to the tremendous increase in Nazi support in 1930.

Human misery may feed the growth of a movement, but deprivation is not sufficient to explain it. Movements require organization. The Nazi Party was really an alternate society in direct competition with the German state, and the Nazi Society was organized along different and more effective principles. The Nazi Party was an independent social structure made of hundreds of thousands of personal relationships. When the party set up soup kitchens to feed hungry Germans, it was not only providing a needed service that the government had failed to provide but also offering the needy the possibility of developing new human relationships. Newcomers would make friends among the party members and then become members themselves (recall the research on conversion in Chapter 3).

Like the Nazis, the German army was another state-within-a-state, for the government could not control its commanders. However, under the terms of the Versailles Peace Treaty, which had ended World War I, the army could not grow beyond 100,000 men. But there were no restrictions on the growth of the Nazis' private armies, the SA (Brownshirts) and the SS (Blackshirts). By 1930 the Nazi military forces had reached 100,000 men, and the Nazi forces soon surpassed the official army in size.

Even the governmental structure of the Nazi party was set up as an alternate state, with district leaders

(Gauleiters) and regional leaders all giving allegiance to Hitler as their highest leader (Führer). When the Nazis took over Germany by stealth and force in 1933, it was a simple matter for their state-within-a-state to become simply the State.

This analysis gives us a valuable perspective on social movement and leads to a conclusion that it is not often stated: Society *is* movements. Social institutions and social movements are not radically different from one another. We might say that social institutions are slow movements and that social movements are merely social institutions that happen to be evolving more rapidly. We defined *collective behavior* and *social movement*, in part, as behavior that is new, unusual, and striking. Obviously, these terms are relative, and our perspective on them depends upon the particular values that we hold as individuals and as members of groups. An entire civilization can be described as a vast movement; the Nazis, on the other hand, actually believed that they were a civilization. All institutions and customs rise from nowhere, and most of them fall back into nonexistence. Change is the only permanent feature of human life. Hitler's Nazi Party is but one of the many movements that grew from almost nothing to become a government of a major nation and then fell into ignominy.

When the Nazis seized power, their first task was to extend their influence into every aspect of the German social structure in order to make it impossible for any other group to challenge Nazi rule.

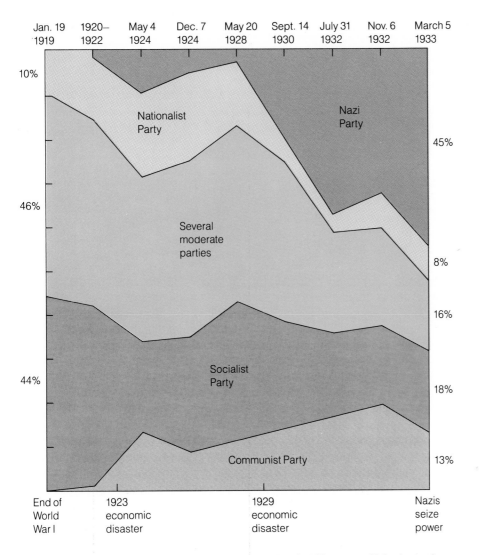

Figure 20-1 / The Nazi rise to power: Strength of different political parties in the German Reichstag (Parliament), 1919–1933.

The Nazi party rose to power over the years shown in this chart, feeding on the dissatisfaction and despair of a nation constantly beset by terrible social problems. In 1923, economic disaster and the French occupation of the industrial region of Germany discredited the dominant Socialist Party, increasing the strength of the Nationalists and Communists, and gave the Nazis their first seats in the Reichstag. The economic situation improved in the mid 1920s, and the radical parties lost ground. The international economic crisis that began in 1929 and became the Great Depression gave renewed strength to the Nazis and Communists. By the end of the period, the moderate parties and Socialists had lost nearly two-thirds of their strength, and the radical movements had come to dominate German politics. In 1933, the Nazis seized absolute power, and elections were no longer held.

Adolf Hitler emerges from a Nazi Party meeting. Uniformed members of his private Nazi Party Army, the Brownshirts, give the Nazi salute. Since the German Army was restricted by the treaty ending World War I to only 100,000 men, the party army soon outnumbered the regulars.

Under the banner of the propaganda word *Gleich-schaltung* ("coordination"), the Nazis dissolved the myriad of organizations that had made up the old society and replaced them with a few completely Nazi organizations. Labor unions, for example, were replaced by the single, Nazi-controlled German Labor Front, which was used to control the workers rather than represent them. The only potential opposition that remained was the German army. When it decided to support Hitler, effective opposition became impossible.

In his book *The Nazi Seizure of Power,* William Sheridan Allen (1965) reported on the experience of a single German town during the Nazi drive to accomplish "the atomization of the community at large." The goal was for each individual to relinquish his or her identity as a member of many interlocking social groups and become an "atom" within the huge, impersonal, Nazi institutions. Outside the context of Nazi mass meetings and organization, the citizens of the town had little opportunity to interact with one another. As one town resident put it, "There was no more social life; you couldn't even have a bowling club" (Allen, 1965).

Once in control of Germany, Hitler moved not only to eliminate his opponents but also to win over the whole society to support the Nazi Party. Here Nazi officers let little boys fire real machine guns during a visiting day at the Berlin barracks. Everyone, including parents, seems to be having a good time.

Recall Mark Granovetter's analysis of the failure of Boston West Enders to organize a movement to stop the urban renewal bulldozers. German citizens were in an equally difficult situation regarding the Nazis. The atomization of social relationships had thrown individuals on their own, and only within the party apparatus or within the army could effective organizations be built. German citizens were unable to organize any kind of serious opposition to Hitler after 1933, and the Nazis had to be toppled from power by outside intervention in World War II.

A successful elite movement: space flight

Not all successful movements are mass movements. Sometimes a small band of dedicated people can cause great changes. Writers on social movements have sometimes made the mistake of considering only movements created by oppressed groups. In fact, many of the most successful movements have been initiated by middle- or upper-class individuals. As we have seen, movements often draw their strength from the misery of some natural constituency. How-

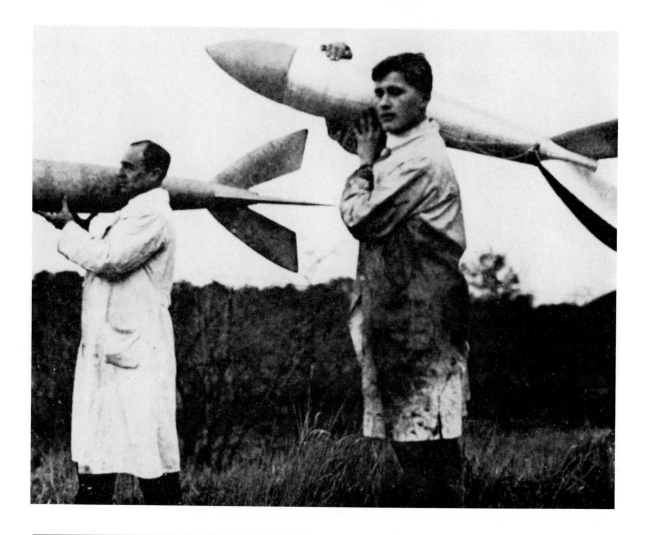

These three photos illustrate the operations of the space flight movement during its purely amateur phase. Above: A teenage Wernher von Braun and another member of the German VfR carry their homemade rockets to the launching pad sometime in 1932. Near right: A member of the American Rocket Society, working in his garage in 1932, readies a homemade rocket for launching. Far right: A homemade rocket is launched by Russian members of GIRD in 1933.

ever, this is not always true: In some cases, a movement grows up around a new opportunity rather than a new problem. Such movements gain power because they satisfy the needs or desires of upper-class, rather than lower-class groups. The "spaceflight movement" was a response to a new opportunity for achievement in the early years of this century. Members of the middle and upper classes perceived this opportunity and supported the movement, which succeeded because it was able to exploit circumstances in three technologically oriented nations: Germany, the Soviet Union, and the United States (Bainbridge, 1976).

Origins of spaceflight For a century before the first actual flight into space, the idea of space travel was

explored and advertised in science fiction stories and popular articles on astronomy. Although astronomers have not as a rule been much in favor of spaceflight, their descriptions of astronomical discoveries for the general public have made the moon and planets seem like exciting places to visit and explore. Three authors of the late nineteenth century—Jules Verne in France, H. G. Wells in England, and Kurd Lasswitz in Germany—wrote influential novels that were read by the early rocket pioneers. Space travel became an idea that was in the air, so to speak, and at least a few people were convinced that it would be a worthwhile goal. This period can be described as one of *cultural preparation* for the later movement.

Throughout the first quarter of the twentieth century, a few far-sighted people independently developed the basic theories and mathematical analyses that would be required. The three most important thinkers were Konstantin Tsiolkovsky in Russia, Robert Goddard in the United States, and Hermann Oberth in German-speaking central Europe. All three worked independently, so their work can be described as parallel behavior. They were highly unusual people who shared a mystical vision and who had the mind and scientific know-how to make that vision practical. Goddard and Oberth came from upper-middle class families. All three can be described as geniuses.

The movement itself was born in Germany after

Oberth published his great book *The Rocket into Planetary Space,* in which he presented a correct mathematical analysis of space rocketry. He had originally submitted it as his doctoral dissertation, but it had been rejected, and Oberth had to pay out of his own pocket to get this revolutionary work published. Young men at the outset of their careers flocked to him, apparently hoping that they could perform exciting creative work in building the first spaceships. Oberth and Max Valier, one of his first converts, wrote articles for magazines and gave speeches all over the country. The two men inspired a few other young men to join together and form a German society for space travel, the *Verein für Raumschiffahrt* (VfR), in 1927.

The space activity in Germany in the 1920s fell into the category of collective behavior. It spread throughout the industrialized nations, and other space clubs were formed like the VfR: the American Interplanetary Society (AIS) in 1930, the Russian *Gruppa Izucheniya Reaktivnogo Dvizheniya* (GIRD) in 1931, and the British Interplanetary Society (BIS) in 1933. The four national space clubs constituted the real beginning of a social movement. They were formal (although amateur) organizations in which dedicated people planned and worked for a stated goal. The clubs were in close communication and attempted to cooperate despite rivalries among their countries. In the transition period from 1920 to 1940, this collective behavior gradually evolved into a social movement.

The rocket clubs tried every possible means to interest the general public, corporations, and governments in spaceflight—and failed utterly. The tiny clubs were attempting to turn their enthusiasm into an international mass movement, but there were no motives compelling enough to inspire many people to join. Spaceflight was not a solution—or even a plausible nonsolution, like Nazism—to any pressing human problem. It had no natural constituency to draw upon for support.

The VfR at its height had only about 1,000 members, and the AIR, GIRD, and BIS had hardly 100 members each. The British club spent about $1,000 on space development in the 1930s. The first liquid-fuel rocket built by the American club cost a grand total of $30.60 and included parts from a saucepan and a beverage shaker.

Max Valier was killed in 1930 when a crude rocket engine he was testing exploded. Oberth, suffering from exhaustion, left Germany and returned to his native Rumania. As the Great Depression deepened, the VfR ran out of money and disbanded. However, in the midst of failure came one crucial success. The young German aristocrat Wernher von Braun, an avid young VfR member, discovered a way to get all the money he needed: He tricked the German army into buying spaceships disguised as long-range missiles.

Success by exploiting political tensions The German army had a problem. Not only had it suffered defeat in World War I, but the peace terms imposed by the Allies had so weakened it that it was unable to defend Germany in case of attack. One of the terms of the Versailles Peace Treaty prohibited the manufacture of conventional heavy artillery in Germany. However, the treaty did not mention long-range rockets: This was a loophole through which you could fire a missile! The army secretly became interested in the rocket work being done by the VfR, and Wernher von Braun was able to convince the military to hire him to develop rocket engines. In 1932, the year before Hitler came to power, 20-year-old von Braun took charge of the fledgling liquid-fuel rocket program of the German army.

Over the next ten years, von Braun and a growing organization of followers outplayed the German army and the Nazi Party in a game of tricks and misrepresentation. Von Braun wanted to build spaceships; the German army wanted long-range artillery. The military, feeling at a disadvantage in the international arena, was ready to snap at any idea that might help them out of their inferior position. Von Braun sold them on the rocket as a way of getting around the restrictions imposed by the Versailles treaty— as a way of outflanking the enemy. Cultural and technological ideas of all kinds often originate as responses to such instances of conflict.

This pattern of events, which was repeated several times in the history of the spaceflight movement, can be represented by a simple interactive model involving a sequence of social interactions between three actors: the spaceman (a leader of the movement), the patron (a military officer or government official), and the opponent (the Allies). (1)

The patron is locked in fierce competition with his opponent. (2) The opponent gains the advantage. (3) The spaceman comes to the patron and presents the spaceman's own favorite project as if it were an ideal solution to the patron's problem. (4) The patron, ignorant in the spaceman's field and under great pressure, accepts the spaceman's "expert" advice and invests in the project.

This same model can be applied to other kinds of movements. The intense needs of some group, either outsiders or (as in Hitler's party), movement followers, are exploited by movement leaders to give the leaders unusual power. Even the most benign leaders typically exploit their followers—at least to the extent of extracting admiration and a livelihood from them.

Without going into the details, we may note that von Braun tricked the military in two ways. First, he misled the German army into believing that long-range rockets were an efficient means of delivering conventional explosives to enemy territory, when in fact his rockets were a far more expensive way of unloading explosives than either artillery or bomber aircraft. Modern ICBMs (the successors to von Braun's rockets) are "ultimate weapons" only because they carry atomic warheads, which were not available to the Germans. Second, the liquid-fuel rockets von Braun designed were best suited for space purposes; the solid-fuel type is generally more appropriate for military uses. The V-2 was really a prototype spaceship crudely adapted to carry explosives. The V-2's were so expensive that they probably cost the Germans much more to develop than the Allies spent to clean up after them. The missiles were also costly to human life on both sides. About 5,000 persons were killed by V-2 bombardments of England and Belgium. But thousands of Germans also died, because the expenditure of something like $1 billion on the V-2 project ate deeply into appropriations for other things, including air defense.

In 1936, von Braun was able to pit the German army against the German air force (Luftwaffe) in order to get the $120 million he needed to construct his Peenemünde test station, the Cape Canaveral of Nazi Germany. In 1943, when he needed money to mass-produce the V-2 so that he could demonstrate its capabilities to the world, he personally went to Hitler and made a successful pitch, using a glowing lecture and dramatic movies of a V-2 launch. Once again, it was the same game—exploitation of the powerful in their hour of need. Hitler's air force had lost command of the air in the midst of the blitz of London, and the Allies had started blitzing German cities. Von Braun sold Hitler the V-2 as a means of continuing the bombing of London.

At the end of the war, von Braun led the scientists and engineers who were the leading members of his movement across the Atlantic. They "surrendered" to the victorious Americans as the first step in a plan to exploit the United States in a similar fashion to produce spaceships. By the late summer of 1945, von Braun was in Boston preparing his conquest of America.

Under Stalin, the Russians had also become very interested in German rocket development by 1947. Stalin felt that he was in an inferior position, just as Hitler did. American air bases encircled the Soviet Union, and only the United States possessed atomic bombs. Stalin ordered a crash program to develop long-range rockets capable of outflanking the American aircraft. Like Hitler, he contributed to the space-flight movement without intending to. The men who took charge of the Russian rocket programs included several who had been avid members of GIRD, the Russian amateur space club. In 1957, a team headed by Sergei Korolyov launched Sputnik I, the world's first artificial satellite. Korolyov, the Russian von Braun, had himself been president of GIRD back in the early 1930s! Both spacemen were leaders of branches of a social movement that had been working away—first outside and then within standard institutions—to achieve an unconventional goal.

Maturity and instutionalization of the movement
Tsiolkovsky, Goddard, and Oberth were first-generation leaders of the movement; von Braun and Korolyov were second-generation leaders. The first generation developed the ideas and values of the movement. The second generation organized it and found the resources necessary to achieve practical success. Sociologist Neil Smelser (1962) has observed, "we may distinguish between two kinds of leadership—leadership in formulating the beliefs and leadership in mobilizing participants for action." Sometimes these two leadership functions are per-

formed by a single individual, but it is usually worth distinguishing the *ideologue,* who invents and spreads ideas, from the *executive,* who builds and guides a social enterprise. When the executives take over a social movement, it is a sign that the movement has reached its maturity.

However, even when a social movement is well established, fresh outbursts of collective behavior in support of the movement are possible. The response of American politicians, journalists, and ordinary citizens to the first Sputnik was striking. A wave of self-accusation, weeping, wailing, and gnashing of teeth swept the United States. How could the Russians have beaten us into space? Many public figures blamed the American educational system, and for a few years there were active attempts to reform the nation's schools and colleges so that they would produce more and better engineers.

However, Sputnik really had nothing to do with any Russian educational superiority; the Russians had simply invested more money in rockets. The United States was actually just about to catch up with them and pass them in missile technology. The hue and cry over Sputnik I was a kind of panic, stimulated both by the spaceflight movement and by educators' chronic desire for more money. The Sputnik panic was largely an instance of movement-instigated collective behavior, or the result of previous action by an organized social movement.

With massive governmental support, von Braun was able to launch his own satellite, Explorer I, ninety days after getting permission. The launch rocket, a direct offspring of the V-2, had been ready for a year and a half, waiting for a go-ahead signal from Washington.

With the sponsorship of the Kennedy, Johnson, and Nixon administrations, space development progressed rapidly. Apollo II took Buzz Aldrin and Neil Armstrong to the surface of the moon in 1969, twelve years after the first orbiting satellite. The lunar module was launched by a huge Saturn V booster, designed principally by von Braun and his team of German-Americans. Now American space missions are carried out by the military and the National Aeronautics and Space Administration, a government agency organized soon after Sputnik. The social movement for space travel has been completely incorporated into standard social institutions.

The spaceflight movement was a success, but as such there is no longer a movement: Spaceflight is not really *moving* much any more. New space-transportation systems like the Space Shuttle are prosaic compared with the first space missions, and the development of space technology has become a gradual affair. The Chinese, the Japanese, the French, and the European space agencies have independently launched earth satellites, and literally dozens of nations have participated in space projects in one way or another. Nearly $200 billion has been spent on space, not including the similar fortune invested in long-range missiles. Manned space programs are continuing, and unmanned deep-space probes have explored all the planets of the inner solar system. Space is big business, and huge government programs remain dedicated to the advancement of space technology.

STUDYING THE SPACEFLIGHT MOVEMENT

This account of the spaceflight movement was condensed from my first book (Bainbridge, 1976), which served as my doctoral dissertation. Unlike most sociological research, it is hard to present a study in social history in a way that allows others to look over the sociologist's shoulder as the research is conducted. Although I did visit rocket installations and interview pioneer members of the spaceflight movement, most of my research was done by sitting in libraries reading books. So rather than have you sit with me in the library and read over my shoulder, perhaps I can best reveal my methods by explaining how I got interested in the subject and found it worth exploring.

As a freshman in college, I planned to major in physics because I was a dedicated spaceflight nut. I still have the junior space cadet certificate I ordered from a TV show when I was 11, and the next year I joined the American Rocket Society. However, it took me only a few months at Yale to discover that I had the wrong temperament for physics. Moreover, I found I was as interested in scientists themselves as in their discoveries. Eventually I found my way to sociology, which has allowed me to do scientific research on people, including scientists.

On July 20, 1969, Astronaut Buzz Aldrin stands at attention after he and Neil Armstrong had planted the American flag on the moon. The Apollo 11 mission to the moon was not the culmination of normal scientific progress but was caused by an international social movement.

I chose to do my doctoral dissertation on spaceflight not only because of my interest in it, but because there had been no serious sociological research on the topic. Also, the spaceflight movement seemed to contradict a major theory of technological change.

Historians have tended to emphasize the unique character of events and to stress the importance of individual actions. Thus, in military history, emphasis is given to how one general outsmarted another. In the history of science, emphasis is given to the genius of a particular person who made a discovery. In contrast, sociologists place much greater emphasis on the social environment in which a general or a scientist operated.

Surely no one could object to sociological suggestions that a famous scientist could not have made a particular discovery had he or she lived a thousand years earlier, or that not even Napoleon himself could have led the Dutch army to victory over Nazi Germany in 1939. However, some social scientists have taken the position that individuals count for nothing in the great scheme of history, and that social forces make everything happen. Thus, a dominant view of social change is called **technological determinism**.

Technological determinists such as S. C. Gilfillan (1963) and Leslie White (1959) argue that changes in technology are the cause of all social change and that technological change is self-generating. That is, technological determinists argue that each advance in technology is the automatic response to previous advances; when technology reaches a certain stage, the next stages must occur. For example, technological determinism holds that if Thomas Edison had not invented the light bulb in 1879, within a few months someone else would have done so, because the times were right for that invention to take place. In this view, the inevitable march of new inventions drives technology forward, taking the rest of society with it.

Technological determinism leaves no room for significant exceptions—for unusually talented and dedicated people to speed up the pace of innovation or even to leap ahead of the times. (They also leave no room for people to slow down the pace or turn the times backward.) I thought that the development of spaceflight might be a compelling counterexample for the technological determinists. If, as I suspected, a few rare individuals had in fact brought spaceflight into existence before the times were right, then we could know that at least sometimes in history individual human actions count. On the other hand, if it turned out that spaceflight was also just the expected outcome of ordinary technological advances, then technological determinism would be further supported. In effect, my study was meant to address the question, Do we make history, or does it make us?

A project such as this could not be done by an experiment or by asking a national sample of Americans whether they thought spaceflight was the result of routine science and engineering. Instead, I had to collect and analyze the history of spaceflight. To do this, I had to acquire two special skills. First, I had to learn to read the languages in which the essential documents were written. In this respect, my study began when I was 13 and read Willy Ley's popular history of the German rocket program, because that inspired me to take German in school. Later I studied Russian, only to discover that the Russian sources were completely useless—nothing but propaganda stories about rockets with very few trustworthy facts about who designed what or why. In addition to languages, I also needed to be able to understand the science and engineering involved in rocketry. Although I had not ended up a physics major, my scientific training proved adequate.

So I began my study. To proceed, I decided to focus on about a dozen major technological advances occurring before spaceflight. Were they the expected outcome of basic trends? Would we have spaceflight today if the amateur enthusiasts of the 1930s rocket clubs had never lived? I am convinced that the historical record says no. There is no evidence of basic trends in technology leading toward space.

During the critical period, conventional scientists and engineers were not even interested in spaceflight, let alone contributing to it. Instead, spaceflight was developed by a few tiny groups of amateur enthusiasts. Later, to further their goals, they consciously deceived military leaders into financing their work by disguising spacecraft research as weapons development. How do I know this? First, because the German rocketeers wrote about what they were doing as they did it; they actually described their involvement in the V-2 programs at the time as a "military detour" to space. Second, the design of the rockets was inappropriate for military use. Had the military simply organized a missile program, the necessary rocket developments for space applications would not have occurred. Finally, we see the role of the spaceflight movement intervening often, in a number of countries, to deflect normal technological trends out toward space.

I intended my book only as the first sociological "space shot." As the first sociological study of this fascinating area, it was meant to be surpassed, corrected, and perhaps even refuted by others. Unfortunately, there are not many practicing sociologists, and we are thinly spread studying a large number of important topics. At the time that I wrote a new preface for my book when it was reissued in 1983, I could not mention any subsequent work on the topic. Indeed, since I, too, have moved on to other topics, at present no one seems to be working on the many questions still to be answered about the implications of spaceflight for human societies. Perhaps one of you will relaunch the sociology of space.

CONCLUSION

In this chapter we have taken a look at why, how, and what happens when people get together to do something new. We have seen how two interrelated concepts—collective behavior and social movements—can be applied. We have focused on whole cases in order to get an overview of basic principles, stressing the historical dimension. Social scientists have used various research methods to study these phenomena and to test narrow hypotheses. We selected an historical approach because it seemed most appropriate for answering our original question, which was really about social change. We have seen that the Nazi movement resulted from social changes that had brought misery and confusion to a great nation. But the Nazis themselves produced social change and laid a basis for other movements like the one dedicated to spaceflight. Thus, the Nazi Party was both the result of social change and the cause.

Collective behavior and social movements are the reactions of numbers of people to social conditions, and these people produce new social conditions to which other people then react. We, as individuals and groups, stand between past events and future ones. The course of human history presents us with circumstances to which we must respond. Our descendents will have the history we give them. To return to a question posed a few pages ago, "Do we make our history, or does it make us?" Clearly, the answer is yes!

Review glossary

Collective behavior Unusual action related to social change taken by a group of people who influence one another but who engage in little planning and do not form an organization. (p. 494)

Social movement An organized group dedicated to causing or preventing social change and acting in unusual ways or outside of conventional channels. (p. 495)

Parallel behavior Several people doing the same thing for the same reasons, but without influencing one another. (p. 496)

Craze Sometimes called a fad; many people suddenly pursuing some new form of behavior, such as when millions bought Hula Hoops. (p. 497)

Panics What occur when many people suddenly seek to evade something they perceive as a danger, such as when crowds flee a burning building or when investors try to sell their stock in a falling market. (p. 500)

Riot A hostile, unplanned outburst in which a crowd threatens or attacks other persons or property. (p. 503)

Luddite A person who opposes technical progress (named for Ned Ludd, leader of the English textile workers who broke their machines to protest poverty). (p. 505)

Technological determinism The belief that technological change is automatic and that when the time is right for the next step forward, it will occur. If Edison, for example, hadn't invented the light bulb in 1879, within a few months someone else would have invented it. (p. 521)

Suggested readings

Allen, William Sheridan. *The Nazi Seizure of Power*. Chicago: Quandrangle, 1965.

Bainbridge, William Sims. *The Spaceflight Revolution*. New York: Wiley-Interscience, 1976.

Gerlach, Luther P., and Virginia H. Hine. *People, Power, Change: Movements of Social Transformation*. Indianapolis: Bobbs-Merrill, 1970.

Smelser, Neil J. *Theory of Collective Behavior*. New York: Free Press, 1962.

Zald, Mayer N. and John D. McCarthy, eds. *The Dynamics of Social Movements*. Cambridge: Winthrop, 1979.

Epilogue

In Chapter 1, I confessed that one purpose of this book was to invite readers to become sociologists. Since I assume that some of you are now considering that option, it seemed useful to add a brief essay explaining how people actually do become sociologists. I have learned from my students that they often have little information about such matters as going to graduate school. For example, many students have worried about how they could afford to go on to graduate school. Clearly, these students didn't know that most graduate students receive full financial support. Nor do undergraduates usually know much about how to select a graduate school.

Since it is difficult to be employed as a sociologist without a graduate degree (in fact, a doctorate is needed for many jobs), I shall devote much of this epilogue to graduate education. Then I shall describe the kinds of employment available to sociologists. First, however, something must be said about being an undergraduate major in sociology.

MAJORING IN SOCIOLOGY

Perhaps the most important thing for a would-be sociologist to know is that graduate schools do not require applicants to have an undergraduate major in sociology. That means you have considerable latitude to select courses that interest you and to take advantage of the strengths of the curriculum offered at your school. If another social science department at your school has a stronger program than the sociology department, you could major in that depart-

Becoming
a Sociologist

ment and still go on in sociology at the graduate school level.

You should also know that leading graduate schools in sociology place little importance on the quality of one's undergraduate college or university. You will not be handicapped if you are not now enrolled in a a well-known institution. In fact, the quality of teaching available to undergraduates is often higher at little-known schools than at famous institutions, where much of the teaching is delegated to graduate students lacking training and experience.

What you major in is not very important in becoming a sociologist; what you learn is. If my son decides he wants to be a sociologist and asks me to help him plan his undergraduate program, these are things I would tell him (depending, of course, on what was offered at his particular school).

It is important to take at least one course in statistics. If possible, do not take this in the math department or in the statistics department. Take it in a social science department, because then it will emphasize the statistical applications that social scientists actually use. If possible, take a second statistics course.

Take introductory economics. If micro and macro economics are separated into two courses, take micro. It is far more theoretical and more pertinent to sociology.

Take a basic course in logic. You may find a good one in the philosophy department or in the speech or communications department. A course that emphasizes the rules of deductive logic may be more useful than a course devoted to modern symbolic logic.

Also, take courses that require you to write. If a good writing course is available, perhaps in the English department, take it. Later in this epilogue, I shall discuss how to learn to write, because sociologists make their living by the written word.

Take some history, especially if you can find a course or two that emphasizes social history.

Take at least one course in research methods if it is offered at your school. Research methods are not simply statistics, although it may be useful to take a statistics course first.

You will notice that I have said nothing about courses in sociology. That is because your sociology department will have a set of courses it recommends or requires for a major. One of these will probably be a course in the history of social thought, and you ought to take it even if it is not required.

But whatever you do, don't specialize in one area of sociology while still an undergraduate. This is the time to sample many different parts of the field in order to discover what you really like and to gain a broad background that can serve as an adequate base for later specialization.

Finally, you may be able to gain some useful experience in doing sociology while still an undergraduate. Check around and see if some faculty members could use a volunteer assistant. Even if it only involves finding things for them in the library, you can learn from doing it, and you can include this experience in your application to graduate school.

GOING TO GRADUATE SCHOOL

Most graduate schools expect students to apply by the end of December for admission in September. Details of admissions procedures can be obtained by writing departments you are considering. That means that by early fall you ought to have a list of schools you think you would like to attend.

Selection

How do you pick graduate schools? The first thing is to know what degree you plan to earn. If you think you want only a master's degree, which will qualify you for some kinds of research jobs (especially in government) and for teaching at some community colleges, you have a choice of many more universities. However, if you think you will aim for a doctorate, which is needed to qualify for most college and university faculty appointments and for most senior research positions, you should enroll in a school that gives a doctorate and that has a "major-league" reputation.

Although the reputation of an undergraduate school has little effect on getting into a good graduate school, the reputation of a graduate school has an immense effect on a subsequent professional career. The general rule is that you will never get a job at a school with a substantially better reputation than the one from which you received your doctorate. So the better the graduate school you attend, the more opportunities you will have.

Fortunately, a number of universities have good reputations. However, the reputation of a university as a whole may not reflect the reputation of any specific department. Thus, some famous schools are not as highly ranked in sociology as some less famous places. Every few years a national study is conducted by the Council on Higher Education to rank departments in various academic fields. You may want to consult the sociology rankings in the latest of these reports (you can find it in most libraries). You can also get plenty of advice from members of your local sociology department. Moreover, you can request information on the recent placement of graduates from various departments you are considering, and this will tell you how well their students are regarded.

Each year the American Sociological Association publishes a Guide to Graduate Departments, which lists all faculty and various specialties of each department. This may help you determine who would be available to work with in any department—you may recognize some people because you know their research.

Be sure to apply to a number of schools, even if your grades and test scores are exceptional. That way you will have a choice. Having been accepted by several schools, you can then telephone the head of admissions at each school and seek further information to help you make your final choice. How much support do they offer? Will you have to pay tuition out of it? (Some schools require relatively high tuitions for out-of-state students; however, this tuition may be waived for graduate students.) You may also want to find out how long it takes the average graduate student to earn a degree at this school.

If you are married and your spouse plans to work while you are in graduate school, you will want to find out the employment situations near the schools you are considering. Usually it will be easier for a spouse to find proper employment in or very near a large city than in an isolated college town. You will also want to find out about housing costs—some cities are very expensive, but that may be offset by the availability of university-owned housing.

Applying

Most departments use their own application forms and have different requirements regarding letters of recommendation and qualifying exams. You should write to each department early in the fall (or even the previous spring) to obtain these materials.

Virtually all good graduate departments require that students take the Graduate Record Examination (GRE) administered by the Educational Testing Service. Your current school will have information on when and where these exams can be taken. It is best to take the GRE as early in the fall as possible so that your scores can be sent to graduate schools in time. Many students have found it helpful to prepare for this text by working through one of the practice guides available. Because undergraduate schools differ so greatly in quality and in grading practices, graduate schools place great emphasis on GRE scores.

Letters of recommendation can also greatly influence graduate admissions committees. The more contact you have with several faculty members while you are an undergraduate, the more able they will be to write you an effective recommendation. That's another reason to volunteer to help some faculty with their research, especially if you are attending a very large school. It is not necessary to restrict letters of recommendation to sociology faculty—any faculty member who thinks well of you will be effective. Moreover, you can sometimes find people not in a college or university whose recommendation will be influential. Be careful, however, to ensure that nonacademics can stress your intellectual ability and motivation, not just your good character. Admissions committees tend to be a bit snobbish and do not react well to students who solicit recommendations from their minister, coach, or manager of the fast-food restaurant in which they were employed.

Succeeding in graduate school

There is a great irony about graduate education. People get into graduate schools by having been good students. They succeed in graduate school by learning to cease being students. Until graduate school, one is a consumer of knowledge—and one succeeds by learning what other people think about various matters. In graduate school, a person must become a producer of knowledge and succeeds by having his or her own thoughts about these same matters.

This is reflected in a whole new style of reading, for example. Rather than reading to understand and to be able to recall what someone has to say on a topic, one now must read to see what the underlying issues are, what remains to be said on that topic, or what is being said that is inconsistent or inadequate. One reads not just to learn, but to find opportunities to contribute.

Nevertheless, the first several years of graduate school will revolve around classwork. A number of courses are required of all graduate students, and it is important to do as well as you can in each. But it is equally important to use this opportunity to get to know faculty members and discover with whom you want to work. For after the coursework is completed, graduate school turns into an apprentice-

ship. Finding the most suitable faculty member to work with as an apprentice will greatly shape your subsequent career.

In negotiating who will be your faculty sponsor in graduate school, you should be guided by several criteria. Ideally, it ought to be someone who does the kind of work you want to do. But that may be less important than finding someone who will train you well, who is interested in working with you, and who is able to place his or her students in good first jobs. Just as departments differ in reputation and ability to place students in top jobs, so do individual faculty members. Young faculty may be easier to approach and even more pleasant to work under, but they may lack the reputation to place students as effectively as senior faculty members. Sometimes, of course, a junior faculty member will be closely linked with a senior member, and thus his or her students will enjoy the sponsorship of the senior member.

In the final analysis, of course, it matters less who works with you than how well you do your work. If you begin to produce fine work, anyone will want to sponsor you, and you will be rewarded with quality job opportunities. What does it mean to produce fine work? Many things. But no matter how original and insightful your ideas, no matter how clever or creative your research, you will produce nothing until you write it down.

ON LEARNING TO WRITE

Perhaps the most disabling myth about intellectual activity is that writing is an art that is prompted by inspiration. Some writing can be classified as art, no doubt, but the act of writing is a trade in the same sense that plumbing or automotive repair are trades. Just as plumbers and mechanics would rarely accomplish anything if they waited for inspiration to impel them to action, so writers would rarely write if they relied on inspiration.

You learn to write by writing, just as you learn to plumb by plumbing. And just as any ordinary person can learn to plumb well, so can any ordinary person learn to write well. If you want to become a good writer, you must write. Regularly! Ideally, you should write every day.

In my teens I began to work for newspapers. Nobody taught me to write. I just began to try to do it every day. At first I was slow, and my prose was not very clear, let alone elegant. But just as one learns to make professional pipe joints as one gains experience, so one learns to write more clearly, cleanly, and easily by writing.

Never wait for inspiration; it seldoms comes. Approach the job of writing just as you approach household chores, as something you do regularly and routinely. For many years I have been in the habit of getting up at the same time every morning; as soon as I have had coffee and read the paper, I settle down to write for about five hours. I never have to ask myself if I feel like writing any more than I have to ask whether I feel like brushing my teeth. It's just what I do at that time of day.

If you write regularly, you not only get better and better at it, but you also get a great deal written. Students often fall into the habit of writing under pressure—of putting on a huge last-minute sprint to get a term paper completed. That's a bad way to write. It mixes writing with anxiety. When you write, you should be able to give your undivided attention to what you are saying, not to impending deadlines. Moreover, when you write regularly, you will find how easy it is to write a lot.

It would have made me a nervous wreck had I tried to write this textbook in a series of crash sessions, trying to avert impending deadlines. The experience would have been so terrible I would have probably tried to avoid writing anything again. But that's not the way I did it. I sat down every morning and calmly knocked out 4 or 5 pages and then quit. That doesn't sound like much, but it is. In just 100 days that adds up to from 400 to 500 pages, or about half this book. Clearly, then I would have been content to average only 2 pages a day (and I write more only because I have practiced so long that I am very fast now).

So if you want to write, you should think of it as a routine task, to be approached regularly and calmly. You will be amazed at how rapidly you improve.

When you write, don't agonize over finding the right word or the best phrasing. Get the ideas down no matter how poor your prose. After you have your ideas on paper, then worry about improving the style. When you have a draft, no matter how crude, you can work on improving the writing without getting sidetracked. You do not risk forgetting where you are going as you seek a word, or wrestle with a sentence. Indeed, what you are doing now is not writing but editing.

If you are considering graduate school, no matter in what department, keep in mind that you are essentially choosing to be a writer. Great ideas do not become great sociology or great chemistry until they are written and published.

SOCIOLOGICAL CAREERS

Colleges and universities are not the only places that employ people to do sociology. Much sociological research is conducted by people working for local, state, and national governments. Many other sociological researchers are employed by private firms. Thus, of the people who went through graduate school at Berkeley when I did, one ended up doing research on aging for the Social Security Administration, one plans new residential communities for a consortium of banks, one does research on drug abuse for the Justice Department, another studied parole and prison policies for New York State, two conduct market research for major advertising firms, one studies TV viewership for a rating company, and one went from research on magazine readership to being founder and publisher of a major new magazine. However, most of them ended up on college or university faculties.

College and university positions involve two very different career lines. The one most visible to students consists primarily of teaching. While virtually all college and university faculty members teach, in most schools faculty are expected to devote their major efforts to teaching. In contrast, faculty at the major research-oriented universities are asked to teach only half or even a third as much as faculty in other schools. The remainder of their time is supposed to be spent on research and writing. That is, these people are hired and promoted primarily to do sociology, not to teach it, and it is to them that the rule "Publish or perish" primarily applies. In major universities, promotion and tenure are awarded almost exclusively on the basis of scholarly publications, with only modest concern given to teaching skills. Many faculty not at the major research universities also do research and publish, but less emphasis is placed on those activities (they are given less time to devote to it, for one thing) and much more importance is placed on their teaching. Most of these faculty members also did their graduate work at major universities, but they primarily chose the career of college teaching.

For people entering graduate schools today, there will be more opportunities for careers in industry and government than when I got my degree. There probably will be somewhat fewer openings in universities and colleges, since higher education was still expanding when I graduated. If you are thinking about being a sociologist, you will have each of these career lines as possibilities. Moreover, during the course of your career, you will probably have opportunities to switch from one line to another.

Before I became a sociologist, I tried some other careers. I enjoyed being a newspaper reporter. I enjoyed being an advertising writer. For several years I even enjoyed being a soldier. But there is a considerable difference between enjoying an occupation and being dedicated to it. Although newspaper writing was an interesting job, I was able to leave it without regret. But for me sociology is different. It is not a job, but a way of life. Being a sociologist is not merely what I do, but what I am.

It is entirely possible for people to do a job very well and to take considerable pride in it without its being essential to their self-image. But if an occupation is based on self-motivation, dedication is essential. Sociology, like any science, is fundamentally a solitary trade. Even when you are part of a research team, the most important work is not done collectively but in private. The basis of all scientific work is thought. It is very hard to force yourself to sit alone and think about things unless you enjoy thinking about them. I am sure I lack the self-discipline needed to force myself to write every morning. Fortunately, the problem never comes up. It never does when you are doing what you want to do. Dedication, then, means doing a job because you love it.

The first and most important thing I look for in graduate students is dedication. How much talent they have is of much less interest to me. The question I truly want a student to answer is, If you were so rich you didn't need a job, would you still be a sociologist? I would. If you would, too, we need you.

References

Ackerman, Nathan W., and Marie Jahoda. 1950. *Anti-Semitism and Emotional Disorder*. New York: Harper & Row.

Adorno, Theodore, et al. 1950. *The Authoritarian Personality*. New York: W. W. Norton.

Albrecht, S. L., B. A. Chadwick, and D. S. Alcorn. 1977. "Religiosity and Deviance: Application of an Attitude-Behavior Contingent Consistency Model." *Journal for the Scientific Study of Religion* 16:263–274.

Allen, William Sheridan. 1965. *The Nazi Seizure of Power*. Chicago: Quadrangle.

Allport, Gordon. 1958. *The Nature of Prejudice*. New York: Doubleday.

Allport, G. W. 1968. "The Historical Background of Modern Social Psychology." In *The Handbook of Social Psychology*, edited by G. Lindzey and E. Aronson, pp. 1–80. Reading, Mass.: Addison-Wesley.

Almond, Gabriel, and Sidney Verba. 1963. *Civic Culture: Political Attitudes and Democracy in Five Nations*. Princeton, N.J.: Princeton University Press.

Anderson, L. S. 1979. "The Deterrent Effect of Criminal Sanctions: Reviewing the Evidence." In *Structure, Law, and Power: Essays in the Sociology of Law*, edited by P. J. Brantingham and J. M. Kress, pp. 120–134. Beverly Hills, Calif.: Sage.

Angell, Robert Cooley. 1942. "The Social Integration of Selected American Cities." *American Journal of Sociology* 47:575–592.

Angell, Robert Cooley. 1947. "The Social Integration of Cities of More Than 100,000 Population." *American Sociological Review* 12:335–342.

Angell, Robert Cooley. 1949. "Moral Integration and Interpersonal Integration in American Cities." *American Sociological Review* 14:245–251.

Arendt, Hannah. 1958. *The Origins of Totalitarianism*. New York: Meridian Books.

Asch, Solomon. 1952. "Effects of Group Pressure Upon the Modification and Distortion of Judgements." In *Readings in Social Psychology*, edited by Guy Swanson, Theodore M. Newcomb, and Eugene L. Hartley. New York: Holt, Rinehart & Winston.

Bainbridge, William Sims. 1976. *The Spaceflight Revolution*. New York: Wiley-Interscience.

Bainbridge, W. S., and Rodney Stark. 1980. "Client and Audience Cults in America." *Sociological Analysis* 41:199–214.

Bainbridge, W. S., and Rodney Stark. 1981a. "Suicide, Homicide, and Religion: Durkheim Reassessed." *Annual Review of the Social Sciences of Religion* 5:33–56.

Bainbridge, W. S., and Rodney Stark. 1981b. "Friendship, Religion, and the Occult." *Review of Religious Research* 22:313–327.

Bainbridge, W. S., and Rodney Stark. 1982. "Church and Cult in Canada." *Canadian Journal of Sociology*. 7:351–366.

Ball-Rokeach, Sandra. 1973. "Violence and Values: A Test of the Subculture of Violence Thesis." *American Sociological Review* 38:736–749.

Baltzell, E. Digby. 1964. *The Protestant Establishment*. New York: Random House.

Bandura, Albert. 1974. "Behavior Theory and the Models of Man." *American Psychologist* 29:859–869.

Baron, Robert A., and Donn Byrne. 1981. *Social Psychology*. Boston: Allyn & Bacon.

Barrett, Richard K., and Martin King White. 1982. "Dependency Theory and Taiwan: Analysis of a Deviant Case." *American Journal of Sociology* 87:1064–1089.

Bell, Daniel. 1961. *The End of Ideology*. New York: Collier Books.

Bell, Daniel. 1980. *The Winding Passage.* Cambridge: ABT.

Benbow, Camilla Persson, and Julian C. Stanley. 1980. "Sex Differences in Mathematical Ability: Fact or Artifact?" *Science,* Dec. 12.

Benedict, Ruth. 1934. *Patterns of Culture.* New York: Houghton Mifflin.

Benedict, Ruth F., and Margaret Mead. 1959. *An Anthropologist at Work.* Boston: Houghton Mifflin.

Benitez, J. 1973. "The Effect of Elite Recruitment and Training on Diffuse Socialization Outcomes." Doctoral dissertation, Stanford University.

Berelson, Bernard. 1978. "Prospects and Programs for Fertility Reduction: What? Where?" *Population and Development Review* 4:579–616.

Berelson, Bernard, Paul F. Lazarsfeld, and William N. McPhee. 1954. *Voting: A Study of Opinion Formation in a Presidential Campaign.* Chicago: University of Chicago Press.

Berelson, Bernard, and Gary A. Steiner. 1964. *Human Behavior: An Inventory of Scientific Findings.* New York: Harcourt, Brace and World.

Berg, E. J. 1966. "Backward-sloping Labor Supply Functions in Dual Economies—the Africa Case." In *Social Change: The Colonial Situation,* edited by Immanuel Wallerstein. New York: John Wiley.

Berger, Peter L. 1963. *Invitation to Sociology: A Humanistic Perspective.* New York: Doubleday.

Berger, Peter L. 1967. *The Sacred Canopy.* Garden City, N.Y.: Doubleday.

Berk, R. A., K. J. Lenihan, and P. H. Rossi. 1980. "Crime and Poverty: Some Experimental Evidence from Ex-Offenders." *American Sociological Review* 45:766–786.

Berkowitz, Leonard. 1978. "Is Criminal Violence Normative Behavior?" *Journal of Research in Crime and Delinquency* 15:148–161.

Bird, Caroline. 1975. *The Case Against College.* New York: David McKay.

Blalock, Hubert M., Jr. 1967. *Toward a Theory of Minority-Group Relations.* New York: Capricorn Books.

Blau, Peter M. 1970. "A Formal Theory of Differentiation in Organizations." *American Sociological Review* 35:201–218.

Blau, Peter M. 1972. "Size and the Structure of Organizations: A Causal Analysis." *American Sociological Review* 37:434–440.

Blau, Peter M., and Otis Dudley Duncan. 1967. *The American Occupational Structure.* New York: John Wiley.

Bloch, Marc. 1962. *Feudal Society.* Chicago: University of Chicago Press.

Blumenfeld, H. 1971. "Transportation in the Modern Metropolis." In *Internal Structure of the City,* edited by L. S. Bourne. New York: Oxford.

Bonacich, Edna. 1972. "A Theory of Ethnic Antagonism: The Split Labor Market." *American Sociological Review* 37:547–559.

Bonacich, Edna. 1973. "A Theory of Middleman Minorities." *American Sociological Review* 38:583–594.

Bonacich, Edna. 1975. "Abolition, the Extension of Slavery, and the Position of Free Blacks." *American Journal of Sociology* 81:601–628.

Bonacich, Edna. 1976. "Advanced Capitalism and Black/White Race Relations in the United States: A Split Labor Market Interpretation." *American Sociological Review* 41:34–51.

Bond, Horace Mann. 1934. *The Education of the Negro in the American Social Order.* New York: Prentice-Hall.

Boudon, Raymond. 1974. *Education, Opportunity, and Social Inequality: Changing Prospects in Western Society.* New York: John Wiley.

Bowers, William J., and Glenn L. Pierce. 1980. "Deterrence or Brutalization: What Is the Effect of Executions?" *Crime and Delinquency* 26:453–484.

Bowles, Samuel, and Herbert Gintis. 1976. *Schooling in Capitalist America.* New York: Basic Books.

Braudel, Fernand. 1981. *The Structures of Everyday Life.* New York: Harper & Row.

Brophy, I. N. 1945. "The Luxury of Anti-Negro Prejudice." *Public Opinion Quarterly* 9:456–466.

Brown, Barbara. 1984. "How the Baby Boom Lives." *American Demographics* 6:5:35–37.

Brown, Roger, and Ursula Bellugi. 1964. "Three Processes in the Child's Acquistion of Syntax." *Harvard Educational Review* 34:133–151.

Brown, Roger, and Richard J. Herrnstein. 1975. *Psychology.* Boston: Little, Brown.

Burchinal, Lee G. 1963. "Personality Characteristics of Children." In *The Employed Mother in America,* edited by F. Ivan Nye and Lois Wladis Hoffman, pp. 106–121. Chicago: Rand McNally.

Burgess, Robert L., and Ronald L. Akers. 1966. "A Differential Association-reinforcement Theory of Criminal Behavior." *Social Problems* 14:128–147.

Burkett, S. R., and M. White. 1974. "Hellfire and Delinquency: Another Look." *Journal for the Scientific Study of Religion* 13:455–462.

Byrne, Donn. 1971. *The Attraction Paradigm.* New York: Academic Press.

Calhoun, J. B. 1962. "Population Density and Social Pathology." *Scientific American* 206:139–148.

Campbell, Angus. 1975. "The American Way of Mating: Marriage, Sí; Children, Maybe." *Psychology Today* 8:37–43.

Cantril, Albert H., and Charles W. Roll. 1971. *Hopes and Fears of the American People.* New York: Universe Books.

Cantril, Hadley. 1941. *The Psychology of Social Movements.* New York: John Wiley.

Cantril, Hadley. 1966. *The Invasion from Mars.* New York: Harper & Row.

Caplow, Theodore. 1968. *Two Against One: Coalitions in Triads.* Englewood Cliffs, N.J.: Prentice-Hall.

Carmichael, Stokely, and Charles V. Hamilton. 1967. *Black Power: The Politics of Liberation in America.* New York: Random House.

Carsten, F. L. 1967. *The Rise of Fascism.* Berkeley: University of California Press.

Chandler, Alfred. 1962. *Strategy and Structure.* Cambridge: MIT Press.

Chandler, David. 1966. *The Campaigns of Napoleon.* New York: Macmillan.

Chase-Dunn, Christopher. 1975. "The Effects of International Economic Dependence on Development and Inequality: A Cross-National Study." *American Sociological Review* 40:720–738.

Chirot, Daniel. 1976. *Social Change in a Peripheral Society.* New York: Academic Press.

Chirot, Daniel. 1977. *Social Change in the Twentieth Century.* New York: Harcourt Brace Jovanovich.

Clark, John P., and Larry L. Tifft. 1966. "Polygraph and Interview Validation of Self-Reported Deviant Behavior." *American Sociological Review* 31:516–523.

Cohen, Lawrence E., and Marcus Felson. 1979. "Social Change and Crime Rate Trends: A Routine Activity Approach." *American Sociological Review* 44:588–607.

Cohen, Lawrence E., Marcus Felson, and Kenneth C. Land. 1980. "Property Crime Rates in the Untied States: A Macrodynamic Analysis, 1947–1977; with Ex Ante Forecasts for the Mid-1980s." *American Journal of Sociology* 86:90–118.

Cohen, Mark. 1977. *The Food Crisis in Prehistory: Overpopulation and the Origins of Agriculture.* New Haven: Yale University Press.

Cohen, Yehudi. 1978. "The Disappearance of the Incest Taboo." *Human Nature* 1:72–78.

Cohn, Werner. 1958. "The Politics of American Jews." In *The Jews: Social Patterns of an American Group,* edited by Marshall Sklare. Glencoe, Ill.: Free Press.

Coleman, James S. 1961. *The Adolescent Society.* New York: Free Press.

Coleman, James S., et al. 1966. *Equality of Educational Opportunity.* Washington, D.C.: U.S. Government Printing Office.

Collins, Randall. 1971. "Functional and Conflict Theories of Educational Stratification." *American Sociological Review* 36:1002–1019.

Cooley, Charles H. 1909. *Social Organization.* New York: Charles Scribner's.

Cooley, Charles H. 1922. *Human Nature and the Social Order.* New York: Charles Scribner's.

Counts, George Sylvester. 1922. "The Selective Character of American Secondary Education." *Supplementary Educational Monographs,* no. 19. Chicago: University of Chicago Press.

Covello, Leonard. 1967. *The Social Background of the Italo-American School Child.* Leiden, Netherlands: E. J. Brill, N.B.

Crutchfield, Robert, Michael Geerken, and Walter R. Gove, 1982. "Crime Rates and Social Integration." *Criminology* 20:467–478.

Dahl, Robert. 1956. *A Preface to Democratic Theory.* Chicago: University of Chicago Press.

Dahrendorf, Ralf. 1959. *Class and Class Conflict in Industrial Society.* Palo Alto, Calif.: Stanford University Press.

Dahrendorf, Ralf. 1968. *Essays in the Theory of Society.* Palo Alto, Calif.: Stanford University Press.

D'Andrade, Roy G. 1966. "Sex Differences and Cultural Institutions." In *Development of Sex Differences,* edited by Eleanor E. Maccoby. Palo Alto, Calif.: Stanford University Press.

Darley, John M., and Bibb Latanè. 1968. "Bystander Intervention in Emergencies: Diffusion of Responsibility." *Journal of Personality and Social Psychology* 8:377–383.

Darroch, A. Gordon, and Wilfred G. Marston. 1971. "The Social Class Basis of Ethnic Residential Segregation: The Canadian Case." *American Journal of Sociology* 77:491–510.

Davis, James A., and Samuel Leinhardt. 1972. "The Structure of Positive Interpersonal Relations in Small Groups." In *Sociological Theories in Progress,* edited by Joseph Berger. Boston: Houghton Mifflin.

Davis, Kingsley. 1940. "Extreme Social Isolation of a Child." *American Journal of Sociology* 45:523–535.

Davis, Kinglsey. 1945. "The World Demographic Transition." *Annals of the American Academy of Political and Social Sciences* 237:1–11.

Davis, Kingsley. 1947. "Final Note of a Case of Extreme Isolation." *American Journal of Sociology* 50:432–437.

Davis, Kingsley. 1949. *Human Society.* New York: Macmillan.

Davis, Kingsley. 1951. *The Population of India and Pakistan.* Princeton, N.J.: Princeton University Press.

Davis, Kingsley. 1955. "The Origin and Growth of Urbanization in the World." *American Journal of Sociology* 60:429–437.

Davis, Kinglsey. 1965. "The Population Impact of Children in the World's Agrarian Countries." *Population Review* 9:17–31.

Davis, Kingsley. 1971. "The World's Population Crisis." In *Contemporary Social Problems,* 2nd ed., edited by Robert K. Merton and Robert Nisbet. New York: Harcourt Brace Jovanovich.

Davis, Kingsley. 1976. "The World's Population Crisis." In *Contemporary Social Problems,* 3rd ed., edited by Robert K. Merton and Robert Nisbet. New York: Harcourt Brace Jovanovich.

Davis, Kingsley, and Wilbert E. Moore. 1945. "Some Principles of Stratification." *American Sociological Review* 10:242–249.

Davis, Kingsley, and Wilbert E. Moore. 1953. "Replies to Tumin." *American Sociological Review* 18:394–396.

Delacroix, Jacques. 1977. "The Export of Raw Materials and Economic Growth: A Cross-National Study." *American Sociological Review* 42:795–808.

Delacroix, Jacques, and Charles C. Ragin. 1981. "Structural Blockage: A Cross-National Study of Economic Dependency, State Efficacy, and Underdevelopment." *American Journal of Sociology* 86:1311–1347.

Demerath, N. J., and Phillip E. Hammond. 1969. *Religion in Social Context.* New York: Random House.

Diaz-Alejandro, Carlos, et al. 1978. *Rich and Poor Nations in the World Economy.* New York: McGraw-Hill.

Doblin, Ernest M., and Claire Pohly. 1945. "The Social Composition of the Nazi Leadership." *American Journal of Sociology* 51:42–49.

Drucker, Peter F. 1946. *Concept of the Corporation.* New York: John Day.

Drucker, Peter F. 1967. *The Effective Executive.* New York: Harper & Row.

Drucker, Peter F. 1969. *The Age of Discontinuity: Guidelines to Our Changing Society.* New York: Harper & Row.

Drucker, Peter F. 1974. *Management: Tasks—Responsibilities—Practices.* New York: Harper & Row.

Drummond, J. C., and Anne Wilbraham. 1957. *The Englishman's Food: A History of Five Centuries of English Diet,* rev. ed. London: Cape.

Durden-Smith, Jo, and Diane deSimone. 1983. *Sex and the Brain.* New York: Arbor House.

Durkheim, Emile. 1897. *Suicide.* Reprint, 1966. New York: Free Press.

Eaton, C. Gray. 1976. "The Social Order of Japanese Macaques." *Scientific American,* Oct.

Edmundson, George. 1922. *History of Holland.* Cambridge, England: Cambridge University Press.

Ehrlich, Issac. 1975. "The Deterrent Effect of Capital Punishment: A Question of Life and Death." *American Economic Review* 397–417.

Eibl-Eibesfeldt, Irenaus. 1970. *Ethology: The Biology of Behavior.* New York: Holt, Rinehart & Winston.

Ember, Melvin, and Carol E. Ember. 1971. "The Conditions Favoring Matrilocal versus Patrilocal Residence." *American Anthropologist* 73:571–594.

Erickson, Maynard L. 1971. "The Group Context of Delinquent Behavior." *Social Problems* 19:114–129.

Erlanger, Howard S. 1971. *The Anatomy of Violence: An Empirical Examination of Sociological Theories of*

Interpersonal Aggression. Unpublished Ph.D. dissertation, University of California, Berkeley.

Erlanger, Howard S. 1971. "Social Class and the Use of Corporal Punishment in Childrearing: A Reassessment." *American Sociological Review* 39:68–85.

Erlenmeyer-Kimling, L., and L. F. Jarvik. 1963. "Genetics and Intelligence: A Review." *Science* 142:1477–1479.

Fair, Charles. 1971. *From the Jaws of Victory.* New York: Simon & Schuster.

Federal Bureau of Investigation. 1982. *Uniform Crime Reports.* Washington, D.C.: U.S. Government Printing Office.

Festinger, Leon, Stanley Schachter, and Kurt Back. 1950. *Social Pressures in Informal Groups.* New York: Harper & Row.

Fischer, Claude S. 1975. "Toward a Subcultural Theory of Urbanism." *American Journal of Sociology* 80:1319–1341.

Fischer, Claude S. 1976. *The Urban Experience.* New York: Harcourt Brace Jovanovich.

Fishberg, Maurice. 1911. *The Jews.* New York: Charles Scribner's.

Flanigan, William H. 1972. *Political Behavior of the American Electorate,* 2nd. ed. Boston: Allyn & Bacon.

Fleming, Joyce Dudney. 1974. "The State of the Apes." *Psychology Today* 7:31–38.

Fogel, John K., and Stanley L. Engerman. 1974. *Time on the Cross: The Economics of American Negro Slavery.* Boston: Little, Brown.

Ford, Clellan S. 1952. "Control of Conception in Cross-cultural Perspective." *World Population Problems and Birth Control. Annals of the New York Academy of Sciences* 54:763–768.

Ford, W. Scott. 1973. "Interracial Public Housing in a Border City: Another Look at the Contact Hypothesis." *American Journal of Sociology* 78:1426–1447.

Frank, Andre Gunder. 1969. *Latin America: Underdevelopment or Revolution.* New York: Monthly Review Press.

Freeman, Derek. 1983. *Margaret Mead and Samoa: The Making and Unmaking of an Anthropological Myth.* Cambridge: Harvard University Press.

Freidson, Eliot. 1973. "Professions and the Occupational Principle." In *The Professions and Their Prospects,* edited by Eliot Freidson. pp. 19–38. Beverly Hills, Calif.: Sage.

Freud, Sigmund. 1927. *The Future of an Illusion.* Garden City, N.Y.: Doubleday.

Fried, Morton H. 1967. *The Evolution of Political Society: An Essay in Political Anthropology.* New York: Random House.

Friedman, Milton. 1962. *Capitalism and Freedom.* Chicago: University of Chicago Press.

Fuguitt, G. V., and J. J. Zuiches. 1973. "Residential Preferences and Population Distribution: Results of a National Survey." Paper presented to Rural Sociological Society, College Park, Maryland.

Galle, O., and W. Gove. 1978. "Overcrowding, Isolation and Human Behavior: Exploring the Extremes in Population Distribution." In *Social Demography,* edited by Karl Tauber and James Sweet. New York: Academic Press.

Gallup, George H. 1972. *The Gallup Poll: Public Opinion 1935–1971,* 3 vols. New York: Random House.

Gallup, George H. 1978. *The Gallup Poll: Public Opinion 1972–1977,* 2 vols. Wilmington: Scholarly Resources.

The Gallup Poll. 1967–1984. *The Gallup Report* (formerly *The Gallup Opinion Index*), published monthly.

Galtung, J. 1971. "A Structural Theory of Imperialism." *Journal of Peace Research* 8:81–117.

Gans, Herbert J. 1962. *The Urban Villagers.* New York: Free Press.

Gardiner, R. Allen, and Beatrice T. Gardiner. 1969. "Teaching Sign Language to a Chimpanzee." *Science* 165:664–672.

Geerken, Michael R., and Walter R. Gove. 1977. "Deterrence, Overload, and Incapacitation: An Empirical Evaluation." *Social Forces* 56:424–447.

Genovese, E. D. 1974. *Roll, Jordan Roll!* New York: Pantheon.

Gerlach, Luther P., and Virginia H. Hine. 1970. *People, Power, Change: Movements of Social Transformation.* Indianapolis: Bobbs-Merrill.

Gerth, Hans. 1940. "The Nazi Party: Its Leadership and Composition." *American Journal of Sociology* 4:517–541.

Gibbons, Don C., and Gerald F. Blake. 1976. "Evaluating the Impact of Juvenile Diversion Programs." *Crime and Delinquency* 22:411–420.

Gibbs, Jack P. 1975. *Crime, Punishment, and Deterrence.* New York: Elsevier.

Gilfillan, S. C. 1963. *The Sociology of Invention.* Cambridge: MIT Press.

Glazer, Nathan. 1971. "Blacks and Ethnic Groups: The Difference, and the Political Difference it Makes." *Social Problems* 18:444–461.

Glazer, Nathan, and Daniel P. Moynihan. 1963. *Beyond the Melting Pot.* Cambridge: MIT Press.

Glazer, Nathan, and Daniel P. Moynihan. 1970. *Beyond the Melting Pot,* 2nd ed. Cambridge: MIT Press.

Glock, Charles Y., and Rodney Stark. 1966. *Christian Beliefs and Anti-Semitism.* New York: Harper & Row.

Goffman, Erving. 1959. *The Presentation of Self in Everyday Life.* New York: Doubleday

Goffman, Erving. 1961. *Asylums: Essays on the Social Situation of Mental Patients and Other Inmates.* Chicago: Aldine.

Goffman, Erving. 1963. *Behavior in Public Places.* New York: Free Press.

Goffman, Erving. 1971. *Relations in Public.* New York: Basic Books.

Goodall, Jane. 1971. *In the Shadow of Man.* Boston: Houghton Mifflin.

Goring, Charles. 1913. *The English Convict.* London: His Majesty's Stationery Office.

Gough, E. Kathleen. 1974. "Nayar: Central Kerala." In *Matrilineal Kinship,* edited by David Schneider and E. Kathleen Gough. Berkeley: University of California Press.

Gouldner, Alvin W. 1959. "Organizational Analysis." In *Sociology Today,* edited by Robert K. Merton, Leonard Broom, and Leonard S. Cottrell, Jr., pp. 400–410. New York: Basic Books.

Gove, Walter R., ed. 1975. *The Labeling of Deviance.* New York: John Wiley.

Gove, Walter R., Michael Hughes, and Omer R. Galle. 1979. "Overcrowding in the Home." *American Sociological Review* 44:59–80.

Granovetter, Mark S. 1973. "The Strength of Weak Ties." *American Journal of Sociology* 78:1360–1380.

Grant, Madison. 1916. *The Passing of the Great Race.* New York: Charles Scribner's.

Gray, Diana. 1973. "Turning Out: A Study of Teenage Prostitution." *Urban Life and Culture* 1:401–425.

Greeley, Andrew M. 1974. *Ethnicity in the United States.* New York: John Wiley.

Green, Richard. 1974. *Sexual Identity Conflict in Children and Adults.* New York: Basic Books.

Guest, Avery M., and Stewart Tolnay. Forthcoming. "Social Variations in School Attendance."

Guest, Avery M., and James A. Weed. 1976. "Ethnic Residential Segregation: Patterns of Change." *American Journal of Sociology* 81:1088–1111.

Habermas, Jurgen. 1975. *The Legitimation Crisis.* Boston: Beacon Press.

Hacker, Andrew. 1983. *A Statistical Portrait of the American People.* New York: Viking Press.

Hale, Oron James. 1955. "Adolph Hitler, Taxpayer." *American Historical Review,* July, p. 837.

Hall, Peter. 1966. *The World Cities.* New York: McGraw-Hill.

Halliday, Fred. 1979. *Iran: Dictatorship and Development.* London: Penguin Books.

Handlin, Oscar. 1957. *Race and Nationality in American Life.* Garden City, N.Y.: Anchor Press/Doubleday.

Harlow, Harry F., and Margaret K. Harlow. 1965. "The Affectional Systems." In *Behavior in Non-Human Primates: Modern Research Trends,* vol. 2, edited by Allan Schrier, Harry Harlow, and Fred Stollnitz, pp. 287–333. New York: Academic Press.

Harris, Louis. 1971. "Political Labels Depend on Who Applies Them." *St. Petersburg Times,* January 18.

Harris, Marvin. 1979. *Cultural Materialism: The Struggle for a Science of Culture.* New York: Random House.

Hatt, Paul K., and Cecil C. North. 1947. "Jobs and Occupations: A Popular Evaluation." *Opinion News* 9:1–13.

Hayes, K. J., and C. Hayes. 1951. "The Intellectual Development of a Home-Raised Chimpanzee." *Proceedings of the American Philosophical Society* 95:105–109.

Hechter, Michael. 1974. *Internal Colonialism: The Celtic Fringe in British National Development.* Berkeley: University of California Press.

Hechter, Michael. 1978. "Group Formation and the Cultural Division of Labor." *American Journal of Sociology* 84:293–318.

Heer, David M. 1980. "Intermarriage." In *Harvard Encyclopedia of American Ethnic Groups.* Cambridge: Belknap Press.

Heider, Fritz. 1946. "Attitudes and Cognitive Organization." *Journal of Psychology* 21:107–112.

Heilbroner, Robert L. 1961. *The Worldly Philosophers.* New York: Simon & Schuster.

Hennig, Margaret, and Anne Jardim. 1977. *The Managerial Woman.* Garden City, N.Y.: Anchor Press/Doubleday.

Heyns, Barbara. 1978. *Summer Learning and the Effects of Schooling.* New York: Academic Press.

Higgins, P. C., and G. L. Albrecht. 1977. "Hellfire and Delinquency Revisited." *Social Forces* 55:952–958.

Hill, Charles T., Zick Rubin, and Letitia Anne Peplau. 1976. "Breakups Before Marriage: The End of 103 Affairs." *Journal of Social Issues* 32:147–168.

Hindelang, Michael, Travis Hirschi, and Joseph G. Weis. 1981. *Measuring Delinquency.* Beverly Hills, Calif.: Sage.

Hirschi, Travis. 1969. *Causes of Delinquency.* Berkeley: University of California.

Hirschi, Travis, and Michael J. Hindelang. 1977. "Intelligence and Deliquency: A Revisionist Review." *American Sociological Review* 42:571–587.

Hirschi, Travis, and Rodney Stark. 1969. "Hellfire and Delinquency." *Social Problems* 17:202–213.

Ho, Ping-Ti. 1959. *Studies on the Population of China, 1368–1953.* Cambridge: Harvard University Press.

Hobbes, Thomas. 1651. *Leviathan.* Reprint 1956. Chicago: Henry Regnery.

Hodge, Robert W., P. M. Siegal, and Peter Rossi. 1964. "Occupational Prestige in the United States, 1925–1963." *American Journal of Sociology* 70:286–302.

Hodge, Robert W., Donald J. Treiman, and Peter H. Rossi. 1966. "A Comparative Study of Occupational Prestige." In *Class, Status and Power,* 2nd ed., edited by Reinhard Bendix and Seymour Martin Lipset. New York: Free Press.

Homans, George C. 1964. "Bringing Men Back In." *American Sociological Review* 29: 809–818.

Homans, George C. 1974. *Social Behavior: Its Elementary Forms.* New York: Harcourt Brace Jovanovich.

Hopkins, Jack. 1983. "Judge's Order Depriving Parents of Son Is Upheld." *Seattle Post-Intelligencer.* June 7. P. 1.

Hoult, Thomas Ford. 1969. *Dictionary of Modern Sociology.* Totowa, N.J.: Littlefield, Adams & Co.

Hout, Michael. 1982. "The Association Between Husbands' and Wives' Occupations in Two-Earner Families." *American Journal of Sociology* 88:397–409.

Howard, John R. 1974. *The Cutting Edge—Social Movements and Social Change in America.* Philadelphia: J. B. Lippincott.

Howard, Michael. 1962. *The Franco-Prussian War.* New York: Macmillan.

Howe, Irving. 1976. *World of Our Fathers.* New York: Harcourt Brace Jovanovich.

Hunt, Morton. 1974. *Sexual Behavior in the 1970s.* Chicago: Playboy Press.

Illich, Ivan. 1970. *Deschooling Society.* New York: Harper & Row.

Inkeles, Alex, and Peter H. Rossi. 1956. "National Comparisons of Occupational Prestige." *American Journal of Sociology* 61:329–339.

Irwin, John. 1970. *The Felon.* Englewood Cliffs, N.J.: Prentice-Hall.

Ismael, J. S., and T. Y. Ismael. 1980. "Social Change in Islamic Society: The Political Thought of Ayatollah Khomeini." *Social Problems* 27: 601–619.

Jacob, Joseph. 1912. *Tulips.* New York: Stokes.

Jencks, Christopher, et al. 1972. *Inequality: A Reassessment of the Effects of Family and Schooling in America.* New York: Basic Books.

Jensen, Arthur R. 1969. "How Much Can We Boost IQ and Scholastic Achievement?" *Harvard Educational Review* 39:1–123.

Jensen, Gary F. 1969. "Crime Doesn't Pay: Correlates of Shared Misunderstanding." *Social Problems* 17: 189–201.

Jensen, Gary F. 1972. "Parents, Peers and Delinquency Action: A Test of the Differential Association Perspective." *American Journal of Sociology* 78:562–575.

Jensen, Gary F., Maynard L. Erickson, and Jack Gibbs. 1978. "Perceived Risk of Punishment and Self-reported Delinquency." *Social Forces* 57:57–58.

Jewkes, John, David Sawers, and Richard Stillerman. 1969. *The Sources of Invention.* New York: W. W. Norton.

Johnson, Benton. 1963. "On Church and Sect." *American Sociological Review* 28:539–549.

Johnson, Paul. 1977. *Enemies of Society.* New York: Atheneum.

Johnson, Paul. 1979. *A History of Christianity.* New York: Atheneum.

Jones, Landon Y. 1980. *Great Expectations: America and the Baby Boom Generation.* Coward, McCann & Geohegan.

Kaiser, Robert G. 1976. *Russia: The People and the Power.* New York: Atheneum.

Kanter, Rosabeth. 1972. *Commitment and Community.* Cambridge: Harvard University Press.

Kantrowitz, Nathan. 1973. *Ethnic and Racial Segregation in the New York Metropolis.* New York: Praeger.

Kelley, Dean. 1972. *Why Conservative Churches Are Growing.* New York: Harper & Row.

Kephart, William. 1957. *Racial Factors and Urban Law Enforcement.* Philadelphia: University of Pennsylvania Press.

Kihumura, Akemi, and Harry H. L. Kitano. 1973. "Interracial Marriage: A Picture of Japanese Americans." *Journal of Social Issues* 29:69–73.

Kitano, Harry H. L. 1969. *Japanese Americans.* Englewood Cliffs, N.J.: Prentice-Hall.

Klein, Malcolm W. 1976. "Issues and Realities in Police Diversion Programs." *Crime and Delinquency* 22: 421–427.

Kohlberg, Lawrence, and Card Gilligan. 1971. "The Adolescent as a Philosopher: The Discovery of the Self in a Postconventional World." *Daedalus* 100:1051–1086.

Kohn, M. L. 1959. "Social Class and Parental Values." *American Journal of Sociology* 64:337–351.

Kohn, M. L., and Carmi Schooler. 1969. "Class, Occupation, and Orientation." *American Sociological Review* 34:659–678.

Kohn, Melvin L., and Carmi Schooler. 1982. "Job Conditions and Personality: A Longitudinal Assessment of Their Reciprocal Effects." *American Journal of Sociology* 87:1257–1286.

Kornhauser, Ruth. 1978. *Social Sources of Delinquency: An Appraisal of Analytic Models.* Chicago: University of Chicago Press.

Kornhauser, William. 1959. *The Politics of Mass Society.* New York: Free Press.

Kowalewski, David. 1980. "Religious Belief in the Brezhnev Era: Renaissance, Resistance, and Realpolitik." *Journal for the Scientific Study of Religion* 19:280–292.

Kramer, Judith. 1970. *The American Minority Community.* New York: Thomas Y. Crowell.

Kroeber, Alfred L. 1925. *Handbook of American Indians of California.* Bulletin 78: Smithsonian Institution, Bureau of American Ethnology.

Landis, Paul H. 1965. *Making the Most of Marriage.* New York: Appleton-Century-Crofts.

Lazarsfeld, Paul F., Bernard Berelson, and Hazel Gaudet. 1948. *The People's Choice.* New York: Columbia University Press.

Leacock, Eleanor. 1978. "Women's Status in Egalitarian Society: Implications for Social Evolution." *Current Anthropology* 19:247–275.

Lemert, Edwin M. 1951. *Social Pathology.* New York: McGraw-Hill.

Lemert, Edwin M. 1967. *Human Deviance, Social Problems, and Social Control.* Englewood Cliffs, N.J.: Prentice-Hall.

Lenski, Gerhard. 1954. "Status Crystallization: A Nonvertical Dimension of Social Status." *American Sociological Review* 19:405–413.

Lenski, Gerhard. 1956. "Social Participation and Status Crystallization." *American Sociological Review* 21:458–464.

Lenski, Gerhard. 1966. *Power and Privilege.* New York: McGraw-Hill.

Lenski, Gerhard. 1976. "History and Social Change." *American Journal of Sociology* 82:548–564.

Levine, Gene N., and Darrel M. Montero. 1973. "Socioeconomic Mobility Among Three Generations of Japanese Americans." *Journal of Social Issues* 29:40–45.

Lévi-Strauss, Claude. 1956. "The Family." In *Man, Culture and Society,* edited by Harry L. Shapiro. New York: Oxford University Press.

Lewontin, R. C. 1973. "Race and Intelligence." In *The Fallacy of IQ,* edited by C. Senna. New York: Random House.

Lieberson, Stanley. 1961. "The Impact of Residential Segregation on Ethnic Assimilation." *Social Forces* 40:52–57.

Lieberson, Stanley. 1963. *Ethnic Patterns in American Cities.* New York: Free Press.

Lieberson, Stanley. 1973. "Generational Differences Among Blacks in the North." *American Journal of Sociology* 79:550–565.

Lieberson, Stanley. 1980. *A Piece of the Pie: Blacks and White Immigrants Since 1880.* Berkeley: University of California Press.

Light, Ivan H. 1972. *Ethnic Enterprise in America: Business and Welfare Among Chinese, Japanese and Blacks.* Berkeley: University of California Press.

Lilly, J. C. 1967. *The Mind of the Dolphin: A Nonhuman Intelligence.* New York: Doubleday.

Linton, Ralph. 1936. *The Study of Man: An Introduction.* Reprint 1964. Englewood Cliffs, N. J.: Prentice-Hall.

Lipset, Seymour Martin. 1963. "Three Decades of the Radical Right: Coughlinites, McCarthyites, and Birchers." In *The Radical Right,* edited by Daniel Bell. Garden City, N.Y.: Doubleday.

Lipset, Seymour Martin. 1976. "Equality and Inequality." In *Contemporary Social Problems,* 4th ed., edited by Robert K. Merton and Robert Nisbet. New York: Harcourt Brace Jovanovich.

Lipset, Seymour Martin, and Reinhard Bendix. 1959. *Social Mobility in Industrial Society.* Berkeley: University of California Press.

Liska, Allen E. 1981. *Perspectives on Deviance.* Englewood Cliffs, N.J.: Prentice-Hall.

Lofland, John. 1966. *Doomsday Cult.* Englewood Cliffs, N.J.: Prentice-Hall.

Lofland, John, and Rodney Stark. 1965. "Becoming a World-Saver: A Theory of Conversion to a Deviant Perspective." *American Sociological Review* 30:862–875.

Lofland, Lyn H. 1973. *A World of Strangers.* New York: Basic Books.

Lombroso-Ferrero, Gina. 1911. *Criminal Man.* Montclair, N.J.: Patterson-Smith.

McClean, Charles. 1978. *The Wolf Children.* New York: Hill & Wang.

Maccoby, Eleanor, and Carol Jacklin. 1974. *The Psychology of Sex Differences.* Palo Alto, Calif.: Stanford University Press.

McCord, William, and Joan McCord. 1959. *Origins of Crime: A New Evaluation of the Cambridge-Somerville Youth Study.* New York: Columbia University Press.

McDougall, W. 1908. *An Introduction to Social Psychology.* Boston: Luce.

McDougall, William. 1932. *The Energies of Men: A Study of the Fundamentals of Dynamic Psychology.* London: Methuen.

McEachern, A. W. 1968. "The Juvenile Probation System." *American Behavioral Scientist* 11:1–10.

McFarland, H. Neill. 1967. *The Rush Hour of the Gods: A Study of New Religious Movements in Japan.* New York: Macmillan.

McGahey, Richard M. 1980. "Dr. Ehrlich's Magic Bullet: Econometric Theory, Econometrics, and the Death Penalty." *Crime and Delinquency* 485–502.

McKenzie, R. F. 1933. *The Metropolitan Community.* New York: McGraw-Hill.

McKinney, William, and Wade Clark Roof. 1982. "A Social Profile of American Religious Groups." In *Yearbook of American and Canadian Churches: 1982,* edited by Constant H. Jacquet, Jr. Nashville: Abingdon Press.

McNeill, William H. 1976. *Plagues and Peoples.* New York: Basic Books.

McNeill, William. 1982. *The Pursuit of Power.* Chicago: University of Chicago Press.

McWilliams, Carey. 1945. *Prejudice: Japanese-Americans.* Boston: Little, Brown.

Mallory, Walter H. 1926. *China: Land of Famine.* New York: American Geographical Society.

Malson, Lucien. 1972. *Wolf Children and the Problem of Human Nature.* New York: Monthly Review Press.

Martin, David. 1981. "Disorientations to Mainstream Religion: The Context of Reorientations in New Religious Movements." In *The Social Impact of New Religious Movements,* edited by Bryan Wilson. New York: The Rose of Sharon Press.

Marx, Gary T. 1967. *Protest and Prejudice.* New York: Harper & Row.

Marx, Karl, and Friedrich Engels. 1848. *Communist Manifesto.* Reprint 1967. New York: Pantheon.

Mead, George Herbert. 1925. "The Genesis of the Self and Social Control." *International Journal of Ethics* 35: 251–273.

Mead, George Herbert. 1934. *Mind, Self, and Society: From the Standpoint of a Social Behaviorist.* Charles W. Morris (ed.). Chicago: University of Chicago Press.

Mead, Margaret. 1928. *Coming of Age in Samoa.* New York: William Morrow & Co.

Mead, Margaret. 1935. *Sex and Temperament in Three Primitive Societies.* New York: Dell.

Meadows, Donella, et al. 1972. *The Limits to Growth: A Report for the Club of Rome's Projection on the Predicament of Mankind.* New York: Universe Books.

Meeks, Wayne A. 1983. *The First Urban Christians.* New Haven: Yale University Press.

Megargee, Edwin I. 1966. "Undercontrolled and Overcontrolled Personality Types in Extreme Antisocial Aggression." *Psychological Monographs* 80:611–617.

Melton, J. Gordon. 1978. *Encyclopedia of American Religions.* Wilmington, N.C.: McGrath.

Meltzoff, Andrew N., and M. Keith Moore. 1977. "Facial Imitation in Infants." *Science,* Oct. 7.

Mendelssohn, Kurt. 1976. *The Secret of Western Domination.* New York: Praeger.

Merton, Robert K. 1938. "Social Structure and Anomie." *American Sociological Review* 3:672–682.

Meyer, John W. 1977. "The Effects of Education as an Institution." *American Journal of Sociology* 83:55–77.

Miles, Betty. 1975. *Channeling Children: Sex Stereotyping in Prime-Time TV.* Princeton, N.J.: Women on Words and Images.

Milgram, Stanley. 1967. "The Small World Problem." *Psychology Today* 1:1–6.

Miller, G. Tyler. 1982. *Living in the Environment,* 3rd ed. Belmont, Calif.: Wadsworth.

Miller, Walter B. 1962. "The Impact of a 'Total Community' Delinquency Control Project." *Social Problems* 10: 168–191.

Millis, H. A. 1915. *The Japanese Problem in the United States.* New York: Macmillan.

Minor, W. William, and Joseph Harry. 1982. "Deterrent and Experiential Effects in Perceptual Deterrence Research: A Replication and Extension." *Journal of Research in Crime and Delinquency* 19:190–203.

Miyamoto, Frank. 1939. "Social Solidarity among the Japanese in Seattle." *University of Washington Publications in the Social Sciences* 2:57–130.

Miyamoto, Frank S., and Sanford M. Dornbusch. 1956. "A Test of Interaction Hypothesis of Self-conception." *American Journal of Sociology* 61:399–403.

Money, John, and Anke A. Ehrhardt. 1972. *Man and Woman, Boy and Girl.* Baltimore, Md.: Johns Hopkins University Press.

Montgomery, Field-Marshall Viscount. 1968. *A History of Warfare.* New York: World.

Mooney, James. 1896. *The Ghost Dance Religion and the Sioux Outbreak of 1890.* Fourth Annual Report of the

Bureau of Ethnology to the Secretary of the Smithsonian Institution. Washington, D.C.: U.S. Government Printing Office.

Morgan, Elaine. 1972. *The Descent of Woman.* New York: Stein and Day.

Morioka, Kiyomi. 1975. *Religion in Changing Japanese Society.* Tokyo: University of Tokyo Press.

Mosca, Gaetano. 1896. *The Ruling Class.* Reprint 1939. New York: McGraw-Hill.

Mowat, Farley. 1965. *Westviking.* Boston: Little, Brown.

Murdock, George P. 1949. *Social Structure.* New York: Macmillan.

Murdock, George P. 1967a. "Ethnographic Atlas: A Summary." *Ethnology* 6:109–236.

Murdock, George P. 1967b. *Ethnographic Atlas.* Pittsburgh: University of Pittsburgh Press.

Myrdal, Gunnar. 1944. *An American Dilemma: The Negro Problem and Modern Democracy.* New York: Harper & Row.

Newcomb, Theodore M. 1953. "An Approach to the Study of Communicative Acts." *Psychological Review* 60: 393–404.

Niebuhr, H. Richard. 1929. *The Social Sources of Denominationalism.* New York: Henry Holt.

Nisbet, Robert. 1980. *History of the Idea of Progress.* New York: Basic Books.

Nordhoff, Charles. 1875. *The Communistic Societies of the United States.* Reprint 1966. New York: Dover.

North, Douglass C., and Robert Paul Thomas. 1973. *The Rise of the Western World: A New Economic History.* Cambridge, England: Cambridge University Press.

Noyes, John Humphrey. 1870. *The History of American Socialisms.* Philadelphia: J.B. Lippincott.

Nozick, Robert. 1974. *Anarchy, State and Utopia.* New York: Basic Books.

Nye, F. Ivan. 1963. "The Adjustment of Adolescent Children." In *The Employed Mother in America,* edited by F. Ivan Nye and Lois Wladis Hoffman, pp. 133–141. Chicago: Rand McNally.

Ofshe, Richard. 1967. *A Theory of Behavior under Conditions of Reference Conflict.* Unpublished Ph.D. dissertation, Stanford University.

Ofshe, Richard. 1972. "Reference Conflict and Behavior." In *Sociological Theories in Progress,* vol. 2, edited by Joseph Berger, Morris Zelditch, and Bo Anderson. Boston: Houghton Mifflin.

Ogburn, William F. 1932. *Social Change.* New York: Viking Press.

Olsen, Mancur. 1965. *The Logic of Collective Action.* Cambridge: Harvard University Press.

Omenn, G. S., E. Caspari, and L. Ehrman. 1972. "Epilogue: Behavior Genetics and Educational Policy." In *Genetics, Environment, and Behavior: Implications for Educational Policy,* edited by L. Ehrman, G. S. Omenn, and E. Caspari, pp. 307–310. New York: Academic Press.

Ossowski, Stanislaw. 1963. *Class Structure in the Social Consciousness.* New York: Free Press.

Paige, Jeffery M. 1974. "Kinship and Polity in Stateless Societies." *American Journal of Sociology* 80:301–320.

Park, Robert E., and Ernest W. Burgess. 1925. *The City.* Chicago: University of Chicago Press.

Parker, J., and H. G. Grasmick. 1979. "Linking Actual and Perceived Certainty of Punishment: An Exploratory Study of an Untested Proposition in Deterrence Theory." *Criminology* 17:366–379.

Patterson, G. R. 1980. "Children Who Steal." In *Understanding Crime: Current Theory and Research,* edited by Travis Hirschi and Michael Gottfredson. Beverly Hills: Sage.

Pearlin, L. I., and M. L. Kohn. 1966. "Social Class, Occupation, and Parental Values: A Cross-national Study." *American Sociological Review* 31:466–479.

Petersen, William. 1971. *Japanese Americans: Oppression and Success.* New York: Random House.

Petersen, William. 1975. *Population.* New York: Macmillan.

Petersen, William. 1978. "Chinese Americans and Japanese Americans." In *Essays and Data on American Ethnic Groups,* edited by Thomas Sowell. Washington, D.C.: The Urban Institute.

Pfeiffer, John E. 1977. *The Emergence of Society.* New York: McGraw-Hill.

Phelps, Edmund S., ed. 1975. *Altruism, Morality, and Economic Theory.* New York: Russell Sage Foundation.

Phillips, David P. 1980. "The Deterrent Effect of Capital Punishment: New Evidence on an Old Controversy." *American Journal of Sociology* 86:139–148.

Piaget, Jean. 1970. "Piaget's Theory." In *Carmichael's Manual of Child Psychology,* 3rd ed., edited by Paul Mussen, pp. 703–732. New York: John Wiley.

Piliavin, Irving, and Scott Briar. 1964. "Police Encounters with Juveniles." *American Journal of Sociology* 70: 206–214.

Pineo, Peter C. 1961. "Disenchantment in the Later Years of Marriage." *Marriage and Family Living* 23:4.

Pirenne, Henri. 1925. *Medieval Cities.* Princeton, N.J.: Princeton University Press.

Powers, Edwin, and Helen Witmer. 1951. *An Experiment in the Prevention of Delinquency: The Cambridge-Somerville Youth Study.* New York: Columbia University Press.

Preston, Samuel E. 1975. "Estimating the Proportion of American Marriages That End in Divorce." *Sociological Methods and Research* 3:435–460.

Quinley, Harold E., and Charles Y. Glock. 1979. *Anti-Semitism in America.* New York: Free Press.

Reiss, Albert J., Jr. 1961. *Occupations and Social Status.* New York: Free Press.

Rhodes, A. L., and A. J. Reiss, Jr. 1970. "The Religious Factor and Delinquent Behavior." *Journal of Research in Crime and Delinquency* 7:83–98.

Richardson, James T., and Mary W. Stewart. 1978. "Conversion Process Models and the Jesus Movement." In *Conversion Careers,* edited by J. Richardson. Beverly Hills, Calif.: Sage.

Robinson, P., Jerrold G. Rusk, and Kendra B. Head. 1968. *Measure of Political Attitudes.* Ann Arbor, Mich.: Survey Research Center, Institute for Social Research.

Ropp, Theodore. 1959. *War in the Modern World.* Durham: Duke University Press.

Rosenberg, Charles E. 1975. "Introduction: History and Experience." In *The Family in History,* edited by Charles E. Rosenberg. Philadelphia: University of Pennsylvania Press.

Rosenberg, Morris. 1965. *Society and the Adolescent Self-Image.* Princeton, N.J.: Princeton University Press.

Rosengren, Karl Erik, Peter Arvidson, and Dahn Sturesson. 1975. "The Barsebäck 'Panic': A Radio Programme as a Negative Summary Event." *Acta Sociologica.* 18:147–162.

Rosenthal, David. 1970. *Genetic Theory and Abnormal Behavior.* New York: McGraw-Hill.

Ross, E. A. 1914. *The Old World in the New.* New York: Century Company.

Rossi, Peter H., R. A. Berk, and K. J. Lenihan. 1980. *Money, Work, and Crime: Experimental Evidence.* New York: Academic Press.

Rossi, Peter H., Richard A. Berk, and Kenneth J. Lenihan. 1982. "Saying It Wrong with Figures: A Comment on Zeisel." *American Journal of Sociology* 88:390–393.

Rosten, Leo. 1968. *The Joys of Yiddish.* New York: McGraw-Hill.

Rubinow, Israel. 1907. "The Economic Condition of Jews in Russia." *Bulletin of the Bureau of Labor,* no. 72. Washington, D.C.: U.S. Government Printing Office.

Sagarin, Edward. 1975. *Deviants and Deviance.* New York: Praeger.

Sanders, Ronald. 1969. *Downtown Jews.* New York: Harper & Row.

Sann, Paul. 1967. *Fads, Follies and Delusions of the American People.* New York: Bonanza.

Sawyer, P. H. 1982. *Kings and Vikings.* London: Methuen.

Schachter, Stanley. 1951. "Deviation, Rejection, and Communication." *Journal of Abnormal and Social Psychology* 46:190–207.

Scheff, Thomas J. 1966. *Being Mentally Ill: A Sociological Theory.* Chicago: Aldine.

Schmookler, Jacob. 1966. *Invention and Economic Growth.* Cambridge: Harvard University Press.

Schoenbaum, David. 1966. *Hitler's Social Revolution.* Garden City, N.Y.: Doubleday.

Schuckit, Marc A., et al. 1979. *The Genetic Aspects of Psychiatric Syndrome Relating to Antisocial Problems in Youth.* Seattle, Wash.: Center for Law and Justice.

Schultz, L. G. 1960. "The Wife Assaulter." *Journal of Social Therapy* 6:103–111.

Schur, Edwin. 1971. *Labeling Deviant Behavior.* New York: Harper & Row.

Schwartz, Richard, and Jerome H. Skolnick. 1962. "A Study of Legal Stigma." *Social Problems* 10:133–138.

Selznick, Gertrude J., and Stephen Steinberg. 1969. *The Tenacity of Prejudice.* New York: Harper & Row.

Selznick, Philip. 1948. "Foundations of the Theory of Organization." *American Sociological Review* 13:25–35.

Selznick, Philip. 1949. *TVA and the Grass Roots.* Berkeley: University of California Press.

Selznick, Philip. 1957. *Leadership in Administration.* New York: Harper & Row.

Sewell, William H. 1964. "Comunity of Residence and College Plans." *American Sociological Review* 29:24–38.

Sewell, William H., Robert M. Hauser, and Wendy C. Wolf. 1980. "Sex, Schooling and Occupational Status." *American Journal of Sociology* 86:551–583.

Shah, Saleem A., and Loren H. Roth. 1974. "Biological and Psychophysiological Factors in Criminology." In *Handbook of Criminology,* edited by Daniel Glaser. Chicago: Rand McNally.

Shattuck, Roger. 1980. *The Forbidden Experiment.* New York: Farrar, Straus & Giroux.

Shaw, Clifford, R., and Henry D. McKay. 1929. *Delinquency Areas.* Chicago: University of Chicago Press.

Shaw, Clifford R., and Henry D. McKay. 1931. *Report on the Causes of Crime,* vol. 12, no. 13. Washington, D.C.: National Commission on Law Observance and Enforcement.

Shaw, Clifford R., and Henry D. McKay. 1942. *Juvenile Delinquency and Urban Areas.* Chicago: University of Chicago Press.

Sherif, Muzafer, and Carolyn W. Sherif. 1953. *Groups in Harmony and Tension: An Integration of Studies on Intergroup Relations.* New York: Harper & Row.

Shirer, William L. 1960. *The Rise and Fall of the Third Reich.* Greenwich, Conn.: Fawcett.

Shirer, William L. 1969. *The Collapse of the Third Republic.* New York: Simon & Schuster.

Shorter, Edward. 1975. *The Making of the Modern Family.* New York: Basic Books.

Silberman, Charles E. 1971. *Crisis in the Classroom: The Remaking of American Education.* New York: Vintage.

Sills, David L. 1957. *The Volunteers.* Glencoe, Ill.: Free Press.

Simmel, Georg. 1905. "A Contribution to the Sociology of Religion." *American Journal of Sociology* 11:359–376.

Simon, Julian L. 1981. *The Ultimate Resource.* Princeton, N.J.: Princeton University Press.

Sjoberg, Gideon. 1960. *The Preindustrial City.* New York: Free Press.

Sjoberg, Gideon. 1965. "Cities in Developing and in Industrialized Societies: A Cross-cultural Analysis." In *The Study of Urbanization,* edited by P. H. Hauser and L. F. Schnore. New York: John Wiley.

Skeels, H. M. 1966. *Adult Status of Children with Contrasting Early Life Experiences.* Monographs of the Society for Research in Child Development.

Skeels, H. M., and H. A. Dye. 1939. "A Study of the Effects of Differential Stimulation in Mentally Retarded Children." *Proceedings of the American Association for Mental Deficiency* 44:114–136.

Slater, Miriam K. 1969. "My Son the Doctor: Aspects of Mobility among American Jews." *American Journal of Sociology* 34:359–373.

Smelser, Neil J. 1962. *Theory of Collective Behavior.* New York: Free Press.

Smith, Hedrick. 1976. *The Russians.* New York: Quadrangle.

Smith, M. D., and R. N. Parker. 1980. "Type of Homicide and Variation in Regional Rates." *Social Forces* 59: 136–149.

Snow, David, and Cynthia L. Philips. 1980. "The Lofland-Stark Conversion Model: A Critical Reassessment." *Social Problems* 27:430–447.

Sorokin, Pitirim A. 1937. *Social and Cultural Dynamics.* New York: American Books.

Sowell, Thomas, ed. 1978. *Essays and Data on American Ethnic Groups.* Washington, D.C.: The Urban Institute.

Sowell, Thomas. 1981. *Ethnic America: A History.* New York: Basic Books.

Sowell, Thomas. 1983. *The Economics and Politics of Race: An International Perspective.* New York; William Morrow.

Spiro, Melford E. 1966. "Religion: Problems of Definition and Explanation." In *Anthropological Approaches to the Study of Religion,* edited by Michael Banton, pp. 85–126. New York: Praeger.

Stack, Steven. 1983. "Religion and Suicide." *Journal for the Scientific Study of Religion* 22:239–252.

Stark, Rodney. 1962. "Policy and the Pros: An Organizational Analysis of a Metropolitan Newspaper." *Berkeley Journal of Sociology* 7:11–31.

Stark, Rodney. 1972. *Police Riots: Collective Violence and Law Enforcement.* Belmont, Calif.: Wadsworth.

Stark, Rodney. 1981. "Must All Religions Be Supernatural?" In *The Social Impact of New Religious Movements,* edited by Bryan Wilson, pp. 159–177. New York: Rose of Sharon Press.

Stark, Rodney. 1984. "The Rise of a New World Faith." *Review of Religious Research* 26:18–27.

Stark, Rodney. Forthcoming. "Correcting Church Membership Rates: 1971 and 1980."

Stark, Rodney, and W. S. Bainbridge. 1980. "Secularizations, Revival, and Cult Formation." *The Annual Review of the Social Sciences of Religion* 4:85–119.

Stark, Rodney, and W. S. Bainbridge. 1981. "American-Born Sects: Initial Findings." *Journal for the Scientific Study of Religion* 20:130–149.

Stark, Rodney, and W. S. Bainbridge. 1985. *The Future of Religion: Secularization, Revival and Cult Formation.* Berkeley: University of California Press.

Stark, Rodney, and Robert Crutchfield. In press. "Intentional and Impulsive Deviance: A Reconceptualization." *Criminology.*

Stark, Rodney, Daniel P. Doyle, and Lori Kent. 1980. "Rediscovering Moral Communities: Church Membership and Crime." In *Understanding Crime: Current Theory and Research,* edited by Travis Hirschi and Michael Gottfredson. Beverly Hills, Calif.: Sage.

Stark, Rodney, Daniel P. Doyle, and Jesse Lynn Rushing. 1983. "Beyond Durkheim: Religion and Suicide." *Journal for the Scientific Study of Religion* 22:120–131.

Stark, Rodney, and Charles Y. Glock. 1968. *American Piety.* Berkeley: University of California Press.

Stark, Rodney, Lori Kent, and Daniel P. Doyle. 1982. "Religion and Delinquency: The Ecology of a 'Lost' Relationship." *Journal of Research in Crime and Delinquency* 19:4–24.

Stark, Rodney, et al. 1971. *Wayward Shepherds: Prejudice and the Protestant Clergy.* New York: Harper & Row.

Stark, Rodney, et al. 1983. "Crime and Delinquency in the Roaring Twenties." *Journal of Crime and Delinquency* 20:4–23.

Steinberg, Stephen. 1974. *The Academic Melting Pot.* New York: McGraw-Hill.

Stinchcombe, Arthur L. 1968. *Constructing Social Theory.* New York: Harcourt Brace Jovanovich.

Sutherland, Edwin. 1924. *Criminology.* Philadelphia: J. B. Lippincott.

Swanson, Guy E. 1968. "To Live in Concord with Society: Two Empirical Studies of Primary Relations." In *Cooley and Sociological Analysis,* edited by A. J. Reiss. Ann Arbor: University of Michigan Press.

Swanson, Guy E. 1969. *Rules of Descent: Studies in the Sociology of Parentage.* Ann Arbor: Museum of Anthropology, University of Michigan.

Taeuber, Karl E. 1983. *Report of the Citizen's Commission on Civil Rights.* Washington, D.C.: Center for National Policy Review, Catholic University.

Taeuber, Karl E., and Alma F. Taeuber. 1964. "The Negro as an Immigrant Group: Recent Trends in Racial and Ethnic Segregation in Chicago." *American Journal of Sociology* 69:347–382.

Taeuber, Karl E., and Alma F. Taeuber. 1969. *Negroes in Cities.* New York: Atheneum.

Tanner, James M. 1970. "Physical Growth." In *Carmichael's Manual of Child Psychology,* 3rd ed., edited by Paul Mussen, pp. 77–155. New York: John Wiley.

Taylor, Ralph B., et al. 1980. "The Defensibility of Defensible Space." In *Understanding Crime: Current Theory and Research,* edited by Travis Hirschi and Michael Gottfredson, pp. 53–71. Beverly Hills, Calif.: Sage.

Thomas, Hugh. 1979. *A History of the World.* New York: Harper & Row.

Thomis, Malcolm I. 1970. *The Luddites.* New York: Schocken.

Thompson, James D. 1967. *Organizations in Action.* New York: McGraw-Hill.

Thornberry, Terrance P. 1973. "Race, Socio-Economic Status and Sentencing in the Juvenile Justice System." *The Journal of Criminal Law, Criminology and Police Science* 64:90–98.

Tittle, C. R., et al. 1978. "The Myth of Social Class and Criminality: An Empirical Assessment of the Empirical Evidence." *American Sociological Review* 43:643–656.

Toby, Jackson. 1965. "Early Identification and Intensive Treatment of Pre-delinquents: A Negative View." *Social Work* 6:3–13.

Toch, Hans. 1969. *Violent Man: An Inquiry into the Psychology of Violence.* Chicago: Aldine.

Trow, Martin. 1973. "The Second Transformation of American Secondary Education." In *The School in Society: Studies in the Sociology of Education,* edited by Sam D. Sieber and David E. Wilder. New York: Free Press.

Truzzi, Marcello. 1968. "Lilliputians in Gulliver's Land: The Social Role of the Dwarf." In *Sociology and Everyday Life,* edited by M. Truzzi. Englewood Cliffs, N.J.: Prentice-Hall.

Turnbull, Colin. 1965. "The Mbuti Pygmies of the Congo." In *Peoples of Africa,* edited by James L. Gibbs. New York: Holt, Rinehart & Winston.

U.S. Department of Justice. 1982. *Sourcebook of Criminal Justice Statistics: 1981.* Washington, D.C.: U.S. Government Printing Office.

U'Ren, Marjorie B. 1971. "The Image of Women in Textbooks." In *Women in Sexist Society: Studies in Power and Powerlessness,* edited by Vivian Gornick and Barbara K. Moran. New York: Basic Books.

van den Berghe, Pierre L. 1967. *Race and Racism: A Comparative Perspective.* New York: John Wiley.

van den Berghe, Pierre L. 1973. *Age and Sex in Human Societies.* Belmont, Calif.: Wadsworth.

Veblen, Thorstein. 1899. *The Theory of the Leisure Class.* New York: Macmillan.

Vogt, William. 1948. *Road to Survival.* New York: Sloane.

von Bertalanffy, Ludwig. 1967. "General System Theory." In *System, Change and Conflict,* edited by N. J. Demerath III and Richard A. Peterson. New York: Free Press.

Waldo, Gordon P., and Simon Dinitz. 1967. "Personality Attributes of the Criminal: An Analysis of Research Studies, 1950–1965." *Journal of Research in Crime and Delinquency* 4:185–202.

Wallace, Anthony F. C. 1956. "Revitalization Movements." *American Anthropologist* 58:264–281.

Wallace, Anthony F. C. 1966. *Religion: An Anthropological View.* New York: Random House.

Wallace, W. L. 1966. *Student Culture: Social Structure and Continuity in a Liberal Arts College.* Chicago: Aldine.

Wallerstein, Immanuel. 1974. *The Modern World System.* New York: Academic Press.

Wallis, Roy. 1975. *Sectarianism.* New York: John Wiley.

Wallis, Roy. 1982. *Millennialism and Charisma.* Belfast, Northern Ireland: The Queen's University.

Walzer, Michael. 1963. *The Revolution of the Saints.* Cambridge: Harvard University Press.

Ward, David. 1971. *Cities and Immigrants.* New York: Oxford University Press.

Webb, Eugene J., Donald T. Campbell, Richard D. Schwartz, and Lee Sechrest. 1966. *Unobtrusive Measures: Nonreactive Research in the Social Sciences.* Chicago: Rand McNally.

Weber, Max. 1946. "Politics as a Vocation." In *From Max Weber,* edited by Hans Gerth and C. Wright Mills. New York: Oxford University Press.

Weber, Max. 1904–05. *The Protestant Ethic and the Spirit of Capitalism.* Reprinted, 1958. New York: Charles Scribner's.

Weed, James A. 1980. "National Estimates of Marriage Dissolution and Survivorship." *Vital and Health Statistics,* series 3, no. 19.

Weis, J. G. 1977. "Comparative Analysis of Social Control Theories of Delinquency: The Breakdown of Adequate Social Controls." In *Preventing Delinquency: A Comparative Analysis of Delinquency Prevention Theory.* Washington, D.C.: National Institute for Juvenile Justice and Delinquency Prevention.

Weitz, Shirley. 1977. *Sex Roles: Biological, Psychological and Social Foundations.* New York: Oxford University Press.

Weitzman, Lenore J., et al. 1972. "Sex Role Socialization in Picture Books for Preschool Children." *American Journal of Sociology* 77:1125–1149.

Welch, Kevin. 1983. "Community Development and Metropolitan Religious Commitment: A Test of Two Competing Models." *Journal for the Scientific Study of Religion* 22:167–180.

Wells, H. G. 1897. *The War of the Worlds.* Reprint 1964. New York: Airmont.

Westoff, Charles F., Robert G. Potter, Jr., Philip C. Sagi, and Elliot G. Mishler. 1961. *Family Growth in Metropolitan America.* Princeton, N.J.: Princeton University Press.

White, Burton L. 1971. *Human Infants: Experience and Psychological Development.* Englewood Cliffs, N.J.: Prentice-Hall.

White, L. A. 1949. *The Science of Culture.* New York: Farrar, Straus & Giroux.

White, Leslie A. 1959. *The Evolution of Culture.* New York: McGraw-Hill.

White, Lynn, Jr. 1962. *Medieval Technology and Social Change.* London: Oxford University Press.

Wilkinson, Karen. 1980. "The Broken Home and Delinquent Behavior." In *Understanding Crime: Current Theory and Research,* edited by Travis Hirschi and Michael Gottfredson, pp. 21–42. Beverly Hills, Calif.: Sage.

Williams, R. M., Jr. 1947. *The Reduction of Intergroup Tensions.* New York: Social Science Research Council.

Wilson, Bryan. 1959. "An Analysis of Sect Development." *American Sociological Review* 24:2–15.

Wilson, Bryan. 1961. *Sects and Society.* Berkeley: University of California Press.

Wilson, Bryan. 1970. *Religious Sects.* New York: McGraw-Hill.

Wilson, Bryan. 1975. "The Secularization Debate." *Encounter* 45:77–83.

Wilson, Bryan. 1979. "The Return of the Sacred." *Journal for the Scientific Study of Religion* 18:268–280.

Wilson, Bryan. 1982. *Religion in Sociological Perspective.* New York: Oxford University Press.

Wilson, Edward O. 1975. *Sociobiology: The New Synthesis.* Cambridge, Mass.: Harvard University Press.

Wirth, Louis. 1928. *The Ghetto.* Chicago: University of Chicago Press.

Wirth, Louis. 1938. "Urbanism as a Way of Life." *American Journal of Sociology* 44:8–20.

Witkin, H. A., et al. 1976. "Criminality in XYY and XXY Men." *Science* 196:547–555.

World Vision. 1979. *Mission Handbook.* Monrovia, Calif.: World Vision.

Wrigley, E. A. 1969. *Population and History.* New York: McGraw-Hill.

Yunker, James A. 1982. "The Relevance of the Identification Problem to Statistical Research on Capital Punishment." *Crime and Delinquency* 28:96–124.

Zborowski, Mark, and Elizabeth Herzog. 1962. *Life Is with People: The Culture of the Shtetl.* New York: Schocken Books.

Zeisel, Hans. 1982. "Disagreement over the Evaluation of a Controlled Experiment." *American Journal of Sociology* 88:378–389.

Zuckerman, Michael. 1975. "Dr. Spock: The Confidence Man." In *The Family in History,* edited by Charles E. Rosenberg. Philadelphia: University of Pennsylvania Press.

Illustration Credits

Page 287, © Abagail Heyman/Archive Pictures
Page 289, Art Resource
Page 290, Bulloz
Page 292, State Historical Society of Wisconsin
Page 294, Alinari/Art Resource
Page 295, Hirshhorn Museum and Sculpture Garden, Smithsonian
Page 297, Henri Cartier-Bresson/Magnum
Page 300, © Ethan Hoffman/Archive Pictures
Page 305, © Gilles Peress/Magnum
Pages 310–11, © Rene Burri/Magnum
Page 312, © Abraham Menashe from *The Face of Prayer,* an Alfred A. Knopf publication
Page 314, © Abraham Menashe from *The Face of Prayer,* an Alfred A. Knopf publication
Page 315, © Ken Heyman
Page 318, © Serge Schemann/NYT Pictures
Page 326, © Jack Prelutsky/Stock Boston
Page 327, © Gerhard E. Gscheidle/Peter Arnold
Page 328, © Abraham Menashe from *The Face of Prayer,* an Alfred A. Knopf publication
Page 334, © Kent Reno, Jeroboam
Page 335, © P.P./Magnum
Page 337, © Burt Glinn/Magnum
Page 339, American Antiquarian Society
Page 341, © Carrie Boretz/Archive Pictures
Page 343, © Benjamin Porter/Archive Pictures
Page 344, © Kas/Picture Group
Page 345, © George Bellerose/Stock Boston
Page 347, National Museum of American Art, Smithsonian Institution 447.83

Page 351, Wide World Photos
Page 355, © Paul Conklin
Page 362, Kansas State Historical Society, Topeka
Page 363, Historical Photography Collection, University of Washington Libraries
Page 366, Library of Congress
Pages 368–9, Library of Congress
Page 373, © Elizabeth Crews
Page 374, © Susie Fitzhugh/Stock Boston
Page 377, © Michael Heron 1980/ Woodfin Camp
Page 386, © Werner Bischof/Magnum
Page 387, left, Mansell
Page 387, right, Neg #326744 Photo:Boltin/American Museum of Natural History
Page 390, © Gilles Peress/Magnum
Page 391, © Marc Riboud/Magnum
Page 393, Neg.# 232240 Photo:D.B. MacMillan, American Museum of Natural History
Page 397, Bulloz
Page 401, Ken Heyman
Page 402, © Philippe Billere/Rapho
Page 403, © Peter Menzel
Page 405, © Marc and Evelyn Bernheim 1981/Woodfin Camp
Page 411, © Bruce Davidson/Magnum
Pages 412–13, Imperial War Museum
Page 416, Popperfoto
Page 417, Bibliotheque Nationale, Paris
Page 418, Bettmann
Page 421, Minnesota Historical Society
Page 424, Library of Congress
Page 427, WHO photo by J. Abcede
Page 428, © John Running/Stock Boston
Page 435, © Elliott Erwitt/Magnum
Page 442, Bulloz
Page 443, Jacob A. Riis Collection, Museum of the City of New York

Page 444, State Historical Society of Wisconsin
Page 445, University of Chicago
Page 447, Art Resource
Page 449, USDA
Page 453, Library of Congress
Page 454, Culver
Page 457, © Bill Owens/Archive Pictures
Page 460, © Rose Skytta/Jeroboam
Page 462, © Gilles Peress/Magnum
Page 465, © Evelyn Hofer/Archive Pictures
Page 471, Bettmann
Page 472, William England. "Niagara Suspension Bridge," 1859. Albumen print, 9½ × 11½". Collection, The Museum of Modern Art, New York, purchase
Page 474, Chicago Historical Society
Page 475, National Gallery of Art, Washington, Ailsa Mellon Bruce Fund 1967
Page 477, © Burk Uzzle 1983/Woodfin Camp
Page 479, March of Dimes Birth Defects Foundation
Page 481, © Richard Kalvar/Magnum
Page 483, Hagley Museum and Library
Page 488, Metropolitan Museum of Art, George A. Hearn Fund, 1956
Page 495, Brown Brothers
Page 498, © John P. Cavanagh/Archive Pictures
Page 501, © N.Y. Daily News
Page 505, Hirmer Fotoarchiv
Page 509, Mansell
Page 514, Imperial War Museum
Page 515, Popperfoto
Page 516, Smithsonian
Page 517, Smithsonian
Page 521, NASA

Name Index

Subject Index/Glossary

A

Abstractions Ideas or mental constructions rather than material objects. All scientific concepts are abstractions. 24

Accommodation Agreement between two groups to ignore differences between them. 29, 248

Achieved status Position gained on the basis of merit (in other words, by achievement). 33, 208

Administrative growth. *See* Blau's administrative theory; Organization

Adolescents, 102–105, 144–145

Adult socialization Processes by which adults are enabled to perform new roles. 135

Age-specific death rates Number of deaths per year of persons within a given age range divided by the total number of persons within that age range. 411

Age structure Proportions of persons of various age groups making up a total population. 414

Aggregate Collection of people lacking social relations. 4

Agrarian societies Societies that live by farming. 225–231

Agricultural revolution, 448–450

Allport's theory of contact Theory holding that contact between groups will improve relations only if the groups are of equal status and do not compete with one another. 249–250

Altruism Behavior alleged to be contrary to self-interest and to occur entirely for the benefit of somebody else. 54–55

Amana community, 211

American dilemma Term used by Myrdal to describe the contradiction of a society committed to democratic ideals but sustaining racial segregation. 251–253

Anarchists Followers of a political philosophy that regards the state as inevitably repressive and unjust; they, therefore, propose to destroy the state and live without laws or government. 213

Animals, 111–116
culture of, 111–113
language of, 113–115
societies of, 115–116

Anomie State in which norms lack definition and force, that is, in which people aren't sure what the norms are and don't greatly care. 161–162, 463

Anti-Semitism Prejudice and discrimination against Jews. 32, 37

Arapesh, 130–132

Arithmetic increase Constant rate of growth (or decline). 419

Ascribed status Position assigned to individuals or groups without regard for merit, but because of certain traits beyond their control, such as their race, their sex, or the social standing of their parents. 33, 208

Assimilation Process by which an individual or a group reacts to a new social environment by adopting the culture prevalent in that environment. 28, 248

Attachment Stable and persistent pattern of interaction between two people. 15, 60, 62, 69
deviance and, 154–157, 159–160

Authoritarian personality, 249

Authoritarian state Undemocratic society that has a significant amount of pluralism. 342, 343

Autonomous divisions Parts of an organization, each of which includes a full set of functional divisions. 483–485

B

Baby boom Brief period of high fertility in many Western industrial nations immediately following World War II. 426, 433–438

Barsebäck nuclear incident, 502–503

Behavior. *See* Collective behavior; Parallel behavior; Political behavior

Behavioral genetics Scientific field that attempts to link behavior, especially human behavior, with genetics. 100–102

Beliefs Our notions about how we ought to act. 161

Bias, 17–18

Bible belt, 321–322

Biophysical development, 119–123

Birth cohort All persons born within a given time period, usually one year. 412–413